Developmental Psychology
A Topical Approach

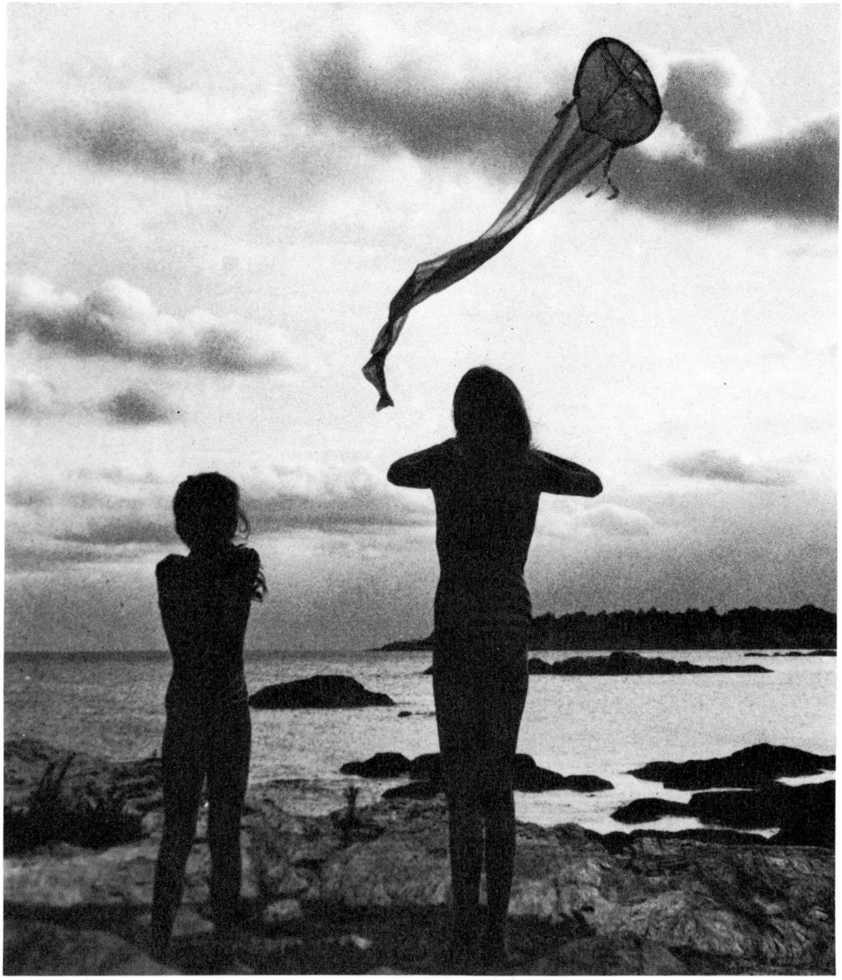

Developmental Psychology
A Topical Approach

David Moshman
John A. Glover
Roger H. Bruning
University of Nebraska—Lincoln

Little, Brown and Company
Boston   Toronto

Library of Congress Cataloging-in-Publication Data

Moshman, David
    Developmental psychology.

    Bibliography: p.
    Includes indexes.
        1. Developmental psychology.   I. Glover, John A.,
1949–   II. Bruning, Roger H.   III. Title.
[DNLM: 1. Human Development.   2. Psychology.
BF 713 M911d]
BF713.M69   1987   155.4   86–21341
ISBN 0–316–58561–0

Copyright © 1987 by David Moshman, John A. Glover, and Roger H. Bruning

All rights reserved. No part of this book may be reproduced in any form or by any electronic or mechanical means including information storage and retrieval systems without permission in writing from the publisher, except by a reviewer who may quote brief passages in a review.

Library of Congress Catalog Card No. 86–21341

ISBN 0-316-58561-0

9 8 7 6 5 4 3 2

HAL

Published simultaneously in Canada
by Little, Brown & Company (Canada) Limited

Printed in the United States of America

Cover art: A Spring Day, By Shannon Vise, Age 8, Charlotte, NC: "My dream is that I would like to spend the whole day with my best friend. We would fly kites and picnic together. Ah, spring!" Art work from the 1984 Crayola® Dream-Makers® Collection, Binney & Smith Inc.

(credits continue on pages 686-689)

Preface

People develop in many different areas. When we study human development we focus our attention on particular areas or aspects such as physical and motor development, intellectual development, emotional development, social development, and personality development. Although it is possible to describe, say, a "typical" toddler, or the usual ways children change between ages 6 and 12, pictures such as these are generalizations.

Actual children, on the other hand, are not generalizations but individuals. One child may show rapid physical development and be slower in developing language abilities. Another child may show advanced strategies for perceiving and remembering but make slower progress in developing reasoning skills. A third may show rapid progress in most aspects of intellectual development but be slower in developing social relationships.

Although developmental psychologists are interested in the child as a whole, nearly all researchers specialize in one or more specific aspects of development and most theories limit their focus to particular topics—for example, language development or moral development. This approach reflects the fact that children develop at different rates in many different areas. In order to understand the developing individual, one must understand the details of development in each of these areas.

Our book, like research and theory in developmental psychology, is thus organized by *topics*. This approach has the advantage of helping you to see the continuity of development within each topic. It is important to keep in mind, however, that the various strands of development are not independent of each other. One's physical maturity affects one's social relationships, for example, and one's intellectual abilities influence one's moral judgments. In order to help you keep this in mind, we will frequently refer to previous or upcoming chapters.

You should make a point of considering how each aspect of development you are reading about might relate to other aspects of development.

Organization

The 16 chapters of the book are divided into five major sections. The first three chapters constitute an introduction to the field of developmental psychology. Chapter 1 presents the history of the field, beginning with early ideas about children and including the rise of scientific study of development. It also discusses some issues that have played a major role in that history and remain controversial today. Chapter 2 presents theories of development. In order to help you see how the various theories relate to each other, they are organized into three major families of theories. The chapter also discusses the nature of theories and their role in science. Finally, Chapter 3 stresses the importance of scientific research in understanding human development, discusses the various methods used by developmental psychologists, and introduces some important practical and ethical considerations.

The second major section of the book covers a variety of factors that influence human development. Chapter 4 focuses on biological factors. It begins by describing the evolution of our species and then discusses the mechanisms of genetics by which traits and tendencies are passed on from each generation to the next. Chapter 5 turns to social factors, including the roles of families, television, schools, and cultures, and the mechanisms by which social learning occurs.

Section III deals with physical and motor development. Chapter 6 focuses on prenatal development, from conception to birth. This is followed, in Chapter 7, by consideration of physical development and the emergence of various physical abilities from infancy through adolescence.

We then turn, in Section IV, to the broad and extensively-researched realm of intellectual development. We begin, in Chapter 8, with a general introduction to the two major theoretical approaches to the study of intellectual development—Piagetian theory, based on the work of the famous Swiss psychologist Jean Piaget, and the information-processing approach, which views the mind as a sort of biological computer. Chapters 9 through 12 then consider in detail the development of four critical aspects of the human intellect—perception, memory, language, and reasoning.

Finally, Section V encompasses personality and social development. Chapter 13 covers the nature and development of human emotions. Chapter 14 discusses the development of social relations with parents and peers. Chapter 15 looks into the development of moral reasoning and behavior. Finally, we conclude in Chapter 16 with a look at the development of sex roles, self-conceptions, and personality.

Special Features

There is obviously a great deal of information about a large number of topics in this book. In writing it, however, we have tried to keep in mind that it is not enough for a book to include extensive and accurate information. No book can *know* anything. Only the person reading it can understand and make use of the material. The measure of an informative book, then, is not how much it includes but how much it communicates.

Our aim, moreover, has been not only to communicate accurate and useful information about human development but to generate interest, to raise unsettled issues and important questions, and to get you thinking for yourself about the psychology of children and the nature of development. In order to further these aims, we have included a number of features in this book. We would like to briefly mention some of these and suggest how you can best make use of them.

First, we have given considerable thought not only to organizing the book as a whole but to organizing the material within each chapter and providing extensive headings and subheadings to indicate that organization. We believe you will learn and remember new information better if you know in advance what is to be covered and how it fits together. We suggest that you glance quickly through each chapter, with emphasis on the headings and subheadings, before reading the material in detail.

Second, we have not tried to cover everything. Developmental psychologists publish and present thousands of books, articles and convention papers every year. It would be impossible to summarize all of these, even briefly. Instead, we have tried to identify the ideas, principles, and issues most important for the beginning student. The emphasis is on general understanding rather than on masses of detail.

Third, we have included a number of application sections in which we make specific recommendations based on developmental theories and research. We think you will find these recommendations useful. In addition, we hope you will consider how we have derived these applications from the material in each chapter and will begin to formulate applications of your own.

Fourth, each chapter contains two types of boxed-off material: Research and Highlights. The research boxes focus attention on key research while the highlight boxes feature significant current issues and topics in the study of development. We have included the titles of the boxes in the detailed Table of Contents.

Fifth, each chapter ends with a summary. This should help in the task of identifying and recalling the major points in the chapter and seeing how they fit together.

Sixth, we have provided a list of key terms for each chapter. These are not simply technical terms to be memorized and defined. Rather, they represent the general concepts covered in the chapter.

Seventh, we have provided a list of suggested readings to follow up on the material in each chapter. In addition, of course, there are references cited throughout, including both classic and recently-published works.

Eighth, each chapter includes one or more application exercises. We hope these will stimulate thinking about important concepts in the chapter as well as understanding how to apply them. Naturally, we would encourage students to work through the exercises before looking at our answers (in the back of the book). In some cases the answers are clear-cut, but in others there is room for a difference of opinion.

Lastly, at the end of the book we have included a glossary of terms. References are also included so that further work can be pursued. We also provide two indexes: name and subject.

It should be clear from the above that we hope you will do more than simply read and memorize this book. Everyone who reads this has been a child, knows children, and continues to experience the process of development. By relating what you read to your own experiences and intuitions, you will understand it at a deeper level and better see how to apply it.

Acknowledgments

Every book is the product of work by many people, and this one is no exception. Our special thanks go to Mylan Jaixen, Senior Editor at Little, Brown, who has worked with us right from the start in conceptualizing, developing, and refining the volume and who has befriended us throughout the effort. We also are grateful to the late Craig Nolte, M.D., who reviewed our materials on genetics, conception, prenatal development, physical growth, and motor development, and who helped us develop realistic applications for parents and growing children. Craig will be sadly missed by all who knew him.

We also want to extend our thanks to several colleagues at the University of Nebraska. George Veomett and Dick Boohar, fine biologists and good friends, helped us keep the biological contents of this volume accurate and current, and Warren Sanger graciously supplied us with karyotypes. Ross Thompson, an insightful and broadly knowledgeable developmental psychologist, enormously aided our understanding of social and emotional development. Our department Chair, Toni Santmire, not only encouraged our work but, as a developmental psychologist, gave us valuable feedback on several chapters.

In addition, we are pleased to acknowledge a very special group of scholars who reviewed various drafts of the manuscript and provided many important suggestions. Our thanks to

> Kitty G. Abraham, The University of Arizona
>
> Lauren B. Adamson, Georgia State University
>
> Linda F. Annis, Ball State University
>
> Earl M. Caspers, University of Arkansas
>
> Roberta L. Corrigan, The University of Wisconsin—Milwaukee
>
> S. V. LeBreque, North Texas State University
>
> Carolyn J. Mebert, University of New Hampshire
>
> Patricia H. Miller, University of Florida
>
> Harold M. Murai, California State University, Sacramento
>
> Gary F. Render, The University of Wyoming
>
> Brenda Robinson, Bunker Hill Community College
>
> James O. Rust, Middle Tennessee State University
>
> Winifred Shepard, State University of New York College at Fredonia
>
> Marion H. Typpo, University of Missouri—Columbia
>
> Suzanne P. Waller, University of Wisconsin—Milwaukee

The transformation from manuscript to book required the talents of many people at Little, Brown. The process was directed by the fine efforts of Sally Stickney, our book editor, and the final product profited greatly from her prompt, careful, and thoughtful work.

We are also grateful to Bridget Franks and Leslie Eastman, two outstanding doctoral students in developmental psychology, for their excellent work in designing and writing a student manual to accompany the text.

Finally, we thank our families and friends, who encouraged and supported us throughout this project.

D. M.
J. A. G.
R. H. B.

Brief Contents

	Prologue	1

PART I An Introduction to Developmental Psychology — 4

CHAPTER 1	Developmental Psychology: History and Issues	6
CHAPTER 2	Theories of Developmental Psychology	38
CHAPTER 3	Research Methods	67

PART II Biological and Social Bases of Development — 104

CHAPTER 4	Evolution and Genetics	106
CHAPTER 5	Social Influences on Development	139

PART III Physical and Motor Development — 186

CHAPTER 6	Prenatal Development and Birth	188
CHAPTER 7	Physical Growth and Motor Development	216

PART IV Intellectual Development — 258

CHAPTER 8	Theories of Cognitive Development	260
CHAPTER 9	Perceptual Development	301
CHAPTER 10	Development of Memory	333
CHAPTER 11	Language Development	368
CHAPTER 12	Development of Reasoning	403

PART V Social and Personality Development — 438

CHAPTER 13	Emotional Development	440
CHAPTER 14	Social Development	483
CHAPTER 15	Moral Development	526
CHAPTER 16	Personality Development	565

Glossary	603
Answers to Application Exercises	627
References	637
Name Index	691
Subject Index	701

Contents

	Prologue	1
PART I	**An Introduction to Developmental Psychology**	4

CHAPTER 1 Developmental Psychology: History and Issues 6
   The History of Children 7
   Influences on the Development of Developmental Psychology 11
   Ideas from Other Fields/Social Forces
      Highlights The Role of Women in Developmental Psychology 16
   Early Developmentalists 17
   Founders of a New Field/The Second Generation
   Current Issues in Developmental Psychology 30
   Heredity vs. Environment/Continuity vs. Discontinuity
      Research The Role of History in Current Research 32
   Elementarism vs. Holism/Directionality of Development/Mini-theories vs. Broad Theories
   Summary 35
   Key Terms 36
   Suggested Readings 36
   Application Exercises 37

CHAPTER 2 Theories of Developmental Psychology 38
   Theories, Data, and the Nature of Science 39
   What is a Theory?/What are Data?/The Relation of Theories and Data/Theories of Developmental Psychology
      Highlights Monty Python's Theory of the Brontosaurus 41

xiii

xiv CONTENTS

The Learning Paradigm — 42
History/Current Learning Theories/Basic Conceptions/Scientific Research Strategies/Practical Applications

The Developmental Paradigm — 49
History/Current Developmental Theories/Basic Conceptions/Scientific Research Strategies/Practical Applications

Research The Role of Theory in Research — 53

The Dialectical Paradigm — 55
History/Current Dialectical Theories/Basic Conceptions/Scientific Research Strategies/Practical Applications

Conclusions — 61
Overview of the Three Paradigms

Applications — 62
Choosing a Paradigm/Combining Paradigms

Summary — 64
Key Terms — 64
Suggested Readings — 65
Application Exercise — 65

CHAPTER 3 Research Methods — 67

Developmental Psychology as a Science — 68
Systematic Observation/Testing Hypotheses About Development/Reliance on Data, Not Belief/Public Sharing of Research

Research Designs in Developmental Psychology — 74

Research Surviving the Cuts: Publishing Research in Developmental Journals — 75

Cross-Sectional Designs/Longitudinal Designs/Cross-Sequential Designs/Comparison of the Three Research Designs

Research Methods in Developmental Psychology — 82
Case Study Methods/Naturalistic Observation Methods/Interview Methods/Correlational Methods/Experimental Methods

Enriching Research: Cross-Cultural Perspectives — 96

Ethics in Developmental Psychology — 97
Right to Privacy

Highlights Research Conferences: Furthering the Work of Developmental Psychologists — 98

Informed Consent/Protection of Participants from Harm

Applications for Ethical Research in Human Development — 100

Contents XV

Summary	101
Key Terms	101
Suggested Readings	102
Application Exercise	102

PART II   Biological and Social Bases for Development   104

CHAPTER 4   Evolution and Genetics   106

About Evolution   108
Principles of Evolution/The Evolution of Humankind

Genetics: Key to Development   115
Basic Concepts in Genetics/How Sex Is Determined/DNA: The Building Blocks of Life

Developmental Behavior Genetics   119
Epigenesis: A Biological Conception of Development/Personality Development/Intellectual Development

  Highlights   Sir Cyril Burt   126

  Research   Commentaries and Rejoinders in Developmental Research   128

Genetic Disorders   129
Problems in Meiosis/Genetic Disorders Based on Recessive Genes

Applications for Life: Advances in Genetics   132
Selecting Children's Sex/Genetic Counseling/Amniocentesis/The Future of Genetic Engineering

Summary	136
Key Terms	137
Suggested Readings	137
Application Exercises	138

CHAPTER 5   Social Influences on Development   139

The Structure of the Ecological Environment   141
Microsystems/Mesosystems/Exosystems/Macrosystems

A Closer Look at Social Contexts   145
Microsystem Influences on Development: Family Members/Microsystem Influences: Family Structure/Microsystem Influences: Par-

enting Styles/A Mesosystem: Relations Between the Home and the School/Exosystem Influences: Parents' Work and Children's Lives/Macrosystem Influences: Cultures and Subcultures

    Research   Comparing Cultures on Their Child-Rearing Methods   166

Macrosystem Influences: The Impact of Television

    Highlights   UNESCO and UNICEF: Two United Nations Agencies with a Commitment to Children and the Family   170

    Research   Children's Television in the United States: A Window on the World?   174

Television's Influences on Development: Applications

Social Influences on Development: Processes   177
Identification/Observational Learning and Imitation/Summary of Identification and Observational Learning

Summary   183
Key Terms   184
Suggested Readings   184
Application Exercises   185

PART III   Physical and Motor Development   186

CHAPTER 6   Prenatal Development and Birth   188

From Conception to Birth   189
The Germinal Period/The Embryonic Period/The Fetal Period/General Factors Influencing Prenatal Development/Negative Influences on Prenatal Development

Application: Guidelines for Expectant Parents   202

The Expectant Parents   203
Emotions in Expectant Mothers/Emotions in Expectant Fathers/Preparing for Parenthood

Birth   207
The Newborn Baby/Hospital Care of the Newborn/Complications in Birth

    Highlights   Alternative Child Birth Methods   210

Premature and Abnormally Small Babies

    Research   Home Intervention with Parents of Low Birthweight Babies   212

	Summary	213
	Key Terms	214
	Suggested Readings	214
	Application Exercise	214

CHAPTER 7 Physical Growth and Motor Development — 216

Patterns of Physical and Motor Development — 217
Cephalocaudal Development/Proximodistal Development/Differentiation and Integration

The Brain and Nervous System — 220
The Peripheral Nervous System/The Central Nervous System/The Growth of the CNS/The Two Hemispheres of the Brain/The Development of a Dominant Hemisphere/Summary of Brain and Nervous System Development

Physical Growth — 228
Normal Rates of Growth/Individual Growth Patterns/Sex Differences in Growth/Adolescent Growth/Psychological Aspects of Physical Growth

    Research Historical Trends in Size and Maturation — 239

Influences on Growth

    Highlights Childhood Obesity — 242

Applications: Facilitating Children's Growth

Motor Development — 246
Reflexes in the Newborn/Later Motor Development/Differences in Motor Development/Motor Development and Self-Image

Summary	255
Key Terms	255
Suggested Readings	256
Application Exercise	257

PART IV Intellectual Development — 258

CHAPTER 8 Theories of Cognitive Development — 260

Piaget's Theory — 261
The Nature of Intelligence/The Process of Intellectual Development

    Highlights Definitions of Piagetian Terms — 264

Stages of Intellectual Development
    Research Development of Object Permanence   268
Genetic Epistemology
    Highlights Beyond Formal Operations   276
Applications/Current Status of Piaget's Theory

Information Processing Theories   **284**
Siegler's Rule Assessment Approach/Sternberg's Componential Analysis/Case's Neo-Piagetian Theory/The Information Processing Paradigm/Educational Applications/Evaluation of the Information Processing Approach

Conclusions   **295**

Summary   **297**

Key Terms   **298**

Suggested Readings   **298**

Application Exercises   **299**

CHAPTER 9 Perceptual Development   301

Vision   **302**
The Eyes/The Development of Vision

Hearing   **313**
The Development of Hearing

Smell, Taste, and Touch   **316**
The Development of Smell, Taste, and Touch

Applications of Perception Research   **317**
    Research Sensory Deprivation   318

Theories of Perceptual Development   **320**
Jean Piaget: A Constructivist Theory
    Highlights The Gestalt Principles   322
Differentiation Theory

Reading Readiness: Applications of Perception Research   **329**

Summary   **330**

Key Terms   **331**

Suggested Readings   **331**

Application Exercises   **332**

CHAPTER 10 Development of Memory — 333

Infant Memory — 334
A Multistore Model of Memory — 337
Sense Receptors/Sensory Registers/Short-term Store/Long-term Store/Implications of the Multistore Model of Memory Development

Levels of Processing Models — 342
Constructive Models of Memory — 345
The Role of Inference in Children's Memory/The Effect of Context Cues/Constructive Processes in Story Memory/Summary of Constructive Processes in Children's Memory

Research Memories that Improve with Time? Piaget's Constructivist Views — 349

A Framework for Memory Development — 350
Knowing/Knowing How to Know/Knowing about Knowing: Metamemory

Highlights Children as Witnesses — 358

Applications of Memory Development Research — 361
Summary — 364
Key Terms — 365
Suggested Readings — 365
Application Exercise — 366

CHAPTER 11 Language Development — 368

Characteristics of Language — 372
Phones/Phonemes/Morphemes/Syntax/Semantics/Pragmatics

Language: What Develops? — 380
Early Speech Production/Early Speech Perception/First Words

Highlights What is the Relation Between Language and Thought? — 383

Early Sentences/Continuing Language Development

Research Do Social Factors Affect Early Language Development? Clues from a Longitudinal Study of Mother-Child Interaction — 392

Language Development: Applications for Parents and Teachers — 398
Summary — 400

Key Terms	401
Suggested Readings	401
Application Exercises	401

CHAPTER 12 Development of Reasoning — 403

Transitivity	404
Logical Necessity	408
Inferential Validity	409
Controlling Variables	412
Controlling Variables in Everyday Life	
Hypothesis Testing	416
Highlights Adolescent Reasoning and Adolescent Rights	418
Understanding Number	420
Metacognition: A Matter of Mind over Mind	423
Highlights Do Fleas Have Metafleas?	424
Philosophical Reasoning	426
Research Development of Reasoning About Knowledge and Reality	429
Conclusion: The Development of Rationality	429
Applications: Developing Reasoning	431
Highlights Should Schools Develop Reasoning?	432
Summary	435
Key Terms	436
Suggested Readings	436
Application Exercise	436

PART V Social and Personality Development — 438

CHAPTER 13 Emotional Development — 440

Biological Bases of Emotion	441
An Evolutionary Perspective on Emotions/The Physiological Basis of Emotions	

Emotional Development in Infancy and Early Childhood — 444
Birth to 1 Month: Insensitivity to Others' Emotions/1 to 3 Months: Turning Toward Others/3 to 6 Months: Positive Affect/7 to 9 Months: Active Participation/9 to 12 Months: Attachment/12 to 18 Months: Practicing/18 to 36 Months: Emergence of Self–Concept

Emotional Development in Childhood and Adolescence — 448

Research Causal Attributions and Emotions — 450

Fear/Anger

Highlights Children's Fears of Nuclear War — 454

Jealousy/Grief/Positive Emotions

Emotional Problems during Development — 460
Phobias/Psychosomatic and Psychophysiological Disorders/Depression and Suicide/Autism/Hyperactivity

Theoretical Perspectives on the Development of Emotions — 466
A Differentiation Theory of Emotional Development/Behavioral Views of Emotional Development/Cognition and Emotions/Other Theories of Emotional Development/A Summary of Theories of Emotional Development

Applications: Dealing with Fears and Anger — 475
Helping Children Deal with Fears/Helping Children Cope with Anger/Seeking Help

Summary — 479
Key Terms — 480
Suggested Readings — 481
Application Exercise — 481

CHAPTER 14 Social Development — 483

The Newborn: A "Sociable" Person — 485
Early Social Skills of Infants/Bonding

Attachment — 491
Individual Differences in Attachment/Long-Term Effects

Highlights Fathers and Attachment — 497

Relations with Peers and Social Development — 498
Origins of Peer Relations in Infancy/Becoming Friends/Children in Groups/Social Play among Peers

The Development of Aggression — 508
The Beginnings of Aggression/Further Development of Aggression/Sources of Aggression

Relationships and Social Development in Adolescence — 515
New Intimacy in Friendships/Same–Sex and Cross–Sex Friendships/Dating/Adolescent Sexuality: A New Dimension of Social Development

    Research   Consequences of Adolescent Sexuality in the United States — 520

Summary — 523
Key Terms — 524
Suggested Reading — 524
Application Exercise — 525

CHAPTER 15 Moral Development — 526

The Study of Morality — 528
The Absolutist Approach/The Relativist Approach/Beyond Relativism: Morality as Social Rationality

The Cognitive–Developmental Approach — 531
Elements of the Cognitive–Developmental Approach/Summary

Piaget's Theory of Moral Development — 534
Specific Developmental Changes/From Heteronomy to Autonomy/Peer Interaction and Moral Development/Research on Piaget's Theory

Kohlberg's Theory of Moral Development — 539
Six Stages of Moral Development/How Moral Development Occurs/Assessing Moral Reasoning

    Research   The Heinz Delimma — 543

Kohlberg's Theory: Research and Critiques — 544
Basic Research on Kohlberg's Stages/Sex Bias and the Scope of Morality/Moral Reasoning, Moral Feelings, and Moral Behavior

Applications: Moral Education — 555

    Highlights   Empathy and Altruism — 556

    Highlights   Are Vulcans Moral? — 559

Summary — 562
Key Terms — 563
Suggested Readings — 563
Application Exercise — 564

Contents xxiii

CHAPTER 16 Personality Development 565

Development of Self-Concept 567
Self–Understanding and Self-Esteem/"I" vs. "Me"/Development of the "Me"/Development of the "I"/Conclusions: The Construction of Self

Sex–Typing and the Development of Sex Roles 573
Stereotypes and Reality/Young Children's Awareness of Sex Roles/ Biological and Cultural Bases for Sex Differences/Theories of Sex–Typing

    Research Adult Reactions to Young Boys and Girls 577

Androgyny/A Dialectical Postscript

A Psychoanalytic Approach to Personality Development 581
Freud's Theory/Erikson's Theory/Marcia's Theory of Identity Formation/Conclusion

A Cognitive–Developmental Approach to Personality Development 589
Stages of Personality Development/The Process of Personality Development

Applications 595

    Highlights The Construction and Limitations of Identity 596

Summary 598

Key Terms 599

Suggested Readings 599

Application Exercises 600

Glossary 603
Answers to Application Exercises 627
References 637
Name Index 691
Subject Index 701

Prologue

Newborn infants are extraordinary creatures. In some ways they seem completely helpless and vulnerable. At the same time, however, they are remarkably effective in attracting the attention of adults and getting their needs met. Very young infants generally strike us as completely naive and ignorant. But research now shows they have sophisticated and adaptive reflexes, actively look and listen, and are capable of learning and developing rapidly.

Over the first 18 months of life, infants change dramatically. They become physically much larger and stronger and become able to turn over, reach for and manipulate objects, crawl, stand, and eventually walk. They increasingly understand that their environments consist of objects located in space and events taking place over the course of time. They become more sophisticated in perceiving the details of objects and events and remembering things that happened earlier. They increasingly understand the language spoken by people around them and even begin to learn words and use them to communicate. The general positive and negative feelings of the very young infant evolve into more specific emotions such as fear, joy, anger, surprise, and distress. Infants become capable of increasingly complex and subtle interactions with other people and develop strong emotional attachments to the major people in their lives. In fact, those who know an infant well can witness the gradual development of what will become his or her unique personality.

Children of 1½ or 2 are so different from newborn infants that we usually refer to them as toddlers. During this period, unsteady toddling becomes walking and even running, allowing the toddler to explore more and more of the environment—and get into more and more trouble! Spoken language skyrockets, moving from individual words to a substantial vocabulary and an impressive ability to put words together into grammatical (though short) sentences. Toddlers begin to relate effectively to children their own age, as well as to adults, and to understand and respond to the feelings of others. If all goes well, toddlers develop a sense of autonomy, perceiving themselves as independent beings with wills of their own.

Preschool children of ages 3, 4, and 5 are remarkably mature compared to what they were like just a few years earlier and yet are still childish in many ways. Physically, of course, they are larger, stronger, and faster than before—and this shows in much of their activity. They can understand and use complex sentences and carry on coherent conversations. They often show accurate and sophisticated reasoning, though there are still sharp limitations on their ability to do this. They form friendships with each other and show increasingly complex play and sophisticated social interactions. They begin to think—albeit simplistically—about moral issues. They see themselves as girls or as boys and show surprisingly accurate awareness of cultural attitudes about sex differences. If all is going well, they are into everything—enthusiastic, playing vigorously, and learning rapidly.

In most modern societies, some sort of formal schooling begins about the age of 6. This is so central to the child's life that the period from about age 6 to 12 is often called "the school years." School-age children learn to read and write, to communicate more effectively, and to reason more systematically. They even begin to think about their own mental processes and to develop strategies for better learning and remembering. Their social environments expand far beyond the family. Friendships become deeper and more meaningful as they learn to understand the feelings of others and to see things from other perspectives. They increasingly think about themselves in terms of their abilities and accomplishments.

Adolescence, roughly corresponding to the teen-age years, is typically seen as the transition from childhood to adulthood. Rapid physical changes dramatically affect one's image of one's own body. Sexual maturity opens up a whole new realm of feelings, challenges, and possibilities. There is increasing ability to think logically about abstract, theoretical matters, to systematically generate and test hypotheses, and to explore alternatives in depth. Peers become extremely important and the moral dimensions of one's social relationships are better understood. As one moves toward adulthood, there is likely to be an active search for an identity of one's own, a sense of who you are as a person.

But development does not necessarily end with achievement of adult status. One does not simply form an identity and enter a long plateau of intellectual and social maturity. Instead, current evidence suggests that at least some adults continue to develop in many ways. They may develop more subtle ways of thinking that go beyond the systematic logic of adolescence, that reflect deeper insights into the complex nature of knowledge and reality. Their moral conceptions may change as they come to better understand the political and social structures of their societies and to consider alternatives to these. Having constructed a firm identity, one may find that new sorts of intimacy are now possible, and this may lead to greater feelings of responsibility to future generations and a deeper sense of one's place in the cycle of life.

The above account raises a number of fascinating questions that deserve to be explored in greater depth. You may have thought of some yourself, but let us suggest several that occur to us.

What specific changes occur in children's bodies and how do these relate to changes in their physical abilities? How do young children perceive and remember things? How do their perceptions and memories change? How do they manage to learn language so rapidly and effectively? What sorts of reasoning develop at various ages?

What emotions develop and what role do they play in our lives? Are there predictable age-related changes in how children relate to their parents and peers? How do young children think about moral issues? Why and how do their moral reasoning and behavior change? How and what do children learn about being male or female? Should we change the way we approach this issue? What do children think about their own personalities? How do personalities change? Do all people continue to develop during adulthood?

On what information do psychologists base their conclusions about the above matters? How do psychologists get new information? What theories are used to organize and explain what is known about development? How accurate are these theories? What issues are currently being investigated?

This book will address all of the above questions and many more. We hope that as you move through the chapters you will agree with us that, at its best, the study of development is as exciting and challenging as development itself.

PART I

An Introduction to Developmental Psychology

The first three chapters of this book introduce the field of developmental psychology: its history and issues, its theoretical perspectives, and its research methods. We will see that developmental psychology addresses a number of controversial and important issues, that it provides a variety of illuminating theories, and that it uses a range of research methodologies to gather new evidence and test those theories. But it would be a mistake to view the field as a fixed set of official issues, accepted theories, and approved methods. On the contrary, just as studying the development of children and adults broadens our understanding of them, we can learn about the field of developmental psychology by examining its collective history.

CHAPTER 1

Developmental Psychology: History and Issues

There is nothing permanent except change.
—Heraclitus

For as long as there have been people, there have been developing children. Developmental psychology as an area of scientific research, however, is only about a century old. In this chapter, we will briefly consider views about children prior to the rise of developmental psychology. Then we will look at factors leading to the emergence of developmental psychology in the late nineteenth century and influencing its development between then and now. Next, we will examine the views of some major early developmental psychologists. We will see that many of the issues they dealt with are much older than developmental psychology, going back to early controversies about how to raise children. In the last section of the chapter, we will examine the form these controversies take in contemporary developmental psychology.

The History of Children

History, as it is usually written and taught in the United States, typically focuses on the political, economic, and military affairs of well-to-do white men in Western society. Historical information about daily life, especially for women, ethnic minorities, and the poor, is harder to find (Zinn, 1980). Information about the treatment of children is even less available and what little exists provides limited insight into what life was like from the children's point of view.

This is an unfortunate situation. Since people's conceptions of children reflect their views about life, humanity, and society, we could learn much about a particular culture by studying its treatment of children. Further, by understanding the experience of children in the thousands of societies that have existed over the course of history, we could gain insight into all of those cultures. Fortunately, historians recently have shown increasing interest in studying the daily lives of ordinary families and children and so information on these topics is becoming more available (Borstelmann, 1983).

Historical accounts of childhood often paint a rosy picture of recent progress. Until the past few centuries, the story goes, children were unloved and harshly treated. Unwanted infants were left on mountainsides to die of exposure. Because families were large and many children died, parents avoided forming emotional attachments to their children. Children were likely to be beaten severely for even minor infractions and were sent to work at very early ages. Today, on the contrary, we are told, parents are highly committed to their children, protect them from harm, value their individuality, and carefully nurture their development.

Although there is some truth in the above picture of historical change (Aries, 1962; Piers, 1978), it is not entirely accurate. Children in ancient Greece, for example, were commonly a loved and important part of the family. Authorities of the time noted the special needs of children for protection, affection, play, guidance, and education (Borstelmann, 1983). And children in the United States today are not all as

In seventeenth-century New England, the Puritans believed children were inherently sinful and should be taught absolute submission to parents and the will of God.

Philosopher Jean-Jacques Rousseau stressed respect for children's natural interests.

well off as the account above suggests. On the contrary, many of them are neglected, exploited, beaten, sexually abused, or even murdered by their own parents.

Thus it is an exaggeration to say that there is a universal historical trend toward better understanding and treatment of children. In fact, a striking aspect of the history of childhood is the recurrence of certain issues that never seem to get resolved.

One such unresolved issue is the nature of the child. Is the child basically evil, basically good, or neither? The view that the child is basically evil has been, and still is, central to the disciplinary practices of many social groups. In the seventeenth century, for example, the Puritans who settled New England saw children as inherently sinful. Children needed to be taught absolute submission to parental authority and the will of God, preferably through reason and love, but, if necessary, through physical force. "There is in all children," admonished minister John Robinson in 1618, "a stubbornness, and stoutness of mind arising from natural pride, which must, in the first place, be broken and beaten down" (Borstelmann, 1983, p. 14).

The view that children are basically good is usually associated with the Swiss philosopher Jean-Jacques Rousseau (1712–1778). Rousseau believed that children's natural tendencies should be understood and respected and, with proper guidance, would lead toward mature intellect and morality. Rousseau's work was widely read and greatly influenced European parents and educators of his period. Interpreters of Rousseau often were highly skeptical of social influences, leading to a view of the child as a flowering seed and of society as a hindrance to the child's natural and proper development.

Finally, the view of the child as neutral is associated with the English philosopher John Locke (1632–1704). He saw the child at birth as a *tabula rasa*, or blank slate, neither naturally good nor naturally evil, but capable of developing in either direction depending on environment and education. Locke's views had enormous influence on other philosophers and, eventually, on psychological theories of learning (see Chapter 2, *Theories of Developmental Psychology*).

As we will see, the controversy over whether children have an inherent nature—and, if so, what that nature is—has taken many forms

Philosopher John Locke emphasized the role of learning from one's environment.

and continues to the present day. Many other questions related to treatment of children over the centuries also have remained highly relevant. Are children simply smaller versions of adults or do they have age-specific characteristics that need to be understood and taken into account? Should we teach children to fit a preordained role in society or should we focus on each child's unique personality and encourage his or her individuality? Should we prepare children to continue the traditions of current society or to be able to adapt to a different future? Should child-rearing focus on moral and spiritual development or on the development of the intellect? How important are early experiences to later development? Various societies have answered these questions differently and there remain strong differences of opinion about these issues within our own society.

Influences on the Development of Developmental Psychology

The history of an intellectual discipline always involves both the internal development of the discipline itself and the external factors that affected it. In this section, we will consider two sorts of external factors that have greatly influenced the scientific study of development: first, important ideas from other fields of study; and second, a variety of societal influences. Then, in the following section, we will trace the internal history of developmental psychology by studying the views of its major early theorists and researchers.

Ideas from Other Fields

Developmental psychology has been influenced profoundly by evolutionary concepts and by the rise of experimental psychology, psychoanalysis, behaviorism, and cognitive psychology. We will consider each of these in turn.

Evolution. A major feature of intellectual life in the nineteenth century was **historicism**, the idea that to understand something in depth one must consider its history (Dixon & Lerner, 1984). With respect to the living world, the historicist perspective involved the view that species evolve over long periods of time. Although Charles Darwin (1809–1882) did not originate this idea, his classic 1859 work, *The Origin of Species*, provided a convincing account of biological evolution and detailed supportive evidence (see Chapter 4, *Evolution and Genetics*). Within a few decades the concept of **evolution** was not only widely accepted but had become the major organizing framework for the entire field of biology—a position it maintains to this day. Moreover, the concept of evolution revolutionized thinking in a number of other fields. In fact, like the earlier discovery that the earth was not the center of the solar system,

The evolutionary perspective led to a view of the human species as part of the natural world.

it forced educated people to reconsider their place and role in the universe.

One of the fields most affected by the evolutionary perspective was the emerging science of developmental psychology (Dixon & Lerner, 1984; but see also Charlesworth, 1986). Darwinism influenced the thinking of early developmentalists in at least seven ways. First, it led to a focus on change as a central aspect of nature. To be always changing is an inherent part of what it means to be a person. People cannot be understood unless we consider how they change across time—that is, their development.

Second, an evolutionary perspective presents humankind not as a special creation but as a species of organism, with ties to other living things. This view led to an emphasis on **comparative research**, in which the psychologist studies a variety of species in order to discover general laws of development. Such research is based on the assumption that human beings, though unique in some respects, are also similar to other species in important ways.

Third, the idea of continuity between seemingly different species led to the idea of continuity between children and adults. Thus it began to make more sense to study children as well as adults and to try to decipher the transformation from child to adult.

Fourth, Darwin's view of evolution stressed that species change in such a way as to become increasingly suited to their environments. This perspective led to an emphasis on the role of various behaviors in helping a person (or other organism) deal with the environment and on the role of the environment in causing behaviors to change.

Fifth, Darwin stressed individual differences within a species as providing the basis for evolution. Those individuals better adapted to their environments would be more likely to survive and pass their characteristics on to their offspring, thus resulting in gradual change in the characteristics of the species. For developmental psychologists, this belief suggested that differences among children could be of great scientific significance.

Sixth, evolutionists in the late nineteenth century believed that **ontogeny** recapitulates **phylogeny**. Ontogeny refers to the development of an individual and phylogeny to the evolution of the species. Thus the phrase "ontogeny recapitulates phylogeny" means that the development of each individual recreates the sequence of events in the evolution of that species. Just as single-celled organisms evolved over many millions of years into fish, then amphibians, then reptiles, and eventually mammals, a mammalian embryo would develop from a single cell to a fish-like state, then to a reptilian state, and eventually show mammalian characteristics. Early developmental psychologists were eager to see whether this sort of parallelism would hold for human psychological development. Would young children, for example, show thinking similar to that of people in "primitive" societies? We now know that the doctrine that ontogeny recapitulates phylogeny, at least if taken literally, is rather naive. Nevertheless, the issue of parallels among individual development, societal history, and evolution of the species remains of great interest.

Finally, an evolutionary perspective gave new meaning to questions about whether there is such a thing as a fundamental human nature (e.g., are children born evil?) or whether development is instead driven by "nurture" (e.g., children are "blank slates" who learn from their environments). As we will see, the issue of whether development is driven by nature (heredity) or nurture (the environment) is still with us.

The Rise of Scientific Psychology. The study of child development has always been influenced by events in the field of psychology as a whole. When Darwin's *The Origin of Species* was published in 1859, psychology was a branch of philosophy. During the 1860s and 1870s, an increasing number of psychologists began to see that their ideas about the human mind could and should be tested through research. The idea that psychological theories should be based on and tested against systematic evidence transformed psychology from a branch of philosophy to an experimental science. By 1879, when the German psychologist Wilhelm Wundt (1832–1920) founded a major psychological laboratory at the University of Leipzig, the science of psychology was well under way.

Wundt himself limited his research to adults and was highly skeptical of the view that serious experimental research on young children was worthwhile or even possible (Cairns, 1983). Other psychologists disagreed, however, and attempted to apply the new methods of scientific psychology to the study of children and development. This work, to be further discussed below, transformed early child study into scientific developmental psychology over the course of the 1880s and 1890s.

Psychoanalysis. As we have seen, Darwin's *The Origin of Species* was a book that not only promoted an important biological theory but also profoundly influenced humanity's conception of itself. A book with a similar sort of impact was *The Interpretation of Dreams*, published in 1900 by the Austrian psychiatrist Sigmund Freud (1856–1939). This book launched **psychoanalysis**, a perspective that profoundly influenced the study of history, anthropology, sociology, literature, and almost every branch of psychology. Today, most people accept, at least to some extent, the idea that much of our behavior is not based on conscious, rational decisions but rather is rooted in unconscious emotional and sexual factors that can be traced back to childhood experiences. In the opening years of the twentieth century, however, this idea was new and radical, and deeply threatened people's basic conceptions of human nature.

Although Freud himself did very little work—and no systematic research—with children, his theory proposed that all children develop through a sequence of psycho-sexual stages and that experiences during the first four or five years of life set the foundation for adult personality, morality, sex roles, and psychological problems. Thus, his work directly suggested the importance of developmental psychology. Freud's followers, including his highly influential daughter Anna Freud, worked directly with children and proposed important ideas about child development. Other theorists modified Freud's ideas in significant ways. Erik Erikson's lifespan theory of personality development, to be discussed in Chapter 16, is a well-known example. Finally, even non-Freudian developmental (and nondevelopmental) psychologists have found a wealth of ideas in psychoanalytic thinking and incorporated these into their own work (Cairns, 1983). Psychoanalytic ideas were a major force in developmental psychology during the 1920s, 1930s, and 1940s, and continue to be important today.

Behaviorism. Psychoanalysis can be seen as having moved psychology below the surface of human thought into the mysterious depths of the unconscious mind. Many considered this an exciting and important direction of inquiry. Other psychologists, however, regarded it as a critical error. For psychology to be a science, they argued, it must abandon the unscientific concept of "mind" entirely and focus on observable behavior. This view became known as **behaviorism**.

The leader of these behaviorists was John B. Watson (1878–1957), whose classic 1913 article, "Psychology as the Behaviorist Views It," has been called the single most important paper ever published in American psychology (Wertheimer, 1978). Watson proposed that psychology should be a completely objective science. Since only behavior can be observed objectively, he argued, scientific psychology must abandon the study of mind and consciousness and focus exclusively on behavior. By the 1930s, many American psychologists had accepted this view and behaviorism became the dominant orientation within American psychology, a position it maintained through the 1940s and 1950s. Many, though not all, American developmental psychologists followed this trend and turned their attention to systematic observations of children's behavior and the effects of experimental manipulations. Research on children's minds continued in Europe but, except for a continuing interest in psychoanalytic ideas, was rare in the United States during this period.

Cognitive Psychology. Beginning around 1960, research on thinking, or cognition, reemerged in American psychology. The limitations of an exclusive focus on observable behavior were becoming apparent and the advent of computers led to a cognitive view of the person as a processor of information. This new perspective, called **cognitive psychology**, extended to developmental psychology and led the field to become once again sympathetic to research on mental development, especially the work of the Swiss psychologist Jean Piaget (see below). Even research on children's social, emotional, and personality development reflected the new emphasis on cognition, which continues to the present.

Social Forces

We have seen how developmental psychology has been affected by intellectual trends within psychology and related fields. We now turn to social influences from outside the realm of science.

Increasing Attention to Education. As societies have become more complex over the past centuries, it has become increasingly necessary for people to be educated systematically. A greater proportion of jobs have required workers with broad knowledge and sophisticated skills. Moreover, democratic self-government requires well-informed citizens ca-

Highlights

The Role of Women in Developmental Psychology

Before about 1970, nearly all work in most scholarly disciplines was conducted by men. It is only since then that, due to changing attitudes about the roles of women in society, substantial numbers of women have received doctorates and made major contributions in most fields.

Developmental psychology, however, is a major exception to the above generalization. Perhaps this is because, even in the days when it was considered odd for a woman to be involved in scientific research, it was socially acceptable for a woman to be concerned with children. In any event, women have always been better represented and far more influential in developmental psychology than in most other fields. As far back as the 1890s, Millicent Shinn was publishing systematic observations of infant development that eventually led to her classic *Biography of a Baby* (Shinn, 1900). By the 1920s and 1930s, there were a substantial number of prominent female developmentalists. Nancy Bayley did major work on the assessment of intellect. Charlotte Bühler studied a variety of topics ranging from young children's social development to adolescent personality. Anna Freud pioneered the field of child psychoanalysis. Florence Goodenough studied a variety of topics and constructed the widely used "Draw-A-Person" test. Mary Cover Jones, an associate of John B. Watson, did experimental research on children's emotions. Dorothy McCarthy investigated the development of language and thought. Myrtle McGraw studied the effects of enriched experience on development. Martha Muchow examined the "life space" of the urban child. Lois Murphy explored young children's feelings of sympathy. Mary Shirley traced various aspects of infant development. Lois Meek Stolz was Director of the Columbia University Child Development Institute and a pioneer in parent education.

The study of development profited greatly from all of this innovative and important work. Today, when women are beginning to have an impact in a wide variety of academic disciplines, female developmental psychologists are a major force, well represented among the most productive researchers, editors of influential journals, and officers of major professional organizations. We will be examining their work throughout this book.

pable of making reasoned judgments about difficult issues. Thus, the proportion of children attending formal schools and the number of years they attend have increased steadily. This has led to more attention to the process of education and to the recognition that to improve education we need to have a better understanding of how children think, learn, and develop.

Over the centuries, philosophers and social theorists have considered educational questions. Many of these scholars tried to deal with these issues on the basis of their views of child development. One particularly important philosopher of education, whose work coincided with the early decades of developmental psychology, was John Dewey (1859–1952). Dewey rejected the traditional view of education in which the teacher is an authority who transmits knowledge and values to children in order to allow them to take their proper place in an unchanging society. Instead, he argued for a humanistic, child-centered approach to education that would enable each child to realize his or her potential as an active thinker and problem-solver. Children should be prepared not to take a fixed role in the existing society but to adapt to a constantly changing society and to play a role themselves in social progress. In short, Dewey argued, the central goal of education should be development. Many early developmental psychologists agreed with Dewey's view of children and with the idea that scientific study of child development should be the basis for education (Davidson & Benjamin, in press).

Child Study Institutes. Another source of support for developmental psychology was the belief that child-rearing in general, as well as education, could profit from systematic developmental research. An Iowa housewife named Cora Bussey Hillis, for example, proposed in 1906 that a research station be established to study and improve child-rearing. "Her argument," wrote Cairns (1983, p. 65) "was simple but compelling: If research could improve corn and hogs, why could it not improve the rearing of children?" The University of Iowa Child Welfare Research Station was established in 1917 and similar child development institutes began operation across the United States and Canada over the next two decades. Cairns (1983) refers to the 1920s and 1930s as a "golden age" of child development research in the United States, marked by the founding of major new journals and magazines, establishment of advanced degree programs, availability of substantial research grants, initiation of long-term developmental studies, and the formation in 1933 of the Society for Research in Child Development.

Early Developmentalists

We have seen that a variety of intellectual and social factors affected developmental psychology. We now move inside the discipline itself and trace the views and activities of its major theorists and researchers. We will begin with those scholars generally seen as establishing developmental psychology as a vigorous area of scientific investigation.

Founders of a New Field

Of the earliest developmental psychologists, four stand out: Wilhelm Preyer, G. Stanley Hall, Alfred Binet, and James Mark Baldwin. Although the four differed greatly from each other in background and approach, they set the tone and direction for the emerging field of developmental psychology.

Wilhelm Preyer (1841–1897). It is usually difficult to pinpoint the origin of a new intellectual discipline since, like a new concept, a new skill, or anything else, a new discipline is rooted always in what came before. Nevertheless, Robert Cairns (1983) suggests that if one must pick a date for the beginning of developmental psychology as a scientific discipline, the year 1882 is a reasonable choice. That was the year in which the German scholar Wilhelm Preyer published *Die Seele des Kindes*, later translated as *The Mind of the Child*. Like the other early developmental psychologists, Preyer was not trained in developmental psychology: There was no such field when he was a student. His original field was physiology and he remained interested in biological issues throughout his life. Under the influence of evolutionary thinking, however, he came to focus more and more on the process of development.

Preyer's developmental research was highly biological. He was very interested, for example, in prenatal development (i.e., development prior to birth). Moreover, he systematically studied and compared development in a number of species. Even at his biological extreme, however, Preyer's focus as a physiologist was not on *anatomy* (the *structure* of the body) but rather on *physiology* (bodily *processes*). From there, it was only one more step to the study of *behavior*; and Preyer took that step, thus moving into the uncharted realm of psychology. Preyer was deeply interested in how the organism's behavior, both before and after birth, is influenced by prior development and in turn affects later development.

The Mind of the Child can be seen as a contribution to the distinguished tradition of "baby biographies." In the century before *The Mind of the Child* appeared, a number of individuals (including Darwin himself) had published careful observations of early development based on their own children. Preyer's book is often considered, however, the first genuinely *scientific* contribution. In part, this is due to Preyer's theoretical breadth and systematic interpretation. He saw the mind of the child as consisting of three major components—Senses, Will, and Intellect—and analyzed the development of each.

Perhaps more notable than Preyer's theoretical breadth, however, was his careful methodology. He insisted that scientists must observe children directly, write down all details before these become distorted, avoid artificial situations and training, include observations that do not relate to theoretical questions of immediate interest, and test reliability by comparing their observations with independent observations made by others. Preyer thus anticipated many of the important methodological requirements of good research that we will discuss in Chapter 3, *Research Methods*.

Preyer's work was an important first step in the establishment of developmental psychology. As Cairns (1983, p. 46) put it, "Preyer demonstrated, by his successful integration of experimental studies of human and nonhuman young, that the investigation of behavioral development could be as much a scientific enterprise as a social, humanistic movement."

G. Stanley Hall (1844–1924). When Preyer's *The Mind of the Child* was first published in the United States, the foreword was written by G. Stanley Hall. During the first four decades of developmental psychology, no one was more active than Hall in bringing European ideas to America and establishing developmental psychology on this side of the Atlantic.

Hall's own research covered a wide variety of topics. With respect to methodology, he was best known for popularizing questionnaire research. He and his followers asked thousands of children questions about a wide variety of topics to determine their knowledge and attitudes at various ages. By modern standards, the data collection was haphazard and the results difficult to interpret. Nevertheless, the ambitious scope of the research was an exciting advance for an emerging field (Davidson & Benjamin, in press).

With respect to theory, Hall was deeply committed to the view that ontogeny recapitulates phylogeny, as discussed earlier. He believed that children's psychological development follows a natural course that recreates the evolutionary history of the species. Fearing that artificial pressures from parents and teachers could be very harmful to the developing child, Hall thus can be seen as somewhat in the Rousseau tradition, viewing the child as a flowering plant that must be permitted to follow its natural course. He believed, however, that this predictable course ends at the beginning of adolescence. Adolescence is thus, according to Hall, a critical time when possibilities open up and development can proceed in many different directions.

Hall's major contribution to developmental psychology, however, was neither his theories nor his research. He was, above all, an open-minded enthusiast. He delighted in learning about and exploring a wide variety of ideas, communicating them to others, and spreading his enormous enthusiasm for the scientific and practical possibilities of developmental psychology (as well as psychology in general). Hall was founder and first editor of the first American psychology journal (the *American Journal of Psychology*) in 1887 and of the first English-language developmental journal (*Pedagogical Seminary*, now retitled *Journal of Genetic Psychology*) in 1891. He founded a child study institute at Clark University in 1891, decades before such institutes became popular. He was the first president of the American Psychological Association (1892) and of the Child Study Section of the National Education Association (1893). He wrote the first textbook ever published on adolescent psychology (1904) and the first American textbook on aging (1922). As the first president of Clark University, he arranged the historic first (and only) visit of Sigmund Freud to the United States in 1909.

Through his activities, Hall interested a number of psychologists in developmental issues and convinced many educators of the relevance of developmental psychology. He is remembered today for his own research and ideas and, even more, for the excitement and enthusiasm he brought to the study of psychological development.

Alfred Binet (1857–1911). Meanwhile, in France, psychology was under the sway of a man of equally wide-ranging interests and equally limitless energy. As Cairns (1983) noted, in 1894 alone Alfred Binet (pronounced Bih-nay') was awarded a doctorate in natural science from the Sorbonne, was appointed Director of the Laboratory of Physiological Psychology there, founded and edited the journal *L'Année Psychologique*, co-authored two books, and published 15 articles. His topics included the extraordinary memories of chessmasters and mathematical wizards, experimental methodologies in psychology, the psychology of aesthetics, suggestibility, the nervous system of invertebrates, children's perception, and the development of memory. His accomplishments in 1895 were comparable. "He maintained this pattern until his death in 1911," added Cairns (1983, p. 47), "except that later in his career he also wrote and supervised several plays that were produced in Paris and London."

Binet believed that a productive research program requires flexible use of a variety of methodologies. He criticized psychologists who relied exclusively on what he saw as limited approaches. He wrote, for example, that the laboratory experiments of Wundt and his followers were narrow in scope and artificial, while the large-scale questionnaires of Hall and his associates were very shallow, typical of "American authors, who love to do things big" (Binet, 1903, p. 299). Binet himself studied large groups *and* individuals, including both normal children and special populations, presenting them with a wide variety of research stimuli and measuring a number of different responses.

Binet's central interest was in cognition, including memory, reasoning, and intelligence. In many ways his work was far ahead of its time. He concluded, for example, that memory is not a passive copying of what one has encountered. Instead, he proposed that children actively reorganize materials on the basis of what is meaningful to them. Binet thus saw memory as an active construction of the mind, a view that did not become popular in the United States until the 1960s and 1970s but now dominates memory research (see Chapter 10, *Development of Memory*).

Binet was interested particularly in individual differences in intelligence. At the time, most psychologists believed that they were based on differences in simple processes such as immediate sensations and perceptions. Binet questioned this view. He suggested that differences in intelligence were linked to complex, higher-level processes, such as reasoning, problem-solving, and use of language.

Around the turn of the century, the French Ministry of Public Instruction became very interested in the needs of retarded children and asked Binet to develop tests to identify such children so they could receive special instruction. In collaboration with Theophile Simon, Binet set to work developing a test that included a carefully arranged set of tasks to assess a variety of complex mental processes. His work was highly successful and resulted in the first IQ test. It is for this work that Binet is best remembered.

Other psychologists further developed methods for assessing intelligence. Interestingly, many came to believe that intelligence as measured by IQ tests is a fixed quantity determined by a person's heredity. Binet himself, however, did not believe this. He argued (as do most current psychologists) that a child's intelligence is greatly influenced by his or her environment and can be improved substantially. Whatever one thinks of IQ tests, there is no doubt they are one of psychology's most influential contributions to twentieth century society.

James Mark Baldwin (1861–1934). In a recent book, John Broughton and D. John Freeman-Moir (1982, p. 2) wrote:

> As the searchlight of inquiry now begins to turn back upon late nineteenth- and early twentieth-century psychology, an imposing figure can be dimly discerned in history's shadows. This mysterious individual developed a genetic epistemology nearly half a century before Piaget, brought into prominence the concepts of cognitive assimilation and accommodation, and proposed a progressive stage-by-stage intellectual development as a continuation and extension of principles of biological organization and adaptation. . . . The shadowy figure who stands at the center of our concerns is James Mark Baldwin.

If, among the early developmentalists, Preyer was the systematic observer, Hall the enthusiastic popularizer, and Binet the multifaceted experimenter, the American James Mark Baldwin was the great systembuilder. Well-versed in biology and philosophy as well as in psychology, he took a broad perspective on development and constructed a cross-disciplinary theoretical perspective to explain developmental phenomena. "Give us theories, theories, always theories!" he proclaimed. "Let every man who has a theory pronounce his theory!" (Baldwin, 1895, pp. 37–38).

Early developmental psychologists were intent on making developmental psychology a genuine science rather than a branch of philosophy or a continuation of pre-scientific child study. They put great emphasis on careful observation and rigorous experimentation. One can almost hear them cry, "Give us data, data, always data! Let everyone who has some data, publish it!"

Although Baldwin recognized the value of such research, he felt most psychologists, by overreacting against philosophical and humanistic speculation, were failing to see the importance of theory. Science, Baldwin argued, is more than the systematic collection of data. Genuine science gives a central role to theories, which are necessary to interpret available data and to guide the collection of new data (see Chapter 2, *Theories of Developmental Psychology*). Baldwin's theories reflected his interests in intellectual, social, and personality development, as well as the relation between individual development and evolution of the species. In addition to his status in developmental psychology, he is considered a founder of the field of social psychology (Broughton & Freeman-Moir, 1982, pp. 2–3) and has been influential among evolutionary theorists.

Baldwin used the term **genetic epistemology** to refer to his broad theoretical approach to the development of knowledge. His general perspective included strong views on some of the central issues of development. He saw development not as just any long-term change but as a *progressive* change, one that moved in a predictable direction. Moreover, he emphasized, developmental changes are *qualitative* rather than just quantitative: That is, the more developed individual has more organized and effective ways of thinking about things, not just more knowledge. Intellectual development can thus be seen as a series of distinct **stages**, each involving a higher level of logic than the preceding one. But new stages do not simply appear; they are actively constructed by the knower. As we will see, all of these ideas are central to the theory of Jean Piaget, who can be seen as Baldwin's most direct intellectual descendent.

As is often the case with the work of intellectual pioneers, many of Baldwin's ideas were far ahead of their time and have only recently been appreciated fully. One idea that now strikes us as very modern is his refusal to accept the position that heredity and environment are in opposition. Baldwin saw no need to argue about whether development is directed by one's heredity or by one's environment. Heredity and environment work together and are both critical; development is a complex interaction of the two. Similarly, Baldwin rejected the simplistic idea that children are passive entities molded by parents, teachers, and others. On the contrary, he asserted, children influence their social environments at the same time that their environments influence them. This idea also has come to be widely accepted only in the past couple of decades.

In later works, Baldwin turned increasingly toward philosophy. Then, in 1909, he was found in a Baltimore brothel in what Dewsbury

Early Developmentalists

(1984, p. 296) characterized as "a position that could not be described as philosophical." American academia was scandalized and Baldwin was forced to resign his position at Johns Hopkins University. He eventually ended up in Paris, where "the French laughed off the whole affair and warmly welcomed him to their country for the rest of his days" (Broughton & Freeman-Moir, 1982, p. 4). His contributions to developmental psychology unfortunately dwindled, though he wrote and worked extensively on political issues and published an autobiography. He had already accomplished more than enough, however, to establish himself as a major figure in the history of developmental psychology.

The Second Generation

During the 1880s and 1890s, while Preyer, Hall, Binet, and Baldwin were founding a new science of developmental psychology, Arnold Gesell was born in Wisconsin, Heinz Werner in Austria, Jean Piaget in Switzerland, and Lev Vygotsky in Russia. By the 1920s, all four had established themselves as important young developmental psychologists, a second generation.

Arnold Gesell (1880–1961). Arnold Gesell grew up in Alma, a small town in Wisconsin. He received his Ph.D. in psychology from Clark University, while G. Stanley Hall was president there. Then Gesell earned an M.D. at Yale, where he founded the Clinic of Child Development in 1911 and spent the rest of his highly productive career.

Psychologists use the term **maturation** to refer to a developmental sequence that is directed by biological factors rather than by environmental influences. Gesell typically is cited as the preeminent maturational theorist. He can be seen as an intellectual descendent of Rousseau, who stressed the idea of a natural developmental course, and of Hall, who emphasized the evolutionary basis of individual development. Gesell believed that children's own self-regulatory processes make them much less vulnerable to environmental variations than one might expect. There are limits to this, of course, but within a wide range of environments, children naturally compensate for external factors.

> All things considered, the inevitableness and surety of maturation are the most impressive characteristics of early development. It is the hereditary ballast which conserves and stabilizes the growth of each individual infant. . . . The inborn tendency toward optimal development is so inveterate that he benefits liberally from what is good in our practice, and suffers less than he logically should from our unenlightenment (Gesell, 1928, p. 378).

Gesell is best known for his work establishing **developmental norms**—that is, average ages for the emergence of various behaviors and accomplishments (somewhat in the tradition of Preyer). He emphasized, of course, that children develop at different rates but believed that the basic sequences are the same for all and that it is helpful to compare individual children to general norms and thus chart their progress. His books about the typical characteristics of children at various ages are classics.

Gesell was also very interested in child-rearing. Before Dr. Benjamin Spock, who was influenced by Gesell's work, published his famous book on parenting in 1945, Gesell was the best-known "baby doctor" in the United States (Crain, 1985). Like Hall before him, Gesell believed parents should respect the natural course of development and not try to push children along too rapidly. Trying to teach a child something she is not ready for is at best a waste of time, in this view, and at worst may yield frustration for both parent and child and interfere with spontaneous developmental processes.

Most psychologists today believe that the environment plays more of a role than Gesell's work suggested. Nevertheless, his work provided a useful corrective to views like those of J. B. Watson, who focused almost exclusively on environmental shaping of the child. As Crain (1985, p. 23) put it,

> In Gesell's hands, Rousseau's idea of an inner developmental force became the guiding principle behind extensive scholarship and research. Gesell showed how the maturational mechanism, while still hidden, manifests itself in intricate developmental sequences and self-regulatory processes. Gesell indicated that there are good reasons to suppose that development follows an inner plan.

Heinz Werner (1890–1964). Heinz Werner (pronounced Ver'-ner) grew up in Vienna, Austria, and went to the University of Vienna to study music. One day, he mistakenly went to the wrong lecture hall and, too embarrassed to leave, ended up hearing a lecture about the German philosopher Immanuel Kant. It sparked his interest and he soon decided to major in philosophy and psychology (Crain, 1985). In 1917 he took a position at the Psychological Institute of Hamburg. Because he was a Jew, he was dismissed in 1933 when the Nazis came to power and fled to the United States. By 1947, Werner was at Clark University, which remained a major center for developmental psychology long after Hall's death.

Werner was very much a theorist. His view of development was in some ways narrower and in some ways broader than that of other developmental psychologists. It was narrower in that he did not consider just any change to be developmental. To count as developmental, a change must have a natural progressive direction. At the same time, his view of development was very broad: He was interested in any progressive change, such as the evolution of a species or the history of a culture, as well as in child development. Obviously, any conception of development intended to apply to fields as diverse as psychology, biology, and history must be very general indeed.

But what does it mean to say that a change has a natural, progressive direction? How are we to identify genuinely developmental changes? Werner's answer to this was to propose what he called the **orthogenetic principle** (Werner, 1965). Development, according to this important principle, is a process of **differentiation** followed by **hierarchic integration**. Consider, for example, your knowledge about developmental psychology. Before taking this course, you probably had a vague sense of what developmental psychologists do. By now, presumably, your understanding is much more *differentiated*. You can distinguish a variety of ideas proposed by developmentalists. If all goes well, as you proceed through the course you will gradually come to see how these ideas fit together. Thus you will succeed in *integrating* the ideas you have differentiated. In putting the ideas back together, however, you will not return to your starting point. Rather, you will reach a higher level of understanding, making this a *hierarchic* integration.

There are several points to be made about the above example that will strengthen your grasp of Werner's theory. First, notice that the example is about your experience in a course, not about child development, evolution, or cultural change. The fact that the orthogenetic principle applies is further indication of how general it is.

Second, notice that your understanding at the end of the course is not simply a matter of learning more facts. Development, as Werner saw it, results in *new ways of thinking or understanding*. Werner, like many developmentalists, believed in qualitative change.

Third, you might argue you would lose something if you learned to think about children in abstract theoretical terms but lost your intuitive sense of how it feels to be a child. Werner would agree. He did not believe it is best to operate consistently at the highest possible level. On the contrary, he believed it important to be able to move back and forth among various levels of understanding. A great artist, for example, would be one who could move easily between abstract artistic principles and a more intuitive awareness of forms, colors, and textures.

Finally, suppose at the end of this course you encountered a child. At first you might simply observe the child, then you might begin to distinguish specific developmental issues inherent in her behavior, and finally you might begin to see how those issues fit together for that child. This is an example of differentiation and hierarchic integration, similar to your overall progress in the course but occurring over a brief period. Werner argued that we typically deal with new experiences by recreating, in a very brief time, developmental changes that we earlier went through over a much longer period. He referred to this as **microgenesis** and viewed it as an important psychological phenomenon.

Werner's theory is so general that it is not clear how one can test it. Because it is applicable to a very wide range of phenomena, however, its influence can nonetheless be detected in many areas of research and in a number of more recent theories. Some still consider it the definitive analysis of what development is really all about.

Jean Piaget (1896–1980). In 1907, the following article (quoted in its entirety) appeared in a Swiss journal entitled *Le Rameau du Sapin*:

> At the end of last June, to my great surprise, in the Faubourg de l'Hôpital at Neuchâtel, I saw a sparrow presenting all the visible signs of an albino. He had a whitish beak, several white feathers on the back and wings, and the tail was of the same color. I came nearer, to have a closer look, but he flew away; I was able to follow him with my eyes for some minutes, then he disappeared through the Ruelle du Port.
>
> I have just seen today in the *Rameau de Sapin* of 1868 that albino birds are mentioned; which gave me the idea to write down the preceding lines.
>
> Neuchâtel, the 22nd of July 1907 (translated by Gruber & Vonèche, 1977, p. 6).

The world of biology was not revolutionized by this observation. At the time, no one could have known that its author, a ten-year-old student named Jean Piaget (Zhon Pee-ah-zhay'), would go on to become the foremost developmental psychologist of the twentieth century.

Piaget was born on August 9, 1896, in Neuchâtel, Switzerland. He was a highly intellectual child with a deep interest in biology. Shortly after he published his observation of the albino sparrow, he began to assist the director of the natural history museum in Neuchâtel and became increasingly interested in mollusks (shellfish: snails, clams, etc.). Beginning in 1909, he published a series of increasingly technical and sophisticated articles using his work on mollusks to address a variety of biological topics, including classification, individual differences, adaptation, and related evolutionary issues.

As a teenager, Piaget actively continued his biological work and also read widely in philosophy and became deeply interested in social issues. In 1915, at the height of World War I, he wrote a long, impassioned essay entitled *The Mission of the Idea* in which he addressed a wide variety of social, political, and religious issues. On the topic of feminism, for example, he wrote:

> Men have made an infamous commerce of politics, corrupting countries; in their insanity they have not prepared a peace; with their narrow logic they have neglected the laws of philanthropy; they are incapable of life, of morality, and of beauty as soon as they are alone at the task.
>
> It is from women's suffrage that will come peace, the death of the politics of interest, patriotic idealism, humanitarian laws, social regenera-

tion, the uplifting of the proletariat. Women will make impossible, once they are conscious of their rights, a gigantic crisis that destroys today everything that was yesterday.

Such is the ideal, and an ideal once stated becomes a duty. Feminism might even compromise the grace of women and the tranquility of the family, [but] a duty would remain a duty and feminism remain the school of sacrifice to the idea, of painful struggle in the vanguard of progress (translated by Gruber & Vonèche, 1977, p. 35).

In January 1918, he combined his biological and social interests in an article entitled "Biology and War." "To struggle against war," he concluded, "is therefore to act according to the logic of life against the logic of things, and that is the whole of morality" (translated by Gruber & Voneche, 1977, p. 41). Later that year he completed a dissertation on mollusks and received his doctorate in biology from the University of Neuchâtel. He also published an autobiographical novel entitled *Recherche*, in which the young hero, Sebastian, struggles with the relations of science, philosophy, morality, and faith.

Of his various interests outside the realm of biology, what most intrigued Piaget was **epistemology**, the branch of philosophy that focuses on the nature of knowledge. Piaget was fascinated with the questions asked by epistemologists: What is knowledge? Where does it come from? How do we know what is true? He was skeptical, however, of philosophical answers to these questions, regarding them as based on pure speculation rather than on rigorous research. He was far more impressed with the scientific methods of biology but wished to use these methods to address broader philosophical issues than biologists typically did. Gradually he began to see the possibility of uniting his biological and philosophical interests to study the development of knowledge using the rigorous methods of the biological sciences.

Piaget's interest in the development of knowledge led him to look into psychology. After completing his doctorate in biology, he went to Zurich to study experimental psychology and psychoanalysis and then went to Paris, where he took a job at the Alfred Binet Institute standardizing reasoning tasks for an IQ test. Piaget did not find the standardization itself very exciting. It simply involved administering the tasks and determining what proportion of children at various ages gave correct answers. Piaget noticed, however, that children of similar ages tended to give similar kinds of wrong answers. Upon questioning them further, he concluded that children are not simply ignorant adults. They not only lack certain information that adults have but think about things in *qualitatively* different ways. Through flexible questioning, one can determine how children of various ages think and see how their ways of thinking change over the course of development. Piaget thus decided that developmental psychology was the field within which he could achieve his aim of scientifically investigating the development of knowledge.

Piaget published his first psychological article, "Psychoanalysis in its relations with child psychology," in 1920 and his first book on psychology, *The Language and Thought of the Child*, in 1923. By the end of the decade, he was one of the world's most prominent developmental psychologists. All of his early works were quickly translated into English and highly regarded on both sides of the Atlantic. He was invited to write a chapter entitled "Children's philosophies" for the first edition of what has become the *Handbook of Child Psychology* (Murchison, 1931) and received an honorary doctorate from Harvard University in 1936. With the rise of behaviorism in the United States, however, Piaget's work came to be dismissed by American psychologists as too mentalistic. Although Piaget continued to work actively in Switzerland, his influence in the United States declined during the 1930s, but rose dramatically in the 1960s as cognitive psychology reasserted itself.

From 1920 until his death in 1980, Piaget and his collaborators studied numerous aspects of children's intellectual development, including language, play, perception, imagery, memory, reasoning, problem-solving, and consciousness, as well as conceptions of time, space, causality, distance, movement, speed, number, quantity, geometry, probability, and morality. Piaget also worked extensively in developing and refining a general theory of intellectual development, including formal models of cognition at each stage and an account of how the child moves from each stage to the next. Never forgetting his guiding interests, Piaget also continued to publish important works on the biology and philosophy of knowledge. Overall, he wrote well over 50 books and hundreds of articles, which were highly diverse in their focus but oriented toward the central question of how we construct new ideas.

Although Piaget's early work is of great historical importance, his theory has contemporary as well as historical significance. We will discuss it in detail in Chapter 8, *Theories of Cognitive Development*, and will consider related work throughout this book. We hope you will emerge with an appreciation for the extraordinary scope and ambition of his life's work. As Gruber and Vonèche (1977, p. xl) put it:

> There are at least three Jean Piagets. There is the austere theoretician, turning the thought of children into formal constructions of logic. There is the playful empirical scientist, who led a whole generation of psychologists into a new way of listening to children. There is the doubter, driven onward to new research by the feeling that he has not yet explained the emergence of novelty, which must lie at the core of any account of the growth of thought.

Lev Vygotsky (1896–1934). Eight weeks after Piaget was born in Neuchâtel, Lev Semyonovitch Vygotsky (Vuh-got'-skee) was born in Orsha, northeast of Minsk, in Russia. In 1917, the year of the communist revolution, he graduated from Moscow University with a degree in literature. Although his earliest works consisted of literary criticism, he became increasingly interested in psychology and education and by 1924 was publishing work in these areas.

The communist revolution profoundly affected all aspects of Russian life, including science. There was pressure to conform one's theories to the views of Karl Marx. Many scientists gave in to these political demands at the expense of their intellectual freedom and creativity. Quotations from Marx became common in the scientific literature. Other scientists refused to compromise and lost their prestige, their jobs, or even their lives.

Vygotsky, however, did not have to make this sort of choice. He sincerely believed that Marx could serve as an excellent basis for important psychological research. He emphasized, though, that Marx was not a psychologist and that one could not create useful psychological theories by simply combining excerpts from his writings. The way to use Marx, in Vygotsky's view, was to take his general conception of human society and his method of analysis and use these as a basis for psychological research and theorizing. "I don't want to discover the nature of mind by patching together a lot of quotations," he wrote. "I want to find out how science has to be built, to approach the study of mind having learned the whole of Marx's *method*" (1978, p. 8, italics in original).

In 1978, four American psychologists published a carefully translated and edited collection of Vygotsky's writings and called it *Mind in Society* (Vygotsky, 1978). The title summarizes Vygotsky's theoretical approach. Vygotsky, like Hall, Baldwin, Gesell, Werner, Piaget, and many other developmentalists, rejected the views of behaviorists, who saw the individual as a relatively passive "blank slate" whose behavior is conditioned by the social environment. He believed, like Baldwin and Piaget, that the mind is active and constructive in producing new knowledge. He argued, however, that Piaget's work gives one a picture of a relatively isolated mind, constructing new knowledge on its own. As a Marxist, he could not accept such an individualistic view. He argued that we must consider the active mind within an equally active society and study how both forces interact to produce cognitive development. In short, we must study *mind in society*.

Although Vygotsky criticized many other developmentalists for not taking a sufficiently interactionist approach, he agreed with them in many other respects. For example, Vygotsky strongly believed that development includes qualitative as well as quantitative changes. Moreover, he took a **holistic** approach, insisting like Binet, Piaget, and others that higher mental processes cannot be understood by breaking them down into their component parts. Any particular perception or image reflects one's general ways of knowing and understanding. Thus, the whole is reflected in *each* part, rather than being the sum of them all. Finally, like many developmentalists, Vygotsky believed that development was not simply one topic within psychology. On the contrary, he believed that development was central to, and necessary for understanding, every aspect of psychology.

Vygotsky used his general approach to study a variety of specific topics. In particular, he is known for his work on the relation of language and thought. Whereas a behaviorist would focus on the conditioning of language behaviors by society (thus ignoring thought) and Piaget focused on the development of individual thought (claiming that language is secondary), Vygotsky saw individual thought and socially derived language as equally fundamental and highly interactive (see Chapter 11, *Language Development*). He also was very interested in the role of play and in educational issues. Whatever he studied, Vygotsky, like Piaget, focused on underlying cognitive processes rather than on whether the child had a correct or incorrect answer.

Vygotsky died of tuberculosis in 1934 at the age of 37. Before his death he had already done enough to firmly establish himself as the founder of Soviet developmental psychology. In the United States, his work, like Piaget's, was mostly ignored during the heyday of behaviorism but became increasingly influential beginning around 1960. In fact, like Piaget, he can be considered a historical figure whose ideas were far ahead of their time and remain influential today.

Current Issues in Developmental Psychology

Heredity vs. Environment

In its simplest form, the heredity–environment issue (sometimes called the **nature–nurture** issue) can be expressed as follows: Is human development a preprogrammed, biological phenomenon determined by heredity (nature) or is it a process of individual change determined for each of us by the environment (nurture)? A defender of the nature position might argue, for example, that all normal human infants engage in babbling behavior and then go through similar milestones in learning to talk, regardless of their environment. A defender of the nurture position, on the other hand, might note that no one learns nuclear physics unless he or she is exposed to nuclear physics in the environment.

Vygotsky saw development as a continuing interaction between child and parent, or, more broadly, between child and society.

At this point, it is tempting to conclude that the whole controversy is silly. Clearly, some things are determined by heredity and others by the environment. So, it would seem that the controversy could be put to rest by determining which human abilities belong in which category.

Unfortunately, the resolution of this issue is not as simple as it first appears. For example, even if certain aspects of language development have a genetic basis, the specific language a child learns and how well she or he learns it depend on the child's experiences. Similarly, even though nuclear physics must be learned from the environment, most people would agree readily that boa constrictors and three-toed sloths do not have the hereditary capabilities to learn nuclear physics, regardless of the quality of their environments. Virtually all important psychological characteristics and abilities seem to be a product of both heredity *and* environment, rather than one or the other. The appropriate question for developmentalists is *how* heredity and environment interact in the ongoing process of human development.

Continuity vs. Discontinuity

Imagine that you put a jar of water in the freezer and check it every few minutes. The first time you look into the jar, it will still contain water. If you take the temperature, however, you will find that it is colder than it was when you first placed it in the freezer. There has been a **quantitative change** (a change in the water's temperature) but not a **qualitative change** (it is still water). At some point in your research, however, you will notice that what once was water has become ice. In addition to quantitative change (cooling) there has now been a qualitative change: Ice is not simply cold water; it is physically different than water.

Human development includes both quantitative and qualitative changes. For example, numerous memory studies have shown that as children develop they can remember a larger number of items and they use different strategies for remembering them. When a child remembers nine items instead of five, she is simply recalling more items—a quantitative change. However, when a child remembers items by mentally grouping them into categories rather than simply repeating them over and over, a qualitative change has occurred.

Research

The Role of History in Current Research

Why study the history of developmental psychology? There are many answers that could be given to this question. Some would argue that it is interesting to learn about the many brilliant individuals who have contributed to developmental psychology over the years. Others might emphasize that the evolution of ideas about child development in itself makes a fascinating story.

But however intriguing the story of developmental psychology may be, one might wonder whether current reserachers really need to attend to it. Wouldn't serious researchers be best off focusing on their research and not worrying about what psychologists were thinking and doing many years ago?

A specific example may help us answer this question. Robbie Case is a noted developmental psychologist who has done extensive research on the development of children's intellectual abilities (see Chapter 8, *Theories of Cognitive Development*). Recently, Case (1985) published a book synthesizing his many years of research and theorizing. One might expect the book would be a systematic presentation of his theory and research.

But although Case does provide such a synthesis, he begins his book with 78 pages of history. Is this just an introduction to whet our interest? Not at all. Case argues that in order to understand his research one must understand the theoretical issues he is addressing. But in order to understand these issues, one must consider Piaget's theory, which is the source of many of these issues. Moreover, he goes back one step further. In order to understand Piaget, he argues, one must analyze the work of James Mark Baldwin, who raised many of the issues Piaget was addressing.

In other words, Case sees his research as falling within a historical tradition that began with Baldwin and extends through Piaget to a number of modern researchers. Of course it would be impossible for every researcher in developmental psychology to write a detailed historical introduction to every study she or he publishes. Due to space limitations, most journal articles provide only a brief review of relevant past research. Nevertheless, good researchers are aware of the historical roots of the issues they are investigating. Only if one understands how developmental psychology reached its present status can one figure out where it is going and how one can contribute to its progress.

Although the existence of both quantitative and qualitative changes is clear, developmental psychologists differ about their relative importance. **Continuity** theorists believe that development is fundamentally a quantitative process. They argue that qualitative changes are relatively superficial and can be explained in terms of quantitative changes. **Discontinuity** theorists, on the other hand, believe that qualitative changes are more fundamental and that these changes explain quantitative changes.

Consider how discontinuity and continuity theorists view memory. A discontinuity theorist might argue that older children remember more items on memory tasks than younger children because the older children use different types of memory strategies. Qualitative change is seen as more basic to development and is the explanation for the quantitative change. A continuity theorist would agree that older children use different memory strategies than younger children. Such a theorist would argue, however, that these different memory strategies require a greater amount of memory capacity. Gradual, quantitative changes in memory capacity result in the ability of older children to use different memory strategies. Continuity theorists explain qualitative changes as resulting from underlying quantitative changes.

The continuity–discontinuity controversy commonly shows up in arguments about developmental stages. Discontinuity theorists such as Piaget talk about distinct stages of development involving qualitatively different types of reasoning. Continuity theorists argue that these apparent stages reflect more basic quantitative changes.

Elementarism vs. Holism

Another continuing controversy among developmental psychologists is whether psychological phenomena should be studied as wholes or reduced to their component elements. Those who take an **elementarist** or **reductionist** approach believe they can best understand phenomena by reducing them to their parts. Elementarists would see the sophisticated reasoning of an older child, for example, as a combination of various simpler thinking strategies. By exploring what those simpler strategies are and how they fit together, the nature of advanced reasoning and how it develops become clear.

Psychologists who take a *holistic* approach believe that such analysis, though sometimes valuable, is not sufficient. They argue that the whole is more than the sum of its parts. Water, for example, consists of hydrogen and oxygen. Although it is valuable to know this, the properties of hydrogen and oxygen do not together yield the properties of water. When hydrogen and oxygen combine, new properties emerge. Studying hydrogen and oxygen is not enough to understand these properties. In addition, we need to study *water*. Similarly, holists argue, we cannot understand complex psychological phenomena simply by reducing them to their elementary components. We need to study them in their own right, focusing on how they function as wholes.

The argument between the holists and the elementarists concerns the proper level of analysis. Clearly, human beings include both simple and complex processes. The question is which of these levels is more fundamental. Elementarists argue that the simple level is more basic and by understanding it fully we can understand how complex processes work. Holists argue that the complex level is more basic and explains the elementary processes that compose it.

Obviously, each of these positions has some validity. Nevertheless, some developmentalists lean toward reductionist analyses and others toward more holistic approaches.

Directionality of Development

Imagine that you observe a child who consistently reaches correct conclusions by using advanced logical strategies and who shows deep insight into other people's perspectives. Some years later, you observe the same child and find that he commonly reaches irrational conclusions due to simplistic reasoning and that he frequently cannot understand others' points of view. Has this person shown development over the past few years?

The answer to this question depends on how we define development. If by development we mean any change taking place over some portion of the lifespan, then the above clearly is a case of development. Many developmental psychologists, however, would be uncomfortable with this conclusion. They would argue that we should restrict the term *development* to those changes that have a progressive character. That is, only those changes that involve better adaptation, more sophisticated organization, greater competence, increased maturity, or, in Werner's terms, differentiation and hierarchic integration, should be called developmental changes. These theorists see development as a unidirectional (one-directional) process. From this perspective, our earlier example would not be seen as development.

Although this might seem like a dispute over a simple definition, the definition of the whole field of developmental psychology is at stake. On one hand, some developmentalists (e.g., Piaget, Erikson) believe that there are important changes in many areas of development that have a natural, progressive direction. It is the study of these changes that should be at the core of developmental psychology. Others (e.g., Bandura) doubt this, arguing that the direction of the change simply depends on the specifics of the environment.

Mini-theories vs. Broad Theories

This final controversy does not concern how people actually develop. Rather, it revolves around how developmental psychologists view the advancement of their own field. Although developmental psychology is theory-based, there is disagreement about the type of theory that should guide scientific progress. For example, is it best to collect a lot of data about a specific topic such as mother–infant relations and then construct a mini-theory about it? Or is it better to formulate a broad theory of development that addresses many topics? Most psychologists see value in both forms of theory, but there are differences in emphasis. Much of the remainder of this book will consider research that was guided by mini-theories. In the next chapter, however, we will first consider several of the broad theories that influence research and thinking about human development.

Summary

Views of children have varied widely over the course of history. For example, Puritans believed children to be inherently evil and needing correction; Rousseau considered them inherently good and urged allowing their natural tendencies to flower; and Locke saw them as "blank slates," capable of developing in any direction depending on the environment.

Developmental psychology has been influenced by ideas from many fields. One important influence has been *evolutionary thinking*, which led to a view of the human species as part of the natural world and an emphasis on change. The rise of *scientific psychology* in the 1860s and 1870s helped those interested in children to see the possibility of turning child study into a field of scientific investigation. The *psychoanalytic movement* launched by Sigmund Freud highlighted the importance of early experience and focused attention on the role of unconscious emotional and psychosexual considerations in development. *Behaviorism* stressed the importance of scientific rigor and temporarily led most American psychologists to focus exclusively on observable behavior. Finally, with the rise of *cognitive psychology* since 1960, developmental as well as other psychologists once again turned to the study of mind.

Social factors also influenced the emerging field of developmental psychology. Increasing recognition of the importance of education led to interest in how children learn, think, and develop. The possibility of improving child-rearing led to the establishment of a number of child study institutes and to a "golden age" of child development research in the 1920s and 1930s. Finally, social attitudes about the role of women kept women out of most other scholarly fields until recently, but the study of child development profited from the work of many outstanding female researchers.

Developmental psychology established itself as an important branch of scientific psychology in the 1880s and 1890s. Central to this emergence were Wilhelm Preyer in Germany, Alfred Binet in France, and G. Stanley Hall and James Mark Baldwin in the United States. Preyer was a systematic observer of early development in many species, including humans, whose book *The Mind of the Child* (1882) marked the establishment of scientific developmental psychology. Hall is remembered for his questionnaire research, his evolutionary perspective, and, especially, his enthusiastic efforts to encourage research, spread new ideas, and popularize the scientific study of development. Binet conducted research on a wide variety of topics, formulated surprisingly modern ideas about the human intellect and its development, and constructed the first intelligence test. Baldwin, combining biological, philosophical, and psychological perspectives, proposed a theory of intellectual development in which the individual proceeds through a sequence of developmental stages by actively constructing qualitatively new ways of thinking.

By the end of the 1920s, four more developmental psychologists had established themselves as major figures: Arnold Gesell in the United States, Heinz Werner in Germany, Jean Piaget in Switzerland, and Lev Vygotsky in Russia. Gesell, interested in biologically directed maturation, used systematic observation to establish developmental norms. Werner was a major theorist who defined development as a continuing process of differentiation and hierarchic integration. Piaget, who came to psychology from a background in biology and philosophy, did extensive research on children's thinking, formulated a general theory of intellectual development, and worked extensively on broader issues concerning the biology and philosophy of knowledge. He was active until his death in 1980; his work remains highly influential. Vygotsky, who also enjoys contemporary as well as historical importance, worked extensively on the interaction between individual development and social forces.

Although the progress of developmental psychology has been impressive, a number of controversies continue. One is the question of how nature (heredity) and nurture (environment) interact to produce development and which (if either) plays the more central role. Another issue is whether quantitative (continuous) or qualitative (discontinuous) changes are more basic to development. A third issue is whether complex psychological phenomena are best studied as wholes or by reducing them to their component elements. A fourth issue is whether development should be defined broadly to include a wide variety of changes or narrowed to include only progressive, unidirectional changes. Finally, some developmentalists prefer mini-theories that focus on specific aspects of development, while others search for more general theories to explain development as a whole. General theories will be the focus of the next chapter.

Key Terms

tabula rasa
historicism
evolution
comparative research
ontogeny
phylogeny
psychoanalysis
behaviorism
cognitive psychology

genetic epistemology
stages
maturation
developmental norms
orthogenetic principle
differentiation
hierarchic integration
microgenesis
epistemology

interactionism
holism
nature–nurture
quantitative change
qualitative change
continuity
discontinuity
elementarism
reductionism

Suggested Readings

Borstelmann, L. J. (1983). Children before psychology: Ideas about children from antiquity to the late 1800s. In W. Kessen (Ed.), P. H. Mussen (Series Ed.), *Handbook of child psychology: Vol. 1. History, theory, and methods* (pp. 1–40). New York: Wiley. This chapter provides an excellent introduction to the history of ideas about children prior to the rise of developmental psychology.

Broughton, J. M., & Freeman-Moir, D. J. (Eds.) (1982). *The cognitive-developmental psychology of James Mark Baldwin: Current theory and research in genetic epistemology*. Norwood, NJ: Ablex. Modern scholars in a variety of fields comment on Baldwin's work and its influence on their own thinking.

Cairns, R. B. (1983). The emergence of developmental psychology. In W. Kessen (Ed.), P. H. Mussen (Series Ed.), *Handbook of child psychology: Vol. 1. History, theory, and methods* (pp. 41–102). New York: Wiley. Cairns treats us to a thorough and thoughtful history of the field, except for the peculiar omission of Werner.

Crain, W. C. (1985). *Theories of development: Concepts and applications* (2nd ed.). Englewood Cliffs, NJ: Prentice-Hall. Crain provides useful treatments of Locke, Rousseau, Darwin, Freud, Watson, Gesell, and Werner, as well as a number of contemporary theorists.

Dixon, R. A., & Lerner, R. M. (1984). A history of systems in developmental psychology. In M. H. Bornstein & M. E. Lamb (Eds.), *Developmental psychology: An advanced textbook* (pp. 1–35). Hillsdale, NJ: Erlbaum. This chapter distinguishes five theoretical approaches to developmental psychology and traces the history of each, emphasizing the influence of Darwin on all of them.

Note: For further reading on Piaget, Vygotsky, Erikson, and other contemporary theorists, see the Suggested Readings in Chapters 2, 8, and 16.

Application Exercises

1-1 Historical Figures

Identify the individual(s) from the following list who best fit(s) each of the descriptions below.

Baldwin	Piaget
Binet	Preyer
Darwin	Rousseau
Dewey	Shinn
A. Freud	Vygotsky
S. Freud	Watson
Gesell	Werner
Hall	Wundt
Locke	

1. Believed development proceeds through a sequence of stages.
2. Saw development as a process of maturation driven by the child's heredity.
3. Viewed the child as a blank slate, ready to be molded by the environment.
4. Focused on intellectual development.
5. Published the first scientific book on child development.
6. Did major work before the rise of scientific psychology.
7. Published *Biography of a Baby* in 1900.
8. Focused on applying psychoanalytic views to children.
9. Known as a psychologist but not primarily as a developmental psychologist.
10. Stressed the continuing interaction of nature and nurture.
11. Strongly biological in perspective.
12. Was primarily a philosopher.

1-2 Current Controversies

For each of the questions below, indicate which of the following controversies is most directly involved: (a) Heredity/environment, (b) Continuity/discontinuity, (c) Elementarism/holism, (d) Directionality of development, (e) Mini-theories/broad theories.

1. Can one study language development without paying very much attention to the development of reasoning or social interactions?
2. Are children basically evil or basically good?
3. Do children get more rational over the course of development?
4. Are the major differences between 5- and 7-year-olds in intellectual ability due to changes in the speed of processing information or to a shift from one strategy to another?
5. Can one mold a child in virtually any way if one has responsibility for him in his first few years?
6. Should one teach a child to pitch a ball by training her in each of the motions involved and then helping her put those skills together?
7. Is an overall theory of developmental psychology possible?
8. Do all developmental changes involve differentiation and hierarchic integration?
9. When perceptions are differentiated and then reintegrated, are they still the same perceptions?
10. How do internal and external forces interact over the course of development?
11. Do children construct qualitatively new ways of thinking over the course of development?
12. Are children essentially small adults?

CHAPTER 2

Theories of Developmental Psychology

Give us theories, theories, always theories! Let every man who has a theory pronounce his theory!
—James Mark Baldwin

In Chapter 1 we discussed the history and current status of the science of developmental psychology. What does it mean to view developmental psychology as a science? We will begin this chapter with a discussion of our definition of science and how science operates through a continuing interplay of theory and data. In the remainder of this chapter, we will discuss the major theoretical views in the field of developmental psychology. Later, in Chapter 3, we will consider the many research methods used by developmental psychologists to test and extend these theories.

Theories, Data, and the Nature of Science

A science is a field of study that focuses on understanding some aspect of the world. For example, physics is the study of the physical world, biology is the study of living organisms, sociology is the study of societies, and psychology is the study of mind and behavior. As we have seen, developmental psychology is a part of the science of psychology that focuses on age-related changes in psychological phenomena. Though sciences differ greatly from each other in their subjects, they all rely on two factors: **theory** and **data**.

What Is a Theory?

All sciences have theories. For example, there are theories about the nature of matter; how microscopic particles interact; why planets stay in orbit; how societies function; how birds fly; why people laugh; and even how the world began. In developmental psychology, there are theories about how language develops; how puberty influences self-concept; how children learn morality; how fathers affect daughters; how stress affects intellectual functioning; why adults have midlife crises; and what role old age plays in the life cycle, to name only a few.

40   CHAPTER 2   Theories of Developmental Psychology

Although theories are extremely diverse, all theories have three things in common. First, they all deal with a range of phenomena; they do not merely express a particular fact. Each theory addresses a broad topic including many different issues to be resolved.

Second, theories do not simply summarize facts; rather, they attempt to explain them. For example, a listing of everything that is known about how infants interact with their parents would not be a theory. A theory of parent–infant interaction would try to explain—to help us understand—what leads parents and infants to interact the way they do, what factors help or hinder these interactions, what purpose such interactions serve, how they change as the infant matures, and what their long-term consequences are. John Bowlby's theory of attachment, to be discussed in Chapter 14, is an example of such a theory.

A third feature of theories is that they attempt to predict new facts. They do not limit themselves to what is already known. Any explanation that makes no predictions cannot be tested and thus has little scientific value. Bowlby's theory of attachment, for example, predicts that certain patterns in the development of attachment will occur for all normal human beings. This can be tested by observing parent–infant interactions in a variety of cultures.

What Are Data?

All sciences have data. Data are what theories attempt to explain. They are the observations that result from research. We use data to test current theories and to serve as the starting point for new theorizing. For example, what color is the ceiling of the room you are sitting in? Your answer constitutes a datum (singular of data) about the room. It is an observation that could easily be repeated by others. How many words are there in this question? How many sentences on this page? How many pages in this book? The answers to each of these questions constitute data about the book. What is the average weight of newborn American infants? The average number of words understood by 2-year-old Nigerian boys? The average number of words in the spontaneous sentences of 4-year-old Russian girls? The answers to these questions are data concerning child development.

The Relation of Theories and Data

As just discussed, all sciences require both theories and data. In fact, neither theories alone nor data alone would be of much use. Why would a theory by itself be of little value? Suppose your neighbor Ralph comes over and tells you his brilliant new theory of how children learn to read. As a scientist, you should immediately ask him some questions about his data. What evidence is his theory based on? What facts does it help to explain? What predictions does it make that we can test through research? These questions are a scientist's way of asking, "Why should I believe your story about how children learn to read?" Some theories are based on stronger evidence than others, of course, and

> ## Highlights
>
> ### Monty Python's Theory of the Brontosaurus
>
> In a classic skit by the British comedy group "Monty Python's Flying Circus," John Cleese (wearing a wig) plays a scientist famous for her theory of the brontosaurus. After several minutes of preliminary fanfare, the scientist finally reveals her theory: The brontosaurus is very thin at one end, *much* much thicker in the middle, and very thin at the other end. The joke is that this doesn't strike us as much of a theory, if indeed it's a theory at all. It doesn't appear to systematize anything, explain anything, or predict anything. Thus, we intuitively feel that this "theory" is simply a fact, an observation about the appearance of the brontosaurus. If someone proposed a systematic set of ideas indicating *why* it was adaptive for brontosauruses to have the shape they did and if this set of ideas could be used to explain and predict the shapes of other animals, then we would have a genuine theory.

some are easier to test than others. But if a theory does not help explain any previous data and does not make any testable predictions, we have little reason to believe it or take it seriously.

If data are so important, why bother with theories at all? If data are our evidence about reality, why don't scientists spend all their time simply gathering more and more data? And why don't textbooks dispense with theory and simply present the data? Why bother with speculations when you can stick to the facts? Here are some facts: The average newborn weighs about seven pounds. Normal human beings have 23 pairs of chromosomes. Eight-year-olds show more logical reasoning than do 4-year-olds. Parts of the reading process can become automatic. People have ten toes. Some people are social isolates.

As you can see, continuing in this vein is useless. If you thought the remainder of this book would consist of simple facts, you would probably close this text. And rightly so. Data alone are clearly of little use. We need theories to organize facts, to explain them, and to help us decide what further data would be useful. Science progresses not from data alone, nor from theory alone, but through a continuing interplay of theories and data.

Theories of Developmental Psychology

There is no shortage of theories in developmental psychology. In the remainder of this chapter we will discuss several of the most important theories in the field. In order to help you grasp how the various theories resemble and differ from each other, we have grouped them into three major **paradigms**, or families of theories.

The first paradigm includes what are generally called **learning theories**. Although these theories are used frequently to explain development over time, they are not specific to developmental psychology. Rather, they are extensions of general theories about how people learn from and are shaped by their environments.

The second paradigm includes what are generally called **developmental theories**. Developmental theorists question whether learning can explain all age-related changes. They have fashioned theories that instead look at long-term development as an internally driven process.

Finally, the third paradigm includes what are generally called **dialectical theories**. Dialectical theorists see strengths and weaknesses in both the learning and developmental approaches. They have attempted to formulate a synthesis of the two.

In order to help you understand each of these paradigms, we will discuss them separately in the next three sections of this chapter. In addition to understanding individual paradigms, however, it is also important for you to realize how the paradigms compare to each other. To help you relate them, we will use the same format in discussing each paradigm. Each of the next three sections will focus on one paradigm and will attempt to answer the following questions: What is the history of this paradigm? What are some of the most important contemporary theories within this paradigm? What basic conceptions about human beings and human development are central to this paradigm? How do theorists in this paradigm approach the scientific study of human development? And what are some of the implications of this paradigm for parents and teachers?

The Learning Paradigm

History

We can learn a lot about a person by looking at that person's childhood and studying his or her development. Similarly, a good way to understand a theory is to explore the history of its basic ideas. Scientific psychology, as noted in Chapter 1, is little more than a century old, whereas most of its central concepts have histories that go back many centuries further.

Three important ancestors of modern learning theorists were the British philosophers John Locke (1632–1704), George Berkeley (1685–1753), and David Hume (1711–1776). These thinkers are commonly called **empiricists**, which refers to their belief that all knowledge comes to us from the outside world through our senses. Empirical knowledge is knowledge of what we have seen, heard, touched, and so on. Wil-

The Learning Paradigm

helm Wundt (1832–1920), who was cited in Chapter 1 as the founder of experimental psychology, was greatly influenced by the British empiricists. Wundt tried to develop scientific techniques for studying the mind through systematic **introspection**, which is the rigorous observation of one's own thoughts.

Early in the twentieth century, introspection came under increasing attack. Behaviorists such as John B. Watson, whose famous 1913 paper was discussed in Chapter 1, argued that observation of one's own mind was much too subjective and uncertain to form the basis for a true science. Behaviorists proposed that psychology should abandon the study of mind and define itself instead as the study of behavior, since behavior is something that can be studied objectively. By the 1930s, behaviorists dominated American psychology. Behaviorism continued the empiricist tradition: It saw the individual as shaped by his or her environment.

Current Learning Theories

Operant Conditioning. Although behaviorism is no longer as dominant in American psychology as it was in the 1930s, 1940s, and 1950s, it remains important. The most influential modern behaviorist is B. F. Skinner (1904–   ). Skinner emphasizes a particular type of learning known as **operant conditioning**. The central idea of operant conditioning is that behaviors become either more or less frequent depending on their consequences. Environmental consequences that increase the likelihood of a particular behavior are called **reinforcers**, while those that decrease the likelihood of a behavior are called **punishers**. Development, according to Skinner, is simply gradual learning through operant conditioning over long periods of time.

An example of how an operant viewpoint can be used to explain an aspect of a child's development can be seen in the following. Suppose that a hypothetical kindergartener, Joseph, is frequently disruptive. Further, assume that our observations of Joseph's behaviors indicate that the teacher pays attention to him primarily when he is disruptive. An operant psychologist such as Skinner would suggest that Joseph's teacher is reinforcing his disruptive behaviors by paying attention to him. In fact, these behaviors were probably learned as a way of gaining attention in other settings. To stop Joseph's disruptive behaviors, then, the teacher should ignore these behaviors and instead pay attention to him whenever he is behaving appropriately. In other words, operant psychologists would emphasize controlling the consequences of Joseph's behaviors.

Although operant conditioning is effective, most psychologists no longer believe it can completely explain human development. Nevertheless, applied psychologists still recognize its great value for dealing with certain kinds of problems.

Social Learning Theory. Another view of development is provided by **social learning theory** (e.g., Bandura, 1977). Social learning theorists accept many of the central tenets of behaviorism (e.g., the effects of reinforcers and punishers on behaviors) but attempt to supplement them with ideas from cognitive psychology, which is the study of thinking. One very important concept emphasized by social learning theorists is **modeling**, which is an extension of the idea of learning by imitation.

To see how social learning theory goes beyond the ideas of operant conditioning, consider a child learning to speak. How does, say, Ellen learn the word "dog?" And once she knows it, how does she learn to use it in a sentence like "The little dog is barking?" An operant theorist might provide the following explanation. Ellen randomly utters various sounds and combinations of sounds in the presence of dogs. When by chance she happens to say "dog," her parents reinforce her, so she learns to utter that combination of sounds more frequently in the presence of dogs. Later, she will randomly put together the words "dog," "little," "is," "the," and "barking" until she happens to get them into grammatical order and gets reinforced for that.

Although this is an oversimplified version of the operant explanation of language learning, it captures the essence of the operant emphasis on trial and error. Social learning theorists argue that learning language this way would take forever. Although they agree that operant conditioning is an important type of learning, they argue that imitation processes are used by the child to learn more efficiently. In the case of language development, children are surrounded by adults who are using language and learn by imitating the words adults use and the way adults put those words together into sentences. Moreover, children not only imitate specific behaviors but are able to abstract general rules, such as putting the adjective ("little") in front of the noun ("dog"). This is what enables children to go beyond what they have heard and produce new sentences of their own. *Modeling*, then, is the term used for a very abstract kind of imitation through which one learns not only specific behaviors but general rules. Development, according to social learning theorists, can be explained as the result of many years of modeling.

Social learning theory has been applied to many different aspects of development and sheds a great deal of light on how development is affected by the social world. We will discuss it in more detail in Chapter 5, *Social Influences on Development.*

Information Processing Theory. We have seen that social learning theory is not purely behaviorist. It goes beyond talking only about behavior and environment and emphasizes that the developing child is always abstracting new concepts. How does she do this? This is what **information processing** theorists ask and, unlike behaviorists, they are willing to go deep into the realm of the mind in order to find answers. Thus, information processing is a **cognitive theory** rather than a behavioral one. It views development as a gradual increase in the individual's mental resources for assimilating new information and solving problems.

The information processing approach has gained rapidly in influence over the past 25 years and is now one of the most important theories in psychology. We will discuss it in detail in Chapter 8, *Theories of Cognitive Development*. Information processing will also play an important role in later chapters on the development of perception, memory, and reasoning.

Basic Conceptions

We have presented three modern theories of learning: operant behaviorism, social learning theory, and information processing theory. Although the three theories differ in important ways, they share certain underlying conceptions about what people are like and how they develop. Let us explore some of these similar underlying ideas.

Level of Analysis. Learning theorists believe that complex psychological phenomena can best be understood by reducing them to their compo-

Social learning theorists stress the role of observing and imitating others.

nent elements. This approach is known as **elementarism** or **reductionism**.

For example, how do children learn morality? A behaviorist would first ask what *specific* behaviors we mean when we talk about morality. The behaviorist would then study how specific environmental consequences such as reinforcers and punishers result in the increasing or decreasing frequency of those behaviors. A social learning theorist would agree with this approach except that she or he would also consider how specific moral behaviors and/or rules are learned from parents, peers, and other models. Information processing theorists would be more interested in how a child *thinks* about a moral issue but would also take an elementaristic approach. They might consider the specific mental processes the child uses for understanding the issue and deciding what to do.

Sources of Knowledge. Notice that both the behaviorist and the social learning theorist in the above example assumed that the source of moral behavior and rules must be the environment. In the case of explaining moral development, the emphasis was on the social environment, that is, the people who provide models of behavior, reinforce appropriate behavior, and punish inappropriate behavior. In other cases, children learn from their physical environments. For example, they learn about gravity by observing what happens when they fall or when objects are dropped. This idea—that people learn things from their environments—is called *empiricism* and is central to learning theories. Although the information processing theorist in the earlier example was most interested in how the child was thinking about morality, that theorist too would probably look to the environment if asked to explain the source of those thought processes.

Role of Person and Environment. Empiricists believe that an **active environment** causes people to change. For example, Skinner writes:

> The runner's heart is said to beat fast before the start of the race because he "associates" the situation with the exertion which follows. But it is the environment, not the runner, that "associates" the two features. . . . Nor does the runner "form a connection" between the two things; the connection is made in the external world (1974, p. 43).

In recent years, social learning theorists (e.g., Bandura, 1977; Zimmerman, 1981) have stressed the active role of the person in choosing his or her environment and abstracting information from it. Information processing approaches go even further in emphasizing the individual's active thinking processes. Nevertheless, compared to the developmental theories that we will consider in the next section, learning theorists put great emphasis on the role of the environment in determining a person's development. The central assumption is that people tend to stay the way they are unless something in the environment causes them to change.

Continuity vs. Discontinuity. Learning theorists generally see development as involving quantitative changes in how much one knows rather than qualitative changes in the *type* of knowledge one has (see the discussion of the continuity/discontinuity controversy in Chapter 1). They typically deemphasize the kind of sharp breaks in overall ways of thinking that most interest discontinuity theorists.

Sequences of Development. Learning theorists believe that sequences of change vary from person to person, depending on environmental circumstances. The grammatical rules a child learns first, for example, depend on what she is exposed to in her environment. According to learning theorists, the sequence could be different for different children.

Generality of Development. Finally, learning theorists stress that people learn how to solve *specific* problems or make sense of *specific* issues. Continuity theorists are dubious of general **stages of development**. Though learning may generalize to new tasks, generalization is not automatically assumed. Just because Bill has learned a solution to one moral dilemma does not mean he will see how to apply that solution to a different moral dilemma.

Learning theorists are uncomfortable talking about cognitive development as an overall process. They prefer to describe how children learn to solve specific problems. According to a prominent information processing theorist, "cognitive development can be characterized as a sequence of increasingly sophisticated rules for performing tasks" (Siegler, 1980a, p. 282).

Scientific Research Strategies

Developmental psychologists working within different paradigms disagree not only in their views about how children develop but also in their views about how science can make the best progress. Thus, learning theorists differ from researchers in other paradigms in their views about the relation of theory and data and in their preferred research methods.

Theory vs. Data. Learning theorists emphasize the empiricist idea that new knowledge comes from one's environment. Consistent with this, they argue that the science of developmental psychology should gain its knowledge about how people develop by collecting empirical evidence. Although learning theorists, like all scientists, acknowledge the importance of theory, they put special emphasis on data. Learning theorists are most comfortable with theories that account for specific sets of data and make clear, testable predictions. They are least comfortable with broad, speculative theories that go far beyond the available data and do not make clear predictions that can be tested.

Preferred Research Methods. Even though learning theorists use a wide variety of research strategies, they typically see the experiment as the ideal type of study. As we will see in the next chapter, an experiment is a type of research in which the investigator manipulates some variable in order to see what its effects will be. Since learning theories emphasize that development is caused by the actions of the environment on the person, the experiment is an ideal way to see the effects of various environmental factors.

Practical Applications

Learning theories suggest certain views about the role of parents and teachers and how one can most effectively perform these roles. Two areas of application are **socialization** and **instruction.**

Socialization. Learning theories stress the role of adults in molding children into acceptable members of society. Each new generation is socialized to resemble the generation before it—a process known as *socialization*—and thus continues the traditions of the society. Operant

A good grade is a strong reinforcement for most students.

and social learning theory, in particular, have a great deal to say about this. In later chapters we will explore the role of adult models in shaping children's behavior with respect to language, sex roles, and morality.

Instruction. From the perspective of learning theory, teaching involves arranging a student's environment in ways that will cause the student to learn. This may involve verbal presentation (e.g., a lecture), modeling (e.g., demonstrating a laboratory technique or a way of thinking), and/or reinforcement (e.g., giving a good grade for a good performance). The term *instruction* captures the emphasis on specific new knowledge produced by one's environment.

The Developmental Paradigm

We have considered several general theories of learning that yield important insights into human development. We now turn to what may be called *developmental theories.* These are a family of theories that are specifically designed to explain psychological development.

History

The most notable ancestor of developmental theorists was the German philosopher Immanuel Kant (1724–1804). In reaction to the British empiricists, Kant argued that the most fundamental knowledge is not learned through our senses. Rather, he emphasized certain inherent categories of mind—such as time, space, causality, and objects—which we impose on reality in order to make sense of it.

This view, as well as the proposals of Rousseau (see Chapter 1), led some early psychologists to the idea that the mind is not simply a passive product of the environment but that it has a developmental course of its own. As discussed in Chapter 1, James Mark Baldwin followed through on this conception around the turn of the century to propose an early theory of natural developmental stages (Broughton & Freeman-Moir, 1982). About the same time, Sigmund Freud also provided a highly influential stage theory. Other developmental theorists included G. Stanley Hall and, later in the twentieth century, Arnold Gesell, Heinz Werner, and Jean Piaget.

Current Developmental Theories

Nativism. As we have seen, learning theories reflect empiricism, the idea that all knowledge comes from the environment. The extreme opposite of this is **nativism, the idea that knowledge is innate (inborn).** Of course, no psychologist would claim that we have complete knowledge at birth or that we learn nothing from our environments. Nativists do claim, however, that we have innate knowledge that makes it possible for us to learn from our environments.

For the nativist, the specific things we learn from our environments are superficial compared to the basic knowledge we all have at birth.

Thus development is seen not as a process of learning but as the unfolding of our inborn human potential. Our innate knowledge and tendencies are viewed as characteristics of the human species that have evolved over the course of millions of years. This makes the topic of evolution a matter of special importance for the nativist.

The most famous nativist of our time is Noam Chomsky, who is an expert on language. Chomsky does *not* argue that anyone is born with the knowledge of his or her native language. Obviously, children learn whatever specific language they are exposed to in their early years. Chomsky does propose, however, that all human languages have certain common patterns and that children are born with innate knowledge of these patterns. This general knowledge of language makes it possible for children to learn the specific languages they are exposed to (see Chapter 11 for a more detailed presentation of Chomsky's view of language development). Other nativists (e.g., Keil, 1981; Lorenz, 1965) propose an innate basis for other aspects of development.

Constructivism. The nativist view that most knowledge and behavior are innate is the most obvious alternative to the empiricist view that most knowledge and behavior are learned. It is not the only one, however. Jean Piaget (1896–1980), a major theorist in the developmental tradition, spent most of his life working out a third possibility. Piaget, like Baldwin before him, believed that the most important sorts of human knowledge are neither learned from the environment nor innate. He argued instead that knowledge is *constructed* by the individual during the course of interactions with the environment. This view, known as **constructivism**, led Piaget to a theory of general stages children go through in the course of their mental development (we will discuss Piaget's theory in detail in Chapter 8). His views have profoundly influenced research on the development of language, memory, reasoning, sex roles, morality, and many other psychological phenomena.

Psychoanalytic Theory. **Psychoanalytic theories** are those that build on the work of Sigmund Freud and emphasize the role of unconscious factors in human personality. The most important modern developmental theory within the psychoanalytic tradition is that of Erik Erikson. Erikson views development as a sequence of eight stages covering the entire lifespan. He is especially known for his work on the adolescent identity crisis. Unlike Piaget, his prime emphasis is on social and personality development (we will consider his theory in more detail in Chapter 16).

Basic Conceptions

Although the various developmental theories are very diverse, they do resemble each other and differ from learning theories in certain fundamental ways.

Level of Analysis. Developmentalists are generally less inclined than are learning theorists to try to understand phenomena by breaking them down into their component parts. They believe that the whole is more than the sum of its parts (**holism**) and that its characteristics are likely to be lost in a reductionist analysis. For example, in Chapter 15 we will consider the theory of moral development proposed by Kohlberg, a follower of Piaget. We will see that Kohlberg is not interested primarily in analyzing a child's morality into a set of specific behaviors, concepts, or processes. Instead, taking a holistic view, he looks at the child's general approach to a variety of moral dilemmas and tries to determine the overall *structure* of the child's moral reasoning.

Source of Knowledge. Developmentalists generally do not agree with the view that all knowledge is accumulated from, and all behavior shaped by, the environment. As we have seen, developmentalists have proposed two alternatives. One, nativism, takes the view that knowledge and behavior, or at least the essential bases for these, are innate. The other, constructivism, emphasizes the continual construction of knowledge through the ongoing interaction between children and their environments.

Role of Person and Environment. Developmentalists question the traditional learning-theory view that changes in the individual are *caused* by the environment. Although environments are undoubtedly important, developmentalists put more emphasis on the active person generating his or her own development. For example, Kohlberg argues that new stages of moral development do not come primarily from the environment but rather are constructed by individuals as they think about moral issues. Development is a natural, ongoing tendency that, although certainly *affected* by the environment, is not *caused* by it.

Continuity vs. Discontinuity. Developmentalists often talk about stages of development to highlight their view that development involves *discontinuous*, qualitative changes. To return to our example of moral development, developmentalists are less interested in the increasing or decreasing frequency of certain behaviors or in the accumulation of moral rules than in an overall change in the way an individual analyzes moral issues. We will see in Chapter 15 that this kind of *qualitative* change is what is involved in moving from one of Kohlberg's stages to another. It is not critical whether the new orientation develops slowly or quite abruptly. What is essential to the developmentalist is that each stage is fundamentally different from the one preceding.

Sequences of Development. What a child learns and in what order obviously is influenced by the environment. Developmentalists believe, however, that there are certain **invariant sequences** (universal paths of development) that all children go through in any normal environment. For nativists, the basis for this universality lies in our shared heredity: Stages of development are genetically programmed. Constructivists, on the other hand, propose that each new stage of development is a transformation of an earlier stage. From either perspective, the environment may speed up or slow down development but it does not alter the basic sequence that all children go through. For example, Piaget's theory proposes that children moving from concrete to formal operations (two of his stages of intellectual development) may be helped or hindered by the environment. But for those who move beyond concrete operations the next stage, regardless of the specific environment, is formal operations.

Generality of Development. Unlike learning theorists, developmentalists focus on *general stages of development.* For example, concrete and formal operations are not behaviors, rules, or techniques for solving particular problems. Rather, they are general stages of development, or overall ways of thinking. Though many developmentalists focus on domains such as moral development or sex role development, in each case they propose general stages of understanding in that area. Of course, a given child may have trouble with a particular task. For example, she may not succeed in applying her understanding of numbers to a particular arithmetic problem. The primary interest of the developmentalist, however, is not what the child does in the specific situation but her broad stage of development.

Scientific Research Strategies

Theory vs. Data. As we have seen, developmentalists see development as a succession of broad stages rather than as an accumulation of information from the environment. This holds not only for how individuals develop but for how science develops. Developmentalists view scientific progress more as the construction of increasingly adequate theories than as the accumulation of data. This does not mean that developmentalists deny the importance of data. Theories can only become increasingly adequate if we test them against empirical evidence. But compared to most learning theorists, developmentalists tend to put more emphasis on theory and less on data. More than most learning theorists, developmentalists try to construct the "big picture" of human development, even if this means proposing broad, speculative theories that go far beyond the available data and are not easily tested.

Preferred Research Methods. No one would deny that changes in the environment can produce changes in the individual. A new teacher, for example, may have a positive or negative impact on a child's learning. Developmentalists, however, unlike learning theorists, do not typically see this as the essence of development. Therefore, developmentalists deemphasize experimental research (in which the researcher manipulates one or more variables and observes their effects). A more typical strategy for a developmental researcher would be to administer a carefully designed set of tasks and interview children about their thinking on those tasks: a **clinical interview**. We could compare the thinking of children at different ages by studying two or more age groups (a cross-sectional study) or by studying the same group two or more times as they get older (a longitudinal study). We will have more to say about all of these research strategies in Chapter 3.

Practical Applications

We have already discussed, from a learning theory perspective, the role of parents and teachers in the socialization and instruction of children. The developmental view does not really disagree, but argues for a broader perspective.

Research

The Role of Theory in Research

People often think of research as a purely objective process. The ideal scientist, according to this view, objectively gathers and presents data. She has no expectations and imposes no interpretation on the evidence.

It should be obvious from the material discussed in this chapter that this is a naive view of psychology or any other science. All scientists have theoretical views that guide their research. In some cases they may specifically design a study to test a particular theory. Even when they are not testing a specific theory, scientists inevitably are influenced by their general theoretical perspectives—that is, they are working within *paradigms*.

Does this mean that research is not objective? The answer depends on what we mean by *objective*. If by objective research we mean gathering and reporting raw facts, then objectivity is impossible. All research, as we have noted, involves some degree of subjective judgment and interpretation.

Perhaps a more useful definition of objective research, however, is research that is not biased. Objective researchers do not simply try to support their biases but, rather, use systematic research techniques to generate valid and reliable evidence (see Chapter 3, *Research Methods*). Ideally, scientists try to overcome their biases as much as possible by careful design and interpretation of their research.

Actual research, of course, does not alway live up to this ideal (Greenwald, Pratkanis, Leippe, & Baumgardner, 1986): No individual can be totally unbiased. Fortunately, science as a whole is a social enterprise. Because scientists have a variety of theoretical perspectives, we can expect that whatever biases an individual has will tend to cancel out for scientific research as a whole. Even if we cannot achieve absolute truth, then, we can move toward increasingly objective knowledge.

The existence of diverse theories makes research in developmental psychology complex. But it is precisely this diversity that ensures that research will reflect a variety of perspectives. Thus, even if any particular study reflects the theoretical biases of the researcher, developmental psychology as a whole can move toward an objective understanding of how children develop.

Piagetians stress the active construction of knowledge by the child. Although physical activity plays a role in this, the emphasis is on mental activity.

Facilitation. Developmentalists believe that children go through a natural, internally driven process of development. From this point of view, the major role of parents, teachers, and other adults is not to *cause* the child to develop but rather to *facilitate* the natural developmental process.

For example, one can often teach children a new intellectual skill by demonstrating it. Stages of intellectual development, however, are much broader than specific skills and, according to developmentalists, cannot be taught through simple demonstration. Each stage represents a general type of reasoning that children have constructed from earlier modes of reasoning. Parents and teachers can facilitate this process by providing the right kinds of environmental input. But the actual construction of new knowledge is done not by adults but by the children themselves.

Disequilibration. Just how *does* one facilitate another person's development? Unlike the learning theorist, whose focus would be on providing the new knowledge or behavior for the child to learn, the developmentalist believes it is the child who constructs new knowledge. The parent or teacher can provide an environment in which the child will see the inadequacies of his or her own thinking. When a child sees that her reasoning is inadequate, she feels uncomfortable and wants to change. This condition is known as **disequilibrium**. The process of inducing disequilibrium is known as **disequilibration**. We will explore this rather indirect approach to education in more detail in Chapter 8 when we consider Piaget's theory of cognitive development.

Similar considerations apply in the realm of social and personality development. For example, Erikson views development as the resolution of a series of "crises" and indicates that each resolution is not something that can be taught. Rather he sees development as internally generated. Of course, Erikson considers the child's environment, including parents and teachers, to be highly influential. He and other developmentalists, however, see parents and teachers as having input into an internal developmental process, rather than being the cause of that process. The developing individual is the source of his or her own development.

The Dialectical Paradigm

We have now considered two contrasting approaches to the study of human development. In recent years a third approach, the dialectical paradigm, has become increasingly influential. Dialectical theorists agree with learning theorists about the active role of the environment but criticize them for viewing people as passive entities shaped by their environments. Conversely, dialectical theorists praise developmental theorists for their emphasis on the active role of the person but fault them for ignoring the equally active role of the environment. Of course, many learning theorists, especially information processing theorists, would respond that they do see the person as highly active; and most developmentalists would stress how critical they consider the environment to be. Nevertheless, dialecticians insist that neither learning theorists nor developmental theorists give enough emphasis to the strong, continuing interaction between person and environment.

History

The two major ancestors of contemporary dialectical thinking are the German philosophers Georg Wilhelm Friedrich Hegel (1770–1831) and Karl Marx (1818–1883). Hegel believed that the mind makes progress through a continual process of generating, confronting, and overcoming contradictions. Marx was much influenced by this analysis but, while Hegel focused on the realm of ideas, Marx emphasized economics and society. Dialectical views have strongly influenced Russian psychology, which in turn has been taken very seriously by American psychologists in recent years.

The opportunity to group and count objects may facilitate a child's intellectual development.

Current Dialectical Theories

Soviet Developmental Psychology. The father of Soviet developmental psychology was Lev Semenovich Vygotsky (1896–1934). Born the same year as Jean Piaget, he died of tuberculosis at the age of 37, more than 50 years ago. Only in recent years, however, has his work had its full impact in English-speaking circles. Thus, as noted in Chapter 1, he can be considered a contemporary, rather than merely a historical, figure.

Although Vygotsky greatly respected the work of Piaget, he could not accept Piaget's view of development as an internally driven process that moves through a series of predictable stages. He was equally dubious of the learning theorists' view that development is nothing more than the accumulation of what one has learned. Instead, Vygotsky (1978) proposed that learning and development can be distinguished but are continually interacting with each other.

Consider, for example, a child learning mathematics. A learning theorist would emphasize the various mathematical techniques (how to count, subtract, take square roots, etc.) that the child learns from the environment (parents, teachers, books, etc.). Development, to the learning theorist, is simply the long-term process of learning all these things.

A developmentalist, on the other hand, would focus on how the child constructs a sequence of underlying mathematical concepts that make it possible to meaningfully learn mathematics. Learning, to the developmentalist, is a relatively superficial change that is made possible by more basic developmental changes in the child's fundamental understanding.

Vygotsky would agree with the developmentalist that there are basic developmental changes that make learning possible. He would add, however, that specific learning can affect the direction of development. From Vygotsky's perspective, learning is indeed constrained by development, as the developmentalist argues, but also serves as its cutting edge, as a learning theorist might argue. The child's underlying mathematical concepts, for example, determine what mathematical techniques she can learn, but the techniques learned are eventually reconstructed at a deeper level as basic mathematical understandings. In essence, Vygotsky is arguing that neither internally driven change (development) nor externally driven change (learning) should be seen as primary. Neither is possible without the other and the two proceed in constant interaction.

American Dialectical Theory. Probably the major influence in increasing American interest in dialectical views was Klaus Riegel (1925–1977), who, as editor of the prestigious journal *Human Development*, actively encouraged research and theorizing within this paradigm. Riegel (1979) viewed development as a continuing interaction of biological, psychological, social, and physical considerations. The influence of dialectical ideas can be seen in a great deal of American research.

Basic Conceptions

Level of Analysis. Dialectical theorists emphasize that all psychological events take place in broader contexts (e.g., in a particular culture, at a particular time in history, in a particular environmental setting, in the company of particular people) and can only be understood in terms of those contexts. This view is known as **contextualism**. Because of their contextualist perspective, dialecticians are uncomfortable with the elementaristic approach of learning theorists. Dialecticians view the learning theorists' efforts to break psychological events down into smaller units and study each unit separately as doomed to failure, since the meaning of a psychological event cannot be understood outside of its context. In their view, one cannot understand morality, for example, by breaking it down into a set of moral behaviors, rules, or thoughts and studying each in isolation.

Dialecticians are equally uncomfortable with the holistic approach of developmentalists, however. For example, each of Kohlberg's stages of moral development represents a broad, abstract way of thinking about moral issues. But this does not consider differences between cultures (e.g., Americans vs. Samoans) or between generations (e.g.,

Americans in the 1950s vs. those in the 1980s) in conceptions of morality. Nor does it deal with the specific application of morality to the unique situations we all must face.

Of course, both learning theorists and developmentalists argue that these criticisms can be resolved within their own theoretical orientations. Dialecticians question this, however. Their preference would be to study the development of morality as a continuing interaction between developing individuals and developing cultures, with special attention to the contexts in which morality is used and elaborated.

Source of Knowledge. Learning theorists, as we have seen, focus on the active role of the environment in development. Developmentalists, on the other hand, say that the environment may facilitate or inhibit development but not control it. They emphasize the active role of the person. Dialecticians believe in both an active person *and* an active environment: This view is called **interactionism**. Development, as they see it, is a continuing *interaction* between the person and the environment. In their view, though all psychologists recognize the idea of interaction between person and environment, most end up emphasizing one at the expense of the other.

Continuity vs. Discontinuity. Like developmentalists, dialectical psychologists believe that qualitative changes (that is, *discontinuities*) are the essence of development. Unlike most developmentalists, however, dialecticians deemphasize the idea of general stages and focus instead on the development of specific concepts in specific contexts. For example, they might study how children in various cultures understand the meaning of time at various points in their day such as school time, bedtime, and so on.

Dialecticians agree with many developmentalists that contradiction is fundamental to development. In dialectical terms, any psychological phenomenon (a behavior, a concept, etc.) can be viewed as a **thesis** and can give rise to its own contradiction, which is called the **antithesis**. For example, consider a child who believes in following authority (thesis). Suppose she internalizes the values of the current authorities (e.g., her parents) and tries to follow those values (which have become a matter of conscience). This alternative view suggests that one should always follow one's conscience (antithesis). But in certain contexts the conflict between thesis and antithesis may become apparent. For example, the child may be exposed to a new authority (e.g., a teacher) who proposes something in conflict with the child's conscience. Should she then follow authority (thesis) or conscience (antithesis)?

The dialectical solution is not to choose between these views but rather to go beyond both. The resolution to a conflict between thesis and antithesis is called the **synthesis**. In the present case, rather than rejecting either authority or conscience, the child may construct a way of thinking about moral situations in which respect for authority and respect for conscience are no longer in conflict. This might, for example, involve a redefinition of authority, or conscience, or both.

Sequences of Development. Dialecticians argue that the specific nature of the child's synthesis is not predetermined. Dialectical syntheses are highly individualized. They are not predictable steps in a universal sequence. Thus dialecticians do not accept the common developmental view of invariant sequences. However, they also differ from the traditional learning viewpoint. In their focus on the thesis–antithesis–synthesis cycle, dialectical theorists are postulating that development does follow a logic of its own rather than mindlessly following the environment. The logic of development yields *progress* rather than simply change.

Generality of Development. Dialecticians believe it is crucial to study development as it occurs in social, cultural, and historical contexts. They fault learning theorists for focusing too closely and uncritically on how children perform specific tasks that are taken out of meaningful context (such as memory for objects in a laboratory). They equally criticize developmentalists for studying general, abstract structures (such as Piaget's, Kohlberg's, or Erikson's stages) that are just as remote from the real world of the child.

For example, a dialectician studying memory would not simply make up some arbitrary memory tasks and see how well children of different ages do and what helps them to improve. Neither would the dialectician propose general stages of memory ability. Instead, the dialectical researcher would see more relevance in matters such as the use of memory in everyday environments, differences between cultures in what it means to remember something, age changes in how memory is used, and so forth.

Scientific Research Strategies

Theory vs. Data. Dialectical thinkers see theory and data as closely interrelated. Scientific progress results from the continuing *interaction* between them. Conflicts among theories, among sets of data, and between theory and data are the basis for the continuing progress of scientific understanding.

Preferred Research Methods. Dialectical researchers are generally not much interested in setting up artificial experiments to see the effects of specific variables on people. Neither are they inclined to generalize across diverse situations and posit some underlying structure to account for them. Instead, they explore the complex paths of change shown by individuals (Lerner, Skinner & Sorell, 1980). For example, a dialectical researcher interested in the development of a sense of identity might be highly intrigued by how today's adolescents are affected by, and effect, changes in society. Careful **observation** of numerous concrete

Dialectical theorists place great emphasis on the social context of development.

details of the adolescents and their environments would be an essential step in any such research. Comparisons across cultures would be seen as particularly valuable.

Practical Applications

Dialogue. The input of parents and teachers is seen by dialecticians as an antithesis. Its specific nature affects the kind of synthesis ultimately constructed. For example, there are many ways to contradict a particular child's ideas about how boys (as opposed to girls) are supposed to behave. A dialectician would suggest that the sort of contradiction (antithesis) one provides will affect the new ideas about sex roles (the synthesis) the child evolves. Thus, the dialectician agrees with the developmentalist that the contradiction will lead to the construction of new ideas, but also agrees with the learning theorist that the nature of the new ideas depends on the specific contradiction. The dialectician views home and school as something less than the *cause* of development but something more than simply input into an internally directed developmental process.

Dialecticians also emphasize that teachers and parents are influenced by the child at the same time as the child is influenced by them. Education is not a one-way street; instead, it represents a continuing dialogue between two (or even among several) people. Adults as well as children are developing individuals in a simultaneously changing world.

Conclusions 61

Context. Dialectical theorists stress the importance of focusing on specific interactions of individuals and their environments. Rather than relying on general principles of learning or development, the dialectician emphasizes the necessity of informed decision-making by parents and teachers in close touch with specific children, home environments, schools, subjects, situations, and societal contexts.

Conclusions

Overview of the Three Paradigms

As we have seen, the learning, developmental, and dialectical paradigms differ in fundamental ways. Table 2-1 summarizes these differences. In order to minimize misunderstanding or oversimplification, however, we should note several important points.

TABLE 2-1 Summary of the Three Paradigms

		Learning	Developmental	Dialectical
History		Locke	Kant, Rousseau	Hegel
		Wundt	Baldwin, Freud	Marx
		Watson	Werner, Piaget	Vygotsky
Current Examples		Operant theory	Nativism	Soviet theory
		Social learning	Constructivism	American dialectics
		Information processing	Psychoanalysis	
Basic Concepts	Level of analysis	Elementarism	Holism	Contextualism
	Source of knowledge	Empiricism	Nativism	Interactionism
			Constructivism	
	Role of person and environment	Active environment	Active person	Interactionism
	Continuity/discontinuity	Continuity	Discontinuity	Discontinuity
	Sequences of development	Variable	Invariant	Variable
	Generality of development	Task specific	General stages	Context specific
Scientific Strategy	Theory vs. data	Primacy of data	Primacy of theory	Theory/data interaction
	Research methods	Experiment	Clinical interview	Observation
Practical Uses		Socialization	Facilitation	Dialogue
		Instruction	Disequilibration	Context

Differences Within Paradigms. In trying to present the essence of each paradigm, we have focused on what the various theories within it have in common. The specific theories within each paradigm also differ in important ways, however. For example, we discussed how operant conditioning and information processing theories differ, even though both were classified within the learning paradigm. Although it is useful to think about the field of developmental psychology in terms of three general paradigms, you should not allow this to blind you to the specifics of particular theories as you progress through this text.

Similarities Across Paradigms. In trying to present three general paradigms as clearly as possible, not only have we understated differences among theories within each paradigm but we have also understated some important similarities among theories in different paradigms. For example, many theories in the learning and developmental paradigms are increasingly emphasizing dialectical ideas. This is especially true of Piagetian theory (Youniss, 1978); information processing theories (Jenkins, 1974; Kintsch, 1979); and social learning theory (Bandura, 1978).

Are There Other Ways of Sorting the Theories? We have just warned that some theories within the same paradigm have important differences and that some theories in different paradigms have important similarities. Are there other ways of sorting the theories that would avoid these problems?

In fact, the numerous theories in the field of developmental psychology are so diverse and have such complex patterns of similarities and differences that no way of dividing them is perfect. The distinction we have made between learning theories and developmental theories is widely used (e.g., Reese & Overton, 1970). The view that dialectical theories constitute a third category is more recent (e.g., Lerner, Skinner, & Sorell, 1980; Moshman, 1982) and more controversial (for a recent criticism, see Overton, 1984). At any rate, you should not allow the three perspectives just outlined to close your mind to other considerations.

Applications

Choosing a Paradigm

Which of these paradigms do you like best? Which might developmental psychologists, parents, and teachers prefer? In general, when we have two or more theories to explain some phenomenon, we try to gather data to test the theories and see which provides the best explanation. Why, then, don't we just look at relevant data and decide which is the best of the three paradigms?

Unfortunately, this isn't so easy. For example, Piaget claims that in early adolescence people develop a new, more abstract kind of reasoning that he calls *formal operational reasoning*. As we will see in Chapter 8, it is difficult enough to decide whether specific theoretical claims such as this one are correct. But even if we had clear evidence in support of this developmental sequence it would not prove the correctness of the developmental paradigm. A learning theorist could still argue that the environment (e.g., schooling) is the central factor that produces formal operational reasoning. And a dialectical theorist could argue that formal reasoning is generated via a thesis–antithesis–synthesis cycle rather than through either learning or internal construction. Similarly, even if there were clear evidence that Piaget's stages were incorrect, this would only show that Piaget's specific theory was incorrect—not that the developmental paradigm is inadequate.

The fact that no single experiment can prove or disprove a paradigm, however, does not mean that any paradigm is as good as any other. Over many years a paradigm may succeed in generating powerful theories that explain important phenomena; on the other hand, it may consistently fail to provide interesting and convincing theoretical accounts that can stand up to the evidence.

The three paradigms discussed in this chapter are all in the first category. Each of them has survived many years of research and remains important in the field of developmental psychology. Each paradigm provides particularly interesting and enlightening explanations for certain phenomena and has more trouble accounting for other data. And their patterns of strengths and weaknesses are mutually complementary. The learning perspective is helpful in analyzing how a child acquires and uses specific skills; the developmental perspective gives a useful overview of the general course of development; and the dialectical view helps us see how internal and external factors interact with each other. Taken individually, however, the learning perspective may blind us to overall developmental tendencies, the developmental perspective may blind us to important environmental influences, and the dialectical approach, though in a sense the broadest perspective, is often too general and vague to give us much guidance. The wise parent, teacher, or researcher can view children from all three perspectives and can be flexible in choosing the most fruitful framework for considering any given question. Anyone who is limited to one of these perspectives will have good insights into certain issues but will have, overall, a narrow scope of understanding.

Combining Paradigms

If all three paradigms have something to offer, it is tempting to try to combine the three into a single "superparadigm." This is easier said than done, however. Imagine trying to produce the ultimate painting by taking the best parts from each of the world's ten best paintings and merging them. The result would certainly not be the world's greatest painting; in fact, it probably would not be a good painting at all. The different paintings each have their own style, and combining them would most likely result in a total jumble.

Similarly, each of the three paradigms we have considered has its own set of basic assumptions about human behavior, cognition, and development. Although there have been some attempts to integrate them (e.g., Moshman, 1982), there have also been some cogent warnings about the traps involved in such efforts (e.g., Reese & Overton, 1970). Whether or not a general synthesis is possible, it is clear that we have not achieved it and will not do so in the foreseeable future.

How should we deal with the existence of diverse perspectives and interpretations? One implication is that parents, teachers, and others who work with children should not view psychological knowledge as a steady accumulation of objective scientific truths. Psychology offers many insights, but it cannot provide cookbook solutions to future problems. What it *can* provide are diverse sources of evidence, useful explanations and perspectives, and some general guidelines. To use these tools effectively, those who work with children must behave as professionals, trying out ideas in new situations and making careful and informed judgments.

Summary

In this chapter we took a preliminary look at current theories in the field of developmental psychology. Like all sciences, developmental psychology includes both theories and data. Progress in developmental psychology, as in any science, comes from a continuing interplay between theories and data.

Theories of development can be divided into three major paradigms, or families of theories. The learning paradigm includes theories such as operant conditioning, social learning, and information processing that are not specific to developmental psychology. Rather, they are extensions of general theories about how people learn from and are shaped by their environments. The developmental paradigm includes theories, such as Piaget's, that focus on long-term developmental changes and internal processes accounting for them. Finally, dialectical theories emphasize the continuing interaction of internal and external factors.

After reading this chapter you should have a better sense of some of the major issues developmental psychologists grapple with and some general perspectives on human development. As you read about specific theories and research results in later chapters you will understand them better by considering them in terms of the three paradigms we have discussed. Moreover, your understanding of the three paradigms will deepen. The broad picture helps you grasp the details, and the details in turn help you better understand the broad picture.

So far we have focused more on theory than on research. If data are just as important to science as theories are, we should certainly consider the methods developmental psychologists use to gather data. These methods will be the subject of the next chapter.

Key Terms

theory
data
paradigm

learning theory
developmental theory
dialectical theory

empiricism
introspection
operant conditioning

reinforcers	experiment	disequilibrium
punishers	socialization	disequilibration
social learning theory	instruction	contextualism
modeling	nativism	interactionism
information processing	constructivism	thesis
cognitive theory	psychoanalytic theory	antithesis
elementarism	holism	synthesis
reductionism	active person	observation
active environment	invariant sequence	dialogue
stages of development	clinical interview	

Suggested Readings

Bandura, A. (1977). *Social learning theory*. Englewood Cliffs, NJ: Prentice-Hall. This book is an introduction to social learning theory by its foremost proponent.

Crain, W. C. (1985). *Theories of development: Concepts and applications* (2nd ed.). Englewood Cliffs, NJ: Prentice-Hall. Crain introduces and compares a variety of theories of development, with emphasis on the contrast between "learning" and "developmental" perspectives.

Kuhn, T. S. (1970). *The structure of scientific revolutions* (2nd ed.). Chicago: University of Chicago Press. This is by far the most widely read and cited work on modern philosophy of science. Though less technical than many philosophical works, it is nevertheless a challenging book open to differing interpretations.

Moshman, D. (1982). Exogenous, endogenous, and dialectical constructivism. *Developmental Review, 2*, 371–384. This article explores the possibility of partially integrating the learning, developmental, and dialectical perspectives.

Quine, W. V., & Ullian, J. S. (1978). *The web of belief* (2nd ed.). New York: Random House. A readable introduction to modern philosophical ideas about theories, evidence, and scientific progress, this work is aimed at students with no background in philosophy.

Riegel, K. F. (1979). *Foundations of dialectical psychology*. New York: Academic Press. Published shortly after Riegel's death, this collection of essays provides a good introduction to the dialectical point of view.

Vygotsky, L. S. (1978). *Mind in society: The development of higher psychological processes*. Cambridge, MA: Harvard University Press. (Original works published in the 1930s.) These recent translations of some of Vygotsky's most important work are edited to be as clear as possible to the modern reader.

Note: For further readings concerning Piaget and information processing theories, see Chapter 8. For further readings concerning Erikson's theory, see Chapter 16.

Application Exercise

2-1 Identifying Theoretical Paradigms

What type of theorist (learning, developmental, or dialectical) would be most likely to make each of the following assertions? (In some cases the answer might be none, two, or all three.)

1. There are certain stages in the development of reasoning that children in all cultures go through.
2. A child's language is shaped gradually by his or her environment.
3. Parents not only influence their children but are simultaneously influenced by their children's behavior.

4. Intelligence may be judged very differently in different cultures.
5. The typical 12-year-old memorizes a list by mentally going through a sequence of steps, each of which is studied through carefully designed research.
6. A little girl's ideas about what is proper feminine behavior can be expected to change over time in response to the different role models she experiences during her development.
7. Children actively construct their identities by continually finding new ways to consolidate their earlier self-conceptions.
8. Theory and data each play important roles in formulating a scientific understanding of human development.
9. A child's performance on a specific task may tell us a lot about his or her general level of development.
10. A specific conflict of ideas may enable an individual to go beyond both to a unique point of view.
11. The environment in which a child develops is only of minor importance.
12. A major purpose of education should be to help a child go through the natural stages of development.
13. Everything we know comes to us through our senses.

CHAPTER 3

Research Methods

The great tragedy of Science—the slaying of a beautiful hypothesis by an ugly fact.
—T. H. Huxley,
   Biogenesis and Abiogenesis

In Chapter 2, we discussed theories of developmental psychology. The basis for theoretical progress in a science is *research*, a systematic process for gathering information and for trying to understand that information. Like other sciences, developmental psychology is founded on its research. This is what we will consider in this chapter.

Developmental Psychology as a Science

Thousands upon thousands of scientific studies have been conducted to study development in humans. Child development researchers have been interested in topics as different as bone growth and changes in moral judgments. In all scientific research in development we find common elements that are the foundations of all scientific studies: (1) systematic observations, (2) development and testing of hypotheses, (3) reliance on data, not belief, and (4) public sharing of the results from the research. Let's look in turn at each one of these elements to get a clearer idea of just how developmental psychology grew to become the broad field it is today.

Systematic Observation

Imagine you are in your local supermarket. There, at the checkout, is a young father holding a small child whom you judge to be about 2 years old. Crying loudly, the child is struggling to be put down. Later that week, you see the same father and child, but this time at the post office. Again, the child is struggling and crying but, as before, the father continues to hold the child and will not put her down. What can you conclude from your observations? Could you say that fathers are not very skilled parents? Could you say that 2-year-olds do not like to be held? That children need to be disciplined in order for their behavior to be improved?

Obviously, any of these conclusions would be rash, because your observations were not systematic, only accidental. What you saw may or may not "mean something," because you have no idea how *representative* your observations are. Are your observations of this father and child typical of parent-child interactions in general? What you saw might be interesting, but it is certainly not the kind of information you would place much faith in!

In contrast to our everyday impressions, research in developmental psychology is based on systematic observation. **Systematic observation** means that certain conditions for observation are present, so that the researcher can be confident that observations are meaningful. These conditions include a focus on variables, selecting representative samples, and use of theory to guide observation.

Variables. Any scientific observation focuses on **variables**, which are factors that can take on different values. Sex is a variable that takes on two values, male and female. Intelligence is another; it has many possible values ranging from low to high. Height and weight are two other obvious examples of variables. Relationships between variables are identified by observing whether one changes as the other changes. For example, as prenatal nutrition is improved for expectant mothers, does birth weight of their babies increase and number of birth-related complications decrease?

Researchers almost always concentrate on some variables while ignoring others. They may be interested, for example, in variables related to speech development (e.g., number of two-word utterances by a child), but not at all in other potentially observable variables (e.g., number of baby teeth, foot size, or hair color). By selecting certain variables, researchers narrow their attention only to those factors of greatest interest and value to the research study.

Some developmental variables are measurable characteristics of children and adults, such as height, weight, or intelligence level. Others are "outside" the child; these are conditions naturally affecting the child or artificially arranged by an experimenter. For instance, a child's family's income or the number of hours of television a child views each day are two variables that might influence development. Similarly, an experimenter might provide two different sets of playthings at a preschool at different times to see if children's actions toward others are affected by the type of toys available.

Variables such as health care during pregnancy that are presumed to affect other variables are called **independent variables**. Variables presumed to be affected *by* an independent variable (e.g., health status of infants immediately after birth) are called **dependent variables**. Scientists predict *from* independent variables *to* dependent variables (Kerlinger, 1979; Seitz, 1984).

The independent variable is the antecedent and the dependent variable is the consequence or outcome. Developmental psychologists have identified many independent and dependent variables that help us better understand children's development. Typical independent variables include mother–child contact immediately after birth, type of neighborhood the child lives in, classroom methods the child is exposed to, ages of brothers or sisters, and early linguistic (language) experience. Important dependent variables are the ability to reason, delinquency, memory ability, level of moral development, aggressive behavior, and infant babbling and early speech. As developmental psychologists study relationships between carefully selected independent and dependent variables (these change, of course, from study to study), they have been able to draw a clearer and clearer picture of the nature of human development.

Representative Samples. Science is aimed at finding out *general* principles or rules about variables. As scientists, developmental psychologists are interested in universal principles or those that are at least true in some definable group of individuals. Taking our example of the father and child in the supermarket, we would have a shaky basis on which to generalize to fathers and children in general. We do not know if the child is representative of all 2-year-olds or even, for that matter, if she is two years old, or even that she may not be a he!

To increase the likelihood that observations extend beyond the children directly observed, therefore, developmental psychologists try to select **representative samples** of individuals to study. A representative sample is a small group that accurately represents some larger group. Researchers interested in understanding more about 3-year-olds in the United States, for instance, would need a representative sample of 3-year-olds to study. Obviously, children from various ethnic, racial, socioeconomic, and geographical backgrounds should be proportionally present in the sample. The researchers can state that their results apply to all U.S. 3-year-olds only if their sample has the same composition as the population of 3-year-olds in the United States. Of course, the results of the study may not be true at all for 3-year-olds in, say, the Soviet Union or in Belize.

Developmental psychologists are seldom interested *only* in the single child or the group of children being studied. They are interested in learning something about *all* children who are similar to those observed. This larger group, to which researchers hope to generalize their findings, is called the **population.** Ideally, careful sampling techniques should be used in developmental studies to ensure that the sample is representative of the population of interest. Many studies, however, are conducted with children who are available to the researcher, but who are not necessarily "representative." Thus, most published studies contain detailed descriptions of the children who did participate (e.g., age, sex, ethnic group) in order to help readers to decide for themselves how far the results can be generalized.

Theoretical Framework. Earlier we mentioned that scientific observation is not random: Some variables are selected for observation and some are not. How do developmental psychologists decide which variables to observe? Often they are guided by theories. As we stated in Chapter 2, *Theories of Developmental Psychology*, theories are sets of ideas. They are attempts to provide explanations and make predictions. To clarify this, let's look at an example of how theories have been used to guide research in developmental psychology.

For many years, we have known that human infants (along with rats, chicks, kittens, lambs, dogs, pigs, and goats) will avoid a *visual cliff*, a space that looks like it drops off suddenly (Gibson & Walk, 1960; Walk & Gibson, 1961). This is an important behavior; without it, humans would be plunging off all kinds of steps, cliffs, roofs, and ledges with predictably disastrous results!

In a typical visual cliff experiment, infants are placed on a large table covered with thick glass. Under one side there appears to be support, but not under the other side. Human infants, when called by their mothers from the other side, will hesitate and refuse to crawl out onto the part of the glass covering the "dropoff." But where does this avoidance come from? How do babies "know enough" to avoid an apparent fall?

One theory or explanation is that this avoidance is instinctive, based in the evolution of the species (see Chapter 4, *Evolution and Genetics* for a detailed explanation of evolution). Supporting this viewpoint is the observation that animals with no prior experience avoid the dropoff (see Rader, Bausano, & Richards, 1980). Others believe that this avoidance in human infants is *not* instinctive (e.g., Campos, Hiatt, Ramsay, Henderson, & Sevja, 1978), but instead learned from early experience. Which theory is more nearly correct? Only systematic observation can answer this question.

Both theories about visual cliff avoidance require observation of how and when infants avoid the cliff. What variables indicate avoidance? In a variety of studies, such dependent variables as heart rate (an indicator of fear or interest), use of a roundabout detour pattern, the time taken to cross, and the time spent to reach the mother were observed.

But what about independent variables? Persons guided by instinct theory tested different species (remember the rats, chicks, goats, and others?) and found that each species avoided the cliff differently, depending on the type of environments that controlled their evolution. Goats, for example, who naturally inhabit rocky, mountainous areas,

Researchers seldom disagree about *what* they observe. They often do disagree, however, on *why* something happens, and their theories play an important role in helping them understand and explain what they have observed.

avoided the cliff one-hundred percent of the time, even though they had no previous experience in moving themselves around (2-hour-old baby goats were used).

In contrast, researchers who held an "experience" viewpoint set up different arrangements. They varied such things as age and crawling experience. Then, noting changes in reactions to the cliff (e.g., older infants tended to avoid the cliff more), they concluded that the infants' experiences in moving themselves around probably was the best explanation for visual cliff avoidance.

While the role of instinct versus experience in visual cliff avoidance is still not completely settled, you can see how these two theories of development each guided what the researchers observed. Those who held an instinct theory looked at species differences; those coming from an experience perspective examined variables such as age to see if they made a difference. Theory helps make the observations of developmental psychologists systematic. Without it, they could not make sense out of their observations. Most likely, they wouldn't even have much of an idea about what to observe!

Most well-planned studies are tests of theory. Theories, of course, are the best current explanations of "the way things are" (see Chapter 2, *Theories of Developmental Psychology*). An explanation or theory is good, however, only as long as it matches the facts that are observed: the data. When a theory no longer fits with observations and it is shown to be false, then it must be modified or abandoned. Progress in developmental psychology has come through testing ideas—theories—through systematic observation and then adjusting or discarding ideas that just don't "match up."

Testing Hypotheses About Development

Developmental theories are broad, global ways of looking at developmental issues. In the visual cliff phenomenon just discussed, "instinct" and "experience" are two general theories that are possible explanations for this rather remarkable capability of human infants (and 2-hour-old goats!) to avoid potentially disastrous circumstances.

Most studies in psychology test *specific* predictions, however, that are *consistent with* a particular theory. These specific predictions of the results of a research study are called **hypotheses**. In the study by Rader et al. (1980), the hypothesis was this: Infants' reactions to the visual cliff would depend on an unlearned link between processing visual information and crawling. Thus, these researchers predicted, infants would avoid the visual cliff while crawling, but not while moving around in a walker (a small chair with wheels and tray).

These researchers did not believe that general experience in moving about was particularly important, nor was the child's understanding that cliffs were places to fall off of. Instead, they took a more instinctual viewpoint—that babies' crawling is guided by a kind of built-in program based on visual information that comes to the infant.

Their data were consistent with their hypothesis. Only 4 out of 22 infants, all with experience in moving around via walker and by crawling, avoided the dropoff of the visual cliff when tested *in their walkers*. When tested while crawling, however, over half of the infants (12) avoided it. Something about crawling made a difference in how likely infants were to avoid the visual cliff.

Since the hypothesis was not shown to be false (Remember that the purpose of research is to test theory and hypotheses to see if they are false!), the theory on which it was based also survived this particular test. An alternative explanation—that experience in crawling and moving about helps develop a "concept" of dropping off—is now less attractive, since all the children had experience, yet with the walker most of them failed to avoid the visual cliff. Still other explanations, however, are possible (e.g., that close versus distant visual contact with the cliff affects crossing) and need to be ruled out. Thus, additional studies are often necessary before issues can be resolved.

Reliance on Data, Not Belief

Developmental theories are not blind statements of belief. Although they emerge from a kind of belief, they are different from other beliefs (e.g., religious beliefs) in that they are deliberately *tested* by observations. We believe them only as long as they are not contradicted by data from systematic observation. Hypotheses that are not true and theories that are not supported must be abandoned. When Einstein first argued that time was relative—that it slows down or speeds up depending on relative motion—this idea was met with disbelief and sarcasm. Experiments, however, later showed this to be the case (clocks traveling at very high rates of speed slow down relative to other clocks not in motion) and physicists' whole concept of time and space had to change. Similarly, scientific study forced us to abandon notions such as that the earth is flat, that it was created 6,000 years ago, and that it is the center of the universe.

If the data of developmental psychology show that a belief (e.g., viewing large amounts of violence on television diminishes children's natural aggressions) is false (in fact, large amounts of television viewing, especially of violent programs, is *associated* with aggressive behavior; see Eron, Huesmann, Brice, Fischer, & Mermelstein, 1983; Ross & Slaby, 1983), then the researcher must abandon it. Abandoning false theories when they do not match the facts (observations) has permitted great advances in developmental psychology. Much of what we know today about the physical, mental, and social development of children has come from this process in which wrong ideas are discarded and knowledge is advanced step by step, study by study.

Public Sharing of Research

The developmental psychologist, like all scientists, has yet another commitment: to share research information with others. Thus, results of studies are published in research journals and are available for anyone who cares to read them. (Examples of such journals are *Developmental Psychology, Child Development*, and the *Journal of Applied Developmental Psychology*.) Researchers publish their results in the belief that knowledge advances only if ideas are scrutinized by others. Another important reason for publication is to permit the research to be *replicated* (repeated). Replication usually confirms earlier results, but sometimes reveals that results may not be as generalizable as earlier believed. When others are able to duplicate earlier findings, confidence increases.

The research and theories published by psychologists are often criticized, sometimes severely, by other psychologists. But criticism often leads to replication, to new studies, to new hypotheses, and to new and better theories. In the example of the visual cliff, simple ideas of "instinct" versus "experience" are replaced by more accurate and sophisticated concepts about how infants do or do not avoid a dropoff.

Research Designs in Developmental Psychology

So far we have talked about the need for systematic research. In the best studies, variables are selected based on theory, observation is carefully planned, and research participants are chosen to be representative of the general population.

Developmental psychology is concerned with the description, explanation, and modification of changes within an individual. It also

Research

Surviving the Cuts: Publishing Research in Developmental Journals

Most of the research cited in this text initially appeared in developmental research journals such as *Developmental Psychology*, *Monographs of the Society for Research in Child Development*, *Child Development*, and *Journal of Experimental Child Psychology*. These and other important developmental journals serve as the primary outlet for developmental researchers hoping to communicate their findings.

Publication in the most highly ranked developmental research journals is not easy, however. Manuscripts must survive an exacting review process in which each study is checked by experts for technical quality, theoretical soundness, and importance to the field. In the most prestigious developmental psychology journals, as few as one in ten manuscripts survive this process and are published. Also, the majority of those that are published undergo at least some revision between the time they are submitted and when they finally appear in print.

The review process begins with the authors' preparation of a double-spaced, typewritten manuscript that describes the research study. This manuscript is carefully written to follow guidelines that appear in the *Publication Manual of the American Psychological Association* (1983), a 208-page manual that outlines details of manuscript preparation, style, and format.

When the authors are satisfied with the description of their research, they send it to the editor of the journal in which they hope it will be published. After an initial scan of the manuscript to determine its general suitability for the journal (many manuscripts are returned at this point with the suggestion to submit it elsewhere), the editor or associate editor typically sends copies to members of the editorial board and to *ad hoc* reviewers who have particular expertise in the area of the research study (e.g., language development, social development). Most often, reviews are blind—neither authors nor reviewers know who the others are. Blind review is important, of course, because it helps assure that publication is the result of scientific merit, and not some other factor such as the prestige of the researcher or the researcher's institution.

As you might expect, editors of the top developmental journals are themselves almost always highly capable and highly regarded researchers. Indeed, they and their reviewers hold the future of developmental psychology in their hands. The standards they set and the articles they select determine the direction developmental research takes. While rejection of a manuscript may indeed be a bitter pill for a research team, high publication standards ensure the continuation of excellent scientific practices in the field and permit other researchers to read the research reports with confidence. For example, when Ross Parke, new editor of the journal *Developmental Psychology*, was asked about his plans for that journal, his first response was to speak of maintaining its high level of quality (*APA Monitor*, February, 1986). This goal is shared by all who assume the high honor and responsibility of editing developmental research journals. Their decisions carry on the scientific tradition of the field and play a crucial role in its future.

---

attempts to explain differences between individuals in change patterns (Baltes, Cornelius, & Nesselroade, 1979; Seitz, 1984). To answer questions about change and individual differences, developmental psychologists ask them within **research designs**. Research designs are logical frameworks used to make key comparisons within research studies. The more careful the design of the research, the more confident researchers can be in their results.

Two research designs—the **cross-sectional design** and the **longitudinal design**—have been used extensively in developmental psychology over the years. These two designs and a combined design are discussed in the following sections.

Cross-Sectional Designs

In a cross-sectional research design, individuals of different ages are observed on the same dependent variable at the same point in time (Baltes, 1968; Seitz, 1984). A simple example we often see in the daily newspaper is the opinion poll, where views on topics such as abortion are contrasted by age group, by religious affiliation, or by gender. Developmental psychologists use the cross-sectional method to compare individuals of varying ages on some dependent variable.

A study by Langsdorf, Izard, Rayias, and Hembree (1983) shows the key features of the cross-sectional research design. These researchers were interested in whether younger versus older infants paid attention to objects differently. Previous research had shown developmental changes in attention and these investigators wanted to test a new measure of interest in which infants' facial expressions were coded and scored.

Four different groups of infants were tested in the study: 2-, 4-, 6-, and 8-month-olds. Dependent variables included the new measure of facial expressions, time spent looking, and degree that the heart rate slowed up (considered to be a measure of interest). A second independent variable in addition to age was the type of thing looked at: a person's face, a mannequin, and an inanimate object. Since prior research had shown that infants prefer to look at human faces, this same hypothesis was made for this study.

The results were as expected: The older the infants, the more likely they were to look at and be affected measurably by the human face. Each successively older group was more "intrigued by" the human face! All groups clearly preferred the human face over the mannequin or the inanimate object.

The main advantage of a cross-sectional research design like this is that age-related or other trends can be assessed quickly and simply. The Langsdorf et al. study, for example, provides important information about the growing attention that infants pay to faces during their first year of life. In this study, the data were gathered in a single study period using different groups of infants.

Using similar methods, researchers over the years have added to the information about mental, physical, and social development through childhood, adolescence, and adulthood. Representative groups at different ages have been tested on such dependent variables as height, weight, intelligence, language skills, and so on to assess general patterns of human development.

The disadvantages of the cross-sectional method, however, are important to note. Comparisons between ages in the Langsdorf et al. study, for example, are not for the *same* children at 2, 4, 6, and 8 months, but instead are for *different* groups of children. Factors other than development (e.g., a biased sample of children at one age level, differences in intelligence, or social background) may actually be the "cause" of the outcomes we think are related to age. For instance, in comparing intellectual functioning at ages 40, 50, 60, and 70, one must keep in mind that current 40-year-olds are likely to have more education than older persons. Thus what might be interpreted as an "intellectual decline" with age actually might just be differences in educational level. The variable of age is *confounded* with the date of birth: changes in educational level may be the reason for "differences across age." Young people's IQ scores may be higher because they typically have more schooling than older people. When using the cross-sectional method, researchers usually strive to assure the comparability of the different groups under study, but they are not always successful in achieving that goal (Nunnally, 1980).

Longitudinal Designs

Longitudinal research designs require that the *same* individuals be studied over a period of time. For example, a psychologist interested in children's self-concept development may select a sample of preschool children, assess their self-concept, and then take measures of their self-concept every second or third year as they move through elementary and then secondary school.

Longitudinal research designs' key strength is *repeated measurement of the same individuals over time.* Thus, changes noted are in the *same persons* and are not potentially confused by differences between groups.

A survey of the field of developmental psychology shows many studies with longitudinal designs (see Mednick, Harway, & Finello, 1984). One such study is by Colby, Kohlberg, Gibbs, & Lieberman (1983). This study spanned a 20-year period from the mid-1950s through the mid-1970s; participants were interviewed every three or four years.

The researchers focused on participants' moral development and observed changes in how their subjects judged right and wrong. The theory underlying this research is that of Lawrence Kohlberg, who has proposed that moral development moves through stages (see Chapter 15). Kohlberg's theory holds that individuals at lower stages of moral development do "what is right" only to avoid breaking rules and to avoid punishment. At higher levels, individuals' moral judgments are guided more by conscience and ethical principles. Six levels of moral development are hypothesized; in Kohlberg's view, individuals move to higher levels of moral development only after they have gone through lower levels.

Colby et al. interviewed their subjects and presented them with dilemmas such as whether a man should steal in order to buy a cancer-fighting drug for his sick wife. Subjects' responses to these dilemmas were then coded by level.

We might ask whether individuals move in a prescribed sequence from one moral judgment level to the next. If this is so, then the developmental sequence should be consistent for each individual studied. Everyone will not reach the same level, but the progression should be successive through levels. No stage-skipping or downward stage movement should occur.

Colby et al.'s results confirmed their ideas about moral judgment development. Only a very small percentage of the subjects showed any evidence of stage-skipping or sequence reversals. Changes from lower to higher levels outnumbered reversals by about fourteen to one (Colby et al., p. 35)

Could we have gotten this information from cross-sectional research? The answer is no because these ideas can be tested only in a longitudinal design. To see if stage-skipping takes place, individuals must be followed over time to see if any of them "jump" over lower levels to go directly to higher stages. In order to know what happens to *each* person, the *same* person must be measured repeatedly. Changes within individuals over time can then be assessed; this is a major goal in the study of development.

No matter how useful they are, all research designs have weaknesses. Longitudinal designs are no exception. The first drawback is that age is confounded with time of testing. Suppose, for example, you were engaged in a study of attitudes toward sex roles that tested women's views over the past 30 years. By the end of the study, your original group of 20-year-olds now would be 50 years old. A finding that the participants' attitudes had become more liberal as the group aged could be due to a general tendency of older people to have more flexible attitudes. The finding might reflect social change, however. Western society has developed more liberal attitudes toward sex and sex roles in the last 30 years. Thus, the difference you observed may not represent a difference between 20-year-olds and 50-year-olds; rather, it might reflect changes from the 1950s to the 1980s.

Other major problems of the design include cost, since projects and data analyses can continue over many years. Also, theories and measures can become outdated. Publication is often long delayed as, in the Colby study, some of the most interesting results become available only after many years. Finally, it can be exceedingly difficult to maintain contact with the original participants over many years. People move or get tired of participating. *Attrition*, or loss of participants, can be a severe problem for the longitudinal researcher (Seitz, 1984). Nonetheless, longitudinal research will continue to play a key role in the study of development (Achenbach, 1978; Mednick, Harway, & Finello, 1984; Nesselroade & Baltes, 1979; Schaie & Hertzog, 1980; Schulsinger, Mednick, & Knop, 1981; Seitz, 1984).

Cross-Sequential Designs

Some developmental researchers have argued that important information is lost in both the cross-sectional and longitudinal designs. A better approach, they say, is to combine the two. Such designs have been called **cross-sequential designs**. In a typical cross-sequential design, individuals of different ages are sampled at the beginning of a study (a cross-sectional approach) and then followed over time (a longitudinal approach). In the study of moral development by Colby et al., an original cross-sectional sample included 10-, 13-, and 16-year-olds in 1955. Each of these groups was then followed longitudinally over a 20-year period.

Schaie (Schaie, 1965; Schaie & Baltes, 1975; Schaie & Hertzog, 1980) has been a particularly strong advocate of cross-sequential designs. In his studies of intelligence in adulthood and old age, he selected eight different groups born in eight different years between 1886 and 1932 and followed each of them longitudinally. These groups were called **cohorts**; a cohort is made up of a group of people born in a given year or beginning a program together. Because this cross-sequential approach combined cross-sectional and longitudinal aspects, it permitted Schaie to answer questions both about cohort effects, or effects associated with the group to which a person belongs (e.g., people born in 1932), and about time-related changes. For example, are people who are now 60 years old different intellectually than those who were 60 years old in 1980? Are individuals who are now 60 years old different intellectually than the same people were at age 54? Only a cross-sequential design allows an examination of both kinds of questions simultaneously.

Cross-sequential designs have drawbacks as well. For example, they can be complex and cumbersome. Also, although they offer insights into how both age and cohort might affect some variables, they do not yield clear-cut answers to all the researcher's questions.

Comparison of the Three Research Designs

Figure 3-1 illustrates how each design can be used to study developmental changes and Table 3-1 summarizes the advantages and disadvantages of each. The key advantage of the cross-sectional design is its efficiency. Through it, studies of developmental trends suspected to change across age or group can be completed quickly and easily. The

FIGURE 3-1 Examples of Key Designs in Developmental Research. Comparing Performance at Ages Two, Three, and Four Using Cross-Sectional, Longitudinal, and Cross-Sequential Designs. Color indicates cross-sectional comparison. Gray indicates longitudinal comparison.

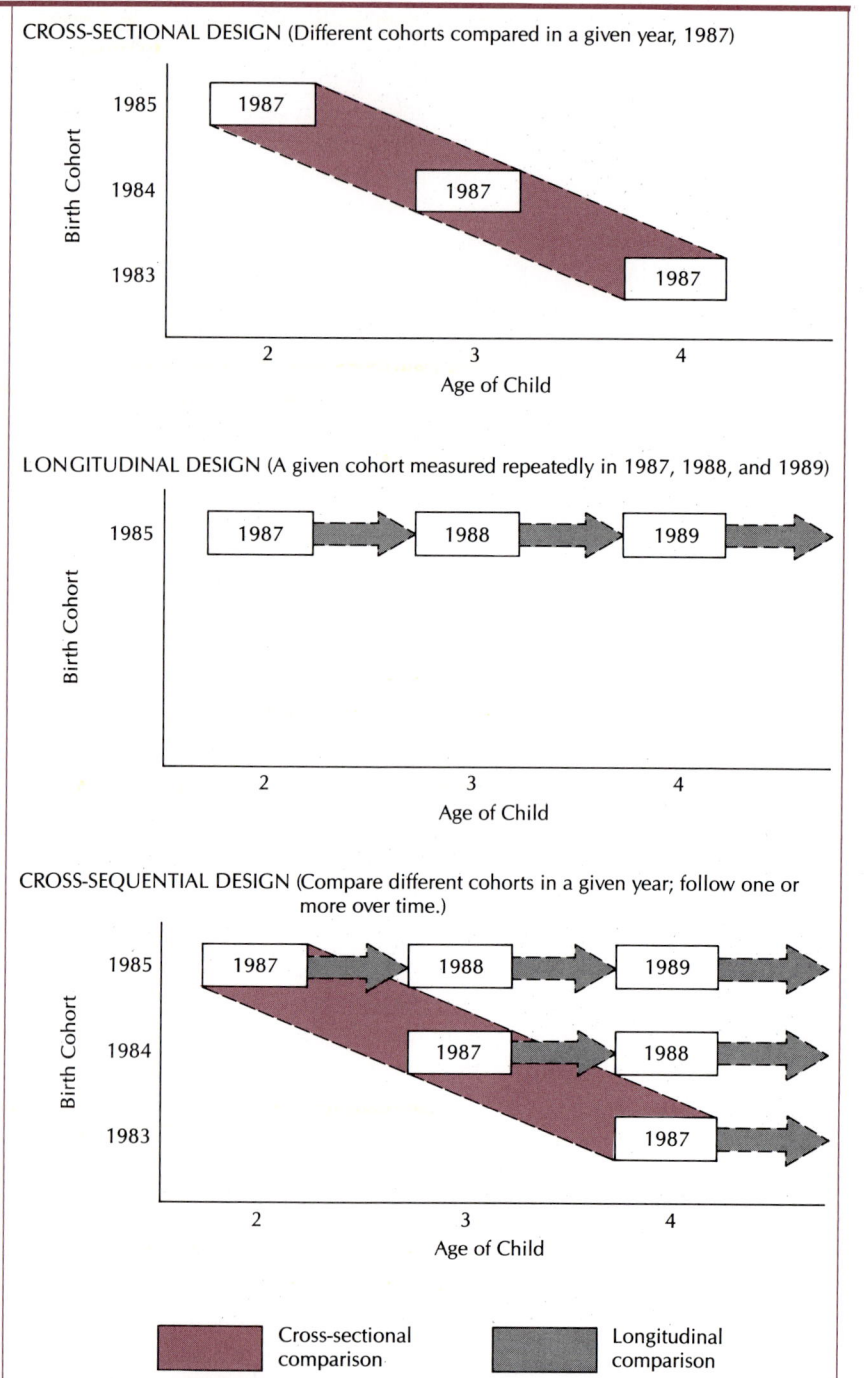

TABLE 3-1 Summary of Research Designs in Developmental Psychology

Design	Key Features	Advantages	Disadvantages
Cross-Sectional	Compares groups of different ages on some variable	Ease of gathering data	Different groups compared Age is mixed up with cohort
Longitudinal	Tests same persons at different times in their lives	Same individuals followed over time	May be impractical, expensive Age is mixed up with time of testing
Cross-Sequential	Combines longitudinal and cross-sectional approaches	Permits examination of both cohort and time of testing effects	May be impractical, very expensive

researcher must keep in mind, however, that other factors can confuse any explanations. In cross-sectional studies of several age groups, for instance, the researcher should remember that individuals are influenced by historical contexts. This contrast in "history," rather than factors related to subjects' age, may account for observed differences.

The longitudinal design seems to more closely meet developmental psychologists' desire to describe, explain, and predict development. Ideally, most developmental studies should have longitudinal characteristics in which the same individuals are followed. Time, cost, and attrition are serious drawbacks, however. Effects caused by repeated testing also can be troublesome; with repeated testing, results sometimes can become invalid.

Although complex and expensive, combined cross-sequential approaches can provide information on both age and cohort-related effects (Labouvie & Nesselroade, 1985). For example, in a study of changes in writing ability over grades 1, 3, and 5, three different classes of first graders in the years 1987, 1989, and 1991 could be followed through the primary grades. Individual changes in writing ability could be traced as the subjects advanced, and differences due to cohort (the year the child entered the first grade) also could be assessed. Research might reveal that the school's writing program is improving, for example; the cohort analysis would enable the researcher to pinpoint this factor correctly.

There is not an "either-or" choice among these three designs, of course. Each design will continue to contribute to the field. Researchers need, however, to select designs that fit the theory under consideration and that permit the most clear-cut tests of hypotheses. Also, practical factors have an impact on the choice of research designs. A good ap-

Research Methods in Developmental Psychology

As we have just seen, research designs provide the general framework for understanding development. Within these designs, however, developmental psychologists have used a variety of specific techniques to describe and explain developmental changes. These methods include: (1) **case study,** (2) **naturalistic observation,** (3) **interview,** (4) **correlation,** (5) **single-subject experimentation,** and (6) **group-based experimentation.** These methods differ in the extent to which researchers impose control over the conditions of the study and have preconceived ideas about which variables they will study. At the most "open" end of the continuum are case study methods.

Case Study Methods

Over the years, many researchers have observed and recorded details of their own children's development. Charles Darwin, for example, studied his child as a naturalist might and wrote anecdotal records about his young son's development. A more recent example appears in the work of Chukovsky (1963) as he describes actions of his children, Liosha and Valen'ka.

> Liosha buried a meat bone under his window and watered the spot regularly to grow a cow. Every morning he ran out to see if the cow's horns had yet sprouted. Valen'ka, observing how her mother watered the flowers, began to water her favorite puppy so he would grow up soon (p. 22).

The key features of the case study method are the intensive study of a single individual and the recording of observations about the individual. Early case studies often were anecdotal and formed a narrative. More recently, however, the case study method has been used more systematically, with careful observations taking place over a period of time.

The case study has provided the science of developmental psychology with some of its most intriguing questions. For example, what is genius and how does it develop? What role do parents play in the social and mental development of the child? How does early experience relate to later development? Questions such as these have stimulated many hypotheses and much systematic research using a variety of methods.

Although case studies are not as prevalent today as they once were, they continue to exert an influence in the study of child development. Their strength is their ability to permit detailed analysis of complex processes within an individual. One example of the use of this method appears in a report by Lawler (1981). As part of his research on development of reasoning, Lawler studied his own children, aged 6 and 8, in great detail. He made extensive observations over a 6-month period, supplemented by well over 100 three- or four-page written "vignettes" that described what the children were doing and learning. Similarly, Chi and Koeske (1983) studied a single child intensively to learn how he understood and organized his knowledge about a particular concept of great interest to him—dinosaurs. Out of such studies has come a detailed, rich set of examples, principles, and theory about cognitive development in children.

The greatest objection to case study information, as Lawler (1981) himself points out, is that the individual child's characteristics may affect findings and conclusions from the study. Although the study is often intensive, the subject may not be typical of other children. Understanding the specific case, however, can sometimes increase our knowledge far beyond what can be obtained from group data, in which individual differences can get lost in averages and generalizations.

Naturalistic Observation Methods

Naturalistic observation simply means observations of events that occur in nature (Seitz, 1984). Naturalistic observation is done in a natural, or nonmanipulated, setting (e.g., children's own homes or neighborhoods) and observers monitor what children do or do not do in their own environments. For example, how do children act when they are playing with other children of the same sex versus children of the opposite sex? Do they act differently in the nursery school classroom than they do on the playground? These are the kinds of questions often posed in a naturalistic observation study.

Naturalistic observation methods can capture the complexity and richness of children's lives better than many other research methods. In naturalistic observation, individuals such as these African children are observed in the actual context of their lives.

A classic study using a version of naturalistic observation methods was done by Barker and Wright (1951), in which an observer attempted to record *everything* a boy did and said in an attempt to make a complete record of how the child and his environment affected each other. An observer followed the child from the moment he woke in the morning until he fell asleep that night. One difficulty with this particular approach is that it can yield a huge amount of information. In the case of Barker and Wright, researchers filled 435 pages with descriptions of one boy's day. Therefore, most naturalistic observation is based on the strategy of choosing only *some* aspects of behavior to record.

In general, the principle in naturalistic observation is to leave things as unchanged as possible (Willems & Alexander, 1980); naturalistic methods are used to discover phenomena that are free of the investigator's influence. Naturalistic observations often can capture the complexity and richness of behavior better than some other methods. Since there is very little interaction between the observer and the child, the child is seen in the actual context of his or her life. For this reason, the approach has sometimes been referred to as an *ecological,* or *ethological,* method.

A basic difficulty of observing in naturalistic settings is establishing causal relationships. In complex settings, it is sometimes difficult to separate cause from effect. For example, when a father interacts with his two children in their home, each person's actions affect the actions of the others. We might ask which is the cause and which the effect. Organizing and quantifying the data gathered also are major tasks. Thus, many naturalistic studies put some degree of *control* on observations, either by the development of behavior coding systems (see Medinnus, 1976; Gottman, 1983) or through time sampling (Seitz, 1984).

Behavior coding methods focus observation; if a behavior fits in a predetermined category, then it is recorded. What is observed also can be limited by choosing only certain times to observe. In **time sampling**, children are observed within specified blocks of time, rather than all of the time. In classic studies of child language development (e.g., Brown & Bellugi, 1964; McNeill, 1970), for instance, children typically were visited at home once or twice a month. Everything the child said or heard was recorded. This record then was subjected to detailed analysis. Much of what we know about language development comes from this kind of naturalistic observation. Another study using a variation of the naturalistic observation method was done by Margolin and Patterson (1975). In their study, observers found that fathers responded more approvingly to their sons than to their daughters. Mothers, however, gave approval about equally to their sons and daughters.

Recent studies often combine elements of naturalistic observation with more standard, structured methods. Frankel and Rollins (1983), for example, in following up on the question of how parents interact

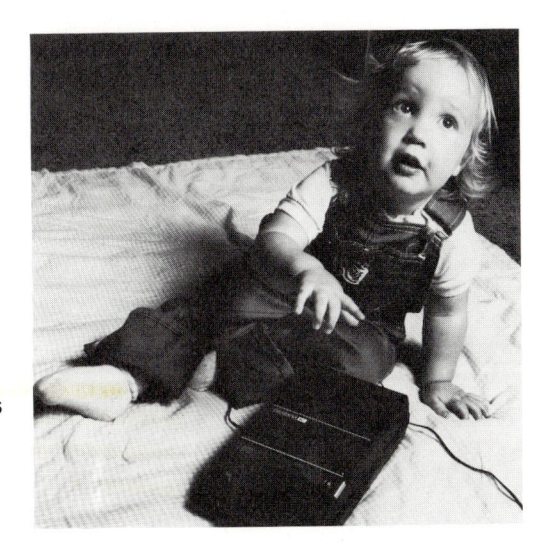

A researcher using time sampling might record this child's speech once or twice a month and then analyze the recordings to study her language development.

with children, arranged situations in which they could interact. Parents were to help their children assemble a jigsaw puzzle and also to teach them to remember picture cards. These two tasks—play and teaching—are common to parent–child interactions. The setting was the home of the parent and child. In contrast to the earlier research, such as that of Margolin and Patterson (1975), these researchers found that mothers and fathers did *not* differ in their interactions with children. In fact, *both* fathers and mothers treated their sons differently than their daughters. Parents were more task-oriented with their sons, giving them judgments about their behavior. With their daughters, however, they participated more actively in the activity. Thus, researchers used a variation of the naturalistic observation method to shed new light on findings from more "pure" naturalistic observation methods.

Interview Methods

In an interview, an interviewer asks an individual a set of questions about some aspect of his or her life. Interviews usually begin with a trained person who contacts the person to be interviewed, asks a standard set of questions, and records the person's responses. The answers to the questions are then analyzed to assess relationships between variables or to determine changes across age.

A well-known study by Kreutzer, Leonard, and Flavell (1975) provides a clear example of the interview method. Their purpose was to find out what children of different ages knew *about their own memory*. This knowledge, called *metamemory* (see Chapter 10, *Development of Memory*), is revealed in answers to questions like the following: "Do you remember things well?" and "Are there some kinds of things that are really hard to remember?" Children must have some awareness of their own memory and their strategies for remembering in order to answer such questions.

Kreutzer and her colleagues interviewed boys and girls in kindergarten, 1st, 3rd, and 5th grades and recorded their answers. The answers were then transcribed and scored. Their study showed that *all* children understood words such as "remember," "learn," and "forget." They also seemed to know that some things are harder to learn than others. Older children, however, had a much greater awareness of how meanings of things to be remembered could be related to each other in order to produce better recall. They were much more *planful* in their approach to studying and recall than were younger children.

By its structured format, the interview permits researchers to gather data systematically. Carefully planned questions and selection of representative groups can result in good tests of developmental hypotheses. A standardized format can be restrictive, however, for persons interested in probing the development of complex phenomena (such as thought processes) over time. In some cases, researchers have used what has been called the **clinical interview** or "methode clinique" to detect subtle aspects of chidren's concepts, thinking, and problem solving. This method was used extensively by Piaget, who contributed greatly to our ideas about the development of children's thought processes. The clinical interview typically uses verbal questions about objects and activities. The interviewer might take two identical balls of clay, for example, have children verify that they do indeed weigh the same, roll one into a sausage shape, and then ask them once again about the weight and for explanations of their answers. Follow-up questions are asked to ensure understanding of their thought processes. As Piaget discovered, children show clear developmental changes in their understanding that shape does not affect weight.

The biggest difficulty with the clinical interview is reporting the procedure accurately enough so that the research can be replicated. Since each child is interviewed individually, this can present a serious problem for other researchers who want to repeat the study. Also, the researcher might unconsciously "lead" the subject to give desired responses. In spite of these problems, however, the clinical interview has been tremendously useful in providing insights about the differences in thinking in children, adolescents, and adults (see Chapter 8, *Theories of Cognitive Development*). The richness of the information gathered depends, of course, on the quality of the questions asked. Piaget's own considerable insights into the nature of development enabled him to use the clinical interview with amazing effect.

Correlational Methods

Questions about *relationships between variables* are at the heart of the study of development. For example, how does intelligence relate to creativity? How do parent attitudes relate to children's attitudes about sex roles? How does early intellectual and physical development (say, at age 3) relate to later intellectual and physical development (at ages 10, 15, and 20, for instance)? Among the vast number of questions about development, it is safe to say that the majority deal with relationships among variables.

A question about relationships between variables in development is usually a question about how variables are associated or *correlated*. Two variables are *correlated* if one varies when the other does; in other words, they go together. A simple example of correlation can be seen in the relationship between people's height and weight. Generally, taller people tend to weigh more and shorter people less. Although the relationship is not perfect, we can say that height and weight are correlated.

Correlational data are gathered by many methods. Among them are *observations* and *interviews* (discussed above), *questionnaires*, and *tests*, which measure intellectual and personality variables. In a typical correlational study, several measures are collected on a group of individuals. For example, assume that we have gathered data such as that presented in Table 3-2 on mothers' and daughters' sex role attitudes: their perceptions of (1) female *competence* to do traditionally male jobs (e.g., car repairs) and (2) their *desire* to do such jobs. Daughters' attitudes are assessed at age 12, with both mother and daughter rating a group of jobs on a 10-point scale, with 1 indicating very low confidence or desire to do a job and 10 indicating a very high confidence or desire. The results for 10 mother-daughter pairs might look like this:

TABLE 3-2 Average Self-ratings of Competence and Desire to Do Traditionally Male Jobs by 10 Pairs of 12-year-old Girls and Their Mothers

Mother-Daughter Pair	Self-Perceived Competence		Self-Perceived Desire	
	Mother	Daughter	Mother	Daughter
1	6	4	5	6
2	2	1	1	2
3	9	9	9	8
4	6	6	4	4
5	7	3	2	3
6	6	7	4	4
7	8	9	9	8
8	4	3	4	5
9	6	8	1	1
10	7	4	6	4

Note: Ratings are on a scale from 1 (low) to 10 (high).

An example of a correlation between two variables is that between children's height and weight: shorter children tend to weigh less, taller children more.

What does this information tell us? In general, we would say that it looks like mother and daughter attitudes are related (alike), but not identical: Mothers and daughters seem to hold similar attitudes. If mothers believe they are *competent* to do so-called male jobs, so do their daughters (see pairs 3 and 7). If mothers do not, neither do their daughters (see pairs 2 and 8). Although most pairs do not rate their competence identically and some (see pair 5) rate it quite differently, there is an apparent association between mothers' and daughters' ratings. A similar association seems to hold for mothers' and daughters' *desire* to do these jobs (Columns 4 and 5 of Table 3-2).

There are obvious limitations to reviewing tables of numbers such as these to determine a correlation between variables. This would be especially true for large groups[1] and for those in which the relationships were not so clear-cut. Fortunately, there are fairly simple measures of association called **correlation coefficients**, which tell us how much two variables are related. They are calculated quickly from data such as those presented in Table 3-2.

The most common correlation coefficient is the *Pearson Product-Moment Correlation Coefficient*. The Pearson Product-Moment Correlation Coefficient is a numerical index that can range in value from +1.00 through zero to −1.00. A *high* **positive correlation** (near +1.00) means that there is a very strong tendency for scores to vary together: If one score is high, the paired score will also be high; if one score is low, the

---

1. Correlational research typically is conducted on groups of at least 30 and often 100 or more. Findings are more stable and generalizable for large groups than for small groups.

other is also likely to be low. The examples in Table 3-2 represent this kind of relationship for both competence and desire. A *moderate positive correlation* means that the same high-high, low-low relationship tends to be present; however, the association is less clear-cut. When the correlation coefficient is near zero, there is little relationship between the variables. A zero correlation means there is no relationship at all.

A **negative correlation** means there is a tendency for a person or pair who has a *high* score on one variable to have a *low* score on the second. Thus a *moderate negative correlation* means that people scoring high on one measure will tend to score low on the other and vice versa; but the association is not a particularly strong one. A *high negative correlation* (near −1.00) is a clear-cut, close association between variables, however. Persons scoring high on one variable almost certainly will have low scores on the other and vice versa. What kinds of pairs of variables in developmental psychology show these relationships? Table 3-3 gives typical relationships for correlations at specified levels.

Cautions About Correlational Research. One of the most common mistakes researchers make in interpreting correlations is to confuse *correlation* with **causality**. Causality, of course, refers to the direct effect that one variable has on another. In the experimental methods discussed

TABLE 3-3 Typical Correlations for Selected Developmental Variables

Value	Range	Some Variables Correlating at This Level
High positive	+.90 to +1.00	IQ scores of identical twins
		Height of identical twins
		A person's scores on two testings on an IQ test
Moderate positive	+.30 to +.70	IQ test scores of siblings
		Age of adult and reaction time
Zero	+.10 to −.10	IQ test scores of unrelated children
		Foot size and degree of honesty
Moderate negative	−.30 to −.70	IQ test scores and level of anxiety as measured on a personality test
		Children's positive self-image and amount of parental criticism
High negative	−.90 to −1.00	IQ test scores and number of errors on the intelligence test

below, researchers try to set up and understand causal relationships by manipulating an independent variable and then looking for effects on a dependent variable.

In most correlational studies, however, variables are not manipulated; they are merely observed. The fact that two variables are correlated (associated) does *not* mean one causes the other. We need to be more cautious in attributing causality. A simple example would be the correlation between husbands' and wives' intelligence quotients (IQs). Generally, intelligence level is correlated in married couples; but it would be silly to say that husbands' IQs are caused by their wives' IQs or vice versa.

Most researchers are careful about inferring causation from correlational research. For example, Mednick, Hocevar, Baker, and Teasdale (1983) noted that the mother's socioeconomic status correlated significantly with both infant weight and health status at one year of age in a large sample of Danish children. But could one say that differences in socioeconomic status *cause* differences in health? The answer must be no. As Mednick et al. pointed out, other factors such as family size, unplanned pregnancies, mothers' employment, and institutional daycare use could be responsible. These researchers concluded that less adult attention seemed to be the common denominator in those children who demonstrated poorer physical status at one year of age. Socioeconomic status was correlated with but was *not* the cause of differences in physical status.

Correlational research often is very useful in explaining the relationships among a large number of variables in a population. By examining the correlations among several measures of, say, personality and selected environmental factors, the researcher can gain valuable insights into how they are related. In many cases correlational research is the only possible research method. No researcher, for example, could or would choose to randomly assign children to different levels of educational opportunity just to observe the effects. Correlational methods, however, let researchers look at the association between educational opportunity and achievement to determine if any relationship does exist. Further, sophisticated modern correlational techniques (see Achenbach, 1978; Cohen & Cohen, 1983) now permit researchers to test assumptions of causality on correlational data.

Experimental Methods

Because researchers often prefer to *create* the event to be studied and to control factors that could interfere with interpretations of causality, they often employ experimental methods. The power of these methods in letting researchers control variables, their versatility in many different settings, and their ability to combine experimenter-controlled conditions with developmental variables (such as age or cognitive level) have contributed to a rise in their use. Two types of experimental research are used: single-subject and group-based experimental methods.

Single-Subject Experimental Methods. During the early years of psychology, *individuals* were studied intensively. Later, however, with increased use of statistics in the 1920s, 1930s, and 1940s, psychology turned more to group-based experimental methods in which one or more groups were compared to others. A number of psychologists, however, continued to advocate intensive study of single individuals as the best way to learn about human beings (e.g., Allport, 1962; Skinner, 1938, 1956). Sidman (1960) summarized many of the methods in his book, which greatly promoted the method of single-subject experiments.

Typically, the single-subject experiment includes the following features: (1) an individual is observed repeatedly; (2) only one or a few simple actions are singled out for observation; and (3) the individual is observed under various conditions, usually when some experimental condition is first *not* present (**baseline**) and then when it is (**intervention**). The effectiveness of the intervention is determined by comparing intervention activities to that of the *same* individual during the baseline period. Repeated measures are the key to assessing change in single-subject experiments. The single-subject experiment is in some senses a longitudinal method, but the period of study is much shorter (usually over periods of days or weeks, rather than over months or years as in most longitudinal designs).

Often single-subject experiments are conducted in field settings, such as schools and other institutions, to determine what methods will best solve a child's problem behavior, such as uncooperativeness, aggression, or hyperactivity. A study by Cataldo, Bessman, Parker, Pearson, and Rogers (1979) illustrates key parts of the single-subject experiment. Their major concern was with the negative personality effects that children sometimes experience when they are hospitalized with a serious illness. Many children in intensive care, the researchers noted, were initially alert but eventually became lethargic and nonattentive.

For eleven of the children in intensive care, Cataldo et al. targeted several behaviors that included: (1) attention to people and (2) interaction with activities. Each behavior was defined carefully so it could be recorded reliably by observers. Next, the researchers observed each child's actions carefully under different conditions: (1) before any intervention took place (baseline), (2) during an intervention (which consisted of a staff member bringing in toys for the child to play with and staying with the child), and (3) during an intervention in which toys were left with the child with no staff member present. Results are presented below for one child, a 7-year-old.

As Figure 3-2 shows, staff members' interactions with the child greatly increased the child's level of interaction. For the child described in the figure, there also were some "carryover" effects to a third stage in which only the toys were available. The child continued to pay attention to people and to take part in activities, two behaviors critical to the child patient's psychological health. As Cataldo et al. stated, this study shows that well-planned procedures for caring for children in intensive care can help avoid "turning a medical triumph into a psychological trauma."

Single-subject experiments such as this have several advantages; probably the most important is that changes in an individual can be studied over time. Another is that they are limited to one or a few participants. Because of this, they are popular among workers in clinics, schools, and institutions, who do not have the resources to do large group experiments. Finally, the variables studied in single-subject ex-

FIGURE 3-2 A Typical Single-Subject Experiment. Changes Occurring in a Child (B. P.) in an Intensive Care Unit in a Hospital. *Example from Cataldo, M. F., Bessman, C. A., Parker, L. H., Pearson, J. E. R., & Rogers, M. C. (1979). Behavioral assessment for pediatric intensive care units.* Journal of Applied Behavior Analysis, 12, *p. 93.*

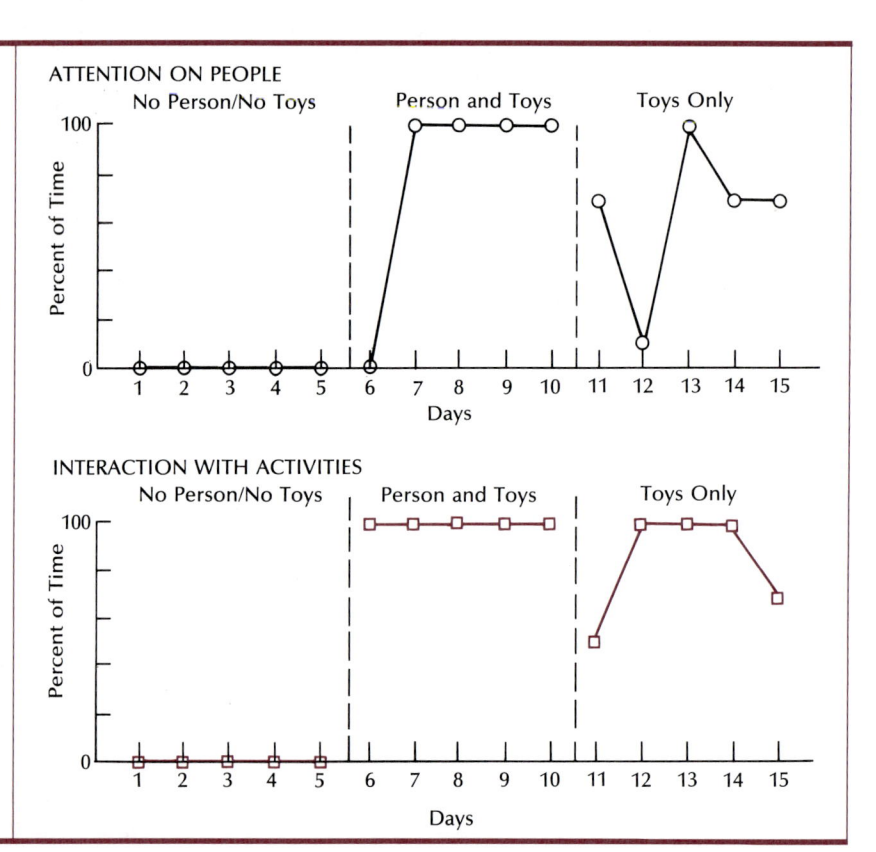

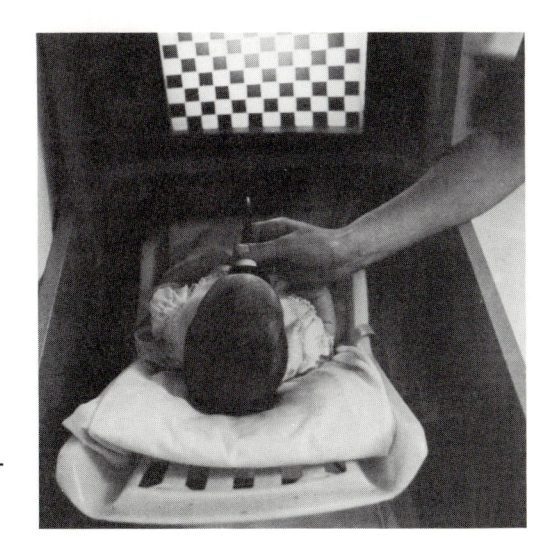

In a group-based experiment, reactions of a number of infants such as this one are studied under different conditions arranged by the experimenter.

periments are usually practical. Thus, single-subject experiments often lead to specific, useful suggestions for practitioners, such as day-care center workers, teachers, nurses, and school psychologists.

The main disadvantage of single-subject experimental methods is generalization of results. Recall that a key to excellent research is to have a representative group to study so that results can be generalized to a population. In single-subject experiments, results are based on just one or only a very few individuals. Generalization of findings to others, therefore, may not be justified.

Because it is not very adaptable to studying several variables in combination, the single-subject experiment seldom is used to study developmental variables (such as age or developmental stage changes) directly (see Hersen & Barlow, 1976). Instead, its contribution to our understanding of development has come from the vast number of single-subject experiments in which preschool and elementary school age children have been studied. Single-subject experiments, therefore, have built our understanding of developmental processes more indirectly than directly.

Group-Based Experimental Methods. Group-based experimental methods are time-honored. In these methods, groups of individuals are compared in two or more conditions set up by the experimenter. The independent variable consists of the conditions the experimenter sets up. The effect of the experimental conditions is measured on some dependent variable.

The study of infant interest by Langsdorf et al. (1983), discussed earlier, is this kind of experiment. These researchers set up three different experimental conditions: (1) viewing a face; (2) viewing a mannequin; and (3) viewing an inanimate object. Infants' interest (as measured by the methods discussed earlier) was compared under these three conditions. As hypothesized, the infants' average interest differed greatly depending on the kind of thing they saw.

In developmental studies, experimental comparisons are often "crossed" with age; that is, children of different ages experience each of the experimental conditions. This was true in the Langsdorf et al. (1983) study. When another independent variable is crossed (Figure 3-3) with age, researchers usually are looking for differences (e.g., in measures of interest) at a given age that might not be present at another.

In group-based experiments, a representative group of children is often selected and then *randomly* assigned to one or another of the experimental conditions. **Random assignment** means that chance is the basis for their receiving a particular condition. Researchers can attribute differences in outcomes to the experimental conditions themselves, and not to some hidden variable.

The greatest advantage of group-based experimental methods is the degree of control it gives to researchers. If experimenters carefully design their study, it can provide a stringent test of a relationship between independent and dependent variables. Experimental research also is

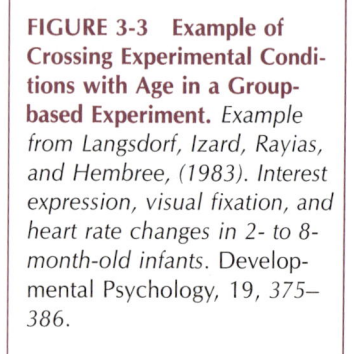

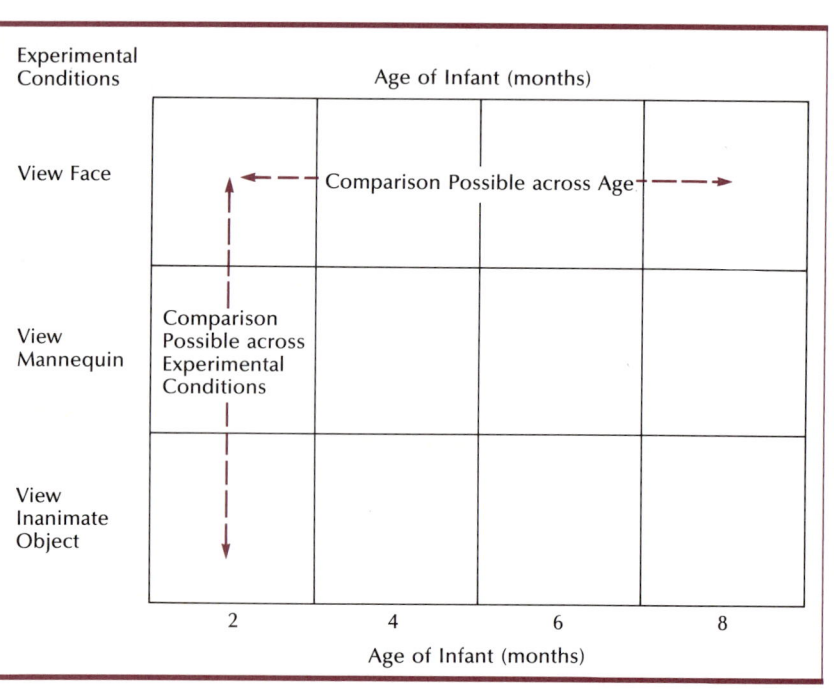

FIGURE 3-3 Example of Crossing Experimental Conditions with Age in a Group-based Experiment. *Example from Langsdorf, Izard, Rayias, and Hembree, (1983). Interest expression, visual fixation, and heart rate changes in 2- to 8-month-old infants.* Developmental Psychology, 19, 375–386.

TABLE 3-4 Summary of Research Methods in Developmental Psychology

Method	General Approach	Advantages	Disadvantages
Case Study	Carefully describe all relevant aspects of a single individual	Intensive study of an individual; Often source of theory and hypotheses	Information is often anecdotal; Child studied may not be typical
Naturalistic Observation	Observe activity in natural settings without intrusion	Provides information from "real-life" setting; Captures complexity of actual behavior	Complexity may lead to confusion; Causal inferences are speculative
Interview	Seek oral descriptions of thoughts, attitudes, and behavior	Systematic data can be gathered; Can detect subtle but important variables	Oral reporting may be inaccurate; Questions may "lead" to certain answers
Correlational	Determine relationships among variables	Can uncover relationships among variables	No real assurance of causality
Single-Subject Experimental	Contrast individual's behavior under two or more conditions	Intensive study of person over time; Practical methods can be studied	Single subject limits generalizability; Cannot be used to study several variables at once
Group-Based Experimental	Compare groups under different conditions	Direct control over variables; Useful in many settings	Results sometimes not generalizable; Sometimes not possible to use

versatile; it has been used in developmental studies with infants, children, and adults. Further, it is applicable in the laboratory as well as in field settings such as homes and schools.

Although group-based experimental methods are powerful and versatile, like all methods they are not without drawbacks (see Table 3-4). First, they often have been criticized as "artificial." The conditions may not reflect natural ones and the results therefore may not be generalizable. Experimental results can be relevant, however, if researchers choose variables and setting (laboratory or field) wisely.

Perhaps a more serious problem is that experimentation is not always possible or even desirable. Serious ethical issues often arise when one group is given a new, experimental method and others are not. Imagine, for example, that an experimenter wanted to test how improved nutrition might affect the intellectual development of preschoolers from disadvantaged families. A field experiment is proposed in which some of the preschoolers in a school would receive nutritional supplements and others would not. Is this study fair to those who do not receive the supplements? Are there possible risks to those who do? Issues such as these often arise when experiments are proposed.

Enriching Research: Cross-Cultural Perspectives

Psychology has a distinctly Western flavor, since it is based mostly on investigations of life in technological, industrialized, modern societies, such as those of the United States, Canada, and Europe. To the extent that researchers focus on development only in certain countries, in a single time and place, developmental psychology remains a study of development in a particular cultural context rather than a study of *human* development in general. Unless we look elsewhere, we can easily be misled into overgeneralizing from our Western experience.

Fortunately, however, developmental psychology has been at the forefront in conducting **cross-cultural research**, research that compares development in different cultures around the world. A primary theme of cross-cultural research is that development is guided by opportunities provided by cultures to learn particular skills and behaviors (Rogoff, Gauvain, & Ellis, 1984). Culture is seen as meshed with development,

Development is guided by opportunities provided by children's cultures. These Nigerian girls are pounding millet; few American children would have this particular experience.

rather than distinct from it. This realization has led many developmentalists into extremely productive cross-cultural investigations.

Cross-cultural research has been particularly valuable in testing the universality of developmental theories: for instance, Piaget's theory of cognitive development. Cross-cultural researchers have shown that there is great variation in the rate of cognitive development and have questioned the ordering of Piaget's stages (see Chapter 2, *Theories of Developmental Psychology*). These researchers also showed the rarity of certain kinds of thinking in some cultures. In response to such evidence, Piaget revised his thinking about certain aspects of cognitive development (Rogoff et al., 1984). Findings such as these sensitize us to the effect cultures can have on development and remind us how complex human beings actually are.

Other cross-cultural research, however, has demonstrated impressive regularities in some developmental processes. For instance, patterns of language acquisition (see Chapter 11, *Language Development*) and of infants' distress at being separated from caregivers (see Chapter 14, *Social Development*) are remarkably similar across cultures.

In general, cross-cultural research in developmental psychology has made us question our assumptions about "human nature." It helps us realize the impossibility of understanding human development without considering the fact that it takes place in the context of a culture. Also, often we are unaware of aspects of children's development until we see them in another context. Only by enlarging our perspectives can we become aware of important factors in our own culture. Through seeing others, we begin to understand ourselves.

Ethics in Developmental Psychology

Whenever we study human beings, we raise ethical questions. Examples of ethical questions are: (1) whether the privacy of individuals is protected, (2) how participation in research studies is arranged, and (3) whether research procedures might cause harm to the participants. Ethical issues are especially critical when children are the subjects of study.

Right to Privacy

In the United States, we consider the individual to have the right to privacy. If we do not want others to know about us, no one need find out what brand of toothpaste we use, which magazines we read, or what kind of cereal we have for breakfast. Of course, people's thoughts, beliefs, and motives likewise are considered to be private. They are available to others only when individuals choose to make them so.

Highlights

Research Conferences: Furthering the Work of Developmental Psychologists

Ask the typical person to imagine a scientist at work and that person likely will conjure up an image of someone working alone—in the library, in the laboratory, or in the field. Scientific research, however, is an activity that thrives only when there is good communication. Research conferences play a critical role in furthering that communication, and conferences focused on research in developmental psychology are no exception.

The American Psychological Association, for example, convenes annually in a major North American city, such as New York, Washington, Toronto, or San Francisco. One of its many divisions is Division 7, Developmental Psychology, and sessions are held at Association meetings in which the latest developmental research is reported. Meetings held exclusively for developmentalists, however, attract an even larger number of developmental psychologists.

Perhaps the most representative of American conferences that are intended especially for developmental researchers is the Biennial Meeting of the Society for Research in Child Development (SRCD). Also drawing many developmentalists are meetings of the Jean Piaget Society and, recently, the meetings of the new Society for Research in Adolescence. At the international level, developmentalists from all over the world attend the biennial meetings of the International Society for the Study of Behavioural Development.

Research conferences are a major attraction for developmental researchers for several reasons. First, they provide a chance to hear about other researchers' latest findings, usually well in advance of the publication of articles (see *Research*, page 75). Also, because of space limitations

Developmental research can intrude on individuals' rights to privacy. Recent issues of developmental psychology journals include studies of intellectual development, social status, attitudes toward sex and drugs, and parental discipline. Each of these issues can be intensely personal; their systematic study can conflict with people's rights to privacy. Therefore, researchers must take care that participants fully understand their role in a research study.

Informed Consent

The term **informed consent** refers to individuals' awareness about any research in which they participate; it also implies that they *formally* agree to participate with full knowledge of the research methods, the possible outcomes, and their personal role in the research.

on the conference program, not everyone who wants to present a paper is able to do so and, to reduce the number, proposals for presentations usually are screened by reviewers. Consequently, work presented at conferences such as SRCD is among the best currently being conducted in the field.

In addition to the opportunity to hear others' latest findings, conferences give developmental researchers a chance to discuss their own work and to receive feedback on it. For instance, those presenting their research or discussing their ideas as part of a symposium often receive feedback from the audience or from a discussant assigned to the session. This feedback not only is valuable as the person prepares the research for publication, but also helps the individual plan future research.

Besides the formal presentations of research by leaders in the field, there are several other important benefits to conference-goers: Publishers exhibit new books and equipment manufacturers often demonstrate their wares at conferences. Also, major conferences provide opportunities for new researchers to interview for positions with interested agencies, colleges, and universities. Finally, a significant side benefit for most conferees is simply the chance to see and visit informally with other scholars from around the country and world. For novice scholars, especially, there is no greater thrill than the chance to meet and talk with a "name" scholar, whose articles they have read in the scientific journals and whose work they have admired. For developmental researchers, as for all scientists, contact with others who share their enthusiasm for research is an important part of their lives as scholars.

In the United States, informed consent is required for participation in most developmental studies. Before including children in a study, researchers must obtain parental consent. Deception almost always is considered inappropriate and is permitted only under rare circumstances. In those circumstances, the researcher must show the necessity of the deception and describe procedures that will be used to prevent any harm to the individual. Clear-cut procedures for informed consent have been outlined by the American Psychological Association (1982) and by the federal government.

Protection of Participants from Harm

A major concern of developmental researchers is to protect participants from harm, either physical or psychological. Therapeutic drugs (e.g., those that control hyperactivity) may have unknown and potentially potent side-effects (e.g., sensitivity to light, loss of muscle control). Similarly, the conditions of a poorly designed experiment or the publication of test scores could potentially cause psychological harm, such as loss of self-esteem, embarrassment, and changes in beliefs about self and others. All research subjects, but especially children, need to be protected from such consequences and fully informed in advance about any potential for harm. Benefits from research must be balanced against possible harm. No intervention should be undertaken in which there is any reasonable possibility that serious or lasting harm could result.

Applications for Ethical Research in Human Development

1. *All research should be reviewed for ethical standards.* Before a study is begun, it should be reviewed for its ethical practices. In colleges and universities, proposals for research typically are screened by a faculty committee and, by law, by an Institutional Review Board (IRB). The IRB permits only research that meets ethical standards and has appropriate safeguards for participants. Some schools and institutions have an individual or committee responsible for checking research for ethics and for giving final approval for the research.

2. *Participants must be fully informed.* All research participants must be informed about important parts of the research. They must also have the opportunity, based on this information, to decline to participate. For young children, written, informed consent from a parent or guardian is required; for older children and adolescents, permission of parent *and* child should be obtained.

3. *Openness and honesty must be a part of any study.* Ideally, research should involve an open and honest collaboration between the researcher and participant. Currently, deception in research is allowable only if the researcher can demonstrate to reviewers that (1) the deception is necessary to do the study, (2) participants will not be harmed by the deception, and (3) participants will receive complete information after the study, including the reasons for the deception. In general, however, deception is inappropriate in research with children because of the unpredictability of its effects.

4. *Participants should be able to withdraw from a research study at any time.* In working with children, researchers need to be especially alert to children's discomfort, fear, or other negative effects that can arise in testing or experimental conditions. Periodic questions by a researcher about a child's feelings about participation are highly ap-

propriate. Of course, if a child does not wish to continue, the researcher must respect that desire.

5. *The research participant must be protected from harm*. Researchers need to *anticipate* possible negative outcomes and do everything in their power to prevent them. If something negative occurs (e.g., a child begins crying because he believes he has failed a test), the researcher is obligated to do everything possible to remove or correct this condition.

6. *Research information is confidential*. Research data are private and must be kept that way. This means that children's test scores, for example, should not be shared. Data should be secured and scores coded by number rather than by name. Test scores from files should be released only by written permission from parents and agency officials.

Summary

The science of developmental psychology has grown out of many years of systematic observation of human development and change. Developmental psychologists are interested in describing, explaining, and predicting change. They also investigate and attempt to understand individual differences in change.

Research designs permit scientific study of change. Two major designs are *cross-sectional* designs, in which individuals of different ages are studied at a single point in time, and *longitudinal* designs, in which individuals are followed over time. These designs and a combined design, the *cross-sequential* design, give different perspectives on development.

To do their field-based and laboratory studies, researchers use a variety of methods. These include: *case study methods, naturalistic observation methods, interview methods, correlational methods, single-subject experimental methods,* and *group-based experimental methods*. Some methods, such as naturalistic observation, intrude very little into the setting in which observation occurs, while experimental methods involve manipulation of conditions. Choice of method depends on the purposes of the research and on the setting in which the research is to be conducted. Cross-cultural studies, using a variety of methods, add an important dimension to research in developmental psychology.

Ethics are an important part of research in development. All researchers must protect children and adults from possible physical, social, or psychological harm. Research participants give informed consent, based on the fullest possible information about the processes and outcomes of the research. Research data must be kept confidential.

Key Terms

systematic observation
variables
independent variable
dependent variable
representative sample
population

hypothesis
research designs
cross-sectional design
longitudinal design
cross-sequential design
cohort

case study
naturalistic observation
interview
correlation
single-subject experimentation
group-based experimentation

behavior coding
time sampling
clinical interview
correlation coefficient
positive correlation
negative correlation
causality
baseline
intervention
random assignment
cross-cultural research
informed consent

Suggested Readings

Achenbach, T. M. (1978) *Research in developmental psychology: Concepts, strategies, and methods*. New York: The Free Press. This volume introduces the reader to several developmental research strategies, including experimental and correlational methods and cross-sectional and longitudinal approaches.

Bronfenbrenner, U. (1979) *The ecology of human development*. Cambridge, Mass.: Harvard University Press. This book gives a thoughtful look at the study of children and offers a plan for child study that is both experimentally rigorous and valid for the child's natural environment. It is considered by many to be a landmark text in the area of developmental psychology research.

Medinnus, G. R. (1976) *Child study and observation guide*. New York: John Wiley & Sons. This volume contains many practical suggestions for observing children and for conducting studies of child behavior and development. It is a good introduction to specific techniques used in many research approaches.

Nesselroade, J. R., & Baltes, P. (Eds.) (1979) *Longitudinal research in the study of behavior and development*. New York: Academic Press. In this edited volume, Nesselroade and Baltes have included chapters on such topics as the history of longitudinal methods, the use of cross-sequential methods, and data analysis. It provides in-depth coverage of topics of interest to the person interested in conducting developmental research using longitudinal methods.

Slavin, R. *Research methods in education*. (1984) Englewood Cliffs, NJ: Prentice-Hall. This general volume on research contains chapters useful to researchers in development, including chapters on group-based experimental methods, single-subject experimental methods, and correlational methods. It also provides guidelines for judging whether a research design is a good one or not.

Willems, E. P., & Alexander, J. L. (1980) The naturalistic perspective in research. In B. B. Wolman (Ed.), *Handbook of developmental psychology*. Englewood Cliffs, NJ: Prentice-Hall. This excellent chapter outlines the ideas underlying naturalistic research and contrasts it with the more tightly controlled, experimental methods. It presents a strong argument for the usefulness of naturalistic research methods in developmental psychology.

Application Exercise

3-1 Methods of Research in Developmental Psychology

For each of the following, decide which of the six methods of research is being attempted.

   (a) Case study method
   (b) Naturalistic observation method
   (c) Interview method
   (d) Correlational method
   (e) Single-subject experiment
   (f) Group-based experiment

1. The ability of 5-year-old children to define and use kinship concepts (e.g., mother, son, aunt, cousin) is related to the variables of intelligence, family size, and birth order of the children.

2. Eighth graders ($N = 20$) are given training in taking a perspective (during training, they were asked to take roles) and compared on several tests to a control group who did not have this training.

3. An 8-year-old child is observed each day for six weeks in a summer school mathematics class to determine how she develops and organizes the arithmetic concept of "carrying." The researcher kept a diary of the child's ideas as she talked about solving these problems. The child also was videotaped unobtrusively as she worked math problems; all her work was copied for later study.

4. Newly enrolled children in a university preschool are observed intensively through a one-way mirror as they interact with each other and with "older" students. In this study, the researcher is attempting to understand the kinds of things that happen in communication as children become friends.

5. A student who is a very slow reader in a second-grade class is asked to read aloud each day for two weeks while the teacher surreptitiously records the number of words he reads per minute. Then the teacher begins to have the child keep a chart of his reading speed. Within two or three days, the child's speed has picked up as both he and the teacher continue to record his oral reading rate on a chart.

6. Mothers from the United States, Japan, and Nigeria are asked a set of 60 questions about their child-rearing practices, including questions about their children's births, their early interaction with their children, early education experiences, and their goals for their female and male children.

PART II

Biological and Social Bases of Development

We are all products of biological and social influences. To say we are products of biology is to suggest that every person, as a member of the species Homo sapiens, is the result of millions of years of biological evolution. To fully understand human development requires that we understand how the human species has been shaped by evolutionary forces and how each of us receives our biological inheritance in the genes passed on by our parents. We explore these matters in Chapter 4, Evolution and Genetics.

But psychological development is not simply programmed in our genes. We grow up in families, in schools, in peer groups, and, most broadly, in cultures. It may be too simple to say that society shapes us, just as it is too simple to say that our genes shape us, but surely the social settings of our childhoods profoundly influence our development. In Chapter 5, Social Influences on Development, we will consider in detail the nature of these various settings and the ways they exert their influence.

Recalling our presentation of the nature/nurture issue in Chapter 1, we could say that Chapter 4 will look at development from a nature point of view and Chapter 5 will consider it from a nurture point of view. But of course we needn't worry about which view is correct: Both of them are. We are prepared by evolution to be social organisms. The development of every child involves a complex interaction of biology and culture.

CHAPTER 4

Evolution and Genetics

In the end, the power behind development is life.
—Erik Erikson,
Harvard Educational Review, *1981*

We typically consider human development to begin at the moment of conception and proceed until death. Yet several factors prior to conception are also important in understanding development. Each new baby is a member of the human species and as such shares a wide range of capabilities in common with every other person. These commonalities, which make our species unique, result from millions of years of successful adaptation to the environment.

Contrary to John Locke's extreme view (see Chapter 1), no newborn enters the world as a "blank slate" on which experience will write. It is true that experience has a profound effect on development, but babies have innate capabilities for a variety of reflexive (unlearned) behaviors. The *rooting reflex*, for example, seems particularly suited to increasing the chances of babies' survival. This reflex occurs when a hungry infant's face is touched, producing quick, jerky head movements until the baby's mouth is aligned with the source of stimulation. Such a reflex, of course, is marvelously adaptive in the feeding process. Similarly, there seems to be an innate tendency for babies to look at those parts of the environment that present the most information (Bornstein, 1984; Haith, 1977).

On a broader level, the human species is characterized by a general tendency to be social, by unique intellectual abilities, and by great facility in the use of language. Certainly, other species (e.g., wolves, lions) tend toward social behaviors but none has attained the complexity of social relations evident in human life. Other species (e.g., chimpanzees and great apes) are also able to reason but still none approach human levels. Where do innate tendencies and abilities such as those we have described originate? The easiest answer—correct in a limited sense—is that we inherit many abilities and tendencies: They are part of the heritage of our species, passed on from generation to generation. But we might ask how that evolved. To explain our innate characteristics satisfactorily, we must step back and consider how the human species itself developed.

The story of human development begins with the appearance of life on Earth. Our physical structure, our intellectual abilities, and our emotional and spiritual lives have all been influenced by the forces that shaped our species. The process of change brought about by these forces is referred to as **evolution**. In the first part of this chapter we examine the principles of evolution and briefly trace the evolution of human beings. A topic central to the understanding of evolution and development—**genetics**—is the focus of the second part of the chapter.

About Evolution

As we noted in Chapter 1, *evolution* refers to the process by which a species becomes progressively adapted to its environment. Modern concepts of evolution date to the publication in 1859 of Charles Darwin's *The Origin of Species by Means of Natural Selection; or the Preservation of Favoured Races in the Struggle for Life* (Fishbein, 1976; Irvine, 1982). In this chapter, we will examine Darwin's basic ideas as well as more recent contributions to our understanding of evolution.

Principles of Evolution

Natural Selection. The major principle of evolution described in Darwin's *The Origin of Species* is **natural selection**. In general, *natural selection is the process in which characteristics favored by the environment become more frequent from generation to generation.*

Darwin noted that organisms generally are able to produce far more offspring than actually survive to adulthood. He also saw that the size of animal populations (a *population* refers to all the members of a group of organisms) typically remains constant over long periods of time. From these two propositions, Darwin concluded that there must be a very low survival rate among the immature members of any species; in other words, only a relatively small number achieve maturity. Darwin further observed that there were great individual differences in any population and that those who survive (presumably because of their characteristics) produce the next generation. From his observations, Darwin concluded that the characteristics of those individuals who survive long enough to reproduce have somehow made them better equipped to survive in the conditions of their environment. Last, Darwin noted that offspring resemble their parents fairly closely but not identically. This observation gave rise to the idea that future generations maintain and improve on those characteristics that aid in survival, with changes in characteristics occurring slowly across generations.

Darwin's three conclusions—that only a fraction of any population's offspring survives to maturity, that those who do survive pass their adaptive traits along to the next generation, and that change is continual and gradual—form the core of natural selection. The implications, particularly for human beings, are clear: Our identity is a direct function of those characteristics in our ancestors that were best suited for survival. The enormous size of the human brain, our upright stance, and our strong emotional reactions, for example, must have contributed to the survival of early humans. Further, the principle of natural selection indicates that human beings are descended from less sophisticated, less well adapted ancestors. This means that at some point in history, our ancestors were different than what could be called human.

Speciation. Biologists consider a **species** to be a category of organisms that represents a natural, self-reproducing group distinct from other groups. Human beings therefore are a species, as are chimpanzees. Despite many similarities (e.g., social behavior, use of tools, 99% of amino acids in common), humans and chimpanzees are two clearly distinct species of organisms. However, the similarities between the species, taken together with the principle of natural selection, suggest that in the distant past humans and chimpanzees had a common ancestor. That is, one species of organisms somehow became two distinct species: humans and chimpanzees. The manner in which a common ancestor results in a new (or several new) species is the process of **speciation**.

Darwin held that the constant pressure of natural selection caused species to diverge and specialize so that life could be eked out of several different environmental locations. In other words, environmental stress is so great that species split up, yielding two or more populations in different environments. At this point, the different environments make different demands on the separate populations. Only those individuals who possess characteristics most favorable to survival in each environment become parents themselves, and so the characteristics of the two separate populations begin to diverge. At first, the divergence is only slight. After many generations of natural selection for those characteristics that best fit different environments, however, the divergence becomes pronounced. Finally, the divergence is so great that the separated populations result in different species (see Figure 4-1) (Dillon, 1978).

The notion of speciation is of interest to us today because it indicates that all living organisms have a basic commonality and that at some point in the Earth's distant history, all life sprang from a common ancestor. The basic continuity among species allows psychologists to use data gathered on lower organisms in their research on various aspects of development. For instance, basic ethical concerns make experimental research on emotionally deprived infants impossible. After all, we cannot randomly choose a group of babies and deprive them of emotional contact to observe the results and study how to construct treatments to counter the effects of early emotional deprivation. Unfor-

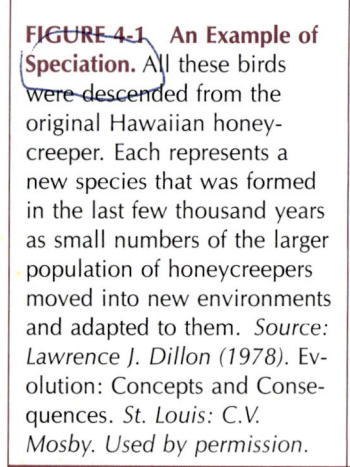

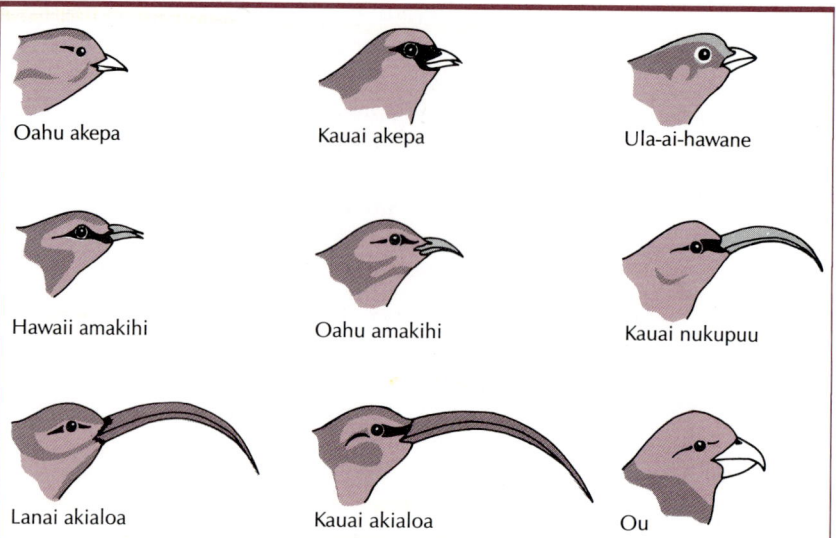

FIGURE 4-1   An Example of Speciation. All these birds were descended from the original Hawaiian honeycreeper. Each represents a new species that was formed in the last few thousand years as small numbers of the larger population of honeycreepers moved into new environments and adapted to them. *Source: Lawrence J. Dillon (1978). Evolution: Concepts and Consequences. St. Louis: C.V. Mosby. Used by permission.*

Oahu akepa   Kauai akepa   Ula-ai-hawane

Hawaii amakihi   Oahu amakihi   Kauai nukupuu

Lanai akialoa   Kauai akialoa   Ou

tunately, however, some babies do grow up emotionally deprived, and we must know more about how to work with them. To increase our understanding, developmental psychologists have gathered data on baby monkeys. The effects of emotional deprivation observed in baby monkeys gives us invaluable data for understanding emotionally deprived human babies. There are also, of course, very real limits to what we can learn about humans by studying other organisms: No matter how carefully we construct a study of other organisms we cannot be certain that their reactions will mirror those of human beings because they are *not* human. A further limitation on studies of other species is the ethical concern involved. Even so, data from studies of the development of a variety of species have had an important place in developmental psychology.

Adaptation. One of the cornerstones of evolutionary thought is the principle of **adaptation** (Gould, 1982). Adaptation can be defined as the changes that occur in a species in order to allow for survival of that species in an environment. Because the world is always changing, old characteristics that previously increased the chances of survival may need to be modified or dropped altogether to ensure future survival (see Figure 4-2).

Psychologists have employed the concept of adaptation effectively in studying individuals in their environments (see Chapter 1). Much of the work in developmental psychology is devoted to the study of how human beings adapt to their environments and how we can alter environments to foster beneficial change. Individuals, as well as species, adapt.

About Evolution

Other Evolutionary Concepts. The principles of natural selection, speciation, and adaptation are the central features of Darwinian views of evolution (Gould, 1982), but other ideas have become important to evolutionary thought in the past 125 years. At the time that Darwin wrote his *The Origin of Species,* scientists did not know much about how characteristics were transmitted from generation to generation. As we will see in the second major section of this chapter, "Genetics," some basic laws of inheritance were worked out in the 1860s, but these did not attract much notice until about 1900. Once scientists obtained a rudimentary understanding of genetics, however, laboratory studies of evolution became possible and resulted in an explosion of knowledge about the process.

One direct result of the early study of genetics was the identification of the phenomenon of mutation. **Mutation** refers to a change in hereditary materials that results in a change in the characteristics of offspring (Dillon, 1978). Mutations occur in the parent organisms and are immediately seen in any offspring; hence, they occur very rapidly. Most mutations are not adaptive and result in an early death of the offspring. When mutations are beneficial, however, natural selection will favor them. Thus over the course of many generations, helpful mutations spread through a population.

Though knowledge of mutations greatly added to our understanding of evolution, mutations account for only a small number of evolutionary changes. A more important conception, which has only recently been developed (see Taylor, 1983), is the idea that *the behavior of organisms influences their evolution* (see also Miller, 1983a; and Piaget, 1978). In the original Darwinian conception of evolution, the behavior of organisms was considered to be a direct outcome of natural selection. Woodpeckers, for example, were thought to peck wood for bugs and to have strong, narrow beaks because the environment required such an adaptation in order for species survival. We now know that the original woodpecker, however, did not have to peck wood to obtain food. The

FIGURE 4-2 **Adaptation of the Horse.** The evolution of the horse provides a classic example of how organisms adapt to their environment in order for the species to survive. Here we see the progressive evolution of the horse from a small, forest-dwelling creature into the large plains animal it is today.

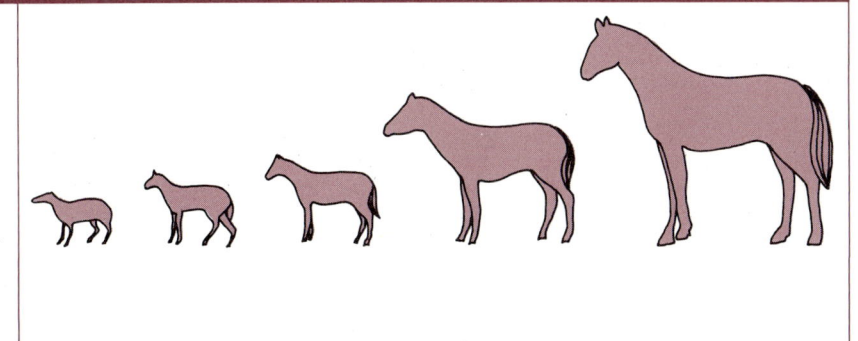

woodpecker could have become a better seed eater or a more efficient chaser of flying insects. Instead, it pecked wood, and this behavior is what led to the evolution of long, narrow beaks. Speaking of this example and several others he provides, Taylor notes, "this convincingly shows that behavior change precedes structural change" (Taylor, 1983, p. 218). Although Taylor takes an extreme viewpoint, the idea that behavior strongly influences natural selection is becoming an increasingly important part of contemporary views of evolution (Gould, 1982).

The Evolution of Humankind

About 3.5 billion years ago, primitive self-duplicating molecules formed in the warm oceans of the Earth. Over billions of years, these evolved into single-celled organisms, then multicelled organisms, and eventually, fish. Then life expanded onto land: This involved the evolution of

FIGURE 4-3 A Family Tree. This chart depicts the ancestry of mammals traced all the way back to ancient fish-like organisms.

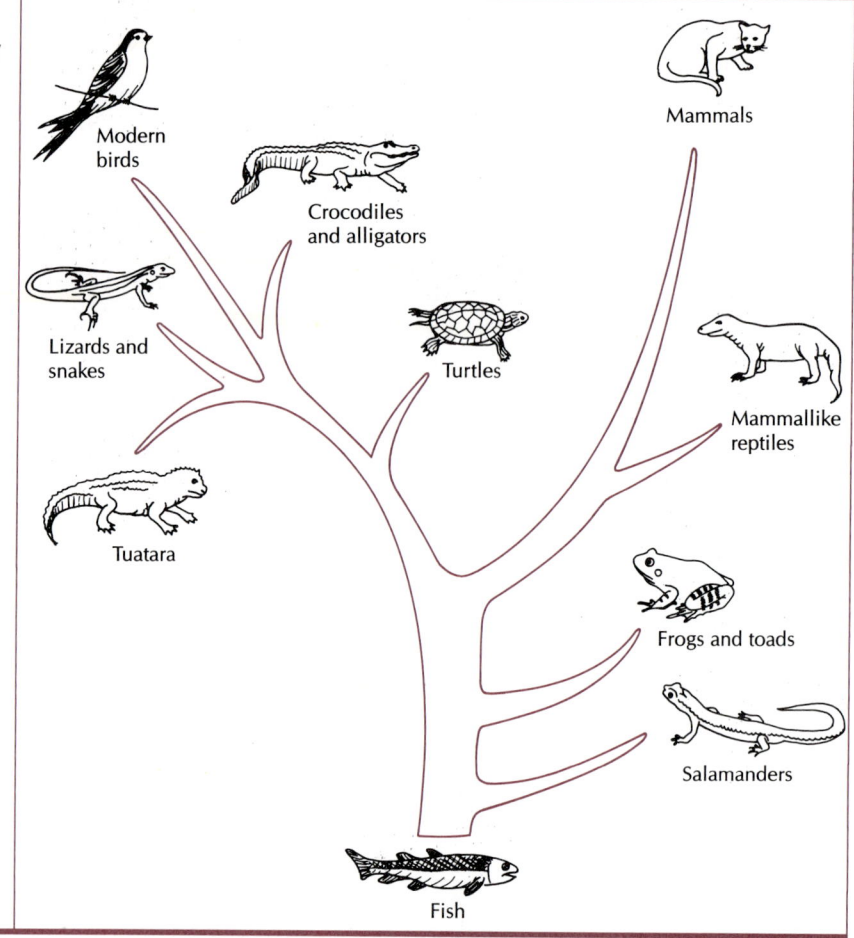

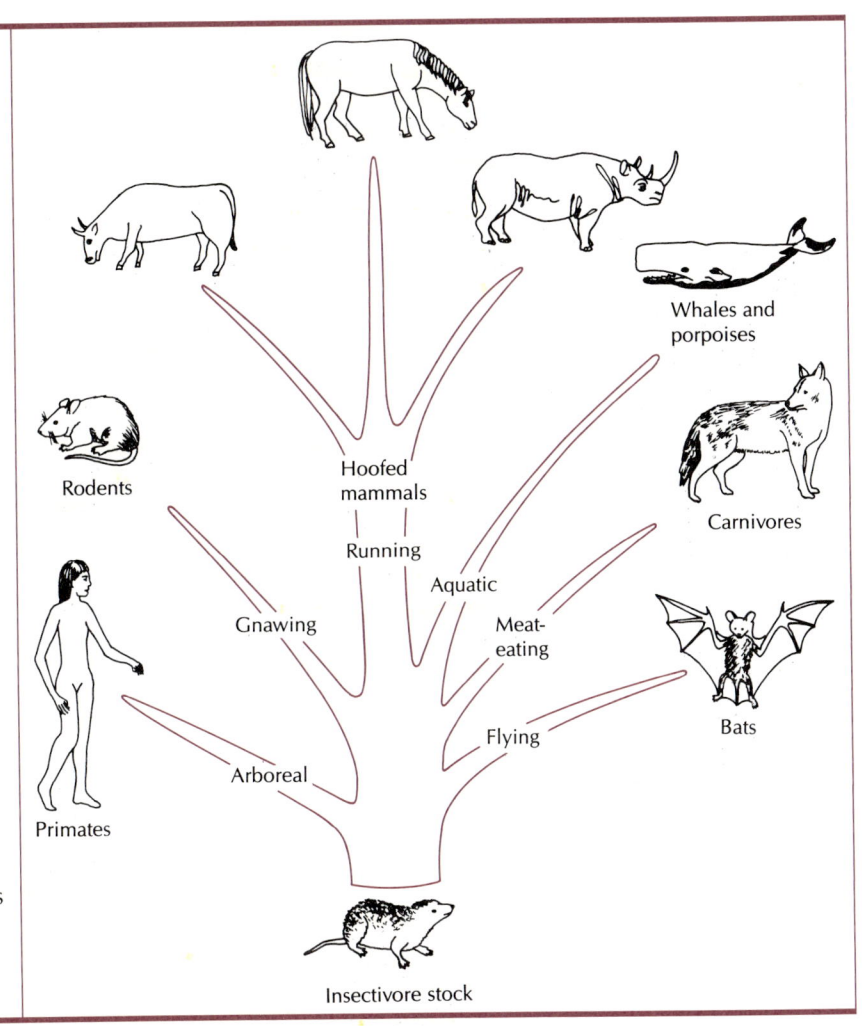

FIGURE 4-4 The Family Tree of Mammals. All mammals are thought to have descended from ancient insect-eaters that coexisted with the dinosaurs for millions of years before the dinosaurs became extinct in a worldwide catastrophe.

fish into amphibians, which in turn yielded reptiles (including dinosaurs such as Triceratops and Tyrannosaurus), which then evolved into birds and mammals.

Early mammals can be dated back to 190 million years ago (Gould, 1983; Priess, 1981). The first mammals, tiny insect eaters, were about the size of small mice. Shortly after the extinction of dinosaurs (about 65 million years ago), the early insect eaters spread to new environments. The process of natural selection soon began to result in many different species, each selected for life in a different form of environment (see Figure 4-3). One of these early species (see Figure 4-4) adapted to an arboreal (tree-dwelling) style of life. These were the ancestors of the **primates**: monkeys, great apes, and humans.

The demands of arboreal living accelerated natural selection and led to important changes (Lumsden & Wilson, 1983). Prehensile (grasping) limbs, binocular vision (vision in which both eyes work together so that the organism has depth perception), color vision, the use of vocalizations to provide simple messages (leaves may block off vision), social behavior, and differentiated functions of the upper and lower limbs are especially adapted to tree dwelling (Lumsden & Wilson, 1983). These changes had the secondary effect of increasing the size of the brain; more capacity was needed for increased visual abilities, vocal abilities, and limb functioning (Jolly, 1985). Another adaptation, not peculiar to arboreal life, was the selection of omnivorous eating habits—in other words, eating meat as well as fruit and seeds—a change that would be very helpful as the next phase of human evolution began.

One group of these early primates occupied a territory that began to change as its climate changed. This area, which was most likely in Africa (Lumsden & Wilson, 1983), became increasingly dryer and gradually transformed huge forests into large, open grasslands. The primates in this area had little choice but to leave the forests for the grasslands or die out. They were poorly adapted to life on the plains, but they did have some advantages over their competitors: They had paws with opposing thumbs that could grasp objects, binocular and color vision, social behavior, and most important, relatively large brains (Leakey, 1982).

Survival on the open grasslands must have taken a terrible toll on our early ancestors, but natural selection worked on the few advantages they did have (Eldredge & Tattersall, 1982). They were small, slight creatures who could not outrun or outfight predators. In order to best defend themselves against predators, early primates underwent two adaptations near the outset: the assumption of an upright posture and greater social cohesiveness (Herbert, 1983). Early primates needed to be upright so that they could spot predators approaching as well as hunt for game. Greater social cohesiveness was important because individual members of this new species could not beat off predators nor hunt large game (Jolly, 1985; Lopreato, 1984). Acting as groups in defense and hunting led to far greater rates of survival among primates (Lumsden & Wilson, 1983).

These two early adaptations had a profound effect on later evolution (Leakey, 1982). Once primates attained the upright posture, their hands were free to learn to manipulate tools. Tools, including clubs, spears, knives, and scrapers, greatly enhanced the odds of survival. The use of tools and the increasing social cohesiveness of our ancestors drastically improved defense against predators and hunting. From this point on, natural selection within the species had a powerful effect. The ability to make tools and to work in social groups was consistently selected for in the struggle for survival (Jolly, 1985; Leakey, 1982). Both of these abilities, of course, depend on the ability to think; this means that natural selection shaped our ancestors over millions of years into large-brained, socially organized tool users.

Our species, *Homo sapiens*, has existed in its current form for about 45,000 years. Whether we shall remain in our present form or continue to evolve is a question that has been pondered by several scholars (Eldredge & Tattersall, 1982). On the one hand, we can argue that it is simply too soon to tell. The 45,000 years of our existence is but the tiniest of bubbles in the stream of time since life began (around 1/100,000 of the time since the first single-celled organism appeared).

On the other hand, our species is the only one ever to have existed that can truly manipulate its own surroundings. We influence our own future by changes we make in our environment. From this perspective, then, the ways in which our species will evolve will be governed by our own choices, not those forced on us by natural selection.

Regardless of our future evolution, each generation will continue to transmit its characteristics to its offspring. In order to relate the development of our species to the development of individual human beings, we must understand how this transmission operates. The study of this process—genetics—is the topic of the next major section of this chapter.

Genetics: Key to Development

Our species has been reproducing itself for the past 45,000 years. The life of a human being begins when a **sperm** cell from the father fertilizes an **ovum** (egg) in the mother. This occurrence is referred to as **conception**. When the joining of the sperm and ovum is complete, a **zygote** has been formed. Only in the last 120 years have we begun to better understand the transmission of characteristics from parents to children. In this section, we briefly outline that process.

Basic Concepts in Genetics

Darwin and his predecessors understood that parental characteristics were transmitted to their offspring but did not know how this process operated. Oddly, the basic principles of this transmission process, genetics, were discovered only a few years after the appearance of Darwin's *The Origin of Species*. In 1866, Gregor Mendel, an Austrian monk, published the results of his painstaking research on the inheritance of traits in the garden pea. Although Mendel's work was available to Darwin and other contemporary scholars, it was published in an obscure journal and so was not widely recognized until the turn of the century.

What did Mendel discover and how are these basic principles of genetics related to human development? In simplified form, Mendel found that specific traits (whether peas are round or wrinkled) were determined by factors (now referred to as **genes**) transferred from parents to their offspring through the sex cells (**gametes**), which are the sperm and ovum in human beings). Mendel also determined that offspring each receive two genes for each observable trait, one from each parent. These genes are called **alleles**. The fact that there is one allele from each parent and that these alleles may contain different kinds of information (for blue eyes or brown eyes, as an example) led Mendel to infer that zygotes may be **homozygotic** for a given trait (containing two alleles that possess the same information from each parent) or **heterozygotic** (containing two alleles that possess different information). Further, Mendel determined that there are **dominant genes** (always expressed in the offspring's appearance) as well as **recessive genes** (not expressed in the offspring's appearance if paired with a dominant allele).

An example of basic human genetics will help illustrate Mendel's ideas. Let's start by considering the alleles for eye color that a brown-eyed male might have, assuming (for the sake of simplicity) that only one gene pair determines eye color. The person could have received one brown allele (B) from each of his parents (BB). In this case, he would be homozygotic for eye color. His outward appearance (**phenotype**) would include brown eyes, matching exactly his genetic constitution (**genotype**).

Our hypothetical subject, however, in fact could have received an allele for brown eyes from one parent (B) and an allele for blue eyes (b) from the other parent. In this case, we would say he is heterozygotic (Bb). His eyes would still be brown because the allele for brown eyes is dominant while the allele for blue eyes is recessive. When a gene pair includes a dominant allele and a recessive allele, the dominant allele is expressed in the person's appearance (the phenotype) while the recessive allele is not. Here, the phenotype reflects the dominant allele and does not directly match the genotype. To have blue eyes, a person must receive an allele for blue eyes from each parent (bb). Recessive alleles are expressed in a person's appearance only when that person is homozygous for the recessive trait.

Let us suppose that our hypothetical male is heterozygotic for brown eyes, which means he has one allele for brown (the dominant allele that gives him his appearance) and one allele for blue eyes (the recessive allele). Let us further suppose that his wife is also heterozygotic for brown eyes. What kinds of eye color possibilities exist for their children? Since the male passes on only one of his two alleles in any sperm cell, his children could receive either the allele for brown eyes or the allele for blue eyes. Similarly, the mother can pass on either her

Genetics: Key to Development

allele for brown eyes or her allele for blue eyes. The possibilities for their children are shown in Table 4-1.

As you can see from Table 4-1, the odds are 1 in 4 that the child of such a union would have blue eyes (homozygotic for the recessive blue) and 3 in 4 for a brown-eyed child. Chances are 1 in 4 that the child would be homozygotic for brown eyes and 2 in 4 that the child would be heterozygotic for brown eyes.

Mendel understood that somehow only one of a parent's two alleles was passed on to the offspring. He did not, however, discover how this process operates. Other researchers in the late nineteenth century began to make headway in this area when they discovered **chromosomes** (structures containing many different genes) in the nuclei of cells. All cells in the human body contain 23 pairs of chromosomes for a total of 46. When a cell divides through a process called **mitosis,** the chromosomes in the cell first double and then are divided into two daughter cells.

The process of mitosis, however, does not govern the formation of gametes (sperm and ova). Instead, gametes are formed through a very special process called meiosis. In **meiosis,** each cell divides twice but the chromosomes are doubled only once. This results in each of the gametes obtaining only 23 chromosomes. Gametes from the male (sperm) and female (ova) join to form a zygote with the normal 23 *pairs* of chromosomes.

TABLE 4-1 A Diagram of the Possible Alleles Passed on to Zygotes from Parents Heterozygotic for Eye Color

	FATHER B (Brown)	FATHER b (blue)
MOTHER B (Brown)	BB	Bb
MOTHER b (blue)	Bb	bb

Note: Each box in the diagram represents the pairing of a set of alleles, one from each parent. As you can see, one of the four boxes contains two dominant alleles for brown eyes (BB). Another box contains two recessive alleles for blue eyes (bb). The remaining two boxes contain one dominant allele for brown eyes and one recessive allele for blue eyes (Bb). In this instance, the chances are one in four that a blue-eyed child will be conceived and three in four that a brown-eyed child will be conceived.

A real breakthrough in understanding the transmission of characteristics occurred in 1902 when W. S. Sutton and Theodor Boveri each independently proposed that genes are contained in the chromosomes. Here, finally, was an explanation for how characteristics are transmitted: Each human gamete contains 23 chromosomes that include genes with specific information governing the development of life. One of each pair of chromosomes, and all the genes it contains, is passed into a gamete. Each member of a chromosome pair has an equal chance of ending up in a particular gamete. The genes a chromosome carries may be what was dominant in the parent (an allele for brown eyes, for example) or what was recessive in the parent (an allele for blue eyes). When the 23 chromosomes in the ovum pair with the 23 in the sperm, the zygote then possesses an entirely new arrangement of 23 pairs of chromosomes with information from each parent.

How Sex Is Determined

Among each person's set of 23 pairs of chromosomes is one pair that carries the sex-determining genes. The male chromosome is labeled Y while the female chromosome is labeled X. All normal males possess an XY pair of chromosomes. During meiosis, the male forms two types of gametes (sperm cells), an X-carrying **gynosperm** and a Y-carrying **androsperm**. All normal ova, on the other hand, contain one X chromosome. Hence, the sex of children is determined by whether a gynosperm or an androsperm fertilizes the ovum. If an XY pairing occurs, the zygote will be male (see Figure 4-5a); if an XX pairing occurs, the zygote will be female (see Figure 4-5b). Several recent advances in knowledge about the properties of gynosperm and androsperm have direct implications for attempting to choose the sex of children. We will discuss these possibilities later in our applications section.

DNA: The Building Blocks of Life

The breakthrough in biological understanding that genes carry the information for the transmission of characteristics from one generation to the next and that genes are contained in the chromosomes greatly aided our knowledge of the origin of life. How the genes carried their information was not completely understood until the structure of genes was determined. During the 1920s and 1930s, biologists discovered that one of the major constituents of genes was deoxyribonucleic acid **(DNA)**. By the 1940s, biologists knew that DNA controlled the transmission of traits across generations in bacteria. However, it was not until 1953 that James D. Watson and Francis Crick of Cambridge University reported their Nobel Prize-winning research explaining the structure and function of DNA.

It turns out that each gene is either a DNA molecule or a part of one. The specific chemical structure of each DNA molecule contains the information transmitted from generation to generation. This information affects what each cell in the body will be (muscle cell, skin cell,

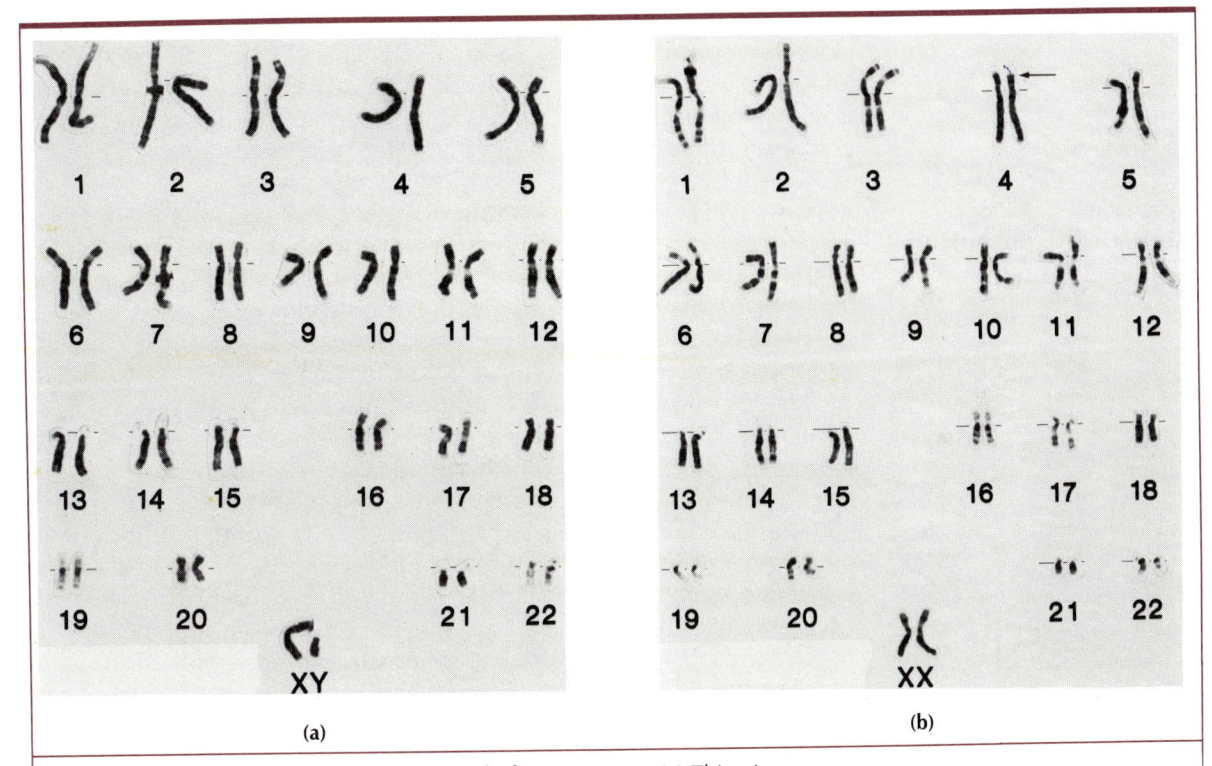

FIGURE 4-5 Illustrations of the Pairing of Chromosomes. (a) This picture shows a normal male's chromosomes. Note that there is one X chromosome and one Y chromosome. (b) This shows a normal female's chromosomes. Note that there are two X chromosomes. Pictures of chromosomes such as these are referred to as **karyotypes**. *(Courtesy of University of Nebraska Medical Center, Meyer Children's Rehabilitation Institute.)*

etc.) and how it will function (Ayala & Valentine, 1979; Kolata, 1985). However, although we often think about genes (DNA molecules) determining eye color, hair color, finger length, lung capacity, and innumerable other factors, genes do not function in a vacuum. The environment also strongly influences development. In the next section, we will examine the interplay of genetic and environmental influences on development.

Developmental Behavior Genetics

So far we have looked at genetics in very general terms. For a psychologist, however, the central interest is the role of the genes in behavior—a field known as **behavior genetics**. In recent years, developmental psychologists have investigated developmental issues in behavior genetics, thus yielding a growing subdiscipline known as **developmental behavior genetics** (Scarr & Kidd, 1983). This section will explore this important area. We will begin with a general discussion of development from a biological perspective and will then apply this perspective in examining the development of personality and intelligence.

Epigenesis: A Biological Conception of Development

As we have seen, the *genotype* is the genetic structure the organism inherits, the product of millions of years of evolution. *Phenotype,* on the other hand, refers to the actual characteristics, both physical and behavioral, of the mature individual. From a biological point of view, development is the process by which the genotype is transformed into the phenotype. The term biologists use for this process is **epigenesis.**

Many psychologists have found it useful to view psychological development from an epigenetic point of view (e.g., Lerner, 1978). An epigenetic viewpoint reminds us that the environment is not solely responsible for the development of adult characteristics. The child is not a lump of clay waiting to be molded by the world around it. As a result of the evolutionary history of our species, every human child has a natural tendency to develop in certain predictable ways. Thus the environment is neither the source nor the cause of development.

In terms of the nature/nurture (heredity/environment) controversy (see Chapter 1), the epigenetic perspective is an important reminder of the limitations of an extreme nurture (environmental) position. There is an equal danger, however, of adopting an extreme nature (hereditarian) position (Kitchener, 1978, 1980; Lerner, 1980). At this extreme, we can get the impression that our adult characteristics are written in our genes and that development is simply the unfolding of an innate program. An accurate conception of epigenesis emphasizes that the genotype is not a set of traits waiting to appear but rather *a tendency to develop in certain ways in certain environments.*

In this modern conception of epigenesis, the common view of development as a "war" between heredity and environment (nature versus nurture) makes no sense. No genotype can produce an adult human being in the absence of environmental influences and no environment can produce an adult human in the absence of a human genotype. In fact, the effects of a person's genes depend on the environment in which they operate and the effects of the environment vary according to the individual's genotype. Development thus is a continuing interaction in which heredity and environment work together to produce a mature organism.

Later, in Chapter 6, *Prenatal Development and Birth,* and Chapter 7, *Physical Growth and Motor Development,* we will focus specifically on how nature and nurture interact in the physical development of human beings. In the next two sections of this chapter, we will focus on the relative contributions of heredity and environment to personality and intellectual development.

The question of whether individual differences in personality and intelligence are due primarily to our heredity or our environment historically has been one of the most interesting and controversial issues in psychological research. It is important to keep in mind, however, that this is not the ultimate question for the developmental psychologist. Some differences among individuals may be due primarily to nature and some to nurture, but virtually all psychological characteristics are due to an interaction of both. The key question for the developmentalist is not whether heredity or environment is the primary influence but how the two interact to produce the continuing process of psychological development.

Personality Development

Recently, research has focused on the interaction of heredity and environment in the development of personality. For example, Thomas and Chess (1977) conducted a longitudinal study in which they followed parents' perceptions of children's temperaments for a 20-year period. In general, their findings indicated that there are innate differences among children in **temperament**—that is, children's natural dispositions to be active or calm, irritable or easy to please, and so on—and that these basic dispositions are shaped by and shape the environment (see also Goldsmith, 1983; Matheny, 1983; Rose & Ditto, 1983; Thompson, 1986a).

Thomas and Chess identified several basic temperaments among infants including "easy," "difficult," and "slow to warm up." Easy children are hungry at regular times, sleep well and at convenient intervals, are usually cheerful, are eagerly willing to try new activities and new foods, and do not fuss much about the common day-to-day frustrations of a baby's life. Not surprisingly, babies with an easy temperament shape an important part of their environment—their parents' behaviors—in positive ways. The highly positive reactions parents elicit from easy babies lead to highly positive parental reactions. Soon, the environment starts to shape babies' personality traits. Very positive parental reactions to cheerfulness, eagerness, and tolerating frustration lead to a strengthening of these and other positive personality characteristics.

Difficult children, in contrast, do not establish convenient or regular eating and sleeping habits; they fuss a great deal over minor frustrations; they do not adjust well to changes in routine; they cry frequently (usually loudly); they seem unfriendly; and they do not like trying new foods or activities. As easy babies do, difficult babies also begin to shape their parents' reactions very quickly. Parental reactions to crying, fussing, and unfriendliness tend to be relatively negative. These negative

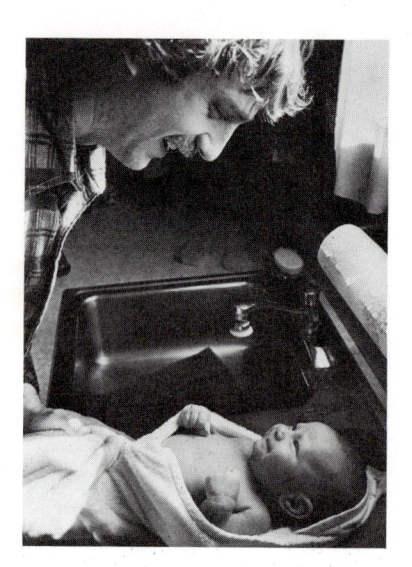

The basic temperament of infants strongly influences the ways in which parents interact with them.

reactions on the part of parents generally further strengthen personality characteristics the parents see as undesirable.

The children that Thomas and Chess referred to as "slow to warm up," tend to fall in between "easy" and "difficult" children in their reactions to things. Slow-to-warm-up children do not immediately enjoy new foods, toys, people, or activities but they usually appreciate them after a little experience. In addition, these children tend to be only partially irregular in their habits; when they do react negatively, these reactions are not strong.

Finding that there were distinct differences in children's temperaments and the ways in which parents responded to them, however, was only a part of Thomas and Chess's (1977) results. They also determined that parental perceptions of these temperaments generally tended to be stable over long periods of time: Easy babies later tended to be viewed as cooperative and highly pleasing children and adolescents; difficult babies were later seen as difficult children and difficult adolescents.

The basic temperament of infants strongly influences the ways in which parents interact with them. It is delightful to parent an easy baby, whereas difficult babies try the patience of parents repeatedly. Apparently, the basic temperament of infants can set up an interaction pattern with parents that can shape the later development of personality. We should also mention, as we will discuss in Chapter 13, that parents can change many of the unpleasant behaviors associated with difficult children and greatly improve the quality of parent–child interactions. Ultimately, children's personality development is powerfully influenced by interactions with the parents and family (Campos, Barrett, Lamb, Goldsmith, & Stenberg, 1983).

Related research has suggested that innate tendencies play an important role in the development of overall activity levels (Scarr, 1966); inclinations to be outgoing or reserved (Gottesman, 1965; Thomas & Chess, 1977; Scarr, 1969); adaptability (Matheny & Dolan, 1975); assertiveness (Vandenberg, 1968); and susceptibility to depression (Miller, 1983a). However, as with Thomas and Chess's findings concerning temperament, these characteristics are strongly influenced by the environment (of which the parents are the most important part). The long-term effects of innate tendencies depend on children's environments, and the effects of any given environment on a child depend on the child's innate tendencies. Personality development is the result of the continuing interaction of heredity and environment.

Intellectual Development

As in the case of personality development, children's intellectual development is the result of an interaction of heredity and environment. Over the years, however, there has been a tremendous interest in the relative contributions of each, and debates about the **heritability of intelligence** (i.e., what proportions of a person's intellectual abilities are due to heredity and environment) have been common.

To understand the research methods used to investigate this question, we must first review some basic information about genetic relationships. Table 4-2 presents a series of genetic relationships among individuals (e.g., parent-child, identical twin to identical twin). As you can see, identical **(monozygotic)** twins, who are formed when a single zygote splits into two identical zygotes, share all of their genetic materials in common. The proportion of genetic materials shared between non-twin siblings (brothers or sisters) is .50: Siblings have half of their

TABLE 4-2 Genetic Relationships and Expected Intellectual Relationships

Relationship	Proportion of Genetic Material Shared	Expected Correlation of Intelligence	Observed Correlation of Intelligence
Identical twins reared together	1.00	1.00	.90
Non-twin siblings reared together	.50	.50	.50
Parent–child living together	.50	.50	.50
Unrelated strangers	0.00	0.00	.02

The study of identical twins, who share all genetic materials, has helped us understand the nature/nurture question but has yielded no final answers.

genetic makeup in common with each other. Similarly, the proportion of genetic materials shared between parents and their children is .50: Each child receives only half of a parent's genetic makeup. Finally, total strangers share no genetic materials (beyond those general to the human species).

These facts led researchers interested in the nature/nurture question to formulate an interesting hypothesis: If heredity were the sole influence on the development of intelligence, the correlation of intelligence test scores among individuals should be highly similar to the proportion of genetic materials they share in common. In other words, since the proportion of genetic materials shared between identical twins is 1.00, the correlation of intelligence test scores between monozygotic twins should also be about 1.00. Likewise, since the proportion of genes shared between non-twin siblings is .50, the correlation of intelligence measures between non-twin siblings should also be about .50. Further, the correlation of intelligence test scores between parents and their children should be about .50, while the correlation of intelligence test scores among unrelated individuals should be close to 0.00 (see Table 4-2).

In practice, things are not quite as simple, however, as the hypothesis described above might suggest. First, even our very best measures of intellectual ability are not perfect (Jensen, in press-a). For many reasons, the same person taking the same intelligence test on two occasions will seldom make identical scores. Typically, when the same person takes the same test several times (or takes different versions of it), the correlation among the test scores is about .90—a very high, but not a perfect, correlation.

Second, genetically related individuals usually live in the same environment. For example, the vast majority of identical twins grow up in the same home, as do most non-twin siblings. Hence, comparing the intelligence test scores of, say, identical twins reared in the same environment does not really help us determine the relative effects of heredity and environment because we do not know whether the similarity in their scores is due to genetic similarities or because they were raised in the same home.

The heredity/environment question can be addressed at least partially by comparing the correlation of intelligence test scores between identical twins reared in the same environment with that of non-twin siblings reared in the same environment. Such comparisons indicate that the correlation of intelligence test scores between identical twins reared together is about .90, just about the same as if one person were tested twice, while the correlation of intelligence test scores between non-twin siblings raised together is about .50 (Loehlin & Nichols, 1976; Newman et al., 1937; Wilson, 1977, 1978). Hence, it appears that heredity plays a relatively important role in determining intelligence.

A better approach to the nature/nurture question in intelligence is to determine the correlation of intelligence test scores in identical twins reared in separate environments. Such an approach should eliminate the environment as a factor in the development of intelligence. Still, studies employing this method have been far from perfect (Jensen, in press-a).

For example, among the widely accepted studies of separated monozygotic twins (e.g., Juel-Nielson, 1965; Newman, Freeman, & Holzinger, 1937; Shields, 1962), there is the problem of the age at which the twins were separated. As we know relatively little about the influence of the environment at different ages on overall intellectual development, the varying ages of twin separation complicates interpretation of the data. This is a relatively minor problem, however, compared to that of the similarity of environments in which separated twins have been raised (Kamin, 1975). Because social agencies try to place children in the best possible situations, the majority of separated twins identified in studies of the heritability of intelligence have grown up in similar environments. However, research focusing on the relatedness of intelligence among various family members other than identical twins has helped us obtain a much clearer picture of the relative influence of heredity and environment.

For example, Joseph Horn (1983, 1985) has reported on a wide-ranging study of the heritability of intelligence that used data from the Texas Adoption Project, one of several projects nationally in which the

Highlights

Sir Cyril Burt

One of the strangest stories in research on the relative effects of environment and heredity on intelligence involves the possibility that a well-known scholar systematically faked his data to fit his political and social beliefs. Sir Cyril Burt, a leading figure in British psychology for nearly sixty years until his death in 1971, was one of the most prolific researchers in the area of intelligence. For many years, his studies provided a primary source of data on the relationship of intelligence in identical twins who had been reared apart. Typically, Burt's studies showed a very high correlation in the intelligence scores of separated identical twins, closely approaching the correlation seen when the same person is tested on two occasions.

In 1975, Leon Kamin very carefully examined Burt's data, and in 1976 accused Burt of having systematically created fraudulent data. A later biography of Burt (Hearnshaw, 1979) provided information supporting this accusation. Burt apparently believed in a genetic basis for social class and racial differences and he may have concocted data to support his point of view.

The truth of the accusation cannot be determined with any absolute conviction so many years after Sir Cyril's death. Some psychologists (e.g., Vernon, 1979) have suggested that Burt's data must be thrown out and not considered in attempts to understand the roles of environment and heredity in shaping intelligence. Other psychologists have not been convinced of any intentional wrong-doing. They have argued that only some of Burt's studies were biased and those biased studies resulted from unintentional errors (Jensen, 1980; Reynolds, 1981).

It would seem that the safest approach to the problem of Sir Cyril's research is to exclude it from any consideration. If his data were fraudulent, they are worthless. If, instead, Burt made unintentional errors in his research, the data are flawed and should not be used in any scholarly analysis. The truth about Sir Cyril Burt's research may never be agreed on, but it is clear that either deliberate bias or unfortunate errors have severely damaged his reputation and caused his life's work to be put in the category of historical curiosity.

---

development of adopted children is being carefully monitored. As a part of this project, Horn obtained intelligence test scores from parents and children in 300 adoptive families as well as from the childrens' biological mothers. Horn then compared the relationship of adoptive parent–child intelligence with biological mother–child intelligence. The results indicated that both the environment and heredity are important factors in determining intelligence in children, although the Texas data seemed to indicate that genetic effects were more pronounced than environmental effects (Horn, 1985). Other recent studies of the relatedness of intelligence support the conclusion that both environment and heredity are important determinants of intelligence (Plomin & DeFries, 1983; Plomin, Loehlin, & DeFries, 1985; Scarr & Weinberg, 1983; Wilson, 1983), although there are still disagreements about the relative contribution of each (Cravens, 1985; Walker & Emory, 1985).

We can conclude that neither heredity nor the environment completely "controls" the intellectual abilities we see among children (Jensen, in press-b) (see Table 4-3). Although the exact contribution of the two factors is unclear, it is well established that a complex interaction of both nature and nurture is responsible for intellectual differences among children and for intellectual development in general.

TABLE 4-3 The Correlation of Intelligence for Persons of Varying Genetic and Environmental Similarities

Relationship	Correlation
Identical twins reared together	.90
Identical twins reared separately	.75
Heterozygotic twins of same sex reared together	.60
Heterozygotic twins of different sex reared together	.55
Non-twin siblings reared together	.50
Non-twin siblings reared separately	.25
Foster parents and foster children	.20
Unrelated children reared in the same home	.20
Strangers	.02

Note: Both genetic and environmental factors are varied in the research. These factors ranged from identical genetic makeup and highly similar environments in the case of identical twins reared together to no genetic similarity and no environmental similarity in the case of unrelated strangers. The data in this table are collated from a variety of relevant studies cited in this chapter.

Research

Commentaries and Rejoinders in Developmental Research

Commentaries on and rejoinders to previously published research have long had an honorable place in developmental research. Typically, a psychologist will write a commentary on someone else's research when she or he disagrees with the original article's findings. The commentary is submitted for publication in the same way as any article sent to a journal and is accepted for publication if the reviewers of the commentary find that it makes important points. The commentary, as a matter of courtesy, usually is shared with the author of the original paper prior to its publication. If this person desires, he or she may write a rejoinder to the commentary. These back and forth dialogues help us better understand the original research and facilitate the open exchange of research ideas.

A recent example of a commentary and rejoinder was published in *Child Development*. Elaine Walker of Cornell University and Eugene Emory of the State University of New York at Binghamton (1985) had read and carefully studied the article Joseph Horn (1983) had published on the Texas Adoption Project (described in the text, see page 125). In Walker and Emory's analysis of Horn's article, they noted that Horn's conclusions concerning the similarity of IQs between biological mothers and the children they gave up for adoption versus the similarity of IQs between adoptive parents and adopted children were based only on correlations (see Chapter 3). In Walker and Emory's judgment, this was an inappropriate way to analyze the data for the conclusions Horn reached (see page 127). Because of this presumed "error" on Horn's part, Walker and Emory (1985, p. 776) asserted that "the report by Horn serves as an example of the subtle interpretative biases that can occur in behavioral science research." In other words, because Walker and Emory found what they considered to be an error in the analysis presented by Horn (1983), they presumed that this error was due to a bias against environmental influences on intelligence.

As one might expect, Horn (1985) took exception to the suggestion that he was biased in his 1983 study. Horn's rejoinder, after describing a great amount of pro-environmental information contained in the original article, stated "What can now be said about Walker and Emory's allegation of bias? . . . it is wholly without substance. . . . It is not difficult to see evidence of an opposite bias in all their [Walker and Emory's] contortions." In terms of the "error" detected by Walker and Emory (1985), Horn stated, "Walker and Emory are simply expressing a preference for a two- rather than one-tailed test of significance [two different ways of testing for statistical differences]. . . . a one-tailed test [the one used by Horn] does seem appropriate."

Who's right, Horn or Walker and Emory? Both. In our judgment, Walker and Emory are correct in suggesting that additional statistical analyses of Horn's data would have been helpful in better understanding his 1983 report. We also believe, however, that Horn's original report was not biased and that he interpreted his results in as straightforward a way as possible. The commentary and rejoinder are both valuable because science only progresses when we question what has been done and seek better and better explanations of research.

Genetic Disorders

Problems in Meiosis

Genetic transmission is such a marvelously complex and fragile process that it should not be surprising that things sometimes go wrong. There are several ways in which genetic transmission can go awry, all of which have unfortunate results. Trisomy occurs when the division process in meiosis is imperfect: An ovum or a sperm is formed that does not contain the normal 23 single chromosomes but instead has 22 single chromosomes and one chromosome pair. When conception occurs, there are 22 pairs of chromosomes and one set of three. The set of three is referred to as the trisomy (literally, three chromosomes).

A particularly common form of genetic disorder that is a direct result of trisomy is trisomy-21, Down's syndrome (see Figure 4-6). Down's syndrome occurs when there is trisomy on the 22nd pair of chromosomes: The label "trisomy-21" is a remnant from early research that incorrectly identified the affected pair of chromosomes. Down's syndrome is usually characterized by mental retardation (it is the greatest single factor causing retardation), although some Down's syndrome children have IQs as high as 100. In addition, children suffering from Down's syndrome tend to have retarded motor development; broad, flat faces; straight hair; oval, upward-slanted eyes; heart defects; a

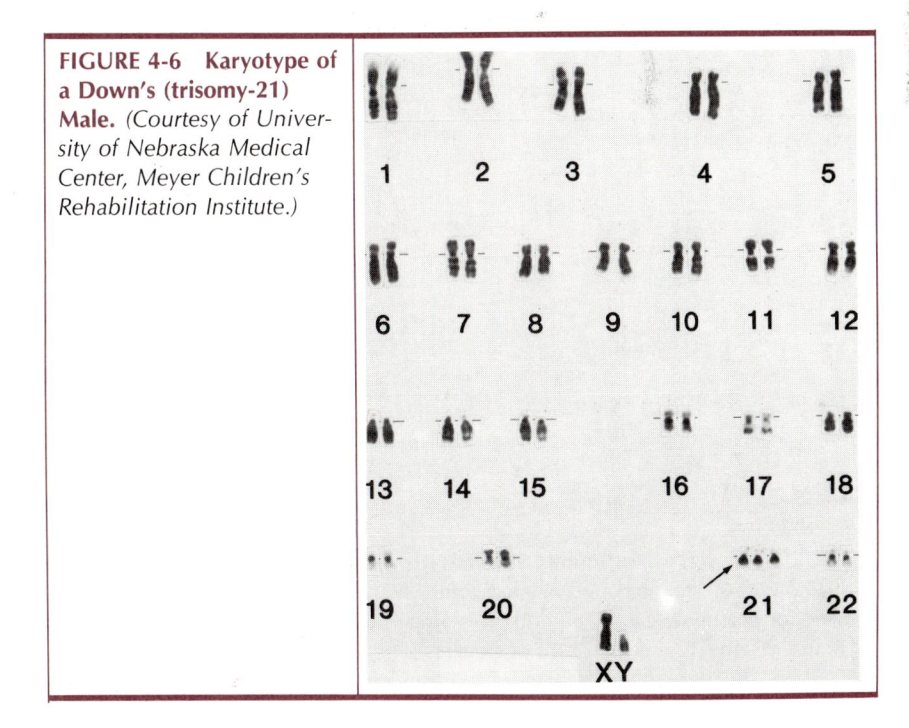

FIGURE 4-6 Karyotype of a Down's (trisomy-21) Male. *(Courtesy of University of Nebraska Medical Center, Meyer Children's Rehabilitation Institute.)*

lengthened fold of the upper eyelid over the inner corner of the eye; and increased susceptibility to respiratory illnesses and leukemia.

Other known forms of trisomy include trisomy-18 (Edwards' syndrome) and trisomy-13 (see Figure 4-7). Both of these conditions result in early death and are coupled with severe congenital problems including profound retardation. **Cri du chat** ("cry of the cat") is an anomaly in which part of the fifth chromosome is absent in the zygote due to chromosome breakage or rearrangement. Children who suffer from Cri du chat are severely retarded.

Several chromosomal abnormalities are associated with the sex chromosomes. These include Turner's syndrome, in which female children receive only one X chromosome; Klinefelter's syndrome, in which male children receive one, two, or three extra X chromosomes; trisomy X, in which female children receive an extra X chromosome; and trisomy Y,

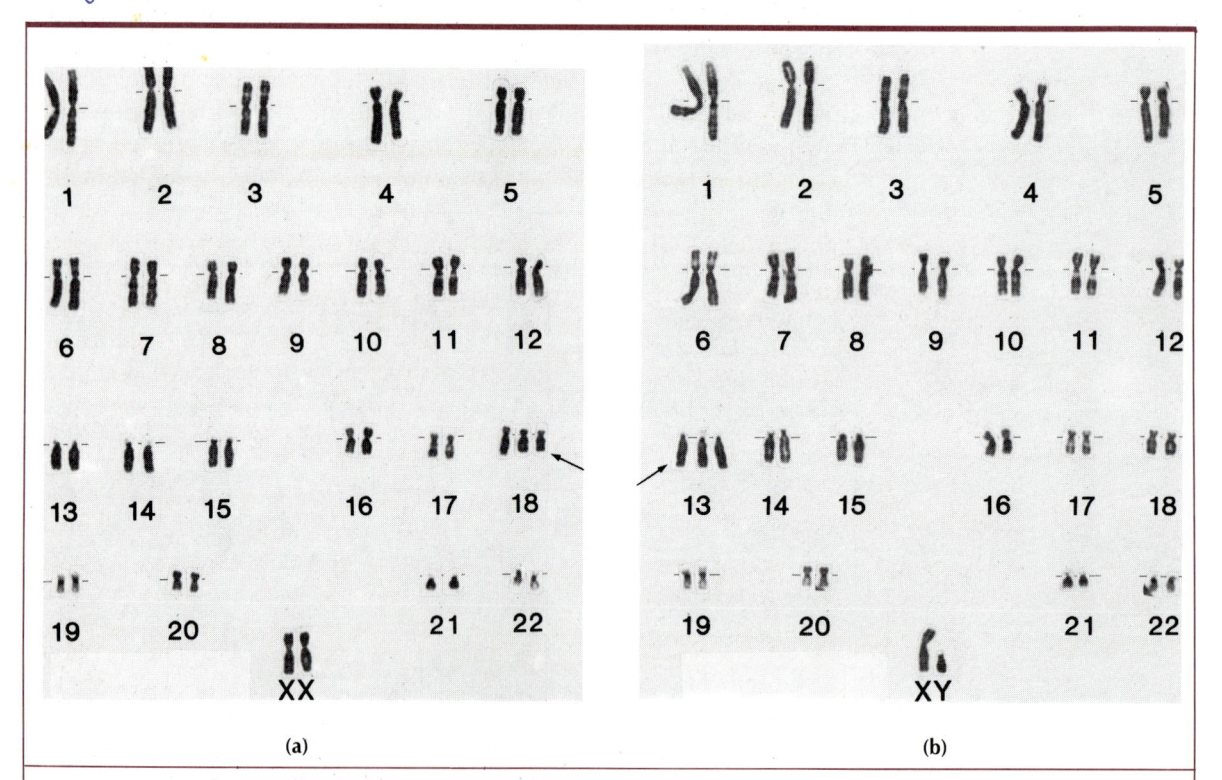

FIGURE 4-7 Infants Suffering from Trisomy. (a) Karyotype for trisomy-18. This condition is almost always fatal within the first year after birth. (b) Karyotype for trisomy-13, a condition that is always fatal. Both trisomy-18 and trisomy-13 are the result of chromosome damage during meiosis. (Courtesy of University of Nebraska Medical Center, Meyer Children's Rehabilitation Institute.)

Genetic Disorders

Down's syndrome results from improper meiosis. Many children suffering from Down's syndrome lead satisfying lives.

in which males receive an extra Y chromosome. All of these conditions are associated with some extent of intellectual impairment.

About one-quarter of chromosomal abnormalities are probably due to improper meiosis in sperm cells. The remainder seem to result from the formation of imperfect ova. All the known instances of imperfect meiosis result in severe consequences for the offspring. It is hard to judge the incidence of such genetic damage, but estimates suggest that as many as one-half of all conceptions involve chromosomal abnormalities with the vast majority resulting in spontaneous miscarriages (Gorlin, 1977; Plomin et al., 1980). In fact, only about 1 in 200 fetuses with chromosomal damage survive until birth.

Genetic Disorders Based on Recessive Genes

The disorders we have described so far result directly from imperfect meiosis. There is also a class of genetic disorders unrelated to problems in meiosis. These are called single gene defects. On occasion, a defective, dominant gene can be passed along in a normal conception. One example of such a dominant genetic defect is Huntington's chorea, which is a neurological disease. However, there are very few defective dominant genes in the human gene pool, presumably because people who inherit such genes do not frequently have children. In contrast to the limited number of defective dominant genes, there are several recessive gene disorders. Because these genes are recessive, they are not manifested in the parents. They show up only when each parent contributes a recessive allele to the zygote.

Recessive gene disorders include phenylketonuria **(PKU), Tay-Sachs disease, sickle-cell anemia,** and **cystic fibrosis.** *PKU* is a serious metabolic disorder in which infants are unable to digest milk and several other foods. Further, the condition results in a buildup of amino acids in the body that literally poison the child's system, resulting in irritability, hyperactivity, and retardation (Reid, 1975). PKU, however, is very treatable through the control of children's diets and can now be diagnosed prior to birth (see Miller, 1983b). Newborns are commonly tested for PKU in most states.

The fact that PKU can be treated so readily provides us with an excellent example of how heredity and environment interact in children's development. In most Western societies, a child who inherits PKU will have an altered environment such that PKU never presents a problem for development. In contrast, children who inherit PKU and grow up in environments in which treatment is not available will suffer serious damage. In the case of PKU, a hereditary factor may or may not influence children's development, depending on the environment in which they are raised.

Tay-Sachs disease is a degenerative nerve disorder, which is found primarily among Jewish people of eastern European ancestry; it also can be diagnosed prenatally. Children who suffer from Tay-Sachs disease typically die in the first three to four years of life. *Sickle-cell anemia* is an occasionally fatal blood disease that primarily afflicts black people. It can be diagnosed prenatally (see Boehm et al., 1983), and treatments for sickle-cell anemia are becoming more and more successful. *Cystic fibrosis* is a fatal disease of the lungs and intestines found primarily among white people. Some children who suffer from cystic fibrosis survive into adolescence, but currently available treatment leaves little hope for prolonged lifetimes in the immediate future.

Other forms of recessive gene disorders are *sex-linked*. That is, they are associated with the sex-determining chromosomes. The most well known of these is hemophilia, a disease that greatly reduces the blood's ability to clot. Until the last few years, only males suffered from hemophilia; this is because males have an X chromosome that carries the allele and no corresponding dominant allele on the Y chromosome to counter it. As modern medical care has allowed male hemophiliacs to lead near-normal lives, marry, and conceive female children, we are beginning to see hemophilia among females.

Applications for Life: Advances in Genetics

Few advances in science have as much promise for affecting human life as the application of research in genetics to medicine and family planning. In this last section of the chapter, we will examine four topics of great interest to prospective parents: selection of children's sex; genetic counseling; amniocentesis; and the future of genetic engineering.

Applications for Life: Advances in Genetics   133

Selecting Children's Sex

The fact that the child's sex is determined by which of the father's sperm cells first reaches an ovum has led to some interesting advances in the possibility of selecting the sex of children. These advances revolve around the fact that gynosperm and androsperm have different physical and behavioral characteristics. Androsperm are more streamlined, faster, more sensitive to acidity, and shorter-lived than are gynosperm. Recent reports indicate that intercourse at the time of ovulation after the female employs a baking soda douche (which reduces the acidity of the uterus) increases the chances of conceiving a boy from about 53 percent to as much as 65 to 68 percent. Similarly, the chances of conceiving a girl increase from about 47 percent to nearly 55 percent if intercourse precedes ovulation by one day and if the acidity of the uterus has been increased through a vinegar and water douche (see Annis, 1979; Whelan, 1975).

Other attempts to determine the sex of children have involved artificial insemination. **Artificial insemination** refers to the process of using a syringe to insert sperm in the vagina at the time of ovulation. If means of identifying and isolating gynosperm or androsperm can be perfected, then the sex of children could be controlled completely. Two methods of separating gynosperm and androsperm have been developed, although neither is foolproof. Dmowski, Gaynor, Rao, Lawrence, and Scommegna (1979) have employed the relative levels of activity of the two types of sperm to increase the percentage of male offspring among their clients to about 60 percent. Fleming (1980) has reported on a sperm separation technique that results in samples of sperm containing as many as 65 percent androsperms, thus greatly increasing the chances of conceiving a male child. As such separation techniques become more refined, the possibilities of choosing the sex of children will increase (Miller, 1985b). Whether or not this is desirable is something that parents and society at large will have to decide.

Genetic Counseling

Genetic counseling is the term for a relatively new field in the health sciences that aims to help prospective parents assess the potential risks of conceptions, pregnancy, and childbirth. Today, genetic counseling is still relatively rare, but it may become as common as choosing a family physician (Miller, 1985a). Couples in at least one of the following circumstances should consider genetic counseling:

1. One or both parents suffer from a genetic disorder.
2. The couple already has had a child who suffers from a genetic disorder.
3. Either the potential father or potential mother has had a child in a previous marriage who suffers from a genetic disorder.
4. The female has had a series of miscarriages.

5. Both members of the couple are from the same genetic stock or are related in some fashion.

6. Woman over 35

None of these circumstances guarantees that genetic problems will appear in prospective offspring, but the odds of genetic damage are higher than normal given such situations. The prudent couple will consider genetic counseling as a means of reducing any potential risk.

When genetic counseling is chosen, blood samples from each potential parent are taken to culture the blood cells and allow for an identification of the chromosomes and their structure. The resulting karyotype can be carefully scrutinized for genetic damage. Genes for Tay-Sachs syndrome, sickle-cell anemia, hemophilia, PKU, and also more obscure genetic disorders such as Lesch-Nyhan syndrome (a form of cerebral palsy) can now be identified via karyotyping procedures.

If both parents carry recessive genes for one of the genetic illnesses, the odds are one in four that their offspring will manifest the illness. While no one can make decisions for prospective parents, this predictive information is important for their family planning. Certainly, the identification of such high-risk parents suggests a very careful monitoring of potential pregnancies. Further, any children of these parents should eventually receive this information.

Amniocentesis

The process of **amniocentesis** involves withdrawing a small amount of amniotic fluid from within the mother's womb and subjecting this fluid to a series of tests (see Figure 4-8). The amniotic fluid contains cells that have been cast off from the fetus. These cells are then grown in a culture and karyotyped. In addition to karyotyping, some of the cells grown in the culture are analyzed for deficiencies related to various genetic disorders. As of this writing, more than 120 forms of single gene disorders as well as the chromosomal problems previously de-

FIGURE 4-8 Amniocentesis. Amniocentesis is practiced by removing a small amount of the amniotic fluid surrounding the fetus. Cells present in the amniotic fluid can be subjected to laboratory tests and chromosome analysis. More than 100 deleterious conditions can now be identified through this process.

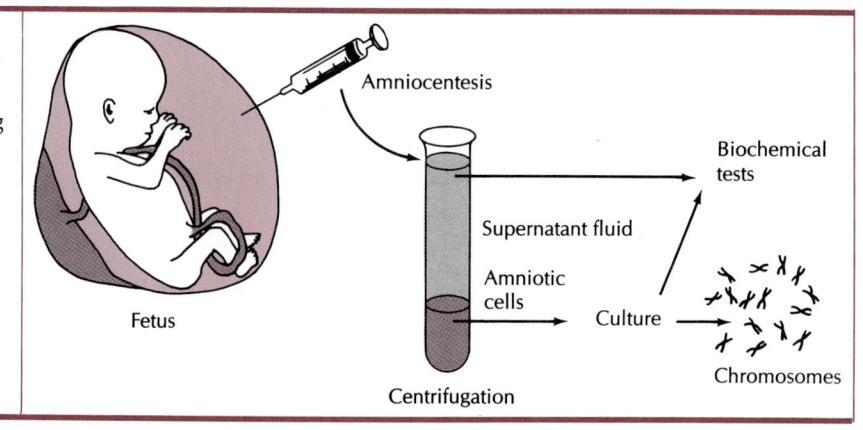

scribed can be identified via amniocentesis. In addition to high genetic risk mothers, women 35 years of age and older may consider amniocentesis as a means of determining potential chromosome damage among fetuses; the risk of improper meiosis seems to increase beyond the maternal age of 35 (Oakley, 1984; Wyatt, 1985).

If the results of amniocentesis show no problems, the parents can feel relief. If there *is* chromosomal damage, parents are informed of its severity and the range of available medical treatments. For example, children with PKU, cretinism (a thyroid disorder that can lead to severe retardation), or abnormal sex chromosomes can often be treated successfully and live fairly normal, productive lives. In contrast, of course, there are abnormalities such as trisomy-18 that guarantee an early, painful death for the infant.

Genetic counseling and amniocentesis do not provide answers; they only help parents better understand the problems they face. Ultimately, parents must decide to either abort the fetus or allow it to continue to develop. This decision is never easy and must be guided by the moral and ethical values of parents. However, despite the great burden that foreknowledge places on parents, those parents who have had severely damaged children without prior warning strongly recommend genetic counseling and amniocentesis for other potential parents.

The Future of Genetic Engineering

Advances in genetics are occurring at a dizzying pace. The conception of children outside the womb is now an accepted practice for parents who have had trouble conceiving. We may soon be able to much more carefully engineer the process. Soon parents may be able to conceive a "test tube baby" for whom an undamaged ovum and an undamaged sperm have been clinically selected, thereby eliminating the transmission of genetic disease entirely.

The concept of genetic engineering poses some profound ethical dilemmas that society has not yet addressed. Although the state of the art of genetic engineering is not yet to the point of applications, recent advances reported by Miller (1983b, 1985a) make the likelihood of genetic engineering seem very real in the not too distant future. For example, researchers have recently closed in on a gene in chromosome 15 that is the likely carrier of a hereditary form of dyslexia, a form of learning disorder (Smith, Kimberling, Pennington, & Lubs, 1983); identified specific genes associated with clotting factors in blood (Ginsburg, Handin, Bonthron, Donlon, Bruns, Latt, & Orkin, 1985); and conclusively identified the gene that carries Lesch-Nyhan syndrome, a serious form of cerebral palsy. Further, in experimental procedures that can only be described as amazingly sophisticated, the gene that carries Lesch-Nyhan syndrome can now be replaced with a normal gene in cultures of human tissue (Miller, 1985a).

Genetic engineering procedures remain experimental, but considered with the recent synthesis of artificial chromosomes that behave almost identically to natural chromosomes (Kolata, 1985; Murray & Szostak, 1983), they give promise that genetic diseases may one day be eliminated altogether.

Summary

In this chapter we surveyed the concepts of evolution and genetics. Evolution—the major process by which a species becomes progressively adapted to life in its environment—is an old concept, dating back to the time of ancient Greece. However, it was not until the time of Charles Darwin that evolutionary thought had a serious impact on intellectual life. Evolutionary theory holds that life on Earth is governed by the processes of natural selection, the process whereby species change across generations as a result of inherited characteristics particularly suited for survival; speciation, the development of new species from a common ancestor; and adaptation, the constant need to change characteristics to fit the demands of the world. In addition, the processes of mutation and structural change resulting from behavioral change also help account for evolutionary events.

The human species is the result of evolution. Our species has existed in its current form for only about 45,000 years, which is a very brief period of time in the cosmic scale of events. Every human capability today is a direct result of what was selected for over many thousands of generations, with only those characteristics most suited to survival being passed on to future generations. The study of how characteristics are passed from generation to generation—genetics—formed the second major part of the chapter.

Life begins at conception, when an ovum and a sperm cell unite to form a zygote. Under normal circumstances, each parent passes along 23 chromosomes in his or her gamete. The new zygote then contains 46 chromosomes arranged in 23 pairs. Each chromosome contains genes, which are the determinants of the structure and function of future cells.

The gametes are formed through a cell division process known as meiosis, while the formation of all other cells proceeds through mitosis. The genes in each cell determine what each new cell will become and how it will function. This information is coded in the DNA molecules that make up each gene.

The sex of children is determined by the type of sperm cell that fertilizes the ovum. If a Y-carrying androsperm joins with the ovum, the child will be a boy. If an X-carrying gynosperm fertilizes the ovum, the child will be a girl.

Genetics plays an important role in physical, emotional, and intellectual development. Heredity can be thought of as providing a basic framework within which development takes place. Environmental influences also strongly affect all of development, however; so it is most appropriate to consider human development as determined by the interplay of heredity and environment.

Given the highly complex phenomenon of the transmission of genetic materials from generation to generation, it is not surprising to find that there are sometimes problems known as genetic disorders. These disorders can be grouped into two classes: (1) those that result from improper meiosis and (2) those that are the result of the transmission of genes for various illnesses. Genetic disorders due to improper meiosis include Down's syndrome, trisomy-13, trisomy-18, and Cri du chat. Genetic disorders based on specific genes may be the result of dominant genes (as is the case in Huntington's chorea, a nervous disorder) or they may be caused by recessive genes (as is the case in sickle-cell anemia). Many of these disorders can be diagnosed during pregnancy and several (e.g., PKU) are highly treatable. Recent advances such as genetic counseling and amniocentesis provide far more information than was historically available on potential genetic disorders. Further, the continued growth of genetic engineering promises to greatly reduce the incidence of genetic disorders in the not too distant future.

Key Terms

- evolution — *process by which species becomes progressively adapted to environment*
- genetics
- natural selection
- species
- speciation
- adaptation
- mutation
- primates
- sperm
- ovum
- conception
- zygote
- gene
- gamete
- allele
- homozygotic
- heterozygotic
- dominant genes
- recessive genes
- phenotype — *outward appearance*
- genotype — *genetic constitution*
- chromosomes
- mitosis
- meiosis
- gynosperm
- androsperm
- DNA
- karyotype
- behavior genetics
- developmental behavior genetics
- twin studies
- epigenesis — *process by which genotype transforms to phenotype*
- temperament — *natural disposition to be calm, reactive, etc.*
- heritability of intelligence — *what part of a person's intellect is due to heredity & what to environment*
- monozygotic twins — *identical twins*
- trisomy — *occurs when the division process in meiosis is imperfect (2 prs of chromosomes & 1 set of 3)*
- Down's syndrome — *extra 21st chromosome — mental retardation*
- Cri du chat — *anomaly in the chromosome leading to severe retardation*
- PKU — *metabolic disorder causing hyperactivity & retardation*
- Tay-Sachs disease — *degenerative nerve disorder (Jew)*
- sickle-cell anemia — *blood disease (black)*
- cystic fibrosis — *fatal disease of lungs & intestines (white)*
- artificial insemination
- genetic counseling — *help prospective parents assess risk of birth defects & childbirth*
- amniocentesis

Suggested Readings

Davies, P. (1983). *The edge of infinity: Where the universe came from and how it will end.* New York: Simon and Schuster. Students who desire a background in cosmology, the study of how the universe evolves, will find this to be an absorbing and well-written book.

Futuyma, D. J. (1983). *Science on trial: The case for evolution.* New York: Pantheon. This book provides a helpful presentation of the creation/evolution controversy and a detailed but highly readable summary of the evidence for evolution.

Gould, S. J. (1983). *Hen's teeth and horses' toes.* New York: Norton. Gould is an excellent writer who has collected a series of his essays originally written for *Natural History* magazine. This volume provides a fine sampling of issues related to evolution.

Irvine, W. (1982). *Apes, angels, and Victorians.* Alexandria, VA: Time-Life. Although actually a dual biography of Charles Darwin and Thomas Huxley, this book presents a marvelous overview of the development of evolutionary thought and the social conditions from which it sprang. The basic tenets of evolution are explained lucidly.

Lumsden, C. J., & Wilson, E. O. (1983). *Promethean fire: Reflections on the origins of mind.* Cambridge: Harvard University Press. This superb volume deals with the evolution of the human mind. It provides an excellent source of additional reading on early humanity.

Plomin, R., DeFries, J. C., & McClearn, G. E. (1980). *Behavioral genetics.* San Francisco: W. H. Freeman. Although somewhat dated, this book provides a very nice overview of basic human genetics, genetic disorders, and research on the heritability of intelligence. It is, however, fairly advanced.

Thomas, A., & Chess, S. (1977). *Temperament and development.* New York: Brunner/Mazel. This book is somewhat technical for beginning readers but it does provide a thorough overview of genetic factors in emotional development.

Application Exercises

4-1 Environmental and Genetic Influences

Although children's development is influenced by the interaction of heredity and environment, some parts of their lives are more influenced by the environment while others are more influenced by heredity. Below is a set of brief descriptions of events in children's lives. Label each as more affected by environmental influences (E) or genetic influences (G). Give your rationale for each of your responses in the space provided.

1. Baby Rachel is 1 month old. She sleeps through the night and is hungry at consistent times through the day. Further, Rachel does not fuss much and seems to be a happy baby almost all the time.

2. Baby Sam is also 1 month old. He awakens frequently at night and is hungry at unpredictable intervals. He howls at the smallest irritation and generally seems to be in a bad humor.

3. Frances' third-grade teacher has worked hard to make arithmetic enjoyable and yet challenging for Frances. Although Frances has not achieved more than average grades in the past, this year she is at the top of her math class.

4. Johnny and Jesse are 18-year-old identical twins who were separated at the age of 3 months when their parents were killed in an automobile accident. Johnny was raised by one set of grandparents in Georgia while Jesse was raised by the other set of grandparents in Boston. As young adults, Jesse has an IQ of 109 while Johnny has an IQ of 120.

5. Angela's weight has become a matter of concern to her parents. At 8 years of age Angela weighs nearly 90 pounds. Her parents have not exercised much control over her eating habits.

6. Despite the fact that Fred was a difficult baby, his parents continually made their interactions with him as positive as possible and eliminated a lot of his cranky behavior by ignoring it and instead attending to his "happier" behaviors. Now, at age 4, Fred is a happy, outgoing child.

7. Monica is 16 and stubborn! "She comes by it naturally," asserts her father. "Both her mother and I were born stubborn and still are."

8. Randy is a 6-year-old first-grader. Every night he takes his "blankie" (a blanket he has always carried with him since he was about 11 months old) to bed with him and sucks his thumb until he falls asleep.

4-2 Choosing Genetic Counseling and Amniocentesis

Below you will see a set of brief descriptions of potential parents. Choose those descriptions for which you would suggest genetic counseling.

1. Rodney's older brother suffers from PKU.
2. Emily is 36 and planning to start her family.
3. Sandra's brother recently died from meningitis.
4. Amy and Joe have been trying to have a baby for three years. Amy has miscarried twice.
5. Ralph and Rhonda (married for three years) are third cousins.
6. Mona, 40, has a surprise pregnancy when her youngest child is nine. All of Mona's previous three babies were healthy.
7. Andrew's brother has been incarcerated as an habitual criminal.
8. Mildred's Aunt Ruth suffered from sickle-cell anemia.
9. Jack suffered from malaria as an adolescent.
10. In Molly's previous marriage, she had a child who died soon after birth from the effects of trisomy-13.

CHAPTER 5

Social Influences on Development

Children have more need of models than of critics.
—Joseph Joubert, Pensées

. . . the very process of living together educates.
—John Dewey, Education as a Necessity of Life

In Chapter 4, we traced the role that evolution has played in shaping the development of human beings. One of the most remarkable aspects of our biological adaptation is the complexity of our interactions with each other. In this chapter, we will examine the effects of these interactions—the social context of human development.

A mother and her child, a crowd of spectators at the stadium, a couple sitting under a tree, a group of teenagers gathered at a fast food restaurant, a family on a picnic, participants in a discussion, children chasing each other on a playgound—each of these instances shows us a different aspect of human social interaction. All the different kinds of contact between human beings are far more than just a source of pleasure. They play a vital role in our survival as individuals and as a species. Without social interactions, no child could survive, no civilization could continue. Each child is raised in a social context that nurtures and shapes it.

Children learn ways of acting, thinking, and feeling, from their families, peers, community, and society. The general name for this process is **socialization**. Socialization is a process that occurs when some individuals in a society share their knowledge, skills, and values with developing individuals. This process takes place within families, neighborhoods, institutions such as schools and churches, and cultural groups and nations. Socialization is a teaching-learning relationship (Tallman, Marotz-Baden, & Pindas, 1983), and each source of socialization is vital to the developing child.

What do children learn during socialization? Tallman et al. (1983) outline several elements, including learning roles for self and others and coming to share the beliefs, commitments, and loyalties of people within groups. Through socialization, children learn how people with given identities act and feel as well as think. Thus children are socialized to understand their roles in the family (e.g., helper, follower of an older sibling) and what to expect from parents (e.g., father puts child to bed, mother takes child to day-care center). Children learn, for example, that

The most important social system for most children is the family, which provides the earliest, most continuous, and most intense social experiences.

both teachers and parents are interested in good behavior in school and that their parents see themselves as caregivers. They may notice that grandparents respond quite differently than do their own parents when they are "cutting up" and that strangers are less likely than parents to be concerned with what they do. They discover that their own families require certain standards (e.g., good table manners, neatness) that are not necessarily required at the babysitter's or vice versa. They learn skills for negotiating with others (e.g., when a child wants to have a snack, but the mother does not approve). They learn what is considered legitimate behavior (e.g., a child makes her bed and is complimented) and what is not (she takes food without asking and is scolded severely). As children interact with the social world, they construct their own identities as well as learn about the identities of others. They also develop ways of perceiving the world.

Of course, parents are not the only social influences on development. Children learn a great deal from interactions with adults other than their parents, with siblings, and with peers. Starting with the family, children quickly become a part of a number of social systems; soon, they must relate to institutions such as schools and become functioning members of the community, state, and country. Each social context—from immediate family through the culture at large—plays a key role in each child's development.

The Structure of the Ecological Environment

Urie Bronfenbrenner, a leading developmental psychologist, has been the most outspoken proponent of the idea that children's thoughts and actions must be understood in relationship to the context in which they occur. He has outlined what has been called an **ecological** (or contextual)

view of child development (Bronfenbrenner, 1979). All human development is contextual; it does not happen in a vacuum. How children perceive, think, and act depends to a great extent on the people and the settings around them.

Consider for a moment the various ways in which children can come in contact with others. Every child is a part of many social settings (contexts) simultaneously: family, school, city, and nation. Children daily move between settings (e.g., from home to preschool to babysitter and back home again). With development, they are forced to move into new settings (e.g., from home to preschool, from preschool to kindergarten), while settings themselves can change (e.g., children's families change with the arrival of a new baby, or the neighborhood changes when new apartments are built). Bronfenbrenner's view is that these social contexts, the interactions among them, and the changes that take place in them have a profound influence on development.

Some contexts affect children directly whereas others exert indirect influences. Bronfenbrenner (1979) outlines four levels of context and children's experiences in them that can have either direct or indirect effects: (1) microsystems (the most intimate level), (2) mesosystems, (3) exosystems, and (4) macrosystems (the least intimate). We will examine each in turn.

Microsystems

The greatest impact on children emerges from the people and settings closest to them. Intimate associates and settings provide the pattern of activities, roles, and interpersonal relations directly experienced by the developing person, called **microsystems** (Bronfenbrenner, 1979, p. 22). These patterns occur in contexts—called *microsystem settings*—in which children can readily engage in direct interactions with others. Perhaps the most important microsystem setting is the family, which typically provides the earliest, most continuous, and most intense experience for almost all children. Other important microsystem settings include relatives' and babysitters' homes, day-care centers, and preschools. Each of these settings has a measurable impact on children's social and intellectual development (Clarke-Stewart, 1984; Scarr, 1984).

The setting (e.g., the home), the objects in it (e.g., furniture, dishes, utensils), and the activities that take place (e.g., talking, reading, washing dishes) all are important parts of an interactive system. Each component affects the others. Most important, however, is how children perceive the setting, materials, and interactions. The *meaning* of children's experiences is more critical for them than the purely objective aspects of the setting. Thus, a familiar blanket, a teddy bear, or the picture on a child's cup are important because of what they mean to children, not because of what they are.

Because microsystems are products of children's experiences of them, a single setting will contain different microsystems for each child.

Children's experiences in a preschool, for example, may create divergent microsystems for each of the children attending the school. Some may achieve success in their activities and capture the favorable attention of adults and peers. Others, however, may not have the necessary skills to interact with others successfully. Still others may experience great distress over being left at the preschool by their parents. Even playgroups have different roles for different children. Depending on the composition of a playgroup, a given child's role may differ greatly. In one group, a child may be a leader whereas he or she is just "one of the crowd" in another. Of course, settings themselves also can vary dramatically. Most children experience love and affection in their families, but some live in conditions of neglect and even abuse. In all cases, however, the roles children learn to play will reflect the conditions they have encountered and how they interpret them. The roles, in turn, exert an important influence on development.

Because children's development occurs within microsystems, developmental psychologists have tried to describe microsystems clearly in order to improve their understanding of development. How do settings in which children spend their time—home, babysitter's home, day-care, nursery school—differ? What, if any, impact does family structure have? How do parents communicate with their children? If there are older or younger siblings, what are their interactions like? What roles do children have in their homes, their playgroups, and their day-care centers and schools? Development, in its great complexity, is a product of all of these factors *and the child's perception of them*. Later in the chapter, we will discuss several aspects of one of the most important microsystem settings, the family. The nature of the family and the changes occurring in it have important implications for the direction development takes (Elkind, 1979; Levitan & Belous, 1981; Maccoby & Martin, 1983).

Mesosystems

Beyond microsystems are **mesosystems**. Mesosystems are the relationships individuals create between two or more settings in which they participate. For example, a mesosystem for an infant may be relatively simple, consisting of the relationships between its family and that of a next door neighbor. These two settings are the only ones the child experiences. For older children, however, mesosystems may be much more varied, with highly complex interactions among several settings. Children who divide their time among home, a preschool, grandparents, extra-family excursions, and occasional family trips, and who are acquainted with children of their parents' friends, for example, have many more contexts to relate to one another.

In school, children's experiences with their peers and with their teachers are each microsystems; the relationship *between* the teacher–child context and the peer group is a mesosystem. Similarly, home and school form a mesosystem for most children, since two of the child's immediate settings are linked (Minuchin & Shapiro, 1983). In Bronfenbrenner's judgment, development is enhanced when persons in different settings in the mesosystem are in close communication. When individuals in home, school, and other settings are all concerned about the developing child, share beliefs about child-rearing, and communicate with each other about the child, the child's developmental potential will be greatest (Long, Peters, & Garduque, 1985).

Exosystems

Exosystems consist of one or more settings that do not actively involve the child, but which include events that *indirectly* affect the child. Later, we will explore in more depth the effect of a parent's place of work, an important exosystem for most children. Even though a child may have no idea what a parent does, the location of a parent's job, the hours, or the demands on the parent may greatly affect the child's life. Parents may become short-tempered or abusive because of work pressures. In contrast, a parent's stimulating job may provide new ideas for child-rearing, opportunities for the child to travel, and many topics for conversation. For the schools, exosystems are at a community or societal level; they determine policies (such as busing or bilingual education) that affect children's experiences in important ways.

Parental activities can create new exosystems for children. If the mother or father plays on a softball team, for instance, time spent at home with the child may be reduced. Participation in a book discussion group may lead to new ideas about child-rearing from which the child will benefit. Although such indirect effects of external settings have not yet been the topic of much research, they nonetheless are important. Conditions such as teacher morale, community leadership, and maternal employment (Hoffman, 1983; Scarr, 1984) each provide some part of the context in which children develop.

Macrosystems

Macrosystems refer to the broad consistencies at the cultural or subcultural levels in micro-, meso-, and exosystems, and also to consistencies in beliefs shared in the culture (Bronfenbrenner, 1979). For example, children in the People's Republic of China are affected by very different micro-, meso- and exosystems than are children in the United States because of cultural differences in family structure, schools, and political systems.

To understand development, we cannot ignore the cultural context. What are the dominant educational and religious values? What are female and male roles like in this culture? What are the common views about children, parents, and grandparents? What characterizes the educational system? If one culture's values and resources differ radically from those of another, children's development may take a different

A Closer Look at Social Contexts

Microsystem Influences on Development: Family Members

course. We will discuss the importance of these cultural and subcultural effects on the developing child in more detail later in the chapter.

Most of us would agree that the family plays a key role in children's development. But what does this mean? Families come in many forms (Scarr, 1984). A family—a system for raising children—can consist of a married couple and children; or it could be a mother and her children; father and children; grandparents, mother and child; collections of relatives and children; or an unmarried person and child. Internal family patterns often change: The addition of a new baby or a fundamental change in family structure, such as divorce, can profoundly alter the family. Finally, there are great differences in the child-rearing practices, or **parenting,** of different parents (Maccoby & Martin, 1983). In the immediate family are several sources of influence on the child—from either or both of the parents (Clarke-Stewart, 1978; Pedersen, 1982), from other adults, and often from one or more **siblings.** Simultaneously, the child is influencing and changing them (Bell & Harper, 1977; Maccoby & Martin, 1983).

In the following sections, we will look at key people in childrens' family-based microsystems—mother, father, and siblings—and how each can relate to a child's development. Next we will examine two prominent patterns of family structure, the two-parent family and the single-parent family, and note similarities and differences. Finally, we will look at four approaches to child-rearing and examine how each affects the development of the child.

Mothers. The mother–child bond is a unique and enduring one (Maccoby & Martin, 1983). Some researchers (Klaus & Kennell, 1976, 1982) have argued that physical contact in the first hours of life between mother and child is particularly critical to developing this bond. Based on the existence of a critical period for bonding in animals (see Chapter 14, *Social Development*) and studies of early contact between human mothers and infants, Klaus and Kennell have contended that mother and infant should be together immediately after birth. Skin-to-skin contact between mothers and infants is, they contend, especially important for creating a close tie between mother and child, which then deepens through continued close association. Others, however, have strongly questioned the idea of a sensitive period in bonding and, indeed, the validity of the entire concept of bonding (Goldberg, 1983; Myers, 1984).

Human beings, they argue, are far more adaptable than other species: Even without early contact, strong ties of affection eventually will develop between mothers and their children. For example, adopted children can develop extremely close ties to their adoptive mothers. All agree, however, that early contact between mothers and newborn infants is likely to be a positive experience for all concerned and applaud recent changes in hospital practices that encourage early, close contact between mothers and their newborn babies (Myers, 1984).

Regardless of the status of the concept of bonding, mothers and children quickly come to coordinate their actions. An integral part of mother–child interaction, for instance, is mutual eye contact, or gazing at one another (Martin, 1981). While making eye contact, mothers and infants tend to link their other actions as well. As they look at each other, for example, the baby may coo while the mother speaks to her. When external objects such as a toy are presented, both infant and mother often look at the same object, most likely because the mother turns to the object the baby is looking at. Mothers also tend to match babies' moods: Positive moods are matched by positive moods and negative moods by negative (Maccoby & Martin, 1983).

Both mothers and children initiate interactions. A large number of studies done both in the laboratory and in naturalistic settings (see Chapter 3, *Research Methods*) have shown that infants take a very active role in initiating social interactions (Martin, 1981). Far from being passive recipients of socialization, infants affect their mothers as well as being affected by them.

Early mother and infant activity is often simultaneous. As children grow older, however, mothers and children begin to take turns in many exchanges, especially as they interact verbally. The following example from Snow (1977, p.12) shows a "conversation" between a mother and her 3-month-old baby in which an elementary form of "turn-taking" is evident:

Baby:	(smiles)
Mother:	Oh, what a nice little smile. Yes, isn't that pretty. There now. There's a nice little smile.
Baby:	(burps)
Mother:	What a nice little wind as well. Yes, that's better, isn't it? Yes. Yes.
Baby:	(vocalizes)
Mother:	Yes! There's a nice noise.

Notice how the mother responds *as if* the baby were intending to communicate. Simple turn-taking like this, developmentalists argue, helps set the stage for conversational and communication skills that will develop later. By the time children are age 1 or so, they clearly can initiate interactions, and their mothers wait for pauses in their infants' vocalizations to make their own contributions. By age 2, children are more equal participants in conversations and partners in interactions.

Fathers. Over the years, most parent–child research has examined the relationship between mother and child. More recently, however, there has been an increasing interest in father–child relationships (see Clarke-Stewart, 1978; Fein, 1978; Lamb, 1977a, 1977b, 1980, 1984; Maccoby & Martin, 1983). As sex roles have changed in our culture and in the family, fathers have become more important participants in child-rearing. But should fathers be more involved in child-rearing? Are they competent in child-rearing? What functions do they have as parents? Are there any negative consequences of fathers' child-rearing activities? Questions such as these have been examined in recent research.

In general, the research has shown that both mothers and fathers are important to the developing child and are competent caregivers, but that mothers and fathers typically adopt somewhat different roles in parenting. Research by Clarke-Stewart (1978), Lamb (1977a, 1977b) and others has shown that mothers seem to be more nurturant and to perform more routine child-care activities than do fathers. Mothers tend to "take care of their children." Fathers, on the other hand, more often

As sex roles have changed in the United States, fathers have become more important participants in child rearing.

play actively with their children (such as bouncing children on their knees or tossing them in the air). The difference in nurturance may be due to the social expectations for girls and women to "mother" children, to a genetic bias in human females that permits them to provide care for children, or most likely, to some combination of social influences and genetics (Maccoby & Martin, 1983).

Although fathers generally are becoming somewhat more involved in child–rearing in the United States (Levitan & Belous, 1981; U.S. Bureau of the Census, 1984), mothers still carry the greater responsibility, as they do in all of the world's cultures. Relatively few two-parent families, for instance, have chosen a family structure in which the father is the primary caregiver. Moreover, when both parents have careers, mothers still have most of the responsibility for child care. Through sheer time spent in contact with the child, mothers are likely to have greater influence on the developing child. It seems likely, however, that paternal participation in child–rearing will increase, as some of the traditional assumptions about fathers' and mothers' family roles change (Hoffman, 1984). The consequences of paternal participation give rise to considerable debate (see Hoffman, 1983, and Thompson, 1983, for discussions of paternal participation in child–rearing).

One area in which fathers seem to have a particular impact is in the development of sex-typed behaviors (Huston, 1983). **Sex-typed behaviors** are those commonly associated with one sex or the other (see Chapter 16). In general, fathers seem to emphasize sex-typed behaviors more than mothers do. For example, in a study of preschool children (Langlois & Downs, 1980), fathers more often rewarded "male" sex-stereotyped play for their boys (e.g., running, jumping, playing with blocks) and punished boys for "female" sex-stereotyped activities (e.g., playing with dolls, asking for help). Fathers also reacted more positively to physical activity by boys than by girls. In general, the study showed that fathers are very likely to engage boys in active, physical play, while they encourage girls to be more dependent and more "feminine." Thus, one effect of father–child interactions may be to teach children to act in ways considered typical of their sex. Of course, the desirability of this outcome is highly controversial, in that many persons feel that rigidly defined sex roles are detrimental to the full development of human beings.

Fathers also tend to interact more with their male than with their female children (Lamb, 1977a; Thompson, 1983; Weintraub & Frankel, 1977). This phenomenon has been observed both in laboratory and home-based studies. The reasons for this bias are not completely clear, however. Possibly, as Maccoby and Martin (1983) have stated, since fathers generally are less involved overall in parenting, they may feel a special responsibility for their son's masculine development. Mothers, in contrast, show much less difference in reaction to their male and female children, perhaps because they have the primary responsibility for *all* of their children.

As mentioned above, current trends in child-rearing in the United States are toward greater male involvement in parenting, although by far the greater responsibility in most families still lies with the mother. The evidence just cited, however, suggests that parents need to consider the *nature* of the father's involvement, not just the *amount* of involvement. In what aspects of child care should he be involved, and how should he interact with his male and female children? These are family-specific questions, since there obviously is no one "right" answer. Many people believe, however, that the demands of modern society are likely to produce significant changes in fathers' roles that will have multiple effects on parents as well as on children (Hoffman, 1983).

Siblings. Siblings—brothers and sisters—also play a major role in development. Older children, for instance, must adjust to a newborn, after a period of being the "only child." For second-born children, in contrast, the family context contains both adults and an older brother or sister from the start. Of course, for children born into larger families, the relationships multiply; sorting out all of the effects becomes very difficult indeed. Some effects are reasonably clear, however.

One factor that has received intensive study is the spacing between siblings. Perhaps this has been highlighted because parents can control this factor through family planning. Are siblings born close together (e.g., 1 year apart) more compatible than those who are farther apart in age? Also, how does the sex of siblings affect their interactions? That is, do same-sex pairs interact differently than mixed-sex pairs? One study of spacing, by Abramovitch, Pepler, and Corter (1982), tried to answer these questions. In the Abramovitch et al. study, children who were 1½ and their older siblings who were either 3 or 4½ years of age were observed in their own homes. Behavior was recorded only when both children were together.

Levels of interaction between siblings in the home were very high; in a typical 2-hour observation period, over 79 interactions per hour for same-sex pairs and over 87 for mixed-sex pairs were observed. Most interactions were initiated by the *older* child in the pair. In a category of interactions called **agonistic behaviors** that included aggression, fighting, loud demands, teasing, tattling, and so on, the older child was the initiator over 80 percent of the time. For **prosocial behaviors** that included cooperation, sharing, praise, approval, and so on, the proportion of initiations by the older sibling was somewhat lower, but still quite high (65 percent).

Thus, older children seem to set the tone for sibling interactions, just as they do in any pair of children of different ages (Hartup, 1983). The younger child, however, also has an important role in maintaining interactions by how he or she responds to the older child's behavior. For example, does the younger child react strongly against aggression or submit to it? A reaction such as hitting back heavily influences the prolongation of aggression. Also, younger children imitate older children significantly more often than vice versa. Imitation is often playful—for example, pretending to be a monster, dancing around the room, repeating words and phrases—suggesting that younger siblings learn both social and cognitive skills from their older siblings.

What differences exist in interactions between boy–boy, girl–girl, and boy–girl pairs of siblings? In same-sex pairs, female siblings had more prosocial activity than agonistic activity, whereas the opposite was true for males. Pairs of boys have more conflict. Older girls in same-sex pairs also were more likely to be nurturant of their sibling than were older boys. Overall, girls initiated more prosocial behavior than did boys, with older boys being the most "agonistic" group.

Eighteen months after their initial study, Abramovitch et al. observed these same pairs again. Younger siblings were now 3 years old, and the older siblings 4½ and 6 years old. Again, high rates of interaction were observed. As before, older siblings continued to initiate most interactions, but now the percentages were not as disparate between younger and older siblings.

A large body of research has often shown boys becoming more aggressive and girls becoming more prosocial with development (see Maccoby & Jacklin, 1974). In the Abramovitch et al. study, however, sex of the children seemed to play little role. Older boys now were no more likely to be aggressive than girls, and older girls were now not observed to be more prosocial than boys. This result was unexpected not only because of earlier research, but also because predictions from theories of modeling and imitation would suggest increases in boys' aggressiveness and girls' prosocial activities as a result of continuing exposure to these sex roles in our culture. Thus further research is needed to heighten our understanding of how these factors develop and to refine theory in this area.

Of course, siblings frequently interact in the presence of an adult or with an actively participating adult. Often, mothers or fathers initiate interaction with one or both children and intercede in quarrels. Interestingly, the majority of mothers (72 percent) in the Abramovitch et al. study believed that their children got along better when they were *not* around and, in fact, observations showed just that: more negative interactions between siblings when mothers were present than when they were absent! Abramovitch et al. speculated that children's negative behavior often is designed to attract the mother's attention, even though mothers in this study were instructed not to intervene.

Mothers, Fathers, and Children. As we examine the role of mothers, fathers, and other children on development, we can see that children's microsystems are very complex and that every family member—mother, father, and siblings—can play important roles. Family members can be teachers, playmates, initiators of activities, antagonists, or helpers. In return, children affect their caregivers and siblings by their actions and reactions. The family unit, no matter what its composition, is best viewed as an interactive network, with each family member being affected by and affecting each other member (Bronfenbrenner, 1979; Clarke-Stewart, 1978; Pedersen, 1982).

Microsystem Influences: Family Structure

Families come in many forms. As Sandra Scarr (1984) points out, the modern American family is not necessarily a heterosexual couple with, as she says wryly, "2.2 children and a white picket fence" (p. 120). In Scarr's view, from a child development perspective, a family is most usefully defined as a system for rearing children. Regardless of whether they are traditional or non-traditional, all family forms have strengths and weaknesses.

Without a doubt, the American family has undergone tremendous change in the years since World War II. Two factors in particular—women's changing roles and the increasing acceptability of divorce—have brought about drastic alterations. Other influences also have had a major impact. Television, for example, has grown from a curious toy to a major industry pervading almost all homes in the United States. Child care, once limited almost totally to relatives or neighbors, is becoming an industry in its own right, available to and used by an increasing number of American families. Also, the American public now is much better educated on matters pertaining to child development than it was in the 1940s, although much yet needs to be accomplished (Scarr, 1984).

In spite of transformations in family structure and views of childrearing, most members of U.S. society still judge marriage and family life to be highly important (Levitan & Belous, 1981). At the same time, there is increasing divergence in family patterns and structures. The proportion of marriages ending in divorce is approaching 2 in 5 (U.S. Bureau of the Census, 1984). The number of children involved in divorces has more than tripled since 1956. Even so, over 70 percent of the children in the United States live with both their natural parents and nearly all with at least one (U.S. Bureau of the Census, 1984). In this section, we will examine the most prominent patterns of family structure and the social context each provides for development. While changes in many different systems have the potential for affecting development (Bronfenbrenner, 1979), those in the family are likely to be the most influential of all.

Children in Two-Parent Families. The **two-parent family** is still the most prevalent family structure in the United States. As mentioned above, over two-thirds of all children live with both natural parents.

Thus, the family settings for most children's microsystems include two parents and whatever material elements the family has. Obviously, in two-parent families both the mother and the father potentially can shape children's development. Of course, two-parent families vary from one another in many ways. In many families, for instance, there may be considerable inequality between the mother and father in child-rearing roles; the "traditional" pattern is strongly biased toward the mother's providing most important aspects of direct child care. In other two-parent families, however, the pattern may be quite different. Parents' roles may be equally shared or, in a pattern that is currently rare but not unknown, the father may assume the role of primary caregiver.

From a developmental standpoint, two-parent families usually are considered to have some advantages over single-parent families. For example, when two adults are involved in child-rearing, the responsibilities can be shared and stresses reduced. Two adults, presumably, can provide more stimulation for the child than one. Further, two-parent families typically are better off economically. The relatively greater level of economic resources available in a two-parent family gives children an advantage when it comes to health care, educational opportunity, stability, and freedom from anxiety. Although specific factors within the family (such as stable adult relationships and child-rearing practices) obviously are more critical than family structure, it seems plausible that children's intellectual, social, and emotional development ordinarily can take place with fewer obstacles in two-parent families.

Children in Single-Parent Families. The number of **single-parent families** in the United States has increased dramatically since World War II. By 1983, over one in five families was headed by a single parent (U.S.

Child care, once limited to relatives or neighbors, is a growing industry used by an increasing number of American families.

Bureau of the Census, 1984). Many single-parent families result from divorce; yet more and more frequently, unmarried women have children. Widows and widowers lead a small, but important, group of single-parent families. Also, in a small number of cases, children are adopted by an unmarried adult.

Two reasons, likely, are most related to the great rise in numbers of single-parent families. First, social pressure to keep marriages going "because of the children" has greatly diminished; more than five of seven adults believe that it is acceptable for married couples with children to divorce if they cannot get along (Levitan & Belous, 1981). Second, there has been a dramatic increase in the number of children born out of wedlock, particularly to teenagers. This phenomenon appears to have resulted from changes in society's attitudes about premarital sex, as well as a greater societal acceptance of unmarried persons rearing children. Between 1980 and 1983, for instance, the proportion of children reared by single, never-married mothers nearly doubled in the United States (U.S. Bureau of the Census, 1984).

The vast majority of single-parent families are headed by women. The proportion of children who live with only their mother is about 1 in 5; only about 1 in 50 children live only with their father (U.S. Bureau of the Census, 1984). Although the bulk of research on families has focused on children in "traditional" two-parent families, recent research has concentrated on single-parent families, most particularly those headed by women. Available evidence on single-parent families headed by men is still extremely sparse, however (Thompson, 1983).

The most noticeable difference with developmental implications between the majority of mother-led families and most two-parent families is economic (Moynihan, 1986). Only 1 of 19 husband–wife-led families is at the poverty level. In contrast, 1 in 9 single-parent families headed by men and *1 in 3* female-headed families are at the poverty level (Levitan & Belous, 1981). The median (mid-point) level of income of female-headed households is *less than half* of that of husband–wife households. Further, a woman's chances of receiving child support from the father are small: About two-thirds of all divorced, separated, never married, or remarried mothers receive no child support from the father (Levitan & Belous, 1981). Women almost invariably show a downward shift in their economic status after divorce. Thus, children in female-headed households are much more likely than those in two-parent families to be economically disadvantaged (U.S. Bureau of the Census, 1984).

Because most female-led families result from divorce, there has been considerable interest in its psychological as well as economic outcomes. Is the psychological impact of divorce on families, and children in particular, as bleak as the economic effect? The research indicates that children's emotional well-being during and after divorce depends on several factors: the amount of hostility in the marriage; the level of preparation the children receive; the children's ages; whether or not the parents use the children as pawns in a fight with each other; and how well the parent retaining custody adjusts to his or her new life.

Even in the best of situations, however, divorce appears to place a great deal of stress on the family system. In a longitudinal study of families following divorce, Mavis Hetherington and her associates (Hetherington, Cox, & Cox, 1976, 1979, 1982) observed interactions of parents with their children on several occasions. In this study, mothers had custody and children were 4 years old at the time legal divorce took place.

In the first year after the divorce, mothers became more "authoritarian," making more direct commands and becoming less responsive and affectionate toward the children. Also, the family routine became more haphazard, featuring irregular bedtimes and mealtimes. In contrast to the mothers' becoming more authoritarian, fathers tended to withdraw. They became less involved in many of the "disciplinary" aspects of child-rearing, such as rule enforcement and management of children's routines; instead, they tended to increase gift-giving. Children, especially boys, became less compliant and more aggressive. Some blamed themselves for causing the parental breakup, while others felt rejected by the parent who left. Still others suffered from depression or become engulfed in feelings of rage expressed as hostility.

By the second year following divorce, however, a kind of balance was reappearing in many of the relationships of parents and children. Mothers were more patient and responsive, fathers stricter, and children more cooperative. Routines were being reestablished. Presumably, as parents adjusted to their new lives, they became more able to function effectively as parents. As the stress of marital conflict and preoccupation with it declined, ability of parents to maintain relationships with their children increased.

Of course, the rate of family readjustment varied greatly, depending on such factors as new intimate relationships by either or both parents and economic conditions of the household. Hetherington et al. (1982) also pointed out that, despite the divorce, continuing support of the father to the family was important. In their sample, mother–child relationships were better under conditions in which fathers not only provided economic support but continued to visit the children and to participate in their upbringing.

Like Hetherington et al., Goetting (1981) has concluded that children's long-term mental health and psychological adjustment seem to depend more on relationships within the family than on the family's actual structure. That is, what happens within the family is more critical to the psychological well-being of children than whether there is one parent or two. Goetting has shown that, in general, developmental problems occur least often in happy intact homes; most often in unhappy intact homes; and somewhere in between in divorced homes. In some cases at least, divorce appears to reduce negative influences on children's development (see Ahlstrom & Havinghurst, 1971), although Hetherington's research indicates this is more true from a long-term than a short-term perspective.

Finally, some feel that the impact of a divorce may be related to how children viewed family life prior to the breakup (Levitan & Belous, 1981). If the marriage was marked by much unhappiness, quarreling, and bitterness, adjustment to divorce is much easier than if children are taken by surprise. Thus, we come back to Bronfenbrenner's observation that the essential characteristic of microsystems is not the purely objective "facts" of the situation, but rather the child's interpretation of it (Bronfenbrenner, 1979).

Microsystem Influences: Parenting Styles

Child-rearing practices vary greatly from parent to parent, from family to family, and from social group to social group. Consequently, much of the research in child-rearing has tried to identify **parenting styles**, or *patterns* of child-rearing, and to link these patterns to developmental outcomes. Maccoby and Martin (1983) have proposed one way of looking at differences in child-rearing practices. Drawing upon early research by Becker (1964) and Baumrind (1967, 1971), their system involves a two-dimensional classification of parenting patterns (see Table 5-1) that provides a way of distinguishing the different contexts parents can create for their children's development.

TABLE 5-1   A Two-Dimensional Classification of Parenting Patterns

	Parent-Centered	Child-Centered
Demanding	AUTHORITARIAN-AUTOCRATIC rejecting unresponsive power assertive	AUTHORITATIVE-RECIPROCAL accepting responsive open to communication
Undemanding	INDIFFERENT-UNINVOLVED neglecting ignoring uncommitted	INDULGENT-PERMISSIVE low control desire accepting responsive

Adapted from E. E. Maccoby, and J. A. Martin (1983). Socialization in the context of the family: Parent-child interaction. In E. M. Hetherington (Ed.), P. H. Mussen (Series Ed.), *Handbook of child psychology: Vol. 4. Socialization, personality, and social development.* New York: Wiley.

Authoritarian-Autocratic Pattern. As the name implies, the **authoritarian-autocratic pattern** involves a high degree of authority or power asserted by the parents. In this parent-centered approach, rules are formulated by the parent and are not subject to negotiation. Strict limits are placed on children's behavior. Children are not allowed to contradict the parents or to challenge their authority. When children's behavior differs from what authoritarian parents require, punishment such as spanking or slapping is often the result. What kinds of outcomes tend to result from authoritarian parenting? In general, children of authoritarian parents tend to lack spontaneity, initiative, and competence with their peers. Further, a controlling parent style is thought to be a factor in the development of poor self-esteem (Maccoby & Martin, 1983).

Many authoritarian parents believe in using physical force in disciplining children. From the parental standpoint, spanking or slapping is necessary in order to curb improper behavior or impulses. Children's views, however, may be somewhat different. They may see spanking or other use of force as merely a form of aggression. Indeed, a large body of research has linked parents' use of corporal (physical) punishment and other punitive methods with children's aggressive behavior (Parke & Slaby, 1983; Welsh, 1985; Wiggins, 1983). Many developmentalists believe that using physical punishment simply models aggressive behavior for children.

When aggression is assessed for parents and children as well, some families typically are much more aggressive than others. That is, not only do children in these families act aggressively, but so do others in the family. It is often difficult, however, to ascertain whether adult aggression such as corporal punishment strengthens childhood aggression or whether children's aggression brings out punitive (punishing) reactions in their caretakers. In other words, parental aggression may inspire child aggression through the mechanism of observational learning and imitation. On the other hand, perhaps a "naturally" aggressive child may stimulate aggressive reactions (e.g., slapping) in parents who would not be aggressive toward another, less aggressive child. Determining the source of aggression is one example of the difficulty that researchers face in attempting to infer causality from correlational evidence (see Scarr, 1984, and Chapter 3, *Research Methods*). In any event, we do know that aggressive children typically live in aggressive home environments.

One interesting finding (Patterson, 1982) is that highly aggressive children may react to punishment very differently than do normal children. When most children's aggression is punished, the chances that they will continue acting aggressively are reduced. With extremely aggressive children, however, the probability of further aggression is actually *increased*. Thus, in some cases, the method most used by parents to cope with their children's aggression may actually worsen the problem!

Indifferent-Uninvolved Pattern. A second child-rearing pattern is called **indifferent-uninvolved**. As shown in Table 5-1, this pattern resembles the authoritarian-autocratic pattern in that it is parent-centered. In this pattern, however, parents minimize the amount of time spent interacting with their children. Children in such homes often have little contact with their parents and few or no rules for their behavior. As a consequence, they may feel unloved and do things calculated to get someone to pay attention to them. In extreme cases, parent neglect can lead to malnutrition, illness, or even death. Of course, uninvolvement can occur in degrees, ranging from infrequent contact to complete neglect. Also, some aspects of children's behaviors are more likely to be neglected than others. For instance, long-term goals (e.g., getting along with others, the child's sexual adjustment, responsible citizenship) may be less central in some parent–child relationships than immediate concerns (e.g., fighting with siblings, breaking a neighbor's window). In many indifferent-uninvolved families, the relationship between parent and child continues at a minimal level, but with little if any attention paid to long-term goals.

Some indifferent-uninvolved families begin as authoritarian-autocratic families. In their desire to maintain control over their children, parents may resort to more and more coercive methods—that is, negative means of control that make extensive use of threats (e.g., "If you're not home by 8:00, you can forget about your plans for this weekend!") and punishment. When parents frequently attempt to coerce children, children learn to interact with their parents in the same way (by whining, threatening to "make a scene," threatening siblings). Because most of the exchanges between parents and children are highly unpleasant, soon parents and children simply learn to avoid one another. In such families, essential socialization processes such as joint problem-solving may fail to occur. Because interactions are either coercive or nonexistent, there is little opportunity to address problems through positive means (Patterson, 1982; Maccoby & Martin, 1983).

Indulgent-Permissive Pattern. The **indulgent-permissive pattern** resembles the indifferent pattern in its lack of rules, but differs sharply in that it is child-centered rather than parent-centered. Permissive parents take a tolerant, accepting attitude toward their children's actions, including social impulses and aggression. They use little punishment and avoid exerting authority or imposing restrictions on their children. There are few rules; children are allowed to make their own decisions wherever possible. Permissive parents make few demands on their children for mature behavior.

In an indulgent-permissive home, for example, young children may be allowed to play with their toys anywhere in the house, create "messes," interact with visitors freely, watch television whenever they like, and so on—actions that would not be tolerated or at least would be very closely monitored in a more authoritarian family. Older children may be allowed to decide on their own dress and choose friends without parents attempting to impose their own values.

In their early work, Sears, Maccoby, and Levin (1957), showed that permissiveness was related to beliefs parents had about children: that children had "natural tendencies" and should be allowed to express them, a seemingly desirable position. On the whole, however, Maccoby and Martin (1983) judge the permissive pattern to have more negative than positive effects on child development. Instead of giving rise to free expression, as parents might hope, it may result in children being impulsive, aggressive, and lacking in ability to take responsibility. The so-called spoiled child may be a product of an indulgent-permissive home in which the child has had difficulty learning self-discipline and concern for others.

Authoritative-Reciprocal Pattern. The **authoritative-reciprocal pattern** is also highly child-centered, but has a much stronger parental involvement than the indulgent-permissive pattern. In contrast to the *authoritarian-autocratic* pattern, a somewhat dictatorial arrangement in which parents have all the control, the *authoritative-reciprocal* arrangement capitalizes on the parents' greater resources (e.g., knowledge, social skills) to promote children's social and cognitive development. This pattern allows for open communication between parents and children and for recognition of children's as well as parents' rights.

Baumrind (1967, 1971) has described the following elements of the authoritative-reciprocal parenting style:

1. *Expectations for mature behavior*. Parents set clear standards and immature behavior is not reinforced.
2. *Firm enforcement of rules*. With clear expectations, commands to action and sanctions are enforced wherever necessary.
3. *Encouragement of individuality*. Individuality of the child is seen as positive and is supported by the parents.
4. *Two-way communication*. Communication occurs from child to parent as well as from parent to child. Verbal give-and-take is encouraged and parents are open to communication.
5. *Respect for children's rights*. Not only do parents have rights, but so do children. Both sets of rights are respected.

In an authoritative-reciprocal home, for example, a young child would be allowed to make decisions, but within limits set by the parent (e.g., "Would you like to have just Carlos and Anne at your birthday party or would you like to invite Bobby too?"). Older children in such a home would have a clear idea of their parents' standards but would feel confident that their opinions counted as well.

Authoritative-reciprocal parenting appears to lead to several quite positive outcomes. Coopersmith (1967), for example, found that children with high self-esteem tended to have parents who set and enforced high standards, who favored "thoughtful" over coercive discipline, and who fostered a more democratic style of family decision-making. Higher levels of children's moral behavior also tended to be associated with the authoritative-reciprocal parenting style. Further, Patterson (1982) has demonstrated that elements of this parenting style can be taught to parents. As parents learn to be less punitive, to develop clear ideas of goals for children, and to pay closer attention, more positive social skills are developed by the child.

Of course, no parent or set of parents fits perfectly into this or any of the other styles of parenting. At one time or another, most parents show some characteristics of all the styles. Also, as Table 5-1 shows, the dimensions from parent- to child-centered and from demanding to undemanding each form a continuum. Thus, many parents would find themselves somewhere "in between" in their parenting, rather than confined clearly within any one style.

Children's characteristics also will have important effects on parenting style. A "hot-headed" child, for instance, is more likely to prompt aggression from parents than one who is not (Olweus, 1980). Likewise, an "easy" as opposed to a "difficult" baby imposes an entirely different set of demands on parents (Bates, 1980). The child's biological organization has much to do with the parenting that child receives (Scarr, 1984). It also is important to note that parents may use similar styles for different reasons. For example, some parents with admirable goals for their children may adopt an authoritarian style of parenting in the belief that it is the best or only way to reach these goals. Other authoritarian parents may have little real interest in their children; they simply may wish to keep children under control with the least possible effort. Thus, a critical factor in development may be how children perceive the parenting style used (Bronfenbrenner, 1979). If they understand that their parents love them and are genuinely concerned about them, even very authoritarian parenting styles may not be seen as negative.

A Mesosystem: Relations Between the Home and the School

Although social influences on children begin and continue in families, children soon begin to interact with individuals, groups, and institutions beyond the home. As you recall from our earlier discussion, in a microsystem children's activities, roles, and interactions with others take place in a single setting. *Mesosystems*, by contrast, involve interrelations among two or more settings in which the child participates and can be thought of as the relations between two or more microsystems. The mesosystem for a young child whose parents are employed, for instance, may consist of the relationship between home and a day-care center. An older child's mesosystem is usually much more complicated, with complex interrelationships among home, peer groups, school, neighborhood, and local business settings.

A critical mesosystem for most children is the one linking the home and the school. Experiences in the home clearly affect children's performance in school; school experiences also have a profound effect on the family life at home (Minuchin & Shapiro, 1983). Children's school schedules, positive or negative experiences in school, and participation in school activities all have far-reaching effects. For instance, a child who has gotten the highest score in a math test may proudly show the paper to parents. Parents, in turn, may use this opportunity to encourage the child in studying. A "bad day" at school similarly may be "brought home" to parents.

According to Bronfenbrenner (1979), children's development is enhanced by mesosystems in which skills can be used in each different setting. For example, a child who has learned to work cooperatively from her parents and siblings and who can accept direction is more apt to "succeed" in preschool or kindergarten, where these same skills are valued. Also, the more *linkages* that exist through communication between the microsystems, the better the chances for successful adaptation. Thus, if older siblings already have attended the school and if parents sometimes visit the school and talk with teachers and administrators, the likelihood that the child will experience successful adaptation is increased.

Not all mesosystems facilitate development, however. For example, a child may find conflict among the roles, expectations, and objectives of his home and those of the school. In the home, for instance, the child may have learned to challenge adult authority or developed attitudes toward education in conflict with those of teachers, administrators, or even other students in the school. In poor and minority neighborhoods, parents may perceive school programs as inadequate or opposed to their children's best interests. Alienation and conflict between parents and school teachers and administrators can create a climate in which cooperation between parents and teachers is all but impossible (Comer, 1980). If discrepancies are too great and linkages between the microsystems of home and school weak, problems are likely to result.

Language is a formidable barrier for many minority children attempting to link home and school. If children do not speak the language used in school, they are cut off from learning subject matter as well as from much of the socializing potential that the school offers. The difficulty of bridging the gap is even greater if the child's parents do not speak the language used in school. Also, in many schools there is a lack of bilingual education, language instruction, teacher familiarity with the child's language and culture, and curricular materials that can link minority children's homes and schools effectively.

Another possible set of barriers between home and school are cultural norms. American schools include a significant number of students from Mexican, Vietnamese, and other minority backgrounds; in many metropolitan areas, it is not unusual to have representatives of as many as 50 or 60 ethnic and language backgrounds in the school system. In an example of the kind of barriers that cultural norms can create, Rogoff and Mistry (1985) describe differences in story telling between Mayan and American children. For Mayan children, it is culturally inappropriate for children to speak freely with adults. When carrying messages to adults, they must add the polite word "cha" ("so I have been told"). When asked to tell a story to an adult, the Mayan children were very bashful and frequently used the word "cha." They responded as if they were being grilled rather than being asked to tell a story. In contrast, U.S. children in Rogoff and Mistry's study required much less prompting and told much less disjointed stories, suggesting that they knew much more about what was being asked of them. A teacher who is unaware of cultural differences such as these might greatly downgrade or misinterpret some children's performance.

Likewise, children in some cultures are socialized to cooperate in learning, while competition is seen as wrong. Children who learn cooperatively would, of course, be at a great disadvantage in classrooms that stress competitive approaches. Intellectual achievement is also valued differently in some families and cultures than in others. These values can lead to greater or lesser support of activities such as regular attendance, homework completion, and course selection. Finally, styles of communication used in families and cultures may or may not match those of the school. Children who speak out of turn, remain silent, or who do not look directly at the teacher may not be "troublemakers," "stupid," or "shy," but simply may be reflecting characteristics of their families or cultures.

Bronfenbrenner believes that the degree of linkage between settings in mesosystems can profoundly affect how easily children learn to function in new settings. Mesosystems can be weakly linked (as when the child is the only link between home and school) or multiply-linked (as when brothers and sisters accompany a child to school, home-school communication occurs, and both teachers and parents have knowledge of the other setting). In Bronfenbrenner's judgment, the more *supportive* links there are between the settings in which children already have experience and any new setting (e.g., between home and school), the greater the developmental potential of the new setting.

Bronfenbrenner (1979) and others (e.g., Comer, 1980) have argued that schools cannot afford to be isolated from the home. For development to be maximized, strong, supportive linkages must exist. As Bronfenbrenner points out, however, the numbers of staff members have increased in many schools, and many staff members commute to rather than live in the local community. In many schools, parents and teachers are unlikely to know one another. Therefore the potential for supportive linkages is reduced. Also, many schools have moved to locations that are physically and socially isolated, Bronfenbrenner points out, while at the same time becoming larger and more impersonal. Where once the school was the center of family, neighborhood, and community life, often now it is not. To Bronfenbrenner, the important parts of the child's life—family, peer group, school, neighborhood—should not be separated. If they are, the result will be increasing alienation and antisocial behavior.

Exosystem Influences: Parents' Work and Children's Lives

Parents' work, educational experiences, social lives, or travel may not be *directly* experienced or even understood by a child, but nonetheless exert a great influence on the child's life. These indirect effects are best understood by referring to the child's *exosystem*. As discussed earlier, the exosystem consists of one or more settings that do not involve the developing child *directly*, but still affect the child's development (Bronfenbrenner, 1979). Exosystem effects occur through links between children's lives and conditions outside the world they directly experience. Parents most often provide the links, but others occur through third persons or indirectly through, say, economic conditions in the exosystem. In this section we will examine one context of parental experience—the workplace—that profoundly affects the lives of most children.

Changes in Parental Roles. The American family has been transformed by changes in the workplace. The traditional family structure, with the husband-father as the provider and wife-mother as housewife, is no longer the dominant family pattern. In 1980, for instance, over 40 percent of mothers with children under 3 were employed, compared with less than 30 percent a decade earlier. This upward trend almost certainly will continue (Zaslow, Pedersen, Suwalsky, Cain, & Fivel, 1985). Through the end of the 1980s and into the foreseeable future, a very large number of both mothers and fathers will be working outside the home, which has important implications for child-rearing and for developmental psychology (Scarr, 1984).

The Need for Child Care. How can parents' work affect children's development? With over half of the mothers of children under 18 working outside the home and the vast majority of fathers also working, substitute child care is almost certain to be a necessity sometime during most children's development (Hoffman, 1984; Scarr, 1984). As Bronfenbrenner (1979) correctly indicates, however, the United States has shown extraordinary resistance to doing what almost all other modern industrialized societies have done—namely, providing large-scale programs of high-quality child care. The result is that many parents are currently unable to find suitable, affordable care. At least 3,000,000 American children under 14 have no child care; some estimates show that more than 500,000 *preschoolers* are left alone for all or part of the day while their parents work (Scarr, 1984). Many children thus spend time in situations that are certainly less than ideal for their development, although almost all parents state a strong commitment to finding the best possible care for their children (Bronfenbrenner, 1979; Long, Peters, & Garduque, 1985)

"Latchkey" Children. The number of children spending large amounts of time alone, especially in the after-school hours, has led to the label **latchkey children**. It is estimated (Turkington, 1983) that by 1990 there may be as many as 5,000,000 latchkey children in the United States, with many children spending two, three, or more hours alone every day. Some people forthrightly have labeled these conditions a national disgrace, which they say will have serious consequences for children. Many former latchkey children report residual fears of being alone, of someone breaking in, or of being hurt in an accident or fire. Latchkey arrangements also can force adult roles on young children prematurely. For instance, many latchkey children, particularly older daughters, are assigned additional responsibilities by their parents, such as cooking, cleaning, and caring for their younger brothers and sisters.

Many parents feel guilty and frustrated about latchkey arrangements but see few alternatives. Children also may be unhappy but feel there is little they or their parents can do. Of course, high-quality, widely available child care is one solution; this might be provided by school-based or employment-based programs. Under the present circumstances, however, with child care unevenly available and dependent almost solely on a family's personal resources, the latchkey phenomenon is likely to remain prominent in American family life and influential in many children's emotional and cognitive development.

Besides affecting the time parents spend with children, the pattern of two-career families appears to have an effect on how mothers and fathers interact with their offspring. For instance, Zaslow et al. (1985) found that, in the evenings when mother, father, and baby were together, employed mothers interacted more (e.g., with greater frequencies of holding, touching, and giving care) with their 3-month-old infants than did the fathers. Nonemployed mothers, however, interacted less. When mothers were with their babies all day, evenings seemed to be defined as "father's time." In contrast, employed mothers desired the evening contact with their babies and fathers seemed to recognize this priority.

Zaslow et al. argue that differences such as these may affect infants' social and intellectual development—particularly if such interaction patterns persist beyond infancy. Clarke-Stewart (1978), for instance, has shown intellectual growth to be related to the duration of play between fathers and infants and the father's attitude toward the child, both of which might be affected by reduced interaction. Of course, the *quality* of the father–child interaction is a critical factor determining the ultimate effect. Also, increased involvement of a mother who cares for, talks with, and plays with her baby more (Pedersen, Cain, Zaslow, & Anderson, 1982) would seem to provide a balance to decreased father involvement.

Economic Effects of Work. A major influence from the workplace exosystem is economic. Well-paying jobs can provide families with resources to buy books, magazines, and newspapers, for example. With more money comes the opportunity for families to travel together or perhaps to provide their children with private lessons in music or sports. Through the mechanism of economics, events occurring in another setting, the workplace, affect the selection and quality of experiences that the child will encounter. If parents have rewarding jobs, for instance, their attitudes toward their own competence and their ability to be parents may be enhanced. As competence and confidence increase, parents become more positive and effective. Conversely, unrewarding work experiences may produce parents who are unhappy, short-tempered, and even abusive to their children. Unemployment can be especially devastating to family life: The economic and emotional stress it produces affects both parents and children.

Summary of Exosystem Effects. Like social influences from other sources, those from the exosystem are critical to our understanding of development. Development is contextual and cannot be separated from factors that, although indirect, greatly influence children's experiences. While other sources of social influence may be more obvious and direct, we cannot hope to completely understand children's intellectual, emotional, and social development without being aware of conditions in their exosystems that affect their lives.

Macrosystem Influences: Cultures and Subcultures

We often speak about "cultural differences," but seldom pause to consider what is meant by the word **culture**. The definition given by Tylor well over 100 years ago (Tylor, 1871) still is frequently cited: culture "... is that complex whole which includes knowledge, belief, art, morals, law, custom, and any other capabilities . . . acquired . . . as a member of society" (p. 1). Thus, culture refers to certain qualities that people possess as members of society. These qualities are not innate but are learned as part of growing up in a given culture.

Cultures are reflections of how people have adapted themselves to their physical environment and to one another. They include the ways humans have agreed to coexist (e.g., through systems of law) and the techniques for survival (e.g., through use of fuels, buildings, food supply methods, etc.). In the United States in the late twentieth century, a child will grow up in a diverse culture that contains a very wide variety of beliefs and tolerates many forms of behavior. At the same time, it still shares some basic traditions and values such as individual freedom and democratic government. In addition, Americans have access to an advanced technology that provides for manufacturing and distribution of goods, widespread communications, and the potential for easy travel from one part of the country to another. In contrast, few if any of these aspects of culture would be experienced by a child growing up in, say, the mountains of central Java or on the steppes of Siberia.

Because child development researchers have been concentrated in the United States and Europe, much of the past research focused on white, middle-class children from these two locations. This makes it tempting to discuss "principles of child development" as if they are universal when, in fact, they were based on narrow studies of some children in some countries of the Western world.

Recently, however, developmental psychologists have realized clearly that we cannot understand child development in its broadest contexts—at the macrosystem level—unless we also know how children grow up in different environments and cultures. In the last 10 years, cross-cultural research has grown (Wagner & Stevenson, 1982) and contributed greatly to a broader picture of child development (see Chapter 3, *Research Methods*).

Studies of cultural differences in the field of developmental psychology have helped us understand much better how child development is affected by the environment in which children live. Because cross-cultural study has been so productive, developmental psychology has broadened its horizons to become international in scope. Organizations such as the International Society for the Study of Behavioral Development and international journals such as *Human Development* and the *International Journal of Behavioral Development* have played important roles in this trend.

Culturally determined patterns in child–rearing are likely responsible for many of the directions that development takes. For instance, in Uganda, adults and siblings talk to and smile at infants much more than is true in most other cultures. Japanese mothers, compared to

Research

Comparing Cultures on Their Child-Rearing Methods

One method for studying cultural effects has been to compare world societies that differ dramatically in their organization and cultural patterns. Super and Harkness (1982), for instance, used this method in studying social and emotional development. They compared child-rearing practices in two radically different cultures, the Kipsigis culture of western Kenya and American culture, looking for similarities in emotional development and for particular ways in which the culture might shape emotional learning. The Kipsigis traditionally have lived by herding cattle and raising crops. To carry out their investigation, Super and Harkness used naturalistic observation methods (see Chapter 3, *Research Methods*) living for 3 years in Kokwet, a Kipsigis community consisting of 54 homesteads spread out over a 3-mile span on a ridge of land formed by 2 streams. They describe the life of an infant born in the Kipsigis village of Kokwet:

> The infant in Kokwet is born into a physical and social setting that is different from the one familiar to most Americans. Until the baby is 3 or 4 months old, the mother is almost always with the child. Most of the time, in fact, mother and baby are actually touching; the baby might be sitting propped up in the mother's lap while she prepares food, riding on her back (secured and covered with cloth) as she goes to the river for water, cradled in her arms for nursing, or straddling her hip as she moves around the yard doing chores.... Unlike many American families, Kipsigis households do not make major modifications in their living quarters or family routines to facilitate infant sleep. There is no baby's room and no nap schedule (pp. 12–13).

Compare this to the pattern promoted as "ideal" in the United States—where infants spend much of their time in a crib, sleep in their own room, are moved to regular schedules as rapidly as possible, and are held mainly while being fed or during periods of play. Super and Harkness argue that emotional expression in each culture moves in a direction dictated by cultural experience. As they state, "The elements of expression are universally human, but they are organized, practiced, and regulated by culture" (1981, p. 19).

Like Super and Harkness, many researchers have focused on child-rearing practices as a likely

American mothers, spend much more time soothing and lulling their infants, compared to the American practice of stimulating infants with active chatting. The American and Japanese mothers' behavior patterns fit within cultural expectations: American mothers tend to share their culture's values of open, expressive, assertive, and autonomous (independent) behavior, while Japanese mothers seek quiet and contented babies, more in keeping with the values of Japanese culture (Super & Harkness, 1983).

The development of intellectual skills also strongly reflects cultural requirements and patterns (Nerlove & Snipper, 1981). For example, Gladwin (1970) noted that Micronesian sailors, who perform miserably source of important developmental differences. For instance, Konner (1981) has summarized a number of important dimensions of child-rearing (a dimension of culture) that differ between nonindustrial societies (those organized around agriculture, raising animals, or fishing) and industrialized nations (those that rely on the manufacturing and distribution of goods). Konner's summary is presented in Table 5-2. As you can see, there are radical differences on several dimensions (e.g., closeness of mother and child, contact with other children) critical to social, emotional, and intellectual development.

One of the important findings of cross-cultural studies of child development, however, is that there *are* certain universals in social and intellectual development. In all cultures and settings, some aspects of infants' emotional and intellectual development appear at nearly the same time and in the same order. Smiling and greatly increased emotional responsiveness, for instance, occur in all cultures around ages of 3 to 4 months. Around one year of age, children everywhere inhibit their activity and retreat when they encounter strange children. Similarly, children 7 to 12 months of age around the world show fear of unfamiliar adults, while anxiety at being separated from the primary caretaker peaks around 12 to 15 months of age in all cultures (Kagan, 1981).

Nonetheless, cultural systems quickly begin to shape even universal responses in particular ways. For instance, children from 7 to 20 months often become very inhibited or distressed when they face an event they cannot readily understand, such as the appearance of an unfamiliar adult, as mentioned earlier. But the specific events that provoke fear vary from culture to culture. In an example from Kagan (1981), 12-month-olds from Fiji often showed extreme fear of a small doll because they had never experienced one; this reaction would be rare among American infants, most of whom have experience with small dolls.

Cross-cultural research is unique in its ability to give perspective to child development principles. On one hand, it has shown us that there are some universal aspects of development that unite all of humanity. At the same time, it helps keep us from assuming that what we observe in Western culture must be true everywhere on the planet. Because of its unique contributions, it is likely to continue to be heavily used by developmental researchers.

on standardized tests, show extraordinary memory, inference, and reasoning skill in sailing from island to island. Serpell (1979), in contrasting Zambian and English children's abilities to copy visual displays, found that each group of children performed better when they were using familiar materials and tasks. When asked to copy two-dimensional figures, the Zambian children were superior in copying figures formed out of strips of wire (an activity that Serpell observed them doing frequently), while English children were superior in copying figures with pencil and paper (a common activity of English but not of Zambian children). In activities to which they had similar exposure (e.g., modeling figures out of clay), there were no differences among the children's

TABLE 5-2 Comparison of Child-Rearing Practices in Nonindustrial and Industrial Societies

Dimension of Child Care	Nonindustrial Societies	Industrial Societies
How Infants Are Carried	Almost constant carrying, often vertical position in sling or cradleboard	Carried much less, usually horizontal
Age at Weaning	Mostly around 2 or 3 years of age	Most weaned by 6 months of age
Mother–Infant Proximity	Same room, often in the same bed	Often in separate rooms or with siblings
Father Involvement in Child Care	Mothers have the primary responsibility	Mothers have the primary responsibility
Contact with Other Children	Often multi-age children's group, with children serving as infant caretakers	Often same-age peer
Learning	Unplanned observational learning, little deliberate instruction	Frequent, planned teaching, modeling, and demonstration
Play	Highly important source of learning	Less important source of learning

Adapted from M. J. Konner (1981). Evolution of human behavior development. In R. H. Monroe, R. L. Monroe, & B. B. Whiting (Eds.). *Handbook of cross-cultural human development.* New York: Garland STPM Press.

performances. Thus, cognitive abilities, like other abilities, are adapted to the requirements of the culture and to the familiar materials and tasks of that culture.

The cultural macrosystem is "the blueprint of the ecological environment" (Bronfenbrenner, 1979, p. 289) for children; their micro-, meso-, and exosystems are embedded in it. Patterns of emotion and intellect of every child are molded by a world view provided by the culture. While some emerging patterns are universal to some extent, all are organized and regulated by culture (Super & Harkness, 1982).

Before we are tempted to overgeneralize cultural effects to all children, we should remember that seldom, if ever, are all aspects of a culture shared by all members of any given society or country. Often, children and their families will be just as profoundly affected by influences in the **subculture**: the cultural ties shared by an identifiable subgroup within the larger culture. In the United States, for example, very strong subcultural groups are organized around religious affiliations (e.g., Catholics, Jews, Muslims), ethnic backgrounds (e.g., Mexican-Americans, Vietnamese-Americans), or regional ties (e.g., Westerners, New Englanders). At times, the values and beliefs held in the subculture may supercede those in the larger culture. Whether or not that happens, however, macrosystem influences at the subcultural level will affect the goals and values of children's families and, ultimately, the direction of development.

Macrosystem Influences: The Impact of Television

Because of its immense cultural impact and its ability to bridge the gap between microsystems and macrosystems, television has been of special concern for developmental psychologists. Nearly every American household (98 percent) has a television set (Parke & Slaby, 1983): American children from about ages 5 to 13 spend more time watching television than in any other waking activity, including attending school (Singer, 1983).

Through television, today's American children have immediate access to worldwide events whereas earlier generations did not. Children everywhere are now exposed to the actions, beliefs, and values of others—both in their own and other cultures. These influences change the way children think, feel, and act.

Compared to American mothers, who tend to stimulate their infants, Japanese mothers spend much more time quieting and soothing their babies.

Highlights

UNESCO and UNICEF: Two United Nations Agencies with a Commitment to Children and the Family

The United Nations, established in 1945 shortly after the close of World War II, is an organization of nearly 150 nations that works toward human welfare and world peace and security. While the United Nations is most often thought of as providing a general forum for discussion and resolution of political problems, it also supports a large number of specialized agencies. Two of these, UNESCO (United Nations Educational, Scientific and Cultural Organization) and UNICEF (United Nations Children's Fund), have been particularly active in promoting the welfare of children and families.

UNESCO, with more than 140 member countries, stresses education, the protection and promotion of culture, and increasing scientific knowledge. As part of its total effort, UNESCO has promoted the establishment of an international network of child research institutions and dissemination of scientific information about children and families. UNESCO's Third International Symposium on *The Changing Family in the Changing World*, held in Munich, Germany, in 1982, and a 1983 followup symposium, *The Changing Family in the African Context*, are examples of activities sponsored by UNESCO as part of this long-term program.

As reported in the newsletter of the International Society for the Study of Behavioral Development (ISSBD Newsletter, 1983, No. 2), the themes of the Third International Symposium included the following:

1. The family is the optimal social system for human development.
2. Social change, particularly in developing countries, affects families by changing patterns of child-rearing.
3. In developing countries, social change often leads to fewer ties within extended families and lessens the role of traditional values.

As a result of presentations and discussions on these themes, several

While television has tremendous potential to educate, socialize, and teach skills in communication (Wright & Huston, 1983), its critics believe that television has serious limitations: It promotes passive rather than active learning, brings about low-level thinking, and takes time away from more stimulating and creative activity. Some (e.g., Singer & Singer, 1983) have worried that television's use of attention-getting techniques in most children's programs (especially in programs such as *Sesame* major needs for research were outlined: study of how migration affects families and children, how values are transformed by urbanization, how changing roles of women and men affect development, and how formal education affects children's social and cognitive development. Intervention programs, based on developmental family research with cross-cultural emphasis, also were urgently called for.

In contrast to UNESCO's attempt to promote scientific understanding of children in families, UNICEF plays a somewhat more direct role by aiding children in its more than 100 member countries. UNICEF (the name comes from the original title of the agency—United Nations International Children's Emergency Fund) provides training for human service workers such as nurses and teachers, and donates supplies ranging from food to medicine in order to aid children in developing countries. It also gives aid for child care and family planning. An especially well-known and popular agency of the UN, UNICEF's funds come from voluntary contributions by individuals and governments. For instance, Halloween trick or treat collections and holiday greeting card sales account for several million dollars each year.

The efforts of both agencies on behalf of children are based on the belief that the family provides an irreplaceable developmental context and on a commitment to preserve and enhance family integrity. No matter which of many forms families may take, maintaining family strengths is essential for humans to cope with today's wrenching social changes. Although historically the family has shown enormous resiliency in the face of many challenges and crises, external support sometimes is needed when stresses become too great. Although the problems that children and their families face in many countries sometimes seem overwhelming, international agencies such as UNESCO and UNICEF help create greater understanding of these stresses and provide assistance wherever possible.

Street) may encourage short attention spans, hyperactivity, and lack of interest in "less exciting" live classroom activities. Probably the most intensely voiced concern about television, however, has involved television violence.

In 1982, the National Institute of Mental Health published results summarizing the effects of entertainment television (National Institute of Mental Health, 1982). This evidence, consisting of a huge body of data gathered by many different research methods, strongly supported conclusions reached 10 years earlier suggesting that television violence leads to aggressive behavior in children (see Rubinstein, 1983). Several aspects of the relationship between televised violence and aggression are important to note.

First, although both adults and children are affected by violence, the impact is greatest on children. Children "act out" what they see in a more direct way than do adults. Second, certain program characteristics especially inspire aggressive behavior. These include live portrayals of violence; suggestions that violence is justified; realistic depictions of violence, especially if the consequences are not shown; suggestions that violence is rewarded or goes unpunished; and violence by a socially acceptable person with whom viewers can identify (e.g., "the good guy") (Parke & Slaby, 1983).

While viewing violence on television increases children's levels of aggression, it also desensitizes viewers to violence in general (Parke & Slaby, 1983). Particularly among young people, watching violence decreases their reactions to violence: That is, the more violence they see, the less unusual or noteworthy it seems to them. Simultaneously, televised violence breaks down children's inhibitions against acting aggressively. Even worse, television portrayals of violence show a pattern of inequality and domination, with the likeliest victims being women, the old, and the young. Children who watch a large amount of television are likely to feel they are living in a "mean," ever-violent world.

In spite of the seriousness of the relationships shown by this evidence, little has changed in television (Rubinstein, 1983); for instance, there has been no reduction in television violence since 1972 when the first report appeared. The average of prime-time violence has stayed at about 5 violent episodes per hour. In children's weekend shows, the record of violence has actually worsened, having risen in the 1982–1984 period from a 17-year average of 20 violent episodes to a record high of around 30 violent episodes per hour!

Cognitive and Social Effects of Television Viewing. While violence has been the most widely studied aspect of television, other influences are also important. For example, children's attention is heightened by such aspects of television as lively music, sound effects, high levels of action, and rapid scene changes. Less understood, however, is television's impact on cognitive development. Although heavy viewing is associated with lower school achievement, the meaning of this finding is unclear. Low-ability students may watch more television, for instance, because they enjoy academic activities less. The extent to which television stimulates higher-level cognitive processes such as memory, concept learning, and problem-solving also is largely unknown, although understanding television is active mental work, particularly for young children (Wright & Huston, 1983). Understanding the context, sequencing and integrating events, inferring events or conditions not shown, and comprehending the motives and feelings of characters all require a great deal of knowledge about the world and about television itself.

Television viewing also influences social relations: For example, a father absorbed in a football game does not hear his child's question. There is little doubt about television's potential to reduce family interactions dramatically. Parents seldom watch television with their children, and most do not supervise their children's viewing (Rubinstein, 1983; Singer, 1983). Family life as portrayed on television is also unfortunately marked by stereotypes (see Research, p. 174). Television families seldom are shown realistically: "Family life on television is either predominantly funny and simplistic or excessively tragic" (Rubinstein, 1983).

Cultural stereotypes also can be conveyed by television, such as in the portrayal of mentally ill persons as violent and dangerous (the vast majority are not); of law enforcement personnel as frequently using violent solutions to problems (most detective work is routine); and of women as incapable of solving problems and interested in little more than diapers, detergents, and deodorants (Rubinstein, 1983). If television serves as the window to culture for American children, it presents an unfortunate picture of the culture that is highly violent, sexist, and simplistic (Rubinstein, 1983). While television undoubtedly has a great *potential* for teaching more about positive social and ethical behaviors (Rubinstein, 1983), the preponderance of violent programming and modeling of low-level solutions to problems make useful learning unlikely. Significant programming shifts to more realistic and constructive depictions of human social relations are needed. At present, television often seems to model the worst that American culture offers.

One critical impact of television is on children's beliefs about the world. As Bronfenbrenner (1979) has noted, the context of child development also includes children's *understanding* of their culture and world. How does television affect understanding of the world "out there"? Heavy viewers, unfortunately, see the world as a scary and frightening place (Rubinstein, 1983), possibly because so many violent and frightening events occur on television. Children also tend to identify much more with the *victims* than with the aggressors. Young children, in particular, may be frightened by what they see.

Television's Potential. Thus far, the overall record of American television as a constructive agent for cultural influence on children is not positive, particularly with the continuation of highly violent and stereotyped programming. Television's potential is undeniable, however,

Research

Children's Television in the United States: A Window on the World?

Children between the ages of 2 and 11 in the United States watch about 4 hours of television every day. With this amount of television being watched, it obviously is a very important part of most children's worlds. Their social and intellectual development, we would expect, might be affected by what they see portrayed on television. Like parents, friends, teachers, and churches, television teaches those things that are to be sought after and valued. It teaches both moral values and practical lessons.

While children obviously watch many of the same programs as adults, children's programs are of special interest to developmentalists. As American children watch the programming directed especially toward them on commercial television, what images do they see of sex roles, of minorities, and of families? Are the images accurate or not?

Data gathered by Earle Barcus in a study funded by the Carnegie Corporation and the Ford Foundation (Barcus, 1983) indicate that the images of our culture, as filtered through children's television, unfortunately are as much or more distorted than those on adult television. In area after area, the content of children's television leaves much to be desired.

Barcus recorded a total of nearly 50 hours of children's programming—all the weekend programming from 6 commercial Boston stations and one day's weekday programming from each of the 6 stations. A total of 225 program segments were identified. Types of programs, characters, and interactions between characters were coded.

Three-fourths of the programs were animated, and over two-thirds were devoted to entertainment. The range of topics, however, was quite narrow. Rivalry between characters, represented by such cartoons as "Bugs Bunny" and "Roadrunner," was the most frequent theme, followed by the subjects of crime, domestic relations, nature, the entertainment world, and science. Fewer than 3 percent of the total were represented by categories of religion, language, war, education, love and romance, business, historical topics, race and nationality, the fine arts, crafts, health, and social relations. As Barcus put it, "In children's television, the focus of attention is indeed quite limited" (p. 13).

Perhaps more disturbing were Barcus's findings that indicate that sex and racial bias are prominent in children's television. For instance, of 1,107 characters identified by sex, 78 percent were male.

and someday may be realized. Television programming *can* show human relationships realistically. It can stimulate children intellectually by offering new information and by helping children organize and think about the world more clearly. By showing contrasting points of view and different ways of solving problems, it can promote better understanding of one's own and of other cultures. Television now accomplishes some of these positive goals; but, on balance, it falls short. Dramatic change seems unlikely in the foreseeable future.

As Barcus states, "there is an implicit message for the child viewer: that males are more often recognized, more visible, and more important than females" (p. 3).

Minorities appear on children's television, but their numbers are scarce. Of all human characters in his sample, 86.9 percent were white, 5.4 percent were black, and 6.2 percent other minorities, a considerable underrepresentation of minorities compared to the United States population. Blacks also were portrayed as younger than whites, but other minorities as older. Both black and white characters were equally likely to be cast as heros or villains, while other minorities were more frequently cast as villains in proportion to their numbers. Further, white characters were more frequently shown as employed (52.2 percent) than either black (36.6 percent) or other minority individuals (34.0 percent).

With respect to portrayals of families, the male and female roles shown tended to depict family relations consisting of male dominance and female nurturing. They also reinforced a traditional pattern of male work and adventure and female domestic activities. On the positive side, however, a significant number of fathers and husbands were portrayed in nurturing roles with respect to their children. Most of these examples, though, were father–son rather than father–daughter relationships. Overall, close father–son relationships were portrayed much more frequently than either mother–daughter or father–daughter relationships. Barcus concluded that the family on children's television is portrayed in "a traditional and stereotyped manner, with parental roles being clearly defined and children having little say or power in family decision making." (p. 154).

Those who are striving to find enlightened models for children to emulate thus find relatively little to comfort them in commercial children's television programming. If goals such as equity between the sexes and among ethnic groups are to be achieved in the United States, it appears that one first must overcome the influence of the television most children watch. Attitudes in families and in many of our institutions have been altered, but it would appear that change is especially needed in children's television.

Television's Influence on Development: Applications

Until television does change, children need to be taught to view television much more critically, and parents need to exercise more control over television viewing (Rubinstein, 1983; Singer & Singer, 1983). Parents and others need to be aware of the negative effects of television on children, as well as of its tremendous potential. The following suggestions drawn from several sources (Eron, 1982; Parke & Slaby, 1983; Rubinstein, 1983; Singer & Singer, 1983) will help adults create conditions in which television's potential can be better realized and negative effects minimized.

1. *Evaluate and screen the programs that children view*. Because programs with violent and stereotyped content will continue to be broadcast and because these types of programs have demonstrably negative effects on children, parents and other caregivers need to exercise control over the programs that children watch.

2. *Set limits on the amount of television viewing*. Research has shown that heavy television viewing is associated with antisocial attitudes and behavior (e.g., Singer & Singer, 1983). Although it is unclear that heavy viewing per se is the cause of these conditions, certainly alternative activities are desirable. While television often is an enticing "babysitter," it is not a substitute for interactions with other children and caring adults.

3. *Watch television with children and discuss what you see*. Adults can help children interpret what they see. They can offer comments (e.g., "I don't think real people act that way") or, better, ask questions (e.g., "Could that really happen?" "What happens to a detective who shoots someone?" "How do you suppose the person felt whose car was wrecked?" "Was it right for him to hit that man?" "Could he have gotten what he wanted in a better way?") Young children, especially, often cannot follow complex plot lines. They may be unable, therefore, to relate actions to their ultimate consequences. By finding out what children think and offering alternative interpretations and information on consequences of actions, adults can help them acquire a more realistic view of life.

4. *Press for alternative programming*. Far too much current programming is violent, intellectually shallow, and stereotyped; its role in development is dubious. Parents and others can contact local television stations and networks to urge them to provide enlightened as well as entertaining programming.

5. *Object to stereotyped portrayals of individuals and groups*. Because of its rigid format (e.g., 30- or 60-minute programs) and commercial sponsorship, television is especially susceptible to stereotyped images of people and groups. Women, ethnic minorities, and members of other cultures are often shown in stereotyped or degrading ways. Insist they not be.

6. *Take advantage of the positive potential of television*. Television has immense potential for stimulating cognitive and social development. Many programs, including some of those on commercial television, are excellent. Adults need, however, to work actively to find such programs and to watch them with children. The key developmental concept is how children *interpret* what they see; adults can be tremendously influential in these interpretations.

Social Influences on Development: Processes

So far we have pointed to several factors—family patterns, parenting styles, and cultural factors—that influence development. Now we will examine *how* development is affected. Cutting across these variables, in the view of many, are two general processes: identification and observational learning. Each has a long research history and continues to figure prominently in developmental psychologists' attempts to understand and explain social influences on development.

Identification

Children tend to adopt the attitudes and values of their families and the culture in which they are raised. They develop habits and ideas about themselves and learn to play certain roles in their families and within society. A number of researchers have argued that children learn many such characteristics through **identification**. Identification refers to a process in which individuals see themselves as similar to another individual in beliefs, attitudes, and values. We can observe identification in children as they adopt the gestures, speech patterns, dress, and attitudes of adults (especially their parents and, most particularly, the same-sex parent). Through identification, children become like the adults with whom they identify.

Originally, the concept of identification was proposed within psychoanalytic theory. According to Freud (1933), identification is motivated by fears and anxiety over the possibility of rejection by the same-sex parent and by the desire to obtain the affection of the opposite-sex parent. Thus, a girl identifies with her mother not only to avoid her hostility and rejection, but to win the affection of her father *vicariously* (indirectly through another person). By identifying with her mother, she vicariously receives the affection that her father shows toward her mother.

Later theorists (e.g., Kagan, 1958) moved away from psychoanalytic explanations of identification and proposed more straightforward ways that identification could occur. Rather than fear of rejection and attempts to receive vicarious affection as key elements, theorists viewed identification as an acquired, internal cognitive process in which some of the attitudes, characteristics, and feelings of a model are adopted by the developing individual. As a girl identifies with her mother, for example, she will begin to react to events that happen to her mother as if they were happening to her herself. Thus, she may become afraid or angry as her mother argues with her father. She may feel proud as her mother is complimented or accepts an award, or she may experience frustration as she sees her mother struggling with a complex problem. As in the Freudian view, identification is thought to occur at a "deep" psychological level. More than simple behavior is involved; in fact, many of the behaviors and values learned through the process of identification cannot be verbalized. For example, the child may not know *why* she feels so proud of her mother; she just knows that she does.

How, then, does identification develop? To children, certain adults appear to have skills and capabilities that they lack and to attain goals that the children would like to attain. Adults also are the ones who take care of and nurture children. Thus, children are motivated to identify with these adults, believing that being like them will help them possess the adult models' positive characteristics. Often, too, there is direct feedback to children that they are like a particular adult. They may be told, "You're just like Aunt Sally—always saying smart things and trying to be funny!" or "When you talk, you remind me of your Dad." Statements like these, argues Kagan, help children learn about themselves and lead to the expectation that being similar to a parent or other person means possessing these positive characteristics.

Children may identify with different models at different times, to varying degrees, and on different dimensions. Thus, they may come to see themselves as like their mothers in certain roles and behaviors, like older siblings in others, and like their fathers or teachers in still others.

Identification seems to be involved in learning what *not* to do as much as it is in learning what *to* do. Children may adopt and practice the prohibitions of parents and others: for example, developing a strong sense of modesty about their bodies or refraining from "hurting anybody by what you say." Children's inhibitions seem to be learned through the process of identification just as easily as things they do.

Observational Learning and Imitation

Imagine a world in which we could learn how to act and think only by receiving feedback on whether an action or decision was correct or not. In this strange world, we could never learn anything by watching someone else do something. We would have to test every possible behavior. In this kind of world, learning how to live within family or culture would be inefficient and, indeed, even hazardous to your health! For instance, if the only way to find out if we treated someone well was to see whether or not we got punched in the nose, our chances of developing a satisfactory social life would be slim indeed. Similarly, if we never saw anyone answer a question or offer an opinion, we might have trouble doing these ourselves. Granted, feedback on our actions is important. Reward and punishment play key roles in learning. Most of our behaviors, however, initially are learned through imitation. By observing others, we learn what actions are appropriate, effective, and safe to perform. **Observational learning** guides what we do and plays an important role in identification (Kagan, 1958; Yando, Seitz, & Zigler, 1978).

Bandura (1977) has argued persuasively that much human behavior depends on observational learning. Because children learn much more easily from examples than they do from trial and error, many actions are performed without needless mistakes. For example, children observe others making requests, talking with each other, hugging one another, playing with toys, or sitting quietly. They see others reading, writing, and attempting to solve problems. They watch still others run, jump, and play games. They do not need to be taught each action, try it themselves, and receive feedback in order to have an idea how to do all of these things. In many cases, they simply can observe the actions and see what the consequences are likely to be.

A number of factors influence the extent of observational learning. Bandura has outlined five that are particularly critical: developmental level, attentional processes, retention processes, motor reproduction processes, and motivational processes (Bandura, 1977, pp. 22–29). Each needs to be considered in determining whether observational learning is likely.

Developmental Level. A general factor in determining the possibility of observational learning is development, which affects the degree of imitation in many important ways. No matter what parents desire, for instance, 2-year-olds are unlikely to produce a good imitation of a complex sentence or to successfully scramble themselves some eggs after watching their parents do so. They might, however, manage to "fix some scrambled eggs" on a play stove or use some of the parents' speech patterns, inflections, and favorite phrases while talking to playmates. Thus, at earlier developmental levels, imitation may be partial. As children become more skilled with increasing development, more subtle aspects of the performance are observed and imitated.

By itself, however, the term *development* is much too broad to explain differences in observational learning. To simply say that observational learning changes with age, according to Bandura, tells us very little. It is useful to focus on changes in subprocesses such as attention that are likely to be affected by development.

Attentional Processes. A major influence on observational learning that changes with development is attention. **Attention** refers to the focus of an individual's cognitive processes on some aspects of the world and not on others. At any moment, for example, children have the potential for perceiving any of the vast number of objects and events in their environment. In order for observational learning to occur, however, their attention must be on: (1) the model, (2) the modeled performance, and (3) the relevant features of the modeled performance. A young child is unlikely to learn how to swing a softball bat correctly, for instance, if the child's attention is diverted from the coach's demonstration by a squirrel in the outfield, a teammate's question, a cloud formation, a passing bicyclist, or even the coach's overly detailed description of how to swing. Of course, some kinds of modeled performances are intrinsically more interesting to watch than others. Television commercials aimed at children, for example, contain carefully selected cues that will capture the average child's attention and lead to imitation and repetition of the commercial jingle and key phrases in the commercial and to later recognition of the product.

Retention. Observational learning requires children to remember what they have seen. Events to be remembered are coded into a symbolic form (see Chapter 10, *Development of Memory*). Two major coding systems are available: imaginal and verbal. **Imaginal coding** refers to the retention of learned behavior in the form of mental imagery. For example, children considering joining others on a playground slide may visualize themselves on it and imagine the sensations of sliding downward. Images from sliding earlier on a smaller slide may also come to mind. **Verbal coding,** on the other hand, is the description of observed actions to oneself in words (e.g., "That slide is *really* tall"; "Gee, that looks like fun"; "They're really going fast"). Either form of coding—imaginal or verbal—allows children to translate what is seen into learning that becomes available for later imitation. "In their mind's eye," children may see themselves successfully going down the slide (imaginal coding) or build up their courage to try the slide by telling themselves that the slide has a railing on the sides of the steps and that they probably will not fall (verbal coding).

How much children notice details of motor performances and how they verbally code them changes with development. Whereas a younger child may describe the activities of a group kicking a ball in terms such as "they're kicking the ball," "they're having fun," or "they're running a lot," older children may recognize and describe the same action to themselves as "they're playing soccer," "the forward is really fast," "I can kick the ball about as well as most of them," or "I don't want to be the goalie because they don't have much to do." Certainly, the form of coding is critical in that it determines what aspects of performances the child imitates. As children come to notice, remember, and recall different aspects of observed behavior, their imitation also will change.

Motor Skills. Another factor in observational learning that varies tremendously with development is motor skills. **Motor skills** are the physical abilities of an individual. Running, jumping, playing an instrument, speaking, throwing a ball, or drinking a glass of water all require motor skills. No matter how well the child codes observations into images or words, they must then be translated into actual performance. While two children both may imitate a disk jockey they have heard on the radio, the older one may produce a much more convincing imitation of the content, tone, timing and inflections because of superior motor skills. Likewise, two 8-year-olds imitating a passage played by their violin teacher may differ tremendously in their ability to actually perform the sequence. Whether children are imitating dancers on television or baseball players or older siblings using scissors, their respective motor skills limit or enhance their ability to imitate.

Motivational Processes. Children do not imitate everything they see. Most imitated behaviors are those that produce or suggest that they will produce desirable consequences. Those that produce negative consequences tend to be avoided. Of course, what children find rewarding or punishing changes as development proceeds. For very young children, tangible, straightforward, and rapidly delivered consequences for behavior are likely to be most effective in maintaining imitated behaviors. Older children, however, respond to more abstract and delayed consequences and can be motivated by, say, the possibility of a field trip or by their belief that their parents will be pleased. In any event, however, observation by itself is not enough: The *consequences* of imitating the behavior are what ultimately determine whether or not the behavior is continued.

Thus, young children may observe their mothers looking at books and may imitate their mothers by bringing their own books and looking at them. Whether they will *continue* to do so, however, depends on the consequences. Are the books interesting to look at? Do the mothers notice their children "reading" and make favorable comments? Positive consequences make it more likely that the behavior, once imitated, will continue. Similarly, young children may make demands that their mothers wait on them in imitation of demands their fathers make. If there are positive responses to such requests, the children may learn to make them regularly; if the responses are negative, the demanding requests will likely cease. Behaviors that begin with imitation typically continue only if they are reinforced.

Reciprocal Determinism. In his discussions of social learning, Bandura (1977) has stressed the concept of **reciprocal determinism**: This is the idea that there is a continuous interchange between the actions of individuals and the controlling conditions of their environments. While children are influenced by others' actions and external physical conditions (the environment), they themselves also *change* the environment in important ways. Consider the following conversation between two small children, for example, in terms of how each affects the other.

Jen: What's that in the bucket?
Jud: A sand turtle.
Jen: Can I hold it?
Jud: No, I'm not 'sposed to let anybody touch it.
Jen: Uh . . . come on, let me hold it!
Jud: No, it might bite you.
Jen: Let me hold it (grabs for the turtle).
Jud: NO! I'm goin' to take it home if you don't leave it alone . . .
Jen: (backs away and peers into bucket)
Jud: (reaches in bucket and picks up turtle to show to Jen)
Jen: Wow, look at them eyes!
Jud: Yeh, he's pretty mean lookin'.
(conversation continues)

Each child plays a vital role in this exchange by providing the environment for the other's actions. Each affects and is affected by the other; questions from one child cue answers from the other. Their actions not only are reciprocal, but determine what the other does. A refusal leads to changes in strategy, such as when Jen decides to grab for the turtle

Through identification, children acquire the behaviors, values, and beliefs of their families and cultures.

and dispense with the formalities of making a request. Her aggressive move (reaching for the turtle) triggers a threat by Jud to remove the object of fascination.

Each child's actions serve as consequences for the other's actions. Of course, a third, unseen element in this whole exchange also is at work: prior learning. How children act in situations like these will depend to a great extent on what they have observed before and been reinforced for doing (see Chapter 2, *Theories of Developmental Psychology*). Another child placed in the same situation as Jen but whose prior history of observation and reinforcement was different than hers might never have tried to grab the turtle. Still another child may just have shoved Jud away and taken the turtle.

Summary of Identification and Observational Learning

Identification and observational learning play major roles in development. To the extent children identify with their parents, other adults, and older siblings, they see themselves as like these individuals in fundamental ways and tend to adopt their attitudes and values. Both learning what to do and what not to do result from identification. Through identification, children adopt the behaviors, values, and beliefs of their families and culture.

Observational learning provides an even more straightforward explanation of how children are affected by family and culture. Because imitation occurs so easily, observation affects social, cognitive, and physical development. Through imitation, children learn to interact with others, to solve problems, and to perform many motor actions. Rewards and punishment then serve to shape the imitated actions. Without observational learning, children would have to learn everything by trial and error, which would prove a slow and (likely) very risky way to learn. Because of their capacity for observation and imitation, children quickly become socially, mentally, and physically capable individuals within their families, communities, and cultures.

Summary

Evolution has prepared us biologically for our physical environment. At the same time, it has shaped us as social and intellectual beings. Each child is born into and develops in a social context that shapes the course of his or her social, intellectual, and physical development.

Bronfenbrenner's *ecological* approach to child development stresses the interaction between children and their environments (Bronfenbrenner, 1979). Four dimensions of context affect children's development. At the most intimate level are *microsystems*, which are patterns of activities, roles, and relationships directly experienced by the child. A second influential level of context consists of *mesosystems*, which link two or more settings in which children take part. A mesosystem for one child might link the home and a day-care center, for instance, while another child's mesosystem could include home, school, and neighborhood areas. Equally important but *indirect* effects are exerted by *exosystems*. These are settings in which the child does not actively participate, but which nonetheless influence development. Parents' jobs, friendship networks, and activities frequently create exosystems that determine important aspects of children's lives. At the most global level are *macrosystems*, patterns or consistencies at the cultural or subcultural level in which micro-, meso-, and exosystems are embedded. These cultural contexts pervade all other levels of context and color events occurring in home, school, and community.

A major vehicle for conveying cultural information to children is television. In the span of a generation, television has grown from a curious toy to a substantial influence on child development by bridging the gap between culture and child. Although television can enhance social and cognitive development, American television unfortunately has moved in directions in which simplistic and sexist portrayals of the culture predominate. Violent models in many television programs lead to aggressive behavior in children, but television also can affect child development in positive ways.

Two broad processes of social influence cut across all of development: identification and observational learning. Identification refers to the process by which children, in seeking to become like adults, adopt adult attitudes, feelings, and behaviors. A second, related process for acquiring skills and values from one's social environment is observational learning. Imitation of models leads to children's rapid learning of many actions modeled by others. During observational learning, children see and acquire behaviors that enable them to function effectively within the contexts of their families, neighborhoods, schools, communities, subcultures, and cultures.

Key Terms

socialization
ecological view of child development
microsystems
mesosystems
exosystems
macrosystems
parenting
siblings
sex-typed behaviors
agonistic behavior
prosocial behavior
two-parent families
single-parent families
parenting styles
authoritarian-autocratic pattern
indifferent-uninvolved pattern
indulgent-permissive pattern
authoritative-reciprocal pattern
latchkey children
culture
cross-cultural research
subculture
identification
imitation
observational learning
attention
imaginal coding
verbal coding
motor skills
reciprocal determinism

Suggested Readings

Bandura, A. (1977). *Social learning theory*. Englewood Cliffs, NJ: Prentice-Hall. This volume is the standard work on social learning theory by its major proponent. Although this is an advanced text, it is worthy of exploration.

Bronfenbrenner, U. (1979). *The ecology of human development: Experiments by nature and design*. Cambridge, MA: Harvard University Press. This is Bronfenbrenner's major work on the role of social context in children's development. Taken with Bronfenbrenner's more recent papers, this volume provides an excellent background in his views on development.

Elkind, D. (1979). *The child and society: Essays in applied child development*. New York: Oxford University Press. This volume collects readable essays on child development in its social context.

Maccoby, E. E., & Martin, J. A. (1983). Socialization in the context of the family: Parent-child interaction. In E. M. Hetherington (Ed.), P. H. Mussen (Series Ed.), *Handbook of child psychology*, Vol.

4. *Socialization, personality, and social development.* New York: Wiley. This chapter provides a thorough and scholarly review of research on the family.

Scarr, S. (1984). *Mother care/Other care.* New York: Basic Books. This book draws on Scarr's personal experience as a working mother and professional experience as a developmental psychologist. The result is a highly readable book about mothers' roles and infants' needs.

Application Exercises

5-1 Identifying Levels of Systems in Developmental Settings

For each of the following, indicate whether the description primarily involves a microsystem, a mesosystem, an exosystem, or a macrosystem.

1. Rachel's parents go to school to talk to her third-grade teacher about problems she is having with her spelling.
2. Roger, a 6-year-old, goes with his parents to Indonesia for a year. He finds himself exposed to many new ideas from his Indonesian teachers, neighbors, and playmates.
3. The babysitter and 3-year-old Chuckie have established a familiar daily routine of games and activities.
4. Twelve-year-old Anne listens to rock music at home, at school, at her friends' homes, and in supermarkets. It is her favorite kind of music.
5. Before Jonas' mother takes him to preschool for the first time, she prepares him for how it will be. When the day comes, she takes him in, visits with the teachers in his presence, and stays at the preschool for a while before leaving.
6. The company for which 6-month-old Andy's father works has a reputation of "taking care" of employees but demands great loyalty from them. Andy's father knows that if he hopes to advance, he must work many nights and weekends.
7. Lynette has joined the Drama Club and spends much of her time rehearsing and putting on high school plays.
8. In the first year of college, Joetta finds living in the dormitory the most novel and interesting part of going away to school.
9. Preston's parents come to the State University for Parents' Day. They stay overnight in his residence hall, attend his classes, and visit with professors and administrators.
10. Policies for the Irving School are made by the Board of Education. Although the rules they follow are affected by these policies, most Irving students do not have any idea who is on the Board or how it operates.

5-2 Observing Characteristics of Television Programming

Although you probably have watched countless hours of television, it is unlikely you have done so systematically. Watch a sample of at least five television shows, including at least two "detective-type" shows. Count the number of incidents involving:

1. violence.
2. stereotyped portrayals of women, ethnic groups, religious groups, etc.

Try to settle on a consistent definition of each variable you observe, and report the number of occurrences per hour.

How do you think children would react to each of the incidents you observed? Would you judge the impact to be negative, positive, or mixed? To validate your judgment, watch at least one of the shows with one or more young children and ask them questions to see what they thought of various incidents you observed.

PART III

Physical and Motor Development

Some of the most dramatic changes that take place over the course of development occur in the physical structure of the body and in related motor abilities. Such changes are not only important in themselves. They also play a critical role in more "psychological" aspects of development—that is, in the development of thoughts, feelings, and personality. In the next two chapters we will describe the typical course of physical and motor development and discuss some relevant general principles. We will also consider potential problems and make some practical suggestions for optimizing development. In addition, we will look into some of the psychological implications of physical and motor development.

We begin our presentation in Chapter 6 with coverage of prenatal development and the process of birth. We then continue to follow the child up to adulthood in Chapter 7.

CHAPTER 6

Prenatal Development and Birth

We must . . . respect . . . this instant of birth, this fragile moment.
The baby is between two worlds. On a threshold. Hesitating. . . .
What an extraordinary thing: this little creature, no longer a fetus, not yet a newborn baby.
This little creature is no longer inside his mother, yet she's still breathing for them both.
An elusive, ephemeral moment. . . .
—Frederick Leboyer
Birth Without Violence

Among parents' fondest memories are the births of their children. In our culture, we celebrate these "birth days" as the signals of new life. A tremendous amount of development, however, precedes the actual birth of a baby.

As we saw in Chapter 4, human development begins at the point of conception, when a sperm and ovum join to form a zygote. The zygote, a cell less than 1/200 of an inch in diameter, contains all the information necessary for the formation of one of the most miraculous of things: a newborn baby. In this chapter, we follow human development from conception through birth.

From Conception to Birth

The Germinal Period

The first two weeks after conception are known as the **germinal period**. Conception typically occurs in the **Fallopian tube** and, with the aid of muscular contractions in the Fallopian tube and the movement of cilia (hair-like strands that line the wall of the Fallopian tube), the quickly growing zygote travels the length of the tube and enters the **uterus** (see Figure 6–1). During its trip down the Fallopian tube, the zygote grows via mitosis (see Chapter 4) from a single cell into a little ball of about 100 cells called a **blastocyst**. The blastocyst is hollow but contains two components: (1) an inner mass of cells that will become the new person and (2) an outer mass of cells that will form the outer sac surrounding the growing person (the **chorion**), an inner sac (the **amnion**), and the connectors to the mother (the **umbilical cord** and the **placenta**).

Within a few days after fertilization, the blastocyst enters the uterus and attaches itself to the uterine wall. The inner cell mass, which will soon be identifiable as a developing person (see Figure 6–2), floats within the amnion, cushioned by amniotic fluid. The only attachment to the mother is through the umbilical cord, which is joined at the other

189

FIGURE 6-1 Conception and Early Cell Growth. The process of conception begins when an ovum leaves the ovary and travels to the Fallopian tube, where the ovum is then fertilized by sperm. The fertilized ovum—the zygote—grows rapidly as it passes into the uterus, where it attaches itself to the uterine wall. Just prior to attachment, the zygote is referred to as a blastocyst.

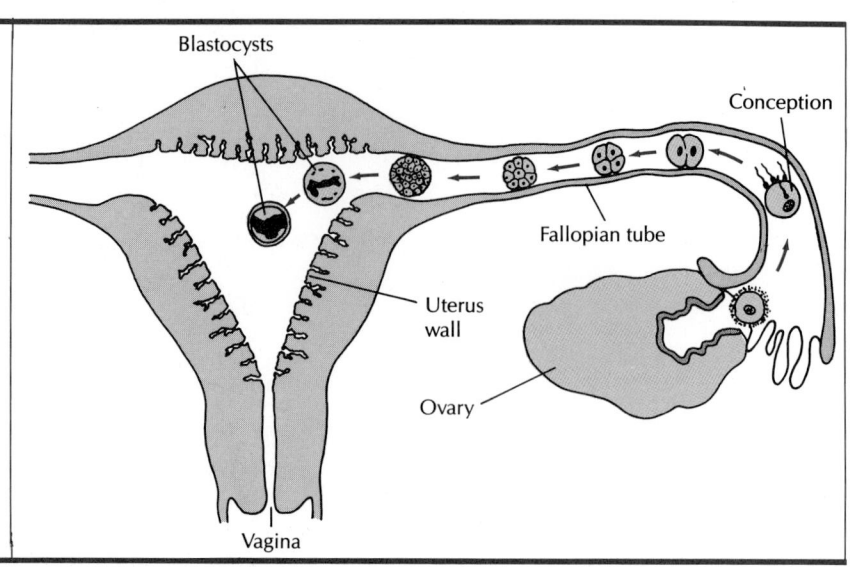

FIGURE 6-2 The Prenatal Environment. The growing child is connected to the mother by the umbilical cord and placenta. The amniotic fluid cushions the embryo. Surrounding the embryo and amniotic fluid, there are two sacs: the amnion (inner) and the chorion (outer).

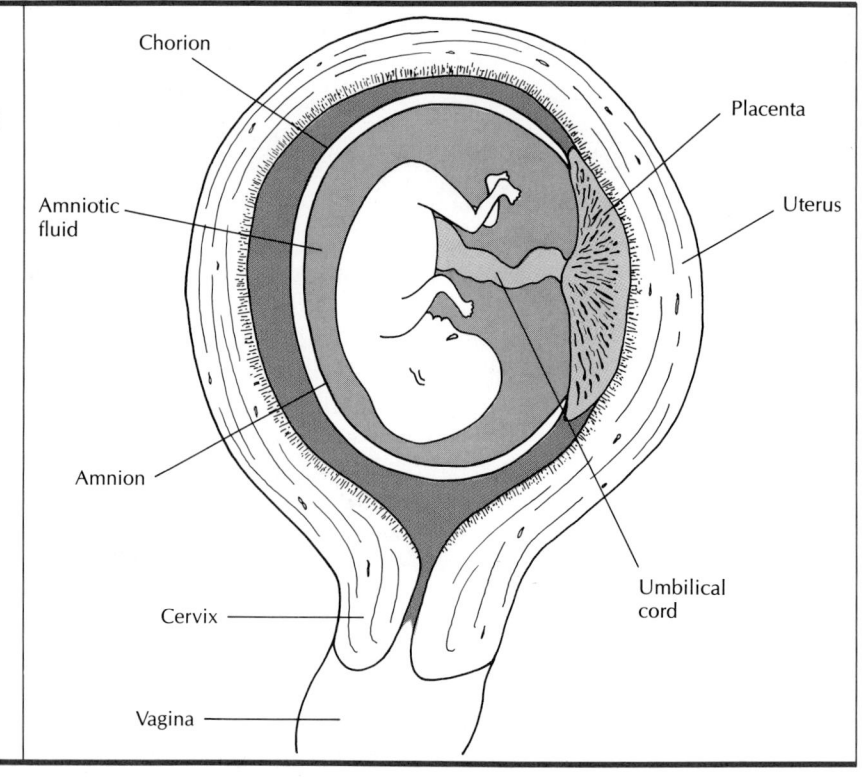

end to the placenta. The umbilical cord is literally a lifeline. This cord rapidly forms veins and arteries that run to the placenta. While the maternal and fetal blood systems do not directly intermix, oxygen and nutrients are obtained from the mother's blood supply at the placenta and carried to the developing child. In return, waste materials are carried from the child to the placenta where these substances are picked up by the mother's system and carried away. During pregnancy, the mother is literally breathing, eating, and discharging waste for two individuals.

The Embryonic Period

The period of growth from two to eight weeks after conception is referred to as the **embryonic period.** During this time, growth (especially the development of organs) is very orderly and rapid. The embryonic period is the time in which the inner mass of cells forms three layers: the **ectoderm,** the **mesoderm,** and the **endoderm.** The ectoderm will ultimately form the skin, sense organs, and nervous system. The mesoderm will differentiate into the muscles, the circulatory system, and the blood. The endoderm soon forms into the digestive system and the remaining internal organs.

At four weeks, the embryo is a little less than a quarter of an inch long (see Figure 6-3). This minute organism, however, now possesses a heart that pumps blood through its own circulatory system and has the rudiments of the brain, the kidneys, the digestive system, and the liver. Growth, as will be explored in greater detail in Chapter 7, is cephalocaudal (meaning from head to tail) and proximodistal (meaning from the center of the body outward—those organs closest to the center of the tiny organism are becoming distinct and growing first. At four weeks, the embryo is almost all head and basic organs.

By eight weeks, the embryo is unmistakably human in appearance, although the head is proportionately much larger than it ultimately will be. At this time the eyes, ears, nose, and jaws are clearly defined. Further, the arms are now rapidly forming and the hands possess tiny fingers. The legs, complete with feet that have extremely small but distinct toes, are easily seen. The nervous system is also developing quickly and the spinal cord is filling out. Almost all of the internal organs are present by the eighth week, although many are still in very basic forms.

The Fetal Period

The period of growth from the eighth week until birth is referred to as the **fetal period.** The fetal period is predominantly characterized by the continued differentiation and refinement of already existing structures as well as changes in the body's proportions. Few new structures appear during the fetal period, although the first bone cells make their appearance during the eighth week and, later, the hair, finger and toe

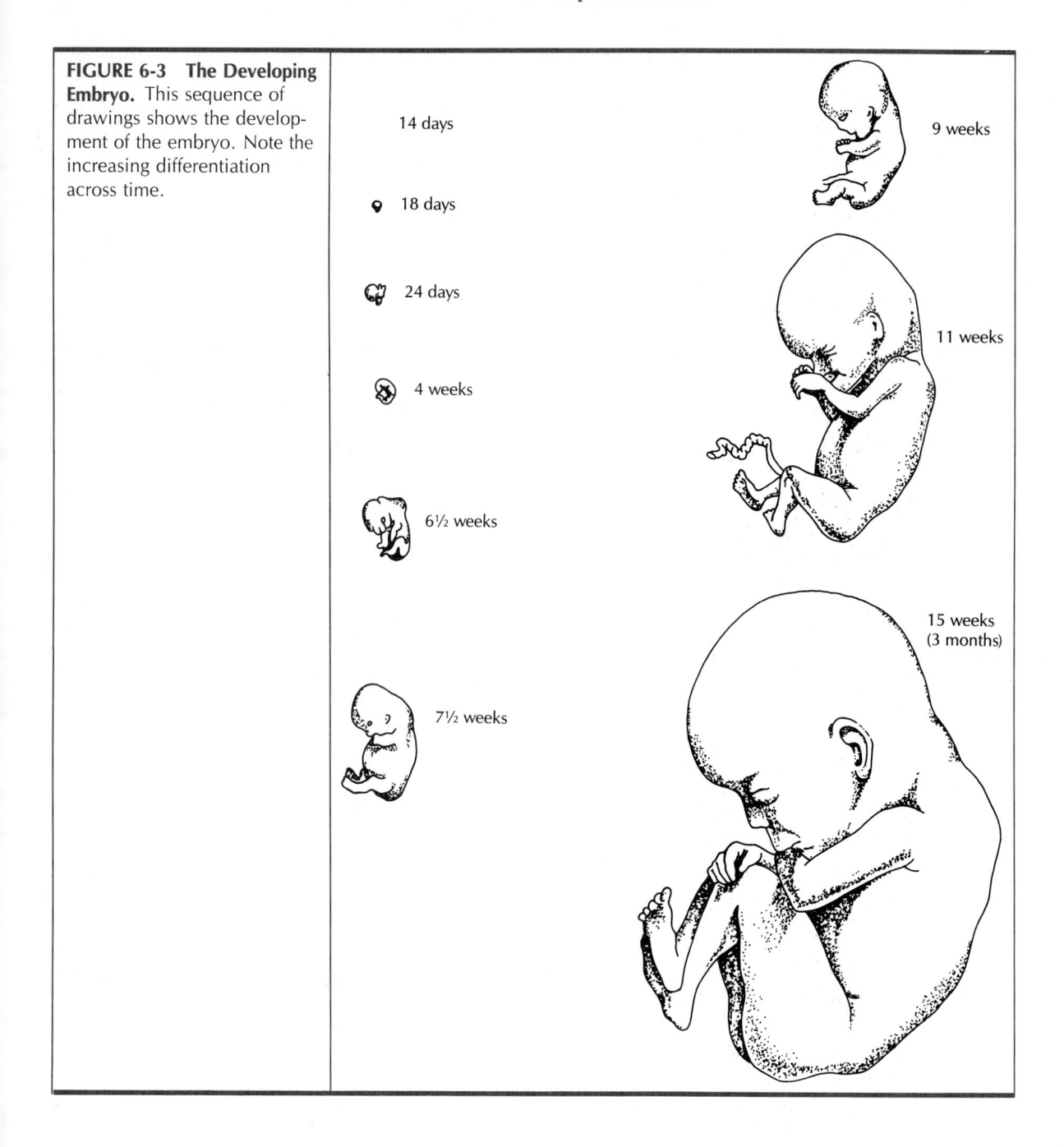

FIGURE 6-3 The Developing Embryo. This sequence of drawings shows the development of the embryo. Note the increasing differentiation across time.

14 days

18 days

24 days

4 weeks

6½ weeks

7½ weeks

9 weeks

11 weeks

15 weeks (3 months)

nails, and sex organs appear. As the fetal period progresses, the bones develop and ossify (harden); lanugo (a very fine form of hair) appears and later dissapears; vernix (a cheese-like substance) appears and covers the body in a protective coating; and the brain develops and greatly refines its folds.

The first month or so of the fetal period is sometimes referred to as the month of initial activity (Hughes, 1980; Rugh & Shuttles, 1971). The fetus begins to move on its own early in this period but the mother is unlikely to feel it until about the sixteenth week. From the sixteenth week on, the mother can feel the fetus wiggle, jiggle, and push. Feeling the baby move for the first time is an exhilarating experience for the mother as the reality of a developing new life sets in. In addition, the baby's movements can provide a time of sharing between the mother and father, who can feel the baby's movements himself by placing his hands on the mother's abdomen.

During the last trimester (the last three months of pregnancy), the fetus prepares to enter the world. Although the lungs cannot function in the amniotic fluid and the mother's system still furnishes all the necessary oxygen for survival, the fetus's lungs begin to move periodically as though breathing were being practiced. Further, a liquid called **surfactin** is produced, which allows the lungs to transmit oxygen to the blood (Hughes, 1980). Also, during this time the hemoglobin (the protein in the blood that imparts its red color and carries the oxygen from the lungs throughout the body) changes form in order to allow the breathing process to work more efficiently. Other changes include the development and perfection of swallowing, the refinement of the urinary and digestive processes, and a gain of fat tissue that smooths out the appearance of the fetus.

A fetus at seventeen weeks after conception.

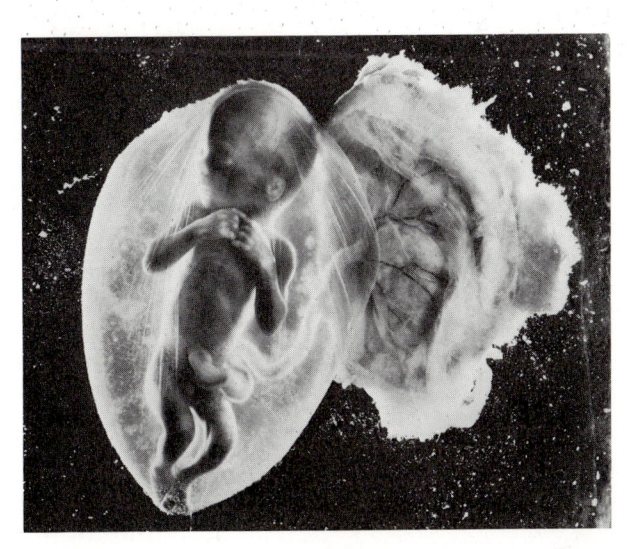

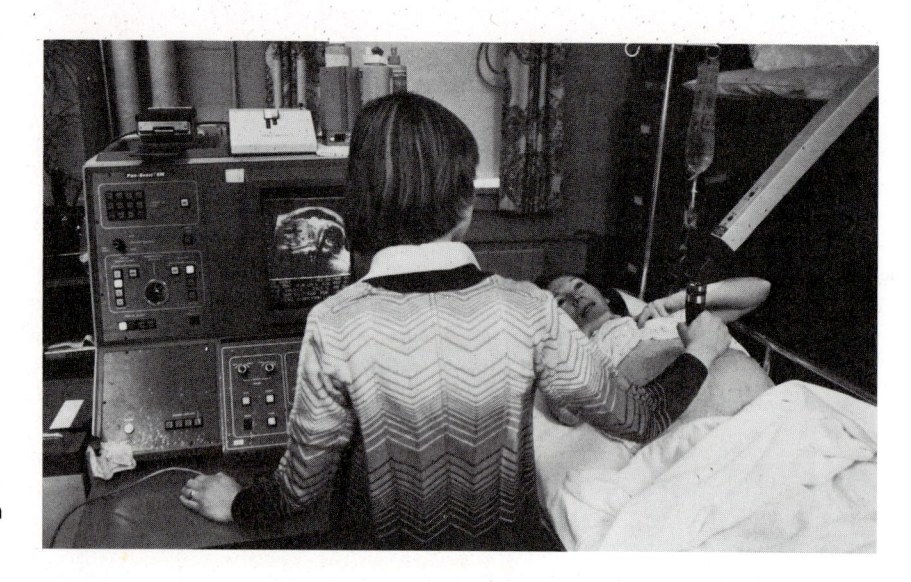

The use of ultrasound can provide valuable information about the developing fetus.

A full-term fetus is ready for birth at about 38 weeks or 266 days after conception—roughly nine months. At birth, the full-term, normal baby is ready to enter the world. It can breathe on its own, its heart is fully capable of keeping its circulatory system operating, and the kidneys and liver are functional. In fact, all the systems necessary to life are now operating effectively.

An average baby weighs about 7 pounds and is about 20 inches long (Hughes, 1980). However, the weight of full-term babies who have developed normally may vary from 5 to 12 pounds and their length may vary from 16 to about 22 inches. Although small size is usually associated with premature babies, about 5 percent of all full-term babies suffer from growth retardation in the womb (Miller, 1983a). These babies have greater health risks than normal babies. Medical science has only recently begun to identify growth-retarded babies as a special category. As yet, there are not good predictors for identifying growth-retarded babies until late in the pregnancy when ultrasound images of the fetus can be produced.

General Factors Influencing Prenatal Development

Prenatal development is influenced by a wide range of factors. Since the mother's body provides the unborn child's total environment, and since chemicals, bacteria, viruses, and hormones are passed from the mother to the fetus through the placenta, the mother's health and her nutritional habits strongly affect the development of the fetus. In this section, we will examine several general influences on prenatal development.

Maternal Nutrition. The fetus receives all of its vitamins, minerals, and nutrients directly from the mother: It is entirely dependent on the mother's nutrition for its own development. The nutritional advice physicians and others have offered pregnant mothers has shifted back and forth over the years. In the 1960s, pregnant women typically were encouraged to gain little weight during pregnancy; so-called common knowledge indicated that the baby would get what it needed from the mother's body. Today, medical science is far more aware of nutritional needs during pregnancy, and physicians are apt to become concerned if mothers do not gain *enough* weight. More important than the quantity of food eaten by mothers, however, is the quality of their diet. Mothers who follow a logical, healthy diet do not need to eat to excess or take large doses of vitamins during pregnancy. In fact, only iron and folic acid are recommended for well-nourished mothers (Hughey & Weber, 1982).

The need to eat properly during pregnancy, however, cannot be overstressed because of the effects of nutritional deficiencies. Nutritional deficiencies are associated with premature birth (Miller, 1983a), small size at birth (Miller, 1983b), stillbirths (Hughes, 1980), and mental deficits (Hughes, 1980). Nutritional deficiencies are serious at any time, but seem to be especially critical during the first trimester, when the organs are forming, and during the last trimester, when the brain and nervous system are undergoing rapid development. Moreover, not only do nutritional deficiencies deny the growing organism the materials necessary to build a healthy body, but they also weaken the mother so that she becomes susceptible to illnesses.

Mother's Socioeconomic Level. A second general factor that seems to influence prenatal development is the mother's socioeconomic and educational level. In general, well-educated, middle- and upper-class mothers bear larger, healthier babies than do poor, poorly educated mothers. There seem to be three general reasons for middle and upper class mothers having healthier babies: (1) the high quality of their medical care throughout life and especially during pregnancy, (2) the quality of their nutrition, and (3) their general knowledge of habits and self-care procedures associated with bearing healthy children. It is also true, of course, that the variables of economic status and level of education are confounded by the fact that many more teenage pregnancies occur among poor and poorly educated families.

Mother's Age. A third general factor influencing prenatal development is the age of the mother. Research suggests that mothers under the age of 20 run a higher than normal risk of improper meiosis, delivering babies prematurely, and bearing babies that die shortly after birth (Miller, 1983a). There seem to be several potential reasons why young mothers run higher than normal risks in their pregnancies. First, the majority of teenage mothers are poor and relatively poorly educated.

Second, mothers under the age of 20 may not possess fully mature reproductive systems and so may not be able to provide the quality of ova or the quality of intrauterine environment that older mothers can furnish (Hughes, 1980). Further, teenage mothers generally have much poorer prenatal care, both nutritionally and medically, than older mothers.

The literature also suggests that as mothers pass the age of 35, the odds of problems in pregnancy begin to increase. The reasons for this trend are not clear. Since all the ova in a mother's body are formed shortly after birth and remain present in an immature form for many years, perhaps the wear and tear on a person's system over the course of 35 or more years simply takes its toll on some of the ova.

Mother's Emotional Health. Although pregnancy is often a time of serenity and joy, emotional stresses may occur. High levels of emotional stress during pregnancy are associated with several problems in newborns: smaller birth size (Hughes, 1980), eating difficulties (Brimblecombe & Barltrop, 1978), greater than normal levels of crying (Dargassies, 1982), diarrhea and vomiting (Copans, 1974), and overall fussiness (Dargassies, 1982). In part, the effects of stress may be due to hormonal factors: Powerful emotions in the mother are associated with heightened levels of hormones such as adrenalin, which can pass through the placenta and affect the fetus. However, emotional stress is also often associated with poor nutrition, poor health, and lack of proper rest—all of which may separately influence prenatal development—so it is very difficult to sort out the specific effects of emotional stress.

Negative Influences on Prenatal Development

Beyond the general factors influencing prenatal development we described above, there are several specific *teratogens* that adversely affect unborn children by crossing the placenta and directly harming the embryo. *Teratogens* are defined as those factors that cause birth defects: drugs, chemicals, radiation, and viruses. The study of teratogens, *teratology*, is a fairly new area of research; thus our knowledge of teratology is far from complete. However, considerable research effort has been devoted to the study of teratogens and several harmful influences on prenatal development have been identified. In this section we will first describe the concept of *critical periods* in which teratogens are most likely to have harmful effects and then review the effects of some specific teratogens.

Critical Periods. During prenatal development, each part of the embryo and fetus has a *critical period* during which it is most susceptible to harm. Usually, these critical periods coincide with the formation of the body parts. For example, malformation of the central nervous system is most likely to occur during the third week after conception while malformation of the heart is most probable during the third, fourth, and fifth weeks after conception. As we have seen, most of the major organs are formed in the first trimester of pregnancy. Hence, the mother's health and nutritional habits are of great importance early in pregnancy since it is then that the major organs are at their greatest risk. As another example, the eyes are most prone to teratogens between 24 and 40 days after conception, the time at which these organs are forming (Hughes, 1980).

The fact that the major organs form primarily during the first trimester and are most susceptible to teratogens during this time has caused some individuals to refer to the first trimester of pregnancy as the critical period of pregnancy. While this statement is generally correct, all of pregnancy is a critical period because teratogens may have an influence at later times during pregnancy.

Specific Teratogens. One of the frustrating things in teratological research is that only a few teratogens are known to affect all embryos and fetuses. Further, two different embryos exposed to the same teratogen at the same stage of development may be affected in different ways. Several variables seem to be involved in determining how teratogens affect embryos: These are genetics, sex, mother's health, social class, and nutrition. In terms of genetics, sensitivity to certain teratogens seems to run in families (e.g., some families seem particularly susceptible to cleft palate), although research in this area is still in its infancy. The sex of the embryo makes a clear difference, with males much more sensitive to teratogens than females. Further, when mothers are in good health and follow sensible nutritional guidelines, their children are more resistant to teratogens.

Keeping in mind that there is a wide range of individual differences in sensitivity to teratogens, we will begin our review of specific teratogens by examining a well-known source, maternal diseases.

Maternal Diseases. Almost any severe infection can result in miscarriage, stillbirth, or premature labor (Vaughan, McKay, & Behrman, 1984). Some specific diseases, however, have been identified as powerful teratogens (see Table 6-1). For example, since 1941 we have known that the rubella virus crosses the placenta from the mother and infects the fetus, giving rise to multiple fetal malformations, retardation, or death (see Brimblecombe & Barltrop, 1978). Infection during the first trimester is extremely serious, but severe effects have also been observed among infants whose mothers contracted rubella as late as the eighth month of pregnancy (Brimblecombe & Barltrop, 1978). The effects of rubella are so devasting that all females of childbearing age should be immunized against it; certainly any woman planning a pregnancy should consider immunization first.

TABLE 6-1 Some Sources of Prenatal Damage

Diseases

Teratogen	Effect on Fetus
Rubella (measles)	Death; blindness; deafness; brain damage; prematurity
Syphilis	Death; blindness; deafness; brain damage
Pneumonia	Possible death
Tuberculosis	Possible death; susceptibility to tuberculosis later in life
Toxoplasmosis	Brain damage; heart damage; death
Mumps	Heart problems; possible death
Scarlet fever	Possible death
Herpes viruses	Mental deficits; malformations

Noninfectious Maternal Conditions

Teratogen	Effect on Fetus
Alcoholism	Death; multiple and severe malformations
Anemia	Possible death; brain damage; small brain; brain damage
Diabetes mellitus	Possible death; respiratory problems
Phenylketonuria (PKU)	Small brain; brain damage

Drugs

Teratogen	Effect on Fetus
Amphetamines	Heart damage; circulatory malformations
Caffeine	Prematurity; small size
Cigarette smoking	Low birth weight; prematurity; slowed cognitive development
Iodides	Hypothyroidism; goiter
LSD	Chromosome damage
Opiates (heroin, etc.)	Multiple malformations; addiction; death
Quinine	Hearing damage; possibility of death
Thalidomide	Severe, multiple malformations

Environmental Factors

Teratogen	Effect on Fetus
Radiation	Death; severe malformations
Mercury	Severe malformations; death; brain damage

Some of the information in this table was drawn from the following sources: Quilligan, E. J., & Kretchmer, N. (1980). *Fetal and maternal medicine*. New York: Wiley; and Vaughan, V. C., McKay, R. J., & Behrman, R. E. (1984). *Textbook of pediatrics*. Philadelphia: Saunders.

Another long-recognized source of fetal malformation is syphilis. Syphilis is a sexually transmitted disease that exerts its severest effects on the fetus during the last trimester (Vaughan et al., 1984). Typically, it causes fetal death; but it may also result in blindness, deafness, severe retardation, or death soon after birth. Syphilis can be detected through a simple blood test, and it is treatable both before and during pregnancy (Brimblecombe & Barltrop, 1978).

Other diseases that can profoundly and adversely affect the fetus include chicken pox, malaria, mumps, poliomyelitis, rubeola, smallpox (now considered to be eradicated worldwide), toxoplasmosis (an infection caused by a parasite found in uncooked meat and cat feces), tuberculosis, gonorrhea, herpes complex, AIDS, and some forms of encephalitis. The effects of these diseases vary from miscarriages and stillbirths to various kinds of malformations. Although any pediatrics text lists still more infectious diseases that can have an adverse effect on fetuses, a few important points can be made on the basis of those we have mentioned here.

First, disease prevention is of great importance: Immunization should be a basic component of family planning. Second, a potential mother's overall health is crucial: Healthy living and nutritional habits must be stressed. Third, competent medical supervision throughout pregnancy is important, especially given recent developments in the treatment of fetal illnesses (see Miller, 1983a).

Endocrine Disorders. Beyond infectious diseases of the sort we have mentioned up to this point, a second class of diseases, **endocrine disorders,** must also be considered. As we saw earlier in this section, hormones can be passed through the placenta to the fetus and affect development. Two important endocrinal diseases affecting prenatal development are: *diabetes mellitus* (common diabetes), in which the mother's pancreas produces too little insulin to break down sugars; and *hypothyroidism,* in which the mother's thyroid gland produces too little of the thyroid hormones that regulate the growth of body cells. Untreated diabetes results in fetal death, stillbirth, respiratory problems, and metabolic disturbances. Hypothyroidism also has severe effects on the fetus. Both diabetes and hypothyroidism can be treated during pregnancy, however, thereby greatly reducing the risks to the fetus. The fact that both of these endocrinal disorders can be so successfully treated underscores the importance of expectant mothers obtaining excellent medical care during pregnancy.

Rh Incompatibility of Mother and Fetus. The Rh factor is a protein, called the **Rh protein**, in the blood possessed by about 85 percent of all people. The problem of Rh incompatibility occurs only when the father is Rh positive (that is, he has inherited this trait), the mother is Rh negative (that is, she did not inherit the trait), and the fetus is Rh positive (that is, the fetus inherited its father's dominant gene for the Rh protein). In this situation, a dangerous set of events can occur if the fetus's blood comes in contact with the mother's. Since the mother does not possess the Rh protein, if her system comes in contact with the Rh protein from the baby, her body will manufacture antibodies to fight the Rh proteins as though they were foreign substances. When this happens, the mother's antibodies destroy the baby's red blood cells, which results in the baby's death or severe mental retardation (Vaughan et al., 1984).

Interestingly, Rh incompatibility only very rarely appears in first pregnancies because the mother's blood and the child's blood do not intermingle in the placenta. However, if the blood of the mother and baby do mix during the birth process, the mother's body may then manufacture antibodies to fight the Rh protein. Because antibodies *can* cross the placenta, a second pregnancy may be risky. Fortunately, however, this whole problem can be prevented by giving the mother an antibody suppression agent called **rhogam** at the birth of the first child (Hughes, 1980).

Maternal Drug Use. Americans use literally billions of painkillers, antacids, stimulants, and sleep aids as a matter of course each year. In the United States there is also a great deal of "recreational" drug use: Alcohol, tobacco, marijuana, cocaine, various opiates, barbiturates, airplane glue, and many other substances are used to achieve "highs." Alcohol and tobacco use are so routine in our society that we often do not even think of them as drugs. And, at least among some segments of our society, marijuana and cocaine are also rapidly achieving similar status. Given this state of affairs, it is not surprising that expectant mothers in the United States consume drugs, often without any idea that these commonplace substances may have harmful effects on their babies.

The average pregnant woman in our society consumes about four different types of over-the-counter drugs, drinks alcohol on occasion, and takes two or three prescription drugs during the nine months of her pregnancy (Hales & Creasy, 1982; Hughey, 1982). About half of all pregnant women in the United States smoke tobacco (Dalby, 1978). Sadly, even these socially accepted drugs have negative effects on fetuses (see Table 6-1).

Because of its widespread use and powerfully negative effects, alcohol causes more problems during pregnancy than any other drug (Abel, 1980; Claren & Smith, 1978; Miller, 1983c). **Fetal alcohol syndrome** is a severe set of malformations that occurs among fetuses whose mothers consume 2 or more ounces of alcohol per day (two to three drinks, typically). Children who suffer from fetal alcohol syndrome tend to have permanent growth retardation (both before and after birth), abnormally small brains, disfigured facial features (primarily the eyes and nose), mental retardation, and heart and liver anomalies (Gofman & DiVitto, 1983; Hughes, 1980). While it was long thought that the greatest risk of alcohol-related damage to the fetus was in the second and third trimesters, recent evidence suggests that alcohol use any time after conception may lead to harmful effects (Miller, 1983c). Further, the adverse effects of alcohol occur not only among alcoholics but also among *moderate* drinkers: Regularly drinking even small amounts of alcohol can lead to severe birth defects.

Tobacco is also a fairly strong teratogen. While the effects of tobacco do not seem to be as powerful as those of alcohol, the increasing use of tobacco among young women is a cause for concern (Hales & Creasy, 1983). Several studies (e.g., Frazier, Davis, Goldstein, & Goldberg, 1961; Ferreira, 1969; Yerushalmy, 1971, 1972) have reported the deleterious effects of maternal smoking on fetal development (see also Berne, 1983, for a review). In general, smoking is associated with lower birth weights, premature deliveries, and slower than normal cognitive development among babies. Apparently, these effects are directly related to the amount of tobacco consumed, with more severe effects seen among heavy smokers than light smokers.

Prescription drugs can also cause birth defects. Thalidomide, a sleep-inducing chemical that was once thought to be harmless, proved to be a terrible teratogen that caused severe birth defects in the 1950s and 1960s. (Vaughan et al., 1984). This example is extreme, but great care should be exercised in the use of any form of prescription medicine during pregnancy. Simply, our knowledge of the effects of many drugs on unborn children is extremely limited (Hales & Creasy, 1983). Perhaps the problem is best summarized by some pediatricians: "In view of the limited current knowledge of fetal effects from maternal medication, no drugs should be prescribed during pregnancy without weighing the maternal need against the risk of fetal damage" (Vaughan et al., 1984, p. 380).

The use of illicit drugs during pregnancy is an almost certain guarantee of birth defects (Brimblecombe & Barltrop, 1978). In general, illicit drugs (e.g., cocaine, PCP or "angel dust," heroin, amphetamines or "speed") used during pregnancy are associated with fetal death, stillbirth, brain damage, nervous system damage, low birth weight, prematurity, hyperactivity, respiratory problems, and digestive tract damage (Hales & Creasy, 1983; Vaughan et al., 1984). There apparently is no safe way for expectant mothers to engage in "recreational drug use."

Radiation. Another powerful teratogen is radiation, which can cause fetal deaths, stillbirths, leukemia, abnormally small brains, visual problems, and very low birth weight (see Gofman, 1981). The dangers of radiation are so severe that many physicians will only schedule abdominal X-rays during or immediately after the onset of women's periods, when they are clearly not pregnant (Hughey & Weber, 1982). X-rays of other parts of the body are not as dangerous, but recent practices include the careful use of shielding materials so that only the target area receives radiation. Even dental X-rays, which are far weaker than those used to examine the remainder of the body, should be taken only when an abdominal shield has been provided (Vaughan et al., 1984).

Teratogens among Fathers. Because of the tremendous importance of the intrauterine environment on fetal development, the vast majority of research on potential teratogens has focused on expectant mothers. It now appears, however, that the father also has an important role in the development of a healthy fetus. Research has shown that several substances consumed by fathers prior to conception—lead, alcohol, caffeine, narcotics, thalidomide, and anesthetic gases—adversely effect fetal development (Kolata, 1978; Vaughan et al., 1984). As yet, research on teratogens among fathers has been limited, but the results so far indicate that it is just as important for fathers to follow healthy living practices as it is for mothers.

Application: Guidelines for Expectant Parents

Our review of the literature on prenatal development suggests that there are some specific principles that should be followed by expectant parents. These principles emphasize the prevention of possible complications and the thoughtful consideration of everyday behaviors.

1. *Women should maintain a well-balanced diet prior to and during pregnancy.* The needs of the developing embryo and fetus are entirely dependent on the mother's eating habits. Women should follow a healthy diet designed to avoid nutritional deficiencies.

2. *Competent medical care should be available throughout pregnancy.* There is no substitute for excellent medical care. If possible, couples planning to have children should consult their family physician well in advance of attempting conception in order to obtain a complete check of both parents' health. In those cases in which a family cannot afford to retain their own physician, city, county, or state welfare agencies should be contacted in order to identify sources of health care available at low or no cost.

3. *Pregnancies should not be planned to occur during anticipated periods of emotional stress.* Events such as moves, job changes, and remarriages are all stressful. And, while unplanned pregnancies may unavoid-

ably occur at times in which levels of emotional stress are high, planned pregnancies should be slated for times at which low levels of emotional upheaval are expected.

4. *Vaccination against illnesses should precede planned pregnancies.* Updating innoculations against diseases such as measles and mumps is relatively painless, inexpensive, and requires little time. There is no reason for a couple planning to have children to run the risk of not being vaccinated. When expectant mothers are not immune to specific illnesses (e.g., chicken pox), they should be very careful to avoid potential infection.
5. *All drug use except that prescribed by a physician should stop during pregnancy.* Tobacco, alcohol, and "recreational drugs" are all harmful to the baby.
6. *Prenatal development is the responsibility of both parents.* Although research on teratogens among fathers is still limited, it is clear that the health and living habits of both the mother *and* the father influence prenatal development.

The Expectant Parents

To this point we have described the normal course of prenatal development from conception up to the time of birth and reviewed several factors that influence prenatal development. In this section, we change our focus and emphasize how pregnancy and the prospect of parenthood affects parents.

For most parents, pregnancy is an emotionally laden experience. The joy of parenthood, the anticipation of loving and caring for a baby, and the excitement associated with changing lives have a tremendous impact (Jessel, 1983). On the other hand, pregnancy may bring tension and stress (Hughey & Weber, 1982). Concerns about finances, the baby's health, becoming good parents, and a long-term change in life-style are often a part of parents' emotional experience during pregnancy.

Typically, the expectant mother and father have similar feelings about the upcoming birth (Jessel, 1983). They may both be elated and thrilled at the prospect of becoming parents, or they both may be frightened or saddened. Feelings fluctuate during pregnancy, of course, but the overall tone generally depends on whether or not the pregnancy was planned and wanted (Jessel, 1983).

Emotions in Expectant Mothers

It is not uncommon for an expectant mother to experience mood shifts (Jessel, 1983). Some of these mood swings, no doubt, are due to the hormonal and physical changes caused by pregnancy (Hughey & Weber, 1982). But others are caused by thinking about the implications of

For expectant parents, pregnancy is a time of joy touched with apprehension about the unknown.

having children. On the positive side is the joy associated with bringing a new life into the world, the fulfillment many women feel in motherhood, and the anticipation of cuddling and kissing the baby. On the negative side are the worries some expectant mothers have about their ability to be good mothers, the new responsibilities of parenthood, and the possibility that the baby may not be healthy. Bringing a new baby into the world is a momentous occasion, and alternating moods in expectant mothers are part of adapting to an important change in their lives.

For most planned pregnancies, the dominant mood among expectant mothers is very positive (Jessel, 1983). A small percentage of pregnant women, however, become depressed, while others become overly concerned with their own physical well-being, that of the father, and especially that of the baby. In fact, a powerful fear of birth defects is common enough that it has been given a formal name, **teratophobia**.

As one might expect, expectant mothers' feelings change as pregnancy progresses (Colman & Colman, 1977; Hughey & Weber, 1982; Jessel, 1983). During the first trimester, many women have mixed feelings. They may be pleased about the prospects of having a baby but worried that they are not yet ready for motherhood. Other women cannot believe they are pregnant, even when they have the results of medical tests in hand. Still others become very concerned about miscarriage or illness (Jessel, 1983).

It is also common for expectant mothers to become closer to their own mothers during the first trimester and to become somewhat less interested in their husbands (Colman & Colman, 1977). In part, this shift may be due to expectant mothers' belief that their own mothers can better understand what they are going through. Further, among some couples, the sexual nature of their relationship declines during the first trimester (Hughey & Weber, 1982).

During the second trimester, expectant mothers' feelings generally become more positive (Colman & Colman, 1977; Jessel, 1983). By now, the discomforts of early pregnancy such as morning sickness and fatigue have usually subsided and expectant mothers feel well physically. Also, the expectant mother can usually feel the baby move by this time, which quells fears of miscarriage.

As things settle down in the second trimester, relations between husband and wife usually improve: The wife becomes more concerned for the husband, sometimes to the point of being overly concerned with his safety (Jessel, 1983). Sexual relations typically improve, and many mothers want to involve their husbands as completely as possible in all aspects of the pregnancy and upcoming childbirth.

Expectant mothers focus on the baby during the final trimester. A lot of time and effort may go into buying the baby's clothes, purchasing toys, preparing a baby's room, picking out just the right furniture, and deciding on the perfect name. Near the end of the third trimester, the

Many expectant women continue to work until about a month before their due date.

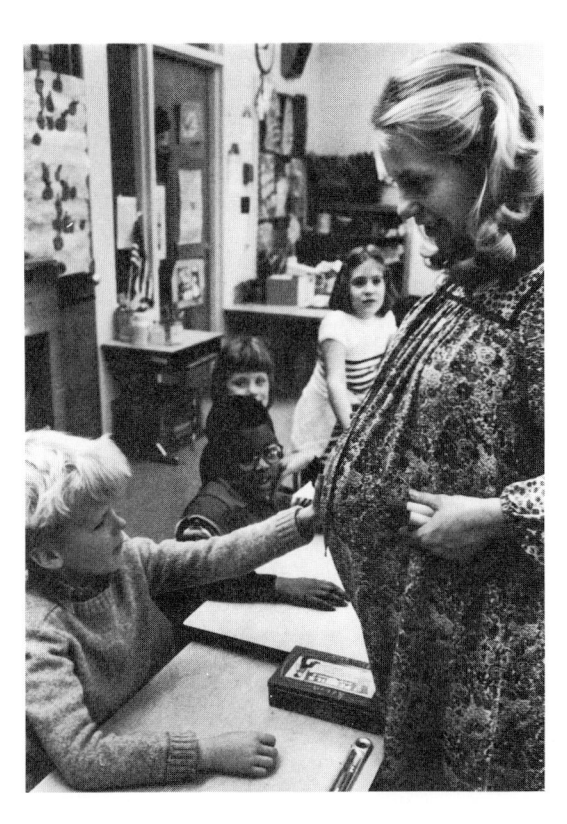

vast majority of expectant mothers are happy to be having a baby, although the physical changes in late pregnancy make it difficult to perform some common tasks such as bending over and stooping.

The thrill of having a new baby culminates near the end of pregnancy. On occasion, the excitement may be so great that parents (especially first-time parents) experience "false alarms": They become convinced the baby is due in moments and call their physicians or rush to the hospital, although birth may still be weeks away.

Emotions in Expectant Fathers

As we have seen, expectant mothers and fathers generally tend to share feelings about pregnancy and parenthood. In fact, many men are so in tune with their wives' feelings that they experience sympathetic pregnancy symptoms (Jessel, 1983). Research suggests that about half of all fathers have some form of sympathetic physical responses to their wives' pregnancy (Jessel, 1983), with as many as 10 to 15 percent experiencing vomiting and abdominal pains.

Unfortunately, not all men react to their wives' pregnancy in caring and concerned ways. Colman and Colman (1977) suggest that many men avoid their wives during pregnancy: They stay away from home, take up with other women, and avoid the responsibility of upcoming parenthood. Worse still, a small minority of men react in destructive ways that may include psychological abuse and wife-beating (Gelles, 1975). Fortunately, though, the vast majority of men react sensibly and responsively to their partners' pregnancies (Jessel, 1983).

Preparing for Parenthood

The months leading up to the birth of a child are an important time for couples to prepare for parenthood (Jessel, 1983). Husband and wife can further strengthen their relationship by sharing their feelings about the soon-to-arrive baby. The months of pregnancy are the time to work out hopes, concerns, and disagreements about the new baby before the responsibilities of actually raising the baby begin.

Pregnancy is also the time to learn how to take care of a baby and to find out about babies' needs. Expectant parents often have to learn everything from how to hold a baby properly, to how to clean and diaper a baby, to what and how to feed a newborn. These tasks should be understood prior to the baby's birth so that the parents do not have to cope with as many new things all at once.

In general, the more expectant parents learn about their feelings with respect to each other and the new baby, the better adjusted they will be as new parents and the healthier and happier their baby will be. Learning about how to provide the new baby with the best possible care is, of course, equally important (Jessel, 1983). Healthy, happy babies pay the parents back for their preparation many, many times over.

Birth

At about 38 weeks after conception, the baby is ready to enter the external world. Birth is usually preceded by **lightening,** in which the fetus turns so that it is head down and prepared for an exit from the womb. This shifting of the fetus relieves pressure ("lightens" pressure) on the mother's diaphragm such that her breathing becomes easier.

The process of **labor,** in which the baby is expelled from the womb, typically begins from a few hours to about two weeks after lightening, although "false labor" may occur earlier (Jessel, 1983). The labor process is initiated by hormonal changes in the mother and is typically considered to involve three stages (Jessel, 1983). In the first stage of labor, the cervix dilates (see Figure 6-4) and, usually, the amniotic sac breaks (colloquially referred to as "water breaking"), which allows the amniotic fluid to run out. This first stage of labor generally lasts from 6 to 12

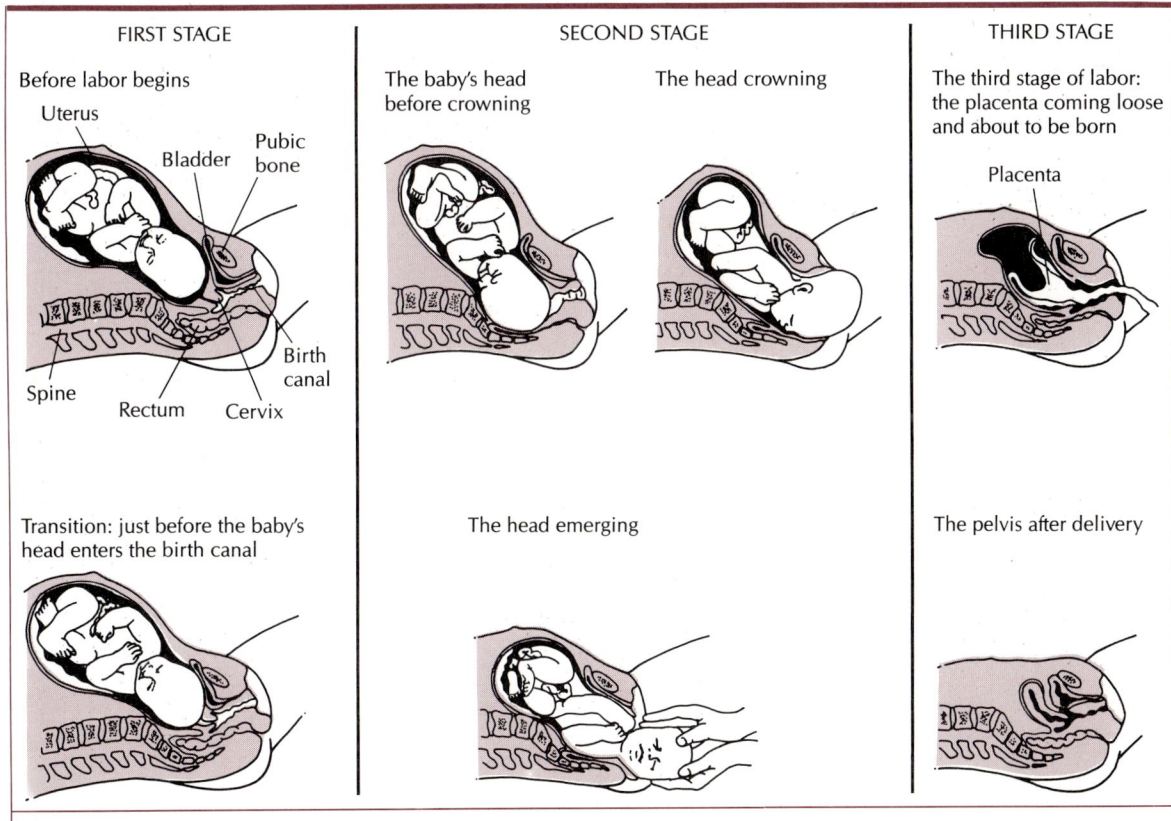

FIGURE 6-4 Diagram of Childbirth. These drawings show the three stages of the birth process.

hours but there are vast individual differences; it is not unusual for the first stage of birth to last 24 hours (Jessel, 1983).

The second stage of birth is the actual emergence of the baby, a process that usually takes from a few minutes to two to three hours. The third stage of labor is the expulsion of the so-called after-birth (the placenta).

The Newborn Baby

Newborn babies usually do not match common preconceptions of babies such as the Gerber baby and other pictures adorning packages of baby food. Newborns have splotchy, wrinkled, or red skin. Some babies are born with a full head of hair, others have facial and body hair, and still others are hairless. Since the bones in the skull are soft and incompletely formed, some babies' heads are malformed because the skull bones were squeezed together to allow the baby to pass through the birth canal. Still other babies have flattened noses or bruises as a result of the birth process.

None of these temporary situations are a cause for concern. Healthy babies' skin will soon clear up, and their facial and body hair will disappear. Babies' heads will take on a more normal shape within a few weeks. The skull is very flexible and the "soft spot" in the top of the baby's head will not solidify for several months. Flattened noses typically straighten out in a matter of days.

Of far greater importance than the baby's appearance at birth is its score on the **Apgar scale.** The Apgar scale (see Table 6-2) rates the health of newborn babies on five dimensions: heart rate, breathing, muscle tone, skin color, and quality of reflexes. As you can see in Table 6-2, each of these dimensions is rated on a 3-point scale (0, 1, 2). Total scores above seven indicate that the baby is in good shape. If the score is between four and seven, the baby needs quick attention to get its

TABLE 6-2 The Apgar Scale

Characteristic	0	1	2
Heart rate	Absent	Slow (below 100)	Rapid (over 100)
Breathing	Absent	Irregular, slow	Good, baby is crying
Muscle tone	Flaccid, limp	Weak, inactive	Strong, active
Color	Blue, pale	Body good, extremeties blue	No blue, all proper color
Reflex irritability	No response	Grimace	Coughing, sneezing, crying

Based on Apgar, V. (1953). A proposal for a new method of evaluation of the newborn infant. *Current Research in Anesthesia and Analgesia, 32,* 260. By permission.

Birth

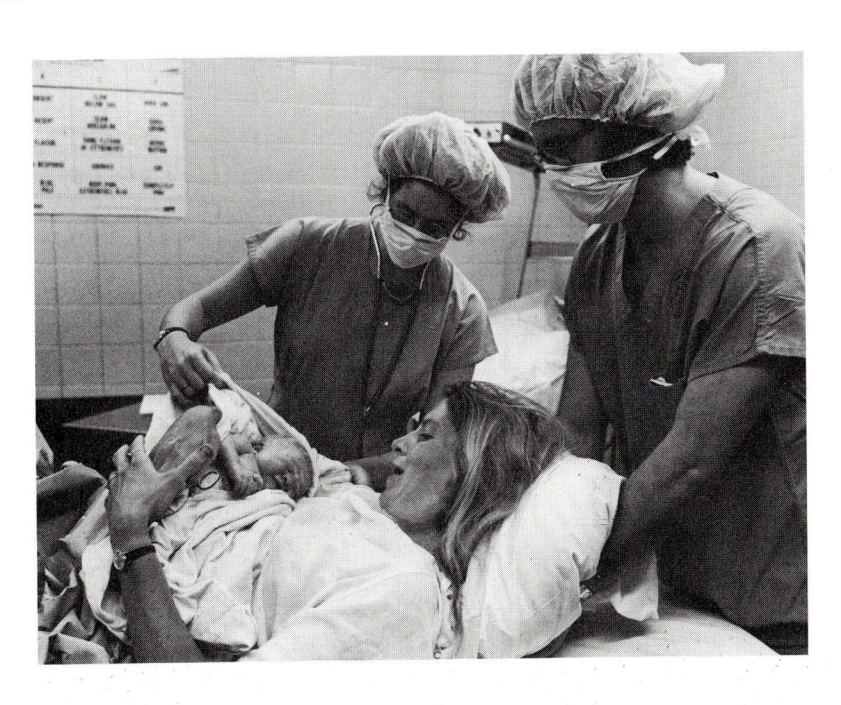

One minute after her birth, a baby is laid on her mother's body, while her father and nurse-midwife look on.

breathing going. If the score is below four, the baby is identified as in critical condition and in need of immediate emergency care. While the vast majority of babies born in the United States are in excellent shape at birth, the Apgar scale identifies thousands of babies every year who need special care.

Hospital Care of the Newborn

Care procedures for newborn babies vary greatly from culture to culture and across settings in the United States. If the baby is born in an American hospital, typical procedures involve cutting the umbilical cord and placing silver nitrate drops in its eyes to ward off possible infection and blindness in case the mother has gonorrhea. The Apgar scale is used immediately after birth and then again about five minutes later. Usually, the baby is washed off, weighed, measured, carefully examined for any deformities, wrapped in a blanket, and given to the mother. Depending on the mother's wishes and the particular hospital's procedures, the baby may then stay with the mother throughout her stay in the hospital, sleeping in the mother's room; or the baby may be taken to a nursery, placed in a warm, comfortable layette, and brought to the mother several times a day. New mothers and their babies usually stay in the hospital three to four days.

Complications in Birth

Although the vast majority of births (90 percent) are not affected by complications, there are some potential problems. One is associated with the position of the fetus at birth. In a normal birth, the fetus is

> ## Highlights
>
> ### Alternative Childbirth Methods
>
> While about 98 percent of all births in the United States take place in hospitals (Jessel, 1983), there are other options available, including the use of midwives. Midwives are women trained in aiding childbirth who, working with well-prepared parents, help deliver babies at home. However, since about one in ten births require medical intervention, parents must be fully aware of any possible complications in choosing alternatives to medical supervision during childbirth.
>
> In recent years, more and more expectant parents have attended various childbirth classes during pregnancy to prepare themselves for the birth process (Jessel, 1983). The *Lamaze* method, developed by a French physician, Fernand Lamaze, has been particularly popular. The Lamaze method employs breathing and exercise routines designed to ready the mother for childbirth. In addition, the father is fully involved in the process and works with the mother in preparing for childbirth, labor, and the birth process itself. The majority of mothers find the total involvement of the father in the birth process very supportive, therefore resulting in much more positive labor and birth experiences (Jessel, 1983; Pawson & Morris, 1972). Approaches to childbirth such as the Lamaze method seem to give parents the best of both worlds—the birth experience is shared and very personal and yet the full range of a hospital's medical facilities are available, should the need arise.

positioned head down (see Figure 6-4) such that the head passes through the birth canal first. About 4 percent of all births, however, are **breech deliveries** (Vaughan et al., 1984), in which the fetus is positioned buttocks down or even diagonally. In such deliveries, the attending physician typically attempts to reposition the fetus and, if this is not possible, employs forceps to extract the baby. Unfortunately, if improperly used, forceps may cause skull damage, leading to severe aftereffects such as brain damage or even death (Vaughan et al., 1984). Because of the danger involved in breech births (and for other reasons as well, see Institute of Medicine, 1985), about 4 percent of all births worldwide occur through **Caesarean section**, in which the baby is removed from the womb through surgical incisions made in the mother's abdomen and uterus.

A second possible complication that can occur during the birth process is **anoxia**. Anoxia (literally, oxygen deprivation) occurs whenever the placenta fails to function properly in providing oxygen to the fetus. This may result from the umbilical cord getting tangled up with the fetus or getting bent, broken, or damaged too soon before birth. Oxygen deprivation causes brain and nervous system damage, resulting in retardation, cerebral palsy, or death.

The effects of anoxia depend on the length of time the fetus is deprived of oxygen. The effects of very brief periods of anoxia are unclear, although prolonged anoxia is clearly associated with severe damage (Vaughan et al., 1984). Not surprisingly, the most important goal at birth is to establish proper breathing in the baby as soon as possible (Vaughan et al., 1984, p. 393).

A third potential problem receiving increased attention is the use of medications during the birth process. Several medications administered to the mother at the time of birth can adversely affect infants (e.g., Kolata, 1978; Yang, Zweig, Douthitt, & Federman, 1976). In general, the more sparingly medications are used, the more likely the baby will be healthy and alert.

Premature and Abnormally Small Babies

Not all babies are carried full term. Babies are considered premature when they are born earlier than 37 weeks following conception (Gofman & DiVitto, 1983; Harrison & Kositsky, 1983). Overall, about 4 percent of the babies born in the United States are premature (Institute of Medicine, 1985; Miller, 1983c), with most being only a week or two early. However, babies born as little as 24 weeks after conception have survived (Institute of Medicine, 1985). In general, **premature babies** have a much greater struggle for survival after birth than do full-term babies, a problem they share in common with abnormally small full-term babies.

Although the care of premature babies has improved in recent years, they still have more difficulty than full-term babies.

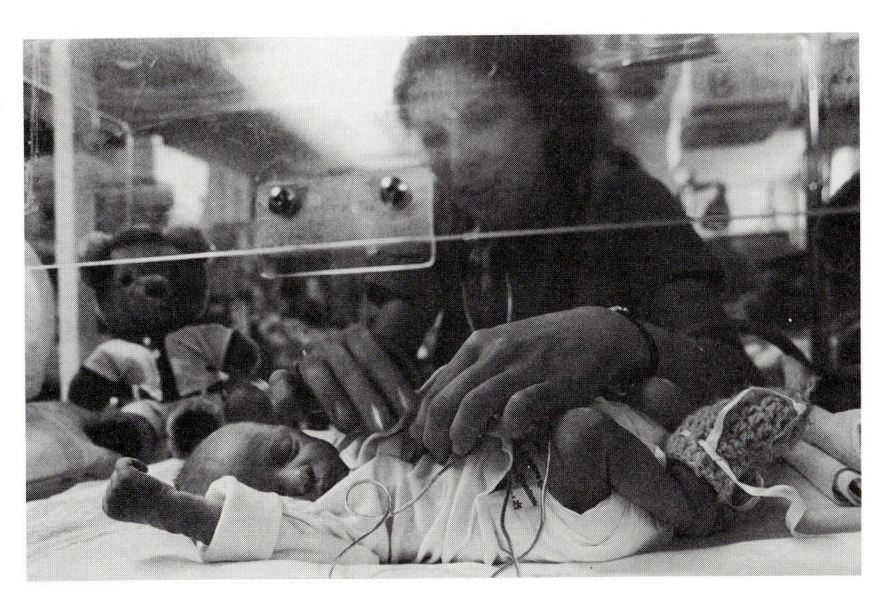

Research

Home Interventions with Parents of Low Birthweight Babies

Low birthweight babies are at much greater risk of developmental disabilities than their normal peers. As a result, considerable emphasis has been placed on strategies for facilitating the development of these babies. Recently Barrera, Rosenbaum, and Cunningham (1986) reported the results of two year-long intervention procedures used with the parents of low birthweight babies. In their study, 24 normal weight babies and their families served as a first control group, 21 low birthweight babies and their families served as a second control group, 22 low birthweight babies and their families were assigned to a parent-infant intervention condition, and 16 low birthweight babies and their families were assigned to a developmental program intervention.

Families in both experimental groups were visited regularly by an infant-parent therapist (once a week for the first four months, once every two weeks for the next five months, and once a month for the last three months of the interventions). Families using the developmental programming intervention were helped to assess their babies' levels of functioning using a formal measure (the Education for Multihandicapped Infants Assessment Scale), and received instructions, encouragement, and feedback from the therapist in working toward enhanced development in "cognition, communication, gross and fine motor development, socioemotional skills, and self-help skills" (Barrera et al., 1986, p. 22). Very specific activities were prescribed for the parents in this group for use with their babies.

Families in the parent-infant intervention group focused on no specific developmental goals, but instead worked toward improving the quality of parent-infant interactions. In this case, parents were helped to adjust their behaviors to their babies' special cues and developing abilities. In addition, the therapist helped parents to design a program to facilitate parent-infant interactions.

The results of Barrera et al.'s study clearly indicated that interventions with the parents of low birthweight babies during the first year of life could make a very real difference in their babies' development. Although never equaling the normal babies in the control group, babies in the parent-infant intervention group experienced significantly greater cognitive development than the low birthweight babies in the control group. In addition, the parent-infant intervention brought about real changes in the home environment and in the parents' and babies' behaviors. Developmental programming brought about similar changes, but these were not as marked as those observed in the parent-infant intervention group.

In reviewing their results, Barrera et al. (1986, p. 31) concluded that

> home intervention focused mainly on parent-infant interaction within a therapeutic problem-solving model is an effective home treatment for [low birthweight] . . . infants and their parents. The effectiveness of the intervention was best demonstrated by measures of the home environment, some behavior changes during mother-infant interaction, and, to a lesser degree, by changes in the cognitive scores.

Continued research on parenting low birthweight babies is needed, but the results of Barrera et al.'s study suggest that parents' interaction with their babies can make a real difference in development.

Summary

Until the mid-1970s, prematurity was defined primarily on the basis of birthweight, with babies under about 5 pounds 8 ounces, (2.74 kilograms) being classified as premature. Recent research, however, has revealed that there is a separate class of babies who are full-term but abnormally small (Institute of Medicine, 1985). Such growth retarded babies make up about 5 percent of all births, with some premature babies also classified as growth retarded. However, growth retarded newborns have certain features that distinguish them from premature babies: They often seem sickly or malnourished but yet alert and more mature than their small size would suggest (Institute of Medicine, 1985; Miller, 1983c).

The causes of retarded growth in fetuses are unclear (Miller, 1983b). One possibility is that somehow the mother's blood vessels near the placenta do not completely form into arteries capable of providing the fetus with adequate nutrition. A second possibility is the inadequacy of the mother's own nutrition. Further research is needed, however, to test these hypotheses. In any event, low birthweight infants—whether premature or growth retarded—have some difficult problems.

More than half of low birthweight babies have at least one physical or neurological impairment (Institute of Medicine, 1985). Of these defects, most (about 40 percent) are related to sight or hearing. Long-term follow-ups of extremely small babies have indicated that these children usually do relatively poorly on intellectual tasks and have significantly lower IQs than their normal peers (see Caputo & Mandell, 1970; Institute of Medicine, 1985). There is also the possibility that the very nature of the intensive care needed to keep tiny babies alive may contribute to later adjustment problems (Institute of Medicine, 1985). The isolation of newborns in incubators (for periods as long as several weeks) deprives them of normal contact with other human beings and ultimately may lead to incomplete mother–child bonding (see Chapter 14). Fortunately, the vast majority of newborn babies are healthy and happy.

Summary

In this chapter we reviewed prenatal development and the birth process. The mother's nutrition, health, and self-care behaviors powerfully influence fetal growth. During the nine months of a normal pregnancy, the baby develops from a single cell, the zygote, to a complete organism capable of surviving in the external environment. Much of the quality of a baby's life, however, is affected by the quality of care taken by the mother and father; several possible teratogens can have serious harmful effects.

Expectant mothers and fathers typically have similar feelings about pregnancy and having children. There are differences, however, as the parents adjust to the impending birth of their child. Mothers typically are ambivalent during the first trimester but become increasingly positive and focused on the baby as pregnancy moves along. Most fathers are sensitive to their wives' feelings and are caring and concerned during pregnancy. A minority, however, seek to escape their responsibilities, and some even respond to pregnancy in destructive ways.

Pregnancy culminates in birth, a three-stage process in which the cervix dilates and the amniotic sac breaks, followed by the emergence of the baby. The birth process is complete when the placenta is expelled. The vast majority of babies are born without complications, but small percentages are breech births, suffer from anoxia, or are adversely affected by medications given to the mother. About 4 percent of all babies are born prematurely, and another 10 percent or so are growth retarded. In the next chapter, *Physical Growth and Motor Development*, we will continue the study of physical and motor development from birth through adolescence.

Key Terms

germinal period — 1st 2 weeks after conception
Fallopian tubes
uterus
blastocyst — cells before implanting
chorion
amnion — forms from blastocyst or wall of uterus
umbilical cord
placenta
embryonic period — 3–8 weeks of week
ectoderm
mesoderm
endoderm
fetal period — 8 weeks – birth
surfactin
teratogens — factors that can cause birth defects
endocrine disorders
Rh protein
rhogam — suppresses antibodies for a few days
fetal alcohol syndrome
teratophobia — pregnant women becomes obsessive by fearful of birth defects
lightening — baby drops
labor
Apgar scale
breech deliveries
Caesarean section — Julia, Michael born
anoxia — no oxygen
premature babies
growth retarded babies

Suggested Readings

Colman, A., & Colman, L. (1977). *Pregnancy: The psychological experience.* New York: Bantam. Although now somewhat dated, this book provides an excellent overview of how expectant parents adapt to pregnancy and the prospect of becoming parents.

Hales, D., & Creasy, R. K. (1982). *New hope for problem pregnancies: Helping babies before they're born.* New York: Harper & Row. This book provides an excellent overview of high-risk pregnancies and some of the medical advances that have provided increased hope for potential parents.

Hughey, L., & Weber, M. (1982). *The American Medical Association book of womancare.* New York: Random House. This book should be required reading for all women contemplating pregnancy. Not only does it furnish the reader with a clear and thoughtful discussion of general self-care, but it also provides very specific guidelines for self-care during pregnancy.

Institute of Medicine (1985). *Preventing low birthweight.* Washington, D.C.: National Academy Press. This excellent book provides overall guidelines for expectant mothers but focuses specifically on the kinds of things that can be done to reduce the possibility of low birthweight babies.

Jessel, C. *The joy of birth: A book for parents and children.* New York: Dutton, 1983. This well-written book is a fine source of information about the birth process.

Application Exercise

6-1 Influences on Prenatal Development

Below is a set of brief descriptions of parents or parents' behaviors. Read each description and determine if there is a potential of a risky pregnancy and, if so, describe the source of the risk.

1. Robyn has already had two healthy babies. Now, as she is finding it hard to keep her weight down in her third pregnancy, she is taking an over-the-counter appetite suppressant.

Application Exercise

2. Alex and Jane are planning their first child. Alex is a moderate to sometimes heavy drinker. He typically has a martini every day at lunch, two or three glasses of wine at night, and sometimes even a "bloody Mary" for breakfast.

3. Ellen is a healthy young woman pregnant with her first child. She has always hated milk and milk products, however. She refuses to drink milk or eat cheese or ice cream.

4. Mimi married the day after high school graduation. Apparently, she became pregnant the same week. Although she is barely 17, she is in excellent health.

5. During the fourth month of her pregnancy, Amy's husband was killed in an automobile accident. Amy has been severely depressed ever since. To complicate things, Amy has made very few friends in the new town she and her husband had moved to.

6. Andrea has never had the measles nor has she been immunized against them. Her brother's family visited at Christmas and, about a day after they left, her brother called to tell Andrea that all of his children had come down with the measles.

7. Nancy is pregnant with her first child. She is Rh negative, but her husband is Rh positive.

8. Laura and Bill are planning to try to conceive their first child. Laura smokes one and one-half to two packs of cigarettes a day.

CHAPTER 7

Physical Growth and Motor Development

I think what is happening to me is so wonderful, and not only what can be seen on my body, but all that is taking place inside. I never discuss myself or any of these things with anybody; that is why I have to talk to myself about them.
　—Ann Frank,
　The Diary of a Young Girl

In Chapter 6, we followed human development from conception to birth. Here, we focus on physical growth and motor development from birth through adulthood. We begin by examining some basic principles of physical growth and motor development. Next, we describe the development of the brain and nervous system. Then, we will examine physical development in some detail and complete the chapter with a review of motor development.

Patterns of Physical and Motor Development

The growth of a newborn baby into a fully functional adult is an intriguing, multifaceted process. As we will see later in the chapter, many variables exert influence on physical growth in subtle and complex ways. Further, there are inevitable individual differences in children's physical growth and motor skill development (Malina, 1980).

Despite the many factors that influence physical growth and motor development and the diversity of individual development, certain basic principles underlie the directions of growth (Smith, 1977). These principles—cephalocaudal development, proximodistal development, and differentiation and integration—determine the overall directions of growth among all human beings.

Cephalocaudal Development

Cephalocaudal means literally "from head to tail." The principle of **cephalocaudal development** states that human development proceeds from head to foot. This pattern of head–foot development is manifested in the order in which parts of the body become larger and their functions more complex. In terms of physical growth, babies' heads develop before their trunks and limbs.

217

A newborn baby's head is about half the size it will be in adulthood. At birth, the head makes up about one-fourth of the body's length; however, by adulthood, the head constitutes only about one-twelfth of a person's height (Bayley, 1956). As we will see later in this chapter, the brain is the most nearly complete organ in newborn babies, although it is only a fraction of what it will become (Dargassies, 1982).

In contrast to the early growth of the head in human beings, the trunk triples in size after birth while the arms and hands increase in size by a factor of four. Even more impressive is the fivefold increase in the size of the legs. In fact, a great deal of children's increases in height are due to the growth of the legs. By adulthood, the legs make up about 40 percent of most people's overall height. Similarly, the development of organs such as the stomach, spleen, and liver is considerably delayed over the brain's development (Smith, 1977). Figure 7-1 presents an illustration of how the proportions of the body change from birth through adulthood.

In addition to the cephalocaudal nature of physical growth, a head to foot pattern of development is also apparent in the progression of motor abilities among children. As we will see in the last section of the chapter, babies gain initial control over the muscles in their heads and necks, followed by the acquisition of control over the arms, the torso, and lastly, the legs. A typically developing baby can hold her head up well before she can sit. Sitting is then followed by standing, walking, and hopping on one foot—all indications of the cephalocaudal nature of motor development.

Proximodistal Development

The meaning of proximodistal is "from near to far." The principle of proximodistal development, then, states that human development proceeds from the center of the body out to its extremities. Generally

FIGURE 7-1 Changes in Body Form Associated with Age. Changes in the body's proportions across the years can be seen easily. Adapted from C. M. Jackson, Some aspects of form and growth, In W. J. Robbins et al., *Growth* (New Haven: Yale University Press, 1929), p. 118, by permission.

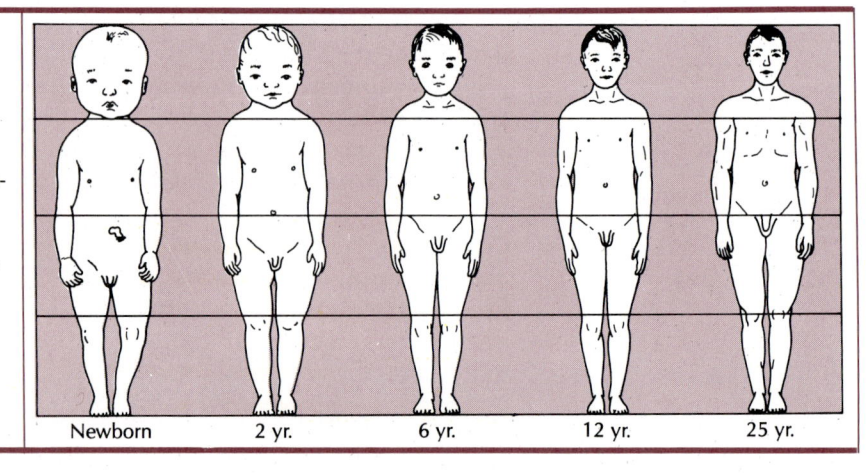

Integration is the coordination of newly differentiated actions.

speaking, babies first gain control of their shoulder muscles followed by their arm muscles; only after about 5 months do they obtain enough control over their hands to start trying to grab objects. The ability to actually grasp objects takes longer still and does not appear until about 40 weeks of age. The same proximodistal pattern is seen in the development of the legs. Babies are able to exert control over their upper legs well before they can manipulate their toes.

Differentiation and Integration

The third general principle governing patterns of growth and development is that of *differentiation and integration* (see our discussion of Werner in Chapter 1). **Differentiation** refers to the fact that babies' abilities become increasingly distinct across time. For example, a baby in a soiled, uncomfortable diaper will thrash all of his body, cry, and show signs of general distress. After a few months, however, the baby is much more likely to shake his bottom and pull at the diaper. Finally, when he is just about ready to be toilet trained, some very sophisticated and clearly differentiated behaviors may allow him to pull off the offending diaper and announce to all who will listen that his bottom needs to be washed. In this example, the baby proceeds from undifferentiated, unfocused behaviors to actions that more and more clearly center on exactly what will provide relief. Further, the nerve impulses that transmit the discomfort to the brain are now transformed into language and allow him to say things such as "dirty bottom."

Integration is the complementary process to differentiation. Where differentiation refers to the tendency for behaviors to become more and more distinct across time, integration refers to the coordination of the newly differentiated actions. For example, after a baby has gained separate control of her head, neck, arm, and lower torso muscles, she can then combine several separate muscle movements into the much more complex action of turning over. Similarly, the act of tying a shoe, a very difficult task for most 4-year-olds, is fairly simple for 6-year-olds because they can integrate a whole series of separate, small actions (eye-hand coordination, pinching movements between fingers, pulling motions with the hands, and so on) into a complex, coordinated skill. Further, many skills reach the level of **automaticity** (LaBerge & Samuels, 1976), such that they require little, if any, conscious attention. Most 8-year-olds, as an example, can carry on a conversation or watch television while tying their shoes—apparently paying little attention to what was once a very difficult process.

The principles of cephalocaudal development, proximodistal development, and differentiation and integration govern human development. These principles, however, provide only the basic framework for viewing the manifold changes that occur during a person's life. We will begin an in-depth examination of these changes in our next section as we examine a critical aspect of development, the growth of the brain and nervous system.

The Brain and Nervous System

One of the most important elements of development is the growth of the brain and nervous system. To appreciate the implications this growth has for children's capabilities requires that we first review some basic information. The nervous system (see Figure 7-2) can be divided roughly into two components: the central nervous system and the peripheral nervous system (D. Jensen, 1980). The **central nervous system (CNS)** consists of the brain and spinal cord while the **peripheral nervous system (PNS)** consists of all the nerve tissue lying outside of the CNS (Winsom, 1985).

In general terms, the nervous system consists of a set of very specialized cells that serves as a very rapid communication system in the body (Ornstein & Thompson, 1984). Stimuli (e.g., light, sound) activate sensors (e.g., the eyes, ears) that send coded electric signals (called neural impulses) from the PNS to the CNS. The nerve impulses are then recorded (when the information reaches the brain and is considered) or directly acted on by the CNS. The CNS then transmits nerve impulses to an appropriate **effector** (a part of the body that can act on the stimulus encountered by the receptor) and an action is taken. For example, if a 4-year-old sips some cocoa that is too hot, the sensors in the roof of her mouth immediately signal pain to the CNS. The CNS responds by sending nerve impulses to the area, causing the child to spit out the hot cocoa.

FIGURE 7-2 The Human Nervous System.

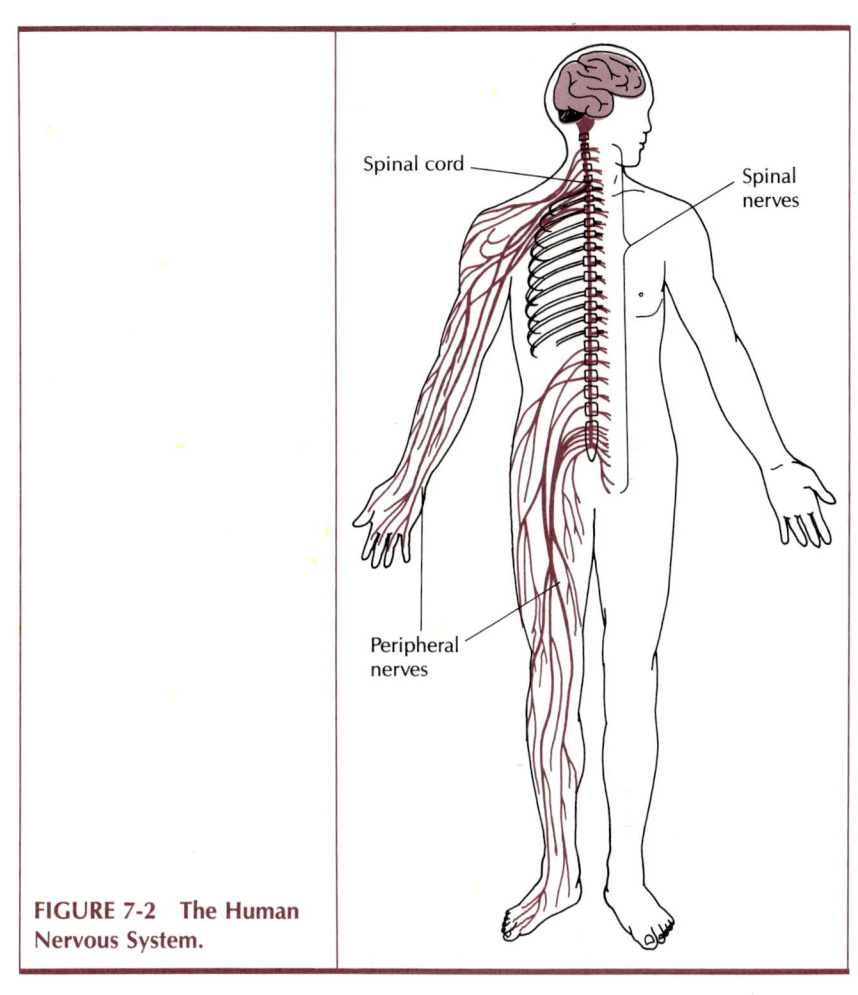

The Peripheral Nervous System

The PNS contains two kinds of nerve fibers: afferent and efferent. The **afferent fibers** serve as conduits of incoming information (from the fingertips to the spinal cord, for example), whereas the **efferent fibers** handle outgoing information (from the spine back out to a fingertip). Some of each of these types of fibers are a part of the autonomic nervous system. The **autonomic nervous system** controls the basic life support functions of the body consisting of the heart muscles, smooth muscles, glands necessary for autonomic responding (e.g., saliva glands, sweat glands, the stomach), and those glands involved in emotions. Nerve fibers in the autonomic nervous system are either **sympathetic** or **parasympathetic**. In simple terms, the sympathetic nerve fibers activate the body systems they serve, whereas the parasympathetic nerve fibers deactivate various body systems (Tortora & Anagnostakos, 1981).

The Central Nervous System

The spinal cord, one of the two major components of the CNS, controls two general forms of activities: spinal reflexes and supraspinal activities. **Spinal reflexes** are muscular and autonomic reflexes to various stimuli. For example, the classic knee-jerk reflex (which occurs when the top of a crossed knee is tapped) is a spinal reflex: The spine handles the response and no conscious thought is involved in the process. **Supraspinal activities** are those actions that are channeled back and forth through the spine to the brain. Walking, for example, is a supraspinal activity.

The brain is the basis for all other neural activity: remembering, creating, solving problems, using language, and making sense of the world. Figure 7-3 pictures a cross-section of the brain with four of its major components identified: the brain stem, the diencephalon, the cerebrum, and the cerebellum.

The Brain Stem. The **brain stem,** which is made up of the midbrain, the pons varolii, and the medulla oblongata, begins as a continuation of the spinal cord. The **medulla oblongata** (or, more simply, the medulla) contains all the nerves that pass from the spinal cord to the brain and back. Interestingly, it is in the medulla that the nerve fibers cross such that information from the left side of the body reaches the right side of the brain and vice versa. In addition, the medulla controls basic heart rate, breathing rhythm, and the constriction of blood vessels. Vomiting, swallowing, coughing, sneezing, and hiccupping are all also apparently controlled in the medulla (Ornstein & Thompson, 1984).

The **pons varolii** (simply, the pons) is situated just above the medulla and primarily acts as a bridge between the spinal cord and the brain, although parts of it are involved in the control of breathing (Winsom, 1985). The **midbrain** appears above and behind the pons and is in many ways an extension of the medulla. In addition to conducting nerve impulses to the upper regions of the brain and back down to the spinal cord, the midbrain is involved as a reflex center for eye and head movements in response to visual and auditory stimuli. Some of the movements of the eyes and fine touch control also stem from the midbrain (Tortora & Anagnostakos, 1981).

The Diencephalon. The **diencephalon** is primarily made up of the thalamus and the hypothalamus (Tortora & Anagnostakos, 1981). The **thalamus** is located above the midbrain and is the point at which all sensory information except smell is relayed to the cerebrum. It is more than just a simple relay station, however: The thalamus also can interpret and respond to stimuli such as pressure or pain. In addition, the thalamus relays information about voluntary motor actions from the cerebrum to the spinal cord and, hence, to the rest of the body.

FIGURE 7-3 View of the Brain and Its Components.

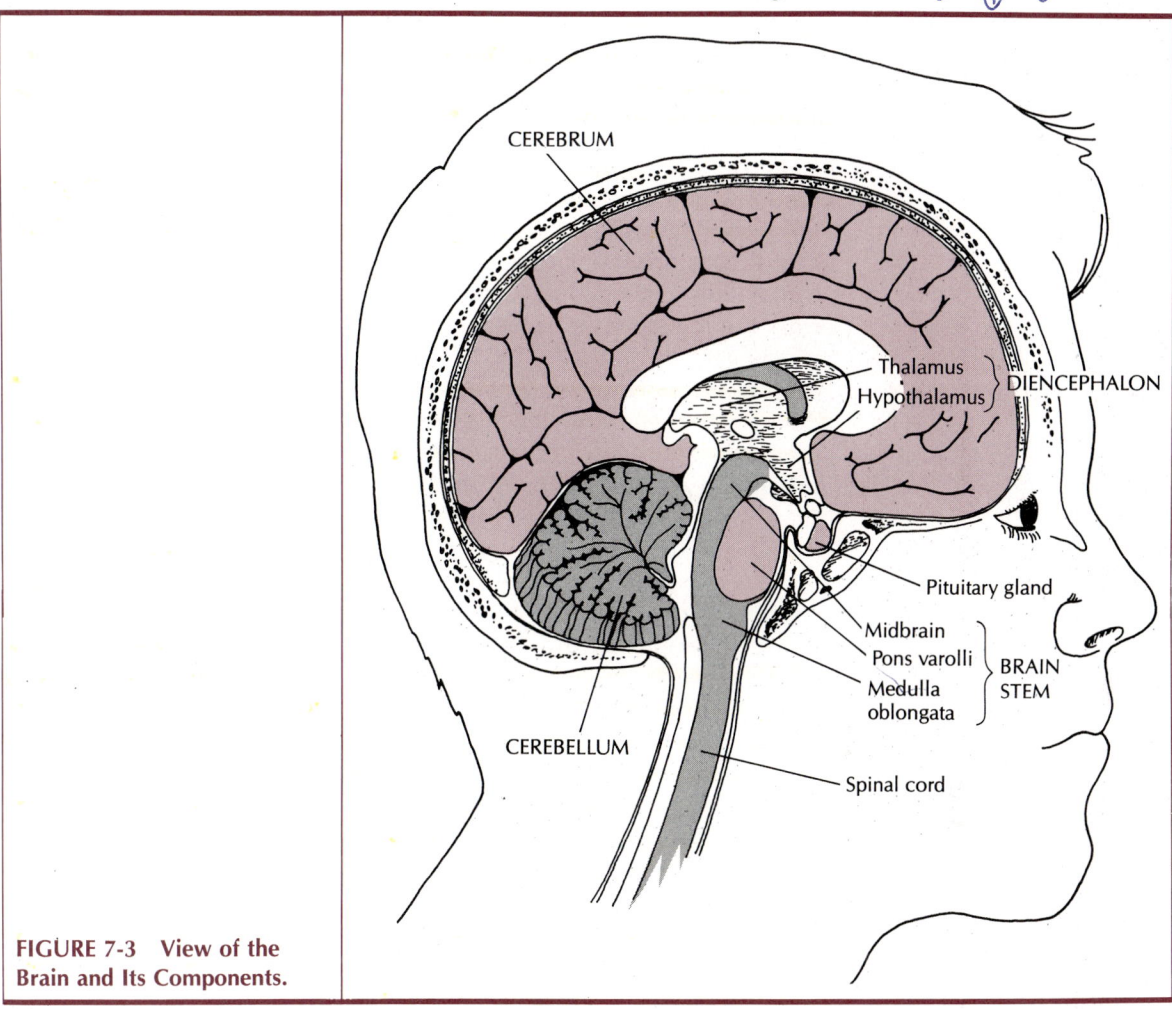

The **hypothalamus,** one of the most important structures in the brain, is below and in front of the thalamus. It controls the autonomic nervous system, receives sensory input from inside the body, integrates functioning with various glandular systems, mediates emotional responses, controls body temperature, regulates hunger and thirst, and influences patterns of sleep and wakefulness.

The Cerebrum. The **cerebrum** is by far the largest part of the brain. The surface of the cerebrum is called the **cerebral cortex:** It is made up of grey tissue. The many folds in the cerebral cortex allow for a great increase in the cortex's surface area without increasing volume. The cerebral cortex is involved in most of the sophisticated functions of the brain, including vision, hearing, taste, smell, motor functioning, thought, memory, and language.

The Cerebellum. The **cerebellum** is the second largest component of the brain and is located behind the brain stem and under the cerebrum. The cerebellum uses feedback from the body to coordinate and maintain balance, posture, and muscle control (Ito, 1984). Although the actual "commands" for voluntary muscle movements come from the cerebrum, the regulation of these movements takes place in the cerebellum.

The Growth of the CNS

At birth, the infant's brain is only about one-fourth of its adult size. The brain and the skull that surrounds it, however, could hardly be any larger and still allow for successful birth. In newborns, the head is immense in proportion to the remainder of the body; larger size at this time would greatly increase the chance of damage as the baby passes through the birth canal.

As a consequence of the relatively undeveloped state of the brain at birth, complex mental processes are not possible and must await further development and experience (Cowan, 1985). Despite the brain's immaturity, all of its nerve cells (called **neurons**) are present at birth. After birth, brain growth occurs primarily though the formation of **glial cells** that provide nutrition for the neurons as well as forming a covering or sheath of fatty material called **myelin** around each of the neurons (Winsom, 1985). The myelin sheath is analogous in some ways to the insulating covering of electrical cords: The sheath keeps the nerve impulses (which are essentially electrical current) contained within neural fibers and reduces the accidental spread of neural impulses from one fiber to another. The extreme importance of myelin can be seen in the effects of diseases such as multiple sclerosis that break down the myelin and result in the loss of motor control.

The brain grows rapidly during the first two years after birth, reaching nearly 80 percent of its adult size (Mehler & Fox, 1985). The growth of the glial cells accounts for most of this change and at about the age of 2 the process of covering the neurons with myelin (called **myelinization**) is nearly complete. Additional growth also occurs as greater numbers of connections among neurons form and the complexity of these connections increases. The growth of the brain and nervous system is not complete until adolescence, however, as some myelinization continues along with further growth of nerve endings in the cortex region (The Diagram Group, 1982).

The brain develops in an orderly sequence determined by genetic structure. The cerebral cortex, which contains the centers for sophisticated thought, memory, language, spatial abilities, and motor skills, is almost completely undeveloped at birth (Vaughan et al., 1984). This absence of cortical development strongly suggests that newborn babies' behaviors are primarily reflexive—consisting of innate, unlearned responses emanating from the diencephalon and the midbrain in response to specific stimuli.

Despite the absence of a developed cortex, the midbrain and diencephalon have developed well enough by the time of birth to allow for the control of all the functions necessary for life. As the cerebral cortex develops, babies' actions become less and less reflexive until only a few innate responses remain.

Cortex development follows the cephalocaudal and proximodistal principles. Those parts of the cortex that govern movement of the head and trunk develop first, followed by elements of the cortex associated with control of the limbs. By the age of 4, the cerebral cortex is fully connected to the cerebellum, allowing for the control of fine motor movements (Ito, 1984). Not surprisingly, tasks requiring fine motor control such as tying shoelaces, writing with a pencil, and correctly using scissors are very difficult for children under the age of 4.

It is no surprise that language generation usually does not get much further than a word or two by the age of 12 months and then accelerates rapidly through early childhood. **Broca's area,** that part of the cortex involved in translating thought into speech, must grow and attain the necessary sophistication to allow for language generation. Further, language generation and language comprehension (following directions, responding to requests, and so on) require memory for language, one of the cortical functions that must await the growth of the brain.

Language, memory, problem-solving, and motor activities all depend on the growth of the brain. Accordingly, brain damage of various forms can result in severe disabilities, from total nonfunctioning and death to very specific handicaps. One such handicap is **aphasia,** the inability to speak, which can be caused by minor damage to Broca's area or to **Wernicke's area** (that part of the brain that generates the thought that Broca's area translates into speech).

The Two Hemispheres of the Brain

Figure 7-4 shows a view of the brain from the top. As you can see, the cerebrum is literally divided into two halves or **cerebral hemispheres.** Not pictured is the cerebellum, which also is structured into two hemispheres. The two hemispheres of the cerebrum are roughly symmetrical but not perfect mirror images of one another. Because of the symmetry of the two hemispheres, we might expect that the hemispheres would perform highly similar functions (Tortora & Anagnostakos, 1981). This is not the case, however.

As we saw earlier, each side of the brain receives neural impulses from and sends neural impulses to the opposite side of the body, with

FIGURE 7-4 View of the Two Cerebral Hemispheres. The cerebrum is divided into two hemispheres. Although they are roughly symmetrical, the two hemispheres perform different functions.

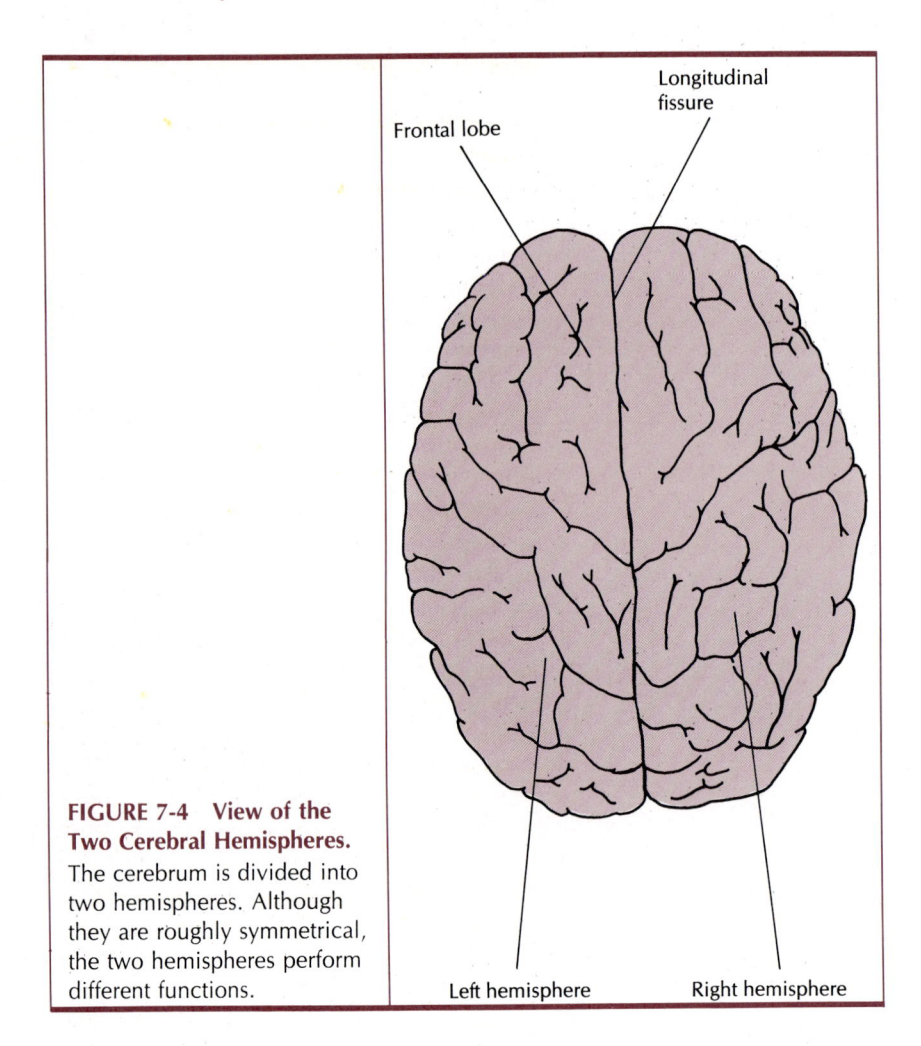

the switching occurring in the medulla. Hence, the *right* hemisphere senses and controls events in the *left* side of the body: The left arm's actions are determined in the right hemisphere of the cerebrum. Similarly, the *left* side of the cerebrum controls the *right* side of the body: The left hemisphere governs the wiggling of toes on the right foot. When auditory stimuli are considered, we see a very similar, although more complex pattern. Each ear is connected to both hemispheres, although the link is strongest to the opposite one. Hence, the stimuli picked up by the right ear are processed by the left hemisphere and vice versa.

The relationship of the eyes to the two hemispheres is still more complex. Each eye is connected to both hemispheres. Visual stimuli detected by the *right* side of each eye are processed by the *left* hemisphere while the stimuli detected by the *left* side of each eye are processed by the *right* hemisphere (The Diagram Group, 1982).

The apparent symmetry of functioning and structure in the two hemispheres, however, breaks down when we consider more sophisticated cerebral activities. Among right-handed individuals, for example, language is controlled in the left hemisphere—primarily in Broca's area and Wernicke's area (Geschwind, 1979; The Diagram Group, 1982; Fincher, 1982). Language is also located in the left hemisphere among most left-handed people, although about 40 percent of left-handed people process language either in the right hemisphere or in both hemispheres (Fincher, 1982).

In contrast to language, musical and spatial perception abilities are primarily controlled by the right side of the cerebrum (Fincher, 1982). Evidence from people who have suffered damage to the right hemisphere or who have had portions of their right hemispheres surgically removed indicates losses of musical abilities, abstract thought, drawing skills, and spatial abilities (D. Jensen, 1980). Damage to the right hemisphere also seems to be associated with an inability to detect emotion in the speech of other people (Geschwind, 1979).

The two hemispheres are joined by the **corpus callosum.** Many kinds of information processing involve both hemispheres. Recent research suggests, for example, that the connection between the hemispheres is important in developing a fully functional memory system (e.g., McKeever & Hoff, 1983). When the corpus callosum is damaged or surgically removed (as is sometimes done in the treatment of severe epilepsy), an odd circumstance exists: The left side of the cerebrum literally *does not know what the right side does* (Daehler & Bukatko, 1985). Hughes (1980) has summarized some of the results of research on children who have suffered damage to the corpus callosum (see also Cowan, 1985; Sperry, 1982). He reported that when visual images are presented only to the left visual area of the eyes (this information would then be processed in the right hemisphere), the patients verbally report not having seen anything. Apparently, the information in the right hemisphere is not available to the left hemisphere (see also Hubel & Wiesel, 1979). The opposite, knowledge in the left hemisphere being unavailable to the right hemisphere, is also the case when the corpus callosum is removed.

The Development of a Dominant Hemisphere

The specialization of the two hemispheres (referred to as **lateralization**) apparently begins as soon as the cortex forms in the fetus (see Cowan, 1979; Sperry, 1982). Lateralization is often complete at an early age and signs of the dominance of one hemisphere over the other can often be seen among infants. For example, greater electrical activity in the left than in the right hemisphere has been monitored in infants being exposed to speech (D. Jensen, 1980). Similarly, even newborns seem to process the sounds of speech more rapidly in their left hemispheres than in their right hemispheres (Molfese & Molfese, 1979). Spatial ability also seems to be lateralized fairly early in life, although the evidence suggests that this process is not complete until about the age of 10 (Flanery & Balling, 1979).

Related to the issue of lateralization is the phenomenon of **handedness.** About 91 percent of the population is right-handed, with the remainder either ambidextrous or left-handed (Tortora & Anagnostakos, 1981). It is unknown why some people are left-handed or ambidextrous, but the distribution of brain functions among left-handed people is clearly different than it is among right-handers (D. Jensen, 1980).

Summary of Brain and Nervous System Development

The growth of the brain and nervous system is a critical aspect of human development. At birth, the brain, which consists of the brain stem, the diencephalon, the cerebrum, and the cerebellum, is only about one-quarter of its adult size. The brain stem and diencephalon, which control basic reflexes necessary for life, are the most complete structures in the brain at birth. The majority of growth after birth occurs in the cerebellum, which coordinates muscle control and balance, and the cerebrum, which carries on the sophisticated processes of thought. This growth is largely due to myelinization and the formation of more and more complex connections between neurons.

In addition to sheer growth, the brain's functions specialize between the two hemispheres, with each taking on different tasks. Elements of the specialization of the hemispheres are evident early in life as babies favor the use of one hand over the other, but specialization is probably not complete, at least for spatial abilities, until the age of 10 or so.

Physical, cognitive, social, and emotional development all depend on the development of the brain and nervous system. As important as the development of the brain and nervous system is, however, it is only one aspect of the more general process of physical development.

Physical Growth

Physical growth is a multifaceted process. In this section, we will highlight normal rates of growth, individual patterns of growth, sex differences in growth, adolescent growth, psychological factors involved in growth, historical trends in size and maturation, and environmental factors influencing growth.

Normal Rates of Growth

The principles of cephalocaudal growth, proximodistal growth, and differentiation and integration govern the overall direction and process of growth. More specific information about how growth typically unfolds has come from large-scale investigations of children's physical growth and motor development. These investigations (e.g., Bayley, 1956; Cattell, 1940; Faust, 1977; Gesell, 1925; Griffiths, 1954; Roche, 1979) have provided us with descriptions of typical patterns of growth and development (called norms) that allow us to identify rates of change and the approximate ages at which various changes occur (Smith, 1977).

Norms are based on the scientific sampling of a population. For example, suppose we wanted to be able to describe the weight of 14-year-old boys in the United States. There are millions of 14-year-old boys, and we obviously cannot weigh all of them. Instead, a much more manageable and yet scientifically sound procedure is to choose 14-year-old boys who represent the same proportion of rural, urban, black, white, Chicano, poor, middle-class, and wealthy boys as exists in the general population. Our measurement of this sample of boys would then provide us with an accurate representation of the weights of the entire population of 14-year-old boys.

Table 7-1 shows the patterns of increase in height and weight among boys and girls from birth through age 19. Care must be taken, however, to remember that norms are merely descriptions of average rates of growth and are not standards or ideals by which to judge children.

At birth, the average baby in the United States is about 20 inches long and weighs between 7 and 8 pounds. During the first few days after birth, most babies lose a few ounces as they adjust to sucking and digesting their own food. The weight loss usually stops at the end of the first week, and babies rapidly gain weight thereafter. The average baby's weight is doubled by the age of 5 months, tripled by the age of 1 year, and quadrupled by the age of 2. The baby who weighed 7 pounds at birth usually weights about 28 pounds on his or her second birthday.

In terms of height, most babies grow 9 or 10 inches during their first year and between 2 and 6 inches from their first to their second birthdays. A 20-inch-long baby may very easily reach 33 inches in height by the age of 2—about half of adult female height. Boys usually reach about half of their adult height at the age of 2½.

Other changes besides sheer growth also take place. A lot of the weight gained by the age of 9 months or so is fat. This gives babies the "roly-poly" look with characteristic dimples and a rounded tummy. From 9 months on, though, normal babies gain less weight as fat and more and more as muscle and bone. So-called baby fat is usually lost during the preschool years as children grow taller and more heavily

TABLE 7-1 Height and Weight of Boys and Girls from Age 1 to Age 19

	Height						Weight					
	Girls			Boys			Girls			Boys		
Age	10th	50th	90th	10th	50th	90th	10th	50th	90th	10th	50th	90th
1	28	29	30	27	29	32	21	23	26	21	23	28
2	32	33	35	30	33	36	24	28	30	24	29	34
3	34	37	39	35	38	40	27	33	35	29	33	37
4	37	39	42	38	41	44	31	36	43	31	37	43
5	39	42	45	40	43	46	34	40	47	35	40	48
6	42	45	47	42	45	48	39	45	54	38	45	54
7	44	47	50	45	48	50	43	52	62	42	52	60
8	46	49	52	47	50	52	47	56	69	47	56	67
9	48	51	55	49	52	54	52	60	78	52	62	74
10	50	53	56	51	54	56	56	67	88	56	68	83
11	53	56	59	53	56	59	63	76	100	60	74	91
12	56	59	62	55	58	62	72	89	112	66	81	103
13	59	62	64	58	60	64	89	105	132	72	90	114
14	60	63	66	60	63	68	100	118	142	87	110	134
15	61	64	67	64	66	70	105	123	148	103	125	152
16	62	65	68	65	67	71	106	125	149	112	134	159
17	62	65	68	66	68	72	107	126	150	116	138	164
18	62	65	68	67	70	72	107	126	151	118	140	166
19	62	65	68	67	70	72	108	127	151	120	141	168

This chart depicts height (in inches) and weight (in pounds) from age 1 to age 19. Note that values are rounded to the nearest inch or pound. Values are given for children at the 10th, 50th, and 90th percentiles. Children at the 10th percentile are as tall (or as heavy) or taller than 10 percent of the children their age. Similarly, children at the 50th percentile are as tall or taller than 50 percent of the children their age. Finally, children at the 90th percentile are as tall or taller than 90 percent of the children their age. The data in this chart were drawn from Smith (1977) and Tanner (1978).

muscled. Bones that are still very soft at the age of 2 **ossify** (harden) and become larger and thicker. In addition, the shape of the face changes as "baby teeth" appear and disappear to be replaced with permanent teeth.

The overall rate of growth slows down from about the age of 12 months to about the age of 3 or 4 and then remains fairly steady until puberty, when the adolescent growth spurt occurs (Smith, 1977). When this spurt ends, very little growth remains to be completed.

Although the onset of puberty is greatly variable, the average girl starts her adolescent growth spurt at about age 10 and the average boy at about 12. The adolescent growth spurt usually reaches its maximum about 2 years after it begins and lasts for about 4 or 5 years. In the United States, the average man is about 5' 10" and about 175 pounds. The average woman is about 5' 4" and 130 pounds.

Physical Growth

We can use norms to make comparisons among groups of children and thereby identify potential sources of growth problems. For example, institutionalized children can be compared to children from normal homes, or children from impoverished environments can be compared to children from middle-class settings. As interesting as growth norms are, they provide us with limited information: simple patterns of how most children progress in size. These data do not provide us any insights into how or why growth occurs; they merely tell us what to expect in the way of normal patterns of growth.

Individual Growth Patterns

Although norms can be useful, they represent group averages that may not be applicable to specific individuals. As discussed earlier, there is a tremendous variation in children's growth patterns. Some healthy children grow much more slowly than average whereas others grow much more rapidly. Some children experience stops and starts in growth, while others follow a smooth pattern of development.

The variability in individual patterns of growth can sometimes be startling to observers. For example, the largest boy in first grade may be the shortest boy in his graduating class while the shortest boy in ninth grade may be 6' 4" at age 19. As we will see, this variability among individuals is also the case in patterns of motor development.

Generally speaking, the amount of physical maturation a child has completed and the amount left to be completed can be determined by maturational "benchmarks." These benchmarks—the eruption of teeth, the ways in which the bones approximate adult shape and form, and the time at which puberty begins (e.g., Smith, 1977; Vaughan et al., 1984)—are usually a part of pediatric examinations. A physician can check these "benchmarks" and provide a reasonable estimate of how much growth children have completed and how much is left.

There usually is no reason for concern if a healthy child's rate and pattern of growth vary from norms. Each child's rate of growth seems to be genetically determined (Hughes, 1980); unless some adverse influence such as severe illness or malnutrition intervenes, there is no reason to try to alter things (see Smith, 1977, for a full discussion of growth-related disorders).

Sex Differences in Growth

There are sex differences in male and female patterns of growth. These variations begin during fetal development and persist until growth is complete. For example, by 20 weeks after conception, the skeletal development of girls is about 3 weeks ahead of boys. At birth, girls are as much as 5 or 6 weeks ahead of boys in terms of skeletal structure. Some of girls' internal organs are also more completely developed. Overall size does not differ, however (Tanner, 1978).

In the first few months of life, boys grow more rapidly than girls. From about 6 or 7 months to the age of 4, however, girls regain the advantage and grow more quickly than boys (Smith, 1977). There do not seem to be any discernable differences in growth rates between the sexes from the age of 4 to the onset of puberty. Boys and girls of this age appear very similar in physique, although girls are more mature in terms of skeletal and organ development. In fact, boys do not catch up in maturity until well into adolescence.

Besides physical maturity, there are some other differences between the sexes. Girls have a greater proportion of **adipocytes** (fat cells) than boys and less muscle tissue. This difference remains consistent across all ages (Smith, 1977). Boys have larger hearts and lungs (Sherman, 1973), whereas girls have lower basal metabolism rates (that is, girls require less energy at rest to maintain their bodies than boys do) (Vaughan et al., 1984). Apparently, there also are differences in brain development: The left hemisphere of girls matures more rapidly than that of boys while the reverse is true for the right hemisphere (Winsom, 1985). These differences in brain maturation may help account for differences in language and spatially oriented tasks among boys and girls early in life. Another difference between boys and girls is in the pace of **canalization**, which is the phenomenon of returning to a normal pattern of growth after serious illness or malnutrition. Girls are apparently more resilient than boys to adverse conditions such as malnutrition. They return to their normal patterns of growth more readily than boys do following adversities (Faust, 1977).

Adolescent Growth

Adolescence is a time of major changes. In addition to cognitive and social changes that will be discussed in other chapters, there are dramatic shifts in physical growth and maturity. Central to adolescence is the attainment of **puberty,** "that time at which one becomes able to beget or conceive children" (Vaughan et al., 1984, p. 123). To fully understand the mechanisms involved in puberty, however, we must first review the endocrine glands and their functions.

Earlier in the chapter, we saw that the nervous system controlled bodily functions through the transmission of electric impulses. Another control system, the **endocrine system** (made up of glands), affects the body through the emission of chemical messengers called **hormones.** As we might expect, the nervous system and the endocrine system coordinate to govern bodily functions (Tortora & Anagnostakos, 1981).

Hormones are chemical substances (either proteins, amines, or steroids) that control the physiological activities of the cells in the body. Hormones may affect the entire body or they may cause changes in a specific organ or group of organs. They are secreted into the bloodstream by the endocrine glands and are then transmitted through the body. Figure 7-5 shows the location of the endocrine glands in the human body.

Physical Growth

FIGURE 7-5 Location of the Endocrine Glands in the Human Body. The nervous system and the endocrine system coordinate to govern bodily functions.

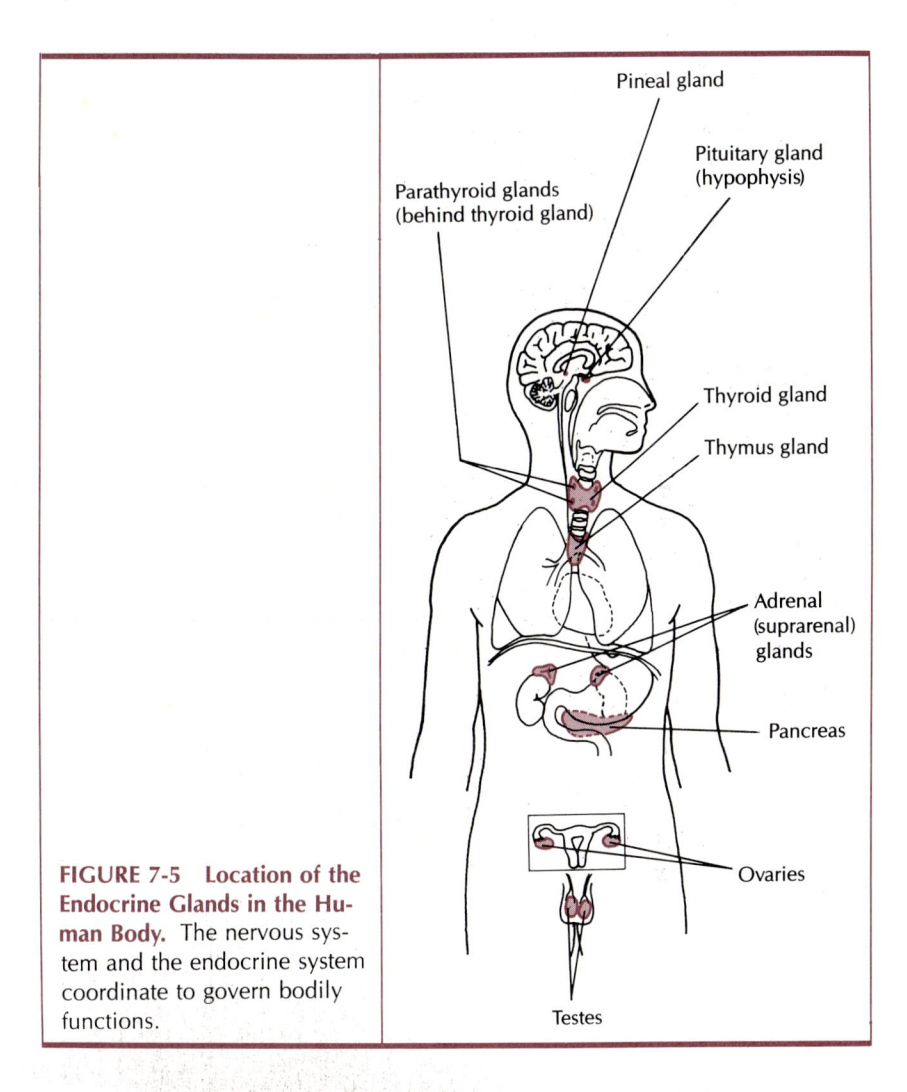

The hormones secreted by the endocrine glands cause the massive changes we see in adolescence. However, the body begins preparing itself for sexual maturity at about the age of 7 through the gradual increase in the production of some hormones by the adrenal glands. About a year or so later, there is also a gradual increase in the production of both **androgens** (male hormones) and **estrogens** (female hormones) in boys and girls. The production of estrogen greatly increases in girls between the ages of 9 and 11 until it reaches adult levels. At about the age of 11, boys undergo a rapid increase in androgen production that will reach adult levels by about the age of 13 (Kaplan, 1984).

At the onset of puberty the pituitary gland (the so-called master gland) stimulates the testes or ovaries. The testes produce **testosterone** while the ovaries produce estrogens. In addition, the adrenal glands' production of androgens greatly increases in both sexes (Vaughan et al., 1984). In both boys and girls the androgens are primarily responsible for the adolescent growth spurt, the appearance of pubic and underarm hair, further muscle development, and the activation of the sebaceous (oil) glands of the skin. In males, the androgens contribute to the development of facial hair and the deepening of the voice. Testosterone stimulates the rapid maturation of the genitals in males while estrogens have this effect in females.

As noted earlier, the adolescent growth spurt in girls usually begins at about the age of 10, reaches its maximum about 2 years later, and ends at about the age of 15. The occurrence of puberty varies widely, however. Some perfectly normal girls enter puberty at 8 years of age whereas other, equally normal girls do not enter puberty until they are 14 or 15 (Vaughan et al., 1984). In girls, the **menarche** (the first occurrence of menstruation) and the appearance of secondary sexual characteristics such as pubic hair and breasts are the benchmarks of puberty. The growth spurt typically precedes the development of secondary sexual characteristics by about 1 year (Kaplan, 1984).

Among boys, the growth spurt usually begins at about the age of 12, although there is also a great degree of variability. Growth in boys usually hits a peak at about the age of 14 and may continue for as long as 5 years. The development of the secondary sexual characteristics in boys follows the onset of the growth spurt. The appearance of a beard,

Adolescents are conscious and often oversensitive observers of their own physical growth.

the lowering of the voice, and the growth of pubic hair are all markers of puberty in boys.

Girls' earlier maturity accounts for their greater stature in the upper elementary grades and at the beginning of junior high school. This advantage in height is soon overcome by boys when they enter their growth spurts. When growth is finally completed, males are, on average, taller and heavier than females.

One of the typical characteristics of adolescent boys and girls is **asynchrony** in growth. Asynchrony refers to the fact that different parts of the body mature at different rates. Adolescent boys, for example, may have disproportionately large feet, which results in temporary awkwardness. Similarly, adolescent girls may complain about outsized noses or hands. As adolescence progresses, the effects of asynchrony become less and less noticeable as the remaining body parts catch up and both boys and girls attain the bodily proportions of adults.

Psychological Aspects of Physical Growth

The ways in which children's bodies grow strongly influence how they feel about themselves (Gollin, 1984). For example, asynchrony in growth may cause even the most stable children to worry about their appearance and to feel self-conscious. A popular, outgoing 12-year-old girl who is worried about her "impossibly big nose" may feel like hiding from everybody if she finds that she must start wearing glasses (Brooks-Gunn & Petersen, 1983). Similarly, a usually outgoing and socially adept boy may avoid interacting with new people for fear that he will once again trip over his "horribly large" feet.

Another common problem associated with physical changes in adolescence is the appearance of pimples. Unfortunately, the eruption of pimples and blackheads almost inevitably coincides with that time in life when young adolescents begin to be very self-conscious of their appearance (Kaplan, 1984). The majority of adolescents may be disgusted by their changing complexions and wish they could avoid social contact from time to time because of pimples that "everybody will see." Typically, complexion problems are transitory and have little lasting effect on adolescents' self-esteem. Sadly, though, a small percentage of adolescents (primarily boys) will suffer from true **acne,** in which the oil glands on the face (and sometimes the neck, shoulders, and back) become severely inflamed. Acne can lead to very large, painful cysts that may leave permanently disfiguring scars. Some adolescents who suffer from acne are relatively unaffected, but others become withdrawn and develop poor self-images. Luckily, most acne problems can be treated by dermatologists.

Size and Physique. Other factors in growth also influence children's feelings about themselves. Overall size and body build are important factors in succeeding at athletic activities and other kinds of play. Not surprisingly, a good deal of the prestige and popularity children obtain from their peers stems from their physical abilities (Borman, 1982; Langlois & Downs, 1979; Mussen, 1973). Beyond the relationship of size and physique to physical success, there is even a relationship between children's size and intellectual ability (Tanner, 1978). Throughout childhood, larger children tend to make higher scores on measures of intellectual abilities than their smaller peers, a phenomenon that lasts into adulthood, although its does diminish gradually (Tanner, 1978).

Mussen (1973, p. 161) described the effects of the body size and physique on personality in direct terms when he stated that

> Small, poorly coordinated, and relatively weak children are inclined to be timid, fearful, passive, and generally worried. In contrast, tall, strong, energetic, well-coordinated children of the same age are playful, self-expressive, talkative, productive and creative.

It is important to note, however, that the relationships we have described between personality and body size are only general trends. A great many small children are confident and outgoing. There is no apparent genetic relationship between physique and personality (Brooks-Gunn & Petersen, 1983). Instead, the different personal characteristics of large and small children seem to be the result of how parents and teachers treat them.

As an example, adults and other children often tend to treat small, slight children as though they were fragile, incompetent, and dependent on others. Of course, small, slight children sometimes do not do very well at sports, confirming others' attitudes and reducing their own self-confidence. One possible result of such a cycle is for slight children to avoid sports and other competitive activities, and in this way perpetuate the lack of physical ability and the responses from other people. Ultimately, such children may begin to form the personal characteristics others expect of them (timidity, dependence, etc.) because of their small size. In contrast, big, athletic children tend to be viewed as competent, independent, and sturdy. The success of such children in sports activities confirms these opinions in other people and strengthens their own self-confidence. This very positive cycle then leads to the development of the personality traits others expect of them (confidence, outgoingness, independence, etc.).

Obviously, parents' attitudes and the way in which parents interact with children make a profound difference in children's development of self-esteem. Thoughtful parents can make up for the relative disadvantages of being small and slight if they provide a supportive environment for children on the one hand and help children learn to strive for success

Parents' attitudes make a profound difference in children's development of self-esteem.

in all areas of life on the other. Parental influences are even more obvious with regard to another aspect of children's size and physique—that is, how closely children approximate a desirable weight.

About 5 percent of all American children are more than 40 percent overweight (Vaughan et al., 1984). These children, who suffer from obesity, face a far more severe stigma than that of small, slight children. Obese children are ridiculed by their peers and have fewer friends than other children. Not surprisingly, obese children often develop very negative self-images and often learn to hate themselves for being fat. As we will see later in the chapter, obesity is almost always due to the kinds of eating habits children acquire and is a problem far better avoided than treated.

Puberty and Adolescence. As we have seen, girls start their adolescent growth spurt at about the age of 10, with boys generally lagging about 2 years behind. Almost any sixth grade classroom in the United States will contain girls who are well into their growth spurts and boys who are still a year or more away from theirs. There are, however, large individual differences in when the adolescent growth spurt occurs among both girls and boys.

In general, early maturing girls and boys have advantages over later maturing children (Brooks-Gunn & Petersen, 1983). At first, early maturing girls may find it difficult being taller than anyone in class and having boys make fun of their height and developing breasts. In fact, it is not uncommon to find fifth and sixth grade girls slouching so that they will not look so tall and wearing bulky shirts so that no one will notice their breasts. It is also difficult being interested in boys and not having peers with whom they can share their interests.

The discomfort of early maturing girls, however, generally lasts for only a year or so until their more slowly maturing classmates catch up (Kaplan, 1984). By seventh or eighth grade, girls who mature early tend to be admired by both boys and girls (Brooks-Gunn & Petersen, 1983). By now, the girls are attractive to older boys and so are envied by their later maturing friends. In addition, they can give advice to later maturing girls about important topics such as menstrual cramps, choosing a bra, and boys.

Early maturing boys also have advantages over later maturing boys. They are taller, heavier, and stronger than their classmates. In addition, they tend to excel at sports and other competitive activities. In general, early maturing boys also tend to be more popular than their later maturing peers and are more likely to become leaders in school and extracurricular activities. As one would expect, early maturing boys also are likely to be interested in girls and acquire social skills for interacting with girls earlier than their later maturing classmates (Kaplan, 1984). Finally, the advantage of early maturing boys tends to last into adulthood as indicated by social and vocational success (Lipsitz, 1979).

Late maturing girls do not experience severe problems, although they do tend to lag behind early maturing girls in the development of social skills. Late maturing boys, in contrast, have some real problems. First, they are outstripped in size by early maturing girls and then by early maturing boys. Late maturing boys have to put up with the snide remarks and scorn of their classmates who themselves have just begun to mature. Studies of late maturing boys (Jones, 1957, 1965; Jones & Bayley, 1950; Mussen & Jones; 1957) indicate that they are less poised and relaxed than early maturing boys and more talkative and restless as well. As adults, late maturing boys, although they tend to reach average or above average size, tend to be less responsible, more submissive, and more prone to feelings of inferiority than early maturers. All is not negative for late maturing boys, however. They tend to be more creative, flexible, and playful as children and as adults. In adulthood, they generally seem to have a better sense of humor and a more balanced perspective on their lives.

Attaining puberty, of course, brings about a whole host of emotional, social, and intellectual changes that drastically affect the lives of adolescents and their parents. We will examine these issues in greater depth later in this volume in chapters specifically devoted to emotional, social, intellectual, and personality development.

Research

Historical Trends in Size and Maturation

Although historical research is not often associated with developmental psychology, some important findings about the nature of human growth have come directly from historical and cross-cultural research. Based on archival research, in which developmental psychologists track through years and years of records, we know that today's average adult is about five centimeters taller than his or her counterpart of 100 years ago. Similarly, foot size has increased about one size per generation over the past 100 years, while the average person's weight has increased significantly as well (Roche, 1979). Further, historical surveys of medical records indicate that today's children mature earlier than previous generations. For example, menarche typically occurred at about age 17 in 1840 and now it usually begins before age 13 (Malina, 1979). Today's boys also reach puberty about four or five years earlier than was the case in the 1840s (Malina, 1979). Another example of maturational differences can be seen by examining the age at which growth stops: Over the past 100 years this age has declined from 23 or 24 to 18 in males and 18 or 19 to 16 in females (Roche, 1977).

Why has this trend toward earlier maturation and overall larger size occurred? Cross-cultural research has yielded comparative data from developing nations that strongly suggests that the trend has been largely due to environmental factors, including the increasing quality and availability of medical care, better nutrition and knowledge of nutrition, and preventative health measures that have greatly reduced the incidence of debilitating diseases (Malina, 1979). Additional data supporting environmental variables as the cause of the trend toward earlier maturation and larger size are also available in studies that examine differences across socio-economic classes.

Generally, these studies find that middle- and upper-class children in the United States mature earlier and attain greater size than lower-class children. Tanner (1978), however, has suggested that genetic factors are also at work in the trend toward greater size. He noted that the genes for tall stature are dominant over genes for short stature. And, since Western society is highly mobile and people interbreed across all of society, the dominance of genes for tall stature may be resulting in an overall increase in the population's height.

Will the trend toward earlier maturity and greater size continue? No absolute answer can be given, but it seems safe to assume that the trend must have a limit and we may have already reached it. For example, data from 1890 to 1970 show a decrease in the average age of menarche by about 3 months every 10 years. No such decrease, however, was noted between 1970 and 1980 (Vaughan et al., 1984). Similarly, the average height of men and women has remained stable since 1960 (Roche, 1979). Roche (1979) asserted that the trend toward greater size and early maturity has stopped in most Western countries and that the trend may, in fact, reverse if adverse components of the environment such as air pollution, water pollution, toxic wastes, and radioactivity are not adequately controlled.

Beyond historical interest, the trend toward earlier maturation has some interesting implications for the social and emotional development of adolescents as well as for society in general. Early sexual maturity carries with it the potential of sexual activity at a time in life when all the consequences of sexuality may not be clearly understood. Teenage pregnancies have increased at an alarming rate over the past several years, as has the incidence of venereal disease among adolescents. Both of these phenomena are serious societal problems, leading many psychologists and educators to stress the importance of sex education in both school and home.

CHAPTER 7 Physical Growth and Motor Development

Influences on Growth

Up to this point, we have focused on physical growth by examining overall trends. Physical growth, however, does not occur in a vacuum. As we saw when we discussed prenatal development in Chapter 6, the environment can have a profound influence on human growth. In this section, we will focus on four specific influences on growth: nutrition, socioeconomic status, illness, and emotional stress.

Nutrition. One of the most common reasons for abnormal growth is nutritional deficiency (Smith, 1977; Vaughan et al., 1984). Malnourished children grow more slowly than well-fed children and, if they suffer severe and long-lasting malnutrition, attain smaller sizes as adults than their adequately nourished peers (Vaughan et al., 1984). In addition, severe malnutrition during the early years of life adversely affects the nervous system. And, while the majority of evidence available on the effects of malnutrition on the growth of the brain and spinal cord has been gained from studies of lower organisms (e.g., Mehler & Fox, 1984; Scrimshaw, 1969), it seems highly logical to conclude that similar effects occur among human beings. In particular, as the brain grows rapidly during the first 2 years of life, malnutrition at this time may have especially profound effects on children leading to lower than normal levels of myelinization and thinner, lighter cerebral cortexes (Vaughan et al., 1984). When malnutrition is neither severe nor of long duration, however, children may catch up to their normal rates of growth (canalization) after returning to an adequate diet (Acheson, 1960; Tanner, 1978).

Beyond general malnutrition, specific types of nutritional deficiencies are also harmful. **Kwashiorkor**, for example, is a very serious disease that children may contract as a result of living on a protein-deficient diet. Typically, this disease is seen among children older than 1 year who are still subsisting primarily on breast milk. Although kwashiorkor has been identified in the United States, it occurs primarily in developing countries (Vaughan et al., 1984). The disease is often fatal because of liver damage, severe diarrhea, and a general weakening of resistance (Hughes, 1980). When children who suffer from kwashiorkor are placed on an adequate diet, their symptoms are alleviated and rapid growth ensues. However, children who have suffered from kwashiorkor never catch up with normal children: Full canalization does not occur.

Another illness tied to a specific nutritional deficiency is **rickets**. Rickets is caused by a deficiency of vitamin D and can lead to the softening and distortion of bones as well as very painful muscle cramps. Severe cases of rickets can lead to uncorrectable skeletal deformities. Other nutritional deficiency diseases include beriberi, pellagra, scurvy, and xerophthalmia. **Beriberi** results from a lack of vitamin B1 (thiamine) and causes damage to the heart and peripheral nerves. Severe beriberi is fatal. **Pellagra** is caused by a deficiency of niacin in children's diets and results in skin lesions, severe diarrhea, and irrational thought. **Scurvy** is caused by a deficiency of vitamin C; it impedes skeletal growth. In addition, scurvy causes softening and swelling of the gums, pain and swelling in the legs, and in extreme cases, pain-induced paralysis. However, when children are placed on a vitamin C-rich diet, the symptoms of scurvy rapidly recede with the exception of the swelling in the legs and gums, which may take several weeks to subside. **Xerophthalmia** is a less well known, but very serious, nutritional deficiency stemming from a lack of vitamin A. This condition can result in permanent eye damage leading to blindness, as well as retardation in mental and physical growth (Vaughan et al., 1984).

The opposite of malnutrition is overnutrition. Not surprisingly, overnutrition also causes problems. Obesity (excessive fat), which was discussed earlier, is almost always due to overnutrition. Only a small percentage of obese people suffer from endocrine or metabolic disorders (see Vaughan et al., 1984). Obese children's bodies form more and larger fat cells (*adipocytes*) than their normal peers. Unfortunately, once new fat cells are formed, they do not disappear, although they may decrease greatly in size (Smith, 1977). There is also a strong tendency for obese children to become obese adolescents and obese adults (Hughes, 1980). The effects of obesity include hypertension, heart disease, diabetes, and gall bladder problems, as well as psychological difficulties.

Realistically, the treatment of obesity must include a physician-supervised diet, increased exercise, and, if necessary, some form of psychological therapy. Unfortunately, "the results of treatment for obesity are poor" (Hughes, 1980, p. 93; see also Spiegler, 1983), although support groups such as Weight Watchers report fairly positive outcomes. It seems that obesity is more effectively prevented than treated.

Illness. Most of the common childhood illnesses have little, if any, prolonged effect on growth. Even when children do suffer from protracted illness, they tend to catch up to their normal levels of growth after recovery (canalization). Despite the generally mild effects of most illnesses on children's overall growth, we must keep in mind that specific illnesses can have powerfully harmful effects on development (Smith, 1977). Even such common infections as the measles, the mumps, and chicken pox can be fatal. There is simply no substitute for prevention. Children must be vaccinated against illnesses.

Emotional Stress. The basic day-to-day emotional stresses children encounter seem to have little impact on growth (Smith, 1977; Tanner, 1978). The upset of losing a pair of mittens or breaking the most expensive lamp in the house is very real but short-term. Generally, homes in

Highlights

Childhood Obesity

In a 1986 workshop on childhood obesity (*Science*, 1986) sponsored by the National Institute of Child Health and Human Development, participants reached startling conclusions that have a direct bearing on child-rearing practices.

Despite our society's tremendous emphasis on thinness, healthy lifestyles, and increasing knowledge of good nutritional practices, more children than ever before are obese. The prevalence of obesity among American children increased dramatically between 1966 and 1986—a 54 percent increase among 6- to 11-year-olds and a 39 percent increase among 12- to 17-year-olds. Worse, the once conventional wisdom that fat children outgrow their weight problems does not seem to be true. *Science* (1986) reported that about 40 percent of obese 7-year-olds go on to become obese adults, while 70 percent of obese adolescents become obese adults.

Given the health and psychological problems associated with obesity, understanding the causes of obesity becomes crucial. True, almost all obesity results from overnutrition, but understanding what leads to overnutrition is a very difficult proposition. According to William Dietz of the New England Medical Center Hospital in Boston, only very slight differences may lead to obesity. He points out that

> Most kids can become obese by eating as little as 50 extra calories per day. That would lead to an excess weight gain of 5 pounds per year. There are no data to support the idea that obese kids are any less efficient in burning off calories and there are no data to support the idea that obese kids massively overeat (*Science*, 1986, p. 20.)

There is a definite hereditary factor involved in obesity, as reported by Albert Stunkard of the University of Pennsylvania at the workshop. His study of adoptive children has shown positive correlations between the weight of biological parents and children they gave up for adoption, but not between adoptive parents and their adopted children. Even so, the evidence provided in the workshop strongly implicates environmental influences as the major cause of overnutrition.

Dietz, for example, analyzed a large amount of data gathered by the National Center for Health Statistics and concluded that "next to prior obesity, television viewing is the strongest predictor of subsequent obesity" (*Science*, 1986, p. 20). As the amount of time spent watching television increased, so too did the odds of becoming obese. Watching large amounts of television, of course, could influence overnutrition in three ways: (1)

children burn fewer calories watching television than they do when engaged in other activities, (2) children tend to eat when watching television, and (3) television communicates the message that if you eat the foods advertised, you will be thin—almost everybody on television is thin.

Other data supporting environmental effects as the major cause of obesity were also presented at the workshop. In particular, the finding that 30 percent of women of the lower socioeconomic level in the United States are obese, as opposed to 15 percent of middle- and 5 percent of upper-class women was a strong argument for environmental effects.

The workshop participants agreed that the environment was the dominant influence on the likelihood of overnutrition, but they also agreed that the exact nature of environmental effects leading to overnutrition are not yet clearly understood. Some direct guidelines for preventing obesity and working with obese children, however, can be drawn directly from the workshop proceedings. First, prevention is best implemented by insuring that proper nutritional practices are followed. Second, all children should be encouraged to be physically active. Watching television should be limited and children should be urged to run, jump, and play ball. In fact, even other "quiet" activities such as reading and playing board games use more calories than watching television. Third, weight loss should be gradual and monitored by a physician. Fourth, special stress must be placed on maintaining a proper weight after weight loss. George Blackburn of Harvard Medical School told the workshop of his research with obese patients who had regained weight originally lost by dieting. He found that each time a patient went on a new diet after regaining previously lost weight, the new weight loss became more difficult. Kelly Brownell and Elliot Stellar of the University of Pennsylvania and M. R. C. Greenwood of Vassar College presented animal research data to support Blackburn's report. In their study, they made rats obese and then put them on a diet in order to reduce them to their normal weight. After the rats reached their normal weight, Brownell and his colleagues once again brought them back to their earlier levels of obesity. Then they put the rats back on exactly the same diet they were put on in the first place. Finally, the rats were once again put on the same high calorie diet that made them obese in the first place. The results were striking—during the first diet the rats lost their excess weight in 21 days and then regained it in 46 days. The second time the rats took 46 days to lose the weight and only 14 to gain it all back! Apparently, weight loss becomes more and more difficult each time a person goes on a diet.

which children are loved and provided with an atmosphere of positive regard are not sources of the kinds of severe emotional stress that can affect growth. However, children reared in environments in which emotional stress is severe may experience a reduction of the growth hormone that can lead to so-called psychosocial dwarfism (Gardner, 1972), a condition characterized by a cessation of growth.

Such stress is most commonly seen in emotionally barren homes or homes in which emotional or psychological abuse occurs (Gottfried, 1984; Steptoe & Mathews, 1984). Fortunately, when children are taken from such extremely stressful environments and placed in emotionally supportive settings, catch-up growth usually occurs.

Socioeconomic Status. The overall patterns of children's growth are related to their socioeconomic class. In general, upper- and middle-class children are larger at all ages than their lower-class peers (Smith, 1977). Causes of the differences in size are partly nutritional, although the incidence of obesity is seven times higher among lower-class children than among middle-class children (Smith, 1977). Nutrition alone, however, does not tell the whole story. Lower-class children generally receive far less medical care than middle-class children do and, as a consequence, they suffer far more illnesses and nagging injuries. In addition, lower-class children generally have poorer sleeping and exercise habits and experience greater levels of emotional stress. Further, basic knowledge of child care is typically more limited among lower-class parents than among middle-class parents.

Applications: Facilitating Children's Growth

The following guidelines were developed on the basis of our review of literature on physical growth. They emphasize the importance of establishing a supportive home environment in which the parents are well informed about health care.

1. *See that children receive adequate nutrition*. As the effects of malnutrition can be very severe, the best approach is to be sure that children eat properly. Information about planning diets can be obtained from county extension agents, nutritionists, family physicians and pediatricians, and the public library. Parents should understand the dietary requirements of children. In the case of children from impoverished families, parents should take advantage of social welfare agencies including Aid to Dependent Children, free or reduced-price lunch programs, and food stamp programs. Private agencies (e.g., church-sponsored social services) may also be sources of aid for feeding children.

2. *Instill proper eating habits*. Having nutritious food available and eating it are often two different things. To avoid nutritional deficiencies,

children should learn to eat well-balanced meals. Further, the amount children eat, when they eat, and the quality of their snacks should be carefully considered. Eating too much in general can lead to problems but so may consuming too much salt, too much caffeine, or too much sugar. In large part, parents can help their children by modeling appropriate eating habits and rewarding children's appropriate choices.

3. *Immunize children.* Normally, a family physician or a pediatrician takes care of this as a matter of course in working with parents. Most city or county health agencies offer immunizations at greatly reduced cost or free of charge.

4. *Arrange for regular medical care.* Most middle-class families work with a family physician and so have readily available medical care. Impoverished families may not be able to establish long-term relationships with physicians, but arrangements can be made through social welfare agencies for adequate medical care. It is important to note that medical care is a part of the prevention of illness as well as its treatment. Parents should follow the guidelines for check-ups suggested by their physicians as a way of preventing problems.

5. *Establish an emotionally secure and supportive home environment.* There is no substitute for high-quality emotional support in the home. Children should feel loved and should not find the home a place of continuing emotional stress.

6. *Be aware of how physical development may influence children's self-images.* As we have seen, children's stature and physiques can have a powerful effect on children's self-images. Parents can counter the negative effects of small stature by reinforcing children's successes and helping children strive for competence in many areas. Parents can also work toward avoiding stereotypes associated with small, slight children and thereby help children avoid the development of personal characteristics such as timidity and dependence. With adolescents, parents need to remain aware that changing bodies can have a profound effect on how adolescents feel about themselves. A warm, supportive psychological environment in the home can make the transitions of adolescence far easier.

7. *Be aware of available social services.* We live in a highly complex world in which many of us are unaware of available services. Both parents and professionals need to know what services are available and how to take advantage of them. Medical care, counseling, and psychotherapy are available at reduced or no cost in almost all areas of the United States.

Motor Development

As important as a knowledge of physical growth is to our understanding of development, we also need to examine how the capabilities of the human body change. The development of motor abilities follows a predictable sequence. Children sit before they can stand and crawl before they can walk. The pattern of motor development is governed by the principles of cephalocaudal and proximodistal change. Babies first gain control over their head, neck, and shoulder muscles. Later, as development proceeds, babies are able to govern the movements of their arms and legs.

In addition to the cephalocaudal and proximodistal nature of motor development, the principle of differentiation and integration is also important. Differentiation can be seen in the fact that children are able to gain gross motor control over large areas of the body before they can attain careful control over small groups of muscles. As an example, 1-year-old children can pick up and hold objects with their hands but they cannot tie a ribbon. Integration is seen as children are able to combine or integrate several independent muscle movements into a larger, more complex, more sophisticated whole. Skipping rope, for example, is an extremely complex activity that requires the integration of a whole host of individual actions.

Reflexes in the Newborn

As we have seen, newborn babies' behaviors are governed by the diencephalon and midbrain and are primarily reflexive (involuntary) in nature. As the cerebral cortex develops, voluntary (nonreflexive) behaviors appear. Some of the more common reflexes in newborn babies described by Hottinger (1980) are the sucking, Moro (startle), grasping, Babinski, and rooting reflexes (see Table 7-2).

The **sucking reflex** is one of the most interesting and complex reflexes in newborn babies. Sucking requires the coordination of a host of separate muscle movements. The baby must pull in its cheeks in rhythmic fashion, squeeze the nipple with its tongue and palate, and, at the same time, coordinate both swallowing and breathing. The complexity and amazing adaptability of this reflex has generated a great deal of research. Piaget (1963), for example, studied it in detail, believing that reflexes formed the basis for cognitive development.

The **Moro reflex** is caused by startling stimuli such as loud noises, a feeling of falling, or sudden flashes of light. This reflex consists of throwing the arms out and away from the body and then bringing them back in again. The Moro reflex is present at birth and lasts through about the first 4 months of life before disappearing, although "a startle pattern continues to exist in adults" (Hottinger, 1980, p. 20).

The **grasping reflex** occurs when the palm of a baby's hand is pressed and the baby's fingers close around the object in its hand. This

Motor Development

TABLE 7-2 Responses of the Newborn Infant

Eyelid Responses.	Opens and closes eyelids; this appears spontaneously and in response to a variety of external stimuli.
Pupillary Response	Pupils contract and expand in response to light. The pupils tend to be consensual (when one is stimulated, the other eye also responds).
Ocular Response	There are pursuit movements, and saccadic movements (quick, jerky movements used later in reading).
	There is coordination of the eyes, with convergence being rare. Eyes in sleep are up and sideways as in the adult.
Tear Secretion	Tear secretion is unusual in the newborn but has been observed during crying and with nasal irritation.
Facial and Mouth Response	Opens and closes mouth; lips move in response to touch; sucking occurs either spontaneously or in response to tactual or taste stimuli; smiles; yawns; frowns; wrinkles forehead; grimaces.
Throat Responses	Crying is usually accompanied by activity of arms and legs. Swallowing occurs in all newborn infants, vomiting may occur, hiccupping may occur, sneezing may occur, and holding the breath has been reported.
Head and Neck Responses	Moves head upward and downward and turns face to side in response to some stimuli. As early as two days of age the baby can balance his head in response to changes in bodily positions.
Head and Arm Responses	Closes hand in response to tactual stimulation of fingers and palm. Arm flexion can be elicited with pricking the hand or a tap on the hand. Rubs his face, and moves his arms. The startle response is evident—throws arms outward if startled.
Trunk Reactions	Arches back—can be produced by pinching the nose.

TABLE 7-2 (cont.)

Trunk Reactions (cont.)	Twisting—head rotates one direction, shoulders and pelvis in the opposite direction.
	Abdominal reflex—draws in stomach in response to needle stimulus.
Sexual Responses	Cremasteric reflex—raising of testes to stimulation of inner thighs.
	Penis erection.
Foot and Leg Responses	Achilles tendon reflex is present in most newborn babies.
	Flexion of leg—this action is accompanied by plantor flexion of the foot.
	Kicking consists of a pedaling action and a simultaneous flexion and extension of both legs.
	Stepping movements occur when the child is held upright with its feet touching a surface.
	Toe phenomenon consists of spreading the toes when the sole of the foot is stroked.
Coordinate Responses of Many Body Parts	Resting and sleeping position—the legs are flexed, fists closed, upper arm straight out from the shoulders with forearms flexed at right angles so they are lying parallel with the head.
	Opisthotonis position—this is a strong dorsal flexion from head to heels (often occurs in crying).
	Backbone reflex—this is a concave bending of a side that is stimulated with a stroke or a tickle.
	Lifting head and rear quarters simultaneously.
	Fencing position—when the baby's head is rotated to one side, the arm toward which the head is rotated will extend and the opposite arm will flex.
	Springing position—this occurs when the infant is held upright and inclined forward. The arms extend forward and the legs are brought up.
	Startle response—this response consists of throwing the arms apart, spreading the fingers, extending the legs and throwing the head back. It sometimes occurs with no apparent stimulation but is usually a response to stimuli which could frighten, such as noise, falling or other sudden occurrences.

TABLE 7-2 (cont.)

Coordinate Responses of Many Body Parts (cont.)	Mass activity—general unrest and crying.
	Creeping—this may occur when newborn is placed in a prone position. The legs and arms are drawn under the body and the head lifted. The legs push and the arms become more active.
	Nursing posture—if an infant is hungry and given a nipple, it begins to nurse and at the same time it flexes its arms so they are pulled across the body with the fists toward the chin. The legs and toes are raised. The position relaxes as the child's hunger subsides.

Abridged from W. Dennis. (1934). A description and classification of the responses of the newborn infant. *Psychological Bulletin, 31,* 5–22. Copyright 1934 by the American Psychological Association. Adapted by permission.

Later Motor Development

reflex is powerful: Babies' grips may be strong enough to allow them to support their own weight for a moment or two (Hottinger, 1980). Anyone who has ever placed his or her index finger on a baby's palm has probably seen the grasping reflex, which is present before birth and typically lasts for only a few months.

The **Babinski reflex** is set off by stroking the bottom of an infant's foot, to which the baby responds by extending and fanning out its toes. The **rooting reflex** occurs when a hungry infant's face is touched, producing quick, jerky movements of the baby's head until its mouth is lined up with the source of the stimulation (Hottinger, 1980). Both the Babinski and the rooting reflexes disappear several months after birth.

From birth to about 6 weeks there is a general improvement of reflexes but little motor learning (Hottinger, 1980). By 6 weeks, however, significant cortical growth has occurred and motor development accelerates rapidly. For example, the grasping reflex is gradually replaced by voluntary grasping, a change clearly apparent by 3½ months. By 10 weeks, a baby can hold its head firmly erect when held at someone's shoulder. By about 2½ months, most babies can sit with support and at about 5½ months they can sit alone for brief periods of time.

Table 7-3 lists some of the landmarks of motor development and the ages at which these abilities typically emerge. As you can see, the tasks indicate the basic cephalocaudal and proximodistal progression one would expect, coupled with increasing differentiation and integration. What are not shown are the hundreds of practice responses that

TABLE 7-3 Landmarks of Motor Development and Ages of Occurrence

Age	Motor Ability
.2 months	crawling movements
.5 months	lifts head at shoulders
1.7 months	arm thrusts in play
1.9 months	head erect—vertical
2.6 months	dorsal suspension—lifts head
2.9 months	head erect and steady
3.4 months	turns from side to back
3.5 months	sits with support
4.1 months	beginning thumb opposition
5.0 months	turns from back to side
5.4 months	effort to sit
5.7 months	sits alone momentarily
6.2 months	pulls to sitting position
6.2 months	sits alone 30 seconds or more
7.0 months	rolls from back to stomach
7.6 months	complete thumb opposition
8.5 months	sits alone with good coordination
9.2 months	prewalking progression
9.3 months	fine prehension with pellet
9.4 months	raises self to sitting position
10.5 months	pulls to standing position
10.6 months	stands up
11.6 months	walks with help
12.5 months	stands alone
13.0 months	walks alone
16.5 months	walks sideways
16.9 months	walks backward
20.3 months	walks upstairs with help
24.3 months	walks upstairs alone
24.5 months	walks downstairs alone
28.0 months	jumps off floor with both feet
29.2 months	stands on left foot alone
29.3 months	stands on right foot alone
30.1 months	walks on tiptoes
32.1 months	jumps from chair
35.5 months	walks upstairs alternating forward foot
27.1 months	jumps from height of 30 cm
37.3 months	distance jump—10–35 cm
39.2 months	distance jump—36–40 cm
41.5 months	jumps over rope less than 20 cm high
48.4 months	distance jump—60–65 cm
49.3 months	hops on right foot less than 2 cm
50.0 months	walks downstairs alternating forward foot

Abridged from N. Bayley (1935). The development of motor abilities during the first three years. *Society for Research in Child Development,* Monograph No. 1, 1-26.

occurred prior to the actual emergence of a motor ability. Anyone who has observed a baby learning to walk, for example, has seen innumerable first steps on shaky, chubby legs followed by a sudden loss of balance or support and the inevitable crash landing on a (hopefully) thick diaper.

Milestones in Motor Development. The first maneuver babies are able to perform that uses the whole body is rolling over. Many babies begin to roll over before 5 months of age and take great pleasure in it—rolling over and over and laughing at their ability. Some babies even use rolling over as a means of getting from one place to another. One of the authors, for example, was reading one evening while his 6-month-old daughter played on the carpet at his feet. When he looked up from his book to check on the baby, she had rolled across the room and was rolling and laughing her way down the hall.

Sitting up is a benchmark in motor development that many parents focus on. Sitting up, like rolling over, requires considerable strength and the coordination of neck, shoulder, back, abdominal, and leg muscles. Many babies are able to sit propped up by pillows or plush toys by about 4 months of age but most are not able to sit independently for long until they are about 7 to 8 months of age.

Not long after they are able to roll over, most babies begin to crawl. In crawling, babies pull themselves along with their hands while lying on their stomachs. Gradually, the arms and legs begin to be coordinated so that the legs push as the hands pull. When the coordination becomes better and better, babies begin to creep—moving around on their hands and knees with their tummies off the floor. Some babies begin to creep as early as 5 months, others do not until they are 9 months or so. Creeping is usually accompanied by attempts to pull up to a standing position. Standing alone, however, usually does not occur until babies are just about 1 year old.

Parents have perhaps taken more photographs of their babies' first steps than photographers have of any other events in human history. Babies can often walk with help when they are as young as 9 months, but most babies take their first independent steps at about 1 year of age. In many ways, walking is the culmination of the first year's motor development, as the separate skills developed in sitting, standing, and crawling coordinate in the sophisticated task of walking.

Practice and Motor Development. Climbing, jumping, hopping, galloping, and skipping all make their appearance in sequence between the ages of 2 and 6 or 7. While these abilities are developing, throwing, catching, and ball bouncing also develop, although these skills are dependent in large part on environmental factors (Hottinger, 1980). Practice is necessary for the complete development of any of the skills listed above: Just consider the relative lack of throwing ability seen in men from cultures that do not emphasize throwing in play and in some Americans who have not had opportunities to play softball or baseball.

Complex motor skills such as hitting a baseball, riding a bicycle, and crocheting all require extensive practice in order for all the involved muscle movements to become fully integrated (Corbin, 1980). Differences in opportunities to practice skills are usually evident among children starting school. In any class of kindergarteners, some of the children will already be able to cut along lines with scissors, fold paper, hold pencils and crayons correctly, and use rulers and templates. Other, equally bright and equally mature children may not possess these skills due to lack of practice (Stewart, 1980).

Practice alone, however, will not ensure the development of physical skills. There is a continued interaction among physical growth, maturation, and skills development. Activities such as skipping, throwing a ball, and riding a bicycle all depend on the continued growth and maturation of the body. Since we are aware that children grow at different rates, it should come as no surprise to find that there are also vast individual differences in the development of motor skills (Lockhart, 1980).

Differences in Motor Development

Many variables seem related to differences in patterns of motor development. Among the most frequently studied are the sex and race of children.

Sex Differences. From birth until about the age of 4 or so, girls typically develop motor skills somewhat more rapidly than boys. However, from about the age of 3 on, boys are usually superior to girls in the performance of skills that require strength, an advantage that becomes more apparent as they progress through school. Girls do continue to retain the advantage in tasks requiring balance and rhythm activities (Malina, 1980).

For years it was thought that these differences between the sexes were due primarily to genetic factors. More recently, however, environmental causes for these differences have been considered. Malina (1980), for example, has argued that boys and girls are encouraged to take part in activities that require very different patterns of physical skills. Boys typically engage in far more rough and tumble play whereas girls spend more of their time in activities requiring finer motor skills. These contrasting patterns of play, of course, represent different kinds of practice and so the possibility exists that the differences we observe between the sexes in motor development may be due, at least in part, to social factors.

Although differences in motor skills have some basis in heredity, environmental factors cannot be discounted.

In fact, for many play activities, differences in strength, balance, and rhythm do not result in advantages for the different sexes so much as they bring about different styles of play. For example, in mixed-league softball, it is not at all unusual to find the infield positions dominated by girls, with boys relegated to the outfield. Although boys may have stronger arms and be able to swing bats more vigorously, girls often have better balance and timing, making them better suited to positions that require these skills. The 10-year-old daughter of one of the authors, for instance, plays second base niftily and can make the pivot at second better than any boy on the team. Her arm, although accurate, is probably weaker than that of any male teammate, and so while she is a real asset at second base, she probably would be a poorer outfielder than most of the boys.

Racial Differences. Several studies have been conducted on differences between blacks and whites in motor development (see Malina, 1980, for an integrative review). The majority of these studies report that black children develop motor skills at a significantly greater pace than white children up to about the age of 3. As is the case in sex differences, both genetic and environmental hypotheses have been offered to account for these differences. It is, of course, possible that the genes associated with the pace of motor development differ somewhat between the races. Possibly differences in development are due to economic conditions, child-rearing practices, parental expectations, or other environmental factors. Malina (1980) suggests that there are no compelling data to support any of these variables as the major source of racial differences in motor development.

Having fun and feeling good about oneself is an important outcome of children's games.

Motor Development and Self-Image

As is the case in stature and physique, there is a relationship between children's self-images and their ability to perform motor tasks. In general, children who excel at physical activities are admired and tend to form positive self-images. Children poor at physical activities may be scorned and tend to form less positive self-images. Of course, children who succeed at physical activities tend to find them rewarding and engage in them more than other children, thereby gaining considerable practice and increasing the likelihood that they will succeed at these activities in the future. In contrast, children who are not good at physical activities are more likely to avoid them, not gain practice, and thereby guarantee failure in the future.

Although sports and other competitive activities are perhaps overemphasized in our culture, having fun and feeling good about oneself is an important outcome of children's games. Parents, of course, can opt to try to keep their nonathletic children away from all sports and other competitive activities, but this does not seem like a completely reasonable solution. Parents cannot control playground activities nor can they keep children from wanting to play games with one another in a neighbor's yard. Instead, it seems that regardless of the activity in question—softball, tennis, basketball, swimming, handball, and so on—children are likely to benefit most when they play in nonpressured situations, with children of similar levels of ability, and when they have a real chance for success. Ultimately, parents need to work with children in developing motor skills, in choosing organized activities appropriate for their children, and in providing a warm and accepting environment that stresses growth.

Summary

In this chapter we reviewed physical growth and motor development. The basic principles of growth and development—cephalocaudal development, proximodistal development, and differentiation and integration—govern all aspects of physical growth and motor development. That is, growth proceeds from head to foot and from the center of the body outwards as parts of the body and their functions first become clearly separate and then integrated.

Overall patterns of growth were outlined with an emphasis on viewing human growth from the perspective of norms. Despite the usefulness of norms, we must keep in mind that each child will have his or her own unique pattern of growth that may or may not match up to tables of norms.

An especially crucial aspect of growth, the growth of the brain and nervous system, was examined in some detail. The nervous system consists of the peripheral nervous system (PNS) and the central nervous system (CNS). The CNS consists of the brain and spinal cord whereas the PNS is made up of all the nerve tissue lying outside of the CNS. The brain has four basic components: the brain stem, the diencephalon, the cerebrum, and the cerebellum. At birth, the cerebrum, which will become the single largest part of the brain, is comparatively small. The limited capacity of the cerebrum and the fairly well-developed nature of the brain stem and diencephalon allow for reflexes in newborn babies but not much in the way of voluntary behavior. Voluntary behavior and sophisticated thinking must await the growth and refinement of the cerebral cortex and cerebellum.

There are general differences between the sexes in terms of physical development. Girls tend to develop somewhat more rapidly than boys and also show a different pattern of brain development in which the left hemispere of girls matures more rapidly than the right, with the reverse true of boys.

One of the most important events in life is puberty, or the attainment of sexual maturity. Sexual maturity is preceded by a growth spurt and is usually marked by the development of secondary sexual characteristics. The onset of puberty is guided by changes in the secretions of the endocrine glands.

We continued our discussion of physical growth by examining historical trends in growth and maturation. In general, today's children mature earlier and grow larger than children did in the past. It does seem, however, that this trend toward increasing size and early maturation is near an end.

The influence of environmental variables on physical growth was reviewed with particular attention given to nutritional deficits, illness, emotional stress, and socioeconomic status. Each child has a genetically predetermined pattern of growth that will be followed if no adverse situations are encountered. However, even severe malnutrition and illness may be overcome by the growth process as we see children return to their normal rates of growth (canalization) after adverse conditions have been cleared up.

The last section of our chapter reviewed motor development. As was the case in physical growth, we saw that motor development also follows the principles of cephalocaudal and proximodistal development coupled with the continued differentiation and integration of motor skills. We then discussed individual differences in motor development and saw evidence for both sex and race differences in motor skills development.

Key Terms

cephalocaudal development
proximodistal development
differentiation
integration
automaticity
central nervous system (CNS)

peripheral nervous system (PNS)
effector
afferent fibers
efferent fibers
autonomic nervous system
sympathetic nerve fibers
parasympathetic nerve fibers
spinal reflexes
supraspinal activities
brain stem
medulla oblongata
pons varolii
midbrain
diencephalon
thalamus
hypothalamus
cerebrum
cerebral cortex
cerebellum

neurons
glial cells
myelin
myelinization
Broca's area
aphasia
Wernicke's area
cerebral hemispheres
corpus callosum
lateralization
handedness
norms
ossification
adipocytes
canalization
puberty
endocrine system
hormones
androgens

estrogens
testosterone
menarche
asychrony
acne
obesity
kwashiorkor
rickets
beriberi
pellagra
scurvy
xerophthalmia
sucking reflex
Moro reflex
grasping reflex
Babinski reflex
rooting reflex

Suggested Readings

Brooks-Gunn, J., & Petersen, A. C. (1983). *Girls at puberty: Biological and psychosocial perspectives.* New York: Plenum. This book presents a readable yet thorough discussion of puberty in girls. No other source pulls together such a wealth of information on this topic.

Hardy, J. B., Drage, J. S., & Jackson, E. C. (1979). *The first year of life: The collaborative perinatal project of the National Institute of Neurological and Communicative Disorders and Stroke.* Baltimore: The Johns Hopkins University Press. Despite its imposing title, this book should be read by all new parents. Nowhere else is there such a thorough and readable description of the first year of a baby's life.

Fincher, J. (1982). *The brain: Mystery of matter and mind.* New York: Scribner. Fincher's book is fine reading on a topic that is of great importance in understanding child development.

Gottfried, A. W. (1984). *Home environment and early cognitive development.* New York: Academic Press. Although the focus of this book is primarily cognitive development, there is a very good treatment of the influence of the home environment on physical and social development.

The Diagram Group. (1982) *The brain: A user's manual.* New York: Putnam. This book is well-written and informative for the lay reader interested in more information about the functions of the human brain.

Application Exercise
7-1 The Brain and Nervous System

Directions: Below is a set of human activities. For each one, identify the component of the brain or nervous system that is most directly related to the activities.

1. remembering yesterday's headline
2. reading this text
3. breathing
4. feeling hungry
5. a baby's Babinski reflex
6. sneezing
7. maintaining balance
8. translating thought into speech
9. responding to pain
10. head reflexes

PART IV

Intellectual Development

In the first three sections of this book we have discussed the history, theories, and methods of the field of developmental psychology; the biological and social foundations of development; and the course of physical and motor development from conception to adulthood. We now turn to a new general topic of equally profound importance. The next five chapters will focus on the development of the intellect. What do children know? How do they learn, remember, think, and understand? How do their intellectual competencies change as they develop? These are the sort of questions that are addressed by specialists in cognitive (intellectual) development.

We begin the new section with a chapter on general theories of cognitive development. In the remaining four chapters, we will consider in more detail the development of four particularly important aspects of cognition: perception, memory, language, and reasoning.

CHAPTER 8

Theories of Cognitive Development

*We are attempting to interpret knowledge in
terms of its own construction.*
   —*Jean Piaget*

Piaget's Theory

Cognition refers to *knowing*. Psychologists who study the development of cognition are interested in the development of children's abilities to perceive their environments, to learn new things, to understand and integrate complex ideas, to comprehend and use language, to recognize the familiar and recall the past, and to think creatively and reason rigorously. Developmental psychologists have conducted thousands of studies on the development of specific cognitive abilities. We will consider much of this work in Chapters 9 through 12. First, however, we will consider cognitive development as a whole. We will focus on **two major theoretical approaches to the study of cognitive development: (1) Piagetian theory and (2) the information-processing perspective.**

Consider the following examples of individuals exploring the physical world:

> Laurent (age 10 months) is lying on his back but nevertheless resumes his experiments of the day before. He grasps in succession a celluloid swan, a box, etc., stretches out his arms and lets them fall. Sometimes he stretches out his arm vertically, sometimes he holds it obliquely, in front of or behind his eyes, etc. When the object falls in a new position (for example, on his pillow), he lets it fall two or three times more on the same place, as though to study the spatial relation; then he modifies the situation (Piaget, 1963, p. 269).

Dei (age 16 years) is exploring the flexibility of a set of rods. The experimenter is Bärbel Inhelder, Piaget's major collaborator. Using Piaget's clinical interview methodology (see Chapter 3), she asks Dei what factors are at work. The conversation proceeds as follows:

Dei: Weight, materials, the length of the rod, perhaps the form.

Inhelder: Can you prove your hypotheses?

Dei compares the 200 gram and 300 gram weights on the same steel rod.

Dei:	You see, the role of weight is demonstrated. For the material, I don't know.
Inhelder:	Take these steel ones and these copper ones.
Dei:	I think I have to take two rods with the same form. Then to demonstrate the role of the metal I compare these two [steel and brass, identical in form, length, and cross-sectional area, with 300 grams on each]. To demonstrate the role of the form, I can compare these two [round and square, identical in material, length, and cross sectional area].
Inhelder:	Can the same thing be proved with these two? [rods varying in cross-sectional area as well as form]
Dei:	No, because that one is much narrower.

(Adapted from Inhelder & Piaget, 1958, p. 60)

Are you struck by the similarities between the two children, or are you more impressed by the differences? Jean Piaget was fascinated by both. He saw significance both in those aspects of cognition (knowing) that change as one's development progresses and in those aspects that appear to be stable. In the pages to follow, we will discuss Piaget's views on the nature of cognition, his ideas about the process of intellectual development, and his proposals concerning stages of cognitive development. You will see how children's thought processes become increasingly symbolic, logical, and abstract over a period of many years.

The Nature of Intelligence

How smart is Suzy? Is Suzy smarter than Robert? These kinds of questions come to mind when we hear the word **intelligence**. They are questions about individual differences: How intelligent is a given person compared to someone else or to people in general?

Piaget did not deny that some people are brighter than others, but this is not what interested him. Even the least intelligent child, in Piaget's eyes, has intelligence. Everyone has knowledge about the world, makes sense of the environment in terms of that knowledge, and improves that knowledge by better organizing it and better adapting it to reality. Instead of emphasizing individual differences, Piaget focused on questions such as: What is knowledge? How is it organized? How do we use it? How does it change?

To understand Piaget's answers to these sorts of questions, reconsider the earlier description of 10-month-old Laurent's behavior. Why was Piaget interested in the childish games Laurent played with his various toys? We can answer this question by considering Piaget's interpretations of Laurent's behavior. In Piaget's view, Laurent was understanding his environment (the swan, box, and so on) by acting upon it (grasping, dropping, and so on). Piaget referred to the actions that Laurent was capable of as **schemes** and the process of using these schemes to make sense of the world as **assimilation**. For example, he assimilates the swan to his grasping scheme. But one cannot grasp a swan and a box in quite the same way. Thus, Laurent must **accommodate** his grasping scheme to the unique characteristics of the swan, the box, or any other graspable object. Moreover, Laurent **organizes** his schemes of grasping and dropping for purposes of his systematic exploration of objects: He grasps and then drops. Finally, we see that Laurent's schemes of grasping and dropping are well-suited for dealing with toy swans and boxes: That is, they are **adapted** to the environment. In observing just a few seconds of infant behavior, we see what Piaget considered some of the major properties of intelligence: It is an *organization* of *schemes* that are *adapted* to the child's environment, meaning that the schemes can *assimilate* the environment and simultaneously *accommodate* to its unique features.

It is clear that Dei, the 16-year-old in the other example, is showing a much more sophisticated level of intelligence. But her systematic isolation of variables (for example, studying the difference between steel and brass rods of the same form and length) can also be thought of as a scheme. Isolating a variable is a highly abstract and sophisticated pattern of thinking, but, like Laurent's grasping scheme, is a way of knowing that can be applied to make sense of a variety of environments. Dei analyzes the properties of rods by assimilating them to her isolation-of-variables scheme, just as Laurent deals with the swan by assimilating it to his grasping and dropping schemes. As Dei assimilates rods to her isolation-of-variables scheme and accommodates to the unique features of each rod, her behavior again shows the organized and adaptive nature of intelligence, this time at a higher stage of development.

The Process of Intellectual Development

We have seen that Laurent and Dei have much in common. But there also are obvious differences in their intellectual abilities. Both show intelligence; but the adolescent, Dei, shows a much more sophisticated way of dealing with the world. How can we explain the dramatic changes in intellectual ability as children mature?

Piaget considered and rejected two obvious possibilities. The first possibility is that new intellectual abilities are learned from the environment. For example, Dei might have been taught a strategy for isolating variables that Laurent has not yet encountered. The second possibility is that all intellectual abilities are programmed in the genes and emerge during the course of maturation. For example, there might be an age at which the ability to isolate variables simply appears in all normal children, regardless of their environments.

Rejecting both of these alternatives, Piaget proposed a middle-ground position which he called **constructivism**. The central idea of constructivism is that individuals construct their own knowledge during

CHAPTER 8 Theories of Cognitive Development

Highlights

Definitions of Piagetian Terms

The originality of many of Piaget's views can make his theory difficult to understand. Because his theory involves many novel concepts, he was forced either to invent new terminology or to give new meanings to old words. To give you a head start, here are brief definitions of some of Piaget's central concepts. All of these terms are discussed in greater detail elsewhere in this chapter. To really understand Piaget, one must grasp how the various concepts interrelate as part of his broader theory.

Accommodation. Fitting or adjusting one's schemes to the particular aspect of the environment that one is assimilating.

Adaptation. The tendency of knowledge to be suited to one's environment.

Assimilation. Fitting the environment to one's schemes in order to make sense of it. This involves mentally or physically acting on the environment.

Centration. A tendency to focus on a single dimension of a problem or situation.

Clinical interview. A methodology for studying thinking through flexible questioning.

Concrete operations. A stage of advanced representational intelligence, postulated to begin about age 7, involving structured, reversible mental actions.

Conservation. An understanding that certain properties remain unchanged when others change.

Constructivism. A theory of knowledge that stresses that the mind actively constructs new knowledge.

Decentration. Consideration of two or more dimensions of a problem or situation simultaneously.

Disequilibrium. An imbalance or inconsistency in one's knowledge.

---

the course of interaction with the environment. Each new scheme is constructed through the coordination of earlier schemes. Such coordinations take place when the environment presents challenges that cannot be resolved using available schemes. For example, a child who fails to isolate variables in exploring the flexibility of rods will get contradictory results. Situations such as this produce **disequilibrium**, a feeling of discomfort that can only be resolved by constructing more adequate schemes. This construction of better-organized and better-adapted new schemes out of earlier ones returns the individual to **equilibrium** and

Equilibration. The construction of new understandings that resolve disequilibrium and restore equilibrium.

Equilibrium. A consistency in one's knowledge allowing temporary cognitive stability.

Formal operations. The final stage of cognitive development, according to Piaget, involving an ability to reason about hypotheses and possibilities.

Genetic epistemology. The study of the origins and development of knowledge.

Hypothetico-deductive reasoning. Making inferences from hypotheses or possibilities rather than known facts.

Organization. The tendency of knowledge to be integrated and internally consistent.

Preoperational stage. The first stage of representational intelligence.

Representation. Something which stands for something else, such as a word or mental image representing a real object.

Representational intelligence. The cognitive level, following the sensorimotor stage, at which one can know things through mental (rather than physical) actions.

Reversibility. A property of mental actions that are part of larger structures, enabling one to grasp the relation between opposite transformations.

Scheme. A physical or mental action that one can perform on the world in order to understand it. (child putting things in his mouth)

Second-order operations. Operations performed on other operations rather than on reality itself.

Sensorimotor stage. The period of infancy, when knowing involves physically acting on one's environment.

is thus known in Piagetian theory as **equilibration**. For example, by constructing and using an isolation-of-variables scheme, the child is now able to get consistent and useful information in studying a variety of situations. Equilibrium is thus restored.

In sum, new knowledge is not a product of genes alone or environment alone but rather is a product of the active mind interacting with a complex and changing environment. Children constantly face circumstances for which their current schemes are inadequate. They respond to such challenges by constructing new schemes, or new modes of understanding. Contradiction and disequilibrium, then, are a normal part of development and the impetus for achieving higher and higher levels of equilibrium.

We have just seen Piaget's account of *how* cognitive development takes place. Now we are ready to survey the four major levels of understanding through which children pass, according to Piaget's theory, on their road to cognitive maturity.

Stages of Intellectual Development

The Sensorimotor Stage. On first observation, infants often seem intellectually unimpressive to the untrained observer. Infants not only do not talk; they also show few signs of mental activity. People who are familiar with infants, however, know that they are very much aware of their environments (via their senses) and capable of responding to them (via overt motor activity). Piaget therefore referred to infancy as the **sensorimotor stage**. Moreover, he believed that infants possess a sensorimotor intelligence and that this intelligence develops gradually over the course of infancy.

How did Piaget reach these conclusions? One possible way to study the development of infant intelligence would be to obtain several observations on each of a large number of infants who vary widely in age. Piaget was concerned, however, about difficulties in interpreting such observations. He wondered how one could interpret a particular behavior in a specific situation without detailed knowledge of the infant in question, its behavior in other circumstances, and its previous experiences. Because of these problems, he decided it would be better to obtain a very large number of observations on a small number of infants than a small number of observations on each of a large number of infants. Therefore, Piaget made detailed observations of the early years of each of his own children: Laurent (the 10-month-old in the earlier example), Jacqueline, and Lucienne.

The results of this research were published in what is now considered a classic series of books: *The Origins of Intelligence in Children* (Piaget, 1936/1963), *The Construction of Reality in the Child* (Piaget, 1937/1954), and *Play, Dreams, and Imitation in Childhood* (Piaget, 1945/1962). In this trilogy, Piaget demonstrated that intellectual development in the first 2 years of life, though often difficult to see on a day-to-day basis, amounts to nothing less than a cognitive revolution.

The infant, according to Piaget, is born with some basic reflexes (sucking, grasping, and so on), which, though critical for survival and later development, are in themselves intellectually unimpressive. A neonate (newborn infant) experiences sights, sounds, smells, tastes, textures, and emotions but has no awareness either of herself or of independent physical and social realities outside herself. But she does have a crucial characteristic: A powerful tendency to assimilate the world to her reflexes, to accommodate those reflexes to the world, and, through the process of equilibration, to construct increasingly sophisticated schemes for intelligent action. Thus, the infant has the foundation for cognitive development.

By the age of about 18 months, the baby is aware of herself, recognizes the existence of people and objects outside herself, and understands that those people and objects continue to exist even when she cannot see or otherwise experience them. She understands **object permanence**. Moreover, she understands that various objects, including herself, exist and interact with each other in space over the course of time. Finally, she can now represent and act on objects and events in her own mind: That is, she is able to *think*. All of these achievements—distinguishing self from other; understanding time, space, object, and causality; and internal thinking—are taken for granted in adults. Piaget's genius emerged in his description of what the world is like for infants and his demonstration of the profound cognitive changes that take place during infancy.

Piaget emphasized, however, that these changes do not take place suddenly. On the contrary, his research on sensorimotor development showed the very gradual nature of that development. Piaget proposed that all infants go through six substages in the development of their intelligence and in the construction of the concepts of time, space, objects, and causality (see *Research,* p. 268). The sixth of these substages, involving the use of mental symbols, marks the start of **representational intelligence,** beginning with the **preoperational stage.**

The Preoperational Stage. An infant who is very strong physically might be able to turn this book upside down. But you, having reached the level of representational intelligence, can do something no sensorimotor infant can do: You can *imagine* turning this book upside down.

The infant knows the cube by assimilating it to his grasping scheme and simultaneously accommodating his grasping scheme to its unique features.

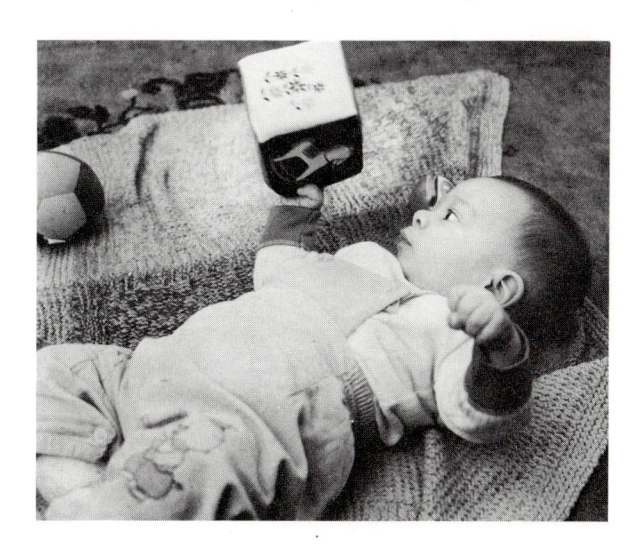

Research

Development of Object Permanence

Suppose you accidentally dropped this book. You would probably look down at the floor to find it. If it were not there, you would be slightly surprised and would probably check to learn whether it had bounced under a nearby chair, desk, or bed. If you didn't find it soon, you would intensify your search to include the entire surrounding area. After a while you might cry in anguish "The #$%&* book has to be *somewhere!*"

Piaget (1954) found that young infants do not share this fundamental conception about the permanent existence of objects. In fact, very young infants do not seem to make any distinction between the *self*, which experiences things, and *objects*, which the self experiences. Only gradually, over the course of many months of interactions with the world, do infants construct the idea that the world consists of objects that continue to exist even when they cannot be seen, heard, touched, tasted, or smelled.

How did Piaget reach these conclusions? His approach was to carefully observe his own infants interacting with their environments. Occasionally, he did a simple experiment, such as hiding an object and observing the infant's reaction. He found that development of the concept of object permanence can be divided into six stages, as follows:

Stage 1 (age 0–1 month): There is no attempt to search for objects. It appears that, from the infant's point of view, sights and sounds simply come and go. There seems to be no awareness of objects responsible for these experiences.

Stage 2 (1–4 months): The infant may turn toward a sound, as if looking for what caused it, thus suggesting some sense that there is coherence in the world.

Stage 3 (4–8 months): The infant may look or search for an object if she was already actively viewing or grasping it, thus continuing schemes that were already in action.

Stage 4 (8–12 months): The infant now initiates active search for objects that have disappeared, thus indicating a stronger concept that objects exist independent of her actions on them.

Stage 5 (12–18 months): Search activities are now more logical. The infant will, for example, look for an object where it has disappeared rather than looking where she previously found it, thus showing a still-stronger sense of its independent existence.

Stage 6 (beyond 18 months): The toddler can often *figure out* where an object will be and thus look in precisely the right place. This suggests that she can mentally represent it and thus think about it even in its absence. This is full-fledged object permanence.

Piaget found that sensorimotor concepts of time, space, and causality, as well as imitation, problem-solving, and other abilities, develop through a similar sequence of six substages. The stages are thus not specific to the developing concept of objects but, rather, reflect systematic general changes in infants' ways of knowing.

Why is the ability to imagine this—rather than doing it—considered such a great intellectual achievement? To turn the book upside down one need only assimilate it to one's sensorimotor scheme of turning things over and simultaneously accommodate that scheme to the unique properties of the book (its shape, weight, and so on). But to do that mentally, you must have an internal (mental) scheme of turning things over. Moreover, since the book itself is obviously not in your head, you must have an internal **representation** of the book that you can assimilate to that scheme. Piaget saw the ability to use mental schemes and representations (rather than being limited to sensorimotor schemes and real objects) as the mark of a major new level of cognition.

How can we tell when a child is moving from the sensorimotor stage to the representational level? If representational intelligence is so important, it should show up in many ways, and, according to Piaget, it does. Toddlers capable of representation can, for example, solve problems mentally rather than through trial and error. We see this when a child looks at a simple problem (such as how to orient a stick so it will fit through an opening) and then proceeds, without trial-and-error, with the correct solution. Toddlers can find hidden objects by mentally tracing a series of invisible movements, such as when an object is hidden in someone's hand and the child only sees the hand move from place to place (see Research box). They can imitate behaviors that are no longer visible to them such as an intriguing little dance performed by a playmate hours earlier. In their increasingly complex play, they can use one object (such as a toy bear) to symbolize another (such as mommy). Perhaps most notable, they begin to develop language: that is, to think and communicate with others by using words to represent objects and events.

Language and other representational abilities develop rapidly. Compared to infants, preschool children (say, ages 3 to 5 years) are very impressive in their intellectual competencies. What, then, remains to

For the preoperational child, a box can represent a house. Symbolic play is not only fun, but plays a critical role in the development of representational intelligence.

develop? Over the course of several decades, Piaget and his collaborators administered numerous tasks to thousands of preschool children. He concluded that they were surprisingly naive in their understanding of self, time, space, causality, the properties of objects, and much more. At first, this seems paradoxical: How can the preschooler be so deficient in precisely those concepts that were developing during the sensorimotor period?

The answer, according to Piaget, is that the rapidly developing concepts of the infant are limited to *direct* sensorimotor interactions with the world. Upon moving to the level of representation, all of the infant's painstaking achievements must be achieved once again in the realm of *mental* understanding, a process that takes many years.

Concrete Operations. Based on his studies, Piaget concluded that representational intelligence begins with a *preoperational stage*, in which thinking is still rather immature, and then moves on to a stage of **concrete operations**, beginning about the age of 7 years. Concrete operational intelligence is still representational, but the child's mental schemes, according to Piaget, are now organized into more complex structures that provide greater logical power and more sophisticated understanding.

Here is an example from Piaget (1941/1965). Figure 8-1 shows a row of six pennies and, right beneath it, lined up one for one, a row of six paper clips. Suppose that we spread the paper clips out so that the row

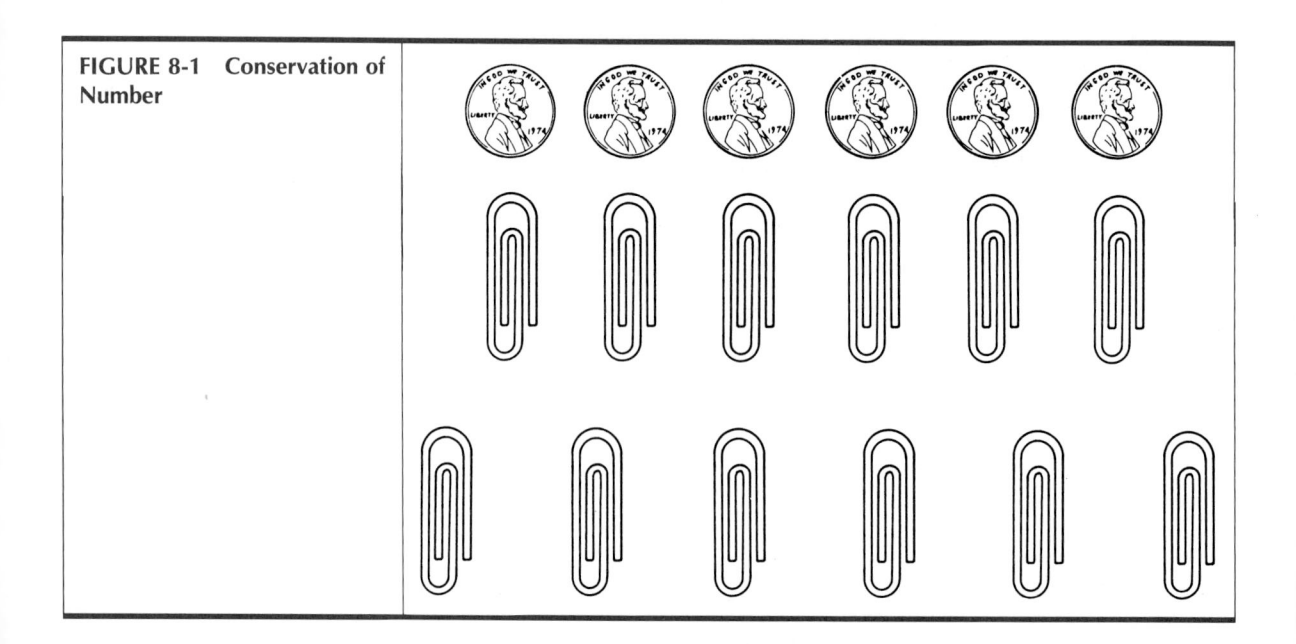

FIGURE 8-1   Conservation of Number

Concrete operational reasoning greatly increases the sophistication of one's operations on reality. These children are creating a structure far more solid than any cardboard box.

of paper clips is somewhat longer than the row of pennies. Are there still the same number of pennies and paper clips or does one row have more than the other? Children who have reached concrete operations respond that both rows have the same number. Preoperational children, on the other hand, believe there are more paper clips. Unlike the concrete operational children, they fail to understand that number is **conserved**: The number of items remains the same regardless of their spacing. How can we account for this? Piaget argued that the difference is *not* that the older child has been taught a simple fact that the younger one has not yet learned. Instead, he proposed that there are fundamental differences in how the two children think about the world. The transition from preoperational to concrete operational thinking, according to Piaget, involves a number of closely interrelated changes:

1. *From a perceptual to a conceptual orientation.* The preoperational thinker is limited to observed realities, whereas the concrete thinker makes more sophisticated inferences that go beyond his or her observations. Thus, in the conservation of number experiment above, the preoperational thinker perceives that the paper clips form a longer row after the transformation and infers that there are now more of them. The concrete thinker, on the other hand, understands the transformation conceptually and can infer that the number remains unchanged.

2. *From centration to decentration.* The preoperational thinker focuses (**centers**) on a single dimension, whereas the concrete thinker can coordinate two dimensions. Thus, the preoperational child con-

cludes that there must be more paper clips because they form a longer row. The concrete child, however, **decenters** from the dimension of length to consider spacing as well. He understands that a longer row may not have more items in it if it is longer only because the items are more spaced out.

3. *From a static to a dynamic focus.* The preoperational child focuses on *states*. She perceives the line of clips before it is stretched out and after it is stretched out, but does not think about the process of transformation. The concrete child, in contrast, is better able to think about *processes* of change and thus understands the relation between the earlier and later row of clips.

4. *From irreversibility to reversibility.* Since the concrete operational thinker understands how the shorter row of clips was transformed into a longer row, he can better appreciate that this process could be reversed, allowing one to return to the starting point. This ability to **reverse** a transformation helps him understand that the number of clips has not changed.

5. *From an empirical to a logical orientation.* A preoperational child might figure out that there are the same number of pennies and clips by counting both rows and thus gathering empirical (observational) evidence. A concrete child, however, would understand that there is no need to count. Since the two rows initially had the same number of objects, and since nothing has been added to or taken away from either row, they must still have the same number. The concrete child has a logical understanding of numbers and transformations that enables her to understand why, in this case, empirical evidence is unnecessary.

Piaget's work on concrete operational reasoning went far beyond the above examples. He demonstrated that concrete reasoners not only understand conservation of number but other forms of conservation as well (see Figure 8-2). For example, if you pour a glass of water into a thinner container, the height of the water is increased, but the concrete child understands that the quantity of liquid is conserved. Similarly, changing the shape of a ball of clay does not alter its weight.

In addition to conservation, Piaget studied a wide variety of other logical abilities, including classification (the class of animals includes the subclasses of dogs, cats, and so on), seriation (if A is longer than B, and B is longer than C, then A is longer than C), and concepts of space, time, causality, and so forth. Although his numerous books explain in detail the development of children's thinking in each of these areas, Piaget consistently emphasized similarities across areas of reasoning. In each case, the observed change could best be understood as a transition from preoperational to concrete operational reasoning.

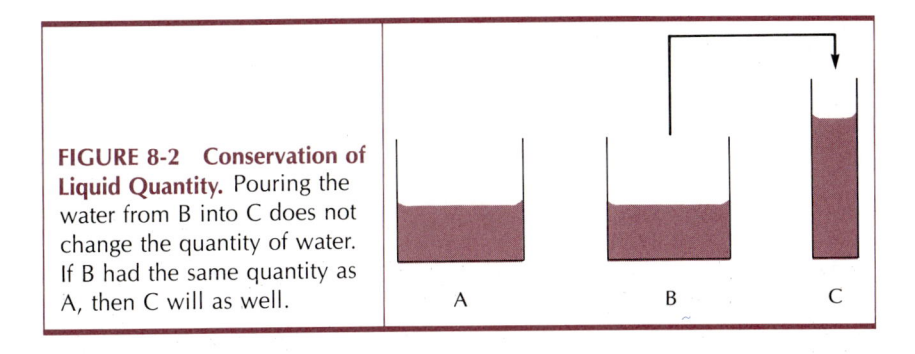

FIGURE 8-2 Conservation of Liquid Quantity. Pouring the water from B into C does not change the quantity of water. If B had the same quantity as A, then C will as well.

By late childhood (say, age 10 or 11), children appear to have an impressive, well-integrated set of logical abilities for understanding the world around them. Their experience is still somewhat limited, of course, and much remains for them to learn. We might ask, however, whether there is any reason to expect further change in their underlying patterns of reasoning and understanding. Piaget proposed that there is, in fact, one further stage of cognitive development.

Formal Operations. The major book on formal operational reasoning (the highest stage of Piaget's theory), is *The Growth of Logical Thinking from Childhood to Adolescence* (Inhelder & Piaget, 1955/1958). It presents a series of ingenious and influential studies of scientific reasoning by Bärbel Inhelder and Piaget's definitive presentation of his theory of formal operations. Piaget proposed that **formal operations** is a single, integrated structure with a number of interrelated facets. Three of the most important facets of formal reasoning are: (1) the inversion of reality and possibility, (2) **hypothetico-deductive reasoning,** and (3) **second-order operations.**

Of these, it is the first—the *inversion of reality and possibility*—that Piaget saw as most fundamental:

> There is no doubt that the most distinctive feature of formal thought stems from the role played by statements about possibility relative to statements about empirical reality (Inhelder & Piaget, 1958, p. 245).

Needless to say, Piaget was not suggesting that young children do not consider possibilities. He did propose, however, that the possibilities considered by young children are merely extensions of, or alternatives to, reality. Only at the formal level does the individual systematically construct sets of possibilities and consider realities within the context of these possibilities. For example, the formal thinker can discern how many license plates could be produced by putting the letters A, B, C,

The mature architect knows that it takes more than careful laying of bricks to produce a house. Hypothetico-deductive reasoning allows her to think systematically about a purely hypothetical building.

and D in every possible order and understands that any given license plate (e.g., C B D A) is one of those possibilities.

To take a less mathematical example, think about the fact that all children learn moral values from the people around them. According to Piaget, preformal thinkers who are exposed to different values are likely to compare them to their own moral realities and conclude that the alternative values are deviant. The reality is taken as the standard for comparison. A formal thinker, on the other hand, is able to construct a variety of possible moral systems, perhaps even including some no society has ever used, and then reevaluate her own ideas from this broader perspective. Her own reality is no longer the ultimate standard for comparison but merely one of many possibilities. At the level of formal operations, there is thus a radical reversal of perspectives: Rather than considering possibilities with respect to reality, reality is considered with respect to possibilities. The central difference between the preformal and formal thinker, then, lies in the ability to spontaneously and systematically generate possibilities and, even more important, to rethink realities in the light of those possibilities.

Closely related to the new use of possibilities is *hypothetico-deductive reasoning*, the ability to pursue a line of reasoning that begins with an assertion that is purely hypothetical—or even false. Consider a simple example (Osherson & Markman, 1975). *Yes or no: If grass is pink, then grass is pink.* A formal thinker is likely to respond "Yes, *if* it's pink, then obviously it's pink." The concrete thinker, missing the internal logic of the statement, would respond "No, it's green."

Consider a more complex example: What would happen if nobody owned things? For the preformal reasoner, the question itself is absurd:

People *do* own things. Formal thinkers, on the other hand, though recognizing that the premise is false, can systematically deduce its consequences. They may raise questions that would never occur to a concrete thinker: If nobody owned anything, would there be such a thing as stealing? Would people be less materialistic? Would they become more materialistic? Would society break down? Would it require a different form of government? Overall, would we be better off? Would we be worse off? Reasoning *hypothetico-deductively* plays a central role in the exploration of possibilities; that, in turn, deepens our understanding of the realities around us.

An additional characteristic of formal operations is that they are operations on operations, or **second-order operations**. To take a simple example: What does it mean to understand a proportion? When we say 6 is to 3 as 4 is to 2, we are indicating that the relation between 6 and 3 (the first number is twice as great) is the same as the relation between 4 and 2 (again, the first number is twice as great). But in asserting that the two relations are equal, we are considering a relation between relations, that is, a second-order relation. Piaget argued that the ability to operate on operations is directly related to hypothetico-deductive reasoning and the systematic elaboration of possibilities. Formal operations, like any other Piagetian stage, is not a collection of skills but a general structure of reasoning.

Genetic Epistemology

So far we have considered Piaget's views on the nature of intelligence, the process of intellectual development, and the stages of intelligence that children progress through. Many psychologists and educators have found Piaget's ideas profoundly important in understanding children and their development and in teaching them effectively.

However, understanding children and improving education were only secondary goals for Piaget. Piaget's primary interest was the study of how knowledge develops. He considered himself first and foremost the founder of a new discipline, **genetic epistemology**.

Epistemology is the branch of philosophy that examines the nature of knowledge. What is knowledge? What does it mean to know something? How do we get knowledge? These are the kinds of questions that interest epistemologists.

Although Piaget was interested in these questions, he was uncomfortable with the way philosophers investigated them. He felt that by focusing on the *development* of knowledge, it would be possible to answer questions of epistemology through empirical research and thus make epistemology a scientific discipline rather than a branch of philosophy. He called this new discipline *genetic epistemology*. The term *genetic* is used here not in the sense of genes (heredity, and so on) but rather in its older sense of genesis—that is, referring to origins and

Highlights

Beyond Formal Operations

Is formal operations really the highest stage? Although Piaget did not postulate a more advanced sort of reasoning, a number of more recent theorists have done so (see Commons, Richards, & Armon, 1984). Many theories of post-formal reasoning argue that abstract logic is not sufficient to deal with the complexities of adult life. Some people, it is proposed, move beyond formal operational reasoning to more flexible modes of cognition better suited to the subtleties and complications they face in the real world of adult relationships and responsibilities. Systematic logic continues to have its place, of course, but intellectually advanced thinkers recognize its limits. They know how to see issues in context, to formulate problems of their own, to deal with seemingly illogical paradoxes, and to resolve contradictions through "dialectical operations" (Basseches, 1985). The following poem by Dave Moshman, though obviously lighthearted, captures the views of many current theorists.

The Stage Beyond

Time was
        when first you'd burst beyond
                the adolescent border
you'd proudly flex your operations of the second order
your oh-so-formal thinking knew no formal inhibitions
to produce a proper proof you'd proposition propositions.
But now your schemes are seeming
        to be scheming
             in your dreaming
metacognitive absurdity has every structure screaming
you're fenced against a Lattice
    by the groping of a Group
your cognitorium is caught within a schizocognic loop:
Conjunction and disjunction
    merit binary ablations
        and who could give a hoot for implication's implications?
        Biconditional relationships
            have failed to set you free
                yet you're incompatible with incompatibility.
        Combinations make you queasy
           permutations make you blue
you never confound variables and yet they confound you
    $\dfrac{\text{correlation is}}{\text{statistical}} \bowtie \dfrac{\text{a meaningless}}{\text{contortion}}$
        $?? = \dfrac{\text{your distrust of all proportions}}{\text{has grown out of all proportion}} = ??$
    And though
beneath it all

                    your INR still comes to C
         you're strangling in your own combinatoriality
                         BUT DON'T DESPAIR! !
                       Don't tear your hair!
                    Don't let your mind grow numb!
         you've not yet reached the terminal disequilibrium.
Just snap those cognivalent cogs
      predialectic bonds
              and start constructing structures
                   of the stage that lies beyond:
A place where contradiction's knock
                         will never leave you vexed
where every dialectic⎯⎯⎯→
                     is a pointer toward the next
where paradox is paradigm!
                       (cognitions all in season)
where thoughts are all self-reinforced
                     and reason is the reason.
You're asked to give colloquia from Paris to New Paltz
    Say everything you've said
        including this
           is truly false.
Or falsely true!
     What difference for a transcendental hero
         who drolly juggles even roots of numbers less than zero?
               Then in a voice
           that's choice to voice
    a choice you once thought grave
you tell of light-wave particles
     particulary waves.
Such epistemic stunts!
                —you laugh! !—
           and now the most unnerving:
              you trace how space
                   (inside black holes)
                       is infinitely curving!
But how is one to move beyond?
    I often am beseeched
How is this stage of metastructuration to be reached?
A triune track to truth pertains
          of which I'll gladly tell:
Assimilate.
Accommodate.
Equilibrate like hell.

From Worm Runner's Digest, *1979, 21, 107–108.*

development. Thus a more modern, and less misleading, name for Piaget's discipline would be *developmental epistemology*.

As a genetic epistemologist, Piaget was interested in all aspects of the development of knowledge, including the evolution of intelligent species, the cognitive development of children, the history of scientific disciplines, and so on. Throughout his long professional career, Piaget emphasized general principles of development that he considered to hold true in all of these domains. He maintained that: (1) Knowledge does not simply *change* but rather *develops* in the sense of becoming increasingly organized and adaptive; (2) this development is not a spontaneous maturation but rather an active construction on the part of the knower; and (3) this construction is not automatic but rather is initiated and sustained by the need to transcend contradictions or disequilibriums that are continually produced by the functioning of knowledge in a complex and changing environment. We cannot fully appreciate Piaget's psychological theory without seeing it in the context of his broader vision of a general developmental epistemology.

Applications

Educators have found Piaget's theory a useful source of guidance for educational programs ranging from preschool (e.g., Forman & Hill, 1980) to college (e.g., Fuller, 1980). We will discuss some of the implications of Piaget's work that have been taken most seriously and been found most valuable.

1. *Treat children as active agents.* Piaget emphasized that children are not simply empty boxes to be filled with knowledge or blank slates on which the truth simply needs to be written. On the contrary, he stressed that children actively make sense of their environments and construct their own knowledge. It would be a mistake, for example, to teach a child multiplication as if the child merely needed to imitate certain mechanical procedures. When children learn multiplication, they already have substantial knowledge of numbers and arithmetic. They assimilate the teacher's instruction to what they already know and actively construct a conception of multiplication. Teachers who are aware of this can use this insight to present the material more effectively and to anticipate and understand the types of errors children commonly make in assimilating the new ideas to their prior knowledge (e.g., concepts of addition) and attempting to construct their own new understandings.

2. *Focus on intrinsic motivation.* Piagetian educators typically put much less emphasis than many others on providing the child with rewards for good performance. According to Piaget's views on equilibration, genuine intellectual development is its own reward: As the child overcomes earlier contradictions, she moves from disequilibrium to equilibrium. A better grasp of mathematics, for ex-

ample, will help a child get consistent and sensible answers to math problems, which leads her to feel the satisfaction of genuine understanding. There may be a role, of course, for encouraging increased effort and better performance by rewarding it. But we should not assume that this is the only, or even the most important, basis for children's learning and development. Teachers should allow children to experience challenge and success.

3. *Recognize the developmental basis for learning.* If children learn by assimilating new experiences to prior concepts, those prior concepts provide the basis for learning, and lack of appropriate prior concepts may make genuine understanding impossible. A child with no conception of what a number is, for example, may learn by rote to get correct answers to addition problems but will probably not understand the point of this. In presenting new material, teachers should ask themselves what prior knowledge students must have to understand that material and determine whether their students have that prior knowledge.

4. *Aim for moderate novelty.* Piagetians, as well as many others, have suggested that children will learn best if presented with concepts slightly beyond their present understanding. If the material presented is already understood, there is obviously nothing to be learned. If, on the other hand, it is too new, the child may be unable to assimilate it without greatly distorting it. Moderately novel material is new enough to present a useful challenge but familiar enough to be assimilated meaningfully. The child who understands addition and subtraction, for example, may be ready for multiplication but not for algebra.

5. *Value the child's point of view.* The child who does not understand things the way the teacher does may not be simply lacking certain knowledge but rather may have an entirely different way of looking at things. From a Piagetian viewpoint it is important to consider not just what the child does not understand but how the child *does* understand things. In fact, the more novel and bizarre the child's viewpoint, the more important it is for the teacher to be aware of it in order to effectively help the child move toward better understanding.

6. *Use clinical interviews.* Although clinical interviews are time-consuming, they may provide insights that standardized tests do not. For example, a child may have trouble with multiplication because she is using a systematically incorrect procedure. By having her solve a series of multiplication problems, observing the steps she takes, and questioning her about each, a sensitive teacher or parent may get better insight into the child's conception of multiplication than would be gained through examining her score on a standardized

mathematics test. This may be especially valuable in working with special populations (e.g., mainstreamed students, minorities) who may be having problems for unique but understandable reasons. The better our understanding of how a child is thinking, the more effectively we can teach.

Current Status of Piaget's Theory

The two most extreme views one could take with respect to Piaget's theory would be complete acceptance or complete rejection. Complete acceptance means believing that Piaget's theory gives a complete and accurate description and explanation of cognitive development. Complete rejection means believing that Piaget's theory has been shown to be entirely wrong. Almost all developmental psychologists agree that neither of these extreme views is warranted. Rather than evaluating Piaget's theory as a whole, it is probably most useful to decide which of his ideas have not stood up to empirical research and which remain important contributions. In this section we will distinguish eight aspects of Piaget's theory, summarize the current thinking of developmental psychologists about each, and speculate about prospects for the future.

Identification of Crucial Cognitive Abilities. Piaget identified and studied the development of dozens of crucial cognitive abilities. Even his strongest critics agree on the importance of the abilities Piaget has identified and have devoted a great deal of time and energy to studying their development (see Gelman & Baillargeon, 1983, for a review of some of this work). It is hard to doubt the importance of recognizing the existence of objects; coordinating multiple points of view; distinguishing conservation from change; being able to classify and order things; making quantitative and probabilistic judgments, or distinguishing variables and testing hypotheses about them. Some psychologists have argued forcefully, however (Gardner, 1979), that developmental psychologists have been too influenced by Piaget to the point of overemphasizing the abilities he studied (e.g., logical competencies) and failing to identify and investigate other sorts of cognition (e.g., artistic ability). It seems likely that in future years psychologists will continue to study the important abilities identified by Piaget but will also identify and study some equally important ones that he overlooked.

Methodology. In addition to identifying important cognitive abilities, Piaget and his collaborators proposed numerous tasks for assessing these abilities, such as the conservation of number task discussed earlier. Many developmental psychologists continue to use the traditional Piagetian tasks and some have argued that they provide the most accurate assessments of children's cognition (Shute, 1983). Many others, however, have argued that the traditional tasks underestimate children's abilities. Some have tried to refine them or suggest alternatives (Tobin & Capie, 1981).

Jean Piaget. New theories will continue to be devised, but Piaget's theory remains a major force in modern thinking about cognitive development.

Piaget also pioneered the flexible assessment technique known as the clinical interview (see Chapter 3). Many developmentalists continue to use this in some form, though most American researchers prefer more quantitative and replicable techniques (such as those discussed in Chapter 3). Our own view is that the clinical interview procedure can provide valuable and unexpected insights into children's thinking, especially when we are exploring a new topic, but must be used with caution and supplemented with other methodologies.

Stage Theory. Piaget is strongly associated with the view that development occurs in general stages (sensorimotor, preoperational, concrete operational, formal operational) and that we can characterize children by determining their current stage of development. The idea of developmental stages implies a certain consistency in children. To say that a child is in the preoperational stage, for example, suggests that she shows preoperational reasoning in most of her activities.

Most developmental psychologists believe that extensive data collected over the past several decades have undermined this aspect of the theory. In fact, many reject the idea of developmental stages altogether.

Those who still consider the concept valuable have become increasingly careful to define just what they mean by stages (Overton & Newman, 1982). For example, some discuss stages of development in particular domains (e.g., stages of deductive reasoning, morality, sex role concepts) but do not believe in consistency across the domains (Fischer, 1980). That is, a child might have developed to a higher level in her ability to use deductive reasoning than in her knowledge of sex roles, while another child might show the reverse pattern. It seems fair to conclude that the evidence has shown cognitive development to be a complex, multifaceted phenomenon. This does not rule out the possibility of general developmental stages but suggests that we must be clear and cautious in our use of that concept.

Age Norms. Piaget's work provides us with indications about the average age at which children reach different stages and achieve various cognitive abilities. Research has shown substantial individual and cultural differences, however. Further, we can obtain different results if we slightly modify the assessment task or the style of administration. Psychologists and educators agree with Piaget that we should not try to teach children concepts before they are ready. We must be cautious, however, about concluding that children below a certain age are incapable of understanding a concept. For example, children under age 6 usually fail Piaget's conservation of number task (discussed earlier), but it is clear that they nevertheless have important numerical competencies (Gelman & Gallistel, 1978). To simply conclude that children below age 6 do not understand what numbers are and are thus not ready for any mathematical education would be a serious mistake (see Chapter 12, *Development of Reasoning*). Piaget himself was always most interested in the sequence of development and insisted that the norms he gave were meant only to give a rough idea of the ages he was talking about and should not be taken too seriously.

Theory of Intelligence. Piaget viewed intelligence as consisting of schemes that assimilate the environment and simultaneously accommodate to it. He often contrasted this view with the simpler behaviorist model of connections between stimuli and responses. Most contemporary psychologists accept Piaget's general way of thinking about these issues. Researchers in the information-processing tradition, for example, emphasize that knowledge is highly structured and use concepts similar to Piaget's notion of assimilation to express how we use our mental structures to deal with our environments. As we will see, however, information-processing researchers commonly view Piaget's discussions of schemes, assimilation, and accommodation as too general and are trying to formulate more specific theories about the structures and processes of cognition.

Theory of Cognitive Change. Piaget extended his ideas about assimilation and accommodation to propose a theory about how new schemes are constructed via the process of equilibration. His ideas about this are viewed by many psychologists and educators as providing brilliant and practical insight into the overall process of intellectual development. Others, however, criticize the idea of equilibration for being too vague to have much theoretical or practical value and have attempted to develop more specific ideas about how children and adults come to have new concepts and intellectual abilities. Piagetians and their critics agree that accounting for cognitive change remains a critical and difficult challenge for all theories of cognitive development.

Paradigm of Constructivism. Piaget proposed constructivism—the idea that the human mind actively constructs new knowledge—as an alternative to the traditional ideas of **nativism** (knowledge is innate) and **empiricism** (knowledge is learned from the environment). This idea has very broad implications for psychology and education and has accordingly been a focus for intense controversy. For many years, the debate was between the Piagetians and the learning theorists (constructivism vs. empiricism). With the rise of information processing views, however, strongly empiricist ideas are no longer as popular. Information processing researchers, as we will see, emphasize the active role of the person in constructing knowledge. In some ways, the major controversy now is between constructivists such as Piaget, and nativists such as Noam Chomsky and Jerry Fodor, whose views have become increasingly influential in recent years (Piattelli-Palmarini, 1980). Piaget's views on constructivism have added an important new dimension to the historical debate between nativists and empiricists, but the debate is unlikely to be settled in the foreseeable future.

Genetic Epistemology. Piaget was interested in broad philosophical issues concerning the origins, nature, and development of knowledge. He emphasized the importance of interdisciplinary collaboration—by psychologists, philosophers, biologists, mathematicians, and other scholars—in exploring these issues and, ultimately, formulating a general science of genetic epistemology. Piaget's breadth of perspective has helped many psychologists and educators see their own fields in new ways and has thus broadened the scope of scientific thinking in psychology and education. Piaget was not as influential as he wished to be among philosophers, although some do take the idea of a developmental epistemology seriously (Kitchener, 1986; Kornblith, 1985). Moreover, interdisciplinary collaboration is still not nearly as common as Piaget thought it should be. The broad vision of genetic epistemology is potentially Piaget's most lasting legacy, but its impact remains to be seen.

Information Processing Theories

In the study of cognitive development, the major alternative to Piaget's theory is what is generally known as the **information processing** approach. Information processing is not a single theory; rather, it is a general approach to research on cognition that has given rise to a number of specific theories. Information processing theorists believe we can understand the mind and its processes by viewing it as a kind of sophisticated computer.

In the following pages, we will consider the work of three theorists—Robert Siegler, Robert Sternberg, and Robbie Case—who have attempted to understand cognitive development within an information processing framework. We will then discuss what these three theorists share in common. Finally, we will examine the educational applications and current status of the information processing perspective.

Siegler's Rule Assessment Approach

Robert Siegler is a developmental psychologist at Carnegie-Mellon University in Pittsburgh, a major center of information processing research. Siegler credits Piaget with identifying many important concepts that children develop and devising ingenious tasks to assess these concepts. Along with other information processing researchers, however, he considers Piaget's explanation of cognitive development overly broad and questionable on many specific points. He suggests that an information processing analysis of performance on Piagetian tasks would be highly valuable.

The specific sort of information processing analysis that Siegler has developed is known as **rule assessment**. Siegler agrees with Piaget that on a given intellectual task we can identify qualitatively different levels of performance and that children progress through these levels systematically. He suggests, however, that Piaget was sometimes vague in how he described children's levels of performance. Siegler also views Piaget's clinical interview method as a rather loose and subjective way of determining a child's level.

Siegler proposes that each level of performance can be seen as a rule. The particular rule a child uses can be determined from that child's pattern of performance on a set of carefully constructed problems. Over the past decade, Siegler and his colleagues have used the rule assessment approach to study children's performance on a wide variety of tasks, most of them drawn from the Piagetian literature.

The Balance Scale Task. If there is a particular cognitive task associated with Siegler, it is surely the **balance scale**. Originally used by Inhelder and Piaget (1958) to assess formal operational reasoning, the balance was the first task to which Siegler (1976) applied his rule assessment methodology. It remains one of his favorite examples and serves nicely as an illustration of his approach.

FIGURE 8-3 The Balance Scale. From Siegler, R.S. (1980b). When do children learn: The relation between existing knowledge and learning. *Educational Psychologist, 15,* 135–150.

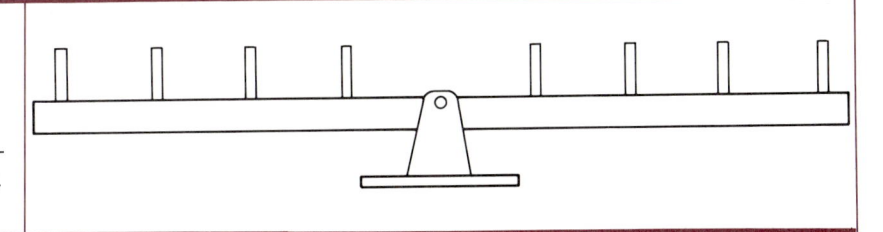

The balance scale is illustrated in Figure 8-3. You will notice that on each side of the center are four pegs on which weights can be placed. A lever prevents the balance from tipping while this is done. The child is then asked to predict, for a given set of weights, what would happen if the lever were released. For example, would the balance tip to the left, tip to the right, or remain level? The task can, of course, be repeated for different sets of weights placed at different distances from the center.

On the basis of Inhelder and Piaget's earlier research and his own analysis of the task, Siegler hypothesized four levels of performance. Each level was formulated as a precise rule, as illustrated in Figure 8-4. As you can see, a child using Rule I would consider only weight. If one side has more weight, that side will go down; if both sides have equal weight, they will be in balance. A child using Rule II is more advanced in that she uses distance in some cases. If one side has more weight, the child predicts that it will go down. If not, then distance from the center is considered: The side with greater distance will go down. If weight and distance are equal, then balance is predicted.

Rule III is still more sophisticated. At this level the child always considers both weight and distance. If the two arms differ only in weight, then it is predicted that the arm with more weight will go down. If the two arms differ only in distance, then it is predicted that the side with greater distance will go down. If the arms differ in both weight and distance, then it is predicted that the arm with greater weight and distance will go down. But what if there is greater weight on one arm but greater distance on the other? The child using Rule III does not know how to resolve this conflict and will, as Siegler puts it, "muddle through."

Rule IV is the most advanced. Instead of muddling through when weight and distance conflict, children who use this rule consider cross products. For example, a weight of 4 units at a distance of 3 units would be seen as equivalent to a weight of 3 units at a distance of 4 units ($4 \times 3 = 3 \times 4 = 12$), so the scale would be predicted to balance.

How can this theory of balance-scale performance be tested? Siegler carefully constructed six types of problems and administered several versions of each to children aged 5, 9, 13, and 17. The problem types were purposely set up so that children using any particular rule would

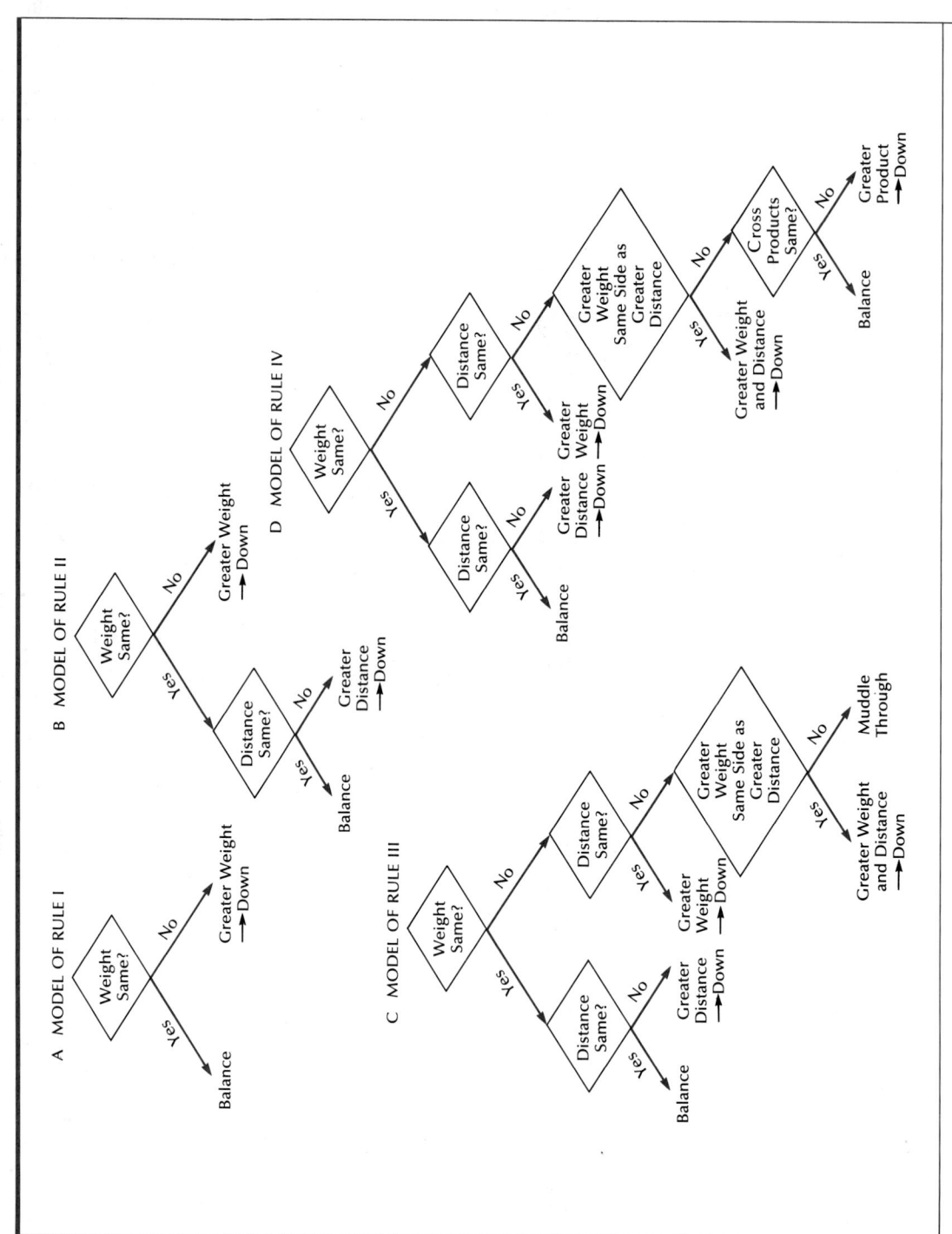

FIGURE 8-4 Rules Used on Balance-Scale Tasks. From Siegler, R.S. (1976). Three aspects of cognitive development. *Cognitive Psychology, 8,* 481–520; and Siegler, R.S. (1980b). When do children learn: The relation between existing knowledge and learning. *Educational Psychologist, 15,* 135–150.

show a pattern of responses different from the pattern of children using a different rule. He found that more than 80 percent of the children at each age showed a pattern of responses fitting one of the four rules. The older children typically used more advanced rules, though Rule IV, involving the sophisticated cross products strategy, was rare even in the oldest participants. Siegler concluded that his four rules accurately characterized children's levels of understanding of the balance scale.

How Do Children Learn? How do children get from one level of understanding to the next? For example, how does a child using Rule II make the switch to Rule III? In more general terms, how do children learn? This has consistently been a central question for Siegler (e.g., 1976, 1980a, 1980b, 1983a, 1983b, 1984). In his view, most theorists have focused on describing **states of knowledge** (what the child knows at a particular point in development) and paid too little attention to **mechanisms of development** (how the child learns). However, he is optimistic that cognitive developmentalists have been increasingly turning their attention to the issue of learning (Siegler, 1983b).

Siegler's analysis of learning stresses three key points. First, he believes that what one learns depends not only on one's environment but also on one's previous knowledge. For example, a child using Rule III on the balance scale might profit from experiences that would be meaningless to a child who only grasps Rule I. The general position that learning depends on the interaction between current knowledge and new experience is widely accepted by developmental psychologists and has been stressed by both Piagetian and information processing theorists.

Siegler's second point is that "children learn most efficiently from experiences that indicate inadequacies in their existing rules" (Siegler, 1983a, p. 264). For example, a child who uses Rule I will be most likely to profit from an experience in which her predictions about the balance scale are proven wrong. This idea closely resembles Piaget's emphasis on the role of disequilibrium in development.

Finally, Siegler proposes that children's ability to **encode** (or mentally represent) information is critical to learning. For example, in some follow-ups to his balance scale study (also reported in Siegler, 1976), he focused on a group of 5- and 8-year-olds who were using Rule I. His efforts to help them move to Rule III were more successful with the older children, despite the fact that the older children were initially at the same level of understanding as the younger children (Rule I). After detailed analysis, Siegler hypothesized that the key difference between the two ages was in encoding. Although all the children were solving the balance scale problems on the basis of weight alone (that is the definition of Rule I), it seemed that the older children were at least aware of distance information and were thus able to profit from new

Sternberg's Componential Analysis

experiences involving distance information. The younger children, on the other hand, appeared to ignore such information entirely.

Siegler (1976) did several follow-up studies to test the encoding hypothesis. He found that when he independently assessed children's observations about the balance scale, the older children (as predicted) were more likely to remember distance information. He also found that when the younger children were taught to encode information about distance, they were then better able to profit from experience and move toward Rule III. In sum, the ability to learn a new rule depended not just on one's current rule but on one's ability to encode relevant dimensions.

Robert Sternberg of Yale University is another major figure in the information processing tradition. Unlike Siegler, who is primarily a developmental psychologist, Sternberg's central interest is in the psychology of intelligence. Sternberg's work on cognitive development is thus only part of his broader interests and reflects his more general information processing theory of human intelligence.

As we noted in our discussion of Piaget, the term *intelligence* makes most people think of IQ tests. In fact, IQ tests are a good place to start introducing Sternberg. A typical IQ test consists of a set of cognitive tasks for children (or adults) to perform. The tasks have been chosen because they are successful in differentiating children on the basis of intelligence: That is, older and/or more intelligent children typically do better on them. The primary goal in selecting such tasks and making an IQ test out of them is to be able to assess academic competence.

If children's performance on IQ tasks improves dramatically with age, it might seem that the tasks used by IQ testers would be of great interest to developmentalists. However, most developmentalists have tended to see IQ tests merely as a practical tool for predicting academic performance. Sternberg disagrees and argues that we should make better use of intelligence tests. A central goal for cognitive developmentalists should be to determine *why* children's performance on IQ items improves. The best way to do that, Sternberg believes, is through an information processing analysis of such tasks.

Sternberg has not been satisfied simply to provide a detailed analysis of children's performance on various intellectual tasks, however. In addition, he has proposed a general theory of human intelligence (1984c, 1984d) and has used this theory as the basis for his views on how intelligence develops (1982, 1984b). Sternberg proposes three major aspects of intelligence: (1) performance components, (2) knowledge-acquisition components, and (3) metacomponents. We will consider each in turn.

Performance components are processes used in doing tasks. Think about the following analogy: Sternberg is to IQ tests as Siegler is to (1)

Hen's teeth; (2) Horse's toes; (3) Piagetian tasks. What processes do you use in selecting the best answer? Sternberg and Gardner (1983) suggest several of the processes (components) involved. One of these is *encoding of information*: You perceive the problem and store the relevant information in your working memory (that is, your immediate storage and focus of attention). Another performance component is *inference of relations*: You infer that the relation of Sternberg to IQ tasks is that Sternberg does information processing analyses of IQ task performance. A third performance component is *mapping of higher-order relations*. You might note, for example, that the relation of Sternberg to IQ tasks is the same as the relation of Siegler to Piagetian tasks: In both cases, the relation is "does information processing analyses of." A fourth performance component is *response*: for example, choosing answer (3) on the basis of these considerations.

The list above is not nearly complete but illustrates what Sternberg means by performance components. Sternberg suggests that some components develop later than others. For example, mapping of higher-order relations involves the sort of second-order relations that Piaget associates with formal operational reasoning. Sternberg's own research with analogy problems (Sternberg & Rifkin, 1979) confirms that this component is a late development and that its appearance results in an important change in how children approach analogies.

In addition to performance components, there are **knowledge-acquisition components**. These are used by people to decide what information is worth learning, to put that information into a meaningful form, and to relate the new information to previous knowledge. The fact that learning involves relating information to previous knowledge has some positive implications for development. The more one knows, the more one is able to learn; but the more one learns, the more one knows, and thus the more one learns, and so forth.

It might seem that performance and knowledge-acquisition components are sufficient. Performance components help us perform tasks and knowledge-acquisition components enable us to learn new things. But how do we use these components? What directs the entire operation? Sternberg proposes that for overall planning and decision making we need a third set of components: **metacomponents**. The metacomponents are "executive processes." They are responsible for such aspects of intelligence as: (1) understanding the nature of the problem; (2) deciding which performance components should be used; (3) selecting a strategy for combining the performance components to solve the task at hand; (4) deciding how much time to spend on various aspects of the problem; and (5) keeping track of what one has done and what remains to be done to solve the problem.

Sternberg suggests that increasing sophistication of metacomponents accounts for much of cognitive development. He also notes that intellectually advanced individuals spend more of their time on meta-componential processing. For example, a sophisticated student is more likely to examine a complex math problem and plan what has to be done rather than plunging into the problem and multiplying or dividing every number in sight. Presumably, global planning is most efficient in the long run, and children learn to put more and more of their intellectual resources into it.

Case's Neo-Piagetian Theory

Robbie Case of the Ontario Institute for Studies in Education has proposed a theory of cognitive development that resembles those of Siegler and Sternberg in making extensive use of information processing concepts. Such concepts are, in fact, so pervasive in his theory that Case is commonly classified as an information processing theorist. On the other hand, unlike Siegler and Sternberg, Case sees his work as emerging from Piaget's. Although his views differ from Piaget's in important ways, he believes that he preserves so much of Piaget's general perspective and approach that his theory should be considered a **neo-Piagetian theory**. In fact, Case has perhaps gone furthest in attempting to synthesize the Piagetian and information processing perspectives in a way that preserves the best insights of each. To understand the nature of this synthesis, let us begin with a simple task.

How many items of information can you hold in your mind while you manipulate them? A rough way to assess this is to have someone read you a string of random numbers. Your task is to repeat the numbers in reverse order. To do this, you must be able to hold all the numbers in your mind while you perform the operation of reversing their order. Most people find that this is not very difficult to do for strings of up to four or five digits but that it gets rapidly more difficult after that. Few people do well for strings of more than nine or ten.

In 1956, George Miller published a classic article entitled "The Magical Number Seven, Plus or Minus Two: Some Limits on our Capacity for Processing Information." He began:

> My problem is that I have been persecuted by an integer. For seven years this number has followed me around, has intruded in my most private data, and has assaulted me from the pages of our most public journals. This number assumes a variety of disguises, being sometimes a little larger and sometimes a little smaller than usual, but never changing so much as to be unrecognizable. The persistence with which this number plagues me is far more than a random accident. There is, to quote a famous senator, a design behind it. . . . (p. 187)

The number, of course, was **seven plus or minus two**. Miller presented evidence gathered from a wide variety of tasks to the effect that most people could hold in their immediate consciousness and actively process somewhere between five and nine items of information. He suggested that this limitation might represent a fundamental feature of human cognition.

The obvious question for a developmentalist, of course, is whether this limitation changes with age. A great deal of research and considerable controversy has been linked with this question. Robbie Case (1984, 1985) has not only done extensive research in this area but has used the results of that research to formulate a new theory of cognitive development.

Case distinguishes between two aspects of **mental capacity: Operating space** and **short-term storage space**. Operating space is used for actually processing information, while storage space is used for holding that information in one's consciousness in order to process it. On the basis of his and others' extensive research, Case argues that mental capacity as a whole does *not* increase with age. Rather, it remains constant. However, operational *efficiency* increases, so that the operating space necessary for basic operations *decreases* with age. This leaves more of the mental capacity available for short-term storage. An older child, for example, who is more efficient in putting words together to form sentences, presumably has more short-term storage space available for holding words and concepts and thus can form longer sentences. It is this increase in short-term storage space, according to Case, that underlies cognitive development.

Why does operational efficiency increase? Case argues that specific practice with particular operations (such as counting) is not the primary reason. Instead, available evidence suggests that the increased efficiency (and the corresponding increase in available short-term storage space) is due either to biological maturation or to very general kinds of experience (or perhaps an interaction of both). One serious possibility is that myelinization of neurons (see Chapter 7) is a central factor.

Case does not suggest, however, that the purely physiological maturation of neurons is the core of cognitive development. He does not believe that new stages of development emerge automatically as the nervous system matures. On the contrary, Case agrees with Piaget that children must actively construct new schemes via their own mental activity. Case's point is simply that such construction cannot take place until the necessary short-term storage space is available. In other words, adequate short-term storage is necessary but not sufficient for achieving any given stage of cognitive development.

Case's specific analyses of the processes children of various ages use in dealing with a variety of tasks are similar in many ways to the analyses provided by Siegler and Sternberg. More than most information processing theorists, however, Case emphasizes an important general constraint on development: short-term storage space. It is this constraint that guarantees that development will proceed at a relatively

The Information Processing Paradigm

slow pace through identifiable stages. And it is this constraint that gives Case's information processing theory of cognitive development its strongly Piagetian flavor.

We have discussed three specific information processing theories of cognitive development. In this section, we will consider what all three of these theories have in common that leads us to classify them together as information processing theories.

One general characteristic of information processing theories is an emphasis on mental representation and process. Information processing theorists want to know how people mentally represent information (e.g., is it encoded in words or pictures?) and how we process those representations. We saw, for example, that Siegler emphasized what children of different ages are able to encode and carefully distinguished different rules for processing information about a balance scale. Information processing theorists view the human mind as a biological computer; they try to determine what programs it uses.

Related to this view is an emphasis on real-time mental operations. The processes Siegler discusses are postulated to occur in the child's mind one after another in precisely the order indicated in each flow chart, with each step taking a specified amount of time. Sternberg, Case, and other information processing theorists similarly postulate models of actual mental events. This is in sharp contrast to Piaget, who focused more on the abstract underlying structure of thinking than on its concrete processes.

Interest in real-time mental processes has led information processing theorists to focus on the limited mental capacity available for these processes. We have seen, in particular, the important role that short-term storage space plays in Case's theory.

Even a young child is far more complex than any modern computer. Nevertheless, information processing theorists believe humans process information via thought processes that operate much like computer programs.

Finally, information processing research is typified by fine-grained analyses of performance on specific tasks. Siegler's detailed work on the balance task and Sternberg's analysis of reasoning with analogies are two examples. Equally detailed analyses of numerous other tasks have been provided by Siegler, Sternberg, Case, and many other researchers in the information processing tradition. To these researchers, development consists of changes in specific skills applicable to particular tasks and contexts rather than the emergence of general structures applicable across the entire realm of cognition.

Educational Applications

A number of information processing researchers have explicitly addressed the implications of the information processing approach for education. In this section we will consider some suggestions made by Case (1978) and Sternberg (1983).

Case's Three Principles of Instruction. Case proposes three general principles for planning instruction:

1. *Begin with a step-by-step description of both the strategy to be taught and the strategies that children spontaneously apply.* For example, consider a child who has trouble with multiplication of multidigit numbers (e.g., 458 × 297). Most adults know a step-by-step strategy for arithmetic problems of this sort. Common sense tells us that if we plan to present this strategy to a child we should first work it out in detail. Case's first point is that this may not be enough. The child may already have his or her own strategy, and it is just as important to understand the child's current strategy as it is to know the strategy we are planning to teach.

2. *Design the instruction so that children will see the limitations of their spontaneous strategies and the need for a new strategy.* Children will learn best, according to Case, if we can convince them that their current strategies are inadequate and that a new one is needed. A student may, for example, be having difficulties because she tends to add when she should multiply. If we can present her with multiplication problems where addition leads to ridiculous answers, she is more likely to attend to and learn a new approach.

3. *Reduce the short-term storage requirements of the learning situation to a bare minimum.* Suppose that a child can only deal with, say, three items of information at a time. We should not try to teach that child a strategy that requires one to deal with more than three items of information simultaneously. Moreover, whatever strategy we teach, we must be careful that no step in the learning process exceeds this limit. If any step requires the mind to hold more than its limit, the instruction will be a failure. A chain is only as strong as its weakest link.

    How can we judge where the weakest link is? Precise specification of the steps in a learning sequence is a very technical matter that requires substantial training. Case suggests, however, that one can roughly estimate how much mental effort each step requires. The step in the learning sequence that provides the most cognitive strain for an adult is the point that is most likely to overload a child. That is where the learning process is more likely to break down.

Sternberg's Criteria for Training Intellectual Skills. Sternberg (1983) suggests that programs for teaching intellectual skills should meet a number of criteria. Some of the most important are as follows.

1. *Begin with a theory of cognition that has received empirical support.* Sternberg is not optimistic about programs based on trial and error, pure intuition, or untested theories.
2. *Use a theory that focuses directly on the mental processes one is trying to teach.* Sternberg does not believe that structural theories such as Piaget's provide an adequate basis for teaching specific cognitive skills.
3. *Use a theory relevant to the sociocultural context of the students.* Different cultures and subcultures have different concepts of intelligence and these different conceptions may affect the results of educational programs.
4. *Focus on both executive processing (Sternberg's metacomponents) and non-executive processing (Sternberg's performance components).* This point follows directly from Sternberg's componential subtheory. Good thinkers, he believes, are skilled both in specific processing of information and in executive processes such as identifying the program, selecting and coordinating specific processes, allocating resources, and monitoring progress.
5. *Make use of individual differences in how information is best processed.* For example, some people do better with verbal representations of information and some excel with spatial representations. A good program will help students learn about their unique strengths and weaknesses and use the former to compensate for the latter.
6. *Furnish links to facilitate generalization from training tasks to real-world behavior.* Teachers must specifically arrange for such generalizations rather than assuming they will occur automatically.

Evaluation of the Information Processing Approach

The information processing paradigm has become a major force in psychology. Information processing theories of cognitive development have advanced rapidly over the past 10 or 15 years to become the major alternative to Piaget's theory. Information processing theorists have provided precise accounts of children's performance on a wide variety of tasks. These accounts are based on a great deal of carefully designed research and make specific predictions that can be tested via further research. They also suggest some important educational applications.

Piagetian critics of the information processing approach have questioned the strong emphasis on specific tasks, however. They are uncomfortable with the information processing view that "cognitive development can be characterized as a sequence of increasingly sophisticated rules for performing tasks" (Siegler, 1980a, p. 282). Consider, for example, the development of children's understanding of the nature of time. To study this, of course, a researcher must devise tasks involving time concepts and observe how children solve them. But a Piagetian would argue that determining the rules children use on such tasks is not an end in itself. Our ultimate goal is to understand how children's underlying conceptions of time are structured at different levels of development and how this relates to their conceptions of space, objects, causal influences, and so forth. In more general terms, the question is whether the information processing approach is too bound to analysis of specific tasks and processes to provide us with a broad view of how children make sense of their worlds and how their conceptions change over long periods of time.

It is possible, of course, that information processing theories will become increasingly capable of providing the sort of broad view of development that Piagetians prefer. At present, however, it appears that the two approaches are complementary. Ultimately, we would all like a theory that provides both the big picture and the details of cognitive development. Currently, it seems that most theorists are forced to go for one or the other. Piaget provided us with a solid overview of the nature and direction of intellectual development from birth through adolescence but was vague or incorrect on many of the details. Information processing accounts are detailed and rigorous in their descriptions of task performance but are less informative about the overall nature and course of development.

The difference between the two approaches has important educational implications. A teacher interested in learning how to teach a particular task would probably find an information processing analysis most helpful. On the other hand, an educator interested in a curriculum to develop more general competencies might find more of interest in Piaget's work. Whether or not a synthesis of the two approaches such as that attempted by Case can give us the best of both worlds remains to be seen.

Conclusions

Although Piaget's theory and information processing are clearly the two major approaches to the study of cognitive development, they are not the only alternatives. Some other important theoretical approaches are skill theory (Fischer, 1980); dialectical theory (Vygotsky, 1978); nativism (Chomsky, 1980a, b; Fodor, 1980; Keil, 1981); social learning theory

(Zimmerman, 1981); and the knowing levels approach (Campbell & Bickhard, 1986). It would be foolish to pretend that all of these theories agree with each other. There are many important differences among them. No one in developmental psychology seriously expects universal agreement on a general theory of cognitive development in the foreseeable future.

Nevertheless, there are some general principles that are now accepted by virtually all developmentalists. The fact that these principles are supported by research conducted from diverse theoretical perspectives and are accepted by nearly everyone in the field is encouraging and important. This does not indicate that developmental psychology has reached the final answers, of course; rather, it indicates that we have learned some fundamental things about intellectual development and have a firm basis for some important educational applications. We will conclude this chapter with a list of some of these basic principles.

1. *Knowledge consists of complex cognitive structures rather than isolated facts.* Psychologists differ about how broad these **cognitive structures** are and how we should describe them, but few seriously doubt that knowledge is highly structured.

2. *We understand our environments by assimilating them to our current knowledge.* Not all information processing theorists use the Piagetian term *assimilation*, and many consider Piaget's use of it too vague. But all accept the general idea that we make sense of things by applying our prior knowledge.

3. *Intellectual performance depends on task content and general context.* People are not consistent across tasks in their level of performance. They may even react differently to the same task in different situations. Piagetians are more likely than information processing researchers to stress general stages of understanding, but even they acknowledge inconsistencies in performance.

4. *Learning depends on current knowledge.* Even young children do not approach their environments as empty receptacles waiting to be filled with knowledge and skills. The principle of assimilation implies that what we learn depends not only on our environments but also on what we already know.

5. *Knowledge is actively constructed by the developing individual.* Again, the idea is that people are not passive receptacles. They actively participate in their own development.

6. *Children show qualitative change in their understanding of many important concepts.* Piagetians are more likely to see different levels of understanding as reflecting general stages of development while information processing researchers such as Siegler focus more on specific systems of rules for performing particular tasks. In either case,

however, it is clear that qualitatively distinct levels of understanding can be identified.

7. *Many qualitative changes occur in predictable sequences.* Information processing researchers have confirmed many of the developmental sequences postulated by Piaget. There remains disagreement as to why those sequences occur and whether they would be the same in different environments or cultures.

8. *Cognitive development involves a complex interaction of biological and environmental factors.* Some theorists stress biological considerations more and some focus on environmental considerations. Few contemporary psychologists, however, take the extreme view that cognitive development is completely programmed in our genes and requires no environmental input; neither do many take the equally extreme view that we are blank slates passively shaped by our environments. Identifying the most important biological and environmental factors and understanding the complex interactions among them remains a major challenge for theorists of cognitive development.

Summary

There are currently two major perspectives on cognitive development: Piaget's theory and the information processing approach. Piaget believes that people of all ages know their environments by assimilating reality to their schemes and simultaneously accommodating their schemes to reality. Schemes are not isolated skills but organized and adaptive ways of knowing one's environment. As new environmental demands produce disequilibrium, the child actively constructs new schemes that are better adapted to the new realities and thus restores equilibrium. Piaget refers to this process as equilibration.

The construction of increasingly sophisticated schemes, according to Piaget, proceeds through four stages. In the sensorimotor stage (including the first 18 or 24 months of life), knowing is directly tied to physically acting on the world. The second stage, preoperations, lasts from about ages 2 to 7. During this time, the child constructs increasingly sophisticated mental schemes, culminating in the logical structures of concrete operations (ages 7 to 11). Finally, beginning about age 11, the child develops formal operational reasoning, which involves the ability to think systematically about hypotheses and possibilities.

Piaget viewed his work on cognitive development as part of a broader program of research on genetic epistemology, a developmental theory of knowledge. Educators using his ideas have emphasized the active nature of the learning process and the role of intrinsic motivation. Although Piaget's theory is vague or incorrect on many details, it is considered by most developmental psychologists to provide valuable insight into the overall nature and course of cognitive development.

The major alternative to Piaget's view is the information processing approach, which is a set of diverse theories sharing some common underlying assumptions about cognition. Three influential information processing theories are those of Siegler, Sternberg, and Case. Siegler has provided detailed analyses of the sorts of reasoning children use on a variety of cognitive tasks. He believes that a child's level of understanding can be characterized as a set of rules. Sternberg discusses intellectual abilities in terms of three sorts of components. Performance components are processes used in doing tasks; knowledge-acquisition components are central to learning; and metacomponents are the executive processes directing cognitive performance. Case has attempted to integrate information processing conceptions with Piagetian theory. He believes that gradual increases in available short-term storage space account for developmental stages in cognitive ability.

Although the three information processing approaches differ in important ways, they share an emphasis on mental representation, real-time processes, limited mental capacity, and fine-grained analysis of performance on specific tasks. Educators influenced by the information processing approach typically use careful analysis of children's current cognitive processes and of the strategy to be learned.

Because information processing research has emphasized details of performance on specific tasks, the information processing approach has been both criticized for its narrowness and applauded for its clarity and rigor.

Theorists of cognitive development agree that knowledge is highly active and organized. We will find both the Piagetian and information processing perspectives immensely valuable as we turn in the next four chapters to the study of development in four crucial areas of cognition: perception, memory, language, and reasoning.

Key Terms

cognition
intelligence
schemes
assimilation
accommodation
organization
adaptation
constructivism
disequilibrium
equilibrium
equilibration
sensorimotor stage
object permanence
representational intelligence
preoperational stage

representation
concrete operations
conservation
centration
decentration
reversibility
formal operations
hypothetico-deductive reasoning
second-order operations
genetic epistemology
nativism
empiricism
information processing
rule assessment
balance scale

states of knowledge
mechanisms of development
encoding
performance components
knowledge-acquisition components
metacomponents
neo-Piagetian theory
seven plus or minus two
mental capacity
operating space
short-term storage space
cognitive structure

Suggested Readings

Ault, R. L. (1977). *Children's cognitive development: Piaget's theory and the process approach.* New York: Oxford University Press. Ault provides an elementary introduction to and comparison of the Piagetian and information processing approaches to cognitive development.

Case, R. (1985). *Intellectual development: Birth to adulthood.* New York: Academic Press. This is the definitive presentation of Case's neo-Piagetian theory.

Furth, H. G. (1981). *Piaget and knowledge: Theoretical foundations* (2nd ed.). Chicago: University of Chicago Press. Originally published in 1969, Furth's book is widely regarded as one of the most sophisticated presentations of Piaget's theory.

Ginsburg, H., & Opper S. (1979). *Piaget's theory of intellectual development* (2nd ed.). Englewood Cliffs, NJ: Prentice-Hall. This is an excellent introduction to Piaget.

Gruber, H. E., & Vonèche, J. J. (Eds.) (1977). *The essential Piaget: An interpretive reference and guide.* New York: Basic Books. Gruber and Vonèche provide 800 pages of Piaget's most important writings, with helpful introductions to each. "This fine volume," wrote Piaget in the Foreword, "seems to me the best and the most complete of all the anthologies of my work."

Sternberg, R. J. (Ed.) (1984). *Mechanisms of cognitive development.* New York: W. H. Freeman. Six major theorists—including Siegler, Sternberg, and Case—each address the issue of how cognitive changes take place.

Application Exercises

8-1 Theorists of Cognitive Development

Identify the theorist—Piaget, Siegler, Sternberg, Case, all four, or none of them—most closely associated with each of the following.

1. Information processing analysis of performance on the balance scale shows that children use systems of rules.
2. Developmental psychologists should only consider overt behavior and not hypothesize about unobservable mental structures or events.
3. Limitations in short-term storage space are a central factor in the limited cognitive abilities of young children.
4. The study of children's cognitive development is central to developing a more general scientific theory of the origins and development of knowledge.
5. Metacomponents serve as the executive processes in human reasoning.
6. Assimilation of reality to one's schemes is accompanied by accommodation of those schemes to reality.
7. What one learns depends not only on one's environment but on one's prior knowledge.
8. The highest stage of development is formal operations.
9. Children actively construct new knowledge.
10. A great deal of human knowledge is innate rather than learned.
11. Cognitive development can be understood as the development of three distinct types of components.
12. Piagetian and information processing theories can be synthesized to give a new account of cognitive development.
13. Children at the same level in their understanding of a task may differ in their ability to encode, and thus profit from, new information.
14. Cognitive development involves increasing decentration and cognitive reversibility.
15. Tasks from IQ tests may be especially useful for the study of cognitive development.

8-2 Assessing Conservation

Many Piagetian tasks require little or no apparatus, are easily administered, and are challenging and intriguing to young children. You might want to try administering a conservation of number task, using the Piagetian clinical interview method, to children between 4 and 8 years of age. You may use the following guidelines for a start, but feel free to alter the technique. This is not a standardized test aimed at getting reliable data but rather a flexible approach aimed at generating some intriguing insights into children's thinking.

1. Tell the child you have a game to play. You might want to start with some other games to develop rapport before getting to the conservation of number task.
2. Spread a row of about six small objects (say, pennies) in front of the child and ask her to place the same number of another set of objects (say, paper clips) in a row below them. Question her and allow her to change her row until she is satisfied the two rows are equal. Even 4-year-olds are likely to succeed on this task.

3. Spread one of the rows apart and ask the child if the two rows still have the same number of objects or if one now has more than the other. Whatever her answer, ask why she thinks that and continue to question (in an interested, non-threatening manner) until you feel confident you understand her reasoning. Was her answer based on counting or on understanding the logic of the transformation? Is her thinking decentered and reversible? Try variations of the task (e.g., more or fewer objects, different objects, different arrangements).

4. If you like, continue with a conservation of liquid quantity task: Place two transparent identical cups of water in front of the child, one empty and one about half full, and ask her to fill the empty one to the same level as the other. When she is satisfied, pour the contents of one cup into a third, thinner cup. The water will now come up higher. Ask if the two cups have the same amount to drink in them or if one has more. Again, question her until you feel confident you understand her reasoning. Is her reasoning similar to her reasoning on the first task, or does she seem to have a better grasp of one form of conservation than of the other? What does she predict will happen if you pour the water back to the original cup? How does she interpret what actually happens when you do this? Do your results seem consistent with Piaget's theory, or are they different from what Piaget might have expected?

CHAPTER 9

Perceptual Development

*". . . we cannot perceive unless we anticipate,
but we must not see only what we anticipate."*
—Ulric Neisser, Cognition and Reality

Perception is the process by which persons assign meaning to stimuli in the environment. Perception is more than sensation, or the simple awareness of stimuli. Rather, it is an active, dynamic process in which children relate every new stimulus they encounter to their previous knowledge. During development, important changes occur in childrens' perceptual abilities. Understanding these changes is crucial to our learning about cognitive development. In this chapter we will first examine the development of visual abilities. In the second section of the chapter, we will focus on the development of auditory perception. Next, we will provide an overview of the development of other perceptual abilities. In the fourth section of the chapter, we present two theories of perceptual development. The chapter closes with a discussion of the applications of perceptual research.

Vision

Most of us take our vision, or sightedness, for granted; yet it is perhaps the most important of the senses. Beyond providing us with information about the colors, shapes, and textures in our environments, our vision helps us gauge the moods and emotions of other people. In addition, thanks to our vision, we have access to a major source of external information—reading. In this section, we will briefly describe the eyes' function and then focus on the development of visual perception.

The Eyes

The eyes are our visual sense receptors. Their primary function is **transduction,** or the conversion of light energy into neural impulses (Cowan, 1985; Spoehr & Lehmkuhle, 1982). The neural impulses are then carried from the eyes to the brain by the optic nerves (see Chapter 7). Figure 9-1 shows comparative cross-sections of an eye and a camera.

As you can see, the structure of the human eye resembles that of a camera. Light reaching the eye is focused on the retina, the back surface

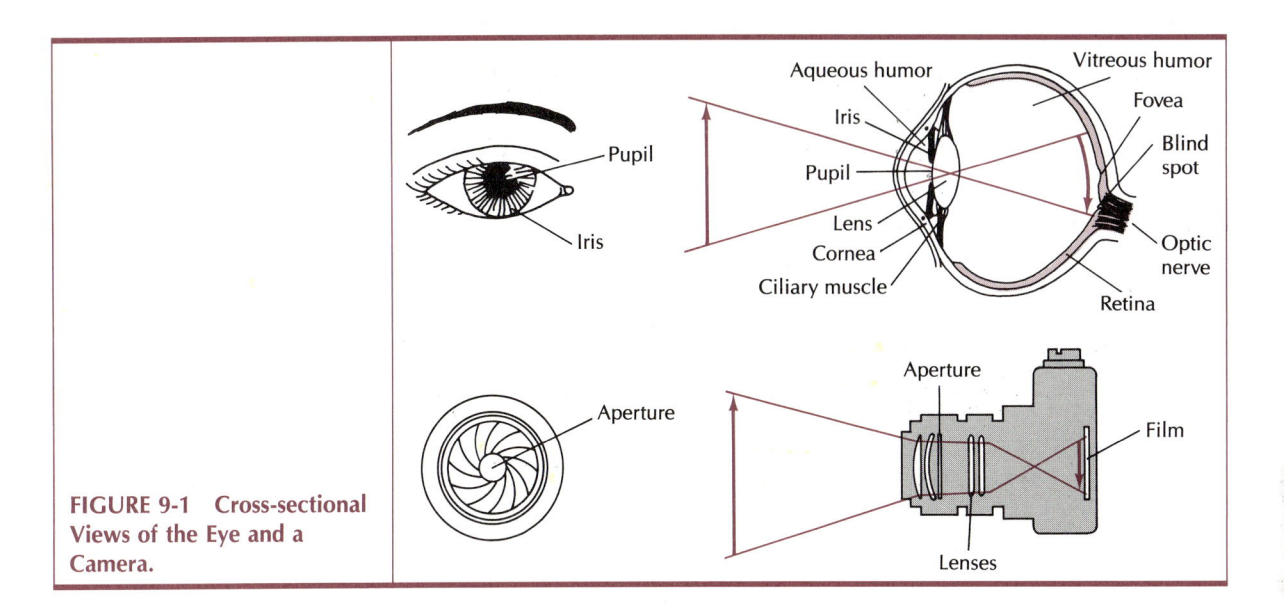

Vision

FIGURE 9-1 Cross-sectional Views of the Eye and a Camera.

of the eye, which contains light-sensitive cells. A camera, of course, also focuses light on a light-sensitive surface, the film. Interestingly, in both the camera and the eye, the image reaching the light-sensitive surface is upside down. The image from the eyes is reversed in the brain.

The eye, however, is a far more complex apparatus than any camera. The visible parts of the eye include the **sclera** (the outer white part), the **iris** (the round, colored part), and the **pupil** (the very dark center of the eye that is formed by an opening in the iris). Most of the eye's components, however, are not readily visible. To understand how these hidden parts of the eye work, we will describe what happens when light reaches the eye.

Light first passes through the **cornea**, a clear covering on the front of the eye. The cornea bends the light to allow focusing. After it is bent by the cornea, the light passes through the **aqueous humor** (a nutritive liquid for the cornea and iris) and then through the pupil. Tiny muscles in the iris control the size of the pupil, allowing different amounts of light to enter the inner eye. The pupils change noticeably when subjected to abrupt changes in light and dark such as when you pass from dark to light rooms (the pupils contract) or from bright to darker places (the pupils dilate).

Once light leaves the pupil, it passes through the **lens** where it is further bent. Light then travels through the **vitreous humor** (a clear liquid that provides nutrients to the inner eye as well as cushioning it against shock) and finally reaches the retina.

The *retina* covers the entire back of the eye except for a spot at which the optic nerve is attached (often referred to as the "blind spot"). The retina contains millions of **receptor cells**: These light-sensitive cells undergo chemical reactions when exposed to light. These chemical reactions, in turn, yield small amounts of electricity that become neural signals which then are picked up by the optic nerve and conducted back to the visual center of the cerebral cortex (see Chapter 7).

There are two kinds of receptor cells: **rods** and **cones**. Rods are very sensitive to light and are primarily responsible for night and peripheral vision. About 120 million (96 percent) of the receptor cells in the retina are rods (Spoehr & Lehmkuhle, 1982). Cones make up the other 4 percent (about 7 million) of the receptor cells. Cones seem to be primarily associated with color vision. They are found mostly in an area of the retina called the **fovea** (Goldstein, 1980), that part of the retina in which the sharpest vision occurs. Unlike rods, cones are not especially light-sensitive: This explains why it is so difficult to see colors at night or in darkened areas (Rivlin & Gravelle, 1985).

The Development of Vision

The Infant's Visual Capabilities. A newborn's eyes contain nearly an adult complement of rods and cones and are functional from the time of birth (Aantaa, 1970; Maurer, 1975). Further, the visual cortex in infants is active, although the pattern of electrical activity differs somewhat between newborns and adults (Ellingson, 1968; Umezaki & Morrell, 1970). By 2 or 3 months, the electrical patterns of babies' visual cortexes closely approximate those of adults (Harter & Suitt, 1970; Jensen & Engle, 1971), with full adult capacities attained as early as age 2 (Ellingson, Lathrop, Nelson, & Donahy, 1972). Additional evidence (e.g., newborns can discriminate between very similar colors) suggests that true color vision is present in newborn babies (Milewski & Siqueland, 1975; Bornstein, 1975) and that reactions to movement also occur (e.g., Harris & MacFarlane, 1974; Schulman, 1973). Further, Bower's (1966, 1971, 1979) work on how infants follow objects with their eyes suggests that "infants are capable of perceiving most of the sensory information that adults do, but they seem to have less of a processing capacity" (1966, p. 92), a conclusion consistent with the work of Case (see Chapter 8). In terms of visual acuity, neonates have about 20/600 vision, which improves to about 20/150 by about 4 months of age (Salapatek, 1977). Normal vision, of course, is **20/20**. In contrast, 20/600 vision means that a neonate sees an object 20 feet away no better than a normal adult sees that object at 600 feet. It seems that babies do not have good distance vision, although their near vision is apparently excellent.

Understanding Perception in Infants. Perception is an active process in which meaning is assigned to stimuli. Studying perception in adults is not difficult since we can ask them what they see. For example, we can show adults an unusual picture and request that they describe it. Infants, of course, cannot describe what they perceive or gesture to indicate that they are thinking about one object and not another. Because of our inability to determine directly what infants perceive, developmental psychologists had to develop methods to allow researchers to infer infants' perceptions. That is, they had to invent indirect methods of studying perception in infants.

One indirect method of determining which elements of the environment are perceived involves discovering what people pay attention to. For example, if we film adults as they watch a computer screen containing many nonsense symbols and very few real words, we will find that most of their attention is devoted to the real words and very little is given to the nonsense. Later, when we talk to the adults, we would likely find out that they had indeed perceived these words but that the rest of the screen made no sense. This relationship between perception and attention has been used by developmental researchers to infer what babies perceive.

The simplest way to measure babies' attention is to give them several things to look at and determine whether they spend more time looking at some things than others. As an example, when three globes are placed above a newborn baby lying on its back, the baby should spend an equal amount of time looking at each. In fact, if the globes are identical, this is borne out. However, if we present three globes—one brightly lit, one moderately bright, and one very dim—newborns spend most of their time looking at the moderately bright globe. This difference in the way babies allocate their attention tells us that they are able to tell the difference among the globes. That is, they have assigned some meaning to (perceived) the globes (Hershanson, 1964).

Researchers have used several methods besides determining where babies look to infer perception (see Banks & Salapatek, 1983, for a thorough review of the research). For example, a baby's pulse rate can be monitored as the child is shown different objects. If the baby's pulse rate increases when certain objects are shown, we can infer that the baby is reacting to seeing the object and that some form of rudimentary perception has occurred. Similarly, the rate at which a baby sucks at a nipple can be measured when the baby is shown different objects. If the baby changes its sucking rate, we can infer that the baby is reacting to what it sees and that perception has occurred (Von Bargen, 1983).

Another method that has allowed researchers to make inferences about the perceptual abilities of babies involves the use of stimuli to which they have become habituated. **Habituation** occurs when a stimulus becomes so familiar that it no longer causes any response. For example, a picture placed in a baby's line of sight may initially cause changes in the baby's pulse rate, breathing rhythm, and so on. However, if the picture is always present, sooner or later the baby will stop reacting to it. After babies are habituated to a stimulus, researchers show them pictures that differ subtly from the first. If babies react to these small changes, the inference is that they can perceive some differences among the pictures (Dannemiller & Banks, 1983).

Studies using different methods of measuring attention and reaction to visual stimuli have given us a great deal of information about what babies perceive. Newborns perceive differences in illumination and prefer to look at moving objects as opposed to those at rest (Haith, 1966; Kremnitzer, Vaughan, Kurtzberg, & Dowling, 1979). In general, it also seems that babies prefer complex stimuli to simple stimuli. For example, Robert Fantz (1965) performed a classic study of infants' perceptions when he followed up on Stirnimann's (1944) findings that even 1-day-old babies prefer patterns to plain surfaces. In his study, Fantz placed babies (aged 2 days to 6 months) in a "looking chamber" in which different objects were placed above them. Fantz confirmed Stirnimann's work: Newborn babies spent more time attending to patterns than nonpatterned surfaces. In addition, Fantz found that as babies became older, they preferred to look at more complex objects such as bull's-eye patterns.

Unfortunately, measures of attention cannot tell us *how* something is perceived. Even though we know that newborn babies perceive differences in illumination, and that they prefer to look at complex stimuli, we cannot infer what babies actually perceive. This inability has led to some interesting debates, especially in the research focusing on how babies perceive complex stimuli.

Infants' Perception of Complex Stimuli. An early study by Fantz (1961) set the stage for recent debates about how babies perceive complex stimuli. In this study, Fantz (1961) exposed 2- and 3-month-old babies to six different kinds of disks: plain white, solid yellow, solid red, a bull's-eye pattern, a disk containing newsprint, and a disk with a drawing of a human face on it. Fantz found that babies greatly preferred to look at the disk depicting a face and that the patterned disks were watched far more than the plain ones (see Figure 9-2).

As interesting as this study is, it caused considerable debate. That is, it did not show whether babies actually prefer to look at faces or whether other, equally complex stimuli would have the same effect. Later research (e.g., Caron, Caron, Caldwell, & Weiss, 1973; Haith, Bergman, & Moore, 1977) seemed to indicate that any complex stimulus array will draw the attention of babies at this age, whether or not it is face-like. More recently, however, Langsdorf, Izard, Rayias, and Hembree (1983) and Sherrod (1978) have provided convincing evidence that, compared to other equally complex objects, the human face is *uniquely* interesting. In the Langsdorf et al. (1983) study, for example, young

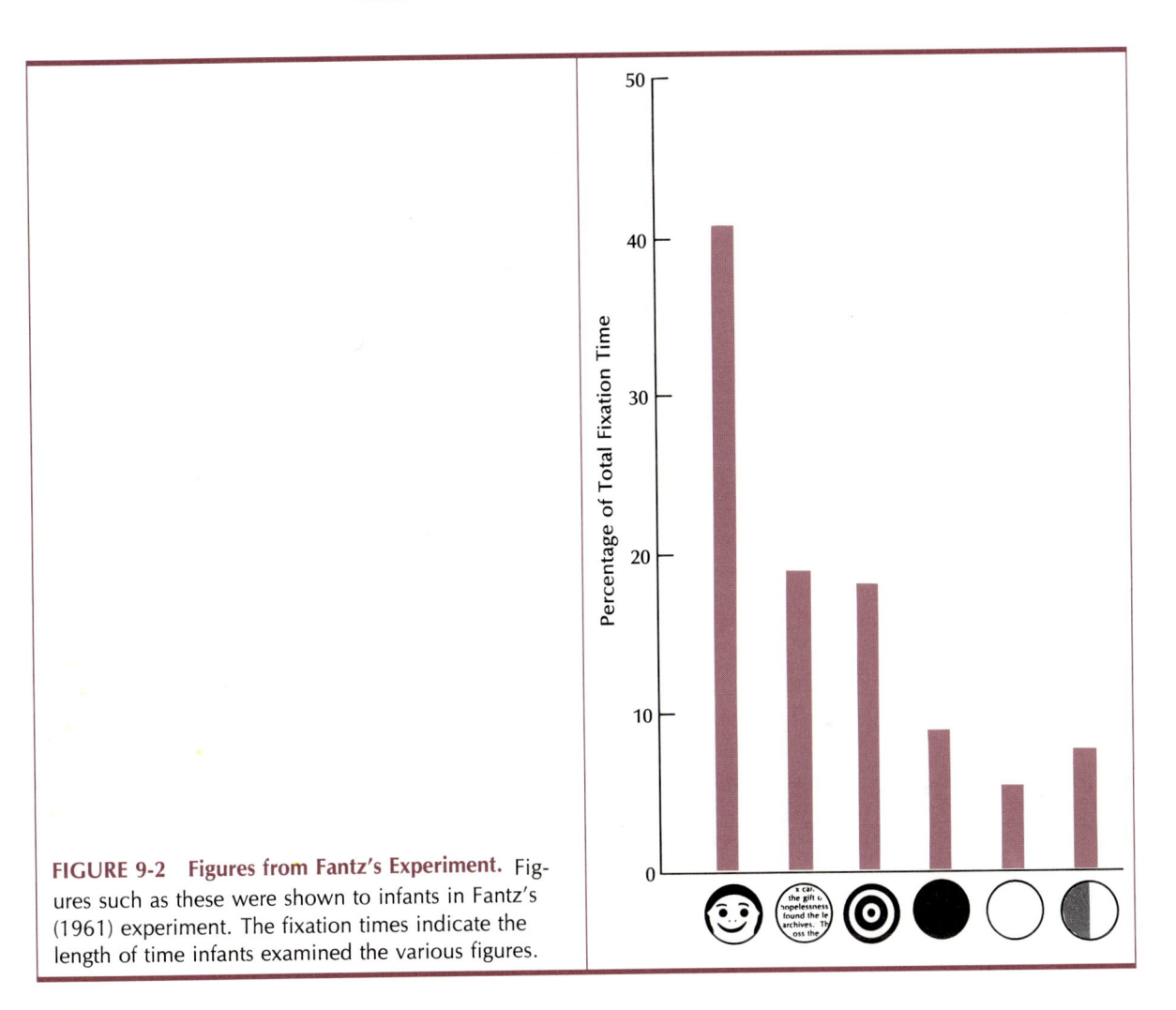

FIGURE 9-2 Figures from Fantz's Experiment. Figures such as these were shown to infants in Fantz's (1961) experiment. The fixation times indicate the length of time infants examined the various figures.

infants were shown real faces, mannequins, and equally complex inanimate objects. The infants spent significantly more time gazing at the real human face than at the mannequin and more time looking at the mannequin's face than at the inanimate objects. The debate is likely to continue, however, because of the problems of defining and measuring stimulus complexity.

Even if the human face is special, it is clear that infants find other sorts of complexity interesting. What is it about complex stimuli that draws babies' attention? Several studies that have employed different methods of tracking babies' eye movements have examined this question (see Figure 9-3). These studies generally have found that areas of contrast such as the edges and corners of triangles are most frequently

FIGURE 9-3 Visual Scanning in Newborn Infants. As seen in (a), babies' attention seems to be drawn primarily to corners. Figure (b) was shown to 7-year-olds in a study by Zaporozhets (1965). The contrast in how newborns and 7-year-olds search for information seems clear.

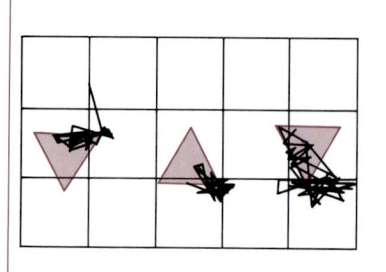

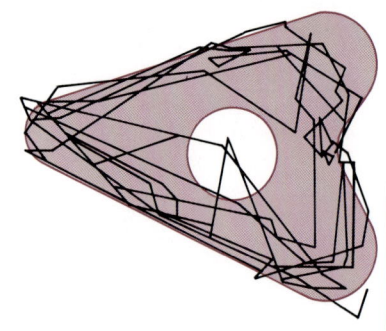

(a) Figure presented to newborns

(b) Figure presented to second graders

attended to (Bornstein, 1984; Hainline & Lemerise, 1982; Salapatek & Kessen, 1966). Similarly, when babies are shown drawings of faces they pay attention to areas of contrast most frequently (Caron et al., 1973; Hainline, 1978; Haith, 1977). In addition, until they are 2 months old, babies tend to stay fixed on one area of contrast and not search for others (Banks & Salapatek, 1983).

The fact that babies' attention is drawn to complex elements of the environment is interesting from an evolutionary point of view. An analysis of almost any environmental setting indicates that complex stimulus situations provide the majority of information. Evolution seems to have provided babies with an innate tendency to attend to those parts of the environment from which they can gain the most information, making this a fine example of how heredity and environment interact to maximize cognitive development.

Depth Perception. We explored the research on **depth perception** in Chapter 3 as a part of our discussion of research methods in developmental psychology. To recap: The results of depth perception studies indicate that babies apparently perceive depth in the first few months of life but do not show fear of falling over edges until they are about 8 months old. As we saw, several theories have been put forward to explain this phenomenon. Hereditary views are currently the dominant theory.

Visual Constancy. **Visual constancy** is the ability to see an object as the same throughout a variety of spatial transformations (Marr, 1982). Two important aspects of visual constancy are **size constancy** (understanding that an object does not change in size because it is nearer or farther away) and **shape constancy** (understanding that an object's shape does not change when it is seen from a new perspective). Both size and shape constancy are complex perceptual processes because they require considerable knowledge on the part of the observer. More information than is actually received by the eye is necessary for this perception and must be supplied by higher cognitive processes.

When do visual constancies develop in infants? Bower (1966) has presented evidence that infants possess size constancy by about 7 weeks of age and that they have the beginnings of shape constancy at about 12 weeks of age. More recent work (see Tighe & Shepp, 1983), however, suggests that visual constancies are not fully developed until about the age of 6 months (see also Banks & Salapatek, 1983). Even so, we know that sophisticated perceptual processes exist at a very early age.

Later Development in Visual Perception. A good deal of research has examined the development of visual perception in childhood. Here, we will emphasize specifically form perception, the perception of illusions, and how children at different ages search for information.

Form perception refers to the ability to identify and discriminate one form from others. Form perception of the letter "F" occurs, for example, when a child can identify the letter "F" and distinguish it from other forms (e.g., "E," "P," "T"). Obviously, form perception is especially important to reading (Bornstein, 1984).

Some of the best known work on form perception has been done by Eleanor and James Gibson. In an early study, they compared the abilities of 6- to 8-year-olds, 8½- to 11-year-olds, and adults to identify a specific form (in this case, a coil-shaped figure much like ⧙). They

Visual constancy enables us to see these two tracks as having the same size and shape, even though they are seen from a different perspective.

began by showing all study participants the form they were to know and then asked them to identify it every time it appeared in the context of an array of very similar forms (see Figure 9-4). As the Gibsons had predicted, the adults performed this task better than the 8½- to 11-year-olds, who were in turn superior to the 6- to 8-year-olds. Clearly, the ability to perceive a complex form improves with age.

A related study by the Gibsons and their colleagues (Gibson, Gibson, Pick, & Osser, 1962) was designed to investigate how 4- to 8-year-old children learn to distinguish letter-like forms. As in the earlier Gibson and Gibson (1955) study, the researchers found that the ability to identify and discriminate forms improved with age. One result of this study, however, was of particular interest: The children most often confused the forms they were to know (e.g., ₹) with left-to-right or right-to-left reversals of the forms (e.g., ₹). One would expect, then, that children learning to read would also have the most trouble with similar letter reversals (e.g., "d" and "b," "p" and "q"). This, of course, does seem to be the case (Gibson & Levin, 1975; Schank, 1982). Bornstein (1984) has suggested that such discrimination errors occur because left-to-right (or right-to-left) reversals are rare in nature and that the

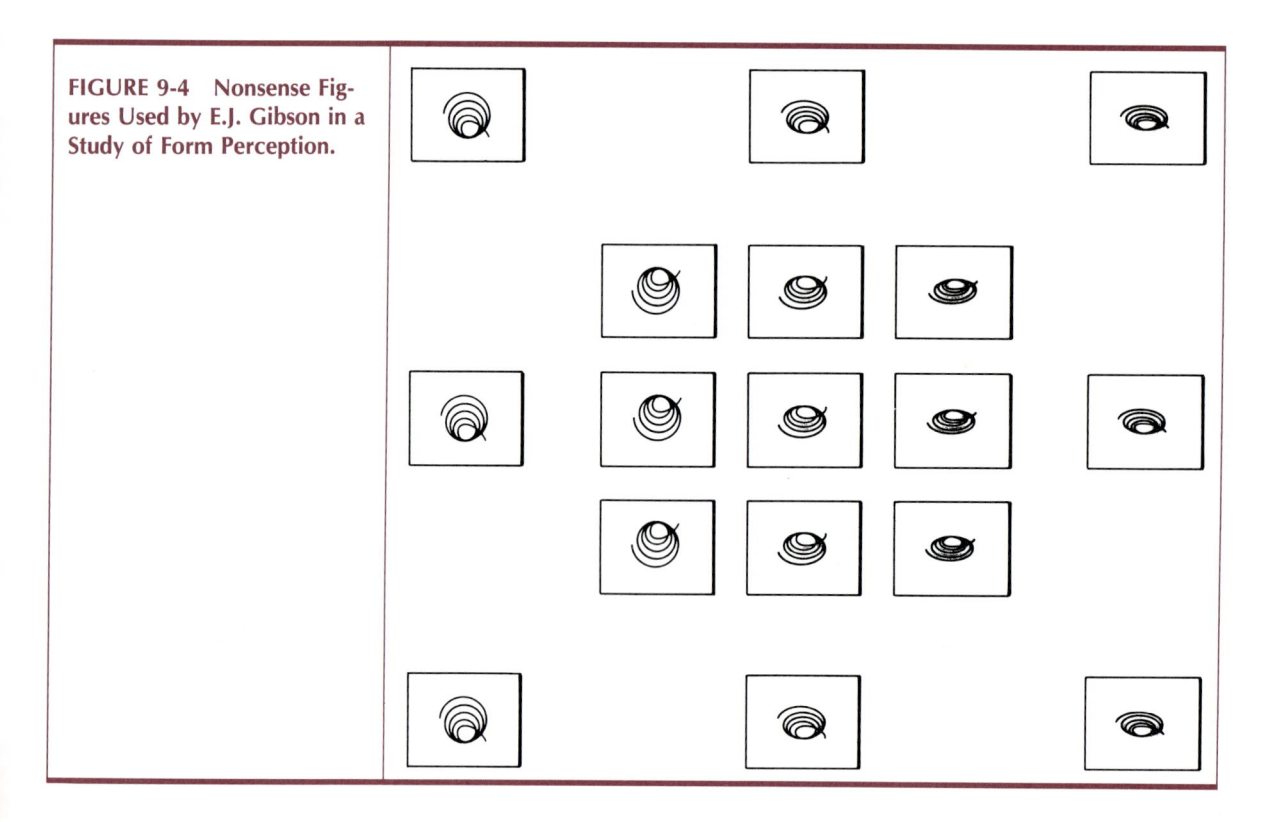

FIGURE 9-4 Nonsense Figures Used by E.J. Gibson in a Study of Form Perception.

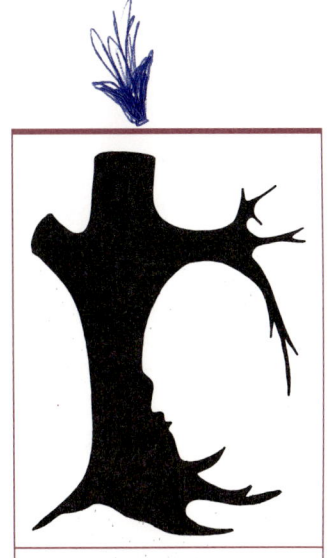

FIGURE 9-5 A Simple Illusion. By about the age of 10, children usually can see both the tree and the face.

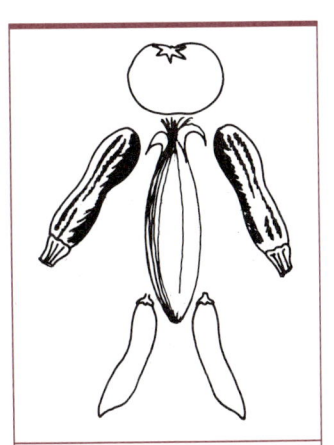

FIGURE 9-6 Illusion similar to that used by Elkind. Older children decenter and see both the vegetables and a "person."

human perceptual system has not evolved in ways sensitive to such reversals. Because children's perceptual systems (and, presumably also the perceptual systems of adults) seem to be relatively insensitive to left-to-right reversals, Bornstein (1984, p. 117) argues that "children must apparently *un*learn a natural perceptual constancy" in beginning reading.

The **perception of illusions** refers to how children (and adults) respond to visual stimuli that can be understood in different ways (Elkind, 1978; Vurpillot, 1976). Figures 9-5 and 9-6 are examples of such visual stimuli. Figure 9-5, for example, can be seen as either a tree or a face. Adults can usually see both images very easily, but 2- to 3-year-old children often see neither. Four- to 5-year-old children typically see the tree but not the face. Seven- to 8-year-olds frequently see both, but sometimes need help in picking out both images. By the age of 10 or so, children seem to attain the adult-like ability to see spontaneously both the tree and the face. Clearly, the visual stimuli in Figure 9-5 are the same for children of different ages. What changes is how the children see the stimuli, which is a direct outcome of cognitive development.

Figure 9-6 is a different kind of illusion similar to that used by Elkind (1975) in a study of how children of different ages perceived figures that could be interpreted in different ways. Elkind's results were highly similar to those previously described and also point to the fact that perception is guided by cognitive development. Elkind (1975) argued that because older children are decentered (from a Piagetian perspective, see Chapter 8) they are able to see both the parts and the whole of the figure.

The results of form perception research and illusion perception research show that perception becomes increasingly sophisticated as cognitive development proceeds. A question that arises from this research is whether or not the actual *search for information* changes as children grow older. That is, do older children look for different information in different ways than younger children? Vurpillot (1968, 1976) has done some interesting research on this question. In one especially clear study, children were asked to look at pictures of pairs of houses and decide whether they were the same or different (see Figure 9-7). Using an eye-tracking methodology that could pinpoint where the children looked, Vurpillot (1976) found that the visual search patterns of younger children were relatively unsystematic. By the age of six, however, visual searches became far more systematic. Not only did the older children examine the key elements of the pictures (in this case, the windows); they also carefully cross-checked the windows in each pair of houses. The results of this study, then, strongly indicate that the search for information changes as children grow older. As cognitive

312   CHAPTER 9   Perceptual Development

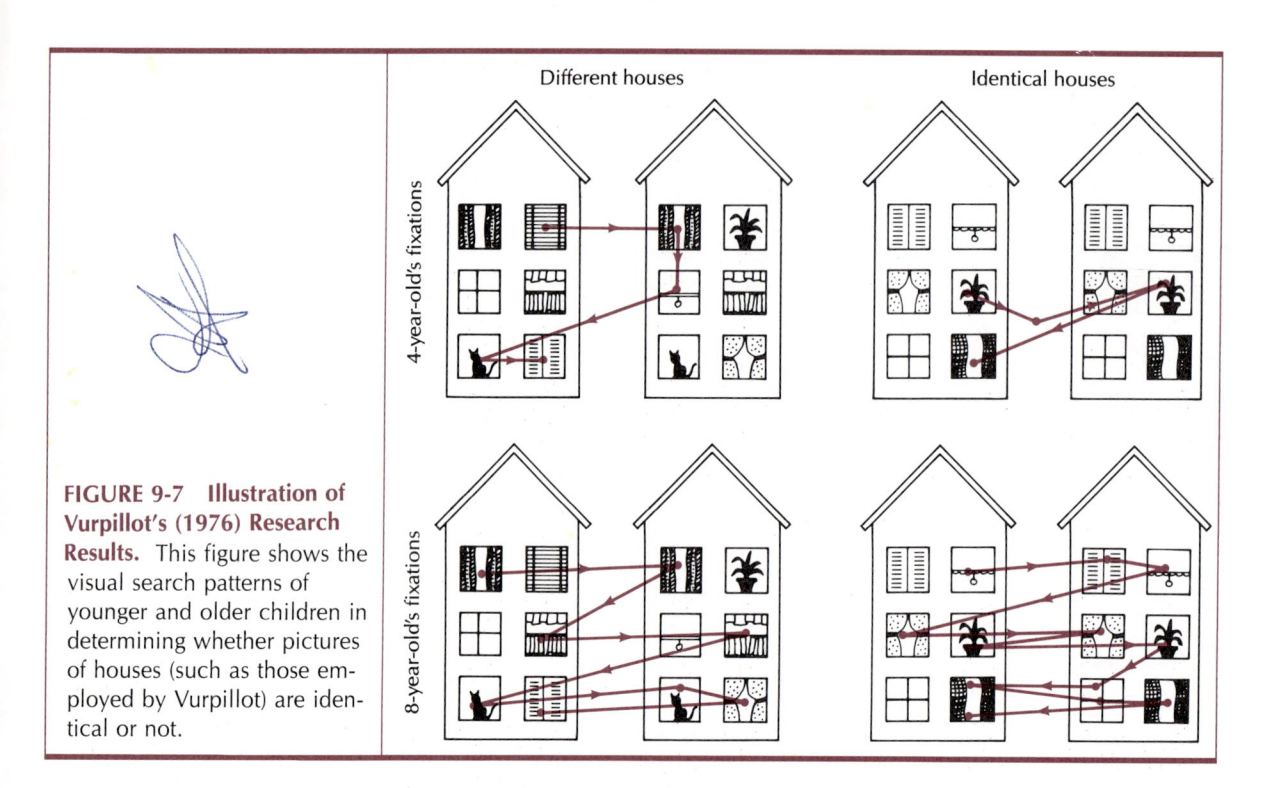

FIGURE 9-7   Illustration of Vurpillot's (1976) Research Results. This figure shows the visual search patterns of younger and older children in determining whether pictures of houses (such as those employed by Vurpillot) are identical or not.

Coordination of the senses is critical to learning.

development proceeds, children's knowledge of the world increases and so does their knowledge of how to gain relevant information about the world (Tighe & Shepp, 1983). As we mentioned early in the chapter, perception is a dynamic process driven by the child's increasing capabilities.

Hearing

We learn a great deal about the world from our hearing. Certainly, the learning and use of spoken language is heavily dependent on how well we hear. Because hearing is so closely linked to language learning, it is important to examine how hearing operates.

The ears are the auditory sense receptors. They translate sound waves (vibrations in air or some other medium) into neural impulses which are then conducted to the auditory center of the cerebral cortex (Goldstein, 1980) via the auditory nerve.

Figure 9-8 depicts the structures of the human ear. The ear has three basic subdivisions: the outer ear, the middle ear, and the inner ear. The **outer ear** consists of the pinna, which is the flap of skin on the side of the head, and the **auditory canal**. The pinna funnels sound waves into the auditory canal, which conducts the sound to the eardrum, or **tympanic membrane.**

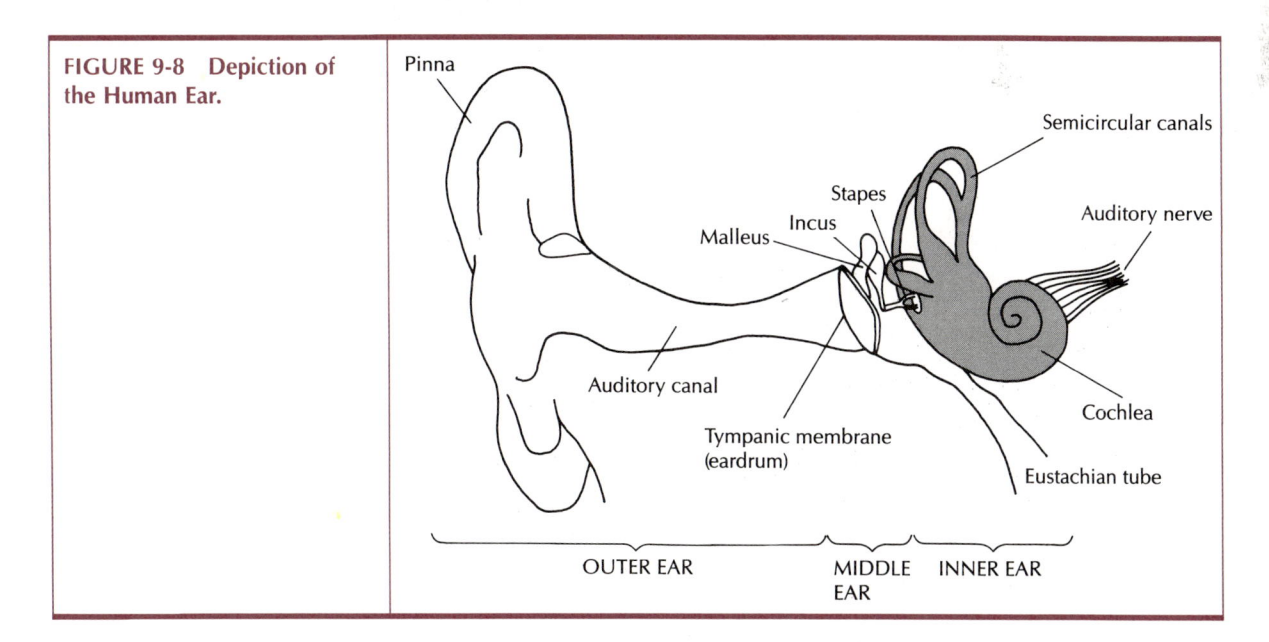

FIGURE 9-8 Depiction of the Human Ear.

The eardrum is the first part of the **middle ear**. When sound waves encounter the eardrum, they cause it to vibrate, much as the head of a drum vibrates when hit with a drumstick. The eardrum is connected to three tiny, interconnected bones (called the **ossicles**): the malleus, the incus, and the stapes. When the eardrum vibrates, it sets these three bones into motion. The motion is amplified as the vibrations move from bone to bone. The stapes, the last of these three bones, hammers against the **cochlea**.

The cochlea, which is part of the **inner ear**, is a hollow bone structure filled with liquid. When the stapes beats against the cochlea, it causes waves of the liquid to form which then travel through the cochlea. These waves bend tiny hairs inside the cochlea. The bending of these hairs translates the mechanical energy of sound waves into neural impulses. The auditory nerve receives these impulses from the cochlea and transmits them to the brain.

The Development of Hearing

During the last few years there has been a dramatic increase in research on auditory development (see Aslin, Pisoni, & Jusczyk, 1983). Despite this, we know far less about the development of hearing than we do about the development of vision. In particular, very little research is being conducted on developmental changes in hearing after infancy (Bornstein, 1984). Our focus here, then, will be primarily on the development of hearing in infancy.

Research on how infants respond to sound suggests that low tones tend to sooth babies whereas very high tones upset them (Eisenberg, 1970; Eisenberg, Griffin, Coursin, & Hunter, 1964). Further, babies as young as 3 days of age show preferences for their mothers' voices as opposed to those of female strangers (DeCasper & Fifer, 1980). In one particularly interesting study of infants' recognition of their mothers' voices, DeCasper and Fifer (1980; see also Kolata, 1984) devised a procedure whereby newborn babies could suck on a nipple in different ways in order to hear their mothers read various stories. The fact that *newborn* babies would suck on a nipple to hear stories is of interest by itself; but more intriguing is the fact that the babies showed definite preferences for stories their mothers had read aloud during the last 6½ weeks of pregnancy! DeCasper and Fifer concluded that such listening preferences for stories among newborn babies could only occur if unborn babies are able to hear their own mothers' voices well before birth and discriminate them from other sounds.

Speech Perception. The development of speech perception, a part of the overall development of language, is discussed in depth in Chapter 11, *The Development of Language*. Here, we wish only to make two points: First, as we will see in Chapter 11, the perception of speech is crucial to all aspects of both cognitive and social development. Second, speech perception is an area of research in which the focus has centered more and more on the relationship of heredity and environment.

On the surface, it seems obvious that the environment would play the dominant role in language development generally and speech perception specifically. However, recent reviews of the development of speech perception (e.g., Eimas, 1985) suggest that inborn mechanisms of speech perception account for the apparent ease with which babies learn to speak and understand language. As Eimas has stated, babies "are richly endowed with innate perceptual mechanisms, well adapted to the characteristics of human language, that prepare them for the linguistic world they will encounter" (1985, p. 46).

As an example of research in this area, several developmental psychologists have examined babies' abilities to distinguish among similar consonants (e.g., the "p" in "pin" and the "b" in "bin"). Eimas, Siqueland, Jusczyk, and Vigorito (1971) determined that American babies were able to make such discriminations very easily. These results have been replicated with Guatemalan (Lasky, Syrdal-Lasky, & Klein, 1975) and Kenyan infants (Streeter, 1976). The apparent universality of babies' abilities to discriminate among different consonants suggests that such "categorization occurs because a child is born with perceptual mechanisms that are tuned to the properties of speech" (Eimas, 1985, p. 49).

Speech perception, however, is not free from environmental influences. Eimas (1985), for example, reports that whereas adult Japanese are seldom able to distinguish between the sounds of "r" and "l" without special training, Japanese babies are able to do so just as well as babies born in the United States. Apparently, since the distinction between "r" and "l" is not important in the Japanese language but it is extremely important in English, environmental effects bring about changes in speech perception abilities. The development of speech perception, then, seems to be the result of the interplay of heredity and environment.

Coordination of Vision and Hearing. A particularly interesting study of newborns' hearing abilities was conducted by Wertheimer in 1961 (Coren, Porac, & Ward, 1979; McBurney & Collings, 1984). Wertheimer tested a *3-minute-old* girl by sounding a toy "cricket" next to either her right or her left ear. Two observers kept track of whether the baby's eyes moved to the left, right, or not at all. The results indicated that the baby's eyes moved in the direction of the clicks 18 out of 22 times.

Wertheimer's study, of course, is extremely limited. Nevertheless, the identification of location (inferred from the eye movements) implies that some rudimentary **coordination of the senses** was occurring. Contrary results on locating sounds, however, have been reported by Bower (1977) and McGurk and Lewis (1974). Their results indicate that the ability to visually locate the source of sounds is developed by the fourth month of life, but is absent in younger children. Similarly, the *Bayley Scales of Infant Development* (a standardized rating scale for measuring developmental skills) gives 3.8 months as the average age at which vision and hearing are coordinated (Bayley, 1969, p. 51).

More recently, Muir and Field have shown that the pattern of how vision and hearing coordinate is more complex than was earlier thought. Their data indicate that newborn babies *do* orient their eyes toward sound but that this coordination ability declines during the second and third month and reasserts itself in the fourth month. Muir and Field argued that the conflicting evidence in the literature prior to their study was due to testing babies who were not always alert, to using brief sounds, and to not allowing enough time for reaction. Apparently, sight and sound can be coordinated very soon after birth with some reduction in this ability (except, it seems, for how babies look for their mothers when they hear their voices) during the second and third month. The coordination of vision and hearing is well established during the fourth month and continues to improve thereafter (Aslin et al., 1983; Bigelow, 1983).

One hypothesis that could account for disparate research results is based on a change in the type of coordination behavior as children develop. That is, visually searching for sounds may be reflexive (inborn) among newborn infants. Such a reflex, however, may be similar to other reflexes present early in life in that it may cease functioning after a few weeks (see Chapter 6). Once the reflex stops working, the coordination of hearing and vision would have to be learned: That is, it would become a voluntary behavior. This reflex/voluntary shift hypothesis would account for the fact that coordination of sight and sound seems to be present at birth but fades out in a few weeks only to reappear at about 4 months.

Smell, Taste, and Touch

The other senses—smell, taste, and touch—also allow us to gain knowledge about the external world. All three senses are reasonably well understood, but developmental psychologists generally pay less attention to them than to vision and hearing. Smell and taste are important, but they are not usually seen as crucial in cognitive development (Walk, 1981). We have all temporarily "lost" our sense of smell and had our sense of taste greatly reduced during bouts with the flu or colds. While enjoyment of eating or drinking is diminished, most of us do not find such information losses to be crucial. The sense of touch, in contrast, is very important to many aspects of cognition. Fortunately, however, loss of the sense of touch is rare, and when it does occur, is usually highly localized (e.g., losing feeling in a finger as a result of an accident).

Because less research has been conducted on the relationship of smell, taste, and touch to cognitive development, we will not examine these senses in depth. In brief, smell depends on chemically sensitive cells in the upper part of the nasal cavity that react to molecules in the air. The cells produce neural impulses that are sent to the brain. Taste operates in a somewhat similar fashion, depending on the chemical stimulation of receptor cells on the tongue, the inside of the cheeks, and the larynx. When these receptors are stimulated (different combinations of stimuli account for different tastes), they produce neural impulses that are then forwarded to the brain. The sense of touch operates through various receptors in the skin that are sensitive to warmth, cold, pressure, and pain.

The Development of Smell, Taste, and Touch

Exactly how the senses of smell, taste, and touch develop is not clear. However, research has shown that month-old babies reject bitter tastes and prefer the taste of milk over sugar solutions (Engen, Lipsitt, & Peck, 1974; Nowlis & Kessen, 1976). In fact, young children are better equipped than adults to taste things in that they possess more taste buds—babies even have taste buds on the inside of their cheeks!

The sense of smell is also present in neonates. Babies react negatively to odors such as vinegar or ammonia and positively to their mothers' scent (Russell, 1976). Newborns do not, however, react to any other pleasurable odors (e.g., flowers, foods) until considerably later in infancy, nor do they react negatively to the smell of human wastes.

Touch perception is present in neonates. Babies can be comforted with hugs or by being wrapped snugly in blankets. After just a few days of life they are quite sensitive to pain, as anyone who has ever slipped with a diaper pin can testify. Babies are also aware of temperature and motion: They prefer warm, comfortable areas and are soothed by being rocked or walked. In fact, as we will see in Chapter 14, contact comfort can play an important role in parent-child attachment.

Applications of Perception Research

A review of the literature on perceptual development yields guidelines for parents and professionals. These guidelines emphasize the importance of identifying perceptual problems early and taking steps to facilitate perceptual development.

1. *Be alert for potential vision problems*. Parents and child care professionals must be on the lookout for excessive squinting, complaints

Research

Sensory Deprivation

Given the relationship of perception and cognitive development, we would suspect that babies raised in environments that provide very little sensory stimulation should lag behind their normally reared peers in terms of intellectual abilities (Walk, 1981). Despite the reasonableness of this assumption, there is little clear evidence available. The reason for this is that when babies experience extremely unstimulating environments, these environments are also likely to be emotionally barren (or even openly hostile) and lacking in parent–child bonds. In other words, severe deprivation usually includes both emotional *and* **sensory deprivation**. It is very difficult to determine what role each element in a deprived environment plays.

Partial sensory deprivation can be found in children without other confounding factors when there are congenital vision defects. For example, some children suffer from **strabismus**, a condition in which the muscles controlling the eyes do not allow the eyes to properly line up. This inability to line up the eyes results in the absence of binocular vision, which allows us to coordinate the information reaching each of the eyes. Without binocular vision, depth perception is greatly impaired.

Banks, Aslin, and Letson (1975) studied gains in binocular vision after corrective surgery. They found that children operated on before the age of three gained full binocular vision whereas children operated on after the age of four did not. These results suggest that early sensory deprivation can be overcome if the correction occurs early. During normal development, the visual region of the cortex forms cells that deal with binocular vision. However, if binocular stimulation is denied past the age of four, no binocular cells form and the ability to coordinate information from the eyes does not develop (see Walk, 1981).

Another form of partial sensory deprivation occurs in **astigmatism**, which is a condition in which the lens is imperfect and distorted images are passed to the retina. Some astigmatics have trouble seeing vertical or horizontal lines. When Mitchell, Freeman, Millodot, and Haegerstrom (1973) completely corrected the astigmatism errors of a group of adults, they found that many still could not perceive some of the lines. Because this impairment was no longer in the eyes, it had to be occurring elsewhere. Mitchell et al. concluded that the absense of sensory stimulation caused by the astigmatism had led to the visual cortex's inability to handle certain information (in this case, certain of the lines the former astigmatics were shown), a result that has been experimentally produced in research on animals.

An hypothesis designed to account for the effects of sensory deprivation on perceptual development may be based on the concept of "critical" or "sensitive" periods of development. In general, a **sensitive period** of development refers to a time in the organism's life at which certain specific stimuli must be encountered in order for a facet of development to occur. The example of strabismus indicates that binocular vision will not develop if children do not receive binocular stimulation prior to the age of four. Because the visual center of the cortex forms prior to the age of four, binocular stimulation after this age will not produce cells designed to deal with binocular stimulation. As we will see later in the text, there appears to be a sensitive period for language acquisition among humans and there may also be sensitive periods related to social development.

about not being able to see, rubbing the eyes, holding objects too close to the eyes, eyes that lack proper muscle control, and eyes that cross. Small children, especially, do not know what "normal" vision is and cannot report difficulties. Because of this, adults must be extremely sensitive to any signs of potential vision problems.

2. *Be aware of potential hearing impediments.* Children under the age of three do not understand what "normal" hearing is. A 10-month-old child, for example, may suffer congestion as a result of a cold or a throat infection and suffer a reduction in the quality of his hearing. Unless there is pain (which sets off crying and fussing), the baby may not know that anything is the matter; and certainly he will not be able to explain his condition. Consequently, parents and child-care professionals need to be very observant during and after children's colds and sore throats. Any changes in sensitivity to sound or any motions that seem to indicate a discomfort in the ears should be investigated. Physicians can treat infected or blocked ears in several ways, thereby reestablishing normal hearing.

3. *Avoid overly loud noise.* Related to problems caused by illness is the potential for hearing loss due to loud noises. Extremely loud noise (whether from heavy equipment, a stereo, or living next door to the elevated railroad) can cause permanent auditory damage without bringing about enough discomfort to result in pain. Adults should carefully monitor children's use of earphones and should keep children from areas where extremely loud noises occur.

4. *Schedule regular vision and hearing checks.* Even if there are no apparent problems, children should have regular examinations of their sight and hearing. These can be part of a routine examination by a family doctor or pediatrician.

5. *Correct vision and hearing problems promptly.* The vast majority of visual and auditory problems are correctable. The sooner perceptual problems are corrected, the smaller their impact will be. If parents cannot afford glasses, hearing aids, or other corrective measures, a social services agency may be able to arrange for low- or no-cost help.

6. *Choose toys for infants that are easily seen and that allow them to coordinate their vision and hearing.* Research has shown that infants are very nearsighted and that they must develop voluntary control over the coordination of hearing and vision. Mobiles (toys that may be placed over a crib) should contain large, colorful elements. Further, mobiles and other toys that make noise provide infants with the opportunity to coordinate hearing and vision. All toys, of course, should be safe for infants as well.

Children are active perceivers and relate new experiences to what they already know.

7. *Make new information meaningful to children.* Children's minds are not little boxes into which we can shove information. They are active perceivers who relate each new thing they see or hear to what they already know. Many factors affect how children relate new information to what they already know, including prior knowledge, interests, difficulty, and familiarity. Parents and teachers should use activities children enjoy and relate new information to things children are already interested in. In many ways, the meaningfulness of information depends on how it is presented to children.

8. *When children begin school, be alert to the possibility of specific perceptual handicaps.* Some children of average or above average ability may have specific perceptual difficulties that interfere with school performance. One well-known category of disability, considered by some experts to be perceptually based, is **dyslexia.** In this condition, otherwise normal children are unable to read successfully. Other children may have perceptual or attentional difficulties that interfere with their comprehension of speech, making it difficult to understand explanations or instructions. Especially in the primary grades, teachers and parents need to be alert to such problems. Early intervention can often minimize the negative impact of perceptual difficulties on academic achievement and self concept.

Theories of Perceptual Development

To this point we have described the development of perceptual abilities, mentioned some of the possible negative influences on perceptual development, and outlined a set of guidelines drawn from research. We now turn to theories that *explain* how perception develops. Although there are a great many theories of perception (see Anderson, 1980; Long & Baddeley, 1980; McBurney & Collings, 1984; Rivlin & Gravelle, 1985; Rock, 1984), most have focused on adults and have not been specifically devoted to how perception develops in children. In this section, we present two major theories of perceptual development: those of Jean Piaget and Eleanor Gibson. We chose these two theories for several reasons. Piaget's theory was one of the first fully articulated theories of perceptual development, and it remains the most influential constructivist (see Chapter 8) theory of perception with influences on many contemporary perspectives (see Rock, 1984). Where Piaget's theory presents a prototypical constructivist perspective, Gibson's is an extreme version of a differentiation theory. Where Piaget's emphasis has been on the construction of reality by individuals, Gibson's has been on the detection of information already present in the environment. Understanding the theories of Piaget and Gibson will give you a balanced perspective on perception and allow you to tie together the results of research in perceptual development.

Jean Piaget: A Constructivist Theory

Jean Piaget (e.g., 1969), whose theory of intellectual development we discussed in detail in Chapter 8, was also concerned with perceptual development. Piaget, we have seen, was a constructivist theorist who emphasized the interaction of children's cognitive structures with the environment. Not surprisingly, the interactive nature of cognitive development also formed the core of Piaget's ideas about perception.

For Piaget, perception is the *construction* of reality: What is encountered in the environment is perceived in terms of children's knowledge about the world. For example, a 4-year-old child attending his older brother's piano recital merely perceives music. He does not have the knowledge to allow him to differentiate among waltzes, minuets, or jazz. In Piaget's view (e.g., 1969; see also Gross, 1985), the boy in our example cannot perceive differences in kinds of music because he has no knowledge about them. His perceptions are based solely on what he does know: that people are playing the piano and that some pieces sound "harder" than others.

Perception is a highly active process in Piagetian theory: Perception occurs when the meaning of incoming stimuli is constructed. The construction of meaning has two components, figurative and operative. The **figurative component** refers to knowledge of what is being perceived. For example, a child who encounters her puppy on the way home from school has a large store of figurative knowledge about that puppy. Her schema for "my puppy" is very detailed and she is capable of very sophisticated and subtle perceptions: She can see whether her puppy is happy, sad, hungry, tired, and many other things that might escape other people's notice.

Highlights

The Gestalt Principles

As children's thinking abilities change, so do their perceptual abilities (Piaget, 1969; see also Daehler & Bukatko, 1985). Piaget did not propose a one-to-one correspondence of perceptual to cognitive development but he did suggest a strong relationship. For example, children's perceptions tend to become less *centered* as they mature.

Piaget's concept of perceptual centration is similar to his ideas about cognitive centration. **Perceptual centration** refers to children focusing on only one aspect of a stimulus they encounter. This centration, Piaget thought, made children especially susceptible to some of the phenomena described in the literature on perception. In particular, Piaget showed that children are more prone to follow the Gestalt psychology principles of continuity, closure, proximity, and similarity.

Gestalt psychology was a very important school of thought originated in Germany by Max Wertheimer, Kurt Koffka, and Wolfgang Köhler in 1912. Their major focus was on perception and, as a part of their research, they described a series of principles that seem to govern how people structure and interpret visual stimuli.

The principle of **continuity** holds that perceptual phenomena tend to be seen as continuous. For example, the zig-zag line in Figure 9-9 is typically perceived as a continuous line rather than as separate lines representing a series of triangles. While most adults can easily make the transition of seeing the zig-zag line in different ways, the results of Piaget's research (see 1969) indicated that children usually centered on the continuity of the lines and did not see them as separate sides of triangles. Children seem especially likely to follow the principle of continuity in their perceptions.

The principle of **closure** involves seeing incomplete figures as complete. For example, the drawings in Figure 9-10 are incomplete but most people see them as a triangle and a square, respectively, although we can shift back and forth in our perceptions. Piaget's work (1969) indicated that children were more likely to follow the principle of closure than adults: Children are less likely to see the incompleteness of figures.

The principle of **proximity** holds that objects or elements of a visual field tend to be grouped together on the basis of their proximity. Figure 9-11 pictures two rows of eight vertical lines each. In row A, these tend to be seen as four pairs of parallel lines because of the proximity of the lines in each pair. In contrast, the vertical lines in row B tend to be seen as three pairs (each pair surrounds a face) with an extra at each end of the row. While adults can decenter from the faces and see the lines, children usually cannot.

The principle of **similarity** refers to the observation that similar objects tend to be perceived as related. Figure 9-12, for example, pictures a set of letters. Because the same letters appear in each column, we tend to see columns rather than rows. While adults can easily switch back and forth between seeing columns and rows, children tend to center on the columns.

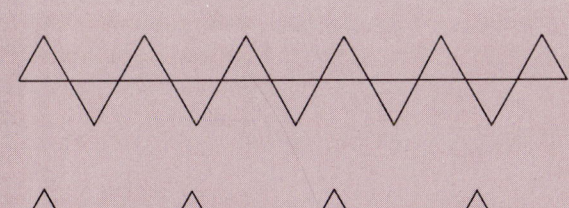

FIGURE 9-9 An Example of the Principle of Continuity. Although adults can see the zig-zag line at the top as both a continuous line and a series of triangles (below), children usually center on the continuous lines.

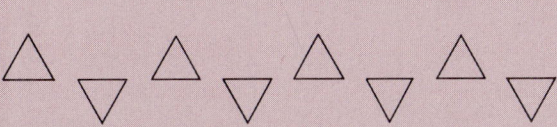

FIGURE 9-10 An Example of the Principle of Closure. Although the drawings are incomplete, most of us see them as a triangle and a square.

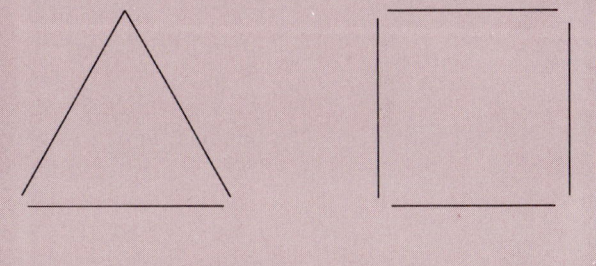

FIGURE 9-11 An Example of the Principle of Proximity. The vertical lines in Row A tend to be seen as four pairs of parallel lines because of the proximity of the lines in each pair. The vertical lines in Row B tend to be seen as three pairs (each pair surrounds a face).

FIGURE 9-12 An Example of the Principle of Similarity. Because the same letters appear in each column, we tend to see columns rather than rows.

A	B	H	R	Y
A	B	H	R	Y
A	B	H	R	Y
A	B	H	R	Y
A	B	H	R	Y

In general, as figurative knowledge about some stimulus is more and more sophisticated (e.g., the schemata an equestrian has about ponies and horses), the more sophisticated and subtle perception is. Where, for instance, we might see an animal and think to ourselves "it's a pony," an equestrian might see the same animal and perceive it as "a five point Connemarra with a blaze." From Piaget's position, then, a critical feature of perceptual development is children's development of figurative knowledge: As figurative knowledge becomes more and more sophisticated, so too does perception.

The **operative component** of perception refers to a different kind of knowledge—that is, knowledge about *how* to perceive. Consider, for instance, differences in operative knowledge about baseball and how these differences influence perception. Let us suppose that we are sitting next to two fans at a ball game, an expert and her granddaughter. As we watch the game, we see a runner on first base start to run as hard as he can toward second base just before the pitcher releases the ball. The batter then hits the ball and it rolls into the outfield between first and second base, advancing the runner to third with the batter reaching first. If we ask the young fan what has happened, she will likely tell us "the batter got a hit." This girl's perception of the event is limited to what she *knows* to look for. In contrast, if we ask her grandmother, we are likely to hear about a far more detailed perception. "The runner was off before the pitch and so the second baseman had to run to cover second base. This took the second baseman out of the play. The batted ball, which normally would have been an easy out because it was hit right where the second baseman was originally positioned, got through the infield. That was a beautiful example of the 'run and hit.' The team got a 'hit' because of the manager's decision." The difference in what the expert fan and her granddaughter saw resulted from what they knew to look for. The expert had far greater operative knowledge—she knew what to look for—and perceived the event very differently than her granddaughter did.

Thus, perceptual development depends not only on the development of figurative knowledge but on the development of operative knowledge as well. In Piaget's view, figurative knowledge is subordinate to operative knowledge, but both types are critical. As figurative knowledge develops, the base of information allowing the construction of meaning increases. As operative knowledge develops, the sophistication of knowing how to perceive increases.

Piaget's theory of perceptual development has received a great deal of interest only very recently (see Daehler & Bukatko, 1985; Gross, 1985). Even so, Piaget's theory has been an important one that strongly influenced other contructivist theories of perception (Rock, 1984). Gibson's differentiation theory, which is in direct contrast to Piaget's constructivism, will be the focus of the next section.

Differentiation Theory

Most closely linked to the work of Eleanor Gibson and J. J. Gibson, **differentiation theory** is related in many ways to the general information processing model we described in Chapter 8 (e.g., Heil, 1983; Pick, 1979). We can best understand differentiation theory by considering a quotation taken directly from Eleanor Gibson (1969, p. 75).

> [T]he environment is rich in varied and complex *potential stimulus information* [emphasis added], capable of giving rise to diverse, meaningful, complex perceptions. . . . [T]here is information in stimuli to be picked up by a sensitive, exploring organism.

This quotation contains the essence of the differentiation theory of perception. That is, the environment contains a great deal of potential information that the developing child is increasingly capable of detecting. An example should help clarify this point.

Consider the book you are now reading. It is full of thousands and thousands of perceivable bits of information: Each word carries meaning (and some of them, out of context, may carry several meanings). As you read through the text, you will perceive those stimuli in much the same way as any literate adult would. Suppose, however, that a copy of the text were suddenly transported to a group of people who neither speak nor read English. If they looked at it, they would no doubt determine that it was a book of some sort and that it contained a great deal of information besides that which they could glean from the pictures. They would not, however, be able to decipher its contents. The book would still contain the same information that you can perceive: Each word, sentence, and chapter would be present. They, however, could not perceive this information. In Eleanor Gibson's terms, this part of their environment would indeed be rich in *potential* stimulus information.

Elements of Differentiation Theory. Eleanor Gibson's theory of perceptual development has four major emphases. First, differentiation theory was designed specifically to account for developmental changes in perception. Second, emphasis is given **differentiation** as an important characteristic of perception. Third, the identification of common patterns is stressed, and fourth, the detection of distinctive features is important. We will briefly examine each of these emphases below.

The emphasis on accounting for developmental differences can be seen in the overall focus of differentiation theory (Goldfield, 1983). Essentially, the theory holds that the world contains far more stimuli than we can perceive and that the way in which we perceive various elements of the environment depends on our ability to detect these stimuli. To return to the book example, suppose that instead of giving the book to the group of non-English-speaking people, we give it to a baby born in Kalamazoo. At first, the baby just experiences patterned

The differentiation theory holds that the world contains far more stimuli that we can perceive. How we perceive various elements of the environment depends on our ability to detect these stimuli.

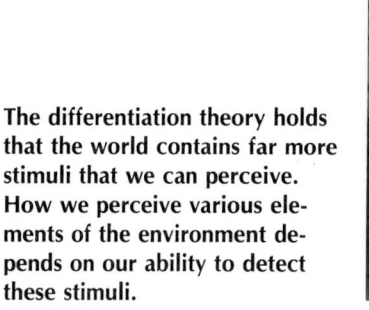

visual stimulation. Later the child will recognize the book as an object separate from the self. Still later, the child will perceive it as a book. When the child is 5 or 6 years old, she will see the book as one that contains many hard words and few that "make sense." Much later, the book will be perceived as a text on developmental psychology. If the baby grows up to attend college, she will see the text as having a particular point of view about a very specific subject area. These changes in perception occur as a result of the development of the child. The book always possessed the same stimulus information, but how these stimuli are interpreted depends on the person's knowledge and ways of understanding the world (Gibson & Spelke, 1983).

Differentiation theory emphasizes differentiation in perception as a sign of increased understanding on the part of the perceiver (Gibson, 1969; Gibson & Spelke, 1983; Goldfield, 1983; Heil, 1983; Pick & MacLeod, 1974; Michaels & Carello, 1981; Pick & Saltzman, 1978; Walk, 1981). That is, as perception moves from gross distinctions ("It's an airplane") to very specific distinctions ("It's a Curtis-Wright XP-32a with a flared nacelle"), it provides evidence that the perceiver knows more about a particular class of stimuli and is able to make very fine discriminations. (Consider also children who move from, "It's a doggie," to "It's a collie.")

The detection of patterns in classes of stimuli is also an important developmental change (Goldfield, 1983). As Gibson has said (1969, p. 81) "Achievement of [increased differentiation] involves the detection of properties and patterns not previously responded to." In other words, for increased differentiation to occur, children must come to know more and more about common patterns and how these patterns are a part of a stimulus event (Gibson & Spelke, 1983). A "nacelle," to return to an earlier example, is one pattern that is a part of propeller-driven aircraft—a separate, streamlined compartment typically housing the engine.

Increasing differentiation involves learning patterns (e.g., a "flared nacelle") within larger stimulus arrays and identifying them. For example, chess masters are, of course, able to identify many different kinds of chess problems (increasing differentiation), but they do so in large part by identifying patterns within the problems they encounter. Much of the expertise seen in chess masters stems directly from their ability to perceive complex situations (Simon & Chase, 1973).

The perception of **distinctive features** of stimulus events is also closely linked to the concept of differentiation. Here, the idea is that increasing differentiation also depends on people's abilities to perceive parts of a large stimulus array as distinctive. Once a larger pattern can be identified on the basis of a distinctive feature (or perhaps more than one), perception can occur more readily, freeing the person to focus on more subtle elements of the stimuli. For example, Buicks could be very easily identified for many years because they all had one very distinctive feature in common: small portholes along the side. A car fancier, then, could easily identify a car as a Buick and then focus in on more subtle parts of the Buick's characteristics (e.g., model, series, size of engine).

Children, of course, also develop more sophisticated perceptions as they learn to identify distinctive features (Gibson & Spelke, 1983). For example, cats' ears are highly distinctive, allowing rapid and easy discrimination from other animals. When such an identification of distinc-

Reading is a skill heavily dependent on the perceptual abilities of children, especially their vision and hearing.

tive elements is possible, children can then focus on other elements (hair length, color, pattern of markings, and so on). Another, more subtle example can be seen in how children learn to identify the various letters of the alphabet. As Figure 9-13 shows, each letter has a combination of distinctive features that make it recognizable. Earlier in the chapter, of course, we discussed the difficulties children face in identifying some distinctive features of letters.

Differentiation theory has continued to grow since the groundbreaking work of Eleanor and J. J. Gibson (see, for example, Goldfield, 1983, and Heil, 1983), influencing theories of cognitive development as well as other theories of perception (see McBurney & Collings, 1984). Differentiation theory has also influenced research on reading. As we

Features	A	E	F	H	I	L	T	K	M	N	V	W	X	Y	Z	B	C	D	G	J	O	P	R	Q	S	U
Straight																										
horizontal	+	+	+	+		+	+								+		+									
vertical		+	+	+	+	+	+	+	+	+					+	+	+	+				+	+			
diagonal /	+							+	+		+	+	+	+	+											
diagonal \	+							+	+	+	+	+	+		+								+	+		
Curve																										
closed																+		+			+	+	+	+		
open V																			+							+
open H																	+		+	+					+	
Intersection	+	+	+	+			+	+					+			+						+	+	+		
Redundancy																										
cyclic change		+							+		+				+									+		
symmetry	+	+		+	+		+	+	+		+	+	+	+		+	+	+			+					+
Discontinuity																										
vertical	+		+	+	+		+	+	+				+									+	+			
horizontal		+	+			+	+								+											

FIGURE 9-13 A Chart Illustrating the Different Features of Various Letters of the Alphabet. Each letter has a combination of distinctive features that make it recognizable. From E. J. Gibson (1969). *Principles of perceptual learning and development.* New York: Appleton-Century-Crofts. Reprinted with permission.

will see in the next section, there are some important guidelines for helping children become good readers that can be drawn directly from work on the development of perception.

Reading Readiness: Applications of Perception Research

One area of perceptual development of great importance to parents and teachers is reading readiness. **Reading** is a complex cognitive skill in which meaning is assigned to written or printed symbols. As such, it is heavily dependent on children's perceptual abilities, especially vision and hearing.

There have been many different definitions of reading readiness (Spache & Spache, 1977; Venezky, 1975). Here, we will focus specifically on a set of perceptually related skills crucial to **reading readiness**.

1. *Perceiving letter orientation.* The ability to discriminate among letters on the basis of their orientations and to do so reliably and easily is an important prerequisite for reading (Gibson & Levin, 1975). For example, some letters (e.g., *m* and *w, b* and *d, p* and *q*) are identical except for their orientations.

2. *Perceiving letter order.* Children are not ready to read until they can perceive differences in the orders of letters (e.g., *no* and *on*).

3. *Perceiving detail in words.* Many words resemble other words except for differences in one or two letters. Reading is very difficult if children cannot yet reliably see such differences (e.g., cold and colt; cut, cute, and cure).

4. *Matching sounds.* Reading depends heavily on linking visual stimuli to the sounds of the spoken language. For example, children need to be able to coordinate the senses of hearing and vision to match the sound of "r" with the appearance of the letter "r." Matching sounds, therefore, is a perceptually based ability children must possess in order to be ready to read. Here, the importance of auditory perception and the ability to relate auditory and visual perception is very apparent. In matching sounds, children should be able to sort pictures of objects by their initial sounds (e.g., cat, car, and cane are grouped together, as are tree, toad, and toe).

5. *Blending sounds.* The ability to blend sounds depends directly on the ability to perceive sound blends correctly. Blending sounds, of course, is related to language production rather than perception, but it is heavily dependent on auditory perception (e.g., the "a" and "g" are pronounced together correctly in bag, rag, hag, lag, and tag).

The five pre-reading skills listed above all are perceptual skills or depend heavily on perceptual abilities. While many reading authorities believe that these skills can be taught directly (e.g., Venezky, 1975), children can best acquire these skills in a broader approach to pre-reading that is reflected in the following guidelines.

1. *Model reading and reading enjoyment*. Children learn a great deal by observing their parents. If parents read frequently and with enjoyment, they communicate an important idea to children: Reading is important and fun.
2. *Have children examined for perceptual problems.* Reading *is* a complex and demanding task that is difficult enough without any handicaps. As we saw earlier in the chapter, the sooner perceptual problems are identified and corrected, the smaller their impact.
3. *Teach children how to pay attention*. We have seen the importance of attention in perception: Nowhere is the need for attention more crucial than in beginning reading. Generally, the use of praise for increasing amounts of attention (within very reasonable limits) coupled with the sensible choice of enjoyable activities is effective.
4. *Read to children often*. Children can learn a great deal about reading by being read to (Smith, 1983). They discover that printed symbols have meaning, that the same patterns always have the same meanings, and that reading is enjoyable. Further, reading to children helps expand their vocabularies.
5. *Use games and activities to foster general skills associated with reading*. Drawing, coloring, scribbling, simple discrimination tasks, and eye-hand coordination activities should all be encouraged.
6. *Don't pressure children to master skills*. As long as children believe that reading is fun, there is an extremely high probability that they will master pre-reading skills. When those activities associated with reading become sources of pressure from the parents, the fun stops and children's enthusiasm disappears.

Summary

The development of perception is an integral part of cognitive development. Perception begins with the senses—vision, hearing, taste, smell, and touch. The eyes translate light into neural impulses that are transmitted to the brain by the optic nerve. The ears transform vibrations in the air into neural impulses which are then passed on to the auditory center of the cerebral cortex. Taste and smell operate through the conversion of chemical reactions into neural impulses, whereas touch works through the stimulation of different receptor cells located in the skin. Any impairment in the sense receptors has direct implications for development. The sooner and more effectively impairments are treated, the smaller their impact will be.

Newborns have effective perceptual abilities. Though nearsighted, they discriminate among objects, and most babies prefer to gaze at highly complex stimulus arrays such as human faces. Further, auditory perception appears to be present before birth. Babies are also able to coordinate their hearing with their vision. We know less about the other senses, primarily because research has focused on visual and auditory perception.

Sensory deprivation has implications for development, but it is difficult to obtain clear-cut evidence of the effect of sensory deprivation in the absence of emotional deprivation or trauma. Available studies of children who have experienced sensory deprivation without other forms of deprivation, however, provide results suggesting that sensory deprivation during sensitive periods of development may limit or totally eliminate the acquisition of certain perceptual skills.

Both Piaget's constructivist theory and E. J. Gibson's differentiation theory help link the research results, emphasize the flexible nature of perception, and show how the person and the environment interact to result in perception. Piaget's theory focuses on the construction of reality during perception and is bound to his general theory of intellectual development. Differentiation theory centers on differentiation in perceptual development, the detection of patterns in stimulus arrays, and the identification of distinctive elements among larger sets of stimuli.

Closely linked to perceptual development, of course, is the development of memory—the topic of Chapter 10.

Key Terms

perception	visual constancy	dyslexia
transduction	size constancy	figurative component
retina	shape constancy	perceptual centration
sclera	form perception	Gestalt psychology
iris	perception of illusions	continuity
pupil	outer ear	closure
cornea	auditory canal	proximity
aqueous humor	tympanic membrane	similarity
lens	middle ear	operative component
vitreous humor	ossicles	differentiation theory
receptor cells	cochlea	differentiation
rods	inner ear	pattern detection
cones	sensory coordination	distinctive features
fovea	sensory deprivation	reading
20/20	strabismus	reading readiness
habituation	astigmatism	
depth perception	sensitive period	

Suggested Readings

Gibson, E. J., & Spelke, E. (1983). The development of perception. In J. H. Flavell and E. M. Markman (Eds.), P. H. Mussen (Series Ed.), *Handbook of child psychology: Vol. 3. Cognitive development* (pp. 1–76). New York: Wiley. This chapter provides a reasonably current overview of E. J. Gibson's views on perception.

Goldfield, E. C. (1983). The ecological approach to perceiving as a foundation for understanding the development of knowing in infancy. *Developmental Review, 3,* 371–404. This review article presents a recent overview of the ecological approach to perception.

Heil, J. (1983). *Perception and cognition.* Berkeley: University of California Press. Heil's book is a very readable, although advanced treatment of perception.

McBurney, D. H., & Collings, V. B. (1984). *Introduction to sensation/perception* (2nd. ed.). Englewood Cliffs, NJ: Prentice-Hall, Inc. This intermediate level text provides a fine overview of human sensory systems and also presents an interesting discussion of perception.

Smith, F. (1983). *Essays into literacy.* Exeter, NH: Hernemann. Frank Smith's collection of essays provides an interesting perspective on perceptual and cognitive skills needed for the development of reading.

Stone, J. (1983). *Parallel processing in the visual system.* New York: Plenum. Stone's advanced book provides a fascinating treatment of mainstream views on visual perception.

Application Exercises

9-1 The Interactive Nature of Perception

Our perceptions depend on our abilities to detect stimulus patterns in the environment. Look at Figure 9-14. What do you see? For many adults, both a mouse (or rat) and a face are present in the figure. Show this figure to several children of different ages and ask them what they see. Very young children may not make out anything. Somewhat older children will probably see either the face or the rat, but not both. Many of these children will be able to see both *if* you point them out but not without help. Finally, most 9- or 10-year-old children will easily see both figures.

FIGURE 9-14 Mouse or Face?

9-2 Perception and Cognitive Development

Look at the object depicted in Figure 9-15. Before reading any further, try to draw the figure. Did you have difficulty? Most people have a little trouble until they see that it is an unreal object that cannot exist in three dimensions. But what do children make of such anomalous drawings? Find out. Show the figure to children of different ages and ask them to try to draw it. What happens? Refer to Eleanor Gibson's theory to explain your results.

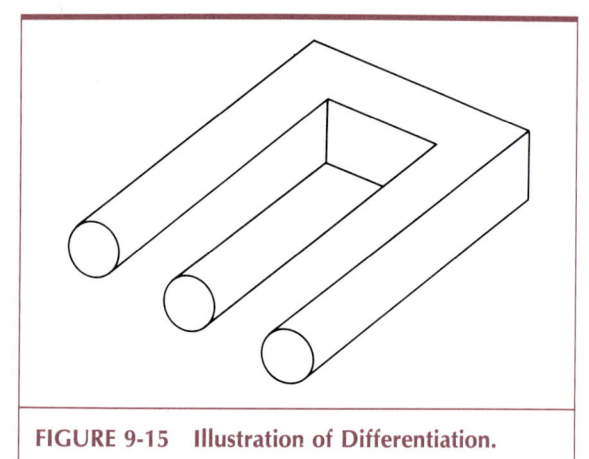

FIGURE 9-15 Illustration of Differentiation.

CHAPTER 10

Development of Memory

Remember that old theory of memory? Well, forget it!
—J. J. Jenkins

*I*n the past 25 years, no other area in developmental psychology has increased more dramatically than the study of memory. Interest has blossomed in infant memory; in how young children come to be aware of their memory; and in the strategies that children, adolescents, and adults use to enhance their memory. The field has expanded from a handful of investigators in the early 1960s to many hundreds of developmental psychologists working in the area today.

Part of this tremendous interest in memory has come from a general resurgence of the cognitive approach in psychology, with its emphasis on thinking and memory processes. A greater influence on the interest in memory was, perhaps, the realization among psychologists that knowing about the *development* of memory is vital to understanding cognitive growth and contributes to a general understanding of human memory and cognition (Brainerd & Pressley, 1985; Ornstein & Corsale, 1979). Some of the clearest insights into human memory and thinking have come from understanding developmental changes in memory and memory processes. Studies of memory in infants have been particularly productive.

Infant Memory

Studying young children's memories presents a great challenge to researchers; this is compounded by children's limited ability to describe what they are seeing or hearing. Infants, of course, cannot talk or even follow directions. How, then, can we possibly know what they are paying attention to, understanding, and remembering?

Although many generations of researchers have been interested in what infants know and remember, it was not until the pioneering work of Fantz and his associates (Fantz, 1958, 1961, 1964; Fantz & Fagan, 1975; Fantz, Fagan, & Miranda, 1975) that reliable methods were in-

Infant Memory

vented that permitted useful study of memory in infants. Their insights helped further fuel interest in the study of memory development in children of all ages.

As we discussed in Chapter 9, Fantz's methods were simple, yet innovative. By presenting something for an infant to look at (a "target"), looking through a peephole at the infant's eyes, and recording how much time the infant spent looking at the target, Fantz found a method for measuring infant perception. Can an infant tell the difference between a plain target and one with stripes, for instance? Fantz's answer was "yes": His early studies showed that infants prefer to look at a patterned surface rather than a plain one. How acute is infants' vision? From a series of studies that compared infants' preferences for similar targets and determined the point when differences became so small that preferences disappeared, we now know that newborns' visual acuity is poor. Vision improves dramatically, however, within the first few months of life (e.g., Bornstein, 1984). Do infants prefer to look at familiar or novel things? When Fantz presented a changing pattern on one side and a static one on the other, infants gradually spent more and more time looking at the changing side (Fantz, 1964). Apparently even infants enjoy novelty.

In early studies, researchers concentrated on infant *perception*. Others soon discovered, however, that Fantz's methods were very useful in memory research. The key to using these methods in the study of memory is **habituation**—when a stimulus is presented over and over again, infants' attention will dwindle as they become adjusted or "habituated" to it (Bornstein, 1984). After habituation has occurred, a new

Studies of infant habituation have shown us that infants can perceive colors, forms, and patterns and that these abilities develop rapidly.

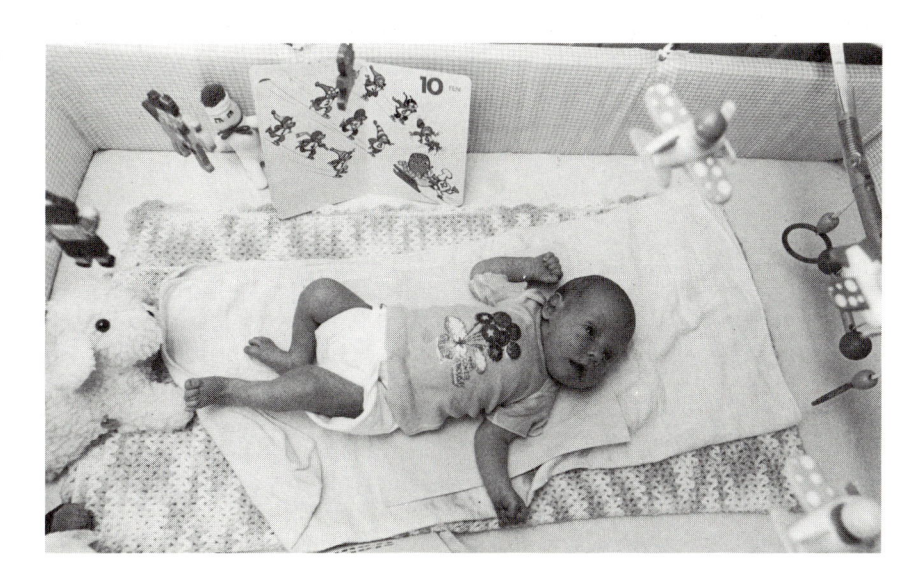

stimulus is then presented that differs in some predetermined way from the old. If infants can distinguish the new stimulus from the old *and* if they remember what they have seen, attention will recover (since the new stimulus will be perceived as a novel one). We now know from many habituation studies that infants can perceive colors, forms, patterns, and faces; this ability develops rapidly through about 6 months of age, when more complex patterns such as faces can be perceived clearly as units (Kail, 1984; see also Chapter 9).

Of course, habituation to any stimulus means that the infant must be *remembering* it: It must become more familiar. Thus, to study memory, one need only put in a delay between the time of original habituation and the time at which memory is tested. Testing is done: (1) on the habituation stimulus and (2) on a novel stimulus. If the infant remembers the original (habituated) stimulus, then she will tend to spend more time looking at the new, novel stimulus than at the old, habituated stimulus. If memory is lost, however, both new and habituated stimuli will appear equally "new" to infants, and no differences in looking time appear.

Habituation studies with infants have shown that they can remember some of what they see over a considerable period of time. For instance, in an early study, Fagan (1973) showed that 5-month-old infants shown a face for only 2 minutes still retained some information about that face after 2 weeks. In a later study (Strauss & Cohen, 1980), 5-month-olds were shown a three-dimensional styrofoam figure and then tested immediately, after a few minutes, and after 24 hours with either the same form or one with a different shape, color, size, or orientation (e.g., upright or turned). Although the infants recognized all four dimensions (i.e., shape, color, etc.), they retained only the color and form after the short delay and only the form after 24 hours. In Strauss and Cohen's view, the reason that form is remembered the longest is that it is the most important in the recognition of objects. Whereas color, orientation, and size may vary, shape is always the critical feature for recognizing objects.

The study of infant memory had a strong stimulating effect on most developmental psychologists. Knowing that even very young infants can remember a great deal of information led developmental psychologists to seek knowledge about how memory continues to develop. In addition, at the other end of the developmental spectrum, exciting research on memory in adults also was contributing to the desire to better understand memory development. Also, older, less productive views of memory were gradually giving way to newer, more accurate understanding of how memory operates. These new conceptions, or **models of memory,** led to greatly increased levels of experimentation and interest in memory and cognition in all of psychology, including developmental psychology. Three of the most prominent models of how memory works used by development psychologists are (1) **multistore models**, (2) **levels of processing models**, and (3) **constructive models**. While all are related and remain influential in the study of memory development, each stresses different but important aspects of memory. We will discuss each model in turn, along with its implications for understanding the development of memory.

A Multistore Model of Memory

As research on cognition increased greatly in the 1960s, researchers tried to develop more accurate descriptions or models of how memory worked. One of the most prominent and productive of the memory models was an information processing approach called the **multistore model** as in Figure 10-1 (e.g., Atkinson & Shiffrin, 1968, 1971). The term *multistore* refers to the belief that information is placed or stored in memory in distinct ways and locations as it passes through the information processing system. The memory system is seen as functioning much like a computer (see Chapter 8).

Probably the best known multistore model of memory was proposed by Atkinson and Shiffrin (1968, 1971). In their model, information is seen as coming from **sense receptors** (e.g., eyes, ears, nose) and passing through three components: a **sensory register**, an initial sensory memory; a **short-term store**, a place where incoming information is thought about and rehearsed; and a **long-term store**, where permanent memories are kept. According to this model, incoming information stays only briefly in the sensory registers before it moves into the short-term store. What is not lost from the sensory registers and the short-term store is transferred into long-term memory. All other information is forgotten.

Sense Receptors

While not actually a part of the memory system, *sense receptors* are critical in that they provide the external information coming into the system. Human sense receptors include the eyes, ears, nose, taste buds, and

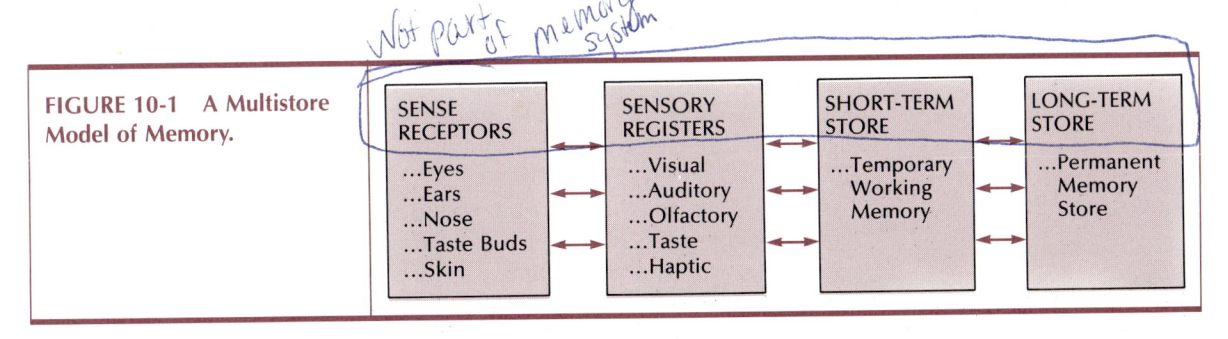

FIGURE 10-1   A Multistore Model of Memory.

SENSE RECEPTORS	SENSORY REGISTERS	SHORT-TERM STORE	LONG-TERM STORE
...Eyes ...Ears ...Nose ...Taste Buds ...Skin	...Visual ...Auditory ...Olfactory ...Taste ...Haptic	...Temporary Working Memory	...Permanent Memory Store

skin. Through seeing, hearing, smelling, tasting, and touching, humans receive information from their surroundings. This information may or may not be remembered, of course. Whether information is remembered depends on what happens in other parts of the memory system.

Sensory Registers

The first component of the multistore model of memory is the sensory registers. Atkinson and Shiffrin (1971) proposed that humans have large-capacity *sensory registers* for each of their sense modalities (i.e., vision, hearing, and so on). Their function is to hold information briefly until it can be picked up and processed by the rest of the information processing system. Atkinson and Shiffrin argued that information is held in the sensory registers in raw, unprocessed form before being moved to the short-term store. That is, it is not changed or transformed from its original state in the sensory registers but is an "exact copy" of the information encountered.

Information decays or fades very rapidly from the sensory registers, however, unless it is further processed and rehearsed. For instance, experiments have shown that subjects can accurately report details from large sets of information (e.g., 4 × 4 arrays of letters) from their sensory registers, but only if the intervals between seeing or hearing and making the report are extremely short. For example, the maximum delay between seeing a large array and being able to report on most of its detail is only about one-half second. This immediate sensory memory for vision called **iconic memory,** appears to be simply "read out" of the sensory registers (Sternberg, 1966). With even slightly longer delays (e.g., 1 second), however, much of the information in the visual sensory registers is lost.

A similar phenomenon exists in sensory memory for things that are heard: **Echoic memory** is a brief memory for large amounts of auditory information in the sensory registers. Although this auditory sensory memory is also short-lived, the loss is not quite as rapid as for visual information; auditory information is retained in the sensory registers for 3 to 4 seconds. Like visual information, however, auditory information is lost if not picked up by other components of the information processing system.

Sensory registers are particularly critical for perception. Since perception is not instantaneous and meaning takes time to be assigned to stimuli, our information processing system needs to have some way of briefly "holding" information until it can be perceived. The sensory registers fulfill this function admirably.

Short-term Store

The second major component of the multistore model of memory is the *short-term store*. The short-term store holds the current contents of consciousness. Attention and rehearsal are required to keep this information alive; otherwise, the contents will be quickly lost. A child who has been reminded of the combination to her bike lock by her mother, for instance, may repeat the combination as she walks to her bike. In the terms of the model, she is rehearsing information in her short-term store. But if she runs into her sister, who asks her a question and diverts her attention, she may quickly forget the combination!

The capacity of the short-term store is limited (Dempster, 1981; Miller, 1956), especially in young children. This capacity, referred to as the **immediate memory span,** usually is measured by the number of items (e.g., numbers) a person can recall accurately in order immediately after having heard them. As you recall from Chapter 8, developmental changes in immediate memory span are important to Case's theory (Case, 1985). Memory span increases steadily throughout childhood, from about 4 or 5 digits for 5-year-olds, to 6 digits for 9-year-olds, to 7 digits for adults (Dempster, 1981). Given a list of 2 or 3 things to get from another room, young children may fare very well. If the list increases to 5 or 6 items, however, their memory span is exceeded and all or most of the information may be lost.

Long-term Store

In the multistore model, long-term memory is seen as a permanent store of unlimited size. New information, rehearsed and circulated within the short-term store, is transferred to the long-term store. Conversely, information already in long-term memory can affect processing in the sensory registers and in short-term memory. As an example of long-term memory, children often will remember faces, names, and skills and recognize or recall them days, weeks, or even months later. What was new information has become a part of long-term memory, or the permanent storehouse of what they know.

Implications of the Multistore Model of Memory Development

Although multistore models initially were developed to help explain adult memory, developmental psychologists quickly recognized their utility for understanding differences in memory performance between children and adults. For example, as mentioned earlier, the number of digits that children can recall increases steadily through childhood (Dempster, 1981). Why does this difference exist? Is it due to differences in the capacity of the memory store, to differences in how material is rehearsed (i.e., because rehearsal is necessary for transferring items from the short-term store to the long-term store), or to some combination of the two? Multistore models have helped developmental psychologists design studies to answer questions like these.

Much attention has been focused on the short-term memory component of the model because children's knowledge and awareness of their own short-term memories seems to play an especially important role in their memory performance (Chi, 1985; Kail, 1984). For instance, nursery school and kindergarten children and even first- and second-graders seem to have little insight about their own short-term memory capacity. That is, they are unaware of the *limits* on what can be kept in mind at one time (Flavell, Friedrichs, & Hoyt, 1970; Yussen & Levy, 1975). Although even 3- and 4-year-olds know that a larger set of pictures will be more difficult to remember than a smaller one (Yussen & Bird, 1979), they are not able to predict accurately how many pictures they actually will recall.

In experiments by Flavell et al. (1970) and Yussen and Levy (1975), for instance, children of various ages were asked to predict how many pictures they could remember. The experimenter first showed children a card with a single picture on it and then covered it, asking them if they could remember it. The experimenter repeated this procedure as the number of pictures was increased up to 10. When the children finished predicting, they were tested for how many pictures they *actually* recalled.

We might ask whether there was a close match between what children *said* they could recall and what they *actually* recalled. The answer is yes—but only for older children. By the fourth grade, children were almost as accurate as adults: Their predicted and actual recall were almost the same. But for younger children, prediction usually exceeded actual performance. Nursery school and kindergarten children, for example, estimated on the average that they could recall around 8 items (beyond the memory limit of most adults!), when in fact their average recall was between 3 and 4 items. Over half of these same children predicted they would be able to recall all 10 pictures! In contrast, only about a fourth of second-, third-, and fourth-graders predicted such exceptional performance, as did fewer than 5 percent of college students.

Young children's unrealistic ideas about their own memories easily can lead them to overload their short-term stores. Also, with no real understanding of how one best remembers something, they are unlikely to rehearse information in the short-term store in an effective way to move it into long-term memory.

Rehearsal Strategies. Ornstein and his colleagues (Ornstein, Naus, & Liberty, 1975; Ornstein & Naus, 1978; Ornstein, Medlin, Stone, & Naus, 1985) have shown that the number of times an item is rehearsed is *not* a good predictor of recall. That is, just repeating an item over and over will not necessarily result in better remembering. More important is *how* material is rehearsed. Quality of rehearsal is more critical than quantity.

There are fascinating developmental changes in how children rehearse materials they are trying to remember. Faced with a list of items to be remembered, for instance, young children simply tend to repeat one or two items over and over again. In contrast, older children often concentrate not only on the newest item to be learned, but also try to rehearse preceding information (Kunzinger, 1985). Gradually, children develop **rehearsal strategies,** techniques used during learning to improve their memory performance.

As an illustration of this kind of difference in rehearsal, Table 10-1 shows two typical rehearsal strategies, one for a third-grader and the other for an eighth-grader. Each child was given a list of words to remember. Note how differently the two children approached the task of remembering the list. Although third-graders repeat each item as many times as eighth-graders, their recall is much poorer. Recall, especially from longer-term memory, is much more affected by the number of times an item appears in *different* rehearsal sets (Kunzinger, 1985). As Ornstein (1978) has pointed out, the evidence now clearly shows that changes in rehearsal strategies are important determiners of changes with age in the ability to recall.

Organizational Strategies. The multistore model emphasizes the necessity of moving information from short-term to long-term memory. One key to success in transferring information is **organizational strategies.** Organizational strategies in memory are methods of clustering information into meaningful groupings for easier learning and recall. For instance, Bousfield showed many years ago (Bousfield, 1953) that adults will take unorganized information and recall it in organized form. When given a long list of things to learn, adults almost invariably will "cluster" the items in some way. Recall is improved when clustering occurs.

TABLE 10-1 Typical Rehearsal Strategies in Children of Two Grade Levels

	Rehearsal Strategy	
Word Presented	*Third-Grader*	*Eighth-Grader*
1. Yard	yard, yard, yard, yard yard, yard, yard	yard, yard, yard
2. Cat	cat, cat, cat, cat, yard	cat, yard, yard, cat
3. Man	man, man, man, man, man, man	man, cat, yard man, cat, yard
4. Desk	desk, desk, desk desk	desk, man, yard cat, man, desk, cat, yard

From Ornstein, Naus, & Liberty, (1975), Rehearsal and organization processes in children's memory. *Child Development, 26,* Experiment 1.

The same principle holds for children. For example, if children are asked to remember a randomly organized set of words that represent several categories (e.g., names, vegetables, and so on), recall will be better for those children who recognize the categories and cluster the items (e.g., Amy, Lisa, Jennifer; carrot, celery, lettuce) in their recall. In general, when materials that can be clustered are used, clustering increases with age and recall performance will improve along with the clustering.

One method for directly assessing children's organizing skills is to ask them to sort items as they study them. A child might be given a set of pictures on cards, for example, and asked to group them (without necessarily being told *how* to group them). Very young children (e.g., preschoolers) often will not be able to sort the pictures in any recognizable way. However, somewhat older children (e.g., third-graders) can sort the pictures, but often form fragmented or partial groupings and change their groupings frequently (Bjorklund, Ornstein, & Haig, 1977; Ornstein, 1978). Older children and adults are much more active in preparing for recall, however. Most look for links between the meaning of items in order to find ways to group them. Grouping seems to imply at least a beginning awareness that grouping will help memory. To some extent, this is true. But the ability to categorize and to group seems to precede the ability to *use* this information to improve memory (Ornstein, 1978). Although even quite young children can group items, they may not realize grouping is useful for remembering things.

Levels of Processing Models

By the early 1970s, psychologists were developing alternatives to the multistore model. In particular, Fergus I. M. Craik of the University of Toronto and his associates were especially creative in devising new ways of thinking about memory. In a classic paper entitled "Levels of processing: A framework for memory research," Craik and Robert S. Lockhart (1972) argued that many differences we see in memory are due to how people go about learning information. In other words, Craik and Lockhart believed that memory depends on what people do when they process information. Storage mechanisms, as emphasized by the multistore model, are less critical.

To illustrate the concept of **levels of processing,** let us assume that we give two 10-year-old children the same paragraph to study. However, let us give each of them different instructions. One child is told we are interested in how well he pays attention to the more detailed aspects of reading materials and that we will test him on his ability to tell us how many "e's" there are in the paragraph. The second child is told that she will have to stand up and tell us about the paragraph in her own words without looking back at it. Then, we give both children (who have about the same level of reading ability) 10 minutes each to do their studying. What do you suppose they will remember? Since this hypothetical situation is very much like a good deal of levels-of-processing research (e.g., Glover, Bruning, & Plake, 1982), we can be quite certain that the child asked to know about the number of "e's" in the paragraph will remember that information very well. It also is likely, though, that he will remember little else. In contrast, the child asked to study the paragraph so that she could tell about it in her own words probably will remember the gist of the paragraph very well but can only guess at how many "e's" there are. What these children remember, and what subjects in depth of processing research remember, depends on how they have processed information.

Although the original levels-of-processing model has been refined as a result of new research (Craik, 1973, 1977; Craik & Lockhart, 1972; Craik & Tulving, 1975; Eich, 1985; Fisher & Craik, 1980; Jacoby & Craik, 1979; Jacoby, Craik, & Begg, 1979), the basic idea of this model remains that memory is a byproduct of perceptual analyses of incoming stimuli. The "deeper" the level of processing, the more likely the recall. **Deep processing** indicates sophisticated analyses of incoming information that focus on meaning (as when the girl in our example put the paragraph into her own words). More sophisticated or "deeper" processing—and thus better recall—occurs as the number of analyses of incoming information increases (e.g., putting a paragraph in one's own words *and* answering questions about the content at the same time), as the complexity of the analyses increases (e.g., drawing inferences from a paragraph as opposed to merely putting it in one's own words), and with the number of decisions (e.g., "Does the author mean . . . ?") one must make about the content (Benton, Glover, & Bruning, 1983; Palmere, Benton, Glover, & Ronning, 1983; Ross, 1981). **Shallow processing,** on the other hand, refers to unsophisticated, superficial analyses of incoming information (as when the boy in our example merely counted the number of "e's" in the paragraph). Information processed in this way quickly will be forgotten.

Now we can examine some additional examples of shallow and deep processing (see Table 10-2) and see how processing influences memory. For instance, a child who has read a definition of an "oar" as a "paddle" might simply repeat "oar-paddle, oar-paddle, oar-paddle" over and over again, a form of shallow processing. As long as the pair of words is repeated, they probably will be retained. Once the repetition is stopped, however, the definition may be quickly lost because the child's analysis of the information was very superficial. This strategy, of course, is much like the one used by the third-grader and to some extent the eighth-grader in Table 10-1.

TABLE 10-2 Examples of Shallow and Deep Processing

To-be-learned Item	Shallow Processing	Deep Processing
Definition of the word "spell" (magical) (sixth-grader)	Repeats phrase, "spell—a magical state"	Repeats phrase, thinks up examples of spells, asks teacher if only witches can cast spells, asks if being made to work by a parent is example of a spell
Textbook paragraph on "erosion" (ninth-grader)	Reads paragraph and rereads	Reads paragraph, writes down key words, underlines them in notes, makes up two questions about the paragraph
Classmates' names (second-grader)	Looks at each classmate, tries to remember each name	Makes up silly phrases, "Apple Amy, Jumpin' Jason, Happy Hillary," forms mental picture, looks for distinguishing features
Steps in running a video camera (eighth-grader)	Watches teacher demonstrate how	Tries each of the the switches, runs zoom control, asks questions about playback, makes a short "practice" videotape
Use of tools by pioneers (fifth-grader)	Listens to teacher tell about early pioneer tools	Draws plan for a tool (e.g., a clamp), cuts out pieces of wood, builds working model of pioneer clamp, uses it to hold her book under her desk
Hitting a softball (fourth-grader)	Watches physical education teacher demonstrate swing	Watches demonstration, asks if stance is okay, swings several times, practices on balls at various speeds and heights
Labeling an object as a "ball" (infant)	Watches as father holds up ball, child says "baw"	Labels different size and color balls as "baw," handles balls, rolls them, puts them in mouth
Naming different colors (nursery school student)	Watches as teacher holds up pink crayon; says, "this is pink"	Uses crayon to color picture, matches pink crayon to shirt, to paint, to wall, says word "pink" to each example
Reading a textbook (college student)	Reads chapters, trying to cover required number of pages	Tries to think of examples, writes key concepts in own words, draws "map" relating important ideas to each other

In contrast, instead of simply repeating "oar-paddle" several times, another child might, for instance, make up a sentence that uses the word (e.g., "The scout lost an oar in the rapids."), write out the word and look at it, or imagine herself as using oars in a row boat. Such deep processing, of course, will result in better memory for the information. The more new information is analyzed and associated with prior meaningful learning, the greater the chances of remembering it.

Table 10-2 shows several examples of shallow and deep processing of the same information by children. As you can see, shallow processing does very little to change or modify the materials to be learned. Rehearsal mainly produces the stimulus "as is" (e.g., repeating a definition over and over). Deep processing, however, involves children's activating their own knowledge, trying to relate the knowledge they have to the new materials to be learned, and their active efforts to *understand* the meaning of the materials.

As was the case in the multistore model of memory, much of the initial levels-of-processing research was focused on adults, not children. Nonetheless, the implications of levels-of-processing model for understanding memory development were soon recognized and the model has guided a great deal of developmental memory research (e.g., Kail & Hagen, 1977; Pressley & Brainerd, 1985). Perhaps the greatest contribution of the levels-of-processing model is the idea that memory for information is determined by what children and adults *do* with that information when they encounter it.

Constructive Models of Memory

With its emphasis on what the developing person *does* in memory, the levels-of-processing framework has had a tremendously important impact on memory research in developmental psychology. While the multistore model helped researchers identify possible components of memory, it is doubtful that all that we now know about children's memory strategy development and their awareness of their own memory skills would have been discovered if the multistore model had remained *the* model of memory. Even the levels-of-processing model, however, has not been without its critics (see Baddeley, 1978; Loftus, Green, & Smith, 1980; Nelson, 1977). These criticisms have led to modification and change. In most criticisms, however, the levels-of-processing view has not been seen as wrong, but rather as difficult to test or somewhat vague. Its major feature—the emphasis on what the learner does in processing information—still is considered to be a key factor in memory performance and also critical to understanding memory development. Further model development, however, has proven useful.

Parallel to the levels-of-processing approaches and to a great extent compatible with them have been the **constructive models of memory**. Such models (see Paris & Lindauer, 1977, for a detailed discussion) stress that new information is *transformed* by social, cognitive, and affective processes in the individual. That is, what individuals remember is as much a product of their existing cognitive structures as it is of the material to be learned. Memory is "constructed by" the individual as information undergoes "blending, condensation, omission, invention, and similar constructive transformations" (Paris & Lindauer, 1977, p. 35). Constructive views of memory are much like those of the levels-of-processing model in their emphasis on the active role of the individual. In constructive views, however, additional emphasis is placed on the *organization* the developing individual applies to the incoming information. New information must be "fitted" to existing cognitive structures (Brown, 1975; Lucariello & Nelson, 1985; Mistry & Lange, 1985; Slackman & Nelson, 1984).

A cardinal principle uniting both early (Bartlett, 1932) and modern (e.g., Bransford, Barclay, & Franks, 1972; Jenkins, 1974) constructive views is that exact reproduction or recall of events is extremely rare; memory usually involves transformation of the input (Paris & Lindauer, 1977). One way in which input is transformed is through *inferences* children make about what they see, hear, or otherwise experience.

The Role of Inference in Children's Memory

In spoken and written language, for example, much information is not stated explicitly, but is inferred by the listener or reader. In the sentence, "The workman dug a hole in the ground," there is nothing to tell us exactly *how* the workman dug the hole. Was it with a spoon, or with a hubcap? Probably not. We ordinarily would *infer* that the hole was dug in the "usual" way, with a shovel. Sentences like this one formed the basis for a study of 7-, 9-, and 11-year-olds by Paris and Lindauer (1976) of how development affects inferential processing and, hence, memory.

Children were given sentences to remember. In some, the instrument was *explicit* (e.g., The workman dug a hole in the ground with a shovel). In others, it was *implicit* (e.g., The workman dug a hole in the ground). Later, Paris and Lindauer cued the children's recall with the instrument (e.g., "shovel") to see if it would help in recall. Younger children were able to use the instrument as an effective cue *only if it had been stated explicitly when the sentence was presented*. Older children, in contrast, used the instrument cues effectively, regardless of the explicit or implicit presentation. In a second study, Paris and Lindauer had 7-year-olds *act out* the sentence. In the case of implicit sentences, the acting out made it necessary for the children to use the imaginary instrument. Under these conditions, differences in the young children's recall disappeared. The instruments were effective retrieval cues whether they were mentioned explicitly in the sentences or not.

Paris and Lindauer concluded that older children stored the inference as part of what is encoded into memory. Younger children, although they knew that shovels are used for digging holes, did not. When the younger children used the relationship in the "acted out" sequence, however, they constructed implied relationships in their memory. These inferential, constructive processes greatly improved access to memory. According to Paris and Lindauer, inferences may occur either voluntarily or spontaneously as automatic "efforts toward understanding" (Paris & Lindauer, 1977, p. 46). These inferential processes improve in frequency and efficiency with development. They allow an individual to expand and enrich given information (Auble & Franks,

1978; Auble, Franks, & Soraci, 1979). Through this enrichment, memory is enhanced, a process not unlike the "deep processing" described by Craik and Lockhart in their levels of processing model (Craik & Lockhart, 1972).

The Effect of Context Cues

Another critical factor in children's understanding and recall of information is the *context* in which information is embedded. Specific features of stimuli serve as **context cues**—indirect clues to the meaning of things. Context clues are encoded according to individuals' perceptions of what is important about those stimuli (Anderson & Ortony, 1975). Thus, a child may look at an unfamiliar word (e.g., *jib*) in a story and conclude that, because the story is about sailing and since "the wind caught the *jib*," and the *jib* was "canvas" and "white," that a *jib* must be some kind of sail. Without a context, the word *jib* would be meaningless. In context, however, *jib* potentially can be understood, providing that individuals make use of the context in which it occurs (Nagy & Anderson, 1984; Nagy, Herman, & Anderson, 1985).

In children's books, context cues often are provided by pictures. Typically, materials written for children contain many pictures in an attempt to give contextual support for the passages and to enhance recall (Lesgold, Levin, Shimron, & Guttman, 1975; Schallert, 1980). Pictures are only one aspect of context, however. Any of a variety of context cues can help individuals combine different sources of information (e.g., a reading assignment, the teacher's discussion, and an audiotape presentation about early colonial life in America). For example, a teacher may describe a new lesson as dealing with the colonists and give directions to note the geographic locations of the colonies and to guess which crops grew in which colonies. Such actions can focus children's attention and help them associate events with one another. Focusing, linking events, and making hypotheses all are constructive transformations of the input. Each allows for better comprehension. The better the context is understood and related to what is being learned, the more it will help children integrate memory traces meaningfully and the better retrieval cue it will be (Paris & Lindauer, 1977).

Constructive Processes in Story Memory

Another important area in which children construct, infer, and integrate relationships is their **story memory**. Constructivist theorists have argued persuasively that children develop an implicit understanding of the structure of stories (Lucariello & Nelson, 1985; Mandler & Johnson, 1977; Mistry & Lange, 1985; Stein & Glenn, 1979). David Rumelhart and Andrew Ortony (Rumelhart, 1980; Rumelhart & Ortony, 1977), in discussing related ideas, have argued that units such as settings, activities, goals, and consequences are common to many experiences. These units form frameworks or scripts for processing stories that are understood

Feats of memory retrieval are a source of pride for students who know the answers to their teacher's question.

by readers. These frameworks are used constructively to transform what is heard or read into what actually is remembered.

In an early study of constructive processes in recall of stories, Stein and Glenn (1975) read two different passages to first- and third-graders. The children were asked to recall all they could immediately and then again a week later. Stein and Glenn observed that the children's recall was highly organized; they recalled important events and their consequences most often. Moreover, they noted a great deal of **elaborative** and **inferential recall**: Often the children "recalled" consequences and goals not actually stated in the stories! Stein and Glenn also found that children elaborated more in their recall after a week than they did immediately: This provided evidence for constructive processes in children's memory for stories. Further, third-graders produced more inferential and elaborative recall then did first-graders, which suggested developmental improvement.

Summary of Constructive Processes in Children's Memory

Several lines of evidence—including the growing role of inference in children's memory, increasing use of context cues, and increasing effects of story structure or "themes" in reading and listening—suggest that constructive processes operate extensively in children's memory and that their use increases with development. These constructive processes transform and enhance memory.

All memory in children involves some transformation of the input. At first, it may be minimal, at the level of a child recognizing different objects and events, but not being able to classify them within a common framework. As children develop, however, cognitive activities and structures exert an increasing influence on memory. New information

Research

Memories That Improve with Time? Piaget's Constructivist Views

Over the years information processing theorists have moved toward a conception of memory as active and constructive. At the same time that American memory research was becoming increasingly constructivist, however, Piaget and his associates in Geneva were becoming interested in memory. The results of their research on this topic were published in a volume called *Memory and Intelligence*, which was translated into English in 1973 (Piaget & Inhelder, 1973).

Piaget saw memory as an aspect of cognition that focuses on reconstruction of the past. "However," he argued, "this reconstruction poses a special problem which the subject cannot solve without reflection, and this is precisely why the memory cannot be divorced from the intelligence" (p. 378). In other words, although memory structures the past rather than the present (perception) or future (decision-making), it nevertheless is an active process intimately related to the rest of cognition.

Piaget's views on memory are consistent with the constructive view of memory, but go two steps farther than most information processing theories. First, if memory is not simply a passive recording of observations but rather is actively constructed by the knower, then children's memories should depend on their level of cognitive development. Second, if remembering is not merely bringing back an image but an active reconstruction, then it should be possible for one's memory actually to improve as the relevant cognitive structures develop.

Piaget and Inhelder (1973) provide extensive evidence in support of these views. In one study, for example, each child was shown an array of sticks arranged in order from largest to smallest. Piaget's conception of memory suggests two predictions. First, concrete operational children, who understand the concept of seriation (arrangement in order from largest to smallest) will be better able to remember what they have seen than preoperational children. Second, if asked many months later to remember what they are shown, children whose scheme of seriation has been developing in the meantime should show *better* memory of the array than they did at the initial testing! The results of the study were consistent with both predictions. Concrete operational and preoperational children did remember differently right after exposure. Most children showed better recall eight months later than they had initially, even though they had not seen the array during that time. Research with a variety of other stimuli yielded similar results.

Piaget's most striking and controversial claim was the idea of long-term memory improvement. Although follow-up research by other investigators has partially replicated most of his findings, the existence of long-term memory improvement remains uncertain (see Liben, 1977). In terms of traditional ideas about memory, it is difficult to see how one's memory of something could improve. We think of a particular memory as a trace in the mind that, if anything, is likely to deteriorate over time. Perhaps in some cases the image might not deteriorate at all, but how could it possibly improve?

From the constructive view of memory, however, Piaget's suggestion is really not that radical, although its does go beyond what most information processing theorists have discussed. Recalling an array is not merely bringing back a static trace of it, but rather an active reconstruction. If children have a more sophisticated understanding of seriation at a later time, they can use it to construct a more accurate memory of the array than they could several months earlier. This doesn't mean that all memories will improve, of course. It merely suggests that under some circumstances certain memories—those tied to developing cognitive schemes—may show improvement.

is changed or embellished by information and structure provided by the children themselves. Often this embellishment is with inferred or implied relationships.

Constructive processes are determined by several factors, including the immediate context, the cognitive abilities of the child, and the particular social and cultural context in which the child lives. What children already know determines what they *can* know. Remembering is not an exact reproduction of an event; it is the *product* of interactions between the individual's existing schemata for organizing information and the new information. Changes occur both in the information encountered and in the cognitive structures to which the material is assimilated.

A Framework for Memory Development

From our discussion so far, it is obvious there are striking developmental changes in children's ability to understand and remember information. Ann Brown, in an oft-cited paper on memory development (Brown, 1975), has pointed out that the kinds of changes we have discussed fall into three major categories: (1) **knowing,** (2) **knowing how to know,** and (3) **knowing about knowing.** Each of these categories is critical to what both children and adults can understand and remember; each develops through childhood and beyond.

Knowing

Adults usually know more than children do. With development come advances in the *amount* known as well as in the organization and structure of that knowledge. To take a simple example, a child of 5 told not to touch the brake in the car may never have heard the word "brake" or even looked at one before. To understand and remember the term is difficult for the child because there is so little information or structure to which to relate this new word. Analysis of the word "brake" hardly can get beyond shallow processing—simple labelling and rehearsal—because there is little in cognition related to it. Remembering the word "brake" therefore is unlikely, even though the child may have some notion he is not supposed to touch something (or anything) on the controls of the car.

On the other hand, a 12-year-old given the same warning will have a much greater store of ideas, images, and associations connected with it. She knows that brakes are parts of cars, that they are critical to safety, that they slow cars down or hold them in place, that "brake" does not mean "break," and so on. Her associations and structures are far different than those of a child of 5. Such "knowing" can have a strong positive effect on memory; information can be processed beyond a simple rehearsal strategy to a much deeper, more meaningful level. Of course, having meaningful knowledge available for deeper processing does not guarantee it *will* be used. Deeper processing requires an active learner. Meaningful knowledge to which the new information can be related only opens up the *possibility* of deep processing.

Michelene Chi of the University of Pittsburgh has reported on a series of unusual experiments that clearly demonstrate just how important background knowledge or "knowing" can be to remembering. Chi (1978, 1985) and others (e.g., Dempster, 1981) argue that memory capacity is constant, at least beyond the age of 5 or so. Chi's assumption is that children and adults differ in memory performance (remember that college students can remember 7 or 8 digits in immediate memory, while a 5-year-old only can remember about 4) because children have less *experience* with the materials they are to learn. Knowing less makes remembering more difficult. Since adults almost always have more knowledge than children, what appears to be more capacity in adults actually is just greater familiarity with the learning materials.

Examining the role of knowledge in memory development is difficult, since knowledge is confounded with age. That is, if one simply looks at age differences, it is impossible to know whether it is age or knowledge that makes the difference: Both vary together (See Chapter 3). However, Chi selected an area of expertise—chess—in which she was able to find children who were far more expert than many adults. Having found young persons who knew a great deal about chess and older individuals who did not, her question was this: Would these third-graders through eighth-graders show better memory for locations on the chess board than the adults who were not chess experts?

As a comparison, she asked both groups to recall digits, with which adults would have had much more experience. Digit recall was assessed by having subjects write down as many digits as they could out of 10 presented to them. In the chess recall, all subjects were given chess positions involving 20 chess pieces placed on the board. The pieces were not placed randomly on the chess board; they were placed in patterns that often occur near the middle of chess games. Thus the patterns would be meaningful to chess players.

The results of Chi's research are presented in Figure 10-2. As she expected from earlier studies, adults were superior in the recall of digits. In their recall of chess pieces, however, the children were significantly superior! They were much better able to place the chess pieces back in their correct positions after seeing them than adults were.

What accounts for this difference? Chi (1978) argued that, for the chess-knowledgeable children, the chess pieces activated many more patterns in memory. According to Chi, some of the differences we

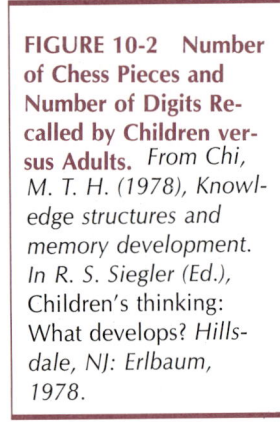

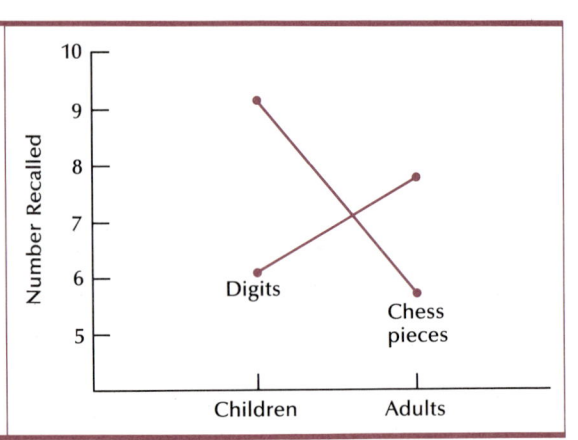

FIGURE 10-2 Number of Chess Pieces and Number of Digits Recalled by Children versus Adults. From Chi, M. T. H. (1978), Knowledge structures and memory development. In R. S. Siegler (Ed.), Children's thinking: What develops? Hillsdale, NJ: Erlbaum, 1978.

typically observe between adults' and children's memory must be due to *knowledge about the stimuli*, or the materials to be learned. As stimuli become more meaningful with greater knowledge, they more easily can be grouped or "chunked" (Miller, 1956), leading to greater ease of recall. As Brown (1975) has stated:

> There must be an intimate relationship between what the child can do or construct at a particular stage in his development and what he can remember or reconstruct. If the to-be-remembered material is meaningful and is congruent with the analyzing structures of the child, then comprehension of and subsequent memory for the essential features of the material will occur readily (p. 116).

Knowing How to Know

Beyond simply knowing more and having more complex cognitive structures within which to organize knowledge, children also show dramatic increases as they develop their use of strategies for memory and recall. According to John Flavell and Henry Wellman (Flavell & Wellman, 1977), "knowing how to know" refers to the vast range of things that people can choose to do voluntarily to improve their chances of remembering something. Repeating lists of things to oneself, paying attention to what is being said, avoiding distractions, and even setting a conscious goal of remembering something all are important strategies that children can develop to improve their memories.

Citing the work of the Russian psychologist Z. M. Istomina (1975), Ann Brown and Judy DeLoache (1978) of the University of Illinois provide us with the following example of how children spontaneously develop procedures for remembering. The task was one that children were motivated to do: to remember a list of items (e.g., food, toys, clothing) that could be purchased at a play store. One at a time, the children were recruited to go get some of the items. The teacher named

A Framework for Memory Development

five items slowly; an assistant at the store then recorded how many items the children actually were able to recall and observed how they tried to remember them.

> Three-year-old Valerik barely waited for the items to be read before rushing off to the store. The 3-year-old's view of the game seemed to be limited to going to the store and returning with items but did not seem to include the notion of bringing back specific items on the list. Four-year-old Igor listened attentively to the shopping list and then tried to carry out his errand as quickly as possible. He even seemed to try to avoid distractions, refusing to stop and talk on the way to the store. Very few 4-year-olds showed more specific mnemonic [memory] behaviors, but between four and five a qualitative shift seemed to occur, and all the older subjects seemed to make active attempts to remember. Many 5- and 6-year-olds actively rehearsed: they were often observed moving their lips, repeating the words to themselves as the experimenter read them and as they walked to the store (p. 29).

In the above examples, except for 3-year-old Valerik, we see much evidence for the *strategies* that children learn to use to minimize the chances of forgetting. In other words, "they know how to know." Igor, for instance, "listened attentively" and then tried to carry out the errand "as quickly as possible." Both are, of course, sensible things to do if one is trying to remember something. He also "seemed to try to avoid distractions," a technique that most of us would identify with as we try to avoid forgetting something. Similarly, older children "seemed to make active attempts to remember" and "actively rehearsed." What each of these kinds of activity have in common is that they are planful

In those areas where a child is an expert and an adult is not—for instance, in chess—the child's memory may be better than that of the adult.

and goal-oriented, or intended to improve later memory. Since the goal of these strategies is memory-related, they can be called **mnemonic strategies** (Kail, 1984).

DeLoache, Cassidy, and Brown (1985) have shown that even very young children (2-year-olds) may use some mnemonic strategies. In DeLoache et al.'s study, as children tried to remember where objects were located in a room, they were observed to point at them, stand close to them, and to spend more time looking at and talking about the objects. Thus, although these children may have had little or no awareness of their own actions, in observing their activities we learn that building blocks for mnemonic strategies may be in place very early (DeLoache, 1986). Full ability to control their use, however, does not develop until much later.

Rehearsal. One of the mnemonic strategies that undergoes the most dramatic changes is rehearsal. When does rehearsal begin? As might be inferred from the study above, many 5- and 6-year-olds use rehearsal as a mnemonic strategy. A more controlled research study by Flavell, Beach, and Chinsky (1966) provides us with better developmental information, however. In this early study, 5-, 7-, and 10-year-old children were shown seven pictures. The experimenter then pointed to and asked them to recall subsets of two to five pictures out loud, either immediately after they first looked at the picture or after a delay of 15 seconds. The experimenter watched the children to see if they were overtly rehearsing. Many were, but the percent increased dramatically with age. Whereas only 10 percent of the 5-year-olds rehearsed, 60 percent of the 7-year-olds and 85 percent of the 10-year-olds did so.

The studies of rehearsal by Ornstein and his associates (Ornstein et al., 1975; Ornstein, 1978; Ornstein et al., 1985), mentioned earlier in the chapter, also shed further light on developmental trends in rehearsal. As you recall, these researchers compared rehearsal in subjects ranging in age from seven to adulthood and found that overall *amount* of rehearsal was about the same. What changed, however, was the *nature* of the rehearsal. The young children simply tended to repeat single words as they were presented, processing the information at a shallow level (see Table 10-1). Older children and adults, in contrast, seemed to try to rehearse and process the information much more actively by using word meanings and reviewing earlier words.

In general, we can conclude that the strategy of rehearsal develops gradually. Before age 7 or so, it is infrequent. Seven-year-olds do rehearse, but often in a rote manner. By age 10, however, many children have become more and more proficient at "memorizing," adopting flexible and adaptive strategies that approximate those used by many adults (Brown, 1983; Ornstein et al., 1975). Some developmental changes in rehearsal, however, continue into adolescence and beyond (Bray, Hersh, & Turner, 1985).

Retrieval. Rehearsal aids in *encoding* and *storage*; that is, in entering the information into the information processing system and keeping it there. Children also develop retrieval strategies aimed at the recovery of information already in memory. Akira Kobasigawa (1974) studied 6-, 8-, and 11-year-olds after giving them pictures from common categories. Individual pictures from a category (e.g., zoo animals) were placed with a larger picture (e.g., a zoo with three empty cages). The children were told that the individual pictures "went with" the larger picture, but that they needed only to remember the smaller pictures. Then when recall was tested, some children were given the larger pictures and told they could be used to help remember the smaller ones. They were not told, however, *how* the larger pictures might be useful. Adults, of course, immediately would see the utility of categories such as "zoo animal" and use them spontaneously to help them recall. The same is not true for children, particularly young children.

Only about one-third of the 6-year-olds used the larger pictures. However, about three-quarters of the 8-year-olds and over 90 percent of the 11-year-olds used them. Moreover, even when younger children used the larger pictures as cues, they used them much less effectively than did the older children. Among those children who used the cues, all of the 6-year-olds and most of the 8-year-olds used each cue to recall only a single word! By contrast, the 11-year-olds' recall per category averaged 2.5 words. The pattern observed in Kobasigawa's research occurs frequently: 6-year-olds are unlikely to use strategies, but by age 11 children clearly possess expertise in using strategies. Eight-year-olds, however, seem to be somewhere in-between. They plainly have some idea that strategies are useful (e.g., in Kobasigawa's research most used the cues to guide their retrieval), but they have not learned to use them effectively (i.e., they used the cues mostly to recall only a single word from each category). Thus, while they see something helpful about using categories, 8-year-olds obviously are not yet capable of using the categories to their greatest advantage.

Knowing about Knowing: Metamemory

A third area in which notable developmental changes occur is in children's awareness of their memory, or **metamemory** (Flavell & Wellman, 1977). Metamemory is one aspect of the broader topic of metacognition, which refers to the ability to think about one's own cognitive processes (see Chapter 12). Included in metacognition are all levels of awareness about one's own knowledge, cognitive abilities, and general mental activity.

Metamemory, however, specifically refers to knowledge about one's own memory or "knowing about knowing" (Brown, 1975). Children

There is much more in our memories than most of us can recall. However, with the "right" cues, such as this woman's images of her family, many long–forgotten events can be retrieved.

have metamemory, for instance, if they realize that some things are easier for them to remember than others. If children see, for example, that they can recall 1 or 2 items but not 20, or that they need to study material longer if it must be remembered for a week instead of only for a few minutes, they are exhibiting knowledge that may be labeled "metamemory." While this knowledge seems to be second nature to adults, children develop it only gradually throughout childhood.

Kail (1984) has divided metamemory into three categories of skills: **awareness, diagnosis,** and **monitoring.** The process of an individual using memory skills, he argues, is much like that employed by a physician in treating an ill patient: Awareness of the problem and its diagnosis leads to a treatment that is then monitored to see how effective it is. If it is ineffective, then the treatment is modified. In the same way, children, after first becoming aware of the need to remember (awareness), learn to assess materials and their own skills to determine what memory strategies likely will work (diagnosis). As strategies are used, their effectiveness is checked (monitoring). If the strategies do not work well, children learn to try other approaches to improve memory performance. In this section, we will discuss each of these three important aspects of metamemory.

Awareness. A basic requirement for effective remembering is knowing when one needs to remember something. For instance, if you were told prior to reading this chapter that you may be quizzed over it or that it will be discussed in tomorrow's class, you instantly see you have been asked to remember the information contained in the chapter. This awareness obviously affects how you read: Depending on the requirements (quiz or discussion), you may spend more time on some sections than on others, reread the chapter, or jot down important points in a notebook.

Even young children, however, realize they need to remember some things: for example, to know what their coats look like in order to find them among all the other coats, the name of a desired toy advertised on television, or the neighbor's dog's name. But when, exactly, does the awareness develop that some things are useful to remember? And how does one measure this awareness?

One method researchers have applied in studying children's awareness of their memories has been to contrast their performance in recalling stimuli: (1) when they are simply told to notice them and (2) when they are instructed to try to *remember* them. If there are differences between (1) and (2) and these differences increase with development, then we have evidence that children understand something about memory problems (Kail, 1984). This technique was used in a study by DeLoache, Cassidy, and Brown (1985) to demonstrate that precursors to metamemory develop very early. It also was employed by Acredolo, Pick, and Olsen (1975) in a group of interesting early studies of memory in natural settings.

Acredolo et al. (1975) took preschoolers and older children on short walks through the hallways of a building. On these walks, the experimenter dropped her keys and then picked them up. Later, the children were asked to remember where the keys had been dropped. In a contrasting condition, the children were taken to specific spots in the building and told to remember the site. With such an instruction, the children's memories were much better than if they had not received this instruction. The improved performance showed that even young children are aware of their own memories and can improve them. Without this awareness, instructions would have had no effect. Of course, realizing the need to remember does not develop all at once; other studies (e.g., Johnson & Wellman, 1980) have shown that metamemory develops gradually through childhood.

Diagnosis. Some memory tasks are more difficult than others. Adults, for instance, know that it is much easier to learn the names of two new acquaintances than those of a roomful of people to whom we might be introduced. This constitutes an *assessment of task difficulty* based on our knowledge that number of items makes a great difference in how hard something is to remember.

Likewise, we can report easily on which of our three friends were at a large gathering, in contrast to testifying to the attendance of three people that we know only slightly. We know that familiarity is important. Similarly, we may worry about our comprehension of a professor who we know presents huge amounts of material at each class but begin feeling more comfortable when we learn that she hands out and

Highlights

Children as Witnesses

With the high crime rates in the United States and with increasing numbers of prosecutions against adults who abuse children, children increasingly are called on to testify in court. Can child witnesses be believed? What do children remember and what do they not? Do they mix imagination and memory? And what psychological harm can come to children who have been victims, but who now need once again to recall traumatic events? Can that harm be reduced?

Historically, children's ability to remember what they have seen and to serve as credible witnesses has been doubted (Goodman, 1984). Particularly, there has been a persistent belief that children do not recall what they have seen accurately and that they are especially prone to mixing fact with fantasy. Also, because their schemata for understanding information are less well-developed than those of adults, children's observations often are not well-organized and coherent by adult standards. Children are also notoriously suggestible, particularly when "led" by a clever interrogator (Dent, 1982).

In reviewing the research on children as witnesses for the *Journal of Social Issues*, however, Marcia Johnson and Mary Ann Foley (Johnson & Foley, 1984) concluded that, under some circumstances at least, children can be surprisingly accurate witnesses. For instance, in a developmental comparison of 6- and 9-year-olds (Foley & Johnson, 1985), they found that children were as good as adults in distinguishing things they did from what they saw others doing (e.g., making gestures, tracing outlines, looking at objects). In other words, the children clearly recalled what they did and what others did. An interesting perspective on these results, though, was provided by another dimension of this study. The children and adults were asked to perform some actions and to *imagine* themselves performing certain actions. Under these conditions, children were much less accurate than adults in remembering what they had done and what they only had imagined themselves doing.

Particularly when children do not understand an event (e.g., an adult conversation), their overall recall is poor. Like adults, if they cannot make sense out of something, then it is hard to recall. In a few instances, however, children's lack of frameworks actually may result in better performance. For instance, in one study (Neisser, 1979), children and adults watched a videotape of a basketball game and were told to pay attention to when the ball was passed between players. At one point in the tape, a woman carrying an umbrella walked through the playing area. Questioned later about whether they had seen the woman, almost no adults recalled seeing her. In contrast, 22 percent of fourth graders and 75 percent of first graders remembered seeing her! In general, it would seem that as children grow older, they pay less and less attention to "irrelevant details." Of course, it may be just these details that become important in the courtroom.

It also has been assumed that children are not skilled at recognizing faces, a critical part of much testimony. Research has shown that this is most true of studies of facial recognition under laboratory conditions (Chance & Goldstein, 1984), but that all subjects, adults included, tend to do relatively poorly under laboratory conditions. Face recognition is quite good in children as young as six years, however, if the face to be recognized is a familiar one and viewing takes place under reasonably favorable conditions. Unfamiliar faces are poorly recognized by children under 10 years, and are better recognized by older children.

Beyond the accuracy of testimony, a special concern when children are called on as witnesses in court is to protect them from psychological harm. It may be extremely traumatizing, for instance, for a child to have to recall a disturbing event, or to face a defendant in a courtroom. If children are not put at ease, their ability to recall accurately and even to testify at all may be impaired (Pyroos & Eth, 1984). Thus, special measures sometimes must be taken both to protect the child witness and to insure maximum accuracy of testimony. Among these are having young children sit on the laps of trusted adults while testifying, not using structured approaches but letting children recount events in their own way, and having children testify by interactive, two-way television, which protects them from the trauma of courtroom testimony, yet also protects the rights of the defendant.

The issue of child witnesses and the accuracy of their recall continues to be a thorny one. As Chance and Goldstein (1984) concluded, we know a good deal less than we would like to about children as eyewitnesses. Most research on witnessing to date has been directed at adults, and research efforts with children are only just beginning. The area promises to be an especially fruitful one, however, for those interested in applications of memory development research. Findings from well-designed research not only can help insure better testimony from children, but can give us new insight into the development of children's memories.

follows an outline. In this case, we know that our memory is affected by speed of presentation and can be overloaded by too much information coming too fast, but that being able to organize it can help ease the memory load.

Even young children are aware of how some of these same variables—number of items, task familiarity, speed of presentation, and organization of information—make memory tasks more or less difficult. As we saw earlier in the chapter, however, young children are not particularly skillful in diagnosing their own memory spans (Kail, 1984; Flavell, Friedrichs, & Hoyt, 1970; Yussen & Levy, 1975): Nursery school and kindergarten children greatly overstated their ability to remember a set of pictures. By fourth grade, however, predicted recall and the children's actual recall closely coincide. Children learn to better match their own abilities to task demands as development proceeds.

Diagnosing *retrieval demands* also is an important part of the diagnostic aspect of metamemory. Retrieval demands refer to the kind of memory performance required. For instance, most of us prepare differently for a true-false or multiple-choice examination than we do for an essay examination because we know the retrieval demands involved are different. Likewise, the expectation that we will need to give a 5-minute talk about a topic may spur us into a great deal of preparation.

Retrieval demands on children vary in much the same way. For instance, do they simply need to *recognize* the information, *recall* it verbatim (word for word), or "tell it in their own words?" By ages 5 or 6, children are beginning to understand these distinctions and to grasp their implications for memory (e.g., Speer & Flavell, 1979). To more closely examine children's knowledge of retrieval demands and their part in metamemory, Kreutzer et al. (1975) told their subjects this story.

> The other day I played a record of a story for a girl. I asked her to listen carefully to the record as many times as she wanted so she could tell me the story later. Before she began to listen to the record, she asked me one question: "Am I supposed to remember the story word for word, just like on the record, or can I tell you in my own words?" (p. 43).

We realize the reason for the child's question: Verbatim recall of an entire story is much harder than simply giving its highlights. But do children comprehend the reason for the question? Young children from kindergarten to second grade mostly did not. Children from the upper grades did understand its significance, however. Most said the girl needed to know because it would affect the difficulty of remembering and the way she would listen to the story.

Another study reported by Kreutzer et al. (1975) tested children's knowledge of how passage of time affects retrieval: Children were asked whether it would make any difference to their recall if, in phoning a friend, they got a drink between the time they were told the number and when they actually called. Again, young children (in kindergarten and first grade) showed less awareness of the need to phone first (although it was still their most frequent choice) than did older children in grades three and five. Thus, like children's knowledge in other areas of metamemory, awareness of the effects of delay on memory develops only gradually.

Monitoring. A final category of metamemory is *monitoring* how well remembering is progressing. Skilled learners decide what is well-learned, what is close to mastery, and what needs additional effort (Bisanz, Vesonder, & Voss, 1978; Goodman & Gardiner, 1981; Kail, 1984). Using this knowledge is vital for successful memory performance in many settings.

As children begin to monitor memory, they can better concentrate their efforts on what needs to be learned. In an interesting early study by Masur, McIntyre, and Flavell (1973), subjects were asked to study a set of pictures for 45 seconds and then to recall them. After recall was completed, subjects (first-graders, third-graders, and college students) were allowed to pick *half* of the pictures to study some more. This pattern was repeated several times, with subjects always picking half of the pictures for additional study. The experimenters' interest was in which pictures subjects would select. Third-graders and college students chose pictures for study that they had *not* recalled. In contrast, first-graders picked about equal numbers of recalled and unrecalled pictures to study. They apparently did not see the usefulness of studying items they did not already know in order to learn the total list.

Summary of Metamemory. Children undergo important developmental changes in their awareness of the need for memory, their ability to diagnose memory requirements and to choose strategies for learning, and their monitoring of the effectiveness of the strategies. Even preschoolers are aware of the need to remember things and have some knowledge about the effect of quantity of information on the ability to remember it. Not until middle childhood, however, do children clearly realize that semantic (meaning) relationships are critical to remembering, that retention requirements (e.g., verbatim or paraphrased recall) create vastly different memory demands, and that some strategies for remembering are more effective than others. The ability to select strategies and to tailor them for maximum memory performance continues to develop into adulthood (Bisanz, Vesonder, & Voss, 1978).

Applications of Memory Development Research

Sometimes memory has been downplayed as an intellectual skill. Rote memorization, in particular, is seen by some as a relatively low-level cognitive activity. Research on memory and cognitive development, however, has shown how critical memory is to all intellectual activity. The following guidelines drawn from the research on memory development should be useful to you in working with children in home, preschool, and school contexts.

1. *Encourage children to use their memories*. Real-life tasks and memory games are good ways to help children develop confidence in using their memories. Such activities give the opportunity to help direct their attention to similarities and differences in things, to teach them to visualize what they have seen, to help them take different perspectives on what they are learning, to diagnose what their memory strengths and weaknesses are, and to teach them effective and versatile ways of retaining new information.

2. *Point out the utility of remembering*. Memory often depends on having a reason to remember. The higher the motivation to remember, the more likely it is that attention will be focused on the material to be learned and that the child will try to remember it. Also, having children think about when the information will be used gives them a better chance of retrieving it when it is needed. Memory, especially for school subjects, usually improves if children make an effort to process it and have a clear idea how the information will be useful.

3. *Help children become aware of their memory strategies*. Children improve metamemory skills by thinking about their own memories. Their developing metamemory will, in turn, improve their memory performance over the long run. Making your own thought processes explicit ("I think I'll probably have to read this a couple of times so I remember it better"); asking questions ("How are you going to

Children who know *why* they need to remember something are much more likely to recall what they have been taught than those who don't understand the reason for remembering.

try to remember this?"); and making suggestions ("Maybe you should mark the spelling words you're missing and concentrate on those" or "Let's make a 'map' of these ideas. What's this paragraph all about?") can assist children in becoming more aware of the need to remember and in developing more effective strategies for remembering.

4. *Create conditions for "deeper" levels of information processing.* "Deeper" processing of information and therefore better recall will result from helping children relate what they are learning to what they already know (e.g., "You told me a papaya was a fruit. Would you like papaya for breakfast? Have any of you ever had papaya for breakfast?"). You can also help them rehearse new information in varied ways (e.g., discussing papayas and where they grow; looking at slides of a papaya tree; looking at photos of street peddlers in Indonesia selling papayas; having them draw and color pictures of papayas, oranges, bananas, and apples). The more varied and distinct the processing, the better the chances for recall.

5. *Aid children in organizing materials to be remembered.* Although many children do not organize information spontaneously in ways that help recall, they often benefit from organization *if it is pointed out or done for them.* This can be accomplished by arranging the materials in logical groupings or by teaching children strategies for grouping the materials themselves.

6. *Assist children in mobilizing relevant schemata.* Children have many schemata that can provide organization for their experiences. To help them better assimilate and retain new information, give them analogies (e.g., a zebra looks a lot like a horse) or otherwise help them associate structures they already have to what they are now trying to remember (e.g., "The kitten was very warm. She was laying in the sun. Have you ever been warm like that? Can you tell me about it?") What seem to us like obvious links from what children already know to what is to be learned may not be nearly so obvious to them. Remember also that the children's backgrounds are vastly different: What may be meaningful to one child may not be to another.

7. *Reduce memory demands in problem-solving tasks.* The chances of children solving problems—in arithmetic, in science, in geography—have been shown to relate to memory span, presumably because problem-solving requires students to keep several things in mind at once. Some information must be stored while other information is being worked on. Thus, some children may seem to be unable to solve problems, when in fact their difficulty is keeping information in mind. Encourage them to spend extra time familiarizing

themselves with the parts of the problem or to use notes or other methods to reduce memory demands.

8. *Realize the limits to children's short-term memory capacity*. The amount of information children can keep in mind at a given time is quite limited, especially for young children. Thus, when speaking to children or giving them directions, adults need to remember that their short-term memory capacity easily can be overloaded. For instance, four or five units of information (e.g., names of animals) at one time easily will go beyond what most preschool children can remember. Only one or two items should be presented at any one time, so the children can rehearse and store them in their long-term memory.

Also, when a teacher gives information orally or makes assignments that have more than a few simple parts, even very capable children may become confused. External aids to memory, such as written outlines, can be very helpful even for older children (and adults!).

9. *Recognize individual differences in memory ability*. Children's memory capabilities change greatly with development; even in children at the same developmental level, memory capabilities can vary substantially. Some children require many repetitions to learn a concept or skill; others do not. Some are much more subject to distraction than others in keeping information in short-term memory. Be prepared to make adjustments depending on the capabilities and developmental level of the children with whom you work. Also, remember that memory ability is closely linked to how much they know about an area. Children's memories are likely to be good for familiar topics, but poorer for unfamiliar material.

Summary

Studies of memory development have greatly increased in number and sophistication in the past quarter century. Much of this interest came from a revitalized cognitive psychology. Also, however, there has been increasing recognition that understanding memory *development* enhances the understanding of all of cognitive development.

Early methods for studying infant memory and memory development began with perception research. Among the most workable were those that used *habituation*, in which infants are exposed to stimuli repeatedly and become used to them. Habituation studies showed that even very young infants have surprisingly durable memories, especially an ability to recognize things they have seen before.

Infant memory studies stimulated great interest in memory development in general and generated several explanatory frameworks or *models* of memory. All are related, but each emphasizes a somewhat different aspect of memory. One, the *multistore model of memory*, depicts human memory as a computer-like system that takes in information from the *sense receptors*; holds it very briefly in raw, unprocessed form in the *sensory registers*; and then passes it on to the *short-term store*, a component that has limited capacity and contains the contents of consciousness. Information in the short-term store must be rehearsed in order to be transferred to the *long-term store*, the location of an individual's permanent memory.

A second prominent model has been the *levels-of-processing model of memory*. In contrast to the multistore model, which outlines the structural components of the information processing system, the levels-of-processing model stresses the *activities* individuals engage in during learning as determiners of recognition and recall. Shallow processing of stimuli leads to poor memory, whereas deep processing leads to better recall.

A *constructive model of memory* holds that information is transformed by cognitive, social, and affective processes in the individual. Memory is "constructed" as information is organized and changed by the cognitive processes and the knowledge structures the individual has. Constructivist views are influential both outside and within the field of developmental psychology.

All three of these models of memory have had a strong impact on developmental psychology. Many investigations of the development of short-term memory have been guided by both multistore and constructivist viewpoints; for instance, children's development of rehearsal strategies has been studied from both perspectives. Memory research based on levels-of-processing and constructivist models has emphasized the critical role of children's knowledge and perspectives.

No matter which model is employed, it is clear that much of memory development occurs in three major categories: knowing, knowing how to know, and knowing about knowing (Brown, 1975; Brown, Bransford, Ferrara, & Campione, 1983; Chi, 1985). Basic knowledge (knowing) greatly affects the ability to remember; as children develop, their knowledge increases and so does their memory performance. Knowing is not always linked to age, however. Even young children may show better recall than adults of information about which they are experts and adults not. With development, children increasingly use strategies for remembering (knowing how to know), such as paying attention and rehearsing. Finally, children gradually become aware of their own memories, how difficult or easy certain things are to recall, and about where to concentrate their efforts to remember (knowing about knowing). This latter category has been called *metamemory*, a form of metacognition focused specifically on knowledge about memory. Changes that take place in all three categories underlie much of memory development. Increased knowledge, improved ways of remembering, and the ability to "know oneself" all help produce better memory performance.

Key Terms

habituation
models of memory
multistore model
sense receptors
sensory registers
short-term store
long-term store
iconic memory
echoic memory
immediate memory span

rehearsal strategies
organizational strategies
levels of processing
deep processing
shallow processing
constructive models of memory
context cues
story memory
elaborative recall
inferential recall

knowing
knowing how to know
knowing about knowing
mnemonic strategies
rehearsal
retrieval strategies
metamemory
awareness
diagnosis
monitoring

Suggested Readings

Brainerd, C. J. & Pressley, M. (Eds.). (1985). *Basic processes in memory development*. New York: Springer-Verlag. This edited volume outlines the fundamental dimensions along which memory develops from childhood through adulthood. For the advanced reader, it examines age-related changes in encoding, retrieval, and cognitive processing.

Chi, M. T. H. (1985). Changing conception of sources of memory development. *Human Development, 28,* 50–56. This brief discussion of research in memory development presents the argument that the knowledge base of the child is a critical variable in memory development. Although strategies and metamemory are important, Chi argues, development in these areas is not sufficient to account for all of the changes in memory.

Kail, R. *The development of memory in children* (2nd ed.). (1984). New York: W. H. Freeman. This paperback, now in a second edition, outlines the relationship between memory development and that occurring in cognition. The book is clearly written and presents a good discussion of memory development in a relatively brief and nontechnical way.

Kreutzer, M. A., Leonard, C., & Flavell, J. H. (1975). An interview study of children's knowledge about memory. *Monographs of the Society for Research in Child Development, 40* (1, Serial no. 159), 1–58. This monograph is a landmark in the field of memory development in that it was one of the first works to clearly highlight the role of planfulness and self-awareness in the development of memory skills in children.

Application Exercise

10-1 Distinguishing among Knowing, Knowing How to Know, and Knowing about Knowing

For each of the following, distinguish whether the memory performance or memory deficit described is most concerned with: (a) the knowledge the individual possesses (knowing); (b) use of strategies for memory in recall (knowing how to know); or (c) awareness of his or her own knowledge, knowledge of task demands, and knowledge of whether memory strategies are working (knowing about knowing).

1. A 7-year-old, told to try to remember the names of her two new friends, Lisa and Emily, is observed looking first at one and then at the other and saying their names to herself.

2. A 13-year-old girl who has helped stock groceries for several years in her parents' neighborhood grocery store is sent to the store to get a large number of items for home. She remembers them all perfectly without needing a list.

3. A 3-year-old is told to go outside and call his older brother and sister for dinner. He steps out, talking to the family cat as he goes. When his parents look out minutes later, he is playing with the neighbor boy. He seems to have completely forgotten about calling his brother and sister for dinner.

4. A boy is reading his science text. Suddenly, startling his parents, he slams down the book, exclaiming loudly, "I just don't get this stuff. I read it, but I'm not remembering any of it. It just doesn't make sense."

5. A 12-year-old boy who has been taught to do needlework by his grandmother and who has entered his work in several shows, remembers all of the needlework prizewinners at the county fair and what patterns, colors, and techniques each winner used.

6. In an experiment, when read a randomly arranged list consisting of three items from the kitchen (e.g., pan, dish, knife), three from the bathroom (e.g., comb, toothbrush), and three from the garage (e.g., hammer), older children recall the items in clusters. For younger children, however, the order of recall seems to be random.

7. Describing his rock collection to his grandparents, Bobby tried to recall exactly what kinds of rocks are in it. As he tells about them, he counts the number of each type on his fingers: "I have . . . let's see, one . . . two . . . three shiny rocks; . . . one . . . two . . . flat rocks; . . . let's see, two, no, three big rocks, and one dusty, dirty rock."

8. A teacher has two kindergarten classes. On a field trip to the local zoo, she told her afternoon group to try to remember as many of the different animals as they could. She had not requested

this of her morning group. The teacher noticed that the afternoon groups asked her to label more animals than did the morning group. Also, when they discussed the zoo trip the next day, her afternoon group used many more animal names as they talked about the trip.

9. A teenager, studying for a social studies examination, concentrates her study on the chapter, "People Cooperating," because she heard the teacher tell another student this was the most important information.

CHAPTER 11

Language Development

The discovery of language during the childhood of every individual is one of the wonders of human life.
—George Miller

BF Skinner - rewards & punishment (conditioning)

Chomsky - born w/ innate ability to learn language
↓
LAD
Language Acquisition Device

Mixture of two is what is shown by current theory.

Steps in Language Development

Earliest example of language function — Crying
Vocalizing — Cooing
Babbling → meaningful sounds.
One word speech.
2 word sentences.

A 1-month-old infant is reclining in an infant seat, a participant in her very first experiment. In front of her is a picture of Raggedy Ann and from a loudspeaker above the picture come computer-generated syllables of speech. Each syllable is the same sound, /b/—the sound that begins the word "bin"—and is repeated over and over, /b/ /b/ /b/.

The infant is sucking on a nipple that contains a pressure-sensitive device to record her sucking rate. As the syllable continues to be presented over and over, /b/ /b/ /b/, her sucking rate gradually slows. But as the sound is shifted for /b/ to /p/, a remarkable change occurs. Her rate of sucking rises abruptly! The infant has recognized the shift between the two sounds.

How can such a young baby distinguish between these two sounds? She certainly has not been trained and she has little, if any, experience to draw on. Nonetheless, she and other infants clearly show this capability for distinguishing speech sounds, leading some researchers (Eimas, 1985) to the conclusion that human infants have an *innate* aptitude for acquiring and using language. This aptitude enables even very young children to make fundamental distinctions between language sounds.

Psychologists study newborns' abilities to perceive language sounds because they offer insights into the astonishing rapidity with which almost every child learns language. The vast majority of children will have learned most of the essential elements of language by age three. How is this achievement possible? How can we explain language development?

One straightforward explanation of how language is acquired is imitation. Superficially, this seems reasonable. After all, Chinese children learn to speak and understand Chinese, just as children in England learn to speak and read English. From this standpoint, language is not seen as a "special" skill. Children learn to speak by copying the lan-

369

guage sounds they hear. Language, like many other skills, is acquired through observation, imitation, and receiving rewards for "correct" speech (Skinner, 1957). Gradually, children's language grows more and more like that of their adult counterparts. Seemingly, language is not very complicated at all. After all, can something that is learned without formal teaching and in such a short time be very complex?

The answer is yes: Human language is one of the most complex and mysterious phenomena that scientists ever have tried to understand. Language defies straightforward explanation (Crystal, 1976; Eimas, 1985). In fact, we know very little about the origins of human language. Since language began so long ago, we likely will never have a definitive answer. The fact that children acquire language so rapidly attests to the remarkable capabilities of human beings for acquiring language. Many researchers believe these special abilities evolved along with other higher functions of human cognition (Chomsky, 1965; Eimas, 1985; McNeill, 1970; Miller, 1981).

One special human ability seems to be that shown by the infant described at the beginning of this chapter, who showed an ability to distinguish critical characteristics of human speech. From studies such as those done by Eimas (1985), it appears that infants are born with many of the underpinnings that permit them to quickly understand and comprehend speech. These inborn mechanisms for speech perception enable children to quickly share in the communication of language.

Other evidence also shows that language is not a simple skill learned through imitation. If imitation were the major principle governing language learning, children would produce quite different speech patterns than they do. Their speech would resemble that of adults and they would not create unique language patterns. This point is illustrated in the following conversation between parent and child, as reported by McNeill (1970):

Child:	Nobody don't like me.
Mother (correcting child):	No, say "nobody *likes* me."
Child:	Nobody don't like me.
Mother:	No, say "nobody *likes* me."
Child:	Nobody don't like me.
Mother:	No, say "nobody *likes* me."
Child:	Nobody don't like me.
Mother:	No, say "nobody *likes* me." (sequence repeated six more times)
Mother:	No, now listen carefully; say "nobody *likes* me."
Child (exasperated):	Oh! Nobody don't *likes* me.

Aside from the fact that the mother *might* have concentrated on the content of what the child was saying and told him that *somebody* liked him, the remarkable thing in this conversation is that he does not use the adult pattern of speech, although he is presented with the correct adult model several times. If imitation were the major route of language acquisition, then a child who makes mistakes and is corrected should pick up the correction quickly. Children would never say an original sentence and would use adult vocabulary and grammar. But of course that is not the case!

Few adults (the ones we know, at least) refer to the dentist as the "tooth-guy," to the mechanic as the "fix man," or tell someone not to "broom their mess" when they do not want their room swept up (Clark, 1985). The fact is that much of what children say is *not* found in adult speech. No adult seriously says, "Nobody don't likes me!" Similarly, few adults would say "all gone kitty," "pussy cat chair," "no play that," "he no bite you," or any of the thousands of other unique constructions common to young children's speech. Children's unique sayings, their **novel productions**, are strong evidence that language learning is not primarily imitative.

Language seems to be "something more" than most human skills. On one hand, it is so rapidly acquired by infants and young children. From early on, we use it every day. We speak, listen, and read unconsciously. Language is entirely familiar to us. On the other hand, however, when we begin thinking about language and its acquisition by the young child, it seems to defy understanding. What is this phenomenon we call language, and how can we hope to comprehend it?

The unique things children say are strong evidence that there is more to language learning than just imitating adult speech.

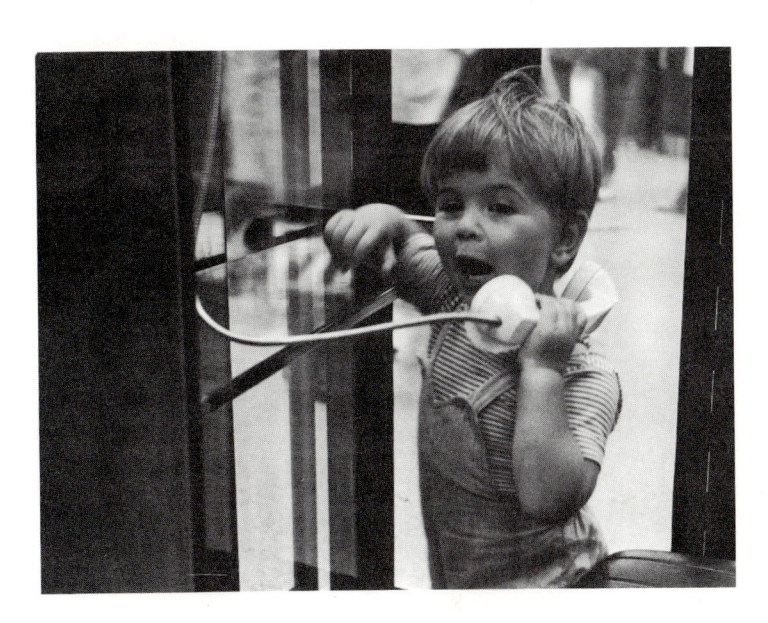

An appropriate starting point for our discussion of language development is a brief description of some of the important features of language, beginning with its building blocks: speech sounds and their perception. Then, we will move on to more global characteristics of language, its words, sentences, and structure. Next, we will consider the *uses* to which language is put and the contexts in which it occurs. Finally, we will discuss the knowledge children have about their language. With this information available, we can then examine the dimensions along which language development proceeds.

Characteristics of Language

All approaches to the study of language recognize three major aspects of any language: its pronunciation, its grammar, and the meaning conveyed by the language (see Figure 11-1). Each of these divisions can be further subdivided: pronunciation—phones and phonemes; grammar—morphemes and syntax; and meaning—semantics and pragmatics.

Phones

The basis for all human languages is the range of possible voice sounds. The technical name for language sounds is **phones**. **Phonetics** is the study of the properties of human soundmaking: how we form, transmit, and hear sounds (Crystal, 1976). Phonetics provides a means of analyzing, recording, and transcribing the sounds made in any language.

Phoneticians, the specialists who study the sounds of speech, have developed a set of symbols for identifying the many sound segments found in given languages (see Table 11-1). One basic distinction in all languages is between **vowels** and **consonants**. Vowels are produced by allowing the airstream to pass in a relatively unrestricted way, whereas

FIGURE 11-1 **The Components of Language.** *Adapted from Crystal (1976),* Child language, learning, and linguistics. *London: Edward Arnold, Ltd., p. 26.*

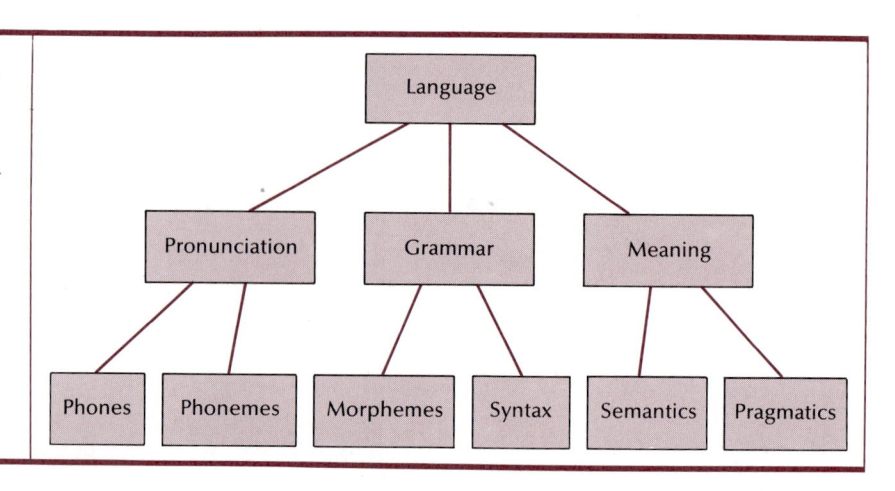

TABLE 11-1 Phonetic Symbols for English Sounds

Consonants		Vowels		Liquids and Semivowels	
Symbol	Example	Symbol	Example	Symbol	Example
p	*p*it, s*p*it	i	h*e*, m*ea*t	l	*l*id, fi*ll*
b	*b*it, ta*b*	I	b*i*d, s*i*t	r	*r*ip, ca*r*
m	*m*it, s*m*all	e	b*ai*t, *ei*ght	y	*y*es, bu*y*
t	*t*ip, s*t*ill	ɛ	b*e*t, *e*xact	w	*w*e, q*u*ick
d	*d*ip, ri*d*e	æ	b*a*d, b*a*t	h	*h*igh, *wh*o
n	*n*ip, pi*n*	u	wh*o*, b*oo*t		
k	*k*in, s*ch*ool	U	p*u*t, f*oo*t		
g	*g*ive, bi*g*	c	b*u*t, *u*tter		
ŋ	si*ng*, thi*nk*	ə	*a*bout, *e*n*e*my		
f	*f*it, rou*gh*	o	b*oa*t, g*o*		
v	*v*at, di*ve*	ɔ	b*ough*t, s*aw*		
s	*s*it, *p*sychology	a	p*o*t, f*a*ther		
z	*z*ip, rou*se*	:	Following a vowel indicates lengthening of the vowel; compare /bae:d/ (bad) and /baet/ (bat)		
θ	*th*igh, e*th*er				
ð	*th*y, ei*th*er				
š	*sh*ip, ra*t*io				
ž	*p*leasure, vi*s*ion				
č	*ch*ip, ri*ch*				

From Anisfeld (1984), Language development from birth to three. Hillsdale, NJ: Erlbaum, p. 140. Used by permission of the author and Lawrence Erlbaum Associates.

consonants are produced by somewhat greater interference by the speaker with the stream of air (Anisfeld, 1984). Vowels can be manipulated most readily by speakers: They can be "lengthened, shortened, clipped, drawled, and so forth. It is for this reason that individual differences in speech are especially evident in vowels" (Anisfeld, 1984, p. 191). A trained phonetician can transcribe the sounds of any language. Using a universal set of symbols and conventions (agreed-upon methods), the phonetician can record the actual sounds being produced by speakers of that language.

Phonemes

Languages are more than just collections of sounds. Sounds become part of language only when used in a meaningful way. Human beings, of course, are capable of making a nearly infinite variety of sounds. We can coo, grunt, warble, chirp, and whistle. Out of the tremendous number of sounds that we are capable of, however, only a few actually are used in any given language. A unique and relatively small set of sound units are perceived as distinctive in a given language. These distinctive sounds, or **phonemes**, are the building blocks of each language. The study of the sound systems of language is called **phonology**.

English, for instance, has about 40 phonemes. We learn in English that /l/ and /r/ sounds are different (they are phonemes in English) because English uses that sound distinction to signify words with different meanings (e.g., "lid" and "rid"). We ignore or do not even hear other distinctions such as the slightly different pronunciations that occur when speakers pronounce /r/. However, we pay attention to the difference between /l/ and /r/ because this difference conveys meaning, while we ignore variations *within* each category because they do not.

What we hear in any language, then, are categories of closely related sounds treated as identical because they mean the same thing. These categories—the phonemes of the language—are really abstractions much like concepts and differ for each language. Spanish, for instance, has several phonemes not found in English; because of this, speakers of English often have difficulty hearing differences between Spanish words that are obvious to native Spanish speakers.

Some phonemes are long, extended sounds, whereas others are quick. Some are hissing sounds and others not. Such differences are differences in **manner**, or how sounds are produced. Other phonemes differ in **place**, that is, where in the mouth they are created (e.g., in the front near the teeth or further back in the throat). Finally, there is **voicing;** some phonemes are voiced (e.g., the /m/ in *m*ill, the /b/ in *b*ill) in that they are said with vibrations of the vocal cords. Others, such as /p/ in "pill" and /t/ in "till," are not voiced. These three dimensions—manner, place, and voicing—form the basis for distinguishing English consonants. Each phoneme differs from every other phoneme along one or more of these dimensions (Lund & Duchan, 1983).

Morphemes

Morphemes can be thought of as minimal units of meaning; they are the building blocks of words. Each word is composed of one or more morphemes. For instance, the word *help* consists of a single morpheme, whereas *helpful* has two, the morpheme for the stem *help* and the marker *ful* for the adjective function. If we added a prefix, *un*, and got *unhelpful*, we would have three morphemes. The discipline that examines the process of word formation is called **morphology**.

Inflections, the changes made in words to indicate their function, form an important aspect of morphology. In English, major types of inflections are possession, past tense, and pluralization. Thus, we change *boy* to *boy's, happen* to *happened*, and *cup* to *cups* by using possessive, past tense, and pluralization morphemes, respectively. As you can see, some morphemes can carry meaning all by themselves. (e.g., *help, bed, sad*); these stem forms are called **free morphemes**. The prefixes and suffixes (e.g., *un, ed*) cannot; these **bound morphemes** must be linked to stems in order to have meaning.

Soon after they begin to speak, children begin to apply morphological rules to convey meanings. Often, children overgeneralize morphological rules (e.g., applying the *ed* bound morpheme inappropriately, as in saying "he goed" instead of "he went"). Such overgeneralizations, which may sound comical or strange to adult ears, indicate that the child is beginning to grasp the morphological rules of the language. This knowledge becomes more sophisticated and detailed as development proceeds.

Syntax

In all languages, words are combined into larger structures, such as phrases or sentences. **Syntax** refers to the structural regularities for combining words in larger meaningful units (Crystal, 1976; Lund & Duchan, 1983). In English, for example, preschoolers would be very unlikely to say "ball the red," "red ball this," or even "this red is ball" in trying to express the color of their ball. Like other languages, English syntax requires that words must be organized in specific ways to convey meaning. Even as children first begin to combine two words, they use them in specific orders, indicating that syntax is acquired very early (Anisfeld, 1984; Crystal, 1976).

The two basic elements of syntax are **clauses** and **noun phrases**. Word combinations that contain verbs are called *clauses* (e.g., Billy *fell*, Brenda *likes* to paint). Clauses are basic language units; utterances can consist of one or more clauses (Lund & Duchan, 1983). A second basic part of the syntax of language is the *noun phrase*. Part of the syntax of any language specifies which words can be used with nouns and which are permissible word orders. In English, a child will say "my little car," "a blue car," or "the beat-up old car," but not "car little my," "car a blue," or "old car the beat-up!" Some word orders are meaningful in English and others are not (although we can sometimes determine what these fractured phrases *likely* mean!).

Syntax obviously is critical to understanding. It makes a tremendous difference whether we are told that "Jenni hit Emily" or "Emily hit Jenni." The words are identical; only our knowledge of English syntactical rules enables us to understand who hit whom. Syntax also reflects speakers' intentions. Different syntactic structures are used to convey information (e.g., "That is mine!"); indicate commands ("Give me my dolly!"); highlight information ("that blue car over there"); ask questions ("How old are you?"); or show politeness ("Could you please pass the pepper?"). Children do not use adult syntactic structures immediately, but they do start showing syntactic regularity from the time they begin to combine words (Crystal, 1976; MacWhinney, 1982). As we will discuss, acquisition of syntactical rules is a major developmental achievement in the area of language.

Semantics

The whole point of using language, of course, is conveying meaning. Children label things, make requests, protest actions of their parents and playmates, and impart information about themselves and their environment to others through words and combinations of words (Nelson, 1973). **Semantics** refers to the meaning of words and word combinations, "the relations of signs to the world" (Ferrara, 1985, p. 138).

Semantics is closely linked to syntax. Each can be clearly distinguished from one another, however. Syntax is only the *vehicle* by which meaning is conveyed, whereas semantics refers to the meaning itself. In the sentences, "Barbara caught the ball" and "The ball was caught by Barbara," the meaning or semantic structure is the same, but two different syntactic structures have been used to convey the same idea.

The nature of meaning is, of course, a complex, philosophical topic (see Clark & Clark, 1977, for an introduction to theories of meaning). One common aspect of meaning, however, is familiar: the meaning of words or, more technically, **lexical meaning**. When we ask what a word means, we are asking about what class of objects, events, beings, or characteristics to which it applies. These objects, events, beings, and characteristics are the **referents** for a word, or what the word means. Thus the words themselves (e.g., "kitten") can be distinguished from their referents (e.g., Allison's pet kitten). Learning that words and their referents are not the same is an important linguistic achievement (Osherson & Markman, 1975; Tunmer, Pratt, & Herriman, 1984).

Much word meaning is **contextual**: That is, words take on different meanings depending on their context. Thus, if a child relates that "then *she* bit Emily," the listener would easily understand who *she* referred to if the child had just said, "Emily took Jenni's toy." In another context, however, *she* might refer to a quite different someone or something—a younger sister or pet poodle, perhaps.

Context is especially important in languages such as English in which many words share the same pronunciation and even the same spelling. Adults use context to convey meaning unconsciously: For example, we have little trouble understanding from a talk with a child that the /rɛd/ in "The flower is red" and "He read a book" refer to distinctly different words, although they are pronounced identically.

Sometimes a great deal of contextual information is needed to distinguish word meaning, as in the example, "They are annoying people." Does *annoying* refer to someone's actions or to a shared trait of a group of people? Only by using context can we clarify the meaning of *annoy*. Usually, however, we do this automatically. So-called garden path jokes play on this ability; for instance, the joke, "I was going to take the plane to Albuquerque, but it was too heavy" takes advantage of our initial understanding of "take" as "catch" to surprise us!

The growth of semantic understanding has been an important issue for developmental psychologists. For instance, how children acquire word meanings is of great interest to many theorists and practitioners (Clark, 1977, 1985; Nagy, Herman, & Anderson, 1985). Similarly, such

Pragmatics

semantic issues as how children come to comprehend and use metaphors (Ortony, 1979) and the relationship of language and thought (Piaget, 1980; Vygotsky, 1962; Waters & Tinsley, 1982) have been the focus of much developmental theory and research.

Traditionally, language forms and meanings were studied as if they were completely independent of the social and physical contexts in which the language occurs. Recent research, however, has demonstrated dramatically just how important context actually is in language use and interpretation (Bates, 1976; Bates & MacWhinney, 1979; D'Odorico & Franco, 1985; Ferrara, 1985; Lund & Duchan, 1983). The study of the effects of context on language is called **pragmatics**. Research on pragmatic aspects of language use has revealed several particularly critical contexts. Among them are the situation in which language occurs, speakers' intentions, listener characteristics, and the language itself.

The Situation. Language often accompanies ongoing physical and social events. Two children playing together in the sand at the beach, for instance, share a common environment that includes sand, sand buckets, toy shovels, and dolls. As they try to make a "house" out of the wet sand, they also share an event. If they are to communicate and to work cooperatively in a setting such as this, they must quickly agree on references for objects (e.g., "pail" for the bucket, "digger" for the shovel, and so on) and to use actions such as looking, pointing, and showing to link words to objects and events (e.g., pounding the sand with the shovel and saying, "bump, bump").

Language is an integral part of play.

While language often is used contextually as an accompaniment to actions (Lund & Duchan, 1983; Ninio & Bruner, 1978), it can be used pragmatically to *establish* contexts. When children say, "Let's pretend," "Let's talk," or even "I got a problem," they are creating **speech events**, or a sense of what the context of an upcoming language interaction will be. Similarly, children may describe ongoing speech events. Children who say "We're playing school," "We're giving our gerbil a bath," or "We're telling jokes" are conveying their ideas of what speech events will be all about and setting the stage for particular kinds of language exchanges. One well-known type of speech event is the *conversation*, which is characterized by information giving, questioning, and taking turns (Dorval & Eckerman, 1984). We will describe language development in this important area later in the chapter.

Speakers' Intentions. If someone asks, "Could you please pass the salt?," we respond by passing the salt rather than by simply saying "Yes." We recognize the speaker's intention as a polite request for salt. Similarly, even preschool children know the meaning of the teacher's statement, "It's VERY noisy in here" as an indirect suggestion to be quieter. Speakers' intentions create contexts for language; in the view of some, every utterance has a function of intention (Searle, 1969).

Children quickly learn to use language intentionally to signal their wants and needs. A baby's cry gives way to single word requests (e.g., "milk" to request a drink of milk). Children adopt more and more intentional uses for language (Ervin-Tripp, 1977), such as informing others (e.g., "My horsie broke"), regulating others' actions (e.g., "Mommy, stay here!"), and even giving orders (e.g., "Come here, Molo"), or giving hints (e.g., "The ice cream is all gone, Daddy," or "I'm thirsty"). Later, we will explore developmental changes in pragmatic uses of language.

Listeners' Characteristics. A third area of context is listeners' characteristics. Most adults automatically adjust their speech to fit their listeners' perspectives and capabilities. Young children, however, develop this ability only gradually. They often cannot understand how others' differing points of view and knowledge might possibly affect the ability to comprehend messages.

One aspect of listener context that affects both children and adults has been studied intensively: This is called **motherese** (D'Odorico & Franco, 1985; Lederberg, 1982; Newport, Gleitman, & Gleitman, 1977). *Motherese* refers to the special characteristics of speech that adults and older children (not just mothers!) direct toward young children (Snow, 1977; Snow & Ferguson, 1977; Wilkinson & Rembold, 1982). This speech has a number of highly distinctive characteristics we all recognize when we hear someone talking to a baby or young child (Lund & Duchan, 1983):

1. Shorter utterances
2. More highly intelligible, fewer "breaks" in speech
3. Better-formed grammatical sentences
4. Lower rate of speech
5. More restricted vocabulary
6. Greater repetition of words, phrases, and sentences
7. Higher and more varied pitch
8. More questions and present tense words

When we hear utterances such as "tum-tum" for "stomach," "choo-choo" for "train," or "Mommy's going to give Boo-boo her dinner," we are hearing motherese. Often these utterances are not only noticeable for the special vocabulary they contain, but also for the way they are said—in a high-pitched voice and with exaggerated intonation.

Whereas there is some disagreement about the exact role of motherese in helping children acquire language (Lund & Duchan, 1983), motherese appears to be a useful and important part of the language context to which young children are exposed. Generally, motherese helps adults encourage children to talk about the things and events they are experiencing (Newport, Gleitman, & Gleitman, 1977).

Language as a Context. Language itself provides a fourth important type of context. Language seldom is a sequence of unrelated statements; instead, sentences usually are woven together by a topic, shared vocabulary, and knowledge held in common by speaker and listener. The exclamation, "I sure would!" only becomes comprehensible when the question that precedes it is known: For instance, "Do you want to play catch with me?"

Language has many mechanisms for linking meaning. These mechanisms, called **cohesive devices**, tie language together. For instance, if you are talking about your neighbor's dog, Farf, and you say "*The* dog bit me," your use of the article *the* signals the listener that you mean a *particular* dog bit you. However, if you had said, "*a* dog bit me," Farf would be off the hook, because you are likely referring to some other (unknown) dog.

Articles are only one of many cohesive devices that enable speakers to make their meanings clear. Some cohesion is produced by repetitions in vocabulary. For instance, textbook writers sometimes repeat certain words to hold their discussions together (e.g., "Paleontologists often study *rocks*. They study all kinds of *rocks*, but they are most interested in studying the kinds of *rocks* that contain fossils. When they find these *rocks* . . ."). Although text writers sometimes overuse vocabulary repetition, cohesive devices generally enhance the ability of the language to convey meaning. They help link utterances or written sentences together into a meaningful whole.

Language: What Develops?

Most people think that children's language development begins at about 12 to 18 months, when they first begin to talk. Actually, language development begins much earlier. Learning to talk is a tremendously significant achievement, true, but one that is built on a vast amount of earlier experience. Well before children start talking, they can understand speech and know how to communicate with those around them.

Two streams of language development—vocalization (making sounds) and communication (sharing meaning with others)—develop side by side during the first year of life. Only in the second year do these two streams converge; vocalization is linked with communication. This linking is the beginning of true language (Anisfeld, 1984; Miller, 1981).

In this section we will examine early language development, beginning with the development of speech perception and production. Then we will examine how speech skills begin to be used in communication as children produce their first words and sentences. Next, we will discuss the growing knowledge children begin to show about their own linguistic capabilities as they become increasingly able not only to *use* language effectively, but to *think about* what language is like.

Early Speech Production

The capability of humans to distinguish and create speech sounds is the basis for all languages. The perception and creation of speech can be divided into two major periods: the **prelinguistic period**, which lasts until around the child's first birthday, and the **linguistic period**, which continues from that point on (Anisfeld, 1984). In the prelinguistic period, speech does not yet convey meaning. Infants vocalize a great deal, but their main language activity is articulating and practicing sounds. Later, in the linguistic period, these skills are applied as meaning becomes linked to speech sounds and to speech production. In the first months of life, however, vocalizations communicate meaning only generally.

Crying is the most obvious form of infant vocalization. Technically speaking, crying is a sound produced during expiration (breathing out) which consists of sounds much like vowels and occurs in series (Anisfeld, 1984). Crying begins at birth; babies cry when they are cold, hungry, uncomfortable, or want to be held. At about 3 months, another form of biologically based vocalization, cooing, develops. **Cooing** refers to sounds babies produce, "usually in response to smiling and talking on the part of the mother" (Stark, 1979, p. 24). Cooing is somewhat closer to speech than crying; it is richer and contains both consonant and vowel sounds (Anisfeld, 1984). In contrast to crying, cooing usually indicates a pleasurable state.

During the next stage of vocalization, **babbling**, infants continue to diversify the sounds made earlier in crying and cooing. Babbling, "playful speech that is devoid of referential meaning" (Anisfeld, 1984, p. 222), becomes prominent for most children between 6 and 12 months of age. Babbling children create an amazing variety of speech sounds. Sound production results from children's trying out their articulatory (sound-making) capabilities; the many different sounds they make are produced by chance. Early in this stage, as was true for crying and cooing, there is little effect of the particular language used in the home. Comparisons across cultures, for example, show nearly no impact of the mother tongue. Thus, babies in England begin to babble in the same "language" as those in, say, Chile or Turkey. In fact, deaf babies, who cannot hear at all, produce vocalizations very similar to those of hearing children at this stage (Crystal, 1976). Soon afterward this changes.

Early Speech Perception

As we saw at the beginning of this chapter, even very young infants can perceive differences in speech sounds (Eimas, 1985). Almost from the beginning, infants also can be soothed by gentle speech (Anisfeld, 1984) and show a preference for their mothers' voices (Mills & Melhuish, 1974). They increase their rate of vocalization when they are spoken to, although actual imitation of sounds usually does not occur until the third quarter of the first year (Anisfeld, 1984). The ability to perceive speech sounds, however, and the fact that adults begin talking to infants almost from the moment of birth (see Rheingold & Adams, 1980; Kaye, 1980) lay the groundwork for linguistic communication with even very young children. As we learned earlier, caregivers use a special form of communication in talking to infants and young children, motherese, which makes speech perception and, hence, communication easier.

As Bruner (1978, 1983) has stressed, adult use of language with infants and young children is bound up in shared activities. Language would mean little without the activities and the activities little without language; each stimulates and complements the other. Adults view infants as social beings right from the start; soon that view is rewarded by children's reactions (Murray & Trevarthen, 1986).

Trevarthen (1979), for example, has shown that middle-class mothers typically respond to children's noises and make a great deal of fuss over them. In the first year at least, parents, not infants, seem to be the imitators! They produce baby talk that comments on their children's activities or repeats and exaggerates their children's vocalizations. A 6-month-old infant may smile, for instance, and the mother may say, "SUCH a BIG smile!" Similarly, an infant may babble, /bi/ /bi/ /bi/ /bi/ /bi/, and the father may imitate these sounds faithfully, /bi/ /bi/ /bi/ /bi/ /bi/. These kinds of interactions help build intimacy between infants and adults (Anisfeld, 1984), and gradually draw them into the social and linguistic community.

First Words

The *linguistic period* begins with a shift from nonmeaningful vocalization (e.g., babbling) to meaningful speech (e.g., a baby's first words). Of course, this shift is not sudden; from about 9 months on, it is more and more possible to identify segments of speech that correspond to words. Also, many infants at this age already have shown the ability to *comprehend* some aspects of speech (e.g., to point to their nose, their eyes, or their Teddy). Further, their speech sounds and patterns are developing clear features of the mother tongue (e.g., English infants are now making sounds of the English language).

As children shift from making "sounds without meaning" to "sounds with meaning," verbal fluency may *drop* dramatically. To some parents, it almost may seem as if their children have stopped talking (Crystal, 1976). This is not the case, however. Babbling babies produce a tremendous range of sounds unrestricted by meaning. When they move to using sounds for semantic (meaning) purposes, many of the sounds of babbling are irrelevant because they are not a part of the language (e.g., English) being spoken around them. Faced with the need to communicate meaningfully, children now must learn to use a *few* sounds in an organized and systematic way. While babbling may be good practice for making sounds, it is not language.

First words are a wonderful milestone of child development, as we can tell from the excitement they produce among parents and other adults! But these earliest words may be very different than adult words; they are usually mispronounced by adult standards (e.g., /dada/ for "daddy"), they may have very diffuse and generalized meanings (e.g., /mik/ referring to milk, water on the floor, and a puddle in the street), and may convey several meanings, depending on context and how the word is said (e.g., /dada/ may be used to identify daddy, to express the need "I want daddy," or to indicate puzzlement, "Is that daddy?"). In some ways, first words can be looked at as one-word sentences, or **holophrases**, used by the child to express a variety of meanings.

First words often are accompaniments to actions and contexts, not true labels for things. Anisfeld (1984) has called this very early use of words **presymbolic**. That is, words are not used as symbols so much as they are things that "go with" certain actions. On the comprehension

Highlights

What is the Relation Between Language and Thought?

One of the continuing issues in language development research is the relationship between language and thought. Do language and thought develop separately? That is, does language acquisition move ahead independently of other cognitive functions or do they affect one another? If language and cognitive development are related, does language acquisition *depend* on thought or does thought depend on language? Theorists have taken quite divergent perspectives on these issues. Some of the key points of view are the following.

Language as Independent of Thought: Noam Chomsky

Noam Chomsky of the Massachusetts Institute of Technology, perhaps the best-known linguist of recent times, has taken an extreme position on the relation between language and thought. Language develops, he has argued, independently of thought. Linguistic categories, in his view, are "hard-wired" into the human brain as a result of evolution. Exposure to language triggers the *language acquisition device* (LAD), with which every human is innately endowed. Thus, language is not learned so much as it unfolds when given the proper stimulation (Chomsky, 1965, 1980).

Language is not a part of thought nor dependent on it; it does not seem to depend substantially on a child's intellectual skills. Because language develops in similar ways for all children at about the same time and language is learned with such remarkable aptitude, it almost seems as if children are "programmed to learn language." To use another metaphor, language is an "independent organ of the mind."

Language as a Determiner of Thought: Benjamin Lee Whorf

Benjamin Lee Whorf, writing in the early 1950's (Whorf, 1952), took a startling position concerning language and thought. Language, he stated, *determines* our thought. Linguistic patterns have a profound impact on how we perceive the world and how we are able to think about it. Language shapes our ideas rather than merely expressing them.

Grammars, to Whorf, are not independent mechanisms or just ways of producing thoughts, but actively help form people's ideas. Although individuals are not conscious of how their language affects their outlook, it nonetheless controls their observations of the world. In Western European societies, for instance, languages have common characteristics that create a "European" perspective of reality—" . . . English terms like 'sky,' 'hill,' and 'swamp' persuade us to regard some elusive aspect of nature's endless variety as a distinct *thing*, almost like a chair or table" (1952, p.

(Box continues on pp. 384 and 385)

What is the Relation Between Language and Thought? (cont.)

21). Time, in European languages (including English), also is described in a particular way, as if it were a ribbon or tape measure with equal segments marked off. Many non-European languages (such as those of Asia or Africa), however, with quite different structures and vocabulary, obligate their speakers to view space and time in a very different way.

Language as Dependent on Thought: Jean Piaget

Jean Piaget took a view contrary to those of Chomsky and Whorf. Piaget, of course, described himself accurately as a genetic epistemologist, which means that his primary aim was understanding the nature of knowledge, not creating a theory of language development. Nonetheless, Piaget's viewpoint has had a huge impact on how the field of developmental psychology views the relation of thought and language.

Piaget argued that language, far from being independent from cognition or a shaper of it, is a *reflection* of it. Children begin with a sensorimotor understanding of the world and then try to find linguistic ways to express that knowledge. Sensorimotor knowledge determines the forms language takes. The development of cognition takes precedence over the acquisition of language; language as it develops simply "maps onto" previously acquired cognitive categories and structures.

Several lines of evidence support these views. First, linguistic categories closely resemble those of nonlinguistic knowledge and the nonlinguistic knowledge appears ahead of linguistic knowledge (Macnamara, 1972; Piaget, 1980; Sinclair, 1975). That is, infants know how to behave intelligently in their environment well in advance of either comprehending or producing speech. Second, what children understand and express linguistically is likely to be based on prior nonlinguistic experience with objects, actions, and events (Clark, 1977). Conceptual categories emerge first; linguistic categories such as nouns or verbs are acquired only if children have mastered the underlying nonlinguistic knowledge (Piaget, 1980). Finally, regardless of the language, children show great consistency in the order in which they acquire certain linguistic distinctions (Brown, 1973; Slobin, 1973). This consistency across languages implies some sequence of cognitive complexity that then is encoded linguistically (Elliot, 1981). Language is acquired *only* within the framework of cognition.

Merging Streams of Language and Thought: Lev Vygotsky

Whereas Chomsky's view tends toward the independence of language and thought and Whorf and Piaget each assigned a clear primacy either to language (Whorf) or thought (Piaget), other theorists have proposed that language and thought are interactive. Possibly the most influential interactionist view is that of the Russian psychologist, Lev Vygotsky (Vygotsky, 1962). In general, his position is that language and thought develop in two parallel streams early in life. They have independent origins and initially are quite separate. On one hand, there is pre-speech intellect (such as in apes or babies); on the other hand, there is preintellectual or nonintellectual speech (such as in parrots or babbling infants). At the point when the child begins to acquire first words and to name objects, however, the two streams begin to merge. Speech ". . . begins to serve intellect, and thoughts begin to be spoken" (Vygotsky, 1962; p. 43). For Vygotsky, thinking and language have different origins, but once they are combined, they mutually influence each other (Elliot, 1981).

Vygotsky did not take the extreme position held by Whorf that our language (e.g., our vocabulary and syntax) determines what we can think about. He did, however, stress how children use language to direct their actions and plan for solutions to problems (Vygotsky, 1978). Language not only expresses children's thoughts, he believed, but can stimulate thought.

As children mature, Vygotsky argued, their thinking becomes more and more verbal in nature. One key process is so-called *inner speech*. Early speech is a precursor to verbal thought, "speech on its way inward." Later, language aids in reasoning and guides actions. When language and thought join, the child's world is changed forever. Language becomes a tool for thought, its symbols powerful ways of representing the world. Concepts like "before," "now," and "after" structure reality; vocabulary words such as "run," "jump," and "fall" describe actions. Other words such as "dog" or "animal" help children classify and relate their ideas. Reasoning becomes linked to language.

The position we have taken in this text is more in the tradition of Vygotsky than that of Chomsky, Whorf, or Piaget. While there seem to be strong innate bases for language development, most researchers today assume an interdependence of language and thought processes. We agree with Piaget and his followers that cognition has a strong impact on language development and with Whorf that language structures affect cognition. We believe, however, that the effects are not so one-sided as either Piaget or Whorf implied. Although these aspects of children's mental lives appear to move ahead independently early in life, by age two they clearly are merged. Each facilitates the other. As children's vocabulary and command of grammar grow, their ability to think and reason advances rapidly.

side, examples of presymbolic uses of words abound. Proud parents love to show off their infants' abilities to touch their noses in response to the request, "Touch your NOSE," or to wave goodbye when prompted to do so ("wave BYE-BYE!"). Adults cue specific action patterns in a particular context.

"True" understanding of the meanings of words is not required to carry out such actions as these, however. In an interesting example, provided by Luria (1982, pp. 47–48), a 1-year-old Russian child was trained to look toward a portrait of Lenin when asked, "Where is Lenin?" But when the portrait was removed and the question was asked again, the child *continued* to turn toward the wall. His association was to the action of head-turning, not to the specific object (the portrait of Lenin).

Childrens' early *productions* of words are often presymbolic, too; they are linked specifically to certain contexts and actions. Greenfield and Smith (1976) have called such utterances "performatives," because they are a part of actions or performances. In an example they cite, at one year and one month of age, Nicky said "bye-bye" as he waved his hand as his father left for work. Not until later, however, did he say "bye-bye" without waving. Saying "bye-bye" was a part of the total pattern of activity when his father left.

Symbolic Word Use. In presymbolic word use, words are used along with childrens' actions. But words gradually come to be more and more free of context, more symbolic in character. They become separated from their referents (Piaget, 1980). Children begin to use words to refer to things and actions other than those in immediate experience; for example, a child might say *cat* when the cat is in another room. Some early "sign words" actually drop out, as children are exposed to greater varieties of contexts.

Words as Personal Symbols. Early **symbolic word use** is highly personalized. Children define words through their own subjective world understanding rather than according to "objective" adult language. One consequence is that early symbolic uses of words are often *overextensions*. In an example provided by Eve Clark (1973, 1977), "mooi" was first used by a child to refer to the moon, but was also then used (in order of occurrence) to refer to cakes, to round marks on the window, to writing on the window, to round shapes in books, to tooling on leather book covers, to round postmarks, and finally to the letter "O." This is quite a journey for a single linguistic unit, but certainly an understandable one. Extensions and overextensions can occur along a variety of dimensions (Clark, 1977), including shape (as in the above example), size (e.g., "fly" used to refer to specks of dust), sound ("oom" used to refer to sounds of busses and then to sounds of all moving machines), and taste ("cola" used to refer to chocolate, then to sugar, tarts, grapes, etc.). In all of these early extensions, it is obvious that the child has a meaning for the "word." This meaning, however, and the dimensions along which the word is extended, belong only to that child!

Although words may have unique meanings, words help children integrate their experiences. For instance, a child may use "dada" to label several things she associates with her father. "Dada" may be spoken, for instance, when she sees her father, when she spies his baseball glove, and when she hears him on the phone. It is as if the child does not have categories, but merely uses the label "dada" to link several parts of her environment together. In each of these things, there is something "father-like" about them.

Words as Socialized Symbols. In order to communicate with others, children need to recognize the social nature of language. Words, they must learn, are "labels for socially defined classes of objects and events" (Anisfeld, 1984, p. 79). When children discover the social and objective nature of language—that is, that words are shared symbols with shared meanings—they confidently begin the task of learning them. There is a period of extremely rapid vocabulary growth, most often in the second half of the second year (Anisfeld, 1984). Whereas a child may acquire only 10 or 20 new words in the first 6 months of the second year, in the second 6 months new words are learned at a phenomenal rate, as many as 60 or more per month (McCune-Nicolich, 1981; Olson, Bayles, & Bates, 1986).

What kinds of words are learned earliest? As one might expect, the majority of early-acquired words pertain to things and actions in children's immediate lives. For instance, looking at the first 50 words of a group of 18 children, Nelson (1973) found most words (64 percent) referred to "things" adults would label by concrete nouns. These include family members, toys, food items, parts of the body, and articles of clothing. Next most frequently labelled are actions (e.g., go, see) and states of being (e.g., allgone).

Many early words have an interesting characteristic in common: They are two-syllable words in which the second syllable is a full or partial copy of the first. Examples are "wawa" (for water), "dada" (daddy), "mama" (mommy) and doh-dohs (a snack cereal). Languages around the world recognize children's fondness for such words. Table 11-2, which contains a number of early words used by a young girl, Hildegard, shows both this tendency to use duplication in choice of labels and the use of these labels as referents for (to refer to) actual objects in her own environment.

Most early words seem to be used for *cognitive purposes*—that is, to name, indicate, or comment. Fewer are used for *instrumental purposes*, such as in making requests or expressing desires (Anisfeld, 1984). Thus a child's first words are more likely to name objects (such as calling a

TABLE 11-2 Examples of Early Single-Word Use by a Young Child, Hildegard

Age	Word	Referent
18 months	titi	cookie, cake, candy cherry, cracker
19 months	titi	cookie, cake, candy, cherry
	gaga	cracker
21 months	titi	cookie
	gaga	cracker
	gig	cake, candy, cherry
22 months	tutis	cookie
	gag	cracker
	geg	cake

Adapted from Werner & Kaplan (1963). *Symbol formation.* New York: Wiley, p. 116.

cookie a "cookie") than they are to express a request (such as asking for a cookie by saying "cookie").

How Are Words Learned? Most adults, as we have seen, intuitively seem to "know how to talk to infants" and how to draw children into social and linguistic interaction. Many also attempt to develop children's vocabulary by using an interaction pattern called **deictic tutoring**. Used especially frequently by middle-class American parents (Heath, 1986), deictic tutoring refers to a pattern of informal teaching in which an object is identified, looked at, and named (Anisfeld, 1984; Ninio & Bruner, 1978). Ninio and Bruner (1978) have carefully analyzed the details of deictic tutoring and found that it typically consists of a routine of five sequential components. The following pattern, adapted from Ninio and Bruner (1978), illustrates these components in a typical parent–child interaction, teaching words from a picture book.

1. *Parent attempts to get child's attention*. The parent looks at a picture of, for instance, a baby chick, points, and says "Look!" to get the child's attention.
2. *Child focuses attention*. Child points at the picture of the chick and looks at the picture.
3. *Parent questions child*. Parent asks the child, "What's that?"
4. *Child makes response*. Child says, "tiky."
5. *Parent gives feedback*. The parent says to the child, "YES, it IS a chicky!"

Deictic tutoring centers around use of the label, which is almost always strongly stressed. Parents mostly give positive feedback in deictic tutoring; in Ninio and Bruner's findings, only 18 percent was negative (e.g., "No, that is not a bin-bin"). Deictic tutoring is a generalized technique; its simple routines are used not only in picture books, but in other contexts as well, such as a trip to the zoo (e.g., mother to child, "Look, Clara, there's a giraffe! Do you see it?"). An especially rich context for deictic tutoring is play, in which parents and children play with toys, label them, and handle them together. Mealtimes also provide numerous opportunities for deictic tutoring, as children are introduced to varieties of foods, table objects, and utensils.

Early Sentences

Children soon move from single word utterances to the **syntactic stage**, in which they begin to produce sentences. At first they say two-word sentences (**duos**) and then move to longer ones. Although some authorities have argued that single-word utterances function as sentences (e.g., McNeill, 1970), most consider children's syntax as developing when they begin to combine two or more words (Clark, 1973; Crystal, 1976). A **sentence** is a structured entity; it is a unit of meaning in which individual words interact to produce more complex, unitary ideas (Anisfeld, 1984; Braine, 1976). Typical first sentences are not elegant constructions, however; "doggie there," "more eat," "where kitten?", and "no mitten" are common examples. Nonetheless, each conveys important *relationships* between ideas and is a unified whole.

Context plays a critical role in sentence interpretation just as it does with single words. Thus, a child may say "daddy shoe" when the child's father is putting on *her* shoe, when she sees him putting on *his* shoe, or when she spies her father's shoe lying on the floor. Later, as children begin to add inflections (e.g., *-ing, -ed*) and better intonation, the meaning of sentences such as these can be more easily determined independent of context.

Children begin using sentences shortly after the "vocabulary spurt." Figure 11-2 shows the rate of increase in sentences for two children, Nicky and Eric. As you can see, once these children started making sentences, their use of sentences accelerated rapidly.

In the period from 24 to 30 months, children's speech becomes more and more elaborate. One phenomenon that often appears during this period is what is called **replacement sequences** (Anisfeld, 1984; Braine, 1971), in which sequences of words are immediately replaced by more elaborate strings of words. The following examples are from Braine (1971):

> Stevie bye-bye car. Mommy take Stevie bye-bye car.
> Fall. Stick fall.
> Noise. Noise car.
> Back there. Wheel back there.
> Plug in. Andrew plug in.
> Want more. Some more. Want some more.

FIGURE 11-2 Rate of Increase in Sentence Use for Two Children, Eric and Nicky. *Adapted from Anisfeld (1984) Language development from birth to three, Hillsdale, NJ: Erlbaum, and used by permission. Data for Eric are from Bloom et al. (1975, p. 7) and for Nicky from Greenfield & Smith (1976), The structure of communication in early language development, New York: Academic Press, p. 38.*

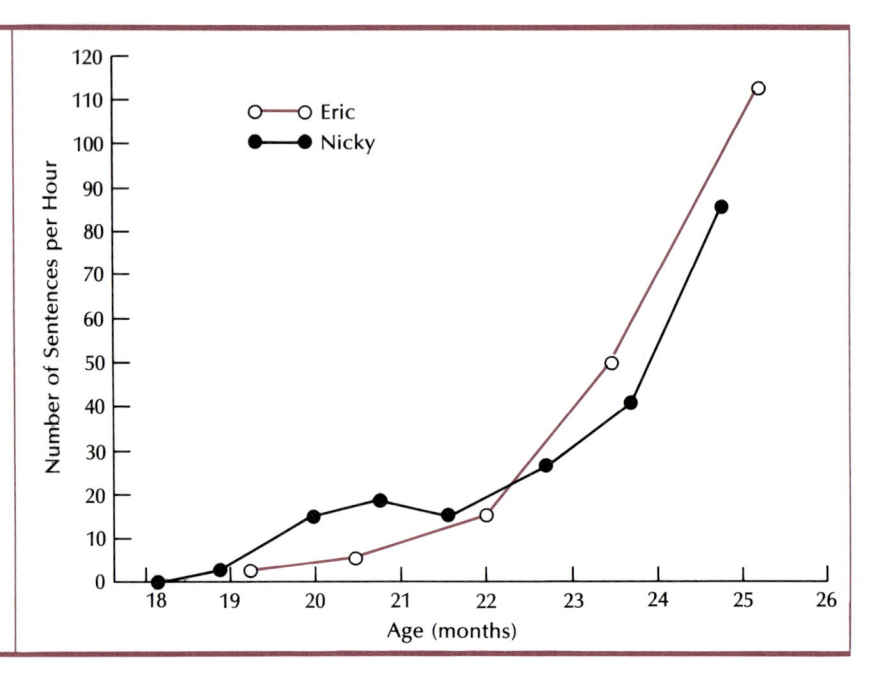

Replacement sequences may be as many as 30 or 40 percent of utterances early in the third year. Anisfeld (1984) argues that they occur partly because the expanded forms are too difficult to do all at once. Gradual *assembly* of sentences is a kind of self-correction and may indicate ways children grope toward producing more complex, difficult sentences.

One of the most firmly established findings of developmental psychology is that early sentences have normal word order (Anisfeld, 1984; Brown, 1973). Children organize sentences in specific orders and seldom, if ever, are these orders violated. As Brown (1973) has stated, "The violations of normal order are triflingly few" (p. 156). Children will say "that daddy" or "see milk" but very seldom "daddy that" or "milk see." In one study (Ramer, 1976), the percentages of children's utterances that violated normal word order were always less than 4 percent; some children had no violations of normal order at all.

Sentences also have other regular patterns: One is **prosodic patterning**. Prosodic patterns are those of stress and intonation, in which words or syllables are emphasized and there is a rising or falling pattern to speech as sentences are spoken. Even before they acquire syntax, children use rising and falling intonation patterns (Wieman, 1976). Although the exact time when children use intonation to express meaning is open to question (Anisfeld, 1984), some authorities (Halliday, 1975) have reported variations in intonation used by children as early as the end of the second year that appear to be used to express different meanings.

Continuing Language Development

By the age of 3½, most children have learned the essential elements of language and use them creatively. Language development does not cease, however. In fact, many aspects continue: further learning of the sound system, better understanding of the grammar of the language, vocabulary growth, attainment of more sophisticated conversational skills, and increasing awareness of language itself.

Increasing Phonological Knowledge. Learning the sound system of a language such as English is a long process, which is not completed until around 7 years of age (Crystal, 1976). Some sounds appear to be more difficult to discriminate and form than others and hence are acquired later. At age 4, children are still learning English consonants such as š (as in *sh*ip), *v*, and *z*; at 5, they are making the distinction between δ (as in *th*at) and θ (as in *th*in); and at 6, they can articulate the consonant ž as in mea*s*ure (Crystal, 1976).

Children's ability to comprehend intonation also increases through the primary grades and even beyond (Cruttenden, 1985). For instance, the distinction in meanings between the following two sentences would cause difficulty for many 8- or 9-year-olds.

1. George gave the book to David and he gave one to Bill.
 (where George gave a book to Bill)
2. George gave the book to David and *HE* gave one to Bill.
 (where David gave a book to Bill)

Such subtleties are clear to adults; however, to many elementary school children, they are not comprehensible. Only in the middle elementary grades do children understand the intricacies of intonation.

Phonological knowledge is an especially critical prerequisite to reading (Ehri, 1985). Speech occurs in a generally continuous flow in a rich context and supplemented with intonation and gesture. Reading, in contrast, requires that children cope with written words, which are separated from one another and presented with few context clues, and minimal information about intonation. The words children see on the printed page are composed of letters that represent the sounds they already know. Naturally, the less children know about language sounds and how they can be divided, the less likely they would be to find reading a reasonable task (Ehri, 1984; Ehri & Wilce, 1985). For example, many children do not have a well-developed knowledge of the concept of *word* when they enter school. Unless one knows what words are, reading them is extraordinarily difficult. Similarly, many kindergarten

Research

Do Social Factors Affect Early Language Development? Clues from a Longitudinal Study of Mother–Child Interaction

In the early days of the "psycholinguistic revolution" in the 1950s and 1960s, much attention was paid to the role of innate factors within children as determiners of language development. As time passed, however, more and more attention was directed to the social and linguistic contexts in which language development takes place. Although it always was obvious that language is learned in a social context (see Chapter 5, *Social Influences on Development*), there was increasing recognition that large individual differences exist in children's language development and that these differences reflect children's social contexts, at least to some extent. Recently, research in this vein has focused on a major influence in the child's language learning environment—the primary caregiver.

Working as a part of a major long-term developmental study of early mother–child interactions, Sheryl Olson, Kathryn Bayles, and John Bates (1986) examined these interactions closely to see what role, if any, they might play in early language development. Three features of the study made it especially noteworthy. First, they investigated both mother–child interactions and language development longitudinally (see Chapter 3, *Research Methods*), permitting them to draw stronger *developmental* inferences from their data. Second, they looked at the mother–child interactions and the children's language in great detail. As they stated, simply to find an overall correlation between mother–child interactions, on one hand, and language or cognitive skills, on the other, does not demonstrate that mother–child interactions play a role in language development. Such a correlation may only indicate that a third variable (e.g., intelligence or child temperament) underlies both. For instance, bright or friendly babies may be more interactive with their mothers and, because they are bright and friendly, more willing to interact with child language examiners, leading to higher language scores. No actual relationship might exist, but a positive correlation still would appear. Detailed correlational analyses, however, can further pinpoint the relevant variables. Third, few previous studies had examined *preverbal* interactions, those that take place prior to the time when children first speak. Do these early interactions provide the building blocks for later language? To address these issues, the researchers made detailed records of mother–child interactions at 6 months of age, as well as later at 13 and 24 months.

When the babies were 6 months old, their interactions with their mothers were observed naturalistically (see Chapter 3, *Research Methods*) in their homes and over 50 variables were coded by observers using small electronic data recorders. Reliabilities of all observations were checked using independent observers. Babies and their mothers also were observed interacting during a separate laboratory visit. Observations were repeated at 13

children have difficulty segmenting (dividing) sequences of sounds into syllable-length and word-length units. They have never considered these concepts before and thus have problems translating the printed symbols they see to the sound-based language system they already know (Nesdale, Herriman, & Tunmer, 1984).

and 24 months, with language and cognitive variables added. Included in the latter were vocabulary measures (mothers' listings of their babies' new words) and cognitive ability measures (the *Bayley Mental Scales of Infant Development*).

Does early mother–child interaction affect language development? Perhaps. Rated at-home responsiveness of the mothers to their infants at 6 months did correlate significantly ($r = +.38$) with vocabulary size at 13 months—in general, the greater the earlier responsiveness, the larger the child's vocabulary. This result did not persist to the 24-month level, however. Because of this and because only a few relationships were found between the 6-month mother–child interaction and later language, the authors called the evidence linking them "marginal" (p. 14).

Much more convincing, however, were their data linking mothers' responsiveness at 13 and 24 months to their childrens' speech. At 13 months, maternal responsiveness to their children's speech was significantly correlated with vocabulary size. At 24 months, vocabulary size was related to the amount of stimulation the mother was providing. Also intriguing were results that showed a strong relationship of (1) social class and (2) mothers' and fathers' educations to vocabulary size. In general, the higher the social class and level of education of the parents, the larger the child's vocabulary. Even when social class and education were controlled statistically, however, maternal interaction still contributed significantly. Thus, although educational and social opportunities are influential, mothers' interactions also continue to play an important, independent role. Another fascinating finding was of parallels between language and cognitive measures (see Highlight on page 383). By age two, language and mental ability were closely related; for example, the *Bayley Mental Scale of Infant Development* correlated highly ($r = +.70$) with vocabulary size at this point.

As we discussed in Chapter 3, *Research Methods*, only a few questions can be resolved by a single study, even a well-designed longitudinal study like this one. Many questions are left unanswered. For example, the study was of mothers only. What about verbal interactions with fathers? Also, the fact that sampling was limited (participants were volunteer white mothers and their children) dictates that similar research be conducted with other groups to determine if the results are generalizable. Other new questions quickly occur to curious researchers. As the authors point out, the effects of early vocabulary content (the kinds of words young children know) and size on later development are unknown. It shouldn't be surprising if they, or other researchers, soon conduct such a study. Thus, in developmental research we again will move ahead question by question, step by step, and study by study, toward a better understanding of development.

Increasing Complexity of Grammatical Structures. Syntax, as we discussed, refers to the structure of the language. Whereas most children have acquired the *basics* of syntax by the time they enter school, there is much still to be learned. Learning about grammar continues until puberty in two major areas (Crystal, 1976). First, children learn to comprehend increasingly complex grammatical structures, such as those using conjunctions (e.g., *although, since, unless*) and those in which some sentence elements are embedded in others (e.g., "The dog the cat bit when it was teased was picked up by its owner."). Children now can begin to appreciate the many jokes and riddles that depend on the ability to detect subtleties and ambiguities in language (Sherzer, 1985). Second, children are learning to *use* new, more complex structures in their own speech: for example, adding clauses; more frequently using modifiers such as adjectives and adverbs; and utilizing "adult" forms of questioning (e.g., being able to use forms such as, "You're cold, aren't you?" or "You're cold?" instead of only the simpler form, "Are you cold?").

Growth of Vocabulary. Estimates of children's vocabulary size vary widely (see Nagy & Anderson, 1984), but there is no question that vocabulary growth continues from early childhood at a high rate well through adolescence and into adulthood (Nagy & Anderson, 1984; Nagy, Herman, & Anderson, 1985). Part of the difficulty in obtaining an accurate estimate of vocabulary size is finding an acceptable definition of what it means to "know a word." Does "knowing" mean that children can comprehend words when they hear them, or only that they can use them correctly? What about words with several meanings? A word may be understood in one of its senses, but not in others.

A number of aspects of vocabulary development are certain, however. Children do not learn words all at once; instead, meanings seem to be built gradually (Mezynski, 1983). Initially, children may have some sense of the meaning of a word, but that knowledge may be only partially correct or even incorrect. Through repeated exposure, however, children's understanding is gradually broadened and extended (Clark, 1973, 1985; Nagy, Herman, & Anderson, 1985; Sternberg, Powell, & Kaye, 1983).

Although vocabulary obviously can be taught directly, most vocabulary does not seem to be learned through formal instruction. Children learn meanings of new words by noticing how they are used in conversation and, later, in what they read (Nagy & Anderson, 1984; Nagy & Herman, 1984, 1985). Certainly, a single exposure would teach little about a word's meanings and uses. More complete knowledge must be added with each additional contact. Part of this knowledge is realizing which words go with which. For instance, as adults we know we do not say "She drove the plane" or "He took out a slice of paper." Because words almost always are used in context, part of our knowledge of their meaning is how they are used in relationship to other words. Obviously, the more children read or are read to, the larger their vocabularies will be. Other things being equal, voracious readers have many more opportunities to learn new words than those who read little or not at all (Wilson, 1985).

Language: What Develops?

Development of Conversational Skills. **Conversational skills**, an important part of language acquisition, also continue to develop well beyond the preschool years. Consider the following conversation among second-graders (Dorval & Eckerman, 1984):

1. Well, we . . . uh . . . have paper plates . . . with turkey on it and lots of (unintelligible). You know.
2. Doo-doo-doo-doo-doo (singing)
3. I don't know what you're talking about.
4. You know what? My uncle killed a turkey.
5. Not frying pan?
6. No.
7. I seen a frying pan at Hulen's store!

As you can see, young children's conversations can be quite disjointed, shifting off topic and often containing many false starts ("The car . . . it was . . . uh . . . the door . . . the kid he pushed on the door . . . They . . . uh . . . he pushed . . . he closed it hard."). Even young children, however, respect the idea of turn-taking. In the study by Dorval and Eckerman (1984), for example, children restored turn-taking order themselves when it was violated. Conversation moved very quickly, as many children wanted to talk and to get the floor. As the example shows, there are often unrelated turns and free associations to topics, which adults might find jarring, but which apparently do not bother the children all that much. Their use of conversations is surpris-

Although turn-taking is prominent in young children's conversations, they often shift off topic. As children develop, however, their conversations begin to stay more and more on track.

ingly varied: They relate their experiences, tell stories, make jokes and word plays, and create fantasies (Garvey, 1977).

As children develop, however, their conversations tend to grow more coherent. Conversations begin to make more sense (in adults' eyes) in that what one child says builds topically on what other children have said. Compared to primary-level students, students later in elementary school show much more awareness of topic. In the conversations recorded by Dorval and Eckerman, for instance, fifth-graders showed "an obvious pleasure in operating within the constraints of topic" (1984, p. 85). The following sample of fifth-graders' conversation shows topical awareness (Dorval & Eckerman, 1984, p. 22):

1. Be quiet! Start off, Billy. What if you was the teacher?
2. OK. If I was the teacher, I'd give us less work and more time to play . . . and I'd be mean to y'all, too.
3. OK. Ann (meaning that it is her turn).
4. If I was the teacher, I'd do work . . . um. I'd sit around and watch TV. I wouldn't assign no papers . . . umm . . .
5. I'd let y'all watch TV stories!
6. I'd turn the TV on Channel 4 at 9:30 to watch "Popeye!"

Adolescents' conversations reveal increasing awareness of the importance of individuals' contributions. They frequently evaluate what others have said and interpret or explain its psychological implications. In other words, they seem to be as much interested in *why* something is being discussed as in *what* is discussed.

By the end of high school, there is greater concern and valuing of "perspective-taking" talk. Students are highly interested in each other's views (e.g., "Why weren't you with Bobby last night? Are you guys getting along?"). Often, in Dorval and Eckerman's study, students at this age would initiate a conversation with a question, abruptly beginning with an attempt to get someone's perspective.

Young adults also like to probe others' perspectives through conversation. The following is one example.

1. I . . . got . . . a small problem. Um . . . simply . . . um . . . after you study all day, don't have anything to do. Especially this summer (4-second pause). Just can't get it together . . . lonely.
2. You miss somebody?
1. Well . . . um . . . like that's part of it. Ronny's back in New York. I'm here alone.
2. You've seemed to be down lately. Got to shake off the blues.

Whereas young adults, like adolescents, often focus on each others' perspectives, they generally are more skilled at being able to maintain their conversations. They also show more tact in initiating topics and seem better able to continue relevant talk. Further, they seem more intuitive about their own and others' feelings and motives.

Development of Metalinguistic Awareness. We have seen that even young children possess a great deal of linguistic knowledge. Their vocabulary grows rapidly, for example, and they show their understanding of the rules of grammar and the basics of conversation. As they get older, however, they increasingly are able not only to *use* language to represent information and communicate with others, but to *think about* the nature of language itself. Just as we used the term *metamemory* to refer to children's knowledge about their own memories, we can refer to children's knowledge about language as **metalinguistic awareness**.

Consider the following paragraph:

> Isn't it interesting that when there were dinosaurs in the world, the word *dinosaur* did not exist (since there were no people talking about the dinosaurs), whereas now that the word *dinosaur* exists, dinosaurs themselves do not. Notice also that we could agree to use a different word to refer to dinosaurs without this having any effect on what dinosaurs were like. The word *dinosaur*, in fact, is not particularly like a dinosaur at all. It is not an especially large word, nor is it a prehistoric word, nor do we find fossils in the earth of those eight letters.

The average 5-year-old probably would be mystified by the above paragraph, even though most 5-year-olds know what dinosaurs are. Many 5-year-olds probably can name more dinosaurs than you and would be happy to tell you all about them. But the above paragraph is not really about dinosaurs. It is about the word *dinosaur* or, more broadly, about the nature of language. To think about the issues raised in that paragraph requires one to get outside of language and think about how it works. This is very difficult for young children.

An intriguing study by Daniel Osherson and Ellen Markman (1975) used a variety of ways to investigate the development of children's conceptions of language. For example, they asked children what would happen to the word *giraffe* if there were no more giraffes in the world. This question was to see if children understood that *giraffe* would still be a meaningful word referring to a long-necked animal. They asked what sound cats would make if they were called "dogs" (the correct answer is that they would still meow). They asked whether the word *nickel* is worth five pennies, whether the word *book* is made of paper, whether the word *bird* has feathers, and whether you can buy bubble gum with the word *penny*.

The investigators found that metalinguistic awareness, as tested by these items, was very rare in 6-year-olds. It gradually increased with age, however. By 11, most children seemed to grasp the concept that words are different than their referents, the things they represent (e.g., the word *giraffe* would not disappear if giraffes became extinct), that they do not share the properties of those things (e.g., the word *nickel* is not worth five cents), and that language connects words to things in arbitrary ways (e.g., the sound of the word *cat* has nothing at all to do with what cats are like).

Metalinguistic awareness develops gradually along many dimensions (Cruttenden, 1985; Saywitz & Wilkinson, 1982; Tunmer, Pratt, & Herriman, 1984). It can involve many different linguistic levels (e.g., phones, phonemes, morphemes, syntax, semantics, pragmatics) and areas of language use. The more experience children have with language and the more they reflect on their use of the language, the greater their metalinguistic awareness.

Language Development: Applications for Parents and Teachers

The following applications for parents and teachers are drawn from the research on language development.

1. *Spend time talking to infants.* It is important to remember that children's experiences from birth prepare them to use language. Even though young babies will not understand *what* you say to them, it is still important to talk to them. As you speak, they learn to associate language with other activities. At first, context is all-important; soon, however, they will learn to understand spoken language both with and without context.

2. *Be responsive to infants' vocalizations.* Most people react naturally to an infant's vocalization. Some adults are more responsive than others, however, and like other human actions, vocalizations are affected by feedback. Your reactions encourage children to continue to vocalize and help them gradually learn how and when to use language.

3. *Read to young children regularly.* Generally, those children who have been read to learn to read earlier and more easily than those children who have not had similar experiences. When adults read to children, they not only expose them to language and create a pleasurable event but convey pragmatic knowledge about reading as a meaningful activity.

4. *Ask children to describe their experiences.* Children develop the ability to express themselves and learn conversational skills by telling

> My Father is a cannibal King
> My Mother is a bell that goes "ding"
> My Brother's a bucket of Paint
> and I'm just a Saint.

> CATS
> I have a cat with soft silky fur and such a roaring purr and when you hold her you no longer say brrr.

While almost any kind of writing aids in language development, poetry—with its rhyming, its images, and its purpose of self-expression—is an especially rich language activity.

about things they have seen or heard. Although very young children may need to be prompted, they soon will express themselves easily. All that is required is an occasional question, the patience to listen, and a respect for what children have to say. Like other language skills, speaking thrives on practice and a nurturing climate.

5. *Encourage children to read.* Reading is a key to a variety of desirable language development outcomes. Other things being equal, for instance, the more children read, the larger their vocabularies are likely to be. Reading also is an important source of metalinguistic knowledge, as children are exposed to different kinds of written language. Later, as children make the transition from "learning to read" to "reading to learn," reading becomes one of the most important and efficient avenues for acquiring new information.

6. *Encourage children's writing.* Like speaking, writing is an expressive language activity that flourishes in a supportive environment. Because it is expressive, writing provides a unique opportunity for cognitive and emotional development. Long writing activities or assignments are not necessary; brief notes or sentence- or paragraph-length reactions often are the most effective in allowing children to express themselves and for building the desire to write.

7. *Help children develop their metalinguistic abilities.* Metalinguistic abilities develop considerably later than linguistic ones; children can use language without necessarily *understanding* it. Thus, they may speak or even write well, but still be unable to analyze what they are doing. Adults' comments and questions can help children develop a sense of language as analyzable.

8. *Provide opportunities for continuing language development.* Learning one's language and learning about language can continue indefinitely. Vocabulary development, for instance, is never finished. Similarly, learning a foreign language provides an excellent opportunity for gaining a deeper understanding of language. Both linguistic and metalinguistic development will continue as long as we focus our attention on our own and others' use of oral and written language.

Summary

Language acquisition is a stunning human capability. Almost from birth, babies can distinguish between important speech sounds and categorize them in the same way adults do. Infants also vocalize, of course. Crying and cooing are two categories of sound-making that seem to be biologically determined. By the age of 3 or 4 months, babies begin to babble, a form of vocalization in which a huge variety of (meaningless) sounds are produced. Soon, however, children make the sounds of their own language; they often produce their first words by the end of their first year. The earliest words tend to be presymbolic accompaniments to actions; only later do they become symbolic and independent of actions.

Children's earliest speech is in single words or *holophrases;* toward the end of their second year most children begin to combine words into pairs that have distinctive new patterns of intonation and regular word order. Grammatical morphemes soon begin to appear, although some may be overgeneralized, such as when children say "I goed" or "two sheeps." A period of very rapid vocabulary growth often occurs around age 2½: Children can learn several words a day, often with only one or two exposures. As children move into their fourth year, they continue to add new vocabulary and to refine their knowledge of grammar, moving closer and closer to adult forms of expression. Most children's vocabulary passes a thousand words. After age 4, children show increasing ability to combine ideas into complex sentences.

A critical development of middle childhood is increased metalinguistic awareness, or the ability to "step back" from language and to see it as a separate phenomenon. During this period, children show increased ability to view language and their language abilities in a detached, objective way.

The relationship of language and thought remains controversial. Some theorists, such as Chomsky, see language and thought as independent and human beings as innately predisposed to learn language. Merely a triggering of a "language acquisition device" is sufficient for language development. Others argue for the primacy of cognition over language or the reverse, however. Piaget, for instance, viewed language as a *reflection* of cognitive development, whereas Whorf maintained that language *determines* thought. Vygotsky represents an interactionist position. He argued that, while language and cognitive development are initially relatively separate, the two streams soon merge and exert profound impact on each other. Thought affects language development; conversely, language gives guidance and structure to thinking.

Key Terms

novel productions
phones
phonetics
phoneticians
vowels
consonants
phoneme
phonology
manner
place
voicing
morpheme
morphology
inflection
free morpheme
bound morpheme
syntax
clause
noun phrase
semantics
lexical meaning
referent
contextual
pragmatics
speech events
motherese
cohesive devices
prelinguistic period
linguistic period
crying
cooing
babbling
first words
holophrases
presymbolic word use
symbolic word use
deictic tutoring
syntactic stage
duos
sentences
replacement sequences
prosodic patterning
conversational skills
metalinguistic awareness

Suggested Readings

Anisfeld, M. (1984). *Language development from birth to three*. Hillsdale, NJ: Erlbaum. This excellent summary of early child language development provides an up-to-date review of all aspects of speech and language development.

Brown, R. (1973). *A first language: The early stages*. Cambridge, MA: Harvard University Press. A still authoritative and highly influential text on the acquisition of language, this book combines a review of studies of early child language with reports of the author's own research.

Chukovsky, K. (1963). *From two to five*. Berkeley, CA: University of California Press. This classic book, translated from the Russian by Miriam Morton, contains charming examples of children's speech and thinking, gathered by a man who saw "the whimsical and elusive laws of childhood thinking" in the children's language that he heard.

Miller, G. A. (1981). *Language and speech*. San Francisco: Freeman. This well-written volume is a highly informative, yet wonderfully readable source on language and language development.

Tunmer, W. E., Pratt, C., & Herriman, M. (Eds.). (1984). *Metalinguistic awareness in children: Theory, research, and implications*. Berlin: Springer Verlag. In this short but scholarly volume, the authors and several associates summarize views of development of metalinguistic skills in children. A strength of the book is the author's attempt to relate metalinguistic skills to educational processes.

Application Exercises

11-1 Distinguishing among Aspects of Language

For each of the following, indicate whether the sample of language-related behavior relates most to: (a) phones, (b) phonemes, (c) morphemes, (d) syntax, (e) semantics, or (f) pragmatics.

1. A 4-year-old says excitedly, "Mommy, Mommy! We saw two *sheepses* on the farm!"

2. A 2-year-old, in his first month of saying duos, combines "two" with 11 other words—two stick, two teddy, two mommy, two dish, and so on. He always says "two" first.

3. A 5-year-old says, "What you eating, Erica?" He looks hungry and you guess he wants some of Erica's cookie dough.

4. An infant has started to babble. His parents hear him "talking" to himself in his crib night and day. They are amused, but of course none of it makes any sense.

5. A first-grader understands that the two sentences, "Jodie was bitten by the dog" and "The dog bit Jodie" mean the same thing. Her younger brother, however, thinks that the first sentence means that Jodie bit the dog!

6. To the 14-month old toddler, "rona" refers to a bean-filled frog. Later, he also calls the cat "rona" and then a poodle he sees on the sidewalk out front.

7. A linguist listens to a tape of a conversation in the Hopi language. Although she does not understand or speak this language, she can transcribe its sounds accurately into a symbol system for study later.

8. "Oh, you said *bad*!" said Gretchen. "I thought you said *bat*! No wonder I got mixed up."

11-2 Identifying Points of View about Language

Using clues in the chapter and the information in the Highlights box on pages 383–385 for each of the following, decide if the quotation is taken from the writings of Noam Chomsky, Benjamin Whorf, Jean Piaget, or Lev Vygotsky.

1. "Specifically, investigation of human language has led me to believe that a genetically determined language faculty, one component of the human mind, specifies a certain class of 'humanly accessible grammars.' The child acquires one of the grammars . . . on the basis of the limited evidence available to him."

2. "The relation of thought to word is not a thing but a process, a continual movement back and forth from thought to word and from word to thought."

3. "You can see my hypothesis: that the conditions of language are part of a vaster context, a context prepared by sensorimotor intelligence."

4. "We cut up and organize the flow of events as we do largely because, through our mother tongue, we are parties to an agreement to do so, not because nature itself is segmented in exactly that way for all to see."

5. "(Thinking) follows a network of tracks laid down in a given language, an organization which may concentrate systematically upon certain phases of reality, certain aspects of intelligence, and systematically discard others featured by other languages. The individual . . . is constrained completely within its unbreakable bonds."

6. "We can see that all the known facts about the functional, structural, and genetic characteristics of egocentric speech point to one thing: It develops in the direction of inner speech. Its developmental history can be understood only as a gradual unfolding of the traits of inner speech."

7. ". . . grammars are represented in the brains of mature speakers, . . . languages are determined by these grammars, and . . . speakers of language can communicate to the extent that languages characterized by the grammars in their brains are alike."

8. "It is at this moment that language appears, and it can profit from all that was acquired by sensorimotor logic and by the symbolic function in the broad sense . . . , of which language is only a particular case. I think, therefore, . . . that there is a link between sensorimotor intelligence and language function. I further believe that the formation of the symbolic function . . . allows the acquisition of language."

CHAPTER 12

Development of Reasoning

*No person can disobey reason, without giving
up his claim to be a rational creature.*
—Jonathan Swift, Gulliver's Travels

$\mathcal{E}$ffective understanding, problem-solving, and decision making usually require that we go beyond what is observable about the present and what we remember about the past. Every day we reach conclusions, evaluate arguments, consider alternatives, weigh probabilities, devise strategies, seek and use evidence, and generalize: In short, we employ **reasoning**. Most psychologists, and nonpsychologists as well, consider reasoning to be a fundamental aspect of intelligence and consider the development of reasoning to be a basic part of intellectual development (Siegler & Richards, 1982; Sternberg, 1982).

Developmental psychologists have studied the development of many sorts of reasoning. This chapter focuses on several of the most interesting and important of these, including some that develop early, some that develop late, and some that develop over a long time span. We will begin each section with a typical research task. We strongly urge you to work the tasks out as you begin each section. You will find some of them quite easy and others very challenging. You may wish to try some of them on your friends or administer some to children of various ages. The more you explore each task independently, the better you will appreciate the subsequent discussion of the type of reasoning the task assesses, the difficulties it presents, and how that type of reasoning develops.

Transitivity

The first task is a simple one:

> David is older than Stan and Stan is older than Bob. What can you infer from this?

You probably did not need to set the book aside to figure this one out. Obviously, David is older than Bob. (No, it wasn't a trick question!)

Transitivity

This is an example of a **transitive inference**. We are told how one thing is related to a second and how the second is related to a third and then are asked to infer how the first is related to the third. Inferences of this sort are usually very easy for adults and older children. But there has been great controversy concerning whether preschool children make transitive inferences.

As is often the case in the study of cognitive development, our story begins with Jean Piaget. Piaget wrote about transitivity and related abilities in many contexts, but we can summarize his analysis briefly. We begin with how adults understand transitivity and then proceed to how young children differ.

An adult who is told that David is older than Stan and Stan is older than Bob immediately understands that she can place these three individuals along a single dimension with respect to age: From oldest to youngest we have David, Stan, and Bob (see Figure 12-1). She understands that David is older than Stan and Bob, that Stan is younger than David and older than Bob, and that Bob is younger than both David and Stan. She also understands that if we came across someone of a different age that person could be put into the lineup in such a way that he would be younger than everyone to his left and older than everyone to his right. In fact, no matter how many people we add to the series, it remains true that each person is younger than everyone to his left and older than everyone to his right. In other words, adults understand the idea of a series. In Piaget's terminology, adults have the concept of **seriation**, or ordering.

Children, according to Piaget, do not understand seriation and thus cannot make transitive inferences until they reach the stage of concrete

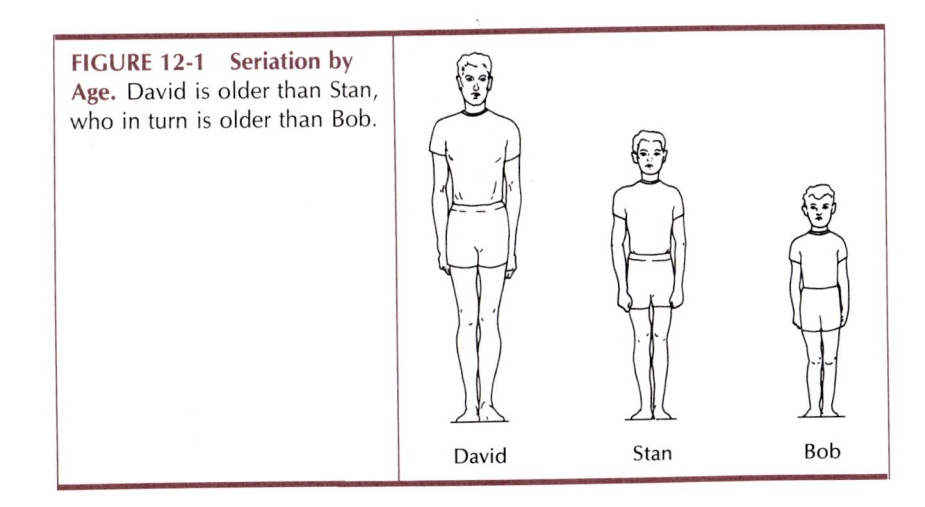

FIGURE 12-1 Seriation by Age. David is older than Stan, who in turn is older than Bob.

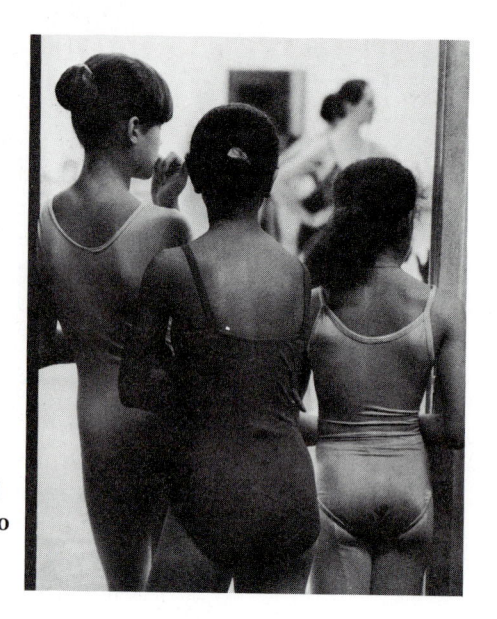

The girl in the middle is short compared to the girl on the left, but tall compared to the girl on the right. To the preschool child this may seem paradoxical.

operations at about age 7. In fact, children under 7 typically do not think in terms of relations at all. If told that David is older than Stan and Stan is older than Bob, they conclude from the first part that David is old and Stan is young and from the second part that Stan is old and Bob is young. Obviously, anyone who thinks this way is going to be rather confused about Stan: How can he be old and young simultaneously? The problem, of course, is that the preschooler is not thinking in terms of relations. He thus fails to grasp the idea that one can be simultaneously older than one person and younger than another. It seems plausible that anyone this confused about relations and seriation will have great difficulty in making systematic transitive inferences.

Although Piaget's numerous studies provided substantial evidence in support of this view (Inhelder & Piaget, 1964), his conclusions have been questioned by many information processing researchers. One major criticism has been that preschoolers may fail transitivity tasks not because they are incapable of transitive inference but because they simply forget the **premises**, or the initial information given. If you cannot recall whether David is older or younger than Stan and whether Stan is older or younger than Bob, you obviously are in no position to compare David and Bob.

Peter Bryant and Tom Trabasso (1971) tested this possibility by training children of different ages on the premises of a transitivity task until they remembered the premises well. They then assessed the children's ability to infer conclusions from the premises. They found that even 4-year-olds did well at this. Bryant and Trabasso suggested that the preschool children in Piaget's research had trouble reaching proper conclusions on transitivity tasks not because they were incapable of transitive inference but rather because they forgot the premises.

Not all developmental psychologists, however, have accepted the conclusion that preschoolers are capable of genuine transitive inference. Another possibility suggested by researchers is that preschoolers may give correct responses on some transitivity tasks without using transitive reasoning. Consider, for example, a child who is presented with the premises *David is older than Stan* and *Stan is older than Bob* and concludes that David is older than Bob. It is not hard to see how a preschooler might think about this problem precisely the way Piaget claimed and yet get the correct solution. She might conclude from the first premise that David is old and from the second premise that Bob is young. Then, when asked to compare David and Bob, she may conclude correctly that David is older without really understanding transitivity, seriation, or even the idea of relations.

Bryant and Trabasso (1971) attempted to rule out this mode of solution by using four premises: A>B; B>C; C>D; and D>E (> means *is bigger than*; A, B, C, D, and E were sticks of different length). After learning the premises, children were asked to compare B with D. This would be a problem for someone who simply used categories of large and small since it had been learned that B was larger than C but also smaller than A, while D was larger than E but also smaller than C. The 4-year-olds were able to make such comparisons, which suggests that they were making genuine transitive inferences.

Not everyone considers the issue settled, however. Over the years, there have been hundreds of studies of transitivity. Piagetians typically attempt to show that solutions by young children do not involve genuine transitivity (Breslow, 1981). Information processing researchers attempt to rule out alternatives and show that preschoolers do indeed understand transitivity (Thayer & Collyer, 1978). Most recently, a variety of very specific hypotheses and theories have been proposed and tested (Brainerd and Kingma, 1984; Halford, 1984; Halford & Kelly, 1984; Oakhill, 1984).

Although the evidence is complex, present data appear to support the information processing view that, at least under ideal circumstances, children as young as age 4 do engage in genuine transitive inference as well as many other kinds of logical inference (Hawkins, Pea, Glick, & Scribner, 1984; Braine & Rumain, 1983). There is also convincing evidence, however, that supports the Piagetian view that there are important differences between how preschoolers think about logic and how older children do so. We will consider one of these differences in the next section.

Logical Necessity

Logical reasoning in children is commonly assessed via simple games that are designed to be intriguing to a child.

> You are playing a game involving a series of logic problems. Each problem involves a rule, a question, and a series of clues. For each problem, you are to answer the question as soon as possible, but not before you are *sure* your answer is correct. You will be penalized for reaching an incorrect answer, so withhold judgment until you have enough clues to be sure of your answer. You will also be penalized, however, for waiting for further clues if you already have enough to reach a definite answer.
> Here are the first rule and question: *If it is a hot day then Judy will wear her blue skirt. Did Judy wear her blue skirt?* Your first clue is *Blue is Judy's favorite color.* Do you wish to answer the question or do you want a further clue?

Obviously the first clue is consistent with an answer of *yes*. If blue is Judy's favorite color, then it is perfectly plausible that she would wear a blue skirt. But we cannot be *sure* that she would. The correct response at this point is to ask for a further clue.

> The next clue is: *It was a sizzling hot day.* Is that enough, or do you want still another clue?

Almost any adult would realize that a logical deduction is possible at this point. If hot, then blue; hot; therefore blue. The conclusion *necessarily* follows from the two premises (the rule and the second clue). Given these premises, it *must* be true. No further clues are necessary.

Children's performance on problems like this one was studied by Carl Bereiter, Suzanne Hidi, and George Dimitroff (1979) of the Ontario Institute for Studies in Education. They found that second-graders typically reached conclusions consistent with the premises but that they showed a strong tendency to choose an answer before they had sufficient clues—that is, before the conclusion was *necessarily* correct. By sixth grade, on the other hand, most children correctly distinguished whether the information available merely *suggested* a particular conclusion or whether it was sufficient to *require* that conclusion. The researchers concluded that the concept of **logical necessity** develops between ages 7 and 11. Even young children can often reach correct conclusions (as we saw in the transitivity research). But only when they are older do they see the difference between (1) a conclusion that is merely *consistent with* the information given and (2) a conclusion *required by* the information given.

As with any study, we can naturally question these results. Perhaps the younger children understood necessity but had trouble with the specific problems used or with understanding the overall task. Because questions of this sort can be raised about any piece of research, developmental psychologists are cautious about interpreting the results of a study until it has been replicated with a variety of methodologies. Studies of logical necessity by other researchers (Byrnes & Overton, 1986; Pieraut-Le Bonniec, 1980; Somerville, Hadkinson, & Greenberg, 1979) have extended our knowledge regarding children's understanding of this important concept. The various studies used different techniques and got slightly different results. Somerville et al., for example, provided evidence that children may have some understanding of logical necessity as early as age 6 (though not before). There seems to be general agreement, however, that: (1) The emergence of the concept of necessity is an important milestone in the development of logical reasoning; (2) logical necessity develops after the more primitive ability to make correct inferences from certain kinds of information; (3) children under 6 do not grasp the concept of necessity; and (4) necessity is well understood by the age of 10 or so.

Does this mean that by age 10 children's logical abilities are fully mature? Or are there important developmental milestones beyond this age? As we saw in Chapter 8, Piaget claimed that there is a qualitative change in reasoning after age 10 as children achieve formal operations (Inhelder & Piaget, 1958). This claim has been a source of major controversy for many years. We will not attempt to provide a general discussion of formal operations in this chapter. In the next section, however, we will consider the issue of a later qualitative change in children's logic.

Inferential Validity

We begin our discussion of later changes in reasoning with seven arguments and an exercise that will get you thinking about them.

1. If elephants are bigger than dogs
   And dogs are bigger than mice
   Then elephants are bigger than mice

2. If adults are older than babies
   And children are older than babies
   Then adults are older than children

3. If dogs are bigger than mice
   And elephants are bigger than mice
   Then dogs are bigger than elephants

4. If dogs are bigger than elephants
   And elephants are bigger than mice
   Then dogs are bigger than mice

5. If babies are older than adults
   And babies are older than children
   Then adults are older than children

6. If mice are bigger than dogs
   And mice are bigger than elephants
   Then dogs are bigger than elephants

7. If elephants are either animals or plants
   And elephants are not animals
   Then elephants are plants

First, consider only the first three arguments. Can you think of a way to sort them—that is, a way that two of the arguments are similar to each other and different from the third? What distinction were you using for your sorting? Can you express it in writing? Now, try to sort the same three arguments in a different way, again explaining your reasoning clearly. Repeat the process of sorting and explaining until you cannot think of any other way to sort the arguments. Check to ensure that you covered all possible divisions of the arguments: 1 and 2 vs. 3; 1 and 3 vs. 2; 2 and 3 vs. 1. If you have not, try any you missed and see if you can think of a meaningful basis for that division of the arguments.

Next try to sort arguments 4, 5, and 6. Again sort them in as many ways as you can think of and explain each sorting. Repeat the process one last time for arguments 1, 2, and 7.

Finally, consider all seven arguments. Which of them seem most logical to you? Try to rank the seven arguments from most to least logical (with ties, if you like). Explain the basis for your ordering.

You might want to administer this task to friends your own age or to children age 8 or more (that is, children who are old enough to read the arguments). It might help, especially with children, to write each argument on a separate index card so your research subjects can physically sort and rank them. Be sure to ask for explanations and ask follow-up questions until you understand what they are doing.

There are many ways to sort the arguments. David Moshman and Bridget Franks (1986) administered these tasks to fourth-graders (ages 9 and 10), seventh-graders (ages 12 and 13), and college students. They found both similarities and differences in what individuals of different ages did. One way of sorting used by almost every student, regardless of age, was to distinguish on the basis of content. For arguments 1, 2, and 3, for example, the student would put 1 and 3 together because they concern animals (or because they concern size) and separate 2 because it concerns people (or age). Another common basis for sorting at every age was truth. For example, 1 and 2 might be placed together because the last line is true and 3 separated because its last line is false (dogs are *not* bigger than elephants).

There was, however, another important way of sorting the cards that was used by the older students only. This was to distinguish arguments with conclusions that followed necessarily from the premises from those in which this was not the case. In argument 1, for example, it is clear that if elephants are bigger than dogs, and dogs in turn are bigger than mice, elephants must be bigger than mice. This is what logicians call a *valid argument*. Argument 2, on the other hand, begins with premises asserting that both adults and children are older than babies. Although we know that the conclusion to argument 2 (*adults are older than children*) is correct, it does not follow from these premises. This is what logicians call an *invalid argument*. Thus argument 2 would be grouped with argument 3, which is also invalid. Similarly, arguments 5 and 6 (both invalid) can be separated from argument 4 (valid). Further, arguments 1 and 7 (both valid) can be separated from argument 2 (invalid). Notice that validity is quite different from "real-world" truth: Argument 7 is valid (the conclusion follows necessarily from the premises) even though its conclusion is false, whereas arguments 2 and 5 are invalid despite their true conclusions.

Moshman and Franks found that fourth-graders did not sort arguments on the basis of validity, whereas many of the seventh-graders and most of the college students did so. They also found that most college students and many seventh-graders picked the three valid arguments (1, 4, and 7) as "most logical" when asked to rank the set of all seven. Fourth-graders, on the other hand, typically picked arguments 1 and 2 as most logical, apparently because each individual statement in those arguments is empirically true. Moshman and Franks concluded that children aged 9–10 typically judge arguments in terms of whether their premises and conclusion are true, whereas older individuals are increasingly likely to think about arguments as logical inferences and evaluate them with respect to whether the conclusion follows logically from the premises. In other words, older individuals have the concept of **inferential validity**: They think about the validity of inferences.

Some further questions could be raised about these results. Why did the younger children not use the concept of validity in distinguishing and evaluating arguments? Perhaps 9- and 10-year-olds do not understand that concept. Alternatively, they may understand it but for some reason did not see how to apply their understanding to the present tasks. Moshman and Franks (1986) explored these possibilities in two follow-up studies by using a variety of different arguments, tasks, and conditions. For example, some students received (1) definitions of validity and invalidity, examples of each, and instructions to use these concepts to evaluate arguments; some received (2) feedback from the experimenter after each of 40 opportunities to evaluate arguments; and some received (3) definitions, examples, instructions, *and* feedback. These conditions improved the performance of the seventh-graders, but most of the fourth-graders still showed little or no understanding of validity.

Why is validity such a difficult concept? The results are consistent with evidence from Osherson and Markman (1975) that children can evaluate statements with respect to their own real-world knowledge but have trouble focusing on the logical connections *within* statements. Imagine, for example, that a researcher holds a single-colored chip behind her back and asks you to evaluate the truth of three statements: (1) the chip is blue; (2) the chip is blue or it is not blue; (3) the chip is blue and it is not blue. Children and adults agree that it is impossible to evaluate the first statement without seeing the chip. Children, however, typically wish to see the chip before evaluating the latter two statements also. An adult would realize that the second statement is necessarily true regardless of the color of the chip and the third statement is necessarily false for any chip of a single color. To grasp validity one must be capable of distinguishing the issue of logical connections from the issue of real-world truth.

The concept of validity is also related to hypothetico-deductive reasoning, which, as we discussed in Chapter 8, is associated by Piaget with formal operations. Hypothetico-deductive reasoning is involved in deducing a conclusion from premises that are purely hypothetical. To evaluate the validity of an argument, we do not ask whether the premises or conclusion are true. Rather, we ask whether the conclusion follows from the premises: that is, whether the conclusion would have to be true *if* the premises were true. In other words, we accept the truth of the premises on a purely hypothetical plane and then deduce their consequences. The results of the validity research are thus consistent with Piaget's views that such reasoning is rare before the age of 11 or 12.

It thus appears that understanding the concept of validity is a rather late development (*cf.* Moshman & Timmons, 1982). Since validity is so central to logic, it seems that children's logical reasoning continues to develop at least through adolescence.

So far we have restricted ourselves to deductive reasoning. Although deductive reasoning is important, it is rather narrow in that it only concerns logical connections *within* arguments. In the next two sections, we will broaden our focus and consider forms of reasoning that are commonly used by scientists and which are crucial to anyone who seeks to explore and understand the real world.

Controlling Variables

The following three problems illustrate scientific reasoning.

You are trying to determine which are more flexible—brass rods or steel rods. You have an 18" brass rod with a square cross-section. You can

FIGURE 12-2 Kuhn and Brannock's Plant Problem. *From Kuhn, D., & Brannock, J. (1977), Development of the isolation of the variables scheme in experimental and "natural experiment" contexts.* Developmental Psychology, 13, 9–14.

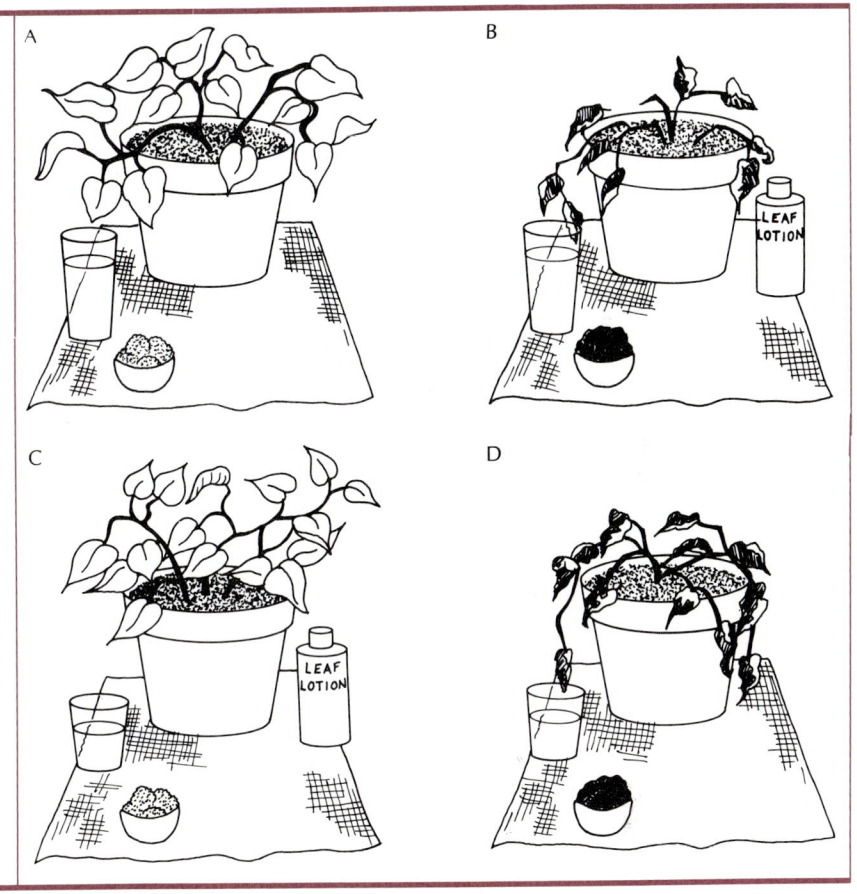

compare it with any of a variety of other rods. Should you choose a 12" rod, an 18" rod, or a 24" rod (or doesn't it matter)? Should it be brass or steel (or doesn't it matter)? Should it have a square or a round cross-section (or doesn't it matter)?

Here's another problem. A psychologist is interested in comparing the verbal ability of boys and girls. She assesses the ability of a group of 4-year-old boys, then assesses a group of 6-year-old girls, and concludes that girls have higher verbal ability. Are you convinced?

One last problem: Imagine you have five plants (Kuhn & Brannock, 1977), all of the same type (see Figure 12-2). Plant A gets a large glass of water each week and light-colored plant food. It is doing well. Plant B gets a large glass of water, dark-colored plant food, and leaf lotion. It appears to be dying. Plant C gets a small glass of water, light-colored plant food, and leaf lotion. It is doing well. Plant D gets a small glass of water and dark plant food. It seems to be dying. Plant E is new. How should you treat it? Should you give it a large or a small glass of water each week? Should you give it light or dark plant food? Should you use leaf lotion? On what basis do you draw your conclusions?

Superficially, these problems may seem very different. One concerns metal rods; another, children; and another, plants. Moreover, the problems differ in the format of the information presented and in the question asked. As you thought about them, however, you may have noticed some similarities. Stop a moment and see if you can formulate more precisely what these three problems have in common.

In all three of the above problems you were asked to work with variables. More specifically, you were asked to consider the role of each of several variables: length, material, and cross-sectional shape in the metal rods problem; age and sex in the verbal ability problem; and amount of water, type of plant food, and use or nonuse of leaf lotion in the plant problem.

The metal rods problem may have seemed a bit familiar. It is based on a study by Bärbel Inhelder and Jean Piaget (1958) that was reported in their classic book on formal operations. We quoted an example of an adolescent working on this task at the beginning of Chapter 8.

Piaget believed that ability to exert **control of variables** is an aspect of formal operational reasoning. To deal effectively with variables we must first determine abstractly what the potentially relevant variables are. Then we must consider the various possible combinations of variables and the possible outcomes. Finally, we must systematically select combinations of variables that will enable us to decide, out of all the possibilities, which variables actually matter. In the above problem, for instance, a formal operational thinker would know that in order to determine the effects of material one must perform an experiment comparing two rods that differ in material but are identical in every other way. Thus, he would compare the 18" square brass rod with an 18" square steel rod. If he found a difference in flexibility, he could attribute it to material: brass vs. steel.

A preformal thinker, on the other hand, might try to vary everything at once: for example, by comparing the 18" square brass rod with a 12" round steel rod. The problem is that we have no way to interpret the results of such an experiment. If, for instance, the first rod is more flexible, is this because steel rods are more flexible, is it because longer rods are more flexible, or is it because square rods are more flexible? The preformal thinker might simply guess or conclude that all of these are true. The formal thinker realizes that there is no way of telling: The experiment did not properly control variables and thus allows no conclusion.

Inhelder and Piaget (1958) found that formal operational control of variables was absent in children younger than about 11 or 12 and well developed by the age of 14 or 15. Subsequent research suggests a more complicated picture. The ability to control variables does increase during late childhood and adolescence but children's performance at any given age depends on the specific task and situation. Children as young as 7 can learn to control variables in certain simple situations (Case, 1974), whereas even college students may have difficulty on more complex tasks (Kuhn & Phelps, 1979).

Understanding the need to control variables is an important aspect of scientific reasoning and plays a crucial role in much scientific research. You probably realized, for example, that the psychologist in our example had no basis for her conclusion about sex differences in verbal ability. Although the girls did show greater verbal ability, they were older than the boys. It might be age rather than sex that was responsible for the difference between the two groups. The proper way to study sex differences would be to study boys and girls of the same age. More generally, the proper way to study the effect of any variable is to vary it and hold everything else constant. This is not always possible, of course, but it remains the ideal of scientific experiments (see Chapter 3).

Controlling Variables in Everyday Life

Most people, of course, do not spend their time conducting experiments. We might ask whether control of variables is relevant to everyday life. Deanna Kuhn and her associates have argued that it is. They believe, however, that in daily life we commonly observe and think about the effects of variables rather than actively manipulate them ourselves. We might, for example, note that some of our plants are growing better than others and wonder what might be responsible. We are unlikely, however, to systematically vary conditions in order to observe their effects.

The plant problem at the beginning of this section illustrates how Kuhn and her associates have studied control of variables. In this problem, we simply observe variations rather than selecting them. Nevertheless, systematic analysis of variables is critical to solving the problem. We must notice that light-colored plant food is always associated with healthy plants and dark-colored food with unhealthy plants, whereas amount of water and use of leaf lotion are not systematically associated with results. We can conclude that the variable *food* is relevant (type of food matters) whereas the other two variables—*water* and *leaf lotion*—are not. Kuhn and Brannock found solid understanding of how to distinguish relevant from irrelevant variables in 15 percent of the fourth-graders they studied, 20 percent of the fifth-graders, 40 percent of the sixth-graders, and 65 percent of the college students. At every age, most had at least a partial grasp of working with variables. Many children, for example, could determine whether a variable was important but did not understand how to rule out an irrelevant variable.

In a follow-up, Kuhn and her associates observed people ranging in age from grade 4 to elderly work their way through a sequence of increasingly complex control-of-variables problems (Kuhn & Phelps, 1979). Over several months, most subjects developed increasingly sophisticated understanding of variables, although progress was typically gradual and uneven. Interestingly, it appeared that the major difficulty was not constructing new strategies but giving up old ones when they proved to be inadequate. It seems that experience working with variables (even without feedback from a teacher or other authority) can result in developmental progress, but that the process is slow and complex. Whether systematic teaching would help or hinder that process is not yet clear.

Hypothesis Testing

In addition to control of variables, scientific reasoning also includes the related ability to rigorously test hypotheses. **Hypothesis testing**, determining the truth or falsity of a hypothesis, is directly involved in the following widely used research task:

> Below are four cards. Each has a number (odd or even) on one side and a letter (vowel or consonant) on the other.

	1	2	A	B
Number	odd	even	?	?
Letter	?	?	vowel	consonant

> Your hypothesis, which may be true or false, is:
>
> If a card has an odd number on it, then it has a vowel on it.
>
> You are going to test this hypothesis by turning over those cards—and only those cards—necessary to determine conclusively whether the hypothesis is true or false for this set of four cards. If you choose to turn more than one card, you must turn them simultaneously. Which card or cards do you need to turn?

After you have pondered this for a while, try it on some friends. It is particularly effective to have a group of college students try to agree on a solution. There are almost always strong, diverse opinions, which can lead to spirited discussion.

This task, usually called the **selection task**, was devised in the mid-1960s by British psychologist Peter Wason and, since then, has been administered to many thousands of college students. In its abstract form (as above), it is surprisingly difficult: Only about 5 percent of college students select the correct answer (Wason & Johnson-Laird, 1972). Most students choose to turn only the *1* or the *1* and the *A*.

Hypothesis Testing

Poor reasoning is not only a problem in school but may hinder social relations as well.

Animal nerds

Probably they choose the 1 because this would support the hypothesis if there were an *A* on the reverse side and choose the *A* with the idea that it would support the hypothesis if there were a 1 on the reverse side. A more sophisticated response is to choose 1, *A*, and *B*. Students who choose this argue that B must be turned because if there were a 1 on the other side it would disprove the hypothesis (which requires that a card with an odd number have a vowel). The correct response, however, is to turn *only 1* and *B*. *A* is not necessary because it would not disprove the hypothesis regardless of what appeared on the other side. The hypothesis requires that a card with an odd number have a vowel on it but not that a card with a vowel have an odd number.

Since this is a difficult insight, let us approach it another way. How should one test a hypothesis? It appears that the proper way is to do experiments that could conceivably prove the hypothesis wrong. Any experiment that could lead to results disproving the hypothesis is relevant. On the other hand, if no possible outcome of a certain experiment would disprove the hypothesis, then that experiment is not helpful.

Consider what could disprove the following hypothesis: *If a card has an odd number on it, then it has a vowel on it*. A card with an odd number and a vowel is obviously consistent with the hypothesis. Moreover, a card with an even number is consistent with the hypothesis regardless of whether there is a vowel or consonant on the other side, since the hypothesis makes no predictions about this case. Thus, only a card with an odd number and a consonant is inconsistent with the hypothesis. Accordingly, we must turn the card with the odd number (1) to see if there is a consonant on the other side and we must turn the card with the consonant (B) to check for an odd number. We need not be concerned about the other two cards because neither is capable of disproving the hypothesis.

We might suppose that developmental psychologists have little interest in a task that even college students generally cannot perform successfully. It might seem pointless to give the above task to children. Research has shown, however, that when college students are presented with more meaningful versions of the selection task they often, though not always, succeed (Griggs, 1983; Wason, 1983). Apparently,

Highlights

Adolescent Reasoning and Adolescent Rights

Should an adolescent who desires counseling or psychotherapy be permitted to arrange for this without parental consent? Should parental consent be required to obtain medical treatment, contraceptives, or an abortion? Should adolescents be allowed to read books or take courses that their parents object to? Should they make their own decisions about participating in research? Should they have the freedom to leave home, get a job, and/or get married? Should an adolescent's parents have the right to commit her to a mental institution or to require her, against her will, to have psychotherapy or medical treatment, or to get an abortion?

Obviously, most issues involving conflict between parents and children are settled, one way or another, within the family. Over the past 20 years, however, issues like the above have increasingly been argued in U.S. courts and have been the focus of much analysis, discussion, and controversy. The questions are indeed difficult ones, and psychologists do not agree on the answers to them. Most psychologists do believe, however, that evidence about the reasoning ability of adolescents is important in making decisions about their rights (Melton, 1983, 1986; Melton, Koocher, & Saks, 1983; Moshman, 1986; Rodman & Griffith, 1982).

Why are parent–adolescent conflicts so difficult for the courts? The reason seems to be that they pit two fundamental principles of our society and legal system against each other (*cf*. Moshman, 1985a). On one hand, we believe that adolescents are people and that, like all people in a democratic society, they are entitled to make their own decisions about their lives, even if we disagree with their choices. On the other hand, however, we believe that adolescents are still, to some extent, children.

many college students are capable of the **falsification strategy**, in which one tests hypotheses by trying to falsify them, though they only reveal this competence under favorable circumstances (O'Brien, 1986). At what age does this strategy develop?

David Moshman (1979a) has suggested that since the falsification strategy involves consideration of hypothetical possibilities (possible outcomes of turning over cards), it requires formal operational reasoning and thus probably develops during adolescence. He presented students with hypotheses such as: *If a person uses fluoridated toothpaste he will have healthy teeth.* He then asked whether it would be better to test this by (a) asking patients with healthy teeth whether they use fluoridated toothpaste or (b) asking patients who do not have healthy teeth whether they use fluoridated toothpaste. The correct answer is *b*, since

---

Since children lack the reasoning ability to act in their own long-term interests, we defer to their parents to decide what is best for them.

How are we to decide whether to treat adolescents as adults or as children? Scientific study of adolescent reasoning ability seems directly relevant. Much of the research reviewed in this chapter shows that a variety of reasoning abilities are developing during adolescence. Most of these, however, involve sophisticated competencies that are imperfect even in adults. Melton (1983) reviews evidence showing that for many sorts of real-life decision-making and problem-solving, older adolescents, and often even younger adolescents, do not differ from the average adult. Moreover, he cites evidence that granting adolescents opportunities to make decisions for themselves increases their decision-making ability. Melton concludes that courts should recognize the personhood of adolescents and society should grant them substantial autonomy.

Research that is discussed in this chapter shows that even young children have some ability to think rationally. Thus the discussion above does not apply only to adolescents. In general, it seems that a reasonable policy for both parents and courts would be to grant children increasing freedom to make their own decisions as their reasoning abilities develop. More research will be needed in order for psychologists to recommend to judges and legislators reasonable age limits for specific rights. Moreover, given the substantial individual differences among children, age limits can never be more than rough guidelines. Obviously, it is best if parents and children can work out their own compromises without resorting to the courts.

only people who use fluoridated toothpaste and do not have healthy teeth disprove the hypothesis. Four versions of this task were presented to 24 students in each of grades 7, 10, and college.

Moshman found that only 25 percent of the seventh-graders ever used the falsification strategy, and none of them used it for all four problems. In contrast, 62 percent of the tenth-graders used falsification somewhat and 25 percent did so consistently. Finally, 58 percent of the college students showed some grasp of falsification and 33 percent were consistent in their use of it.

It appears that at least some people develop the concept of testing hypotheses by attempting to falsify them. This seems to be a much more difficult aspect of scientific reasoning than control of variables, however, since performance on falsification tasks is far from perfect, even among college students. Research in social psychology (Snyder & Campbell, 1980) suggests that many adults focus on verifying information and ignore falsifying evidence, a tendency that may lead to stereotypes about other people being maintained even when the stereotypes are obviously false. As we noted in connection with control of variables, most people rarely design experiments. But we do need to be able to think scientifically about information. Research on use of the falsification strategy in testing hypotheses suggests that some forms of scientific reasoning remain difficult even for intelligent adults (Moshman, 1979b).

Understanding Number

The task in the last section was very challenging, but now we turn back to a much simpler one.

> Imagine six pennies placed in a row. If you spread them further apart, will there still be six? How about if you move them closer together? How about if you rearrange them in a circle?

You may recognize this as a Piagetian conservation of number task. Obviously, there will still be six pennies no matter how they are spaced or arranged. As we saw in Chapter 8, however, this fact is not obvious to children younger than about 6 years old. They seem to believe that superficial perceptual changes affect the number of objects. It appears that preschool children do not understand the concept of number, at least not the way adults do (Halford & Boyle, 1985).

As Piaget's findings became increasingly known in the United States during the 1960s, some educators argued that we should not teach math to children under age 6. Since these young children have no concept of number, they are unable to comprehend any mathematical instruction and will either be confused and anxious about math or will learn mechanical procedures without genuine understanding.

But can we really say that because a child fails a number conservation task he has no mathematical understanding? Rochel Gelman thought not and, along with other researchers, has provided convincing evidence that preschoolers know much more about math than their poor performance on Piaget's task suggested (Gelman, 1980; Gelman & Gallistel, 1978; Gelman, Meck, & Merkin, 1986).

In one line of research, Gelman and her associates exposed preschool children to sets of objects and then observed whether the children noticed and were surprised by various changes in these sets. They found that by age 3 or earlier, children know that addition and subtraction change the number of items but that changing the length of the array, the color of an item, or the type of item does not. Moreover, children understand that addition and subtraction can cancel each other out. They also can determine whether two arrays have the same number of objects and, if not, which has more.

Of course, there are important limits to children's abilities in these areas. Not surprisingly, young children do not seem to understand mathematical concepts in the abstract. Their competence is limited to specific, countable arrays of two to five items. Nevertheless, the abilities documented by Gelman and her associates represent an important basis for further development of mathematical reasoning.

Gelman's work led her to believe that counting is fundamental to young children's understanding of mathematical concepts. By counting, Gelman does not mean running through the sequence 1, 2, 3, 4, and so on by rote. In Gelman's analysis, successful counting involves coordinated application of five **principles of counting**.

The first is the **one-one principle**. In counting an array, each item must be tagged with one and only one unique tag (number name). For example, to count the number of words in this sentence, you apply the tag *one* to the word "for," *two* to the word "example," *three* to the word "to," and so on. You must not skip a word, or skip a tag, or apply two tags to the same word, or apply the same tag to two different words.

The second principle is the **stable-order principle**. You cannot apply the tags *one, two, three,* and so on in a different order every time you count. You must have a stable, consistent list.

The third principle of counting is the **cardinal principle**. If asked how many words there are in the first sentence of this paragraph, you use your one-one and stable-order principles and get up to the tag *nine* corresponding to the word "principle." You respond that there are nine words in the sentence. You understand that the last tag is the cardinal number of the array: the number of items it contains. That is, if the last word is the ninth counted, then there must be nine words in the sentence. This is the cardinal principle.

Fourth is the **abstraction principle**. Any set of items can be counted. They need not be the same color, shape, or type. If we have a psychology textbook, a phone book, a daffodil, and two armadillos, then we have five items. It may be unclear what, if anything, they have in common, but that does not stop us from counting them.

Finally, the **order-irrelevance principle** informs us that the order in which the items are tagged is irrelevant. Whether we begin counting with the textbook or one of the armadillos, we need only follow the other principles for our counting to be correct.

Having learned all this about counting, you may feel like the centipede who has just learned he has 100 legs. He wonders how he manages to walk, and you may wonder how you manage to count. In fact, you have already known all of the above about counting and have successfully applied these principles for many years, although they may seem new to you because you have rarely thought explicitly about them.

It is clear from this analysis that there is much more to counting than simply reciting the standard number list of one's language. Genuine counting is quite a sophisticated ability. Do young children know how to count?

It appears that they do. Gelman (1980) summarized evidence that preschoolers understand all five of the above principles and use them in their counting. Not surprisingly, 3-year-olds have more trouble than 5-year-olds, especially with large arrays. Nevertheless, even 3-year-olds seem to understand all five of the principles.

Gelman notes that children of 2 or 3 may not yet have learned the standard number sequence: *one, two, three,* and so forth. Even though they may use their own unique sequence, however, they show their grasp of the stable-order principle by their consistency in using that sequence. Gelman reports a case of one child whose number list was 1, 2, 3, 4, 5, 6, 7, H, I, J!

We saw in Chapter 11 that when a child incorrectly uses "goed" for the past tense of "go," psychologists take this to show an impressive grasp of grammar, since the child is using a general rule for forming past tenses. Gelman suggests that, similarly, when a child consistently uses a personal number sequence like *2, 6, 10* we should not emphasize his ignorance of the correct sequence but rather should be impressed with his understanding of the stable-order principle.

Although the mathematical understanding of preschoolers is impressive, this does not mean that overall mathematical competence is an early development (Kaye, 1986). In fact, there are important mathematical competencies such as estimating correlations and reasoning about probabilities that do not develop until much later and that, unlike

Young children love to count and, as Gelman and others have shown, have impressive competence in this skill.

counting, remain difficult even for adults (Evans, 1983; Halpern, 1984). Nevertheless, young children's numerical competence and motivation are astonishing. They certainly provide a firm basis for continuing development. "I am struck," wrote Gelman, "by the general willingness of preschoolers to count almost anything" (1980, p. 62).

Metacognition: A Matter of Mind over Mind

We turn now to a topic central to all aspects of reasoning.

> Think about your thinking: How did you solve the various problems introducing the earlier sections of this chapter? What were you thinking as you worked on them? What were you aware of?

As we have seen, whenever we count we put into practice a number of mathematical principles without explicitly thinking about them. Similarly, logical and scientific reasoning involve cognitive processes that we are not aware of. But are *all* the processes and principles we use in reasoning unconscious? Don't we know something about our own thought processes? Don't we use that knowledge to direct and control our thinking? Doesn't *consciousness* play a role in reasoning?

Most psychologists avoid questions about consciousness. We know that we will never have a complete understanding of how the mind

Highlights

Do Fleas Have Metafleas?

Metacognition is an important topic in the study of cognitive development with major implications for the development of reasoning. But there is also a fanciful side to the world of "metas." Thinking about other metas can be a mind-expanding exercise that may help you understand at a deeper level what metacognition is all about.

Do you ever think about what theories are and how they work? If so, you might come up with a theory of theories, or a metatheory. What if your house burned down and the insurance company, instead of paying up, informed you it was bankrupt? That would be a problem, unless you had insurance against an insurance failure, or metainsurance. Did you ever see a button that reads "Wearing Buttons Is Not Enough"? If so, you were reading a button about buttons, or a metabutton. Of course, the machines that make buttons are only one of many types of machines. If you had a machine capable of constructing a variety of machines, it would be—you guessed it—a metamachine.

The rules that determine how the American legal system works—found in the Constitution—are laws about laws: metalaws. There are even rules for amending the Constitution: meta-metalaws. Perhaps the ultimate in bureaucracy is when an organization has so many committees it needs a committee to regulate its various committees, or a metacommittee.

Why did the chicken cross the road? To get to the other side. That's not funny at all. But its unfunniness is what is supposed to be funny about it. It is a parody of a joke, a joke about jokes, a metajoke. Why did the punkrocker cross the road? Because he was stapled to a chicken. That is a joke about punkrockers. But it is also a metajoke: A joke about chicken-crossing-the-road jokes.

---

works without somehow coming to terms with the issue of consciousness but, at the same time, we do not know how to deal with consciousness in a rigorous, scientific fashion.

For many years, American psychology was under the sway of behaviorism and refused to deal with the issue of consciousness at all, dismissing it as outside the realm of science. Since the rise of cognitive psychology in the 1960s, however, it is once again acceptable to talk about the mind, including processes and principles of reasoning. Most psychologists still avoid the term *consciousness* but do attempt to deal with the sort of issues raised by that term, usually under the heading of **metacognition**.

We have addressed certain aspects of metacognition earlier in this book. We saw in Chapter 8, for example, that Sternberg's information

> Did you ever dream that you were having a dream? If so, you were metadreaming, dreaming about dreaming. Would you like to write a book about all the great books of the world? The book about books would, of course, be a metabook. Do you ever feel anxious about the prospect of experiencing anxiety? Your anxiety about anxiety is meta-anxiety.
>
> Ask someone whether it is okay to ask him a question: "May I ask you a question?" This is a question about questioning, a metaquestion. If you have so many lists of things to do that you lose track of them, you need a list of your lists, a metalist. Some dogs have fleas, but are the fleas, in turn, infested with tiny flealings? Such creaturettes, whether fictional or not, are metafleas.
>
> As for metacognition itself, when you read and think about metacognition, isn't that *meta*-metacognition? But if you think about *that*, you are now engaging in *meta*-meta-metacognition. And if you think about *that* ... well, you get the idea!
>
> Just in case your mind is not yet fully boggled, let us conclude with a metalimerick, or a limerick about limericks.
>
> A limerick writer from Dryzing
> metacognized her own limerizing:
> "A A B B A
> is the limerick way!"
> And that's metalimericizing.

processing theory of cognitive development puts great emphasis on the development of what he calls *metacomponents*, or executive processes that direct other aspects of thinking. We then saw that children not only develop better memories but develop better understanding about how memory works and better control over their own memory strategies (Chapter 10). Finally, we described how children learn to use language and logic *and* to think about the nature of language (Chapter 11) and the nature of logic (earlier in this chapter).

In general, metacognition refers to cognition about cognition, or thinking about thinking. This includes both our knowledge about what we know and, closely related to that, our ability to regulate our own processes of knowing, understanding, learning, remembering, and reasoning. Because so much is included under the heading of metacognition, simple questions such as "When does metacognition develop?" are impossible to answer. Metacognition includes many facets, some of which can be seen in preschool children and some of which are rare even in adults (Brown, Bransford, Ferrara, & Campione, 1983). It is widely agreed, however, that metacognition is an important aspect of cognition and that reflection on one's thinking plays an important role in cognitive development.

As a student, you undoubtedly have considerable metacognitive ability and use it regularly. You estimate the difficulty of various assignments, for example, and decide how much time to allot to each. You decide which things you should memorize by rote and which you need to understand at a deeper level. You assess how well you are grasping various ideas and, if necessary, figure out how you can learn more effectively in the future.

Most students, however, probably can profit from further metacognitive development. Wagner and Sternberg (1984) argued that training people in metacognitive skills should be a major goal of education. "Metacognitive theorists," they write, "have in common their belief that teaching specific strategies just won't work in the long run: One must teach general principles and how to apply them over a variety of task domains" (p. 202). They reviewed extensive evidence indicating that metacognitive skills are important in cognitive performance and academic success; that students are often lacking in important metacognitive skills such as estimating task difficulty, apportioning study time wisely, and determining how well they understand material; that metacognitive skills are rarely taught in schools; and that instruction in metacognitive skills can have results that generalize across settings.

Wagner and Sternberg noted reasons for caution. We do not always know, for example, which metacognitive skills to teach, how to get children to learn them, or how to get children to apply what they have learned. Nevertheless, Wagner and Sternberg concluded that "everything considered, the main implication of recent information-processing research would seem to be the advisability of teaching metacognitive as well as cognitive skills" (p. 205).

Philosophical Reasoning

Which of the following examples shows a more sophisticated kind of reasoning?

Interviewer: Is it a good idea to teach metacognitive skills?
Student A: Yes.

I: On what do you base that point of view?
S: It says so in my developmental psych text.
I: Is that sufficient reason?
S: They quoted Wagner and Sternberg.
I: Is that sufficient reason?
S: Yes.
I: Why?
S: They're experts on metacognition.

Interviewer: Is it a good idea to teach metacognitive skills?
Student B: Yes.
I: On what do you base that point of view?
S: Ideas discussed in my developmental psych text.
I: Is that sufficient reason?
S: There is some convincing evidence supporting those ideas.
I: Does that prove the ideas are right?
S: No. Further evidence could lead me to change my mind. But for now, the view that one should teach metacognitive skills seems well-reasoned and well-supported.

Although students A and B both believe in teaching metacognitive skills, they differ greatly in how they justify their points of view. But what exactly is the difference? Is it possible to classify different kinds of justifications consistently? Are some justifications better than others? These questions address the issue of people's philosophical reasoning—their conceptions about the nature of knowledge, truth, reality, and the justification of ideas.

After a detailed study of college students at Harvard University, William Perry (1970) concluded that students differ in their level of philosophical understanding and that many make progress toward more sophisticated philosophical reasoning during their college years. Perry viewed this progress as a gradual, developmental transition. Increasing philosophical sophistication might be due at least partially to the broad intellectual experience of a college education but was not a matter of simply taking philosophy courses or learning techniques of reasoning.

Of course the ability to think about philosophical issues is not limited to college students. John Broughton (1978) extended the study of people's philosophies by interviewing individuals ranging in age from 5 to 26 on a wide range of issues. As we might expect, the youngest children typically showed little understanding of the issues involved. This is illustrated, for example, in the following attempt by Broughton to raise basic questions about the nature of knowledge and reality with a 5-year-old:

Question: How do you know that chest is really over there?
Answer: They put it there.
Question: How do you know that house is over there?
Answer: That's where they built it (1978, p. 79).

Broughton reported that young children did not have trouble understanding philosophical questions but failed to see their point. They considered truth absolute and knowledge automatic and thus viewed Broughton's questions "with wonder or suspicion" (p. 79). Broughton found steadily increasing philosophical sophistication over a period of many years.

Anecdotal reports by Matthews (1980) suggest that children spontaneously raise philosophical issues and at least occasionally have surprising insights. Seven-year-old Michael, for example, says

> I don't like to [think] about the universe without an end. It gives me a funny feeling in my stomach. If the universe goes on forever, there is no place for God to live, who made it. . . . It's nice to know you're *here*. It is not nice to know about nothing. I hope [the universe] doesn't go on and on forever. I don't like the idea of it going on forever because it's obvious it can't be anywhere (pp. 34–35).

Despite such examples, however, available data indicate that much of the development of philosophical understanding takes place during adolescence and early adulthood. Although various theories about the later development of philosophical conceptions differ on many details, there is substantial agreement about the general direction of development. There seems to be a trend from absolutism to relativism to rationality.

At the level of **absolutism** (including Student A above), the individual believes that reality and knowledge are absolute. The truth is thought to be either inherently known or learnable from the proper authorities (e.g., "but the teacher said . . ."; "It's written right here that . . ."). Recognition that some things are not known even by the authorities leads ultimately to the level of **relativism**, at which knowledge is viewed as personal and subjective. Truth is relative: It depends on one's point of view, and anyone's view is as good as anyone else's. But is 2 + 2 = 4 no more justifiable than 2 + 2 = 5? Increasing recognition that some views really *are* better than others leads to the level of **rationality** (e.g., Student B above). At this level, the individual believes that, even though we cannot obtain an absolute and final

Research

Development of Reasoning about Knowledge and Reality

Karen Kitchener and Patricia King (1981), extending the work of Perry, Broughton, and others, proposed that the development of philosophical understanding proceeds through seven distinct stages. Each stage includes a conception of reality, a view about the nature of knowledge, and ideas about how knowledge is justified. The general direction of development is toward increasing understanding of rational criteria for reasoning about complex matters.

To test their theory, Kitchener and King interviewed 20 high school students, 20 college students, and 20 graduate students about four dilemmas. Each dilemma involved a set of conflicting opinions—for example, chemical additives to food are/are not safe. Kitchener and King were primarily interested not in students' opinions about these dilemmas but rather in how they reasoned about them. Therefore each dilemma was followed by questions designed to probe students' justifications for their views.

Kitchener and King found it was possible to reliably classify different levels of philosophical reasoning by using their seven stages. For most students, reasoning spanned two or three stages, indicating that people usually have a range of typical reasoning rather than fitting neatly into a single stage. As expected, the average level of reasoning was highest for the graduate students and lowest for the high school students, suggesting that philosophical development continues well beyond adolescence, at least for some people.

An important limitation of Kitchener and King's study is that it was *cross-sectional:* It compared three groups of students differing in age (see Chapter 3). But can we really be sure that the results reflect developmental changes in individuals? To rigorously test this, we need to do a *longitudinal study* (see Chapter 3), one in which the same students are retested to see if they have changed over a period of time.

Elizabeth Welfel and Mark Davison (1986) recently did precisely that. They used the same interview techniques as Kitchener and King to assess 32 first-year college students and then reassessed as many as they could (25) four years later. Almost all students were found to score higher at the later testing, though the difference was usually not very great. Welfel and Davison concluded that development of concepts of knowledge and reality moves slowly but surely through the stages proposed by Kitchener and King.

knowledge of reality, we can nevertheless improve our knowledge through proper use of evidence and reasoning. Thus, even if none of our knowledge is the last word, some ideas are indeed better justified than others on the basis of rational standards. It should be emphasized that most people do not fit neatly into a single level of philosophical understanding. A person may, for example, be absolutist on some issues and relativist on others, or relativist on some issues and rational on others.

Conclusion: The Development of Rationality

We have considered many different sorts of reasoning in this chapter and have seen that development takes place not only in childhood but in adolescence and adulthood as well. As a logician, the preschool child appears capable of reaching correct conclusions from a variety of premises. During later development, she shows increasing understanding of the nature of logical arguments.

But there is more to rationality than logical inference. The rational thinker also can get outside logical arguments and understand the world scientifically by effectively controlling variables and testing hypotheses. We have also seen how related mathematical skills emerge, beginning with the surprisingly sophisticated mathematical competence of the counting preschooler.

Mature rationality goes still further, however. We have seen how people become increasingly aware of their cognitive processes and increasingly able to use this knowledge to direct their own thinking. Finally, we have looked at the developing person as a philosopher, constructing increasingly sophisticated views about the nature of knowledge and reality.

In considering the development of knowledge in various domains, some general patterns emerge. With increasing age, there is an impressive increase in the ability to focus on abstract logical connections, to interpret information appropriately, to systematically test hypotheses, to reason about large numbers and probabilistic situations, to understand and direct one's own reasoning, and to make defensible judgments on the basis of sophisticated conceptions about the nature of knowledge and reality. In short, development seems to involve a continuing increase in rationality.

Does this mean that young children are essentially irrational and that adults are fundamentally rational? It does not. To avoid reaching an oversimplified conclusion, let us consider in greater detail the evidence for rationality or irrationality in children and adults.

It is quite easy, of course, to find a wide variety of tasks on which preschoolers exhibit naive or even bizarre responses. Nevertheless, with a little ingenuity, it can be shown that preschoolers can make correct transitive inferences, understand the basic principles of counting, and show equal rationality in their approaches to a wide variety of other tasks (Gelham & Baillargeon, 1983). To label them irrational would be incorrect.

We must beware, however, of overreacting to the evidence of preschool competence and jumping to the extreme position that preschoolers are no different than adults. Preschoolers' rationality is limited in various ways. For example, they reason best about observable, concrete objects and small, countable sets. More abstract strategies and concepts, such as holding variables constant or looking at the validity of arguments independent of empirical truth, appear to develop later.

However, we have also seen that many aspects of rational thinking, such as testing hypotheses by looking for disconfirming cases or holding mature conceptions about the nature of knowledge, are not fully developed even in most adults. Research with adults has shown numerous departures from standards of rationality. Psychologists have disagreed about what these results mean and there have been vigorous debates in the the literature about whether adults are fundamentally rational or irrational (Cohen, 1981; Evans, 1982, 1983).

It seems quite clear from scientific evidence as well as from daily observation that even adults do not consistently deal with issues in a rational manner. Again, however, we must be wary of leaping to the opposite extreme and concluding that most people are fundamentally irrational or that adults do not differ from young children in their reasoning. The evidence discussed in this chapter shows that adults, at their best, are capable of types of reasoning that are simply not seen in young children (Moshman, 1985b).

Thus we cannot conclude that young children are entirely irrational, that adults are entirely rational, or that the development of reasoning is a simple progression from irrationality to rationality. There is evidence at all ages of some degree of rationality and some limitations on the ability and/or willingness to use that rationality. It does appear, however, that as development proceeds, people use increasingly sophisticated forms of reasoning in an increasingly wider variety of circumstances. Development moves in the direction of rationality.

Applications: Developing Reasoning

It has been suggested by many that reasoning should be considered the fourth R of schooling—as important as Reading, 'Riting, and 'Rithmetic. There is much that a teacher (or parent) can do to encourage the development of reasoning.

1. *Ask students for reasons, not just answers*. Make it clear to them that how they think about a problem or reach a solution is at least as important as their ultimate answer.

Highlights

Should Schools Develop Reasoning?

Educators and psychologists have devised and implemented numerous programs for developing the reasoning ability of students at all levels. Although there is considerable debate over what educational strategies are most effective for this purpose, most professionals assume that the development of reasoning should be a major goal of education (Kuhn, 1986). Some, in fact, have argued that it should be the *central* goal (Kohlberg & Mayer, 1972).

Not everyone agrees, however, that schools should attempt to develop reasoning, and some parents and concerned citizens are highly threatened by a developmental approach (Franks, 1986; Hentoff, 1980; Moshman, 1981; O'Neil, 1981). In most cases, those who object are people who believe they know what is intellectually and morally correct. The proper role of schools, they argue, is not to develop reasoning but rather to transmit certain "absolute and unquestionable" truths to the next generation. Students should be shielded from unacceptable ideas or points of view and discouraged from formulating their own ideas and expressing their own opinions. Some who take this approach have denounced public schools for fostering what they call "secular humanism," the concept that one's own reasoning can be a legitimate source of knowledge and development.

Although only a minority of parents and citizens support this indoctrinative view of education, they have had considerable impact on the public schools in many communities. This is because they are very active, vocal, and organized and because public schools are highly vulnerable to political pressures (Franks, 1986). In some cases, the impact is clear and direct, such as when textbooks are rejected for political reasons or when books by such well-known authors as Kurt Vonnegut or Judy Blume are removed from school libraries because they challenge students to think about things some parents find threatening. In other cases, the effects of community pressure are harder to detect, such as when teachers censor their own lesson plans in order to avoid trouble. As a ninth-grade history teacher in Plano, Texas, put it, "I think about what I'm doing twice. Is there anything controversial in this lesson plan? If there is, I won't use it. I won't use things where a kid has to make a judgment" (Moshman, 1981, p. 10).

Most psychologists and educators are dubious of this indoctrinative approach to education for a variety of reasons (Siegel, 1986, 1987). For one thing, we live in a pluralistic society where people hold widely diverse political and religious views. Even if we wanted to teach "the truth and nothing but the truth," how would we choose which truths to teach? Second, today's students will be living most of their adult lives in the twenty-first century, facing issues we are not even aware of today. Won't an ability to reason intelligently serve them better than a set of facts and values that may no longer be relevant? Third, many people believe schools should prepare students to be voting citizens of a democratic society in which freedom of speech is highly valued. If so, shouldn't we present a diversity of ideas and encourage free expression and active decision making? Finally, current theories propose that exposure to diverse ideas, thinking about the resulting conflicts and contradictions, resolving disequilibrium, making one's own judgments, and discussing one's opinions with others are crucial to intellectual and moral development (Bearison, Magzamen, & Filardo, 1986; Berkowitz, 1985). Limiting these sorts of opportunities means limiting the development of students toward greater rationality.

As with all conflicts, those between educators and parents are best resolved by open communication. When parents understand what schools are trying to do they are often less threatened by it. Nevertheless, conflicts over the education of children can be highly emotional and difficult to resolve (Moshman, 1985a). Many have resulted in legal cases and some have gone all the way to the U.S. Supreme Court. In most cases, courts have found indoctrinative approaches to education inconsistent with the First Amendment guarantee of freedom of speech. Students have a right to be exposed to a diversity of ideas and to form and express their own views. "In our system," the Supreme Court ruled in its 1969 *Tinker* decision, "students may not be regarded as closed-circuit recipients of only that which the state chooses to communicate. They may not be confined to the expression of those sentiments that are officially approved" (Hentoff, 1980, p. 6). In the words of the late Supreme Court Justice William O. Douglas (Hentoff, 1980, pp. 27–28),

> What else can the School Board now decide it does not like? How else will its sensibilities be offended? Are we sending children to school to be educated by the norms of the School Board or are we educating our youth to shed the prejudices of the past, to explore all forms of thought, and to find solutions to our world's problems?

One can help students develop their reasoning abilities by regularly asking for reasons, not just for answers.

2. *Encourage students to think about their own thinking.* Even young children are capable of some metacognition; their problem-solving and development will benefit if you can get them to use and improve this ability.

3. *Encourage critical thinking.* Asking children for reasons is a good start, but we do not want students to remain dependent on good questions from others. Encourage them to ask themselves for reasons, to spontaneously question ideas that are presented to them, and to scrutinize their own ideas. Help them get in the habit of looking for relevant evidence and analyzing the validity of arguments.

4. *Examine tasks and assignments with respect to the specific reasoning required.* If, for example, a science lab requires students to control variables, students who fail to understand the logic of working with variables will have trouble. Working on this concept may help them eventually deal with the lab assignment. For the teacher, of course, focusing on specific reasoning may be more difficult than just assuming a student is doomed to fail because of, say, low IQ. It is often worth the trouble, however.

5. *Make students part of the process of developing reasoning.* Good reasoning is not merely a set of skills that can be put into a student in the same way that a new program can be put into a computer. Students

will do better if they know that you are trying to help them develop their reasoning abilities and they are interested in working toward that goal.

Summary

Reasoning is a crucial aspect of intelligence. Psychologists interested in the development of reasoning have studied the performance of numerous children, adolescents, and adults on a wide variety of reasoning tasks.

One sort of reasoning is transitive inference. As adults, for example, we know that if David is older than Stan and Stan is older than Bob, then David is older than Bob. Evidence shows that even preschool children can make inferences of this sort, though there is still controversy about how they do so.

Mature understanding of logic, however, involves more than simply reaching correct conclusions. It also involves distinguishing conclusions that are logically necessary—that is, required by the information given—from those that are merely likely or plausible. For a child who understands logical necessity, it is clear that if David is older than Stan and Stan is older than Bob, then David *must* be older than Bob. It appears from several studies that an understanding of logical necessity begins to develop about age 6 and is well-established in most children by the age of about 10.

Even 10-year-olds, however, seem to have trouble dealing with the logic of arguments in a purely abstract way, independent of the actual truth and falsity of the statements within them. This can be seen, for example, in arguments with false premises and conclusions, such as: *If babies are older than children and children are older than adults, then babies are older than adults.* Most 10-year-olds would reject this argument, whereas beginning about age 12 adolescents are increasingly likely to understand that the conclusion does follow logically from the premises, although it is factually incorrect.

Although logic is important, the above example shows that it is not sufficient to guarantee factual truth. In addition to developing logical reasoning, children develop an ability to reason the way scientists do in trying to understand the world around us. One type of scientific reasoning that has been extensively studied is the ability to control variables. In order to understand how a given factor affects some outcome (e.g., is water or plant food more important for healthy plants?), one must consider the effects of one variable at a time, with other variables held constant. Research has shown that even 7-year-olds can learn to control variables in simple situations but that the understanding of how to deal with variables continues to develop over many years and is incomplete even in many college students.

An even more difficult scientific concept is the importance of testing hypotheses by seeking information that could disconfirm them. It appears that this ability develops to some extent over the course of adolescence, but most college students have difficulty with this sort of reasoning.

Understanding of mathematical concepts also develops over a long age range. Preschool children show an impressive understanding of the principles of counting, though more sophisticated mathematical concepts (e.g., probability) develop much later.

Although much of our logical, scientific, and mathematical reasoning is unconscious, an important aspect of sophisticated reasoning is the ability to think about and direct one's own reasoning processes. Psychologists refer to this as metacognitive ability and have argued that the gradual increase in metacognition during childhood and adolescence is an important aspect of cognitive development and should be encouraged strongly in educational programs.

Not only are children and adolescents increasingly aware of their own reasoning but they construct increasingly sophisticated views about the general nature of reality and knowledge. These intuitive philosophical conceptions are important in making rational judgments. Overall, the development of reasoning moves in the direction of greater rationality in reaching conclusions, testing hypotheses, solving problems, and making decisions.

Key Terms

- reasoning
- transitive inference
- seriation
- premises
- logical necessity
- inferential validity
- control of variables
- hypothesis testing
- selection task
- falsification strategy
- principles of counting
- one-one principle
- stable-order principle
- cardinal principle
- abstraction principle
- order-irrelevance principle
- metacognition
- absolutism
- relativism
- rationality

Suggested Readings

Braine, M. D. S., & Rumain, B. (1983). Logical reasoning. In J. H. Flavell & E. M. Markman (Eds.), P. H. Mussen (Series Ed.), *Handbook of child psychology: Vol. 3. Cognitive development* (pp. 263–340). New York: Wiley. This chapter presents a technical but comprehensive review of the literature on the development of logical reasoning.

Gelman, R. (1980). What young children know about numbers. *Educational Psychologist, 15*, 54–68. Gelman provides a very readable summary of her landmark work in this area.

Kitchener, K. S., & King, P. M. (1981). Reflective judgment: Concepts of justification and their relationship to age and education. *Journal of Applied Developmental Psychology, 2*, 89–116. This paper begins with a clear presentation (with numerous examples) of Kitchener and King's theory of the development of concepts of reality, knowledge, and justification.

Matthews, G. B. (1980). *Philosophy and the young child*. Cambridge, MA: Harvard University Press. Matthews argues that children are more sophisticated in their reasoning about philosophical issues than is generally recognized. Whether or not one is convinced, the numerous quotes and anecdotes are intriguing and entertaining.

Moshman, D. (Ed.) (1986). *Children's intellectual rights*. San Francisco: Jossey-Bass. In this edited book, six authors, representing the fields of law, philosophy, psychology, and education, address the question of what rights children and adolescents have to use and develop their reasoning abilities.

Application Exercise

12-1 Identifying Types of Reasoning

For each of the following examples, indicate which of the following types of reasoning is illustrated: (a) transitive inference; (b) logical necessity; (c) validity; (d) isolation of variables; (e) falsification strategy; (f) principles of counting (specify which); (g) metacognition; (h) absolutism; or (i) relativism. Indicate whether the example illustrates a failure to apply one of the above.

1. If we are comparing three study techniques to see which produces better learning, we should ensure that the students using each technique are comparable in age and intelligence.

2. Ips are bigger than Bips and Bips are bigger than Blips. Therefore, Ips are bigger than Blips.

3. George Washington was a great man because it says so in my history book and the teacher told me it was true. Anyone who disagrees is mistaken.

4. We can study whether Ips are bigger than Blips by looking for large Ips and small Blips and seeing if the Ips are indeed larger.

5. If all Eps are Beps and all Beps are Bleps, then there cannot be an Ep that isn't a Blep.

6. In solving a problem one should determine what the desired goal is and stop after each step to consider whether one is closer to that goal.
7. In determining the number of points on a star, it doesn't matter which point one starts with or whether one counts clockwise or counterclockwise as long as one keeps track of where one started.
8. What one person considers good reasoning may be considered bad reasoning by another. It's all up to the individual. No one has the right to judge the reasoning of another.
9. From a strictly logical point of view, the following two arguments are equivalent: (1) Either bears fly or birds fly. Bears do not fly. Therefore birds fly. (2) Either bears fly or frogs fly. Bears do not fly. Therefore frogs fly.
10. It is proposed that all Ips fly. To test this hypothesis, we should look for nonflying Ips.

PART V

Social and Personality Development

Children's increasing abilities to perceive, remember, communicate, and reason are critical to their development. But our discussion of these topics in the previous section raises still further questions. Obviously, there is much more to child development than the development of cognition. How do children's feelings develop? What do we know about their developing relationships with their parents and with other children? How do they come to appreciate moral standards and principles? How do they think about themselves as girls, as boys, and as people? How do their personalities develop?

These are the sorts of questions we will address in this last section of the book. We will see that, although cognition is a critical part of development, there is much more to be said in order to round out our picture of the developing person. In this last section we will explore the development of emotions, social relationships, moral orientations, self-concepts, sex roles, and—finally—the personality as a whole.

CHAPTER 13

Emotional Development

Fear cannot be without hope nor hope without fear.
  —Spinoza, Ethics

motions are central to our lives. We all experience amusement, joy, and contentment, as well as anger, fear, and grief. To fully understand human development, we must understand how emotions develop.

[**Emotions** may be defined as subjective experiences acccompanied by physiological changes] (Candland, 1977; Lewis & Michalson, 1983; Sroufe, 1979a). Emotions affect all aspects of life. In discussing emotional development, we will recognize the complex interrelationships among emotional, cognitive, physical, and social development (Mandler, 1980). We begin by examining the biological bases of emotion. Then we will trace the course of emotional development during infancy and early childhood. Next we will focus on the normal development of emotions among children and adolescents. In the fourth section of the chapter, we will discuss emotional problems among developing children. Then we will examine some theoretical frameworks for understanding emotional development. The chapter closes with a review of the applications of research for helping children cope with fears and anger.

Biological Bases of Emotion

In order to fully understand emotional development, we must review briefly why we have emotions and how they operate. As we saw in Chapter 4, human beings have been shaped through the process of evolution. In this section, we will briefly review the evolution of emotion in our species. Then we will examine the physiological foundations of emotion.

An Evolutionary Perspective on Emotions

Although many scientists have focused on the role of instinct in emotinal behavior, Robert Plutchik, a developmental psychologist, has focused most strongly on the evolutionary basis of emotion. Plutchik (1980a, 1980b, 1983) proposes that emotions have been highly adaptive in human (and lower organism) survival.

441

Consider, for example, negative emotions (i.e., those usually considered unpleasant) such as anger or fear. During strong negative emotional reactions several physiological changes take place, including an increase in pulse rate, blood pressure, sweating, and secretion of hormones from the adrenal glands. In addition, blood vessels near the surface of the skin are constricted and the capacity of the lungs is increased. These changes, in essence, equip the human body to rapidly flee threatening situations or, if necessary, to engage in a struggle for survival.

The physiological changes that occur during powerful negative emotions, however, must be short-term. When negative emotions continue unabated over long periods of time (such as in situations of chronic tension or anxiety), the body suffers. Ulcers, hypertension, and heart disease are only some of the potential side effects of prolonged emotional stress. The human body is not equipped to remain in a highly "energized" state over long periods of time. Negative human emotions evolved as *short-term* physiological states that allow the human body greater strength, endurance, and resistance to damage when faced with threatening situations (Plutchik, 1983).

Our early ancestors lived in a harsh, untamed world. An encounter with a predator (stumbling into the presence of a large, irritated bear, for example) required strong reactions such as fleeing or fighting if survival was to occur. Millions of years of evolution resulted in natural selection of ancestors who had powerful emotional reactions. Those with weak emotional reactions did not survive threats and, hence, did not pass their genes along. Apparently, the ability to quickly become "energized"—ready to flee or fight—was an adaptive trait.

Since survival in threatening situations is an adaptive trait, we might wonder why we simply were not selected for greater size, strength, and endurance, rather than for emotional strength. The answer can be seen when we consider other aspects of emotion, particularly the highly adaptive function of positive emotions (those typically considered pleasant) (Plutchik, 1983). In particular, a mother's love for her infant makes it far more likely that she will protect it and make strong nurturing efforts. Similarly, babies who display very positive emotions toward their parents are more likely to be well cared-for than infants who reject their mothers.

Love, of course, is also adaptive in male–female pairings. Two people are far more likely to work toward caring for and protecting each other if they love each other. Further, when male and female parents cooperate in nurturing and protecting their children, they greatly increase the odds of their children's survival and, hence, the survival of their own genes.

On a broader level, positive emotions such as love, caring, and concern for others increase the possibility of successful social structures.

Biological Bases of Emotion   443

Early human beings could protect themselves, hunt, or gather food far more effectively as a group than as separate individuals. The evolution of positive emotions facilitated mutual cooperation and, thereby, our species' survival.

Our emotions, then, can be seen as part of our evolutionary legacy. Negative emotions helped our ancestors survive threats and help us respond to dangers today. Positive emotions allowed greater nurturance of our ancestors' babies and the development of social functioning. Today, positive emotions are critical in maintaining families and facilitating the functioning of larger social units.

The Physiological Basis of Emotions

One obvious aspect of emotions is the body's reactions. Nearly everyone, for example, has been anxious at one time or another about a job interview, taking a test, or making a presentation. You can probably remember your body's changes when you felt such anxiety: sweaty palms, a queasy stomach, thirst, a pounding heart, and, perhaps, trembling hands. How and why do these changes occur?

Figure 13-1 presents a simple model devised by Leshner (1977) for describing emotional responses. Leshner's model depicts some external stimulus as the cause for an emotional response. (We will see later that this is simplistic: Emotions also can be elicited by a variety of *internal* events). This stimulus is perceived and processed. The processing influences both physiological and behavioral responses that together determine the person's new state. For example, suppose a baby sees a stranger (i.e., the external stimulus is perceived). In Leshner's model, parts of the cognitive processing system identify this stimulus (i.e., the stranger) as a "to-be-feared" part of the environment. This determina-

FIGURE 13-1 Leshner's Model. Leshner's model presents a straightforward approach for describing emotional responses. *From Leshner, A. I. (1977). Hormones and emotions. In D.K. Candland, J.P. Fell, E. Keen, A.I. Leshner, R. Plutchik, and R.M. Tarpy (Eds.), Emotion. Belmont, California: Wadsworth. Used by permission of Wadsworth Publishing Co., Inc. and the author.*

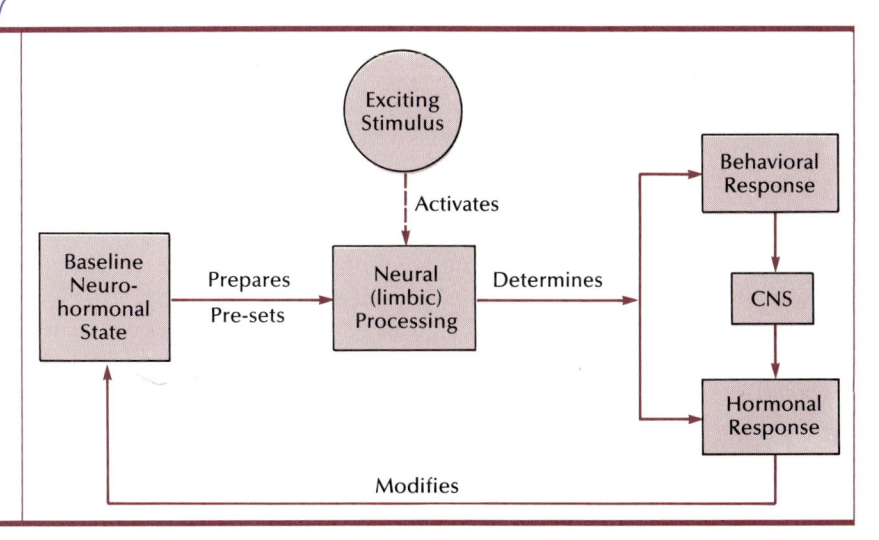

tion then activates the **limbic system** (the part of the brain involved in emotion), the central nervous system (CNS), and the endocrine system (see Chapter 7), bringing about physiological changes in the baby. Simultaneously, the baby responds with a set of behaviors (e.g., crying, turning toward the mother). This heightened level of emotion is the state in which the baby will respond to new stimuli (e.g., a frightened baby may cry at a minor provocation that a happy baby would ignore).

Even though our emotions are based on physiological functions, they are more than simple neural and hormonal reactions. Emotional development involves much more than physiological and neurological growth. It is a complex process intertwined with all other aspects of development. In the next section we will trace emotional development from birth to age 3.

Emotional Development in Infancy and Early Childhood

We have seen (see Chapter 7) that newborn babies are marvelously complex and capable of a large number of sophisticated actions. We also know, however, that the physical, perceptual, and cognitive capabilities of neonates are rudimentary compared to those of older children and adults.

What emotions do newborn babies have and how do these emotions change with time? Several recent reviews of the research on early emotional development (Brazelton, 1983; Izard et al., 1984; Sroufe, 1979a) have shown a striking consistency of findings on the emergence of the different aspects of emotions. Here, we will follow the lead of Sroufe (Motti, Cicchetti, & Sroufe, 1983; Sroufe, 1979a, 1979b; Sroufe & Wunsch, 1972) by organizing early emotional development into a series of seven stages. These stages are merely convenient benchmarks for considering early emotional development and do not represent a lockstep sequence. However, they do allow us to describe the typical emotional reactions of average infants and small children at different ages.

Birth to 1 Month: Insensitivity to Others' Emotions

In general, the first month of life is characterized by a lack of sensitivity to the emotional milieu. Neonates seem to be unaware of the emotional states of their parents (e.g., joy, sorrow) and there is little evidence that the emotions of others influence neonatal behavior (Brazelton, 1983). This lack of sensitivity to emotional stimulation is often considered to be an inborn phenomenon designed to protect newborns from overstimulation (Izard et al., 1984). However, an equally plausible explanation is the relatively unsophisticated state of cognitive development at this time (Mandler, 1980). That is, newborn babies have no knowledge or experience to draw on for reacting to the emotions of others.

The first month of babies' lives, however, is not unemotional, as any parent can verify. Babies respond to a wide range of aversive stimuli (e.g., loud noises, bright lights, a feeling of falling, empty stomachs, soiled diapers, errant safety pins) with crying, thrashing, and jerky movements of the arms and legs. Parents awakening in the middle of the night at the sound of a baby's cries are aware that some emotion is being expressed, although the form of the emotion is unclear.

Babies, however, rapidly develop generalized positive reactions (e.g., wiggling or "burrowing in" when hugged) and negative reactions (e.g., crying, fussing). As we will see later in the chapter, developmental psychologists disagree about the explanation for the appearance of new emotions (Buechler & Izard, 1983), but a clear pattern of increasing specificity does begin to emerge during the first month of life.

1 to 3 Months: Turning toward Others

The second stage of emotional development is characterized by turning toward the external world. During the second and third months of life, babies become very sensitive to others' emotions and begin to reflect the moods of those around them: smiling when smiled at, appearing stern in response to sad faces (Sroufe, 1979a). At this point in development, distress is a clearly distinguished emotional response that consists primarily of crying. Babies at this age, however, have little or no expression accompanying their crying. Further, despite stereotypes to the contrary, tears seldom accompany crying; real tears as a sign of emotion do not usually appear until the fourth or fifth month of life.

The crowning achievement of this second stage of emotional development is the appearance of the **social smile** (Sroufe, 1979a). The social smile is a "real" smile that is used by babies to convey their positive feelings in seeing others. Prior to about 6 weeks of age, smiles often do not seem related to pleasure or social interactions. The social smile, however, clearly is associated with people and pleasurable events (Murphy, 1983). By the age of 3 months, babies regularly react to faces and pleasant surprises with genuine smiles and real laughter.

3 to 6 Months: Positive Affect

During the **positive affect** ("affect" means feeling or emotion) **stage** there is a general awareness of the environment. In addition, 3- to 6-month-old babies can anticipate some aspects of their world. Of course, their anticipations are not always met, causing frustration and its resulting emotions, rage and wariness (Lewis & Michalson, 1983). This stage, however, is primarily characterized by positive emotions. At this point, the early fussiness of most babies is over and they are able to take some actions to avoid unpleasant situations (e.g., clamping the mouth tightly shut to keep out that dreadful oatmeal). Most important, the social smile and laughter tend to increase positive interactions with parents and other people. That is, a big smile is met by smiles and hugs from adults, which bring on more of the baby's smiles, and so on.

The social smile conveys positive feelings in seeing others.

The positive affect stage of babies' emotional development is one of the most pleasant times for parents. Play and vigorous stimulation evoke great pleasure in babies (and, of course, big smiles, laughter, and chortling). In fact, the mere presence of the parents can evoke highly visible pleasure among 3- to 6-month-old babies (Murphy, 1983). There are few things in life more pleasant than walking in the door to a baby's squeals of delight! Not surprisingly, positive affect on the part of babies begets positive affect on the part of parents: a cycle of highly pleasant emotional interactions characterize the stage of positive affect.

7 to 9 Months: Active Participation

The active participation stage of emotional development represents a continuation of social awakening (Sroufe, 1979a). During this stage babies begin to participate in social games and make real efforts to bring about social responses in others. "Peek-a-boo," "this little piggy," various kissing and hugging games, and a whole host of baby–parent interactions bring about highly pleasant emotional responses. More than participating, however, babies at this age begin to *initiate* social interchanges with parents, siblings, and even other babies. The active nature of emotional development also becomes clear when babies begin to explore parents' bodies (e.g., peeking in pockets, playing with buttons) and testing things in the environment (e.g., pushing the oatmeal off of a high chair tray and laughing at the outcome).

Emotional development during the active participation stage, however, is not limited to positive emotions. Six- to 9-month-old babies often show a hesitancy when presented with novel objects and they may show only somber faces to strangers; this is the beginning of fear of strangers. At this age babies also may be uncomfortable in strange surroundings, for example, refusing to eat in a neighbor's house or to nap on the baby bed at grandmother's house. Further, **separation anxiety,** a fear of being separated from the mother (or other well-known adults), typically begins during this stage.

Perhaps most importantly, during this stage babies begin actively seeking out stimulation leading to positive emotions and avoiding situations that might lead to negative emotions (Offer & Sabshin, 1984). By the end of the stage of active participation, the emotions of joy, surprise, fear, and anger are clearly delineated.

9 to 12 Months: Attachment

The fifth stage of emotional development is referred to as the **attachment stage** (a complete discussion of attachment and its importance to development appears in Chapter 14). Although babies still show a general tendency toward highly positive emotions at this time, the attachment stage is characterized by a very strong preoccupation with the primary caregiver. Wariness of strangers is now fairly strong, showing an increase from the mildly negative reactions during the previous stage.

The attachment stage can be viewed as a time in which babies pull back from the external world and focus primarily on the mother. At this time, babies seem to be highly possessive of their mothers. They may actively try to push other people away while holding tightly to their mothers. The stranger wariness also serves to focus babies on the well-known and the comfortable. More than a preoccupation with the primary caregiver and a wariness of strangers occurs during this stage, however. Feelings become more and more finely graduated and the communication of moods and feelings becomes much more effective.

12 to 18 Months: Practicing

In contrast to the cautious nature of babies during the attachment stage, the stage of **practicing** is characterized by an ebullient exploration and mastery of the inanimate environment (Sroufe, 1979a, pp. 27–28). The firm emotional base developed during the attachment stage allows babies to move away from the comfort of their mothers and to explore the world. In addition, wariness of strangers generally drops off considerably during this stage (Lamb, 1984), although some researchers have observed an additional peak of this wariness occurring at about 18 months (Scarr & Salapatek, 1970).

18 to 36 Months: Emergence of Self-Concept

The beginning of the seventh stage of emotional development is characterized by another pulling-back phase, as toddlers start to become aware of their separateness as persons. This beginning sense of self-identity or self-concept causes toddlers to want the safety and security

The three-year-old is a marvelously competent person, capable of a broad set of subtle emotional responses. Emotional development, however, is far from complete at this age.

of their mothers, but to need to explore the world independently to allow for the development of a separate self. Not surprisingly, many 2-year-olds swing back and forth between independent, nearly obstinate actions and dependent, baby-like behaviors. From the child's perspective, the world is not the safe place it once was. Yet the world must be independently experienced in order to allow for the development of the self (see Chapter 16).

By the end of the **self-concept stage**, a wide range of emotions, often with subtle nuances, is present. Several shades of positive emotion are available to 3-year-olds: love, joy, pride, contentment, and pleasure. Negative emotions (discussed in more detail later in the chapter) include fear, anxiety, anger, shame, and guilt (Murphy, 1983; Sroufe, 1979a). There are also the beginnings of **empathy**, which is the ability to infer and experience the feelings of others.

The 3-year-old is marvelously competent, capable of a broad set of subtle emotional responses. Emotional development, however, is far from complete at this age.

Emotional Development in Childhood and Adolescence

In the last section, we saw that by about the age of 30 months children are beginning to infer other people's emotional states and understand their own. As we might suspect, these abilities play an important role in later emotional development. In particular, children's increasing knowledge of *why* they and other people feel as they do is crucial (Thompson, 1986b; Weiner & Graham, 1984).

Consider the following situation:

> Ellen's fourth-grade teacher was asking the children in her room questions about a story they were to have read. Ellen had not read the story. When it was Ellen's turn to answer the teacher's question, she guessed at the answer and got it right. Ellen knew that the reason for her success was good luck. How do you think Ellen felt?
> a. stunned
> b. thankful
> c. surprised
> d. happy

If you look at the options presented above, you can see that they fall into two basic categories: **outcome-dependent** (D. happy, in this case) and those that require a more subtle understanding of the situation (A–C). These more subtle alternatives can be referred to as **causally linked**.

Outcome-dependent emotions are determined wholly by the *results* of some event such as feeling happy when a test is passed, a new toy is obtained, a question is answered correctly, a hug is received; or feeling sad when a toy is broken, a question is answered incorrectly, or a test is failed. Although all of us have such emotional reactions, they are relatively unsophisticated because they focus only on the outcome of events. Causally linked emotional responses center not just on outcomes but on *why* outcomes occur (Weiner, 1982; Weiner & Graham, 1984; Weiner, Kun, & Benesh-Weiner, 1980).

Imagine, for example, how you might feel if you were in Ellen's situation. You would probably feel happy, but wouldn't surprise or thankfulness be a more accurate description of your state? After all, luck accounts for the question being correctly answered. Likewise, let us suppose that you forget to study for your next test in this course (purely hypothetical, of course) and fail. You would probably feel sad (an outcome-dependent emotion), but more likely you would describe your emotional state as one of shame or anger (at yourself). Rather than simply feeling sad because of the outcome, it is likely that you would focus on the *cause* of the outcome: forgetting to study.

As development proceeds, a shift from outcome-dependent to causally linked emotions occurs in children's emotional reactions to events (Graham, 1982; Weiner & Graham, 1984; Weiner, Graham, Stern, & Lawson, 1982). In early childhood, emotions are outcome-dependent. Children are happy if the outcome is positive, sad if it is negative, or angry if their intentions are blocked. By middle childhood, however, the emphasis increasingly is on the causes of outcomes (e.g., hard work,

Research

Causal Attributions and Emotions

We might suspect a relationship between the age of children and the categories of emotions (outcome-dependent vs. causally linked) they choose in describing how they and others feel in various situations. In fact, a very clever study has shown that this is the case. Weiner and Graham (1984) presented situations such as the one we described for Ellen to three groups of participants: a middle childhood group (average age 6.4 years), a late childhood group (average age 10.4 years), and a group of adults. Some of these situations described positive outcomes (such as Ellen's), others described negative outcomes. In each instance, an outcome-dependent decision could be made or participants could choose the more sophisticated causally linked emotions. The use of outcome-linked emotions was found to decrease with age and the use of causally linked emotions increased (Weiner & Graham, 1984, p. 174). Similar results have been reported in studies by Thompson and Paris (1981) and Thompson (1986b).

Another study by Weiner (1980b) will help you get a direct sense of how causal attributions influence emotional reactions. Weiner (1980b) examined how causal attributions influenced college students' emotional reactions. The participants in this study were randomly assigned to one of three conditions and asked to read a description of a hypothetical event. The descriptions Weiner used (1980b, p. 677) are presented below:

1. At about 1:00 in the afternoon you are walking through the campus and a student comes up to you. He says that you do not know him, but that you are both enrolled in the same class and he has happened to notice you. He asks if you would lend him the class notes from the meetings last week. He indicates that he needs the notes because he skipped class to go to the beach.

2. At about 1:00 in the afternoon you are walking through campus and a student comes up to you. He says that you do not know him, but that you are both enrolled in the same class and he has happened to notice you. He asks if you would lend him the class notes from the

luck); by adulthood emotional reactions are primarily based on the causes of outcomes.

The change from outcome-dependent to causally linked emotional reactions is due largely to cognitive development. More than the continued differentiation of emotions we saw in the first 3 years of life, later emotional development depends heavily on children's increasing abilities to understand why things happen. As children's insights into events improve, their emotional reactions change. The 3-year-old who is told that his mother will not play with him may react with anger. A 6-year-old in the same situation may also react with anger. If the 6-year-old understands that her mother has a terrible headache, however, she may be angry but the anger is now likely to be tempered with pity. A 9-year-old who has his request denied may not experience anger at all; instead, disappointment coupled with pity for his mother's headache may be the reaction.

meetings last week. He indicates that he needs the notes because he was having difficulty with his eyes, a change in type of glasses was required, and during the week he had difficulty seeing because of eye-drops and other treatments.

3. At about 1:00 in the afternoon you are walking through the campus and a student comes up to you. He says that you do not know him, but that you are both enrolled in the same class and he has happened to notice you. He asks if you would lend him the class notes from the meetings last week. He indicates that he needs the notes because he was having difficulty with his eyes, a change in type of glasses was required, and during the week he had difficulty seeing because of eye-drops and other treatments. You notice that he is wearing especially dark glasses and has a patch covering one eye.

When the participants had finished reading the passage to which they were assigned, they were asked to imagine that the event had actually occurred and to describe their emotions toward the student trying to borrow class notes. (At this point, you might describe your own feelings about the three "note-borrowers.") Not surprisingly, the most positive emotions were generated by the last situation, in which the "note-borrower" was wearing very dark glasses and an eye-patch. The least positive emotions were generated by the "note-borrower" who had been to the beach.

The kinds of causal attributes made by the students in Weiner's study were fairly sophisticated with many expressing skepticism about the "note-borrower" with eye trouble ("Is he faking to get sympathy?") and others looking for hidden motives ("What does he really want?") in the "note-borrowers." Such sophisticated reasoning, of course, is common in adults but not in young children. As children develop, their abilities to make causal attributions improve apace with their cognitive development.

As adults, our emotional reactions typically are determined by how we understand situations. For example, we may feel anger if someone steals money from a store. If we find out that the thief is destitute and stealing in order to feed her children, however, it is much more likely that we would feel pity. In another instance, a person's pride in finding out that he or she is to be included in *Important People in America* may turn to anger if being listed in the book depends only on ability to pay the publisher.

Our analyses of situations for which we seek "why" answers are referred to as **causal attributions** (Weiner & Graham, 1984). As development proceeds, children's abilities to make causal attributions improve. As a result, emotional reactions depend increasingly on our interpretation of events rather than on the events themselves. As we will see, the pattern of emotional development in childhood and adolescence parallels that of cognitive development. In the following sec-

Fear

tions we will examine the development of fear, anger, jealousy, grief, and positive emotions and see how they follow the developmental trend of increased differentiation and sophistication.

By the age of 3, fears common in infancy (e.g., fear of strangers, unknown situations, bright flashes of light, a feeling of falling, loud noises) decrease, but fears of "imaginary creatures, the dark, and being alone or abandoned increase" (Jersild, 1968, p. 333). Although the basic work on age changes in fears was done many years ago (Jersild & Holmes, 1935), the general pattern of fears shifting from tangible and immediate situations to those requiring cognitive analyses still appears valid (Bauer, 1976).

During the preschool years, children increasingly understand the nature of their world and begin to see the possible implications of events. For example,

> A 4-year-old insisted that his father, not his mother, walk him to nursery school every day. After considerable questioning, he explained that many of his classmates "have no daddy living at home and I'm scared that will happen to me" (Brozan, 1983, p. 20).

Many early childhood fears may result from having some, but not enough, knowledge. In the previous example, it is clear that the boy understood and greatly feared the possibility that his father could leave home and not return. However, he probably did not understand the idea of divorce, the stable relationship between his own parents, and the extremely low likelihood that his own parents would separate. As another example, some children fear dogs, even though they have had little experience with them. In part, these children fear dogs because dogs are loud and (comparatively speaking) large and because the children know that some dogs bite. However, if the children knew more (e.g., as the result of having a gentle family dog), the fear might not appear at all or at least be more specific (e.g., being afraid of "bad" dogs).

Fears tend to become more realistic as children move through middle childhood and into adolescence. In 1968, Jersild was able to write that there is

> on the whole, a *decline* in fears relating to personal safety . . . There is also in general, a decline in the fear of animals . . . On the other hand, fears pertaining to school (including worries about grades, fears of teachers, stage fright) in general *increase* from age nine to about age twelve and a slight but uneven decline sets in thereafter. There is also . . . an increase in fears pertaining to social relationships and in fears classified as 'economic and political' including worries about money, allowances, getting jobs . . . (p. 335).

Although many of the general trends observed by Jersild still seem accurate, times have changed. In terms of personal safety, for example, research by Dabbs shows that "for New York city school children, the main fear is that they will be mugged—by other children" (cited in Brozan, 1983, p. 20). Similarly, Dabbs' work indicates that many elementary school-age girls fear rape.

A representative letter written by a 12-year-old girl to the House Select Committee on Children, Youth, and Families read as follows:

> It seems that there is no safe place anymore, even the home, where most murders and robberies are committed. We are afraid to be home alone because of this constant fear. Some children are even afraid of their parents. The divorced parent might kidnap their [sic] child or the sick parent might abuse them [sic] (Brozan, 1983, p. 20).

Fears of losing a parent through separation, divorce, or death have increased markedly in recent years to become the single most often named fear among preadolescents (Brozan, 1983). Another common fear that did not show up in early research on emotional development is the fear of nuclear war (see *Highlights*, p. 454).

Anger

As we have seen, 3-year-olds can experience anger, frustration, and rage. Research has shown that temper tantrums and other angry outbursts usually peak at about the age of 2 and decrease thereafter (Jersild, 1968; Goodenough, 1931; Walters, Pearce, & Dahms, 1957). This early anger is often manifested in crying, wailing, and hitting. It is, in a sense, a very unsophisticated anger precipitated solely by outcomes such as being hurt, having intentions blocked, and so on.

At about 3 years of age, anger becomes much more focused. That is, rather than crying, screaming, and indiscriminately hitting, children become much more oriented toward revenge. If a 4-year-old has a toy taken away by another child, he may lash out directly at the transgressor or get back at him by taking one of his toys away. In addition to the increase in retaliatory behavior, children from 3 to 5 also are more likely to threaten ("I'll break your toy," or "I'm gonna tell"), scold ("You're very mean," "That's not being nice"), insult ("You're yucky"), or use other verbalizations to express their anger (Jersild, 1968).

Not all attempts at retaliation, of course, are direct. Jersild (1968) has indicated that several forms of indirect revenge such as overturning furniture, engaging in forbidden behaviors (e.g., running into the street), or making comments such as "I wish I had a mother like Mary's" (1968, p. 368) are used by children. In some instances, indirect retaliation may be self-directed such as when children bite, scratch, or hit themselves (Jersild, 1968).

The shift in anger from fairly undirected to focused and retaliatory reflects changes in cognitive abilities. Sources of anger are identified

Highlights

Children's Fears of Nuclear War

Children have always had fears. Many contemporary fears are probably no different than those experienced by children thousands of years ago. Many children today, however, have a relatively new fear: fear of a nuclear holocaust. Recent data suggest that the concern may be deeper and more widespread than most adults had realized and that it is rapidly increasing (Beardslee & Mack, 1986; Yudkin, 1984).

In 1983, the U.S. House of Representatives Select Committee on Children, Youth, and Families was sufficiently concerned about the evidence of children's fears that they held hearings about the issue (Mirga, 1983). "It's scary to think about the world being destroyed, and nothing is left," testified 11-year-old Jessica. Ursell, age 16, said, "I think about the bomb just about every day now. It scares me about my future. I really want to have children and a family some day, but then I'd feel fear for them, too. It makes me wonder whether I should have kids at all."

John Mack, a psychiatrist at Harvard Medical School, told the committee that comments of this sort are not atypical. He summarized the results of a recent study commissioned by the American Psychiatric Association:

> Approximately 50 percent of the high-school-age students said nuclear advances had affected their thoughts about marriage and their plans for the future. A majority said nuclear advances affected their daily thinking and feeling. . . . There were vivid expressions of terror and powerlessness, grim images of nuclear destruction, doubt about whether they will ever have a chance to grow up, and an accompanying attitude of "live for now." Some expressed anger toward the adult generation that seemed to have so jeopardized their futures (Mirga, 1983, p. 13).

Children's knowledge of and feelings about nuclear war depend partly on their age. Young children who are aware of the issue are likely to view it in relatively personal terms, often with an emphasis on abandonment and isolation. Rosa, an 8-year-old quoted by the International Physicians for the Prevention of Nuclear War, says, "If I did survive, even if there was enough food I'd probably kill myself or just die of sadness because my family and all the people I love would die." Older children are more likely to see the broader issues involved. In 1982, more than one-third of a sample of high school seniors at 130 high schools around the country agreed with the statement, "Nuclear or biological annihilation will probably be the fate of all mankind within my lifetime" (Yudkin, 1984).

Recent studies of children in Belgium, Canada, Finland, Japan, the Middle East, New Zealand, the Soviet Union, Sweden, and Great Britain reveal similar fears. A study of Soviet children by Eric Chivian, John Mack, and their associates, sponsored by International Physicians for the

Prevention of Nuclear War and the Harvard Medical School Department of Psychiatry, involved interviews with a number of Soviet children. Sveta, age 11, told them, "I can imagine . . . how bombs fall on my village, and sometimes at night I cover myself with a blanket because I'm afraid." Elena, age 13, says that a nuclear war "will be absolutely terrible. . . . Everything, everything around will die." "The entire earth will become a wasteland," says 13-year-old Alexei.

How should adults respond to such fears? There seems to be agreement on several basic points (Engel, 1984; Myers-Walls & Fry-Miller, 1984). First, adults should encourage children to express their thoughts and fears and genuinely listen to them. Some children, especially young ones, may not express themselves directly, so we must be prepared to watch their play (e.g., war games) and read between the lines of what they say. Second, we should communicate our own thoughts and fears openly. Obviously, we cannot dismiss nuclear concerns as immature or irrational (comparable, say, to fear of ghosts). Nuclear war would very likely be at least as devastating as children imagine and is indeed a genuine possibility. This is a difficult issue for many adults to think about themselves, much less discuss with a child. Nevertheless, adults' inability to talk about this issue may be more frightening to a child than a frank discussion would be. Third, we should provide accurate information. For very young children, this may be a matter of correcting childish misconceptions, such as the idea that there is a nuclear bomb at home or school or that their own misbehavior could cause a nuclear war. For older children, there are an increasing number of books and nuclear war curricula aimed at educating them about the issues. Fourth, children need to know that many people are working to avoid nuclear war and that they too can be involved (e.g., by drawing pictures or writing letters to officials about their views). Such involvement gives children a feeling of control and helps avoid a sense of helplessness and despair.

The long-term effects of fear of nuclear war are unknown. Psychiatrist Eric Chivian suggests that the problem is potentially very serious: "What is it like to grow up without believing that you will? It's hard to expect kids who feel that way to work hard in school, develop deep relationships or do anything that has a future element" (Yudkin, 1984, p. 22). On the other hand, fear of the prospect of nuclear war may be a necessary first step to doing something about that possibility. As 14-year-old Denise Thomson (1984) writes:

> We must be international in thinking and not let differences of political ideology, religion, or thought deter us from the goal of peace. The records we keep as historians of our future must turn out to be false—their portrait of holocaust no more than a nightmare we had the misfortune to dream while wide awake.

and means of getting even are considered and tested. These are changes that require some basic analysis and planning skills. Consider the following example:

> Robert, a 5-year-old, wandered into the living room from his bedroom and looked out the window. He saw his friend Bill playing tag with another neighbor child. He then asked, "Dad, can I go over and play with Bill?" Robert's father, who was just taking the meat loaf out of the oven responded by saying, "No. It's time to get ready for supper. Go wash your hands." Robert responded, "But Dad . . ." "No," said his father. Robert then knocked his father's pipe rack (containing what Robert knew were his father's favorite pipes) on the floor, ran into his bedroom, and slammed the door.

In this scene, Robert clearly understood who the source of his anger was—his father. He retaliated by knocking down what he knew were his father's prize possessions. This action required the ability to foresee what would hurt his father and allow Robert to "get even." As childish as such an outburst of anger may seem, it is far more selective and sophisticated than the anger of a 2-year-old (Weiner, 1980a, 1980b).

From the approximate age of five through adolescence, causal attributions become increasingly important in determining anger. Whereas a 5-year-old may become angry with her parents for canceling picnic plans because of rain, a 7- or 8-year-old is likely to feel only frustration and disappointment because she is able to attribute the cause of the canceled plans to something beyond anyone's control. In general, as children's abilities to form causal attributions improve, anger responses become less frequent and more realistic (see Weiner & Graham, 1984). Emotional responses to negative outcomes continue, of course, but they are less and less outcome-oriented and tend to be causally linked instead.

Interestingly, the onset of puberty may be accompanied by temper tantrums not unlike those seen during early childhood. These tantrums, however, are not the result of an inability to understand situations and their causes. Rather, they often seem to be associated with understanding how little can be done to alter an event. For example, if a 13-year-old girl is excluded from a party by her peers at school, she may very well become angry. But what can be done right at that moment to rectify the situation? If no reasonable answer appears, a tantrum may at least work off some of the emotion.

Sources of anger also change during the course of development. Early in life, most anger results from parents' efforts to keep children on a schedule for eating, sleeping, going to the bathroom, and so on (Feshbach, 1956, 1970). From the age of 3 to about 6, the majority of anger responses tend to be directed at playmates (Feshbach, 1970).

During middle childhood, the focus is typically on peers and school situations, with teasing, sarcasm, unfair treatment, being bossed, having a brother or sister take something, and failed plans among the major sources of anger. During adolescence, anger is still most likely to be centered on school and social issues. In addition, unfair accusations, unwelcome advice, being contradicted, failure, and the interruption of typical activities (e.g., interrupted sleep or study) also bring about anger (Jersild, 1968).

Another change often seen during development, as we mentioned earlier, is the shift away from physical manifestations of anger (hitting, etc.) to verbal attacks. As cognitive abilities become more sophisticated among older children and adolescents, revenge is more likely to take the form of sharp sarcasm and ridicule. Further, planning for revenge becomes more evident as adolescents bide their time waiting for the proper moment to ridicule or humiliate the person who is the source of their anger (Jersild, 1968). The shift from physical to verbal expressions of anger seems to vary somewhat between the sexes with boys remaining more physical throughout development than girls (Jersild, 1968).

Jealousy

Jealousy is a complex emotional state involving elements of anger, self-pity, grief, dejection, and fear (Jersild, 1968; Rosenhahn & Seligman, 1984). Children become jealous if they feel threatened when attention or affection they want for themselves is bestowed on someone else. Apparently, jealousy (particularly of siblings) first appears at about 18 months (Sewall, 1930; Neisser, 1951). From then until school age, jealousy is most often shown in relations between siblings. Later, during middle and late childhood, the frequency of jealousy decreases and its focus broadens (e.g., a child may be jealous of classmates and acquaintances in addition to siblings). During adolescence, jealousy over boyfriends and girlfriends appears. Finally, among well-adjusted adults, jealousy becomes a fairly uncommon emotional response (Rosenhahn & Seligman, 1984).

The role of causal attributions in jealousy can be seen in the changes between middle childhood and adulthood. During middle childhood (and earlier) jealousy is outcome-oriented; children respond to the fact that someone else is receiving the attention or affection they think they should have. Hence, a child may respond to the attention a sister gets during an illness by feigning illness herself or engaging in other behaviors likely to gain attention. Such jealous behavior becomes less frequent as children move to causally linked emotional responses. Where a 6-year-old may feel jealous of the attention his sick sister is getting, a 10-year-old is much more likely to understand the cause of this attention and respond with pity (Weiner & Graham, 1984).

During adolescence, there seems to be an increase in jealousy, centered on members of the opposite sex—the "desire for exclusive possession of another's affection" (Jersild, 1968, p. 377). In the past, increases in jealousy (and, as we saw earlier, anger) were often taken as evidence for "heightened emotionality" among adolescents. It seems, however, that the increase of adolescent jealousy and anger is not due to an overall increased tendency to be emotional. Instead, increased jealousy and anger occur because adolescents have entered a new social milieu for which their social skills are still insufficient. When a 16-year-old boy is jealous because his girlfriend talks to another boy, it is an indication that he does not yet understand how mature social relations operate: Causal attributions in such situations must await further social development.

Grief

Grief refers to a sense of loss. We all experience grief at the loss of loved ones and, to a lesser extent, at the loss of pets or favorite objects. Grief is predominately sadness, but it also contains elements of fear, anger, and pity (Malatesta & Izard, 1984). Grief has not been widely studied in development (Murphy, 1983), although more attention is now being given to the related emotional state of depression (Kaslow & Rehm, 1983; Schultebrand & Raskin, 1977).

Grief appears early in life, as can be seen in "the young infant's crying at loss of his or her bottle or of a favorite toy" (Murphy, 1983, p. 22). Some authors have suggested that separation anxiety may be an early form of grief (e.g., Murphy, 1983). True grief requires an understanding of the loss and its consequences. Such an understanding, however, as in the case of the death of a loved one, takes sophisticated cognitive abilities. It does seem clear that by the age of 3, a powerful, if simple, form of grief accompanies the loss of a parent or sibling (Schultebrand & Raskin, 1977).

Grief seems to be influenced by causal attributions: for example, when a family grieves at the death of a loved one who has died in a car accident. If they discover that this person was intoxicated while driving, the family's grief may become interwoven with anger. As another example, the family of a 90-year-old great-grandparent who is suffering from very painful cancer may experience relief or even gratitude mixed with grief when the person dies. Helping a child understand the suffering involved in the illness and emphasizing that the person lived a long, productive life would likely temper the grief.

Positive Emotions

The development of positive emotions after the age of 3 has not received a great deal of research attention. One reason for this lack of research, of course, is that no one complains about being happy. Nonetheless, there has been some work on age trends in positive emotions.

By late childhood, events such as extracurricular activities are frequently cited as sources of pleasure.

In early childhood, pleasant emotions are largely outcome-based (holidays, birthdays, and other festive occasions) (Weiner & Graham, 1984). Between the ages of 6 and 9, causally linked positive emotions become more frequent, but Jersild (Jersild, 1968; Jersild & Tasch, 1949) found that the primary sources of positive emotions were still outcome-oriented. By late childhood, other kinds of events such as being with a friend or the return of a family member after an absence, are more frequently cited sources of pleasure. In early adolescence, there is a marked drop in citing festive occasions as the source for happiness. At this age, outcomes are less important determinants of emotional states than causal attributions. Relationships with peers, school-related activities, and extracurricular activities become more frequent sources of pleasant emotions. Older adolescents tend to emphasize recreation, travel, self-improvement (including educational successes), relations with peers and family, and events benefitting others as sources of pleasure (Jersild, 1968; Jersild & Tasch, 1949).

Thus the development of positive emotions follows the trends of cognitive and social development. Early in childhood, special occasions are important sources of pleasure, with the primary focus on the outcome of the event. Birthdays, for example, have myriad meanings to adults, but for most American 6-year-olds they certainly mean presents, candy, cookies, or other tangible outcomes. By late adolescence, birthdays are evaluated far differently. Outcomes do not lose their ability to give us pleasure (it is always nice to receive a birthday present). Their effects, do, however, become tempered by an increasing understanding of the significance of events.

Emotional Problems during Development

In the last section, we traced the course of emotional development followed by average children. Unfortunately, some children experience severe fears; some seem unable to cope with even minor frustrations; and still others are much less happy than their peers. Further, there are some children whose emotional reactions differ so much from most children that we identify them as having emotional problems.

Phobias

Fears are a normal part of emotional development. In fact, fear can be a very reasonable and healthy response to environmental threats (Rosenhahn & Seligman, 1984). For example, if you decide to wash some second-story windows, you should be afraid of falling and take reasonable precautions to keep that from happening.

Not all fears, however, are rational or realistic. **Phobias** are fears strongly out of proportion to the actual threat (Rosenhahn & Seligman, 1984). Phobias do not seem reasonable or rational to observers and may become severe enough to interfere with day-to-day life. Morris and Kratochwill (1983, pp. 54–55) provide the following example of a phobia in a 6-year-old girl:

> When Mary was 6 years old, her parents decided to have an alarm system installed . . . Mary asked her parents many questions concerning the new alarm system—especially . . . why it had to be turned on at night. Her parents explained to her about . . . recent robberies in the neighborhood . . . The first night after the alarm was installed, there was a false alarm at about 2:00 A.M. The alarm woke up Mary and her parents. Mary began yelling and crying, and Mr. and Mrs. Frank started walking nervously throughout the house. After deciding that it was a false alarm, they returned to Mary to comfort her. To help Mary fall back to sleep, Mrs. Frank allowed Mary to keep the light on next to her bed for the whole night. This continued for the next several days, with Mary going to bed at night with her lamp on next to her bed.
>
> Whenever Mrs. Frank tried to have Mary go to sleep without her lamp on, she would cry and become upset. As a result, for the next three months she was allowed to sleep at night with her lamp on in her bedroom—afraid of being in her room alone when it was dark. Her fear of the dark was found to transfer to movie theaters and to going out on Halloween night (activities that she had always previously enjoyed doing). She also became

Emotional Problems during Development   461

fearful of sleeping at a friend's house, because she was concerned that she could not have a light on at night.

These behaviors on Mary's part continued for another two months, until her parents sought professional help.

In Mary's case, the fear was not reasonable and curtailed many activities she had previously enjoyed. About 5 to 7 percent of all children experience phobias or severe fears at some time (Graziano & De-Giovanni, 1979; Morris & Kratochwill, 1983. Although there are many different types of phobias (e.g., blanchophobia is fear of snow; triskaidekaphobia is fear of the number 13), most are fairly rare. The most common phobias seen in the United States are fears of crowded places (including schools), open places, dealing with other people, specific animals (spiders, snakes, dogs), specific situations (e.g., dark places, enclosed areas, high places), specific substances (e.g., dirt, fecal matter), and illness, injury, or death (Rosenhahn & Seligman, 1984).

Psychosomatic and Psychophysiological Disorders

Generally, **psychosomatic** and **psychophysiological disorders** may be defined as conditions in which the body or body functions are affected adversely by the person's emotional state (American Psychiatric Association, 1980). Although there are a wide range of such disorders, here we will restrict ourselves to briefly describing those most common in childhood and adolescence: eating disorders, eliminative disorders, and asthma.

The most serious form of eating disorder among adolescents is **anorexia nervosa**.

> This disorder is characterized by a refusal to eat and extreme weight loss (at least 25 percent of original body weight) without any organic causes . . . It poses a grave danger to the patient, with estimates of mortality as high as 15 percent (Dally, 1969). The onset of this disorder is typically during adolescence with most cases occurring by young adulthood. It occurs most frequently among females . . . (Siegel, 1983, pp. 258–259).

The causes of anorexia nervosa are unclear (Rosenhahn & Seligman, 1984) and some researchers question whether it is a psychophysiological disorder. Some writers, however, have argued that our society's overemphasis on thinness (especially for females) is at least partly to blame for the increasing number of anorexic patients today (Rosenhahn & Seligman, 1984).

There is, however, an intense preoccupation with body size and body image among anorexics, coupled with a great deal of anxiety associated with eating and getting fat. About 1 in 200 girls between the ages 12 and 18 suffer from anorexia nervosa. A related disorder, **bulimia**, also affects girls primarily and is similar to anorexia nervosa in that bulimarexics are overly concerned with their body image. It differs

CHAPTER 13 Emotional Development

A victim of anorexia nervosa being weighed by a psychotherapist at Dieter's Counseling Service, N.Y.C.

from anorexia in that it is characterized by cycles of gorging followed by purges of vomiting or using laxatives. While not having the mortality rate of anorexia, bulimia is a serious disorder that can cause irreparable damage to the digestive system and teeth.

Elimination disorders typically are found in early to late childhood and, while frustrating and embarrassing, are not dangerous. **Enuresis** involves the involuntary release of urine at an inappropriate time in the absence of any organic cause (Siegel, 1983). All children wet their beds or lose control of their bladders at some time or another. Enuresis does not refer to such common "accidents." It is diagnosed only after children are 3–4 years of age and when there is a *consistent* pattern of inappropriate wetting over a period of time. About 20 percent of children wet the bed at the age of 5 and about 10 percent at the age of 10. Enuresis is twice as common in boys as it is in girls (Siegel, 1983). The exact cause is unclear. However, about 10 percent of children who have trouble with bladder control suffer from some biological problem (Siegel, 1983). Anxiety seems to be associated with a majority of the remaining cases.

A much less common elimination disorder is **encopresis**. "Encopresis is defined as any voluntary or involuntary passages of feces that results in soiled clothing or occurs in a socially unacceptable place. This disorder occurs beyond the age of 3 or 4 and in the absence of organic pathology" (Siegel, 1983, p. 270). Encopresis is also associated with anxiety and typically occurs in early to middle childhood and primarily affects boys. It is diagnosed only when there is a *consistent*, long-term pattern of inappropriate bowel movements.

Asthma is the third disorder we will discuss. Although it may seem very far removed from eating or eliminative disorders, at least one-third of all asthma cases are due to emotional stress (the remainder are caused by allergies or infections) (Weiner, 1977).

> Asthma is characterized by periodic difficulty in breathing because of the constriction of the bronchial passages of the lungs . . . Wheezing, coughing, gasping for breath, and, during a severe attack, a sensation of suffocation and tightening of the chest are common symptoms . . . Hospitalization and emergency medical treatment may be required during prolonged episodes of an asthma attack (Siegel, 1983, pp. 275–276).

Asthma typically begins before the age of 10 and affects about twice as many boys as girls. When asthma is due to emotional stress, it seems to be a byproduct of the child–parent relationship (Rosenhahn & Seligman, 1984). The effectiveness of anxiety-reducing psychological treatments in countering asthma indicates a strong link between emotional stress and asthma attacks (Siegel, 1983). Although problems such as enuresis and asthma may result from emotional stress, emotional problems are not always the cause. In fact, enuresis and asthma, rather than being an *outcome* of emotional problems, may instead be the *cause* of emotional difficulties. Readily available techniques based on classical conditioning are highly effective in many cases.

Depression and Suicide

Depression. **Depression** can be defined broadly as an all-pervading sense of loss. It is the single most commonly reported emotional disturbance among adults, with one in three people suffering from clinical (i.e., needing treatment) depression at some time in their lives (Rosenhahn & Seligman, 1984). Whereas once it was thought that depression occurred only among adults, it is becoming clear that it is a serious problem among children and adolescents (Kaslow & Rehm, 1983). Depression is characterized by very low moods (primarily sadness) and the loss of enjoyment of once-pleasurable activities. Further, children suffering from depression think of themselves in very negative terms (e.g., worthless, guilty). Depressed children also lose their motivation to accomplish things and, in severe cases, may suffer from sleep problems, loss of weight, and lack of energy (Rosenhahn & Seligman, 1984).

The causes of depression in childhood and adolescence—as in adulthood—are not clearly understood. Apparently, however, it may be the result of a bodily disorder, stressful life events, or a combination of the two. The most commonly cited stressful events leading to depression are loss of a parent through death, separation, or divorce, loss of a sibling (see Turkington, 1984), rejection by a loved one, failure at school, and physical illness. Among adults, women are twice as likely as men to suffer from depression. Among children and adolescents, no clearcut data point to differences between the sexes.

We all experience depression from time to time. For example, the high school boy who does poorly on a history test the same day his girlfriend breaks up with him may feel very low for a few days. Similarly, the 9-year-old who finds out that his family is moving to another town may feel blue for several days as he contemplates the loss of friends. Such brief periods of low mood are not diagnosed as clinical depression.

Suicide. Depression must be taken seriously. Of all emotional problems, "it is depression that most frequently results in irreversible harm: death by suicide" (Rosenhahn & Seligman, 1984, p. 349). Suicide is the second leading cause of death among high school and college-aged people and it is a significant, though not clearly documented, cause of death among children (McKnew, Cytryn, & Yahraes, 1983).

The overall rate of suicide among adolescents has increased dramatically in the past 30 years, having reached a level of nearly 20 per 100,000 among males (*Science News*, 1984). The rate among females is lower, at about 5 or 6 per 100,000. Available data suggests that the difference between males and females is due to the methods they choose: Males are far more likely to shoot or hang themselves, crash an automobile, or jump from a building. Females, in contrast, are more apt to employ drugs, poisons, or wrist slitting—techniques that allow for a greater chance of survival. When *attempted* suicides are considered, however, far more girls than boys try to take their own lives. Although no clearcut data are available, estimates suggest that as many as 2 in 100 children and adolescents attempt suicide at some time (McKnew et al., 1983).

Precipitating events (e.g., the breakup of a romance, a pregnancy, the loss of a loved one) often seem to account for suicide. However, they are usually only "the straw that breaks the camel's back." The majority of adolescents who attempt suicide suffer from depression, are alienated from their parents, and suffer overwhelming feelings of loss, hopelessness, and isolation (McKnew et al., 1983).

If a child has mentioned suicide or seems depressed (persistent low mood, appetite disturbance, sleep disturbance, loss of enjoyment of normal activities, feelings of worthlessness) professional help should be sought. Severe depression is not something that parents should attempt to treat themselves; a mental health professional must be involved in the process. In a later section, we discuss guidelines for seeking professional help.

Autism

Autism is characterized by gross impairment in interpersonal relationships and communication (Rosenhahn & Seligman, 1984). Further, autistic children have bizarre reactions to their environment. Apparently, they are uninterested in people and do not form attachments. In infancy, this is seen in a continued failure to cuddle, an avoidance of eye contact, and a general aversion to affection and touching. Language may not develop in autistic children; if it does, it is often **echolalic**, or the simple repeating (echoing) of what is said to them. In its most severe form, autism is a shutting out of the world and the people in it (see Schriebman, Charlop, & Britten, 1983).

Autism occurs in about 2 to 4 cases per 10,000 children (Rosenhahn & Seligman, 1984). Despite its rate of occurrence and the amount of research devoted to the problem, its causes are poorly understood. Theories designed to account for autism have stressed the emotional climate in the child's home and biological abnormalities. That our theoretical understanding of autism is still crude can be seen in the fact that the treatment of autism has not been highly successful. Only 1 in 6 autistic children grow up to be able to hold down a job; even these people are usually socially handicapped (Lotter, 1978).

Hyperactivity

Hyperactivity is not, in the strictest sense, an emotional problem. However, it causes enough difficulties for parents, teachers, peers, siblings, and the child that a brief description seems appropriate. Hyperactivity is characterized by inappropriately high levels of activity accompanied

Autistic children appear uninterested in people and do not form attachments.

by a low attention span and impulsive behavior. Typically, parents and teachers describe hyperactive children as not listening, not completing their work, easily distracted, unable to sit still, and "into everything."

Boys suffer from hyperactivity far more often than girls. About 3 to 5 percent of school-age children are diagnosed as hyperactive (Barkley, 1983). The causes of hyperactivity are unclear, but the fact that the vast majority of children outgrow hyperactivity and that both chemical and psychological treatments are effective suggests that the causes of hyperactivity are likely to be linked to both the child's social environment and physical state (Barkley, 1983).

Theoretical Perspectives on the Development of Emotions

To this point, we have reviewed the biological basis of emotions, described the development of emotions from birth through adolescence, and examined problems in emotional development. As yet, we have not dealt directly with theoretical underpinnings for our understanding of emotional development. In this section, we will examine several different theoretical positions and see how each contributes to our overall understanding. We will begin our review with an accounting of differentiation theory, the theoretical perspective that has been implicit in our previous discussion.

A Differentiation Theory of Emotional Development

The best known theory of emotional development is **differentiation theory**. Originally proposed by Bridges in 1932, differentiation theory has been elaborated by several researchers (Sroufe, 1976). In general, differentiation theory "holds that by a process of differentiation the separate emotions derive from a single emotion or arousal state" (Izard & Buechler, 1980, p. 173). That is to say that all the emotions experienced by adults are the result of the differentiation of a **generalized excitement response** present in newborns.

From this perspective, emotions quickly differentiate into generalized pleasant and unpleasant emotional responses. The generalized unpleasant emotional response then further differentiates into rage, frustration, anger, fear, and so on. Although the original version of differentiation theory has been criticized (Izard & Buechler, 1980), recent theorists (Sroufe, 1979a) have reemphasized its importance.

In particular, Sroufe (1979a) has argued that emotional development depends on cognitive development, and he has used Piaget's stages (see Chapter 8) as benchmarks in exploring the unfolding of emotions. In a somewhat similar fashion, we have seen that Weiner (1980) and Thompson (1986b) have employed the concept of causal attributions to deal with emotional development in childhood and adolescence.

The argument that emotional development proceeds through differentiation as a result of cognitive development seems very reasonable. In addition, of course, physical and motor development (see Chapter 7) are also involved closely. That is, as the CNS and endocrine systems develop more and more completely, responses to situations can become more differentiated and sophisticated.

There are, however, several alternative theoretical views of emotional development. Differentiation theory is well accepted but it is only one viewpoint. We will begin our exploration of alternative theoretical views by reviewing a learning theory approach, behaviorism.

Behavioral Views of Emotional Development

As we saw in Chapter 2, behavioral psychology focuses on observable events, what children do and say. It is the study of behavior as it interacts with the environment. In terms of emotions, behaviorism emphasizes how emotional responses are affected by elements of the environment. To understand fully how behavioral psychologists see the development of emotions, it is necessary for us to examine three different behavioral traditions: early behaviorism, contemporary behaviorism, and social learning theory.

Early Behaviorism. The roots of behaviorism are found in the pioneering work of Ivan Pavlov, a Russian physiologist, and John B. Watson, an American psychologist. Both stressed a form of learning that has come to be called **classical conditioning.**

Classical conditioning involves the pairing of a **neutral stimulus** (a stimulus that has little, if any, effect on behavior) with an **eliciting stimulus** (a stimulus that brings forth an unlearned, reflexive response) until the neutral stimulus by itself acquires the ability to elicit the reflexive response. A classical conditioning view of the development of emotions assumes that emotions are reflexive behaviors (i.e., innate and unlearned) brought forth by specific eliciting stimuli (e.g., a loud noise causes a reflexive fear response in infants).

Pavlov began his work on classical conditioning with a very simple eliciting stimulus, meat powder given to dogs. Meat powder, of course, elicits the reflexive response of salivation. What Pavlov did was to pair a neutral stimulus (e.g., the sound of a buzzer) with the meat powder. After several pairings, Pavlov observed that his dogs would salivate to the sound of the buzzer alone, although no meat powder was provided.

A diagram of the process of classical conditioning appears below:

Step 1: An unconditioned (eliciting) stimulus elicits a response.

> Unconditioned stimulus (meat powder) → Unconditioned (reflexive) response (salivation)

Step 2: A neutral stimulus is paired with the unconditioned stimulus.

> Neutral stimulus (buzzer) + Unconditioned stimulus (meat powder) → Unconditioned response (salivation)

Step 3: After several pairings, the neutral stimulus becomes a conditioned stimulus, eliciting the response on its own.

Conditioned stimulus (formerly the neutral stimulus) (buzzer) → Conditioned (reflexive) response (salivation)

Later research by John B. Watson built on Pavlov's ideas by demonstrating that fear could be conditioned in small children. In his classic book, *Conditioning of Fear Responses* (1919), Watson described the conditioning of fear in an 11-month-old boy, "Little Albert." Essentially, Watson paired a stimulus (i.e., loud noise) that produced a fear response with the presentation of a white rat (i.e., a neutral stimulus that had not caused Little Albert fear prior to the experiment). Not surprisingly, after a few trials Little Albert reacted to white rats (and other, white fuzzy things) in the absence of loud noises with the same fear response: Little Albert had learned a fear.

As useful as classical conditioning is for describing the formation of some specific fears, this theory has weaknesses as an explanation for emotional development. First, although Watson claimed that several different emotions could be classically conditioned (Watson, 1919), later work has provided little evidence to support his views. Second, the formation of fears is often a far more complex process than simple classical conditioning (Rosenhahn & Seligman, 1984). Despite classical conditioning's considerable insight into how some fears are formed (and, perhaps most important, into the treatment of fears), it is too limited to do more than hint at the processes that underlie emotional development.

Contemporary Behaviorism. **Contemporary behaviorism** recognizes the importance of classical conditioning but places its primary emphasis on *voluntary* rather than reflexive behavior. B. F. Skinner, a central figure in the formation of contemporary behaviorism, has argued that most behaviors are controlled by events that precede and follow them, a process called **operant conditioning.** According to this view, emotional behaviors are thought to begin as reflexive responses to the environment, but they are also seen as becoming voluntary behaviors.

Skinner postulated that behaviors are strengthened by some consequences (called **reinforcers**) and weakened by others (called **punishers**). Further, children learn to react to different situations on the basis of whether behaviors are likely to be reinforced or punished. That is, a situation may serve as a "signpost" that a specific behavior is likely to be reinforced (an S_D—"ess-dee," in behavioral parlance), while another stimulus may signal that a specific behavior is likely to be punished (an S_Δ—"ess-delta"). These S_Ds and S_Δs do not cause reflexes in the way that eliciting stimuli do. Rather, they are cues that certain voluntary behaviors will be reinforced or punished (e.g., a red traffic light is an S_D for stopping your car but an S_Δ for accelerating).

For example, a 3-year-old sitting in a grocery cart may be denied his request for candy. The boy may recognize this situation, however, as one in which a temper tantrum will be reinforced. That is, having a request denied is an S_D for temper tantrums: In the past his parents have given in to his outbursts as a means of "quieting him down." The same child may be denied a request for candy at his grandparents' home but recognize that this situation is an S_Δ for temper tantrums: His grandparents do not give in to temper tantrums.

Three additional concepts central to operant theory are generalization, discrimination, and extinction. **Generalization** refers to the performance of a behavior in a setting other than the one in which it was originally learned. For example, if the boy described above starts to attend a preschool, his tantrums likely will generalize. That is, he is likely to try temper tantrums as a means of responding to denied requests at school. After all, they work at home, why shouldn't they work at school? He may, however, learn that they do not get him anywhere at school (his teachers have seen a great number of tantrums and ignore them). If he then learns to have tantrums only at home and not at school (because he is not reinforced for them at school), we say that **discrimination** (distinguishing among situations and behaving differently in the presence of each) will have occurred. Finally, if the parents learn to ignore the tantrums completely (withholding all reinforcement from them), the tantrums will become extinct. **Extinction** is the cessation of a response due to the removal of reinforcement.

Despite its strengths, operant conditioning, like classical conditioning, is too limited to deal with the broad scope of emotional development. Emotions seem to be learned through other mechanisms. One behavioral approach that has attempted to deal with other means of learning emotional responses is social learning theory.

Social Learning Theory: Social Influences on Emotion. As we saw in Chapter 5, **social learning theory** goes beyond operant theory by positing that a great deal of learning occurs through the imitation of models. Many developmentalists agree that imitation plays a role in how children learn to express emotions (Buck, 1983; Cicchetti & Hesse, 1983; Harlow & Mears, 1983; Plutchik, 1983).

Pawlby, for example, reports a wide variety of emotion-related actions that are imitated by infants, including smiling, frowning, laughing, and pursing lips. More than simply imitating the gross actions of adults, however, small children actively imitate the behavioral nuances involved in emotional expression (Plutchik, 1983). For example, one of the authors was attempting to remove the blade from a lawn mower one summer when his hand slipped and he smacked his knuckles into the mower's side. With his usual aplomb, he jumped up and down, tightened his hands into fists, cursed a few times, kicked the mower,

Cross cultural studies show that the facial expression of different emotions is innate. We don't have to speak her language to know that the girl with the cymbals is happy.

and then muttered some expletives under his breath. Only after his display of immature behavior did he notice a very wide-eyed 4-year-old watching him. After apologizing to his daughter for "acting badly," he thought no more of the episode until later in the day when the 4-year-old and a 6-year-old neighbor were arguing over who would use the backyard swing. As the author watched, his daughter lost the swing; she proceeded to jump up and down, clench her fists, utter some very familiar curses, kick the swing, and walk off muttering under her breath. Her means of expressing anger apparently had been learned in one observation. The father, incidentally, spent the next several days talking to his daughter about "how to act when angry."

Despite the fact that imitation plays a role in the expression of emotion, a great deal of cross-cultural research seems to show that facial expression of different emotions is innate (Ekman, 1972, 1973; Ekman & Friesen, 1971, 1975; Ekman, Sorenson, & Friesen, 1969; Gnepp & Hess, 1986; Russell & Bullock, 1986). In the experiments by Ekman and his colleagues, people from different cultures are shown photographs of facial expressions and are asked to identify the emotions expressed in each instance. Surprisingly, there is a high rate of agreement across very divergent cultures. In fact, in the most striking of these studies (Ekman & Friesen, 1971), people from New Guinea who had never seen movies or television, spoke no English, and had almost no contact with other cultures could identify the emotions expressed in photographs of Americans (with the exception of distinguishing fear and surprise) at the same level as American college students (see Table 13-1).

TABLE 13-1 Judgments of Emotion in Five Literate Cultures

Percentage Agreement in How Photograph Was Judged across Cultures

	United States (N=99)	Brazil (N=40)	Chile (N=119)	Argentina (N=168)	Japan (N=29)
	97% Happiness	95% Happiness	95% Happiness	98% Happiness	100% Happiness
	92% Disgust	97% Disgust	92% Disgust	92% Disgust	90% Disgust
	95% Surprise	87% Surprise	93% Surprise	95% Surprise	100% Surprise
	84% Sadness	59% Sadness	88% Sadness	78% Sadness	62% Sadness
	67% Anger	90% Anger	94% Anger	90% Anger	90% Anger
	85% Fear	67% Fear	68% Fear	54% Fear	66% Fear

From Ekman, P. (1973). Cross-cultural studies of facial expression. In P. Ekman (Ed.), Darwin and Facial Expression. New York: Academic Press, p. 207.

Since facial expressions for basic emotions seem to be consistent across cultures, imitation must then be limited to ancillary elements of emotional expression such as kicking inanimate objects or muttering curse words. However, imitation plays a different kind of role in the development of emotions when we consider the *objects* of children's emotions.

For example, the daughters of one of the authors exhibit highly positive emotional reactions toward baseball. They like to play baseball, go to games, watch games on television, read about baseball, and talk about it. Of course, there is no innate reason for anyone to like baseball (despite the protestations of true fans). These girls have acquired their positive feelings about baseball primarily because both their father and mother like baseball and have modeled their enjoyment. Of course, reinforcement also plays a role. The imitation is fairly obvious (e.g., shouting at the umpire), but so is the reinforcement. For instance, the parents are more likely to agree to a family excursion to a ball game than a movie; more willing to go outside and play with the kids when baseball is involved; and enjoyable interactions about baseball are plentiful. ("You're right. They should have put on the hit-and-run".) In another family, soccer, tennis, handball, or any number of activities might be the source of positive affect.

The objects of negative affect also can be acquired through much the same process. For instance, parents who are prejudiced against a

"Now remember—roar just as you leap.... These things have some of the greatest expressions."

particular ethnic or racial group may model their feelings and reinforce the expression of similar emotions in their children. Similarly, parents, who model specific fears and reinforce fear responses in their children are fostering the development of specific emotional reactions. Of course, as we saw in Chapter 5, social influences on development go far beyond the microsystem of home to include the school, community, subculture, and culture. All of these elements of children's social environments contribute to the development of emotions.

When we combine the behavioral traditions of classical conditioning, operant theory, and social learning theory, we have a reasonably effective perspective from which to understand the learning of emotions. Still lacking, however, is an exploration of the role of cognition.

Cognition and Emotions

George Mandler (1980) has put forward the major cognitive theory of emotion. In this view, emotions are seen as the coming together of biological responses, "cognitive analyses of the current state of the world, and interactions with other cognitive processes . . ." (Mandler, 1980, p. 222). Generally, Mandler is an information processing theorist (see Chapters 8 and 10) who has emphasized the relationship of physiological and cognitive reactions.

From Mandler's perspective, emotional states arise in one of two ways. First, an autonomic nervous system (ANS) response interrupts thinking. The person then becomes aware of her internal reactions and evaluates them and the current environment. This evaluation involves matching the current situation to previous experiences. When a correct match is made, the person then assigns herself an emotional state and behaves accordingly. This process usually occurs so rapidly that it is unnoticed. For example, if someone elbows you during a "pick-up" basketball game, you have a rapid ANS response and your cognitive processes almost immediately determine that you are in a state of anger.

At times, however, the cognitive evaluation component that Mandler speaks of can be seen clearly. For example, most of us have felt a general sense of unease from time to time and have had difficulty identifying the source of our emotion. In such situations, we may spend considerable time and effort trying to understand our feelings (e.g., "Could I be anxious because finals are coming up?" or "Maybe I'm irritated because Jane hasn't returned my notes").

Sometimes emotions begin with cognition. That is, thoughts themselves may bring about an accompanying ANS response. For example, a child may remember the death of his grandmother during a conversation about another child's grandparents. Recalling the event and how he felt at that time may act as an ANS stimulus that provokes an emotional state of grief. Similarly, remembering an irritating event may induce anger, recalling a frightening situation may induce fear, and so on.

Mandler's information processing theory is valuable because it allows us to place cognition at center stage as we consider emotions. Clearly, his theory helps us account for phenomena that behavioral theories do not. Mandler's views are not developmental, however, and have some limitations for the study of how emotions change over time. Even so, his strong emphasis on cognition supports developmental perspectives such as Sroufe's (discussed earlier).

Other Theories of Emotional Development

Although the theories described in this chapter shed considerable light on the development of emotions, there are several other competing theories. One that has gained fairly widespread support is psychoanalytic theory, originally formulated by Sigmund Freud (1938). This theory outlines the development of emotions in some detail, but it is much broader than a theory of emotional development. Psychoanalytic theory is a theory of personality, personality development, emotional development, and treatment of mental illness. Because of its breadth, we will consider it in Chapter 16.

Building on an evolutionary perspective, Izard (Buechler & Izard, 1983; Izard, 1977; Izard et al., 1984) has proposed what he calls a **discrete emotions theory.** He argues that "each emotion develops as a discrete system. . . . Izard proposes that . . . (emotions do) not evolve in a continuous process from 'precursor' emotions but emerge . . . at a distinct point in development. According to [this] . . . view, there are separate, innate neural programs for the expression of each of the fundamental emotions" (Buechler & Izard, 1983, p. 299).

In other words, Izard believes that emotions do not differentiate from a generalized excitement response. Rather, each emotion appears at a specific time in development that has been determined genetically: "when it becomes adaptive in the life of the infant" (Buechler & Izard, 1983, p. 299). In Izard's view, anger, for example, motivates activities that allow people to remove restraints or circumvent barriers. Izard argues that such an emotion would be of very little value before infants are able to move about and manipulate elements of their environment. "If anger emerged [earlier than about 5 months of age], . . . it could only result in mounting frustration . . . and negative exchanges with the world" (Buechler & Izard, 1983, p. 299).

A Summary of Theories of Emotional Development

None of the theories addressing emotional development presents a complete picture. Each, however, adds to our understanding. Based on an evolutionary and biological foundation, emotional development proceeds through several processes. Some sources of fear, for example, may be classically conditioned as a neutral stimulus is paired with a fear-eliciting stimulus. Other emotional reactions may come under operant control as the consequences of behavior strengthen or weaken it.

Some aspects of the expression of emotions are learned through modeling, although the facial expressions associated with basic emotions seem to be innate. Modeling also helps account for the objects of children's emotions, as when children imitate parents' feelings about specific events or people.

Cognition is an integral part of emotional behavior. It is not so much environmental situations that produce emotions as it is how we think about them. We may account for the increasing differentiation of emotions in children through a combination of cognitive and physical development. As cognitive development proceeds, thought processes necessary for different emotional states emerge and finer and finer gradations of emotions appear. Like development in general, emotional development moves from the general to the specific and from the simple to the sophisticated.

Applications: Dealing with Fears and Anger

A vast quantity of literature has been written on how to facilitate the healthy personal, social, and emotional development of children. In this section, we present a set of guidelines for facilitating development in two areas that have been widely researched and that are specific to emotional development: fear and anger. Then we close the section and chapter with guidelines for parents concerned about the possibility of emotional problems in children.

Helping Children Deal with Fears

As we have seen, fear is a normal, often beneficial response to environmental threats. Most children, however, will acquire inappropriate fears from time to time. By applying the following guidelines, many of these fears can be overcome.

1. *Help children understand their fears.* As one example, a sizable number of children fear thunder. This fear can interfere with sleep at night, naps, play activities, and cause a surprisingly large number of disruptions in daily life. One method that may reduce such fears is to explain their source: Thunder is caused by lightning when air rushes in to fill the space where lightning has passed. Understanding what is feared often reduces children's anxiety.

2. *Model appropriate behavior.* Children's fears are often reduced when they see a model dealing with the fear-provoking situation (Spiegler, 1983). In particular, children are most likely to benefit from watching a model their own age acting unafraid. For example, Melamed and Siegel (1975) were able to greatly reduce children's fears of surgery

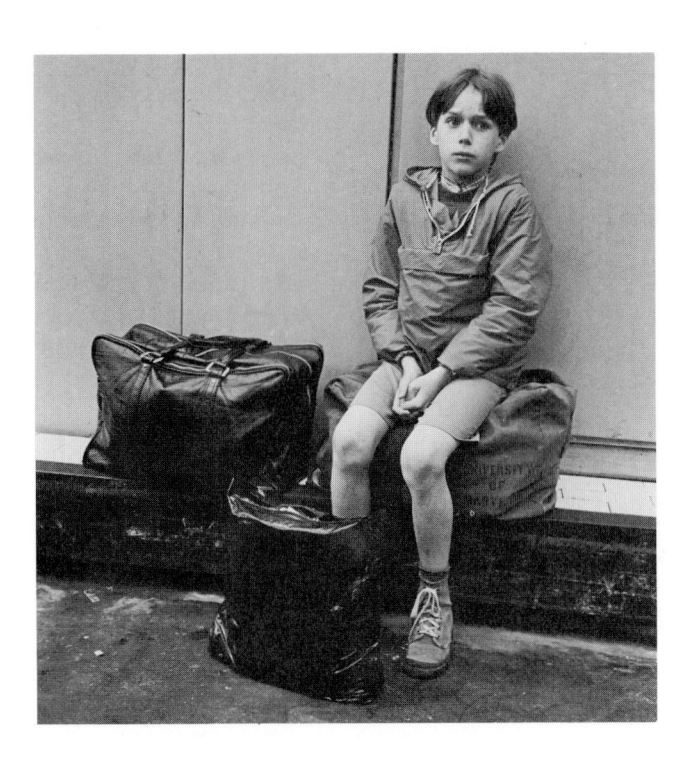

This little boy is lost and afraid. Fear in such a situation is normal but parents can help children be better prepared for such events by teaching them coping strategies such as checking with the information desk, asking questions at the airline terminal, or getting a guard to help.

by having them watch a brief film depicting how a 7-year-old managed his fears in preparing for surgery. Similar modeling approaches have been used to reduce fears of going to the dentist, fears of animals, and fears of the dark (Spiegler, 1983).

3. *Help children gradually confront fear-provoking stimuli.* The classic treatment of fear is known as **systematic desensitization.** Basically, the caregiver seeks to identify some level of exposure to a fear-provoking stimulus that is still comfortable to the child and to *gradually* approach it a little at a time without making the child uncomfortable. For example, if a child fears cats, a parent could help him overcome this fear by first identifying some point at which the fear response would not occur (e.g., looking at a kitten through the window of a pet shop). If no fear occurs, the parent and child could *gradually,* over the course of several visits, come closer and closer to the kitten until the child actually pets it without fear.

Such a procedure must be employed carefully, and professional therapists are best equipped for the job. Often, they use a form of relaxation therapy in conjunction with the systematic desensitization such that the child is trained in how to relax in different situations. For minor fears, though, parents may wish to try this approach. The key idea for parents to keep in mind is patience.

4. *Build children's confidence in dealing with fear-provoking situations.* One way of helping children cope with fears is to increase their feeling of control. A child who is afraid of dogs might first be desensitized to puppies as described above and then given a puppy to care for. Similarly, a child who is frightened of the water might first be desensitized and then be given swimming lessons. When a child believes that he or she has control, fear is usually greatly reduced.

5. *Prevent unnecessary fears.* Two keys to preventing the formation of unnecessary fears are honesty and the avoidance of surprise (Jersild, 1968; Spiegler, 1983). To infants and small children, almost anything surprising can be frightening. When new objects or people are to be introduced to small children, do so gradually, after adequate preparation.

   Honesty also is important. If a child is going to have dental treatment for the first time, many dentists encourage visits first and ask that parents tell the children the truth about the possibility of minor discomfort. A child who knows the dentist, knows the office and staff, and understands that there might be discomfort is not likely to be surprised and is far more likely to manage his or her fear.

   Of course, honesty goes far beyond the preparation of children for visits to the dentist, doctor, or a hospital. We live, unfortunately, in a society in which children must be wary of strangers and even of well-known relatives and family friends. On the one hand, none of us wants our children to be easy prey for potential child molesters. On the other hand, we do not want our children to be so fearful that they view the world as a terrible place. There appears to be no substitute for open and direct discussions of when and why wariness is needed and how children should handle threatening situations.

Helping Children Cope with Anger

Anger is a natural part of life, yet there are appropriate and inappropriate ways of dealing with it. The following guidelines have been taken from research.

1. *Do not reinforce temper tantrums.* Although most children grow out of temper tantrums, such behaviors can become a very real difficulty if children are able to use them to gain their wants. Children who have temper tantrums are best ignored until they calm down (Spiegler, 1983). Small children need to learn that losing their tempers does not get them what they want.

2. *Reinforce efforts to settle disputes through reason.* Children will have innumerable disagreements with their siblings and playmates over the years. There are many ways of settling such disagreements—

fighting, yelling and screaming, running away in a huff, or reasoning things through. Parents and other adults should make efforts to reward children's attempts to resolve conflicts through reasonable means. If children are rewarded systematically for attempts to deal with conflicts through discussions, compromises, and other reasonable approaches, they will be far more likely to employ such methods in the future and avoid inappropriate behaviors (Glover, 1981).

3. *Model appropriate anger.* In addition to rewarding children for appropriate methods of dealing with anger, parents need to demonstrate them. When parents find themselves in anger-provoking situations, they will help children learn how to deal with anger by explaining their actions. For example, "Even though I'm feeling angry, the best thing to do is remain calm. I'm sure the manager will exchange our purchase if we explain the problem to her correctly. If I shouted and yelled, it would only make her angry too, and less likely to help us."

4. *Help children make causal attributions.* Understanding the reason for other people's actions is one way to defuse anger. For example, a parent could ask, "Why do you think the lifeguard made you get out of the pool? Was the lifeguard's reason a good one?" Guiding children's reasoning in this way helps them learn to look beyond the surface of events for their causes.

Seeking Help

There are no clearcut rules for deciding when to seek help for children. Standards of acceptable behavior vary from family to family, from subculture to subculture, and from culture to culture. There are, however, some general suggestions we can make for parents who are concerned with their children's emotional behavior.

1. *Do not be afraid to seek help.* Regardless of what the problem is (fears, aggression, and so on), parents should not worry about going to others for help. No professional helping person will ridicule parents. If parents have been overly concerned about minor problems, they will receive reassurance. If the problem needs treatment, the professional will either provide it or make a referral to someone who can.

2. *Begin with a physical examination.* A great number of physical problems can be manifested in emotional behaviors. Allergies, illness (e.g., liver dysfunctions), and injuries can all result in behavioral changes. Beyond the potential diagnosis of physical problems, medical personnel should be informed sources of information about child behavior and should also be able to provide appropriate referrals.

3. *Prepare a detailed description of the problem.* Before visiting a professional, parents should compile a careful description of the problem. This description should include the severity of the problem, its onset, contributing factors (i.e., precipitating times, places, events), and specific examples of the problem. Any change in routines, diet, or family structure should also be included.

4. *Choose a therapist carefully.* Parents should feel comfortable with the professional they consult. There are many successful approaches to the treatment of children's emotional problems and many different professionals are available. Parents should choose a therapist with whom they feel a rapport.

5. *Be committed to the treatment plan.* There is no sure way to predict how long the treatment for various emotional problems may take. Some specific fears may be overcome in a matter of a few weeks. Similarly, tantrums and aggressive behavior in small children can often be overcome in a brief period. Other problems (e.g., autism) are not so amenable to treatment and may involve years of work. Then, too, some problems are more difficult to treat in older children and adolescents than in small children (e.g., aggression). Parents should obtain a realistic assessment of the potential length of treatment, the form it will take, a rationale for the treatment, and a description of their involvement. Parents may wish, of course, to obtain a second opinion. However, regardless of the treatment method ultimately chosen, parental commitment is necessary for success. Realistic expectations, of course, are an integral part of this commitment.

Summary

Emotions are subjective experiences accompanied by physiological changes. Human beings have emotions because emotions were highly adaptive during evolution. Negative emotions enhanced survival by increasing our ancestors' abilities to flee or fight. Positive emotions also had a highly adaptive function, allowing for greater nurturance of infants, love in human bondings, and the likelihood of successful social structures.

The physiology of emotions is complex. In general, stimuli (either external or internal) are processed by the limbic system, which then acts on the autonomic nervous system (ANS). The ANS, which is made up of sympathetic and parasympathetic fibers, activates or deactivates various body systems. In particular, the activation of the endocrine system brings about many of the physiological changes associated with emotion.

During the first 3 years of life, emotional development proceeds from a generalized excitement response to several clearly differentiated and sophisticated emotional states. The first month of life is typically characterized by insensitivity to others' emotions, although neonates do express generalized emotional responses. The second and third month of life are characterized by increasing sensitivity. The major achievement of this period is the social smile. From 3 to 6 months of age, babies are typified by high levels of positive emotions, although wariness, frustration, and rage begin to emerge. The 7- to 9-

month-old is also characterized by positive emotions but at this age babies begin to actively initiate social interchanges. It is also at this time that separation anxiety (a fear of being separated from the primary caregiver) appears.

Nine- to 12-month-olds also exhibit high levels of positive affect but tend to become preoccupied with their primary caregivers. Fear of strangers is usually pronounced. The practicing stage (12 to 18 months) is usually characterized by a decline of wariness of strangers and greater exploration of the environment. The emotional development of children from 18 to 36 months of age is typified by the emerging self-concept.

Emotional development during childhood and adolescence is interwoven with cognitive development, particularly children's increasing abilities to make causal attributions about events. As children become able to analyze situations for which they seek "why?" answers, emotional reactions increasingly depend on the interpretation of events rather than the events themselves.

Some children experience difficulties in emotional development. Anxiety problems include phobias (fears out of proportion with the threat), anorexia nervosa (a severe eating disorder characterized by a refusal to eat and extreme weight loss), bulimia (an eating disorder typified by cycles of gorging followed by purging), enuresis (the involuntary release of urine), encopresis (bowel movements at inappropriate times), and asthma. Other emotional problems seen during development include depression and autism.

Several theories of emotional development have been proposed over the years. Differentiation theory posits that the separate emotions seen in adults result from the differentiation of a basic arousal state. In contrast, behavioral views of emotional development suggest that emotions are learned through classical conditioning, operant conditioning, and imitation. Recently, more and more emphasis has been put on the role of cognition in emotional development in theories such as that developed by Mandler.

Parents and other adults can help children deal with fears and anger through straightforward guidelines drawn from the research on emotional development. Parent–child interactions, of course, are a major topic to be addressed in the next chapter, *Social Development*.

Key Terms

emotions
limbic system
social smile
positive affect stage
separation anxiety
attachment stage
practicing stage
self-concept stage
empathy
outcome-dependent emotions
causally linked emotions
causal attributions
phobias
psychosomatic disorders

psychophysiological disorders
anorexia nervosa
bulimia
enuresis
encopresis
asthma
depression
autism
echolalia
hyperactivity
differentiation theory
generalized excitement response
classical conditioning
neutral stimulus

eliciting stimulus
contemporary behaviorism
operant conditioning
reinforcers
punishers
S_D
S_Δ
generalization
discrimination
extinction
social learning theory
discrete emotions theory
systematic desensitization

Suggested Readings

Harvard Educational Review. (1984). *54* (3). The entire August 1984 issue of this distinguished journal was devoted to the topic of "Education and the Threat of Nuclear War," including articles by numerous educators and researchers interested in children's knowledge and feelings about nuclear issues.

Jersild, A.T. (1968). *Child psychology* (6th ed.). Englewood Cliffs, NJ: Prentice-Hall. Although quite dated, Jersild's work remains the most thorough on age trends in children's emotional development.

Lewis, M., & Michalson, L. (1983). *Children's emotions and moods*. New York: Plenum. This volume provides an excellent overview of children's emotions and problems in emotional development.

McKnew, D. H., Cytryn, L., & Yahraes, H. (1983). *Why isn't Johnny crying?* New York: Norton. This book presents a highly readable treatment of childhood depression.

Sroufe, L. A. (1979). Socioemotional development. In J. D. Osofsky (Ed.), *Handbook of infant development*. New York: John Wiley and Sons. Sroufe's chapter presents a thorough accounting of emotional development in infancy. Sroufe also has a new volume on emotional development in preparation at the current time that is expected to be a major work in the area.

Weiner, B., & Graham, S. (1984). An attributional approach to emotional development. In C. E. Izard, J. Kagan, & R. B. Zajonc (Eds.), *Emotions, cognition, and behavior*. New York: Cambridge. This chapter presents a thorough discussion of the role of causal attributions in emotional development.

Application Exercise

13-1 Attributions and Emotional Development

Below is a set of six situations. Each describes an event and then lists some potential emotional responses. Have children at different ages respond to them (you will have to read them to younger children). After each child completes that task, review the responses and ask the child to explain his or her reasoning. Describe the kinds of attributions made by the children and detail any age trends you notice.

1. Jamie forgot to study her spelling words last night. Jamie's teacher asked different children to spell words from the list. When it was Jamie's turn, she shut her eyes and guessed at the spelling. Jamie guessed correctly. Jamie knew she had spelled the word correctly because of good luck. How do you think she felt?
   a) proud   c) surprised   e) sad
   b) thankful   d) happy

2. Bill's parents had promised to take him to the zoo today. Bill was looking forward to going and was watching the rain when his father came and said, "We can't go to the zoo today. It's raining too hard. We'll go next Saturday." How do you think Bill felt?
   a) angry   c) sad   e) pleased
   b) surprised   d) disappointed

3. Paul was not supposed to try to pour the milk from the carton by himself. But he was thirsty and his mother was in the basement. Paul poured himself a little glass of milk anyway, but spilled a lot of it on the floor. He quickly put away the carton and drank his glass of milk. He then put the glass in the dishwasher and mopped up the floor with a wet rag. Just when Paul got the last of the milk up and was using a clean rag to dry the floor, his mother came up the stairs and saw Paul working. She must not have seen the milk because she gave him a big hug and said, "What a good helper you are—cleaning the kitchen for me!" How do you think Paul felt?
   a) sad   c) guilty   e) surprised
   b) happy   d) angry

4. Sally was supposed to have learned a song for her Bluebird meeting. She forgot and, when the

girls sang the song, Sally did very poorly. How do you suppose she felt?
a) surprised   **c)** sad   **e)** afraid
b) ashamed   **d)** angry

5. Robert's name has been put on the list of "best scientists" on the teacher's door. Robert found out, though, that this happened because the teacher didn't grade a part of his science work that had many mistakes. These same mistakes kept Robert's friend, Sally, from being put on the list. How do you think Robert felt?
a) sad   **c)** surprised   **e)** ashamed
b) afraid   **d)** happy

6. Susie forgot to bring in her paper dolls last night. It rained hard most of the night and her dolls were ruined. How do you think Susie feels?
a) angry   **c)** ashamed   **e)** afraid
b) sad   **d)** surprised

CHAPTER 14

Social Development

So closely interwoven have been our lives, our purposes, and experiences that, separated, we have a feeling of incompleteness—united, such strength of self-assertion that no ordinary obstacles, differences, or dangers ever appear to us insurmountable.
—Elizabeth Cady Stanton
Eighty Years and More

Human beings are social beings. Most of us (with the exception of an occasional hermit or two) interact with other people in our homes, our schools, at work, and a thousand other places. We need this interaction for our psychological pleasure and well-being as well as for our very survival. Without social connections, society could not function, families could not exist, and individuals could not survive. **Social behavior**—how people relate to other people—is key to human life.

Because of its centrality to our lives, social behavior always has been one of the major concerns of psychology. Relationships between parents and children, husbands and wives, and teachers and students are only a few of those singled out for special study by the field. Developmental psychology has focused on *changes* in social behavior and especially on the relationship of adult social behavior to that of infancy and childhood. Why is it that some children grow up to be well-adjusted adults, able to get along well with other people, whereas others seem unable to fit in? Why do some children grow up able to form warm, intimate relationships, whereas others cannot? Why do some become good parents themselves, carrying out their roles with great skill and responsibility, whereas others adapt very poorly to parenthood, neglecting and even abusing their own children? Many developmentalists have sought to trace the roots of these adult behaviors to the experiences of childhood.

Social development—the changes that take place from infancy to adulthood in how individuals interact—is a fascinating topic: Infants mature rapidly from nearly helpless beings into independent persons capable of intentionally influencing others. Children quickly form attachments to significant persons and make friends with peers. As childhood proceeds and children become adolescents and then adults, their social behavior becomes tremendously complex and versatile. Their social understanding increases greatly and they become capable of effective interaction in many situations and contexts.

In this chapter, we will examine social development. Two contexts of social development will be examined in depth: the family and the peer group. We will first discuss the role of infants in stimulating "caregivers" to take care of them and examine the concept of bonding between newborns and their mothers. We will then look at the process of attachment, the development of strong ties between children and their primary caregivers.

Next we will examine the formation of relationships with peers, especially how children learn to interact with other children and how this interaction changes with development. We will stress how children make friends, learn to take roles in groups, and come to understand others as they move through childhood to adolescence and adulthood. We will also examine in detail the development of aggression.

The Newborn: A "Sociable" Person

Superficially, there seems little about newborn human infants that is "sociable." Babies spend most of their time sleeping; awake, they seem mostly indifferent to their surroundings and show little potential for communication. After all, they can neither speak nor understand human speech. Nor can they move around and initiate physical contact with others. All in all, they seem to be remarkably poor candidates for the label "sociable."

Because of infants' apparent deficiencies in receiving and making contact with the world, it was easy for a generation of social scientists to view and describe infants as socially isolated, virtually cut off from most meaningful interaction with the world. Only biological needs such as food, warmth, and comfort matter to the newborn, it seemed—social interaction must wait until later. Infants appeared to be passive recipients of adult attention.

The truth, however, is far different. As we shall see, psychologists' ideas of infants as social isolates have been replaced with far more accurate views of infants as active partners (almost from birth) in social interactions. While infants obviously do not have the social skills of adults, they have a surprising set of abilities to prompt behaviors from the adults who take care of them, their so-called caregivers (Damon, 1983; Hay, 1985). These behaviors, many of which are reflexive and have their source in our evolution, have been critical to the survival of the human race. Because of the extreme dependency of human babies on others to provide for their needs, infants somehow must be able to stimulate adults to care for them. Otherwise, they could not survive.

In this section, we first will examine some of the social behaviors of very young infants and their probable effects on adults. Then we will look at the other side of this reciprocal interaction, the strong, early attraction that mothers can develop for their infants, bonding. We will see how the social behaviors of infant and caregiver quickly become intertwined and form the basis for later human interaction.

Early Social Skills of Infants

Although babies obviously do not have adults' range of social behaviors, they nonetheless have a remarkable repertoire of abilities for communication. As we saw in Chapter 11, newborns have extraordinary sensitivity to the critical sounds of human language. But they also have important ways of communicating on their own through their actions. Three of the most prominent are: (1) gaze, or eye fixations, (2) head movements, and (3) facial expressions (Stern, 1977).

Gaze. From the moment of birth, babies' visual systems are available and working (see Chapter 9). Newborns can see and, without any previous experience, follow a moving object with their eyes and head and look at it. Learning is not necessary; this ability to **gaze** is innate and can be demonstrated easily in most alert newborns (Stern, 1977).

One limitation, however, is that babies can focus well only on very close objects. Their sharpest vision is at a distance of only 8 inches; the rest of their world is fuzzy. This limitation in vision actually turns out to be a plus for social development. During normal breast or bottle feeding, a stimulus that is almost exactly 8 inches away is the mother's face! Since the mother spends about 70 percent of her time facing and looking at her infant during feeding (Stern, 1977), her baby is most likely to see her face and, especially, her eyes.

Infants have a special fascination for complex visual elements (e.g., lines, curves, and so on) such as those in the human face (Fagan, 1979; Sherrod, 1981; Spelke & Cortelyou, 1981). Babies seem prepared by evolution to find the human face interesting. At the same time, mothers naturally seem to attract as much attention as possible to their faces by their facial expressions, their looking at, and their talking to their infants. Thus newborn infants' skills and the caregivers' actions naturally combine to lay the groundwork for a developing relationship.

As early as 6 weeks of age, infants not only look at the mother, but focus specifically on her eyes and mouth (Haith, 1980). According to Stern (1977), at this point mothers begin to feel that they and their babies have a "real" relationship; they now are really connected as persons. Also, infants' focal distance now expands, and they can watch their mothers come and go. By the age of 3 months or so, infants have almost complete control over their visual system. They now can be effective partners in a relationship and true social interaction can begin.

Head Movements. Gaze is coordinated with **head movements**, which turn out to be potent signals used by infants to affect caregivers' behavior. For instance, when infants point their faces directly at their mothers, or bring their heads forward and tilt their faces up, almost all mothers find this tremendously appealing (Stern, 1977). Newborns turn their heads away, however, as part of an innate avoidance reflex when objects loom in their faces. This reflexive action quickly becomes social in nature as infants learn to turn their heads away from overstimulation or from, say, hated foods. The stronger the turning away reaction, the more mothers assume their babies do not like something. Thus, as with gaze, an innate reflexive reaction becomes a "signal" in infants' relationships with their mothers. Mothers try to keep their babies facing toward them and avoid actions that result in their babies turning away.

Facial Expressions. Gazing and head turning are two relatively straightforward ways babies use to communicate. Babies also have a surprising ability to directly convey emotions such as pleasure, anger, fear, joy, and disgust through their facial expressions. Like gaze and head movements, **facial expressions** are innate. For instance, reflexive *smiling* can be observed in neonates during sleep in the first 2 weeks of life. Similarly, there are many associated reflexive expressions of *displeasure*, such as "sobering" of the face, frowning, grimacing, and, of course, crying. Like babies' other reflexes, however, these expressions soon become increasingly linked to the external world. As we saw in Chapter 13, by 6 weeks or so of age certain sights and sounds—the human face, a high-pitched voice, a mother's gaze, or tickling—can coax forth a smile. Even earlier, of course, expressions of displeasure can be brought out by such stimuli as bad-tasting food, a wet diaper, hunger, or overstimulation. Infants soon move to *instrumental* (purposeful) uses of these expressions of emotion (Stern, 1977; Damon, 1983). That is, they begin to use them to get desired reactions from others. For example, smiles now become truly social, as they are used to coax smiles from others. The smiles themselves have not changed, but now they are being used by infants as a part of genuine social interaction with those around them.

As Stern (1977) and others (Damon, 1983; Maccoby, 1980; Maccoby & Martin, 1983) have pointed out, gaze, head turning, and facial expressions are not separate, discrete elements. Instead, they are a part of integrated packages of responses. The sight of her mother, for instance, may elicit baby's gaze, coordinated with head turning and an expression of delight. Also, the baby may move her head forward and lift her head and face toward her mother while gurgling excitedly. Babies do not need to *learn* to link these actions; they are naturally coordinated. Like the separate units, these coordinated packages of behavior change with development from simple reflexes to instrumental actions that are a part of true social relationships. But perhaps the most important aspect is that for mothers (or other caregivers), these actions by their babies are critical stimuli that naturally lead to changed perceptions and to "caring" actions. While parents sometimes may overinterpret a very young baby's expressions and actions (e.g., "Oh, look how happy Baby is with his new mobile!"), the baby's actions and parents' reactions quickly become the real thing, building blocks upon which later social interactions are constructed.

Bonding

Whereas the early months of life are critical times for social development, developmental psychologists, prospective parents, and others have recently grown more and more interested in what happens to mothers and their newborns in the period right after birth. At the heart of this interest is the concept of **bonding**. Bonding is defined as a process in which a mother forms an affectionate attachment to her infant immediately after birth (Myers, 1984a). Bonding is thought to be facilitated by early contact between mothers and their newborn babies, especially by extended skin-to-skin contact, suckling, and looking at one another.

The concept of bonding is not new; processes much like it have long been observed in the animal world (Rosenblatt & Siegel, 1981). For instance, in sheep and goats, the bond between a particular mother and her newborn normally is formed within a very few *minutes* after birth. If the mother and newborn are separated during this brief time, the mother usually completely rejects her offspring and will butt or kick it away. For instance, in one study (Klopfer, 1971) 15 mother goats were allowed 5 minutes with their offspring right after birth before they were separated. A second group of 15 mothers and kids were separated immediately. Mothers in the first group accepted their offspring up to 3 hours later. In the second group, however, 13 out of 15 would have nothing to do with their offspring. There seem to be two aspects to this attraction (or rejection): (1) hormonal influences in the mother related to giving birth, and (2) stimulation of the mother by the offspring (Rosenblatt & Siegel, 1981). As Myers (1984a) has pointed out, however, many questions remain concerning how applicable these findings are to humans and other primates.

One reason the concept of bonding attracted so much interest is that, in the United States and in many European countries, hospitals traditionally have separated mothers and newborn infants just after birth. The babies are cared for in a nursery, while the mothers are kept in a maternity ward. Contact often has been quite limited, involving only feeding times and perhaps a few other times as the mother "recovered." If bonding occurs in humans, and especially if there are

The bond between the newborn infant and mother is strengthened by skin-to-skin contact, nursing, and gazing at one another.

critical periods for bonding between mothers and their babies, then this mode of care that separates mothers and infants could be very harmful to a critical process in the social development of children.

The strongest case for the concept of human bonding was made by two pediatricians, Marshall Klaus and John Kennell (1976, 1982), who observed many babies in hospital units for both regular and premature newborns. Premature infants, they noted, often failed to thrive when they were released and had to be returned to the hospital. The researchers' clinical judgment led them to believe that these babies' isolation from their mothers and other caregivers in intensive care units might be a causal factor.

Drawing on their observations and on animal research that showed strong influence of hormonal and physiological factors on bonding, Klaus and Kennell made a radical proposal: For humans, just as for many other animal species, the first hours (and even perhaps minutes) after birth are critical in forming a bond between mother and child. Contact between mother and baby right after birth, particularly extended periods of skin-to-skin contact, is crucial, they argued, for creating intimacy. Mothers and children who have this opportunity demonstrate and feel greater closeness to one another, even months later.

In support of this argument, Klaus and Kennell (1976, 1982; Kennell & Klaus, 1984) supplied experimental evidence based on several studies.

In the 1976 study, 14 mothers were given "extended contact" with their infants and compared to 14 mothers having a traditional hospital experience. Observations during their babies' physical examinations at 1 month of age showed that mothers who had extended contact tended to stand by the examination table and to soothe their infants more if they cried. Also, they showed more face-to-face contact and gave their babies more physical affection during feeding. Similar differences were present, Klaus and Kennell reported, a year later (although no differences existed on most measures). Their interpretation of the data was that there may be a critical bonding period based on hormonal influences and physiological factors that has lasting consequences for the development of ties of affection.

This strong claim has not been accepted uncritically, however (Egeland & Vaughn, 1981; Goldberg, 1983; Myers, 1984a; Maccoby & Martin, 1983; Svedja, Campos, & Emde, 1980; Taylor & Hall, 1979). Most later studies have either failed to replicate Klaus & Kennell's findings or have questioned the notion of a hormone-based *critical period* in bonding. Also, as Maccoby (1980) has written, unless we want to claim that whole populations (such as that of the United States) are impaired in their capacity for affection, most handicaps created by separation after birth (e.g., such as those that may be created by traditional hospital practices) are overcome by normal care over time. Klaus and Kennell too have pointed out the problems in attributing all manner of consequences to just the single process of bonding. As they stated in their reaction to a critique by Myers (1984a):

> We have speculated that there might be a sensitive period of several hours or days after birth during which contact with the baby might enhance a mother's relationship and bond with her baby. We have never suggested that early contact for additional hours or days after birth is the sole determining factor that will produce a certain maternal behavior or change in child development at some point far off in the future, independently of anything that might happen in between. . . . We stress repeatedly . . . that the many complex factors in the bonding process cannot be considered in isolation (Kennell & Klaus, 1984, p. 276).

Perhaps the reaction of Myers, a strong critic of the idea of a critical period in human bonding, best captures the most prevalent feeling about the work of Klaus and Kennell among child development specialists:

> The humanizing changes seen in American birthing traditions in the last 15 years—prepared childbirth, drug-free deliveries, father's presence, early contact, rooming-in, increased support for breast feeding—have been a blessing to millions of new families. These changes are beneficial whether you "believe in bonding" or not. We owe a debt of gratitude to Kennell

and Klaus for their contribution in drawing attention to the importance of making childbirth a natural, family affair rather than a stark medical event. Whether the research evidence supports the notion of bonding or not, Kennell and Klaus' clinical judgment was keen in noting that the conditions for childbirth could be improved (Myers, 1984b, pp. 286–287).

Attachment

While the evidence for biologically based human bonding in critical periods right after birth is mixed, the research on another process in the social development of children is not. This process is **attachment**, a relatively enduring emotional tie to a specific person, usually the mother. There is an almost universal tendency for infants to become increasingly focused on a specific person. Babies are happy in the presence of this person and unhappy in his or her absence. Biology is not critical in this: Babies can become attached to fathers as well as mothers and to adoptive mothers as well as biological ones. Infants who are secure with one parent are not necessarily secure with the other. Although there is usually one primary attachment, additional attachments can be formed. In general, attachment is shown in infancy and early childhood by the child's: (1) seeking to be near the other person, (2) showing distress on separation from the other person, (3) expressing joy or relief at reunion, and (4) being oriented toward the other person even when he or she is not close by (e.g., by listening for the person's voice, watching the person's movements, or calling out) (Bretherton & Waters, 1985; Lamb, Thompson, Gardner, Charnov, & Estes, 1984, 1985; Maccoby, 1980).

Originally formulated by Bowlby (1969/1982, 1973, 1983), the concept of attachment has been much clarified and amplified by researchers such as Harriet Rheingold (e.g., Rheingold & Eckerman, 1970) and Mary Ainsworth (Ainsworth, 1967; Ainsworth & Bell, 1969; Ainsworth, Bell, & Stayton, 1971; Ainsworth, 1978; Ainsworth, Blehar, Waters, & Wall, 1978). Ainsworth and her colleagues and others (see Lamb et al., 1985 have used a particularly productive research procedure called the **strange situation** to examine how attachment develops. In the strange situation, a mother and infant are brought into an observation room filled with toys. The mother puts the infant down and sits down in a chair. In a few minutes, an unfamiliar woman comes in, talks to the mother, and then attempts to play with the child. While the stranger is doing so, the mother quietly departs but leaves her handbag on the chair as a signal she will be back. While the mother is gone, the child is observed and his or her reaction to the stranger is recorded. When the mother returns (and she *does* return), observers record details of the reunion. Subsequently, the mother again leaves, but this time the child

In many families, children can become just as attached to the father as to the mother.

is left alone. The child's reactions are observed again as is the reaction when the mother returns a second time.

The strange situation is especially instructive because it exposes infants to three experiences that potentially can be upsetting: unfamiliar surroundings, contact with a stranger, and separation from the caregiver (usually the mother). Because of the way the experiences are arranged, it is possible to look at their effects both independently and together, as well as to examine their *cumulative* impact. The strange situation also very closely parallels many "real life" situations, so that children's reactions to it tend to be much the same as to their everyday experiences.

Maccoby (Maccoby, 1980; Maccoby & Martin, 1983) reports the following predictable characteristics in many children's reactions to the strange situation.

1. Infants stay fairly close to their mothers during the first few moments in the strange environment. They soon move away, however, to explore and to play, but stay in contact by returning occasionally.

2. Entrance of a stranger causes children to go to their mother. Often they may cling to her, stand behind her, or simply sit close to her. The mother seems to be a "safe haven."

3. Most children will warm up to a stranger but are more comfortable with the mother present. Some children continue to cling to their mothers.
4. Separation from the mother has a noticeable effect on almost all children. Most become less involved in play. Many cry or show some other sign of disturbance. Some will go to the door or wait, immobile, at one spot, as if their normal activities have been suspended.

Of course, the process of attachment undergoes a great deal of change with development. Figure 14-1 shows data from Kagan (1976) on how two groups of children reacted when their mothers left the room. One group (day-care group) had been spending 5 full days a week at day-care centers, while the other (home-care group) had been spending these days at home. These children were observed at regular intervals from the time they were 3½ months old until they were 29 months old. Fussing and crying, distress indicators, were among key reactions observed.

As Figure 14-1 shows, the protests (fussing and crying) of the two groups of infants did not differ, which was somewhat surprising since the day-care group had been separated almost daily from their mothers.

FIGURE 14-1 Changes with Age in Children's Distress When Separated from Their Mothers. Note the similar patterns in the home and day-care groups. *From J. Kagan (1976). Emergent themes in human development.* American Scientist, 64, p. 190.

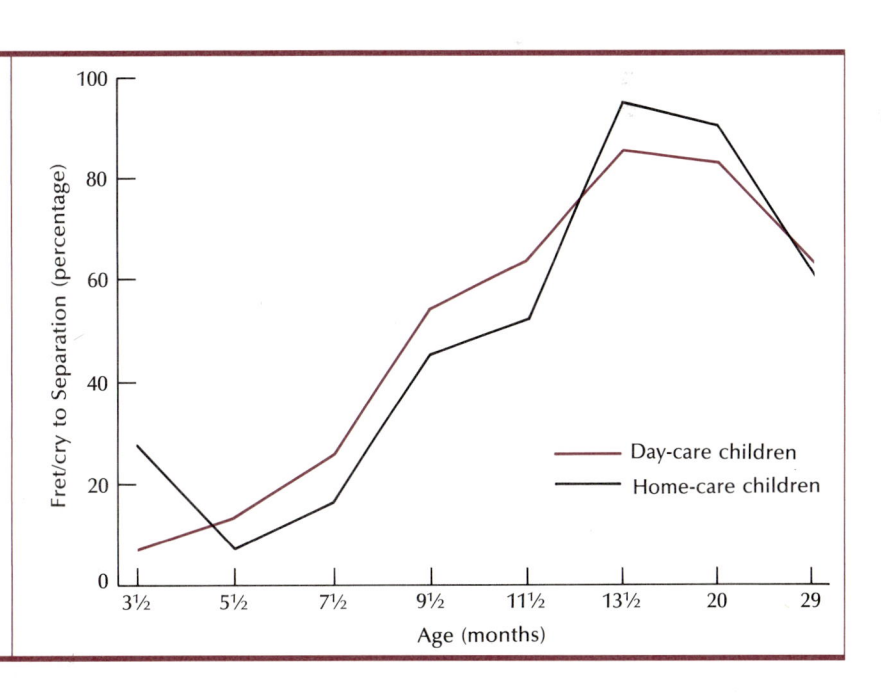

In this new, unfamiliar setting, however, their reactions were almost identical to those of the home-care group.

Separation reactions such as these seem universal (see Chapter 13), peaking early in the second year of life (Ainsworth et al., 1978). Although attachment does not disappear as children grow older, it becomes less intense and is transformed over time (Martin, 1981). Whereas children still regard their mothers as their secure base, they become more and more independent. In a study by Bronson (1975), for instance, by the end of the second year children "visually checked" their mothers only half as often as they had a year earlier. "Shadowing" the mother, or following her wherever she goes, also declines as children become more independent. A few children, however, seem to hang on to their need for physical contact and do not move as easily toward the secure but autonomous state of the well-adjusted child.

As most mothers and children become less attached physically, they become closer conversationally, talking to each other more to maintain contact. As children become more competent in their thinking (e.g., able to remember, to represent events and relationships mentally), they begin to understand their caregivers' goals, feelings, and intentions (Damon, 1983). Consequently, more complex relationships are possible. Furthermore, as attachment to a single caregiver wanes, other attachments—to brothers and sisters, friends, grandparents, and others—can form or further develop. As children move toward adulthood, their relationships become richer and more varied.

Individual Differences in Attachment

Whereas attachment is a universal phenomenon, individual mother–infant pairs show different patterns that are generally consistent over time. Three general patterns have been identified: securely attached, avoidant, and resistant (Ainsworth, Bell, & Stayton, 1971; Ainsworth, Blehar, Waters, & Wall, 1978; Ainsworth, 1982; Hay, 1985; Lamb et al., 1984; Maccoby, 1980; Maccoby & Martin, 1983; Sroufe & Waters, 1977; Waters & Sroufe, 1983).

Securely attached infants react positively to strangers and use their mothers as "secure bases" from which to explore their environments. These children are obviously distressed when they are separated from their mothers. They show pleasure at their mother's return, desire interaction, and are comforted by her presence. Not all infants are securely attached, however: Two groups of **insecurely attached infants** have been identified. The first group, called **avoidant** (about 25 percent of middle-class American children), seem relatively unconcerned about their mothers' whereabouts during exploration. On reunion after separation, these infants often ignore or avoid their mothers. In general, they do not seem particularly distressed by separation. The second group of insecurely attached infants, however, acts quite differently.

These infants, called **resistant** (about 10 percent of middle-class American children), are uneasy in new situations and have difficulty using their mothers as secure bases when they explore. When they are reunited with their mothers after being separated, they act unusually: They seem to simultaneously seek and *resist* contact. That is, they run to their mothers and hold out their arms to be picked up, but when picked up immediately begin struggling to be put down. They also have a distinctly angry emotional tone.

Ainsworth and her colleagues (Ainsworth et al., 1978) and others (Clarke-Stewart, 1973) have shown that these attachment patterns and the intensity of the attachment are related to patterns of mothering; that is, securely attached infants have mothers who are the most *responsive* to their babies. These mothers tend to notice their babies' signals, to accept the necessary ties of caring for their babies, to show concern and respect for their babies' activities, and to be available to them. Figure 14-2 shows this relationship with data from a study by Clarke-Stewart (1973) in which she ranked children along a dimension of *intensity* of attachment (based on assessment in the strange situation) and also rated their mothers' behaviors from observations during a home visit. As can be seen, positive emotions, responsiveness, and amount of social stimulation provided to their infants are highest in mothers of *securely attached* children and lower for mothers of both unattached (analogous to the *avoidant* group) and malattached infants (the *resistant* group).

Long-term Effects

In his early writing, John Bowlby (1951) claimed that the caregiver–child relationship had long-term effects and that serious psychological damage could result from its disruption. As Damon (1983) points out, at that time the claim must have seemed speculative at best. Over the past decades, however, this assumption has been accepted by many experts in child development.

For example, Matas, Arend, and Sroufe (1978) provided evidence that infants who were securely attached at 12 or 18 months approached problems presented to them as 2-year-olds with greater enthusiasm and interest than did avoidant or resistant children. Similarly, Waters, Wippman, and Sroufe (1979) showed that securely attached children later tended (during nursery school) to be social leaders who were more active, sought out by other children, and rated by their teachers as self-directed and eager to learn. This latter study is particularly interesting because it was a *prospective* study; after the assessments of attachment, predictions were made concerning which children would later show the greatest competence with peers. Other researchers, however, have argued for caution in interpreting the research on attachment (Kagan, 1984; Lamb et al., 1985). They point out that the research has shown

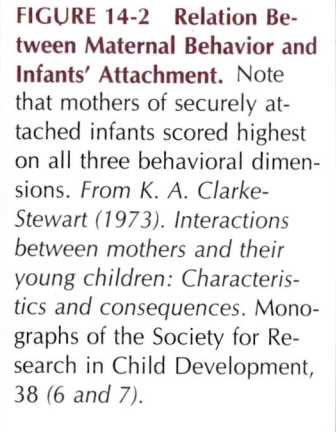

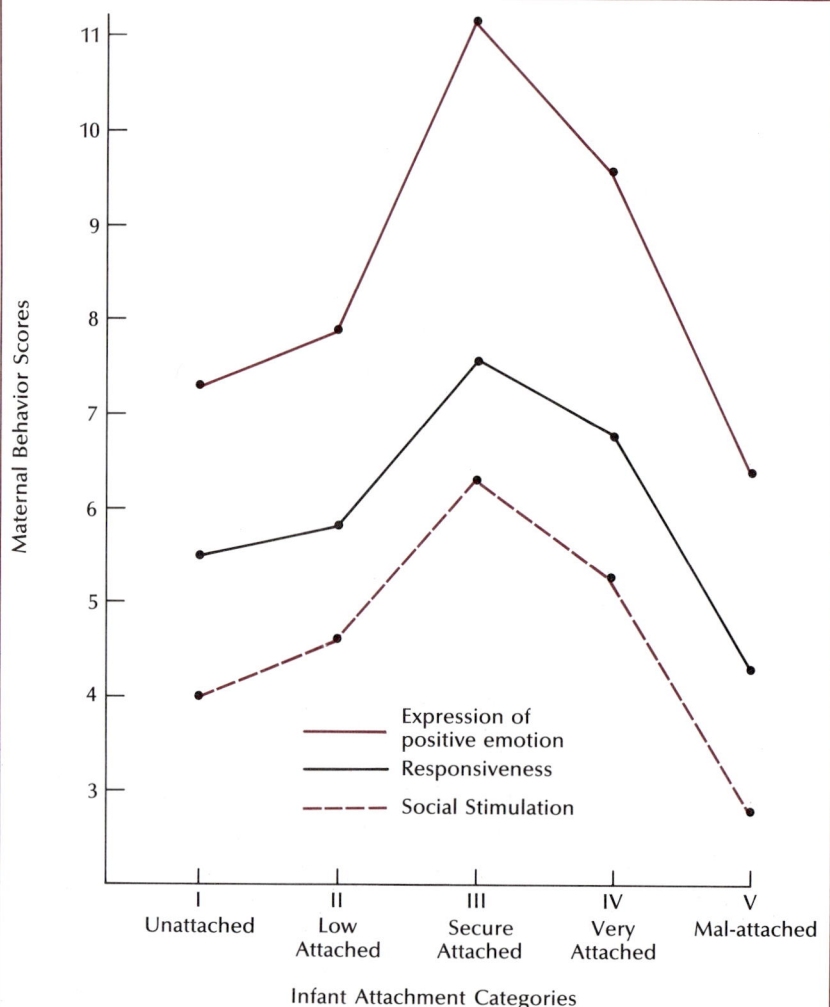

FIGURE 14-2 Relation Between Maternal Behavior and Infants' Attachment. Note that mothers of securely attached infants scored highest on all three behavioral dimensions. *From K. A. Clarke-Stewart (1973). Interactions between mothers and their young children: Characteristics and consequences. Monographs of the Society for Research in Child Development, 38 (6 and 7).*

consistent effects of attachment only on *some* of the variables studied and that family stability may exert an important influence on attachment patterns. Furthermore, cultural factors and temperament may affect how children react to separation, leading researchers to misinterpret behavior they observe.

Are the consequences of adverse experiences and poor early attachment permanent? Probably not, at least in the sense that children's social behavior and personality might be determined once and for all by the caregiver–child relationship. Work with primates, for instance, has shown that, although monkeys reared in *total isolation* as infants are notably defective in their later ability to interact socially with other monkeys (e.g., they were unusually aggressive, frightened, and so on), they could be rehabilitated to some extent (Suomi & Harlow, 1972). In humans, of course, such extreme conditions seldom, if ever, occur. Moreover, there are multiple influences on human social development, such as the presence of several caregivers in many families, social customs, the child's own temperament, and family stability (Lamb et al., 1985). Also, some authorities (e.g., Kagan, 1984; Kagan & Brim, 1981; Werner & Smith, 1982) have provided evidence that the potential for development, including social development, is surprisingly resilient.

Research

Fathers and Attachment

A common stereotype is that mothers are the primary and even the *only* attachment figures. In many families, however, the father is just as important as the mother as an attachment object. Lamb (1977a, 1977b, 1980; Lamb et al., 1985) has shown, for instance, that babies can become equally attached to their fathers as to their mothers. During their second year, girls were observed to interact equally with their fathers and mothers, whereas some boys actually preferred interacting with their fathers. If both parents are present and interacting with the infant, attachments will be formed to both.

Although attachment occurs with both fathers and mothers, several reliable differences that may affect attachment appear in the specific ways that fathers and mothers interact with their infants. Fathers, for instance, often play with their babies in a physically stimulating, vigorous way, such as by tossing their babies in the air and playing "rough and tumble" games. Mothers, on the other hand, more typically play quietly with their infants, emphasizing verbal exchanges over physical ones (Clarke-Stewart, 1978, 1980).

Also, interactions with caregivers usually occur as part of a **family system**, in which all individuals are interacting. Thus mothers and fathers not only have *direct* influence through the attachment process but may also affect their infants *indirectly* through their relationships with one another (Damon, 1983). For instance, mothers may interact differently with their infants when the babies' fathers are around than when they are not. Similarly, when mothers are around, fathers direct less of their attention to their infants. The possibilities for attachment and the quality of attachment may change depending on family context.

Attachment does not seem to be an "exclusive" process. It involves both fathers and mothers and can extend to other caregivers, such as a day-care worker. It most often occurs in a family system, however, in which there are many avenues through which the infant and caregivers influence one another. Fundamental to attachment is that truly social ties to specific individuals have been formed. The child uses these individuals as a "secure base" from which to explore and for comfort and protection when distressed (Bretherton & Waters, 1985). When separated from them, the infant will protest strongly. As Lamb (1984) points out, "missing" either parent shows that infants have the cognitive and emotional capacity to react to the *absence* of a person, a person who has assumed a role of considerable importance in their lives.

Although difficulties in attachment may increase the likelihood that social adjustment and personality problems will arise later, they by no means ensure this. There are many paths to social maturity. Whereas attachment is an important process, early problems in this area by no means doom unlucky children to lives of maladjustment and unhappiness.

Relations with Peers and Social Development

Although families usually are the first arena for many of the processes of social development (both prosocial and antisocial), children's experiences with other children—their **peers**—are among the most significant they will have. The unique aspect of their relationships with peers is the relative "developmental equivalence" between participants (Hartup, 1983; Hay, 1985). Peers are equals, so to speak. Thus relationships are likely to be quite different than those with parents or other adult caregivers.

Both laypersons and developmentalists conventionally use the term *peer* to refer to children who are similar in age to one another. Most of the research on child–child interactions (about 90 percent) is indeed conducted on age mates or peers, children within 12 months of one another. Often, however, other interactions occur that are not, strictly speaking, peer interactions. In reality many children interact regularly with younger or older siblings, and in some settings (e.g., a small rural school) no other children a child's own age may be present. Social interactions vary considerably depending on whether a given child is with a younger child, an age mate, or an older child.

Origins of Peer Relations in Infancy

Many children come into contact with their peers in their first months of life. According to Vandell and Mueller (1980), over half of all babies 6 to 12 months of age have contact with other babies at least once a week. For the youngest infants, social behavior with peers largely is confined to crying when other babies do. By 3 or 4 months, however, babies will reach for and touch one another; by 6 months, many will smile at each other (Vandell & Meuller, 1980; Vincze, 1971). Between 6 and 12 months, social interaction with other babies continues to increase. Relative to total time infants are together, however, their "social" actions are still quite infrequent. When infants (with their mothers present) are placed together (e.g., in a crib or playroom), an expected rate of contact is about once every 2 minutes—not a very lively social exchange! Many infant-to-infant overtures are not reciprocated (Hartup,

1983). Even when there is a response, a single pattern of overture-response (e.g., a child holds out a toy and the other child takes it) usually constitutes the entire interaction. Multiple exchanges, in which each baby responds in turn more than once, are extremely rare before 1 year of age.

Between age 1 and 2, the amount of interaction increases somewhat, but social skills remain basic. Most baby–baby exchanges are emotionally neutral, although smiling and laughing are more common among 2-year-olds than 1-year-olds. Social interest is present at this time, but the skills for long-term social interactions are not (Hartup, 1983). As children move into the preschool years, however, their capacity for sustained social relationships increases. Real friendships now become possible.

Becoming Friends

From preschool on, children greatly treasure their social relationships with their friends. They want to be with Amy or Troy, not just with any child.

Interviewer:	Why is Caleb your friend?
Tony:	Because I like him.
Interviewer:	And why do you like him?
Tony:	Because he's my friend.
Interviewer:	And why is he your friend?
Tony:	(with mild disgust) Because . . . I . . . choosed . . . him . . . for . . . my friend (Rubin, 1980).

Friends are special persons, and friendship in some ways resembles attachment: It is specific to a given person, separation from the person is disturbing, and reunions are occasions for joy (Hartup, 1983). In their friendships, children learn about others. They also learn about their own feelings, the need to invest in others, and perhaps about the fragility of human relationships. As Hartup (1983) points out, friendships can be as intense and significant in children's development as are attachments in the family.

How do children become friends? Are there certain actions or processes that lead to children "hitting it off"? An extensive analysis of children's interactions by John Gottman of the University of Illinois would seem to indicate so. Gottman (1983) studied children ranging in age from 3 to 9 and identified six important aspects of initial interactions between two children: (1) connectedness (2) information exchange, (3) establishing common ground, (4) conflict resolution, (5) positive reciprocity, and (6) self-disclosure.

In their friendships, children learn about others. They also learn about themselves, the need to invest in their friends, and the importance of frienship.

The aspect of **connectedness** refers to the extent to which two children are able to interact effectively with one another. Are they talking *to* each other or just talking? Are requests for clarification (e.g., "Which car do you want?") followed by appropriate information (e.g., "The big red one")? This aspect also refers to the extent to which children are able to convey their intentions clearly to one another.

Information exchange is the degree to which children are able to ask for and receive relevant information. For example, an exchange between two boys might go as follows, as information is requested and received in a regular pattern:

(Chris comes into room where Tyler is sitting with his mother.)
Chris: (to Tyler) Hey, you know what?
Tyler: What?
Chris: I got a new bike!
Tyler: Wow, what kind is it?
(The conversation continues about the new bike.)

As you can see, Chris initiated an exchange, Tyler responded, Chris provided more information, and the exchange continued.

Establishing **common ground** involves two aspects: (1) children finding something that they can do together and (2) exploring how they are alike or different. Children who succeed at the first are able to find

Relations with Peers and Social Development

a common activity that both will enjoy:

(Nick and Yolanda sit at the kitchen table.)
Nick: Let's pretend we're baking stuff, O. K.?
Yolanda: O. K.
Nick: There's some pots in the stove.
Yolanda: Let's get some real big ones.
(Nick and Yolanda assemble several pots and dishes for "baking.")

In contrast, other pairs of children will fail to establish common ground:

(At preschool, Shawn moves over to a toy piano in a play area.)
Shawn: (to Kari) Hey, come here! Watch me!
Kari: Let's go over here (points to toybox).
Shawn: Ding, ding, ding (sings and plays).
Kari: Let's go.
Shawn: Ring, ding, ding (keeps playing).
Kari: I'm gonna get my colors.
Shawn: Why don't you be a singer (continues to play)?
Kari: Don't want to (goes to toybox).

Many times children disagree on how they should go about something and conflicts result. **Resolution of conflict** refers to children's ability to deescalate conflicts by such methods as giving in to reasonable requests, using politeness, or stating reasons for disagreeing. Failures in conflict resolution may be shown by **disagreement chains**. If these chains appear frequently in children's conversations, they signal that conflicts are not getting resolved.

(Eric and Jane pretend to taste food.)
Eric: This tastes yukky!
Jane: No, it doesn't!
Eric: Does *SO*.
Jane: Does *NOT*.
Eric: Does *SO*.
Jane: Does *NOT*.
Eric: Does *SO*.
Jane: You're dumb.

An exchange of positive behaviors in which partners please one another is referred to as **positive reciprocity**. Chains of jokes, gossip, or fantasy (e.g., *Samantha*: "Let's pretend we're on top of the Glass

Mountain!" *Jeff:* "Oh, Oh! I'm starting to slip!" *Samantha:* "Don't fall, I've got you!") are examples of such exchanges.

Finally, **self-disclosure** is the extent to which children express their own feelings (e.g., "I'd be scared if my Mom left, wouldn't you?") over the course of their contact with one another.

Gottman's research has shown that these six variables, measured in initial contacts between previously unacquainted children, can be used to predict with high accuracy whether they will become friends. In other words, friendship seems to depend on the processes measured by these variables. In general, if children are to become friends, they need to interact in a connected way and to exchange information successfully. They also need to find a joint, common-ground activity and discover ways to resolve conflict. As the relationship develops, friends-to-be show more skill at clarifying communication than children who will not be friends. As their friendship grows, information exchange, finding common ground activities, exploration of similarities and differences, resolution of conflict, and self-disclosure also become even more important than they were initially.

As Gottman points out, these processes are not exotic. Nonetheless, they predict the extent to which children will progress toward becoming friends. Observations of how well newly acquainted children can exchange information, find mutually enjoyable activities, reduce conflict, and reciprocate joking, gossip, and fantasy are highly predictive of later friendship. However, Gottman is careful to point out that his is a correlational, not an experimental, study (see Chapter 3). Relationships were observed, not manipulated. While the observed variables may be *indices* for important processes and *predictive* of others (i.e., the formation of friendship), more studies are needed before we can be completely assured that *interventions* based on these variables will lead to greater friendship formation.

Gottman does believe, however, that some children are more skillful than others in forming friendships. Further analysis of his data indicated that some children show more of these processes (e.g., message clarification, conflict resolution) with *both* friends and strangers. They are better at "being friendly." Thus, while more research is needed, the above variables may be an excellent starting point in designing ways to help socially unskilled or isolated children develop friendships.

A common thread in the variables identified by Gottman is **reciprocity**, the give and take between two individuals. Reciprocity is a critical factor in children's friendships, just as it is in adult relationships. Those who will be friends or already are friends engage in more reciprocal interactions. "I" gives way to "we." Reciprocity is shown in the cooperation and closeness of childhood friendships; it also is a key building block for mutual emotional support, which becomes especially strong during adolescence (Hartup, 1983).

Children in Groups

Many of children's social interactions occur in groups of two, three, or more peers. A **group** is a social unit to which individuals have a sense of belonging. A group shares certain values and supports attitudes members should have about each other. Clusters of friends form groups. Similarly, a softball team is a group: Interaction occurs (playing the game, talking, and so on), values are shared ("I hate playing right field, don't you?"), and group values are transmitted (e.g., the coach tells them, "O.K., Kristi's up! Let's give her some encouragement!"). Mrs. Smith's second-grade class or the Kantorei, a junior high vocal music organization, also are groups if they share activities and values. Membership in groups can be on the basis of age, sex, ability, or almost any other variable. Young children initially do not have much of an idea of "groupness": Their focus is on their relationship to single individuals (Hartup, 1983). By middle childhood and adolescence, however, the peer group becomes a real community and provides the setting in which social and intellectual development takes place.

Children's groups are formed in many different ways; they may emerge spontaneously or may be created for children by adults. Soon, patterns of friendship and division of labor will develop (Hartup, 1983). Groups also quickly develop **norms**, standards that govern their conduct. These characteristics of groups are illustrated in a well-known experiment conducted many years ago by Muzafer Sherif and his associates (Sherif, Harvey, White, Hood, & Sherif, 1961). In this study, a group of fifth-grade boys was recruited to a summer camp, divided into two subsets, and moved to separate campsites. They did the usual camp activities, including hiking, crafts, organized games, and building. Using a combination of naturalistic observation and experimental methods (see Chapter 3), the investigators observed the boys, occasionally arranging situations and watching their reactions. For example, when faced with only the raw ingredients for an evening meal (the staff had not prepared dinner) and left on their own, the boys quickly divided the labor and solved the problem cooperatively, with some cooking, some setting tables, and so on. Leaders and followers quickly emerged. Both groups adopted names (the Rattlers and the Eagles). A definite identity had been created within each group.

An especially interesting aspect of the Sherif et al. study occurred when the two groups met and competed in activities such as baseball and tug-of-war. The reactions to losing within each group were very strong: Anger, blaming others, and grumbling were common in both groups. Soon, however, the groups became more solid internally and new norms developed, as members of each group reaffirmed their unity and their separateness from the other group. Each group believed itself to be the "good guys" and the other the "bad guys." The rivalry between the groups increased, intensifying to open conflict. In fact, the experimenters needed to intervene before the conflict got out of hand.

By arranging several situations in which members of the groups were forced to cooperate toward a common goal (e.g., all of them trying to find out what was wrong with the water supply, which broke down on a hot day), much of the conflict was defused. Mutually desired goals and cooperative activity were the keys to reducing tension. In contrast, when members of the two groups had been together in pleasant circumstances but *without* a common goal and need for cooperation, hostility was *not* reduced, but actually seemed to increase.

Group Structures. A universal characteristic of groups is **group structure**: Different children have different levels of power and influence. Group structure usually is **hierarchical**—that is, a top to bottom structure, in which some individuals are dominant and others are submissive. Children's roles will not necessarily be the same in all groups to which they belong, however. Individuals' power depends to a great extent on the type of group. A girl who is athletically but not academically talented, for example, may be a leader on the volleyball team but not in any of her classes. **Leadership** is closely related to the match between an individual's skills and the purposes of the group.

Leadership. Group structures and, hence, leadership tend to change with development. Leadership generally is reflected in the ability to influence, guide, and direct others in groups. In early childhood, group leaders tend to be children who can hold onto possessions and use them effectively (Hartup, 1983). By middle childhood, leaders are those who are skilled at directing play and games. By early adolescence, leadership positions tend to shift to those who have matured early, and who have athletic and social skills. Later in adolescence, the highest status positions in groups often go to those who are well-liked and intelligent, traits that are related to adult leadership as well.

Leadership must be earned and cannot be assigned arbitrarily. When children without the necessary skills are put in leadership positions (e.g., one of the least skilled boys is assigned to be "team captain" on a soccer team), children quickly perceive that this authority is not legitimate and resist it. In general, leaders at all ages usually are those whose social and intellectual skills help the group meet its objectives (Hartup, 1983). Most child leaders, however, interact vigorously with their peers; they also are generally successful in influencing other children.

Overall Impact of Groups. It is hard to overestimate the impact peer groups have on children's social development. The necessary skills of sharing, giving, and helping are learned in groups; group judgments shape self-concept. Children learn to lead and follow in groups. Ideas of fairness and justice evolve out of transactions in groups (Damon, 1983), while peers serve as models for behavior and provide reinforcement for actions, ways of thinking, and group conformity. The myriad

Social Play among Peers

of interactions that occur and a groups' abilities to establish and enforce norms make them a potent force in the socialization of most children.

Few adults are interested in sipping pretend tea for hours on end, jumping off a bed thirty times in a row, or making the roaring sounds of a motor while "driving" a cardboard box in the front yard. While adults can and do play with children, and exert important effects on children's social and intellectual development, there is a special quality of play among peers simply because they are peers.

At first, children's play is not oriented toward peers. Infants tend to engage in **object play**, involving specific items such as balls, spoons, or cups. They may hold, bang, and mouth an object; early social contact often tends to involve mutual interest in the same object. Around the age of 1, however, children begin to use objects *representationally* as symbols for other things. A pot may become a hat or a block of wood a car. This shift to **pretend play** can be dramatic. Pretend play begins to mimic real-life activities (Rubin, Fein, & Vandenberg, 1983).

In its earliest forms, pretend play frequently is solitary, but during the preschool and kindergarten years it becomes increasingly social. In **social play,** children are mutually engaged in activities that both understand are pretend; that is, the significance of the activities is not in the activities themselves but in what they represent to the children (Garvey, 1977). Two developmental changes, in particular, make social play possible. The first is children's growing cognitive capabilities. Being able to see that events can represent something beyond themselves opens up tremendous possibilities for play and for social interactions in general (Damon, 1983). Second, children begin to see themselves in stable relationships with other children. Pretend play is built on this sense of continuity. As relationships develop and children become friends, favorite play themes that have a particular structure and sequence that is repeated each time children play often emerge. Some children's favorites include taking domestic roles ("I'll be Mother; you be Baby"); danger and rescue ("Look out! It's a deep cave. Oh, we've fallen in!"), and shared deviance ("My hand is the *bad hand*. Watch out for it!").

Social play often has a ritual-like quality, in which reality is suspended and there is turn-taking, assigned roles, and mutual expectations about what the format of activities should be. Take the following example:

(Donie comes running into the house from the back.)

Donie: The squirrel just talked to me!

Lissa: (turns to her) Really?

Donie: (grins) No, just pretend.

Lissa: (smiles) Can I talk to him, too?

Children's play is often highly organized and ritualistic, with assigned roles and mutual expectations about how the activities should go.

In this exchange, reality is suspended by Donie's comments and this is quickly recognized by Lissa.

Skill at turn-taking is illustrated clearly in the following exchange.

(Dante and Tobie are discussing their feelings about school.)
Dante: I hate school, don't you?
Tobie: Yeah, 'cause it's just like a jail.
Dante: Yeah.
Tobie: Yeah, 'cause it's got bars and everything.
Dante: And it has guards and mean people and . . .
Tobie: And they keep you all locked up all the time.
Dante: And they don't give you nothing to eat.
Tobie: Yeah.

As Dante stated a theme, Tobie quickly became aware of it and amplified on it. Of course, this kind of ritualistic dialogue does not necessarily mirror reality. Neither will it always make much sense to adults.

(Two preschoolers are "making soup," talking as they do.)
Mia: I'm Bo Bo.
Rob: I'm Be Be.
Mia: I'm Ya Ya.

Rob: I'm Pa Pa.

Mia: I'm Ick Ick.

Rob: I'm Uck Uck.

(Routine continues through several more sequences.)

Even in this sequence, however, we see the same important aspects of social play: the suspension of reality and taking turns.

Simple ritualistic play such as this decreases with age, however, and tends to be replaced by more elaborate sequences of pretense for which preparation is required and roles assigned (Rubin, Fein, & Vandenberg, 1983). The following example of more elaborate pretense in social play is illustrated by another example, adapted from Garvey (1974):

(Todd, preparing to "talk on phone," addresses Kris.)

Todd: Pretend you're sick.

Kris: O. K.

Todd: (speaks into phone) Hey, Dr. Wren, do you got any medicine?

Kris: Yes, I have some medicine.

Todd: (to Kris) No, you aren't the doctor, remember?

Kris: O. K.

Todd: (speaks into phone) I need some medicine for the kids. Bye (turns to Kris). He hasn't got any medicine.

Kris: No? Oh, dear.

Vygotsky (1976) pointed out that *sets of rules* underlie all play. In addition to turn-taking (a kind of rule), children learn what is appropriate to certain roles ("Come on! Captain Mylan's not like that [Child knocks blocks down.] He's *tough*!"). Often, too, there is a shared development of a theme, with each child contributing his or her conceptions in turn.

(Wade and Kari are playing house.)

Wade: Ugh, this tea is bad!

Kari: Mine too! I want some milk.

Wade: I'll go get it.

Kari: No, baby, you're too small to carry it. You'll spill it.

Wade: No, I'm big enough, Mommy.

Kari: Here, let me help you.

As play becomes more complex, themes are negotiated and agreed upon prior to play. Children often discuss or argue at length about the roles to be filled (e.g., "I'm Big Sister," "I get to be Daddy," and so on), where the pretend situation is taking place ("Let's pretend we're in a dark old cave!"), and what various objects represent ("Here, I got me a snake catcher!").

Later Play. Piaget (1962) contended that, with increasing cognitive competence, children gradually become able to engage in more complex forms of play—play governed by rules. In games with rules, children compete with each other and participants' behaviors are governed by codes or prior agreements. Piaget believed pretend play gradually gives way during concrete operations (approximately 7 to 11 years of age) to participation in games that are formal and rule-governed. Later research has, in fact, confirmed that there is some decline in the "pretend play" of earlier childhood as children move into elementary school (Rubin et al., 1983), while participation in games with rules increases during the same period.

The Significance of Play for Social Development. Most researchers agree that play has a critical role in social development (see Rubin et al., 1983). Usually, play does not occur when children are fearful, uncertain, or distressed. Because it is pursued for the sake of pleasure, it provides a unique occasion for positive social interaction with peers. Also, play almost always repeats or elaborates on previously learned behavior (Rubin et al., 1983). Thus it offers an unusually rich opportunity for children to practice previously learned cognitive and linguistic skills and for children to learn new social-interactive skills in their give and take with others.

The Development of Aggression

Few topics in developmental psychology have attracted as much attention as **aggression**. We worry a great deal about conflict, particularly when it escalates into actions that cause physical harm. Developmental psychology has had a large stake in trying to understand how aggression develops. At the same time, few topics have provided greater challenges and frustrations for developmental researchers.

One of the biggest stumbling blocks has been the difficulty of defining aggression (Parke & Slaby, 1983). For example, we might observe a teenage girl yelling and banging on her 10-year-old brother's door, because she believes he has used all the hot water for the shower. Is she being aggressive? Later, at school, we hear this same girl making "smart-alecky" comments under her breath when her math teacher gives a big assignment. Is this aggressive? Still later, at a clothing store, we see her returning a blouse in which the seam was not sewn right. She is firm, but polite, in her insistence that she should get a new blouse. Is this aggression?

Clearly, judgments about what constitutes aggression can vary tremendously. A behavior may be labeled aggressive in one situation and not in another, by one person and not another, or in one community or social group and not in others. Finding a good operational definition of aggression (see Chapter 3) is not easy. As Parke and Slaby (1983) have pointed out, however, this recognition of individually and culturally determined "changing standards" for judging aggression actually may help us understand more about aggression. In our discussion here, however, we will follow Parke and Slaby's lead in adopting what may be the simplest definition of aggression: "behavior that is aimed at harming or injuring another person" (Parke & Slaby, 1983, p. 550).

The Beginnings of Aggression

It is hard to conceive of an aggressive newborn, particularly when one considers that very young infants can do little that is (1) intentional or (2) directed specifically toward another person. As babies develop, however, they begin to understand the concepts of cause and effect and to realize that other people, such as their parents, can frustrate them. Thus, by 7 or 8 months of age, an infant may begin to push a parent's hand away in order to reach, say, a shiny spoon. Although infants at this age may direct their behavior to remove obstacles, a part of aggression, they probably have no intention of hurting their parents in the process!

Maccoby (1980) has argued that there is a close relationship between cognitive development and aggression. In order to be aggressive, children must be able to (1) distinguish themselves from other persons, (2) be aware that others can feel distress, and (3) recognize that they can cause that distress. Obviously, this is a complicated set of knowledge involving self-awareness, information about others, and understanding cause and effect. At first, children have little awareness of these factors. Although they might hurt someone, they could not be said to be acting aggressively. Gradually, however, the cognitive abilities that underlie aggression develop.

For example, Bronson (1975) observed children between 1 and 2 years of age in play groups of 3 or 4. Their mothers were present to provide security but were not involved otherwise. Children this age do not interact at length; most of their disagreements were brief and consisted of one child's trying to take a toy from another. Although the number of disagreements did not change over a year's time, the emotional intensity of their reactions did. As the year progressed, children showed more anger and frustration when toys were taken from them. They became increasingly concerned with ownership ("That's *mine!*"). Fairly often, Bronson noted, children struggled over toys neither played with either before or after the encounter! The fact of possession had become important: They seem to have developed concepts of "I" and "mine" and loss of a toy became an offense to their ideas of self. This aggression, however, was focused more on the toy than on the other person. In contrast to later, "true" aggression, conflict was not aimed toward hurting or frightening others, but only toward "staking out a claim" (Maccoby, 1980).

Further Development of Aggression

Between the ages of 2 and 4, there is a decrease in **physical aggression** and an increase in **verbal aggression**, as children begin to substitute words for direct physical action. In a well-known and still-cited study conducted over a half-century ago, Florence Goodenough (1931) asked 45 mothers to keep daily diaries of their children's outbursts. The children ranged between 7 months and 7 years of age; most were 2 or 3 years old. Angry outbursts peaked between the ages of 1 and 2 and then declined rapidly. Youngest children's outbursts were mostly tantrums; later, focused anger such as retaliation for a parent's or child's action became more frequent. The outbursts of infancy usually occurred in reaction to physical discomfort, whereas "habit training" (e.g., finding a regular bedtime) often brought outbursts in the second and third years. In 4-year-olds, a major cause of aggression was conflict with peers.

Thus, as children mature, the form of their aggression changes. **Instrumental aggression** is the earlier and more basic form, resulting simply from children's being blocked from goals. With increasing cognitive skills, however, comes the ability to react with **hostile aggression**. Hostile aggression (Hartup, 1974) is based on (1) a perceived threat to the child's ego or sense of self (e.g., "He can't do that to me", "He's making fun of me") and (2) an inference that the aggressor is acting *intentionally* (e.g., "He did that *on purpose!*"). Hartup noted that instrumental aggression decreased from preschool through the early primary grades. The frequency of hostile aggression did not change much, but the nature of the hostile response did. Whereas younger children might respond to an insult by hitting, older children were more inclined to respond *in kind*: Insults merited insults, hitting would bring on hitting back, and so on. Older children's shift from instrumental to hostile aggression may be based on their increased ability to infer hostile intentions on the part of the attacker (Ferguson & Rule, 1980) and seems to become more and more a matter of attempting to restore balance to relationships after one child has attempted to "harm" the other.

Sources of Aggression

Why are human beings aggressive? Is aggression part of the natural state of human beings, linked to our evolution and to our biology? Or is aggression more of a social phenomenon, conditioned through children's upbringing in particular families and cultures? The answer seems to be both.

Biological Determinants of Aggression. Some authorities argue that there are strong **biological determinants of aggression**. Taking an evolutionary perspective, these researchers point out the close parallels between the developmental patterns for aggression in children and in other species, particularly primates. Konrad Lorenz, a Nobel Prize winner and author of *On Aggression* (1966), defined aggression as "the fight instinct in man and beast." Aggression, he argued, is an adaptive, instinctual system that has played an important role in the survival of the human species (e.g., the need to defend self and others from attack). Aggression develops naturally in each human because of our evolutionary history.

Taking a biological perspective, Suomi (1977) has pinpointed the development of aggression in monkeys, with infant monkeys first showing only curiosity to novel stimuli; at about 3 months of age a fear response; and then, at 6 to 8 months, an aggressive pattern. The appearance of the aggressive pattern can be seen in a change from the rough and tumble play of infant monkeys to actual fighting. At this point, Suomi observed, some animals become dominant, a kind of social structure appears, and fighting declines. Like other animals, human beings have an evolutionary history. The pattern of aggression in children shows strong parallels to the kinds of patterns seen in other animals, such as those observed by Suomi. From this point of view, it makes sense to argue that aggression is unlearned, basically following the course of a genetically determined time schedule.

This view is supported by the fact that biology also seems to have an important role in sex differences in aggression. For instance, several researchers (Olweus, Mattsson, Schalling, & Low, 1980; Persky, Smith, & Basu, 1971) have found links between levels of the male hormone, testosterone, and levels of aggression, such as aggressive responses to provocation and threat. Boys are many times more likely to be arrested for violent crimes (Cairns, 1979) and, in reviewing a large number of studies of children under 6 years of age, Maccoby and Jacklin (1974) found "clear sex differences in aggression," with boys being consistently more aggressive than girls. Both physical and verbal aggression differ in frequency. According to Maccoby and Jacklin, the universality of sex differences such as these lends support to a view that biology provides basic conditions for development of sex differences in aggression. As they state, "It is conceivable, but unlikely in our opinion, that cross-cultural universality [of sex differences] could occur with no biological rootedness at all" (Maccoby & Jacklin, 1974, p. 971).

Social Determinants of Aggression. While biology plays an important role in the development of aggression, there is also ample evidence for **social determinants of aggression**. For example, sex stereotyping (e.g., belief that boys are "hardier," or girls more "delicate") begins in earliest infancy (Condry & Condry, 1976; Rubin, Provenzano, & Luria, 1974) and continues into later childhood (Block, 1978; Izard, Kagan, & Zajonc, 1984). Parental attitudes (e.g., "Come on, Jennifer, quit wrestling around!"), child-rearing practices (such as the greater likelihood of using physical punishment with boys than girls), and modeling (such as seeing one's mother and father argue in characteristic ways) can socialize aggression differently for boys than for girls. The differences in aggression between males and females noted above, for instance, may stem from these socialization differences as well as from biological factors.

Certain families, social groups, and cultural characteristics likewise can exert an important influence on how aggression develops and the form it takes. Whereas "turning the other cheek" may be an ideal for a child in one family, "an eye for an eye" may be the norm in another. Whereas holding back aggression would be rewarded in one social group ("I'm glad you didn't hit back; that was very grown-up of you"), this same action might be frowned upon in another ("Don't be such a sissy—if he hits you, hit him back!"). Some cultures also may condone some forms of aggression, such as threats or arguing, but not approve of others, such as use of physical force. Similarly, peers in a given group may tolerate only certain kinds of aggression. For example, some children may ignore insults directed toward them (e.g., "You're dumb") but react aggressively by hitting and yelling when their parents are insulted (e.g., "Your Dad is a BIG dummy!"). Thus children quickly learn to channel their aggressive feelings in ways allowed by their families and social groups.

How, specifically, do social factors affect the development of aggression? Perhaps the most prominent explanation of the development of aggression has been the **social learning theory** of Albert Bandura, a Stanford psychologist and former president of the American Psychological Association. According to Bandura, humans learn much of what they know, including aggression, through **observational learning** (see Chapter 5). By seeing parents and peers act aggressively and by observing many other aggressive models in the media (especially on television) children readily learn a wide variety of aggressive actions (Parke & Slaby, 1983).

As discussed in Chapter 5, developmental level, attention, retention processes, the ability to imitate actions, and motivation control the potential for imitation. Imitation of aggressive responses is no exception. Once aggressive responses are imitated, however, their continued use depends on reinforcement. Aggression (such as a threat) may produce the desired results in some instances (the other child drops the desired toy), but provoke unpleasant reactions in others (the other child bops the aggressor on the head with the toy when threatened). Aggres-

The possibility of aggression depends on the interpretations children make of others' actions. Some children have a special sensitivity to being provoked, while others do not.

sion, in the view of the social learning theorists, begins with modeling and is shaped by the consequences of the aggressive behaviors.

Social learning theory has been a tremendous stimulus for research on how children's environments affect the occurrence of aggression. With few exceptions (e.g., Yando, Seitz, & Zigler, 1978), however, it has not particularly emphasized the *developmental* aspects of aggression—that is, how the developmental levels of children can affect learning of aggression and other social responses. As a consequence, researchers on aggression have recently turned to what has been called a **social cognition theory** of aggression (Dodge, 1980; Dodge & Frame, 1982; Parke & Slaby, 1983), which has many similarities to the concept of causal attribution described in Chapter 13. Social cognition theory draws on social learning theory but particularly emphasizes children's processing of information, especially information about what constitutes a provocation and what are appropriate retaliations for certain aggressive actions. For example, if a child is hit in the face by a basketball thrown in bounds during a game at school, she may first try to determine the passer's intentions: Was it an accident or "on purpose"? If all the cues point to an accident (e.g., the boy who threw the ball looks startled, begins apologizing, comes over to comfort her), she will not respond aggressively. On the other hand, if the boy is laughing and pointing at her, she may decide that retaliation is called for. She then needs to find an appropriate response. If the boy looks considerably bigger and meaner than she, she may settle for glaring and muttering a few angry words. A smaller and less menacing antagonist, however, may get the ball thrown back at him or be chased and hit.

The critical variable is how children *interpret* others' intentions. Their interpretations affect the degree of aggressiveness in children, and determine the extent to which children avoid or are involved in aggressive encounters. These interpretations are shaped by the family, society, and culture in which a child lives. As development proceeds, children become more and more able to infer others' intentions and tend to respond to aggression only when they infer aggressive intent. Some children, however, seem to have a special sensitivity to "being provoked" and interpret situations as provocative that most other children would not. Because of their tendency to react aggressively to many situations, these children may find themselves living in an increasingly hostile world as others react in turn to their aggressive behavior with aggression of their own. As Dodge (1980) has pointed out, peers who have become recipients of negative outcomes such as being hit, yelled at, or taunted are likely to attribute hostile attentions to an aggressive child. They come to view the child as being inappropriately aggressive in general, are more likely to interpret future behavior as hostile, and to become aggressive themselves. A cycle of increased hostility, aggressive behavior, and social rejection of the aggressive child can thus develop.

In sum, both biological and social factors appear to be influential in the development of aggression. Human aggression follows a developmental course similar to that observed in other species, but the expression of aggression is strongly affected by children's family interactions and cultural expectations. In our society, for instance, children are exposed to many aggressive models through television, a factor many authorities believe is extremely influential in developing aggressive responses in children (see Chapter 5). Some families, too, provide models and reinforcement for aggression. With development, aggression becomes increasingly "cognitive" as children become more able to infer others' intentions. By late childhood and adolescence, most children learn to respond aggressively only when they infer aggressive intent.

Obviously it is useful to understand aggression and its role in the problems of society. However, we also must understand **prosocial behavior**, behavior carried out for the benefit of others. Just as aggression has survival value for humans, so do prosocial behaviors. Infants cannot survive unless they are cared for, and the early relationships between infants and their parents, described earlier, provide a stable base for ensuring that care. Family life, institutions, and societies are built on human ability to cooperate and help others. In fact, most human achievement has been the result of people working together in positive ways and expressing care and concern for others (see Chapters 13 and

15, for discussion of prosocial behaviors as aspects of emotional and moral development). Whereas studying aggression helps us identify problem areas, thinking about prosocial behavior focuses our attention on our goals for children's social development.

Relationships and Social Development in Adolescence

Peers, strong figures in childhood social development, become even more important in adolescence. Through their peer group, adolescents learn about themselves and about how to get along with their own and the opposite sex. To many adolescents, "fitting in" with their peers is one of their highest values: Clothing styles, behavior, and ways of speaking are all chosen in relationship to their peer group.

An especially critical developmental task of adolescence is the development of **autonomy**, or independence. Adolescents need to resolve the conflict between dependence on their family, on one hand, and the new demands and privileges of independence, on the other. The peer group provides the setting in which this independence truly can be tested and autonomy developed. Peer interactions allow for an exchange of ideas and activities that would be extremely unlikely to occur with adults. In many ways, the adolescent peer group provides its own culture, with shared ways of looking at the world and norms for behavior. It is a transitional community for teenagers as they move toward adulthood.

Adolescent groups are quite different from the groups of childhood. They tend to be broader, drawn from wider geographical and social spectra. Many also are more formal, organized around activities such as music or sports and linked to institutions such as schools or clubs. Structural changes also are evident, in that the same-sex groups of childhood and preadolesence give way gradually to the familiar patterns of adolescence—the **crowd**, the **clique**, and individual friendships.

The broadest and least personal group of adolescent peers is the *crowd*. Crowds are groups of people who meet because of a mutual interest in *activities*, not because of any special interest in one another. Groups of adolescents who regularly attend concerts or basketball games, for instance, are drawn together mainly by the activity. "Our old crowd" is a phrase describing such a loosely knit group who went many places and did many things together. *Cliques*, in contrast, are smaller, more tightly knit groups who come together on the basis of similar interests and social values (Santrock, 1984). In contrast to the relative impersonality of crowds, cliques are much more intimate and their members have much more in common.

In many schools, cliques are well-defined and generally identifiable. For example, students may label other as "preppies," "freaks," or "jocks" on the basis of members of a clique sharing common dress, behavior, or values. Each clique offers the adolescent its own subculture; membership in one often precludes membership in another. The choice of which clique, if any, to be a part of, may greatly affect the course of a particular adolescent's social development.

Cliques obviously are not fixed entities for all times and places. In one high school in the 1970s, the following cliques were identifiable (Hartup, 1983). *Sporties* participated in and attended sports activities; they also drank beer. *Crispies* were students who used drugs, were the best football players, and did not work very hard in school, while *workers* were students who had jobs, were motivated by earning money, and owned cars and structured their lives around them. *Musicians* were students who spent much time in the music room and in various performance activities. Finally, *debaters* were those who read a lot, got good grades, took part in "intellectual" clubs, and drank Pepsi-Cola at their parties! While this particular arrangement of cliques existed only in a single high school at one point, similar cliques are part of almost every school.

Adolescent cliques (especially in early adolescence) can exert tremendous power over their members. For the younger adolescents, at least, there seems to be some truth to the stereotype that individuals are especially likely to conform to peer standards not favored by adults (Damon, 1983; Hartup, 1983). Often, definite **cross-pressures** exist, in

Primitive peer pressure

which parents or other adults may disapprove of adolescent dress, grooming, or actions, while peers endorse them.

Conflict between peer and adult standards tends to lessen, however, with further development. By the end of high school, most adolescents are becoming more independent-minded and less affected by peer pressure. Moreover, most adolescents are unlikely ever to be completely separated from their parents' values, even during the period of peak opposition (Hartup, 1983). In general, adolescents' values are not terribly discrepant from those of their parents, especially on important issues. In fact, parents appear to exert relatively *more* influence than peers in some areas, such as job expectations and educational aspirations (Santrock, 1984). While critical adults may speak of adolescents as "irresponsible," "always getting into trouble," and "driving them crazy," (especially if the adult–adolescent relationship has deteriorated), most adolescents eventually are able to accommodate both their parents and their peers successfully.

New Intimacy in Friendships

Childhood friendships are rarely as close or intense as those that begin to appear in early adolescence; there is a distinct change in friendship patterns as **intimate friendships** begin to arise. In these intimate friendships, adolescents are likely to share private thoughts and personal knowledge (Santrock, 1984; Selman, 1980). In a study by Diaz and Berndt (1982), for example, fourth- and eighth-graders did not differ in what they knew about the external and observable features of their friends, but eighth-graders knew more intimate things about their friends. The intimate friendships of adolescence offer this potential for learning about one another.

Selman (1980) has argued that such changes from child to adolescent friendship patterns result from general cognitive development. "Friendship awareness" and expectations for friends are tied in to such cognitive abilities as conceptualizing themselves and taking others' perspectives. The expectations in childhood friendships—sharing and reciprocity—are relatively simple, and do not require a high level of conceptual development. However, more is expected of adolescent friends, such as sensitivity, trustworthiness, loyalty, and self-disclosure. Adolescent girls, especially, seem concerned with intimate qualities such as these and are likely to describe their best friends in such terms. For instance, a 14-year-old girl wrote the following postscript to a note to her best friend.

> P. S. In youth club at church we had to say just why our best friend was our best friend and I said my best friend is you because I can trust you and talk to you if I have problems and you always try to help me out and I can trust you with anything.
> P. P. S. I just thought I'd tell you 'cause I love you. Well, gotta go!

Same-Sex and Cross-Sex Friendships

During childhood, most peer relationships are with members of the same sex. In early adolescence, with its rapid and even bewildering physical and psychological changes, same-sex friendships still predominate. There even may be considerable antagonism toward the strange, "different" members of the opposite sex! Some authorities (Conger & Peterson, 1984) feel that these antagonisms may be linked to a deep self-consciousness of the adolescent and to anxiety about one's own sexual awakening. Thus the same-sex friendships may create a useful avoidance of heterosexual relationships with which the young adolescent is not yet prepared to cope.

As maturation proceeds, however, cross-sex interest increases and the earlier antagonisms fade. Nonetheless, many adolescents continue to be very self-conscious, and many heterosexual interactions are superficial and gamelike. Heterosexual contact often is limited to group activities such dances, parties, and athletic contests, where adolescents can explore heterosexual relationships from the comparative safety of their groups. Gradually, through a succession of such experiences, most individuals learn a variety of ways to relate to the opposite sex, building the groundwork for dating and intimate involvement with another person.

Dating

A stereotype with considerable basis in reality is one of a tongue-tied teenager calling up someone for a first date. Even though **dating** is now much more relaxed and informal than it once was, many of the anxieties that have accompanied adolescent heterosexual relationships through-

In the U.S. at least, dating plays a critical role in adolescent social relations and is a primary way of learning about intimacy. It also serves as a source of status and achievement.

Table 14-1 Frequency of Dating for U.S. High School Seniors (percent)

	Male	Female
Never	13	13
Once a month or less	20	18
2 or 3 times a month	21	17
Once a week	18	14
2 or 3 times a week	20	24
Over 3 times a week	8	14

From: L.D. Johnston, J.F. Bachman, & P.M. O'Malley. (1983). Monitoring the Future: Questionnaire responses from the nation's high school seniors. Ann Arbor, MI: Institute for Social Research. Used by permission.

out history remain ("Will he go to the dance with me?" or "What if she turns me down when I ask her?"). Perhaps the major reason for this anxiety is that dating is still the key social institution in the United States for fostering heterosexual relationships.

Dating plays an extremely important role in adolescent social relations in the United States. Most girls begin dating at about age 14 and most boys somewhere around 14 or 15. By the time they are seniors in high school (see Table 14-1), almost half of the boys and over half of the girls indicate they date at least once a week. Around one-third say they date 2 or 3 times a week. Girls tend to date boys somewhat older than themselves.

Although some worry that the American dating ritual may produce some undesirable results in relationships between the sexes (e.g., superficiality, lack of genuine caring, dishonesty), it has an undeniable role in providing a structure for learning to interact with members of the opposite sex (Conger & Peterson, 1984). It serves as recreation, a source of status and achievement, and helps adolescents learn to get along with others. However, it still retains its traditional function as a means of courtship and eventual mate selection (Skipper & Nass, 1966). It is also a way of learning about intimacy. Going steady, an indicator of more "serious" involvement, increases progressively with age, from around 10 percent in 13- to 15-year-old boys and 20 percent in 13- to 15-year-old girls, to around 30 percent of 16- to 18-year-old boys and 40 percent of 16- to 18-year-old girls.

Adolescent Sexuality: A New Dimension of Social Development

In American social life, dating provides the arena for increasing intimacy and is a testing ground for the emerging sexual behavior of adolescents (Santrock, 1984). Sexuality, of course, adds a significant new dimension to peer encounters. In many ways, it is the critical dimension in the heterosexual relations of adolescence. Certainly, many adolescents are concerned with their sexuality and with what is or is not "appropriate"

Research

Consequences of Adolescent Sexuality in the United States

According to the Alan Guttmacher Institute (1985), sexual activity among unmarried teenagers has been increasing since the 1940s. For instance, between 1971 and 1982, the proportion of sexually active teenagers grew from 28 percent to 43 percent. More young people have sexual relations during adolescence than not; 8 in 10 men and 7 in 10 women have had sex by the time they are age 19. Although the trend toward increasing sexual activity seems to be leveling off, the number of sexually active adolescents remains high. Out of 28 million teenagers, nearly 12 million have had intercourse, with the average age of initiating sex being 16 (Alan Guttmacher Institute, 1984).

One of the most vexing and persistent problems stemming from adolescent sexual activity is unwanted pregnancies. By the time they reach age 20, nearly 4 in 10 women will have had at least one pregnancy, while 2 in 10 will have had at least one birth. More than 1 in 7 will have had at least one abortion. Perhaps most sobering, however, is this: over three quarters of these pregnancies are unintentional.

As can be seen in Figure 14-3, the rates of adolescent pregnancy in the United States are far higher than those in similarly developed countries—Canada, France, the Netherlands, Sweden, and Great Britain, for example. Over 83 of every 1000 white American women become pregnant between the ages of 15 and 19, a rate over twice as high as Great Britain, the country with the second highest rate (*Newsweek*, March 25, 1985). Similarly, the abortion rate among adolescents is twice as high in the United States as in Sweden and France, and nine times as high as in the Netherlands. Further, rates seem to be *increasing* in the United States.

Why are these rates so high in the United States? One possibility is that American teenagers are more sexually active than adolescents in other

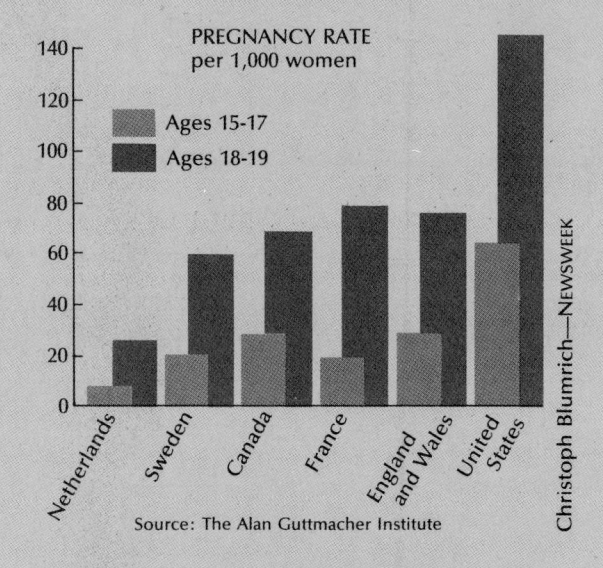

FIGURE 14-3 Rates of Adolescent Pregnancy. *From* Newsweek, *March 25, 1985, p. 91. Copyright 1986, by* Newsweek, *Inc. All rights reserved. Reprinted by permission.*

sexual activity at various stages of dating. Table 14-2 presents *desired* sexual behavior in three age groups. Both with increased age and increased involvement with dating, a greater number of both males and females desire physical involvement.

Most research into adolescents' social relationships and sexuality reveals an evolving pattern of increasing intimacy (Damon, 1983). First, countries but this is not the case (*Newsweek*, March 25, 1985). More likely, the high adolescent pregnancy rates stem from conflicts in our values and their effect on teenage attitudes toward sexuality. Although American children and teenagers are heavily exposed to models in advertising and entertainment media showing the desirability of sexual activity, our society seems largely unwilling to deal with sexuality openly. While sexual activity is encouraged on television, in movies, and in popular music, there is a kind of prudishness in American culture about possible consequences of sexual activity, such as venereal disease or pregnancy. Adolescents are pushed toward sexual activity on one hand, but they are left largely to their own devices in dealing responsibly with their sexuality.

As a consequence, when adolescents initiate sexual activity, most are unprepared (Kisker, 1985). Many adolescents report that planning somehow seems "wrong," since it indicates an intention to become sexually involved. Frequently there is also the naive trust, "It won't happen to us." Unfortunately, it often does and often to those just beginning to be sexually active. Over a third of all teenage pregnancies occur in the first three months of sexual activity. When adolescents do seek family planning/birth control advice, the vast majority (85%) do so *after* they have been sexually active a year or more, many because of a "pregnancy scare" (Alan Guttmacher Institute, 1985). By the time knowledge is available, it is frequently too late.

While a few people think sex education *causes* increased sexual activity and pregnancies, especially if it includes birth control information, most Americans believe there should be comprehensive sex education programs in the schools. Over 7 in 10 Americans favor sex education and over 80 percent of these would include information on birth control and venereal disease (Gallup, 1985). Although about 7 in 10 students receive some sex education before leaving school, most is narrowly focused and occurs as a unit in other courses. Fewer than 10 percent receive comprehensive courses in sexuality education and only a handful of states require sex education. While parents potentially are excellent sources of information on sexuality and most parents believe it is their responsibility to talk to their children about sex-related issues, many feel uncomfortable and wait too long. Most want assistance (Alan Guttmacher Institute, 1985).

Where sex education has been systematically evaluated (e.g., Zelnik & Kim, 1982), the data seem to show that it can be highly effective—reducing pregnancy rates and making contraceptive use more likely. At the same time, the data strongly support the claim that the decision to engage in sexual activity is *not* influenced by whether or not teenagers had sex education in schools. If anything, increased knowledge and accurate information is likely to lead to greater, not less, responsibility in adolescents' sexual behavior.

there is a "hesitant" emergence of sexuality in the mid-teens. Intermittent experimentation then gradually gives way to more sustained relationships. For many adolescents, increasing physical intimacy accompanies increasing emotional intimacy. The majority of adolescents report having been in love (Gallup, 1985), with percentages increasing for both boys and girls throughout the teenage years.

TABLE 14-2 Sexual Behaviors Desired by Males and Females in Three Age Groups at Three Stages of Dating (percent)

| | 16–17 Years ||||||| 19–20 Years ||||||| 24–25 Years |||||||
| | First Date || Several Dates || Going Steady || First Date || Several Dates || Going Steady || First Date || Several Dates || Going Steady ||
Behavior	M	F	M	F	M	F	M	F	M	F	M	F	M	F	M	F	M	F
Hand holding	89	96	93	100	95	100	92	76	97	98	100	98	83	75	90	87	90	87
Light embrace	94	91	94	100	97	100	92	73	97	98	100	98	79	75	93	100	93	100
Light kissing	96	94	93	97	89	98	92	79	89	92	94	90	83	87	90	92	90	87
General body contact	76	48	98	93	100	100	69	29	94	92	97	100	65	33	94	96	100	100
Necking	67	31	84	79	77	94	50	25	75	62	78	82	21	25	69	75	75	92
Deep kissing	60	31	89	79	97	90	58	25	83	73	97	98	45	29	79	71	90	100
Light breast petting	55	18	85	55	87	76	50	19	86	67	94	80	45	25	86	83	93	92
Heavy breast petting	27	3	67	15	93	49	45	6	58	42	86	77	31	8	27	58	86	96
Light genital petting—female	36	2	67	15	87	52	36	8	58	44	83	77	38	12	83	54	90	83
Heavy genital petting—female	20	2	53	12	80	30	33	2	58	21	78	69	24	4	62	37	86	83
Nude embrace	9	6	40	9	70	31	45	4	53	19	78	71	28	4	69	46	93	92
Simulated intercourse	16	3	44	12	60	31	25	4	47	29	65	57	24	8	55	33	65	55
Mutual masturbation	18	3	45	12	76	31	36	8	61	27	81	75	24	4	55	37	79	79
Oral stimulation																		
Female genitals	24	6	44	7	75	31	45	10	61	21	72	50	24	4	48	46	79	87
Male genitals	13	3	27	6	64	31	36	6	56	21	75	58	3	4	55	29	83	83
Intercourse	16	0	27	4	62	19	31	2	47	8	78	58	24	4	52	37	86	87

From M. P. McCabe and J. K. Collins, Sex role and dating orientation (1979). *Journal of Youth and Adolescence, 8,* 407–425. Used by permission.

During adolescence, stable and committed long-term relationships are the exception rather than the rule, however. Much more often, adolescents have intense, but short-term, experiences. Even though relationships may not last, they nonetheless appear to be just as powerful and the consequences of a "break-up" just as devastating for adolescents as for adults. The claim, "I'll never smile again," expresses the feelings of many teenagers, grieving over a broken love affair. Fortunately, most adolescents in time go on to new and satisfying relationships.

Summary

Human beings are social animals. Our social behavior is the key to our very survival. The changes that take place in social development from infancy to adulthood are indeed dramatic.

The roots of human social development are present from birth. Newborn infants are born with a surprisingly effective array of skills for influencing their caregivers. Babies' gaze, their head movements, and their facial expressions all profoundly affect adults. Also, drawing on observations of other species, some researchers have proposed that there is a biologically based process of bonding occurring in a critical period shortly after birth. Others disagree, however.

Strong evidence exists for attachment. Universally noted in all cultures, attachment is an enduring emotional tie of an infant to another person. Attachment is shown by the infant's seeking to be near that person, showing distress on separation, and expressing joy or relief on reunion. To explore these and other dimensions of attachment, many researchers have used the experimental arrangement called the "strange situation" which shows clearly such attachment phenomena as wariness of strangers and the infant's use of the mother as a secure base for exploring.

Not all infants are securely attached, however. Some insecurely attached infants are avoidant, showing little emotional closeness to their caregivers, whereas others are resistant, simultaneously seeking and rejecting contact. Patterns of attachment have been shown to be related to the care they have received. Generally, those infants most securely attached are those whose mothers have been most responsive to their needs.

While parents foster early social development, peers quickly begin to assume more importance. Contacts between babies often focus on objects in which both have interest. Social interest in other children develops quickly, however, and smiling and laughing become relatively common by age 2. By preschool, real friendships are possible and continue to develop through childhood.

Also developing in childhood is aggression, a social behavior that has concerned many developmentalists. Aggression is an intentional act aimed at harming another person. Young infants cannot be said to be aggressive, but instrumental and then hostile aggression soon develop. Both biological and social factors seem influential. Social learning theorists have pointed to modeling and imitation of aggressive behavior as affecting its development. In particular, American television provides a rich source of models for aggressive behavior. Social cognition theorists, building on social learning theory and using information processing models, emphasize the role of children's perceptions about others' intentions to be aggressive. Some researchers, however, have concentrated on prosocial behavior instead of aggression, contending that, while aggression may have evolved in humans because of its survival value, prosocial behavior may have equal or greater survival value today.

As children move into adolescence, friendships take on a greater intimacy. Adolescent crowds and cliques provide a relatively safe haven in which adolescents can begin to explore heterosexual relationships. Early, hesitant exploration gradually gives way to more intimate contact. In the United States, dating provides the major vehicle for this contact. The frequency of both psychological and physical intimacy increases as early, more superficial relationships are replaced by the "real thing," the experience of being in love. Although adolescent relationships are not usually permanent, they are serious, and have all of the intensity of joy and sorrow experienced by adults.

Key Terms

social behavior	information exchange	physical aggression
social development	common ground	verbal aggression
gaze	resolution of conflict	instrumental aggression
head movements	disagreement chains	hostile aggression
facial expressions	positive reciprocity	biological determinants of aggression
bonding	self-disclosure	social determinants of aggression
critical periods	reciprocity	social learning theory
attachment	group	observational learning
strange situation	norms	social cognition theory
securely attached infants	group structure	prosocial behavior
insecurely attached infants	hierarchical structure	autonomy
avoidant infants	leadership	crowd
resistant infants	object play	clique
family system	pretend play	cross-pressures
peers	social play	intimate friendship
connectedness	aggression	dating

Suggested Readings

Damon, W. (1983). *Social and personality development.* New York: Norton. This book gives a clear account of social development during infancy, childhood, and adolescence, and relates social development to individual personality.

Gottman, J. M. (1983). How children become friends. *Monographs of the Society for Research in Child Development, 48* (2, Serial No. 201). This study describes the processes that are operating when children become friends. Although a technical report, this monograph provides a comprehensible overall picture of how children progress toward friendship.

Maccoby, E. E. (1980). *Social development.* New York: Harcourt Brace Jovanovich, Inc. This paperback book draws on Eleanor Maccoby's long-time experience as a leading developmental psychologist and deals extensively with the family's contribution to socialization: the processes by which children acquire the knowledge, values, and goals of adult society. Although topics are treated rigorously, the book is very readable.

Myers, B. (1984). Mother-infant bonding: The status of this critical period hypothesis. *Developmental Review, 4,* 240–274. This review article outlines issues relating to the concept of mother–infant bonding and provides a critical analysis of the status of the concept of bonding.

Rubin, Z. (1980). *Children's friendships.* Cambridge, MA: Harvard University Press. Rubin's book provides a fascinating account of the nature of children's friendships and their development.

Application Exercise

14-1 Identifying Patterns of Attachment

For each of the following, indicate whether the behavior of these 1-year-old infants shows that they are (a) securely attached, (b) avoidant, or (c) resistant.

1. Latisha stops playing and begins crying when her mother leaves the room. When her mother returns, however, Latisha smiles, gurgles delightedly, and begins playing again.

2. Tracy shows no particular fear of strangers. When she cries, she is just as easily comforted by them as by her mother.

3. Marta's mother has been visiting briefly with the day-care center director. When she returns and approaches Marta, who is playing with blocks, Marta looks away. She seems barely to notice that her mother is back.

4. Burton, visiting the Happy Baby Day-Care Center for the first time, will not leave his mother's side. Even though she sits down in a chair and shows no indication of leaving, he clings tightly to her leg and whimpers softly.

5. Mac screams as his parents open the door because it appears he is going to be left with a teenage babysitter. When his mother comes back in and holds him, however, he kicks and struggles angrily.

6. While his mother visits with another mother in the pediatrician's office, Curtis moves around the waiting room, handling magazines, touching other babies, and smiling at some adults. He occasionally glances at his mother and returns to her side now and then.

7. When Mr. Jackson, a new neighbor, enters the room, DaShan hides behind his father. During the 10-minute conversation between his father and Mr. Jackson, DaShan shows continual anxiety at Mr. Jackson's presence.

8. Trying to crawl up on the couch, Laurie tumbles backward and hits her head on the coffee table. Crying loudly, she holds her arms open as her mother rushes to comfort her. After some hugs and kisses, Laurie becomes calm and begins playing again when put down.

CHAPTER 15

Moral Development

Everyone is aware of the kinship between logical and ethical norms. Logic is the morality of thought just as morality is the logic of action.
—Jean Piaget, The Moral Judgment of the Child

The following clubhouse rules of a gang of 10-year-old girls appeared on September 18, 1954, in *The New Yorker*:

1. Do not tell a white lie unless necessary.
2. Do not hit anyone, except Ronny.
3. Do not use words worse than "brat."
4. Do not make faces, except at Ronny.
5. Do not make a hog or pig of yourself.
6. Do not tattle, except on Ronny.
7. Do not steal, except from Ronny.
8. Do not be a sneak.
9. Do not destroy other people's property except Ronny's.
10. Do not be grumpy, except at Ronny.

"This particular decalogue," noted Robert Kegan (1982, p. 167), "is not exactly a triumph of the Golden Rule." Nevertheless, we cannot simply assert that these children had not yet learned morality. Quite clearly, they had a morality, though as adults we may see their rules as reflecting a somewhat primitive conception of what morality is. Children's morality has long been a major interest among developmental psychologists and an active and exciting field of research.

We will begin this chapter with an introduction to some major issues in the study of morality. This will lead to a presentation of the major theoretical perspective in the modern study of moral development, the cognitive-developmental approach. We will discuss the cognitive-developmental approach with respect to its basic assumptions, and the work of its two major theorists, Jean Piaget and Lawrence Kohlberg. The chapter includes extensive discussion of research and criticism related to Kohlberg's theory and recent modifications of his theory. We will conclude with a discussion of moral education.

The Study of Morality

How should we study moral development? Where do we begin? Psychologists do not agree about the nature of morality. Not surprisingly, researchers with different views of morality have done different sorts of research and reached different sorts of conclusions.

The Absolutist Approach

Let's try a commonsense approach. First we will decide what the most important moral virtues are. Then we will study children's beliefs and behavior with respect to our list of virtues.

Consider, for example, the list at the beginning of this chapter. Some of the rules do seem to reflect important moral values. For example, we might decide that morality includes not lying, not hitting others, not stealing, and not destroying other people's property. We can study children's awareness of these norms and whether they behave consistently with them at various ages. Do children become more truthful as they get older? Do they become less likely to hit or steal? Do they learn to respect other people's property?

Early studies of moral development took this absolutist approach, viewing moral development as the emergence of a set of specific virtues (Hartshorne & May, 1928–1930). There is a major problem with absolutism, however. Who decides what the moral virtues are? To go back to the girls' ten rules, is it immoral to be a sneak or a pig? Is it immoral to tattle or make faces? Is it immoral to be grumpy or to use a word worse than "brat"? And what about poor Ronny?

Of course, a psychologist, like anyone else, has the right to decide what his or her moral values are. But if psychologist X studies the development of what *she* considers the proper moral virtues, she cannot claim to be studying moral development. The reason is that other people have different views of what morality consists of. No one can be sure that his or her morality is the "true" one. There is no simple list of absolute moral virtues every moral person must accept.

The Relativist Approach

How then are we to study moral development? Some psychologists have argued that research on moral development should begin with an orientation known as **ethical relativism**. Relativism has become an increasingly influential viewpoint in Western society over the past several centuries (Kurtines & Gewirtz, 1984). Relativists argue that there are no absolute moral truths. Morality is relative to one's culture. What is considered moral in one culture may be considered immoral in another.

From the relativist point of view, there is no need for moral development researchers to decide what *really* is moral. Researchers need only observe what people in a particular culture consider moral and how children in that culture learn those values. Whether the cultural values are moral or immoral is meaningless. The values of a culture are

The Study of Morality

moral *for that particular culture*. To judge them by the standards of any other culture would be illegitimate. Moral development, then, simply involves learning the norms of one's culture.

This relativist approach underlies the behaviorist view of moral development:

> What a given group of people calls good is a fact, it is what members of the group find reinforcing as a result of their genetic endowment and the natural and social contingencies to which they have been exposed. Each culture has its own set of goods, and what is good in one culture may not be good in another (Skinner, 1971, p. 128).

The major relativist approach to moral development today is social learning theory, an intellectual descendent of behaviorism (see Chapter 2). Social learning theorists argue that children gradually learn to behave in whatever ways are considered moral in their society by imitating the behavior of adult members of society and responding to rewards and punishments (Liebert, 1984). They do not see anything unique about moral development and thus have not proposed a specific theory of moral development. On the contrary, they view moral development as directed by the general processes of observational learning that we discussed in Chapters 5 and 14.

Social learning theorists argue that children gradually learn to behave in whatever ways are considered moral in their society by imitating the behavior of adult members of society and responding to rewards and punishments.

Ethical relativism is an important advance over the simplistic absolutism described earlier. It recognizes the dangers involved in assuming that one's own moral views or those of one's society are the proper moral standards for all people and all societies. It points out that societies differ in what they value and that psychologists must recognize these differences.

Nevertheless, total relativism raises serious problems. Ethical relativism suggests that learning the values of one's society is moral development regardless of what those values are. In a society where certain races or religions are scorned, moral development would consist of learning to discriminate against people of those races or religions. In a society that believes women should not be educated or permitted to have jobs, it would be considered immoral for a woman to try to develop her intellectual abilities or live an independent life. It would be moral in such a culture to prevent women from obtaining jobs or education. In a society where stealing, cheating, or killing are considered acceptable, moral development would consist of learning to steal, cheat, or kill in socially approved ways.

There is something intuitively disturbing about this. Extreme ethical relativism leads to the view that children simply learn the norms of their societies and that those norms themselves cannot be evaluated. The idea of moral development seems to evaporate from this perspective. Morality becomes arbitrary.

Beyond Relativism: Morality as Social Rationality

Neither absolutism nor extreme relativism seems to provide an adequate conception of morality or a useful basis for studying moral development. Absolutism asserts without justification that the moral standards of a particular person, a particular society, or a particular group within a society are the final and correct standards of morality for all people and all societies. Relativism goes to the opposite extreme of asserting that any society can do as it pleases since there is no basis for judging its values.

Most moral philosophers (philosophers who specialize in morality) reject both of these approaches and have tried to formulate a middle-ground position (Boyd, 1984; Rawls, 1971, 1980). Such a position argues, in contrast to relativism, that it is possible and proper to evaluate the standards of an entire society with respect to morality. However, it is critical not to do this by simply judging those standards by the standards of our own society or some other set of standards we happen to prefer (as an absolutist might do). Instead, we must move beyond our societies and our personal preferences to develop general principles of moral judgment that any rational person from any society would have to agree with.

This perspective has been highly influential in the work of both Piaget and Kohlberg, the two major figures in the study of moral development. Both take an approach generally known as **cognitive-developmental**. In the next section, we will consider the cognitive-developmental perspective on moral development, with an emphasis on how it attempts to move beyond the limitations of absolutism and relativism. Then we will look more specifically at Piaget's theory and then Kohlberg's theory.

The Cognitive-Developmental Approach

The *cognitive-developmental* approach is not a particular theory. Rather, it is a **paradigm**, a general way of thinking about issues of human development that has been useful in understanding moral development (as well as other aspects of development). In this section, we will consider ten closely interrelated facets of the cognitive-developmental approach to moral development.

Elements of the Cognitive-Developmental Approach

Focus on Cognition. Theories of moral development differ in their central focus. Behaviorist theories such as social learning theory focus on the actual *behavior* of children: Do they lie, cheat, steal, help others, and so on? Psychoanalytic (Freudian) theories focus on moral *feelings*: When, why, and how do children begin to feel guilty about certain things? The cognitive-developmental approach focuses on moral *cognition*, or the judgments children make about moral issues and the reasoning that produces those judgments.

Developmental Perspective. You may recall that in Chapter 2 we distinguished three different paradigms: the learning approach, the developmental approach, and the dialectical approach. As you might expect from its name, the cognitive-developmental approach takes a developmental point of view. (For a thoughtful analysis of how this relates to a learning perspective on moral development, see Gibbs and Schnell, 1985.)

Stages. One aspect of the developmental point of view is the idea that children go through a succession of stages in their moral reasoning. Each stage is considered to be more advanced than the one preceding it. A person reasoning at a higher stage makes finer distinctions among moral issues, understands how different issues are related, and takes a broader and more stable perspective on moral conflicts and on the nature of society. Consider, for example, a boy disagreeing with his friend about who gets to use a toy. If the boy is at a more advanced stage of moral reasoning, he is more likely to understand the difference between his point of view and that of his friend and to find a compromise that takes both views into account.

Structure. The difference between higher and lower stages is not simply a matter of rejecting one set of values in favor of another. Two children with very different values might be judged to be at the same stage of development if the *underlying reasoning* they use to justify those values is the same. Alternatively, two children with very similar values might be judged to be at different stages if they justify those values differently. For example, two children might both believe that they should share their toys with another child. Upon questioning, however, it might turn out that one child believes in sharing with others because they will then share with you, whereas the other believes in sharing because mother will punish you if you do not. A cognitive-developmentalist would say that the morality of these two children is the same in *content* (both believe in sharing) but different in the *underlying structure* of their reasoning (the cognitive bases for their beliefs are quite different). Although content is important, cognitive-developmentalists consider structure to be more critical.

Morality as Justice. Morality, as we have seen, can consist of a lot of things and not all psychologists agree about what it should include. Cognitive-developmentalists see the above example of sharing as a typical moral dilemma: It involves deciding on the fairest way to resolve a conflict (or potential conflict) between two or more people. In other words, the essence of morality is **justice**.

Constructivism. Where does a child's morality come from? Common sense suggests that it comes from one's parents, other adults, or society at large. Social learning theory and psychoanalytic theory essentially agree with this view. Psychoanalytic theory emphasizes the parents, arguing that at a very young age the child identifies with the same-sex parent and internalizes his or her moral values. Social learning theory takes a broader perspective, arguing that anyone in the child's environment can serve as a model from whom the child will gradually learn the values of his or her society. The most obvious alternative to these views would be to suggest that morality is innate to human beings: Our inherent goodness simply reveals itself as we get older.

Cognitive-developmentalists do not believe morality is innate or that it is simply learned from one's social environment. Although they do not deny the importance of parents and other models, they emphasize the role of the child's active reasoning. Children do not passively imitate or internalize whatever they see. They actively think about moral issues and *construct* their own ideas about these issues. Thus progress from stage to stage depends on the creation of increasingly sophisticated moral reasoning structures. In Piaget's words, "From the moral as from the intellectual point of view, the child is born neither good nor bad, but master of his destiny" (1932, p. 99).

Social learning and psychoanalytic theorists consider morality to consist of values learned from one's social environment.

Social Interaction. No one would argue, however, that the construction of morality can take place in social isolation. Since cognitive-developmentalists define morality as justice in social interactions, they insist that a truly isolated human being could never develop any concept of morality. Morality may be constructed by the active mind, but it is only in the context of interacting with others that such construction is possible.

Perspective-taking. Social interactions can be difficult and lead to conflict because of people's different perspectives. In cognitive-developmental theories, higher stages of moral understanding involve more sophisticated awareness of differences in perspective. Solutions to moral dilemmas come from putting oneself in others' shoes and finding the fairest resolution. Of course, sophisticated **perspective-taking** can be extremely difficult, which is why moral development is a slow process that continues over many years.

Rationality. Morality is the rational coordination of different social perspectives. This is different from the Freudian view that morality is primarily an emotional matter separate from cognitive development. Cognitive-developmentalists believe that the reasoning involved in resolving a moral dilemma may be as difficult as the reasoning involved in the most complex sorts of mathematical or logical problems. Morality is social rationality. It is, as Piaget put it, "the logic of action" (1932, p. 398).

Universality. No one would deny that human societies differ from each other in important ways. Cognitive-developmentalists argue, however, that there is also substantial **universality**. For example, all cultures involve social interactions, which invariably cause moral conflict. Resolution of such conflict requires coordinating diverse perspectives and thus development tends to move toward increasingly rational and effective ways of achieving this. Of course, such development may be more difficult in a culture in which opportunities to interact with one's peers and to take various perspectives are in some way restricted. People in such cultures may not progress as fast or as far in their moral development. Cognitive-developmentalists believe, however, that the *direction* of development and the ideal highest stage nevertheless will be the same in any human society. The essence of morality lies not in particular customs that may vary from culture to culture but rather in "the permanent laws of rational cooperation" (Piaget, 1932, p. 72).

Critics of the cognitive-developmental approach (Emler, 1983; Liebert, 1984; Vine, 1983) have suggested that in rejecting relativism the cognitive-developmentalists have returned to absolutism. Aren't Piaget and Kohlberg merely taking their Western values about justice and imposing them as a moral standard for all societies? Cognitive-developmentalists respond that their approach differs from absolutism because it does not simply take a set of particular values and claim they are proper for all societies. Instead, it finds universality in general principles of human interaction (Kohlberg, 1984).

Summary

We have seen that cognitive developmentalists view moral development as the development of structured modes of reasoning about justice that appear in a series of stages. These stages are constructed by the developing individual through increasingly rational coordination of perspectives during his or her social interactions, leading ideally to a universalist conception of morality that goes beyond any particular culture. In the next two sections we will examine in more detail the cognitive-developmental theories of Piaget and Kohlberg, which incorporate these principles.

Piaget's Theory of Moral Development

Piaget's research on moral development was published in his classic 1932 book, *The Moral Judgment of the Child*. On the basis of clinical interviews with hundreds of Swiss children, Piaget suggested a number of specific developmental changes, all of which he saw as aspects of a more general developmental trend. We will first discuss some of the specific changes and then consider the general direction of moral development.

Specific Developmental Changes

Conceptions about Rules. Believing that rules are a basic aspect of morality, Piaget began his research by watching children play marbles and asking them about the rules of the game. Piaget found that children up to the age of about 3 typically used only **motor rules**, or purely personal habits of arranging and throwing the marbles. Beginning about age 3, the child increasingly recognizes **coercive rules**. These are seen by the child as obligatory rules, formulated by the authorities, that have always been the same and can never be changed. Fal (age 5), for example, said that he learned the rules of marbles from his brother, who in turn learned them from their father, a highly authoritative individual who Fal believed was born before Fal's grandfather and was older than God. Interestingly, Piaget observed that children like Fal, despite their immense respect for rules, did not understand the actual rules they thought they were playing by and frequently violated them unknowingly.

With increasing age, children in Piaget's study began thinking in terms of **rational rules**. They saw the rules of marbles as useful for guiding cooperative play, understood that the rules had evolved over time, and said it was acceptable to change the rules as long as everyone agreed. Older children, perhaps because of their more sophisticated ideas about the nature and purpose of rules, better understood the actual rules of marbles and were more likely to follow them consistently.

Consequences versus Intentions. One of Piaget's main techniques for studying moral judgments was to tell stories about two different children and ask which child was naughtier. Here is one of his most famous story pairs:

> A. A little boy who is called John is in his room. He is called to dinner. He goes into the dining room. But behind the door there was a chair, and on the chair there was a tray with fifteen cups on it. John couldn't have known that there was all this behind the door. He goes in, the door knocks against the tray, bang go the fifteen cups and they all get broken!
>
> B. Once there was a little boy whose name was Henry. One day when his mother was out he tried to get some jam out of the cupboard. He climbed up on to a chair and stretched out his arm. But the jam was too high up and he couldn't reach it and have any. But while he was trying to get it he knocked over a cup. The cup fell down and broke (1932, p. 122).

Piaget found that young children (ages 6 and 7) were likely to compare the stories on the basis of **consequences**: John was naughtier because he broke more cups. One 6-year-old, for example, was quite clear in deciding the proper punishments: "The one who broke the fifteen cups: two slaps. The other one, one slap" (p. 125). Older children were more likely to judge on the basis of **intentions**. Henry was naughtier because he, unlike John, purposely did something wrong.

Young children's tendency to ignore intentions was also seen in their views about lying. Most defined lying as simply a matter of saying something untrue. Older children better understood that if one believes the truth of what one is saying then, although it might turn out to be a mistake, it is not a lie. Something is only a lie if one *intends* to deceive the listener (Wimmer, Gruber, & Perner, 1985).

Moral Realism. Young children have difficulty distinguishing products of the human mind from physical reality. They often think, for example, that what they dream about is physically in the room with them. Similarly, they fail to grasp that the word "cat" is merely a sound that speakers of English use in talking about cats; it is not a property of cats in the same sense that having four legs and a tail are properties of cats (see Chapter 11). Piaget used the term *realism* to refer to the young child's tendency to interpret products of the mind as if they had an objective physical existence.

In failing to understand that morality, like dreams or language, is a human product, the child exhibits **moral realism.** Young children seem to think that rules coming from their parents are not made up by people but rather are directly based on some objective physical reality. They do not see the distinction between a moral rule, such as not hitting your sister, and a physical rule, such as the law of gravity. Piaget suggested this is why they interpret moral rules so literally and believe so absolutely in the unquestionable rightness of those rules. This does not mean, however, that children always follow the rules. Because the rules are perceived as coming from outside them, children do not see themselves as having a personal stake in those rules and thus, paradoxically, may violate the very rules they so naively respect.

Immanent Justice. Because rules are seen as part of the physical universe, punishment may be seen as automatic. Piaget referred to this as **immanent justice.** Children interviewed by Piaget suggested, for example, that a bridge might collapse under a child to punish him for stealing apples. As children overcome their moral realism they gradually realize that punishment for moral violations must come from human beings. Such punishment is not built into the world in the same way as, say, the consequence of defying the law of gravity.

Human Justice. How should people dispense justice? Piaget described three stages in the emergence of a sense of justice. Children up to age 7 or 8 tended to see justice as submission to authority and believed in strict, often surprisingly harsh, punishment. (Remember that they themselves were not about to be punished. They were responding to hypothetical stories involving other children.) Between ages 8 and 11, by contrast, children were more likely to refer to standards of fairness and equality (independent of any authority) and to favor punishments logically related to the offense. For example, rather than suggesting that the boy who broke a cup be slapped, the older child would be likely to suggest that he pay to replace the cup. Finally, beyond age 11, Piaget found an orientation he called **equity**. The older children realized that even equality could be unfair if applied too strictly. For example, it would be moral to give special consideration to a child who was younger or in some way handicapped.

From Heteronomy to Autonomy

Piaget argued that the age-related changes discussed above were all closely interrelated and could be seen as parts of a more general trend from a **heteronomous morality** to an **autonomous morality**.

Heteronomous morality is a morality of duty and obedience. What is morally right is an absolute imposed from the outside (most directly, from one's parents). It is a morality of **unilateral** (one-directional) **respect** for authority, a morality of **constraint**.

With increasing age, the child moves gradually toward an *autonomous morality*. Autonomous morality is a morality of self-determination. But this does not mean one can do as one pleases. Morality is a matter of behaving in a socially appropriate manner that not only reflects one's own autonomy but equally respects that of others'. What is crucial is that the others are not seen as authorities but rather as equals. Through interaction with them, one constructs what is morally right. Autonomous morality is a morality of **mutual respect,** a morality of **cooperation.**

Piaget emphasized that moral development does not consist of a sudden shift from a consistently heteronomous morality to a consistently autonomous morality. Quite the contrary, he emphasized that elements of both moralities can be found in individuals of all ages. His data indicate that autonomous morality is rare in young children and becomes increasingly frequent as they develop; heteronomous morality, though not totally disappearing, becomes less frequent as children get older. Whether a given individual shows autonomous or heteronomous responses depends not only on his age but on his culture, his personal characteristics, his history of social experiences, and the specific moral issues he is dealing with. As Piaget put it, "there is an adult in every child and a child in every adult" (p. 85).

Peer Interaction and Moral Development

Why do children develop toward an autonomous morality of mutual respect and cooperation? Piaget was highly interested not only in describing children's development but in accounting for it. His explanation is of great importance in that it somewhat contradicts many people's views.

It is commonly believed that parents are central to moral development. Parents can, for example, model morally correct behavior, reinforce children for behaving morally, punish them for behaving immorally, and/or explain to them the cognitive rationale for moral behavior. Peers, on the other hand, are more likely to model and/or reinforce deviant behavior and thus work against the morality instilled by parents.

Piaget (1932) argued that the relative contributions of parents and peers to moral development are precisely the reverse of what is stated above. Even when parents try to reason with their young children they are perceived as authorities to be obeyed. Young children are much better able to learn their parents' rules than to grasp the explanations for those rules. The child may learn, for example, not to take toys from another child but may fail to understand the explanation about seeing things from the other child's point of view. Thus parents typically are accorded unilateral respect and viewed as sources of constraint.

According to Piaget, then, parents may teach rules. But, despite their best intentions, their efforts are more of a hindrance than a help to the child's moral development. Piaget saw peer interaction, not parental constraint, as the major factor allowing the child to construct more sophisticated conceptions of rules and justice. Only when the child is interacting with peers can there be mutual respect among equals, thus allowing the development of genuine cooperation and autonomous morality.

Research on Piaget's Theory

Beginning in the 1960s, a great deal of research followed up on Piaget's theory of moral development. As in other areas of development (see Chapter 8), there is much evidence that (at least under favorable circumstances) preschoolers are more competent than Piaget suggested (Shultz, Wright, & Schleifer, 1986; Smetana, 1985; Turiel, 1983; Wimmer, Gruber, & Perner, 1985). In general, however, the results have supported Piaget's views about the direction of moral development, have been consistent with Piaget's conclusion that the moral concepts he studied do not emerge in clearcut stages, and have given us a more detailed picture of how specific aspects of moral dilemmas influence children's judgments (Rest, 1983). Piaget's emphasis on peer interaction remains highly influential (Bearison, Magzamen, & Filardo, 1986; Berkowitz, 1985), although parents may be more important than he suggested (Leon, 1984; Rest, 1983). A challenge for future research will be to provide a more precise picture of how parental influences, peer interaction, and the child's own reasoning interact in determining the course of moral development.

Kohlberg's Theory of Moral Development

As a graduate student at the University of Chicago in the 1950s, Lawrence Kohlberg thought Piaget had provided a fruitful general perspective for studying moral development. He believed, however, that Piaget's work was limited in several respects and that it was important to move beyond it. For one thing, Kohlberg thought that moral development *does* proceed in strict stages. He believed that Piaget had failed to find such stages because he had not looked abstractly enough at the structures of reasoning underlying children's judgments. Kohlberg also believed that the autonomous morality described by Piaget as common in 8- to 10-year-olds, though an important advance over their earlier heteronomous morality, was not fully mature. Kohlberg attempted to develop a theory corresponding to his view that moral development continues at least through adolescence.

Consider the following individuals: Al Capone, Lee Harvey Oswald, Jack the Ripper, Socrates, Ghandi, and Martin Luther King (Rest, 1983). This may seem an odd list, but in fact all six men share something. Each deviated so greatly from the conventional norms of his society that society saw fit to punish him (e.g., through imprisonment). If we define morality as conformity to the norms of one's society, each of these men was an immoral individual.

Something seems intuitively wrong about this conclusion. Kohlberg would argue that the six individuals did deviate from **conventional morality,** but in significantly different ways. Al Capone, Lee Harvey Oswald, and Jack the Ripper probably never achieved a genuine understanding of conventional morality. We can call them **preconventional.** Socrates, Ghandi, and King, on the other hand, did understand conventional morality but rejected it, not for their own selfish purposes but in the name of higher moral principles. Their morality can be considered **postconventional.**

In his 1958 dissertation, Kohlberg argued that moral development proceeds through three general levels: from preconventional to conventional to postconventional. He further divided each of these levels into two stages, thus yielding a total of six stages. In the next subsection we present Kohlberg's (1984) current formulation of these six stages of moral development.

Six Stages of Moral Development

Stage 1: Heteronomous Morality. The stage 1 child perceives moral behavior as what does not get punished. Obedience is right for its own sake. Immoral actions are punished because they are immoral and immoral because they are punished. Although there is respect for the superior power of authorities, the child does not distinguish the authorities' perspective from his own. Goodness or badness are inherent in acts (moral realism). Tattling is wrong, for example, in the same sense that the sky is blue. If asked why it is wrong to tell on someone, the child is likely to reply, "Because it's tattling" and see that as settling the issue.

Stage 2: Individualism and Exchange. Moral behavior is acting to further one's interests and letting others do the same, or **individualism and exchange.** There is recognition that others have their own interests that differ from and may even conflict with yours. To get what you want from other people, you must recognize and respond to their needs. Morality includes arranging fair deals and equal exchanges with others.

Stage 3: Mutual Expectations and Interpersonal Conformity. Stage 3 marks the emergence of conventional morality. Other people are not merely there to serve your purposes. Relationships with others, based on mutual trust and loyalty, are important for their own sake. You should live up to the expectations of those close to you and fulfill your various roles (e.g., be a good sister). You are moral because you genuinely care about others, want them to think of you as a good person, and want to consider yourself a good person. **Mutual expectations** and shared moral norms take primacy over individual interests. You put yourself in the other person's shoes.

Stage 4: Social System. The stage called **social system** is still within the conventional level but is more sophisticated than stage 3. One's acceptance of moral conventions is based not on immediate interactions with others but on an abstract understanding of society as a whole. The social system defines appropriate roles and rules. Of course, individual relations are still important, but they are understood from the point of view of the entire social, legal, or religious system. Morality means upholding the law, fulfilling one's social and/or religious duties, and contributing to society and its institutions. You should do what is right in order to meet your obligations and preserve the social structure. Antisocial behavior is wrong because it potentially contributes to the breakdown of the system.

Stage 5: Social Contract. Why follow the law? Because it is determined by society? But why accept the conventions of society? Most people, according to Kohlberg, never fully face these questions. Those who do, however, move beyond conventional morality to stage 5, which is the first stage of postconventional morality: **social contract.** The stage 5 thinker adopts a **prior-to-society perspective.** Rational individuals existing with no social arrangements (if this were possible) would set up a society because this would benefit all of them (through mutual protection, division of labor, and so on). They would agree to fair procedures for deciding on laws and would agree to abide by those laws. The stage 5 thinker believes one should usually follow the law because it is the result of a social contract. As an autonomous individual, she understands the basis for social commitments and freely accepts them. Laws and social duties should, however, be based on rational calculation of "the greatest good for the greatest number" (the principle of **utility**) and should respect absolute rights such as life and liberty. Thus, although laws are generally to be obeyed, a given law or even an entire social structure or religious system may be rejected as violating the intrinsic worth and dignity of individuals or failing as a rational social contract. The social system, though highly important, is not the last word. From the prior-to-society perspective, societies themselves can be evaluated morally.

Stage 6: Universal Ethical Principles. The basis for morality is a set of universal principles of justice, or **universal ethical principles,** involving respect for the equal rights of all people and the dignity of every individual. These principles are explicit, forming a coordinated, self-conscious structure, or a formalized moral philosophy. Particular laws or social agreements are usually consistent with such principles, but when they are not we should reject the law or custom and act in accord with the principle. We are committed to these principles because they are rationally determined.

Martin Luther King is often cited as an example of someone who acted on the basis of postconventional moral principles.

How Moral Development Occurs

Why does a child move from one stage of moral judgment to another? Why do some people progress further than others in Kohlberg's sequence? Kohlberg accepts the basic ideas of the cognitive-developmental approach in accounting for moral development. He agrees that moral dilemmas and the responses of other people to those dilemmas result in cognitive conflict (disequilibrium), which can be resolved by constructing more sophisticated moral structures. He also proposes that general cognitive abilities may be important. Stage 4 reasoning, for example, involves a highly abstract grasp of social structure, whereas stages 5 and 6 involve the even more abstract concept of moral values existing prior to society. General cognitive development (such as reaching formal operations) does not ensure advanced moral development but may be necessary for it (Walker, 1986a). Kohlberg also accepts Piaget's views concerning the importance of peer interaction.

Kohlberg's particular emphasis in accounting for moral change is the increasing ability to take other perspectives. He argues that each of his stages requires more sophisticated perspective-taking ability than the stage before. Stage 2, for example, involves some recognition that other people have perspectives different from one's own, whereas stage 3 requires a more sophisticated coordination of the different perspectives. Stage 4 involves taking the perspective of society as a whole, whereas stage 5 is based on a still more abstract perspective outside of and logically prior to society. Finally, Kohlberg frequently cites the work of moral philosopher John Rawls (1971), who describes the ultimate perspective-taking of stage 6. Opportunities to develop one's perspective-taking ability are thus seen by Kohlberg as critical to moral advancement.

Assessing Moral Reasoning

How can we determine a person's level of moral reasoning? Kohlberg uses a Piagetian clinical interview procedure (see Chapter 3). In a Kohlberg interview, the subject is presented with a moral dilemma and is then asked a series of questions to determine how she or he is reasoning about the dilemma. Kohlberg's dilemmas typically involve resolving conflicts between values. In one dilemma, for example, a 14-year-old saves money from his paper route to go to camp. But then his father, who had told him he could go to camp if he saved the money, changes his mind and demands that the boy give him the money so he, the father, can go on a fishing trip. Should the boy follow his father's orders or refuse? Another story involves a woman with terminal cancer who is in great pain. She asks her doctor to give her enough morphine to kill her. The doctor cannot relieve her pain without killing her but knows that mercy-killing is illegal. What should he do? Kohlberg's most famous interview story is the Heinz dilemma. See *Research,* p. 543, for the story of Heinz and some of Kohlberg's followup questions.

Research

The Heinz Dilemma

In Europe, a woman was near death from a special kind of cancer. There was one drug that the doctors thought might save her. It was a form of radium that a druggist in the same town had recently discovered. The drug was expensive to make, but the druggist was charging ten times what the drug cost him to make. He paid $400 for the radium and charged $4,000 for a small dose of the drug. The sick woman's husband, Heinz, went to everyone he knew to borrow the money and tried every legal means, but he could only get together about $2,000, which is half of what it cost. He told the druggist that his wife was dying, and asked him to sell it cheaper or let him pay later. But the druggist said, "No, I discovered the drug and I'm going to make money from it." So, having tried every legal means, Heinz gets desperate and considers breaking into the man's store to steal the drug for his wife.

1. Should Heinz steal the drug?
2. Why or why not?
3. Does Heinz have a duty or obligation to steal the drug?
4. Why or why not?
5. If Heinz doesn't love his wife, should he steal the drug for her? (*If subject favors not stealing ask:* Does it make a difference in what Heinz should do whether or not he loves his wife?)
6. Why or why not?
7. Suppose the person dying is not his wife but a stranger. Should Heinz steal the drug for a stranger?
8. Why or why not?
9. Is it important for people to do everything they can to save another's life?
10. Why or why not?
11. In general, should people try to do everything they can to obey the law?
12. Why or why not?
13. How does this apply to what Heinz should do?

From Kohlberg (1984). Optional questions used in some interviews are not included here.

It is important to emphasize that the subject's stage of moral development is determined not from her solution to the dilemma (e.g., yes, the boy should give his father the money; no, he shouldn't) but rather from the reasoning she uses to justify her solution. This is consistent with the theory itself, which is not a theory of *what* people think is right but one of *why* they think it is right. Unfortunately, determining a person's level of moral reasoning through this method is very difficult. One must learn to administer the interview properly and to score the responses according to the very detailed criteria worked out by Kohlberg and his colleagues (the latest version of the scoring manual is hundreds of pages long). Not surprisingly, there has been great interest in developing simpler techniques for assessing and doing research on morality.

The best-known alternative to Kohlberg's interviews is the **Defining Issues Test** (DIT) designed by James Rest (1979, 1983; Schlaefli, Rest, &

Thoma, 1985). The DIT is based on the idea that people at different stages of moral development will differ in what they see as the central issues in resolving a moral dilemma. The test presents 6 dilemmas (including 3 of Kohlberg's) and 12 issue-statements for each. For the Heinz dilemma, for example, one issue-statement would be, "whether a community's laws are going to be upheld," whereas another would be, "Isn't it only natural for a loving husband to care so much for his wife that he'd steal?" Presumably, a stage 4 subject would see the first of these issues as central, whereas a stage 3 subject would focus on the second. By asking subjects to rate and rank the importance of the various issues for each dilemma, each person's level of moral development can be determined. Even though this method differs from Kohlberg's clinical interviews, the issues presented and the analysis of subjects' choices are based directly on Kohlberg's stages.

Kohlberg's Theory: Research and Critiques

Kohlberg's theory has generated a great deal of empirical research and theoretical criticism. In this section, we will consider three sets of responses to the theory. First, we will review basic research on development through Kohlberg's stages. Then we will discuss the controversial work of Carol Gilligan, who has claimed that Kohlberg's theory, by focusing exclusively on morality as justice, ignores moral issues of care, compassion, and responsibility that are particularly salient for girls and women. Finally, we will look into the thorny question of whether and how moral reasoning—the focus of Piaget's and Kohlberg's cognitive-developmental work—relates to the actual feelings and behavior of children and adults in real-life situations.

Basic Research on Kohlberg's Stages

Cross-Sectional Research. The most obvious prediction of Kohlberg's theory is that older children will show more sophisticated moral judgments than younger children. Thus we should find that stage of moral development is positively correlated with age. This can be tested by giving Kohlberg interviews to children of different ages (a cross-sectional study, see Chapter 3) and comparing their moral judgments. Numerous studies have done this and the results are consistent: Level of moral sophistication increases with age (Rest, 1983).

Although these results are consistent with Kohlberg's theory, cross-sectional studies do not put the theory to a very rigorous test. Kohlberg's theory claims that not only do children, on the average, reach higher stages of moral development as they get older, but that each *individual* child goes through the stages one at a time. It is not predicted that all children will progress at the same rate or that every child will reach the highest stage, but it *is* predicted that no child will skip a stage or regress to an earlier one. These predictions cannot be tested in a cross-sectional study, since, although the children vary in age, each child is tested only once. A stronger test of Kohlberg's theory requires that we follow the moral development of a set of children over a span of several years—that is, that we do longitudinal research.

Longitudinal Research. The results of early longitudinal investigations of Kohlberg's stages confirmed the findings from cross-sectional research that development generally moves in the direction he postulated. There were, however, indications that some individuals might skip stages (Holstein, 1976) and that regression was possible. In particular, Kohlberg's own research suggested that students who are at stage 4 or 4/5 (a mixture of stage 4 and 5 thinking) in high school often regress to stage 2 in college. Kohlberg and Kramer (1969) noted, however, that regressed stage 2 students (unlike stage 2 children) still *understood* higher-level reasoning. This suggested that the regression to self-centered preconventional morality was merely an exploratory phase related to questioning and reconsidering their identities and commitments (a common phenomenon at this age—see the discussion of Erikson's "identity crisis" in Chapter 16). The data indicated that the regressed individuals eventually returned to the more mature reasoning they had earlier developed.

This interpretation, however, weakened the idea of developmental stages and, moreover, did not resolve other problems raised by the longitudinal data. Kohlberg (1973) and his associates (Turiel, 1974, 1977) decided that their scoring system needed to be revised to focus less on the superficial content of what subjects said and more on the underlying structure of their reasoning. Upon re-scoring the data with the revised system, they changed their conclusions about moral development in two important ways. First, they found that stage 5 thinking was an adult development not found in high school students. Second, what seemed to be a regression to stage 2 reasoning actually was different from genuine stage 2 reasoning. Instead, it was a transition phase (stage 4½) between stages 4 and 5, in which students rejected conventional morality but had not yet constructed a postconventional morality to replace it. Since these students had rejected conventional standards but had no postconventional principles to replace them, their moral thinking was highly relativistic ("Do whatever you want; there are no standards"). This had earlier been scored as a self-centered stage 2 orientation but was now seen as a more sophisticated relativism that inevitably led to the construction of stage 5 principles of social contract.

More recently, Kohlberg has come to believe that relativism is not limited to the transition between stages 4 and 5. It can arise whenever an individual rejects one moral orientation (stage) on the way to constructing another (Colby, Kohlberg, Gibbs, & Lieberman, 1983; Kohlberg, 1984). The current scoring system, known as **Standard Issue Scoring**, represents Kohlberg's latest efforts to refine his system to get at the underlying structure of reasoning (Colby & Kohlberg, 1986).

The broadest and most rigorous test of the current formulation of Kohlberg's theory is the continuing followup of Kohlberg's original dissertation subjects (Colby et al., 1983). The results now include up to 6 interviews (typically about 4) with each of 58 subjects over the course of about 20 years. All data were analyzed using Standard Issue Scoring.

The results are impressive. Regression was extremely rare and no subject ever skipped a stage. For a typical subject at a given time of testing, most reasoning was at a single stage and nearly all reasoning was within two adjacent stages. Thus, it appears that virtually all subjects moved one step at a time through Kohlberg's stages, with each stage gradually dropping out as the next developed.

As the scoring system has increased its emphasis on structure over the years, the criteria for attainment of the higher stages have become substantially more demanding. According to the current system, stage 2 reasoning is predominant in 10-year-olds, with some reasoning at stages 1 and 3 also found. In adolescence, stage 3 reasoning becomes increasingly dominant; stage 2 reasoning declines; and stage 1 reasoning disappears. Stage 4 reasoning begins in some individuals early in adolescence but does not become predominant until well past age 20. Stage 5 reasoning does not appear until after age 20 and remains rare even in the oldest subjects (age 36). Stage 6 reasoning was not observed at all. Kohlberg now considers it an ideal end point of moral development and suggests that research on stage 6 will require specially designed dilemmas and subjects selected as likely to be at a high level of moral sophistication (e.g., judges, theologians, or moral philosophers).

Experimental Research. In the longitudinal and cross-sectional work discussed above, the researcher interviews subjects to *assess* their moral reasoning but does not attempt to *influence* their reasoning through manipulation of potentially relevant variables. Obviously, there is great value in studying the natural progression of moral reasoning without attempting to manipulate it. There is also much to be learned, however, through systematic experimentation.

Experimental research has enabled researchers to investigate issues that could not be resolved through interviews alone. Questions asked have included the following: Do people understand the moral reasoning involved in stages below their own? Do they understand stages above their own? Given a choice, do they prefer reasoning at, below, or above their own stage? How will they respond to models who use reasoning at, below, or above their own stage?

Research on understanding and preference has yielded fairly consistent patterns (Walker, de Vries, & Bichard, 1984). People generally understand the reasoning of stages below their own as well as reasoning one stage above their own. They do not, however, understand reasoning two or more stages above their own. When asked to evaluate examples of moral reasoning, they tend to prefer the highest stage they can understand. This pattern is easily explained in terms of Kohlberg's theory. People understand lower stages because they have been through them, but reject such reasoning as inferior. Kohlberg argues that recognition of the inferiority of lower-stage reasoning is precisely what motivates people to construct more sophisticated moral reasoning.

How do people respond to models of reasoning illustrating stages above or below their own? Many studies have considered this. Lawrence Walker (1982), for example, assessed the moral reasoning, perspective-taking ability, and general cognitive development of 101 children ranging in age from 10 to 13. He then chose 50 students who, on the basis of their cognitive development and perspective-taking scores, seemed ready to advance in moral development. These were randomly divided into five groups. Children in four of the groups were exposed to moral reasoning either two stages above their own, one stage above, at their own stage, or one stage below. A fifth (control) group was not exposed to any reasoning. The effects on the moral reasoning of the subjects were assessed one week later and then again six weeks after that to determine whether the changes were lasting.

On the basis of the earlier discussion, one might expect that exposure to reasoning one stage above one's own would be most effective. Lower-stage reasoning would be rejected as inferior, same-stage reasoning provides no reason to change, and reasoning two stages above would be misunderstood and thus ineffective. Walker's study showed that exposure to reasoning one stage above resulted in moral development that lasted through the delayed post-test. Exposure to reasoning two stages above, however, was just as effective, while no other condition brought about changes. An important aspect of the results is that children who progressed always moved to the stage one above their own, regardless of whether they had been exposed to a model one stage above or two stages above.

Thus children were not simply imitating the reasoning they were exposed to. One way of interpreting these results is in terms of equilibration theory (see Chapter 8). Models at or below the student's stage induce no disequilibrium and thus have no effect on development. Models illustrating higher-stage reasoning do cause disequilibrium. Rather than simply learning the reasoning they have been exposed to, however, children resolve the disequilibrium by *constructing* a new mode of thinking. Regardless of whether the model was one or two stages above them, their new moral orientation is always one stage above their present one.

Cross-Cultural Research. All the research discussed so far has involved Americans. If Kohlberg's theory accounted only for the moral development of Americans, that would itself be a worthwhile accomplishment. Kohlberg claims, however, that his stages apply to individuals in all cultures. To test this requires data concerning moral development in cultures that differ radically from that of the United States.

Research on Kohlberg's stages has been conducted in a wide variety of cultures and has generally supported his theory (Snarey, 1985). The two most extensive investigations of moral development outside the United States have been longitudinal studies of moral development in Turkey (Nisan & Kohlberg, 1982) and Israel (Snarey, Reimer, & Kohlberg, 1985a). In both of these cultures, subjects proceeded through Kohlberg's stages in the same invariant sequence as American subjects. This universality is impressive in that the three cultures sampled were quite different: The American subjects were mostly Christian city-dwellers; the Israeli subjects were Jews raised in *kibbutzim* (collective communities involving communal child-rearing and economics); and the Turkish subjects were Moslems living mostly in small villages.

There were, of course, differences as well as similarities among the cultures. Only in the American and Israeli samples, for instance, was much stage 5 reasoning observed. Moreover, close analysis of stage 5 kibbutz reasoning suggested some interesting differences from stage 5 American reasoning: For example, there was greater emphasis on community, social solidarity, and collective happiness. Research in India, Taiwan, New Guinea, and Kenya also has revealed instances of moral reasoning difficult to score within Kohlberg's system (Snarey, 1985). The concept of a universal sequence of stages does not rule out important differences between cultures in the rate of development, the highest stage commonly attained, and the way the stages are expressed.

Sex Bias and the Scope of Morality

The cross-cultural data collected on Kohlberg's stages provide at least a partial answer to those who claim that his theory is culturally biased. Closer to home, however, the theory has faced a serious charge of sex bias. A number of psychologists have suggested the theory is biased toward males and provides a distorted picture of the moral development of girls and women.

The best-known example of the sex-bias charge is the work of Carol Gilligan (1982), a colleague of Kohlberg's at Harvard. Gilligan and her associates interviewed a number of women, in some cases using Kohlberg's hypothetical dilemmas and in others focusing on real issues in the women's own lives (e.g., in one study the subjects were pregnant women deciding whether or not to have abortions). She concluded that women and men differ in their orientations to morality. Men, she argued, focus on morality as justice—abstract, rational principles for respecting the rights of others. They view people as individuals, each of whom is entitled to be treated fairly and not be interfered with. Deciding what is the correct solution to a moral dilemma is a matter of objective analysis and calculation. It is, in the words of an 11-year-old boy, "sort of like a math problem with humans" (Gilligan, 1982, p. 26). Women, by contrast, see morality as essentially a matter of care, or a compassionate concern for human welfare. The focus is on relationships and one's special responsibilities to those with whom one is intimately interconnected. Resolving moral issues from women's perspectives is primarily a matter of sensitivity to the social context.

Gilligan cited research by Kohlberg and Kramer (1969) and Holstein (1976) showing that women, on the average, score lower than men on Kohlberg's measure of moral development. Specifically, female development often seems to end at stage 3 whereas males go on to stage 4. Kohlberg and Kramer (1969) had argued that this difference is due to sex roles in our society. They suggested that women have less opportunity than men to play important roles in social institutions. Therefore, women remain at the face-to-face morality of stage 3 whereas men—because society allows them more opportunity to see things from a broader, societal perspective—are more likely to move on to a stage 4

Carol Gilligan has suggested that women typically think about morality in terms of care and compassion while men are more oriented toward rights and justice. Many have disagreed with her claim that males and females differ in their conceptions of morality.

morality. In a society with more equal opportunities, according to Kohlberg's theory, the sex difference would disappear.

Gilligan, in contrast, argued that the sex difference observed in research using Kohlberg's stages reflects fundamental differences between men and women. She disputed the idea that women's morality is less sophisticated, however. Kohlberg's theory, she suggested, is set up to assess male morality. The dilemmas used and the criteria for scoring them focus on justice rather than care. Responses focusing on interpersonal concern and responsibility are therefore mistakenly seen as a stage 3 morality inferior to that of the mature man.

How does female morality develop then? Gilligan suggested that it moves through three levels, though not all women necessarily reach the third level. The first level involves a concern only for the self. A redefinition of the self in terms of attachment and responsibility to other people leads to a level 2 morality of self-sacrifice, in which care and compassion for others become primary. But what about caring for oneself? The third level is reached when a woman recognizes she is responsible for herself as well as others and succeeds in integrating her responsibilities to self and other.

Do boys and girls really develop along two separate tracks and reach two distinct kinds of adult morality? One response to Gilligan's work has been tremendous interest in the issue of sex differences in morality, including new research and systematic reviews of existing evidence. As noted above, there have been some studies showing sex differences in moral development (see also Baumrind, 1986). The vast majority of studies, however, show no differences in the stages of development attained by males and females (Brabeck, 1983; Broughton, 1983; Gibbs, Arnold, & Burkhart, 1984; Kohlberg, 1984; Nunner-Winkler, 1984; Pratt, Golding, & Hunter, 1984; Smetana, 1984; Snarey, 1985; Snarey, Reimer, & Kohlberg, 1985a; Thoma, 1986; Walker, 1984, 1986a, b), especially when Kohlberg's current scoring system is used.

This evidence presents a serious problem for Gilligan's theory. To a large extent, her work is devoted to explaining why women score lower than men on Kohlberg's measure of moral development. If women do *not* score lower than men on Kohlberg's stages, then the phenomenon Gilligan was trying to explain simply does not exist. In that case, what remains of her theory?

Even if Gilligan is entirely wrong about sex differences, there may still be value in her work. Perhaps her main contribution to psychology is not a better understanding of women but rather a broader sense of the scope of morality. Morality is indeed more than justice and rights—it *does* include care, compassion, and responsibility—and psychologists need to pay more attention to aspects of morality outside the realm of justice (Baumrind, 1986; Brabeck, 1983; Nunner-Winkler, 1984). Kohlberg himself, although denying that his stages are sex-biased, acknowledges that his theory focuses primarily on the development of the concept of justice. Although he considers justice central to morality, he agrees with Gilligan that a general theory of moral development would need to be much broader and would have to include research on the sorts of issues Gilligan has raised (Kohlberg, Levine, & Hewer, 1983). He suggests, however, that the development of justice (fairness, respect for rights, and so on) and the development of care (compassion, responsibility, and so on) are not two separate tracks but rather are closely interrelated. The Golden Rule of the New Testament, he notes, is formulated in two ways corresponding to these two orientations: "Do unto others as you would have them do unto you" and "Love thy neighbor as thyself."

In sum, Gilligan has proposed that morality includes not only the concept of justice (as studied by Kohlberg) but also an orientation toward care and responsibility. In addition, she has proposed that men are more oriented toward morality as justice and women toward morality as care. Available evidence does not support her views about the different orientations of males and females. Nonetheless, her emphasis on the morality of care is a useful corrective to Kohlberg's focus on morality as justice. Mary Brabeck (1983) expresses what is probably the current view of most psychologists:

> There is an essential tension between autonomy and interdependence, between the requirements of justice and the demands of mercy, between absolute moral principles and situation specific moral action, between reason and affect. To resolve this tension by assigning half to males and half to females when evidence does not support that division is to reduce the complexity of morality, to cloud truth with myth, to do an injustice to the capacities of both sexes, and to lose an opportunity to revise and modify our theories of morality (p. 287).

But if we can get beyond the issue of sex differences, Brabeck continues, there is much value in Gilligan's work.

> When Gilligan's and Kohlberg's theories are taken together, the moral person is seen as one whose moral choices reflect reasoned and deliberate judgments that ensure justice be accorded each person while maintaining a passionate concern for the well-being and care of each individual. Justice and care are then joined; the demands of universal principles and specific moral choices are bridged and the need for autonomy and for interconnection are united in an enlarged and more adequate conception of morality (p. 289).

Moral Reasoning, Moral Feelings, and Moral Behavior

Although Gilligan's work may be seen as expanding our conception of moral development by considering aspects of morality other than justice, it still focuses on people's *reasoning*—that is, how people *think* about moral issues. But what about moral feelings, our guilt at having done wrong or pride at having done right? And what about moral behavior? Clearly, a theory of moral development should address what children actually *do* and how their behavior changes over time.

Kohlberg (1984) acknowledges the importance of moral feelings and behavior. He indicates that he has focused on moral reasoning not because feelings and behavior are unimportant but because moral reasoning is most fundamental. We must understand how people think about moral issues in order to predict their feelings and actions.

Using Kohlberg's stages of moral reasoning to predict behavior is not a simple matter, however. The stages are not meant to be a simple scale of morality with higher stages directly corresponding to increasingly moral behavior. For one thing, Kohlberg's theory indicates that two people at the same stage may make different choices (though they use the same sort of underlying reasoning), while people at different stages may make the same choice (but for different reasons). For example, one child might say that Heinz should steal the drug because his wife's relatives will punish him if he does not, whereas another child might say he should not steal the drug because the druggist will punish him if he does. These are opposite judgments, but the underlying reasoning is stage 1 in each case: avoid punishment. An adult at stage 5 might agree with the judgment of the first child—steal the drug—but have a much more sophisticated reason.

A second problem in predicting behavior from stages of moral reasoning is that people might not always reach the same decision when facing a real-life issue that they do when responding to a hypothetical dilemma. Real-life issues, for example, are likely to be more complex and their moral aspects not as obvious as the moral aspects of one of Kohlberg's dilemmas. Third, even if people's real-life decisions did correspond in a simple way to their stage of moral reasoning, we all know people do not always do what they know is right (Locke, 1983a; Straughan, 1983), a problem philosophers call "weakness of will." We can see, then, that it is a long way from one's stage of reasoning about hypothetical dilemmas, to one's choices of correct action for those dilemmas, to one's choices of correct action in real-life situations, to one's actual behavior in those situations. Considering all of this, we might wonder whether Kohlberg's stages would predict actual behavior at all.

In fact, available evidence shows that moral stage predicts actual behavior to some degree, but not perfectly (Blasi, 1980; Gibbs, Clark, Joseph, Green, Goodrick, & Makowski, 1986; Rest, 1983). Kohlberg has interpreted these results as showing the relevance of moral reasoning to behavior and has attempted to expand his theory in ways that will further clarify how reasoning leads to behavior (Kohlberg & Candee, 1984). It does appear, however, that for a complete theory of moral development one must look beyond the confines of Kohlberg's stage theory.

One radical alternative would be to focus exclusively on behavior. Perhaps reasoning is simply verbal chatter and rationalization that has no effect on our actions. Why not simply study the moral and immoral behaviors of children and observe how these change with age and experience?

This strictly behaviorist approach has a number of problems, however. Perhaps most important, how do we determine whether a given behavior is moral? Suppose Sally locks Jim in a room. One is tempted to call this immoral. But if Sally does it at great risk to herself in order to prevent Jim from murdering Joe, it may be a highly moral action. If she does it as part of a game, it may be a morally neutral behavior, neither moral nor immoral. We cannot judge a behavior without knowing its underlying reason. More broadly, we cannot study morality without considering intentions and reasons (Kohlberg & Candee, 1984; Locke, 1983b).

What we need, then, is not to replace the study of moral reasoning with something else (such as the study of moral behavior), but rather to develop an expanded model that puts reasoning into a broader context. James Rest (1983, 1984) has attempted to do precisely that. He

Theorists such as James Rest and Augusto Blasi have considered the relation between what one decides is moral and what one actually does.

suggests that moral action involves four components. Component 1 involves *interpreting a situation*. This includes determining what actions we can take and evaluating how each course of action will affect the welfare of others. Component 2 encompasses *figuring out the moral thing to do*. This is where our stage of moral reasoning ability is relevant. Component 3 involves *choosing among moral and nonmoral values* to decide what we actually intend to do. This might include deciding not to do what you have determined is the morally correct action because other motives are more important. Component 4 is *carrying out our intentions*. This component is necessary because even if we intend to take the morally correct course of action we may fail to do so.

Rest's model agrees with Kohlberg's view that to engage in genuinely moral actions requires adequate moral reasoning. The same behaviors, if performed accidentally or for immoral or amoral purposes, would not be considered moral actions. In Rest's model, however, moral reasoning is only one of four components. In order to behave morally, we must not only reason morally (component 2) but must also recognize moral aspects of real-life situations (component 1), decide to do what is morally right (component 3), and follow through on what we have decided (component 4).

Although Rest's ordering of the components seems logical, he stresses that the determination of moral action is not this straightforward. Complex interactions occur among the components. What one identifies as morally relevant aspects of a situation (component 1), for example, may depend on one's stage of moral reasoning. Moreover, if the personal costs of moral action are very great (component 3), one may reconsider the situation (component 1). Rest has reviewed research related to each of the components and some research looking at relations between certain components. He suggests that further research considering complex interactions of the components is needed. In fact, he promises a Nobel Prize to the first researcher able to determine how all four components interact to produce behavior!

The Rest model is a framework for integrating studies of moral reasoning, feelings, and behavior. It is useful for seeing how current research fits together, what the major gaps are, and what further research would be most helpful. Another, perhaps even broader, approach is provided by Augusto Blasi (1980, 1983, 1984).

Blasi's theory begins with some basic questions. Why should I be moral? Why not just do what is best for me (selfishness) rather than what is best for others (morality)? Even if I can determine what is morally right (Rest's component 2), why not just ignore that and do what is best for me instead (component 3)? If I do not end up actually doing what I know is morally right (component 4), why should I feel guilty?

Blasi suggests these sorts of questions cannot be answered if we stay strictly within the domain of morality. We must look more broadly at the person's entire sense of self, the development of his or her personality. People will choose to do what they know is morally right if they see themselves as moral persons, if being moral is central to their identities. As Blasi (1984, p. 132) put it:

> The individual who lacks a moral identity will still understand and use moral speech, will be able to make moral judgments and to engage in discussions about the appropriateness of certain moral decisions and the validity of certain moral criteria. However, a moral perspective will play no significant role in his or her life, in the decisions that really matter, in the fundamental outlook on the world and on history, or in eliciting strong emotions and deep anxieties.

In other words, the difference between the person who has a moral identity and the one who does not is *not* a difference in the ability to *decide* what is morally right (Kohlberg's stages; Rest's component 2). Rather, it is a difference in the commitment to *doing* what is morally right when it conflicts with other goals or desires (Rest's components 3 and 4). Of course, having a moral identity is not an all-or-none matter. The more important morality is to your deepest sense of self, the more likely it is that you will do what is morally right, even when this conflicts with other considerations.

If morality is central to one's identity, moral action is not a matter of putting aside one's own interests but instead being true to one's deepest self. To be immoral is to betray one's identity. The resulting feeling of guilt is a direct effect of perceiving one's inconsistency, one's lack of intactness and wholeness, one's lack of integrity.

Blasi argues that moral understanding ideally plays a central role in the development of one's self-concept and sense of identity (topics that will be discussed in detail in Chapter 16). Thus, although moral understanding is itself a cognitive matter (as is $2 + 2 = 4$), it can become part of a broader sense of who you are that links reasoning with emotions and behavior. To the extent that this happens, the conflict between self-interest and moral concern for others tends to disappear. We are at our moral best when thought, feeling, and action unite, when our behavior is guided by a synthesis of reason and emotion, when we are driven by what Peters (1981) calls "the rational passions."

Applications: Moral Education

Moral development is a fascinating topic in its own right and one with highly important practical relevance. Since morality of some sort is probably necessary for people to live together, every society has a critical

Highlights

Empathy and Altruism

It is easy to think of moral behavior in purely negative terms, as following a set of "Thou Shalt Nots." Clearly, however, there is more to morality than *not* doing harm. Intuitively, it seems that a person who has no impact on others could be judged as more moral than one who harms them but as less moral than one who *helps* others. In other words, there is more to morality than refraining from anti-social behavior. Morality also includes **altruism,** behavior that helps others.

Psychologists have long been interested in altruistic behavior. There are many studies of how likely children (as well as adults) are to behave altruistically (e.g., to share with another child or to help someone in distress) and under what circumstances altruistic behavior is most common. Available evidence indicates that altruistic behavior is quite frequent in preschool children and that examples of caring for others or comforting someone in distress occur even in children under age 2 (Bridgeman, 1983; Eisenberg, 1982; Iannotti, 1985; Levitt, Weber, Clark, & McDonnell, 1985; Radke-Yarrow, Zahn-Waxler, & Chapman, 1983). Although the evidence is widely accepted, there are differences of opinion about how to explain it.

One potential explanation is that the altruism of young children is rooted in their ability to understand the feelings of others and experience those feelings themselves (Denham, 1986). If you see someone crying and immediately share his distress, you may be motivated to help relieve that distress. Psychologists use the term **empathy** to refer to an emotional reaction to someone else's feelings in which you tend to share those feelings or at least to feel something that has more to do with the other person's situation than with your own.

The view that empathic distress is central to altruism has been argued vigorously by Martin Hoffman (1975, 1984). Hoffman proposes that empathic distress is present at all ages but that it changes dramatically as the child's cognitive abilities develop. On the basis of current evidence, he proposes four levels of empathic distress.

During the first year or so, a baby may feel global distress as a result of another's distress. However, she does not grasp the distinction between herself and the other person. Hoffman (1984) gives an example of an 11-month-old girl who saw another child fall and cry. Looking as if she were about to cry herself, she put her thumb in her mouth and buried her

---

interest in the morality of its members. Children's moral education (and perhaps adults' as well) is therefore a topic of great interest (Berkowitz & Oser, 1985). Many difficult questions, however, arise with respect to moral education. Is it really possible? Who should be responsible for it?

head in her mother's lap, exactly what she typically did when she herself was hurt.

During the second year of life, related to the development of object permanence (see Chapter 8), the child increasingly grasps the distinction between self and other. The child now understands when it is another child, not himself, who is in distress. However, he does not really understand the difference in perspective between himself and the other. Hoffman (1984) describes an incident in which an 18-month-old boy observed a crying friend. Although both his mother and the friend's mother were present, he fetched his own mother to comfort the other child. Although he apparently understood that it was his friend, not himself, who needed to be comforted, he did not understand the difference in perspectives well enough to figure out who would be the best comforter.

Children of age 2 or 3 begin to understand that other people have their own feelings, needs, and interpretations of events. They gradually become able to empathize with an increasing range of emotions, including subtle feelings such as disappointment or a sense of betrayal. In late childhood, as children come to see themselves and others as people with continuing identities, they begin to see beyond immediate feelings to understand the broader context of a person's life—for example, feeling bad for a child who is chronically ill. This can ultimately lead in some adolescents to a more abstract concern for entire groups of people, such as the poor or oppressed, and to moral or political ideologies based on that concern.

Hoffman (1984) makes some useful suggestions concerning the sorts of experiences that may be helpful in developing children's empathic abilities. First, children need the opportunity to experience a variety of feelings. Obviously, it is difficult to empathize with someone who is experiencing an emotion you yourself have never felt. Second, it helps to explicitly direct the child's attention to the feelings of others (e.g., "How do you think Mary felt when you took her toy?"). Third, giving children a lot of affection helps them be open to others rather than absorbed in their own needs. Finally, children can learn empathy from models who not only show altruistic behavior but verbalize the empathic feelings that underlie it.

How should we go about it? Our discussion of moral education will focus on school settings, though it is also relevant for parents.

At the beginning of this chapter we discussed absolutism and relativism as approaches to the study of moral development, considered some problems with each, and proposed the cognitive-developmental approach as a possible solution. We can do a similar analysis of perspectives on moral education.

An absolutist approach involves deciding the correct moral rules for children and then training them to use those rules. We might, for example, have them read and repeat certain rules each day, provide models who follow these rules, reward children when they follow the rules, and punish them for deviating from the rules. This approach is rife with problems, however. One of the most obvious questions is very basic: Who decides what rules to teach? Should it be up to each teacher? Should a school principal decide? Should a school board vote on the moral rules for an entire school district? Should a majority vote (51 percent) of parents be the deciding factor? Should Congress pass a law determining the correct moral virtues to be taught to all American students? Obviously, none of these are very good solutions. The absolutist approach breaks down because there is no basis for deciding that certain rules are correct for all people. An absolutist approach becomes a sort of moral indoctrination. (See *Highlights*, p. 432, *Should Schools Develop Reasoning?*, for a discussion of some closely-related issues).

One alternative is to take a relativist approach. From a relativist point of view, students should simply decide for themselves what rules to follow, since all rules and values are equally good. Some families or societies may prefer certain values, but these are arbitrary choices with no rational justification. From a relativist perspective, there is no basis for trying to change students' values, since the values they already hold are just as good as anyone else's. Thus the whole concept of moral education becomes meaningless.

The cognitive-developmental approach rejects both of these extreme positions. In the view of Kohlberg and his followers, we do not have to choose between (a) indoctrinating students in a single set of moral rules or (b) accepting any morality as being just as good as any other. As we have seen, the cognitive-developmental approach holds that, although there is no simple set of absolutely correct rules, some forms of moral reasoning are better than others and people tend to construct increasingly adequate forms of moral reasoning. The issue for moral educators, then, is whether we can assist this natural process.

The emphasis of cognitive-developmental theory on social interaction and cognitive conflict suggests that discussion among peers might be a useful way to approach moral education. Blatt and Kohlberg (1975) found that having students discuss moral dilemmas with each other was an effective technique, a finding that subsequent research has supported (Berkowitz & Gibbs, 1983; Rest, 1983). As Kohlberg's theory predicts, however, students do not leap to new stages in a few weeks. The effects of moral discussion are usually found to be very gradual, appearing only over the course of many months.

Highlights

Are Vulcans Moral?

In an episode of the old TV show *Star Trek*, Captain Kirk meets a bearded version of Mr. Spock, his ultra-logical Vulcan First Officer, in a parallel universe. The alternative Spock turns out to be one of the few ethical people in a world inhabited by vicious brutes. Kirk tells the bearded Spock that he is an honorable man in both worlds.

And Mr. Spock is indeed an honorable man, by almost any earthly—or unearthly—standard. Why is Spock moral? One gets the impression that all Vulcans, in addition to their famed logicality, are highly moral. As they see it, morality is simply a matter of course for the rational individual. There is no logical alternative. To behave immorally would simply be illogical.

So far, the Vulcan orientation would seem to support the cognitive-developmental view that morality is simply the rational coordination of various people's actions and points of view. The totally rational person, for whom there is no emotional interference, would be totally moral. But are logic and emotion really the opposite ends of a single dimension? Does being highly rational necessarily mean being unemotional? And is Mr. Spock really as unemotional as he claims to be?

The true *Star Trek* fan knows that Mr. Spock is in fact quite emotional. But he keeps his emotions strictly in check. Why? Because Vulcans are socialized to do so and being a Vulcan—not merely in ancestry but in ideology—is highly important to Spock. Spock is totally committed to being logical. One might even say he is *emotionally* committed to logic, and thus to morality.

As Spock sees it, then, to behave immorally would not merely be illogical but would violate his emotional commitment to the Vulcan way, his fundamental sense of his own identity. Thus, Mr. Spock, famous for his intense logic, provides an excellent example of Blasi's view that morality is rooted in a complex integration of thoughts and feelings, a deep cognitive *and* emotional sense of who you are.

Should we set up morality classes in which students meet for one or more periods each week to discuss Kohlbergian dilemmas? Kohlberg and his associates think not. Such an approach to moral education would give students the impression that morality is a special topic of study, like chemistry or French, and that moral reasoning is simply a skill one works on in school for a certain number of hours each week. Kohlberg's followers believe it would be much better for all teachers to lead moral discussions, not only on hypothetical dilemmas but also on topics in their own classes (Reimer, Paolitto, & Hersh, 1983). Morality is, after all, directly relevant to the study of literature, history, politics, science, and almost every other subject.

Even integration of moral discussion into the entire curriculum of a school might not be adequate, however. No matter how accomplished students become at discussing moral dilemmas, their moral development might be hindered if they are in a school environment in which they are subject to the whims of teachers and administrators, required to follow arbitrary rules they have no say about. People do not live and make moral judgments in a vacuum. Their social contexts—homes, schools, and societies—provide a moral atmosphere that can help or hinder moral development (Higgins, Power, & Kohlberg, 1984; Snarey, Reimer, & Kohlberg, 1985b).

To modify moral atmosphere, Kohlberg and his associates have arranged **just communities**, initially in a prison setting and more recently in a variety of schools. The just community is a small society in which the prisoners or students have democratic control over important aspects of their lives (e.g., in setting disciplinary policies or school rules). Many consider the concept of moral discussion integrated into school curricula and taking place within a school that functions as a just community to be the state of the art in moral education (Reimer et al., 1983). Others worry that Kohlberg's approach may in fact be merely a new and more subtle form of indoctrination into American middle-class values (Feldman, 1980).

Kohlberg himself (in press) acknowledges that no single current theory can be the basis for a complete program of moral education. Moral education is a complex matter. Nevertheless, it is possible to provide some guidelines for the teacher interested in moral education (see Reimer et al. (1983) for elaboration of these ideas). Such guidelines can be useful, provided one understands their basis, applies them flexibly, pays attention to results, and modifies one's approach as necessary.

1. *Create cognitive conflict.* Have students discuss hypothetical dilemmas (like Kohlberg's) or real issues that come up in school or elsewhere in students' lives. Ask questions that will help students to identify the moral conflicts involved.

2. *Focus on moral reasoning.* Discussion may move to nonmoral aspects of dilemmas or students may propose resolutions that sidestep the moral issue. Redirect discussion to keep the moral dimension central. Students may also simply state opinions without justifying them. Ask "Why?" questions to get them to think about and verbalize their reasoning.

3. *Stimulate social perspective-taking.* Encourage students to see an issue from the point of view of various people involved. Also, as the views of different students become known to the class, encourage

students to reconsider the issue from others' perspectives. Especially with younger children, it may help to have them actually play the roles of some of the characters in the dilemma. For example, have one student be Heinz and another be his wife; let them discuss what Heinz should do and why. Some teachers have literally had students get into each other's shoes to explore other points of view!

4. *Encourage student–student interaction.* Even when many students are participating, they may tend to address their comments to the teacher. Encourage them to talk *to each other.* Use of small groups or rearrangement of seats in a circle can help.

5. *Avoid being "the authority."* This is easier said than done. Students, especially younger children, have a strong tendency to think of the teacher as the authority who will sooner or later tell them the correct answer to the dilemma. Even if you never do this, you may unintentionally direct their ideas in subtle ways. This problem usually cannot be solved by simply staying out of the discussion. As noted above, the teacher has an important role to play in helping students focus on the critical issues, getting them to state their reasoning, and keeping them on track. It takes much experience to walk the fine line between insufficient guidance and overdirection.

6. *Keep the students' level of moral development in mind.* This does not mean precisely determining the stage of every child. Most children will tend to use a mixture of two or more stages. By having a rough idea of students' developmental levels, however, you can recognize when they are interpreting the entire issue differently than you do and can more effectively question them in ways that move them toward slightly more sophisticated views.

7. *Help students generalize to new content.* Moral development is not simply a matter of going from one stage to the next. Students who show a trace of stage 3 reasoning are probably not yet ready to move on to stage 4. They need to consider a variety of issues and gradually figure out how their new forms of reasoning can be applied to these issues. A student who can reason at stage 3 about Heinz, for example, may not yet be able to apply stage 3 reasoning to a disturbing issue in her own life, such as her father's alcoholism.

8. *Create a supportive atmosphere.* Moral development is a risky business for students. As a teacher, you are purposely exposing them to conflict and encouraging them to question and possibly abandon established modes of thinking. Stimulation and challenge are important but should occur within a classroom atmosphere of cooperation and trust. Help students understand that disequilibrium can lead to further development and that to question someone's reasoning is not to question his or her value as a person.

Summary

Three approaches have been taken to the study of moral development. The absolutist approach defines morality as particular virtues and behaviors and looks at children's adherence to this code. The relativist approach views morality as relative to one's society and looks at children's increasing conformity to cultural norms. Post-relativist approaches maintain that morality is neither an unquestioning conformity to absolutes nor a blind adherence to cultural norms. Instead, they define morality in terms of rational standards for social interaction in any society.

The cognitive-developmental paradigm of Piaget and Kohlberg takes the latter perspective. Moral development is seen as the development of structured modes of reasoning about justice that appear in a series of stages. These stages are constructed by the developing individual through increasingly rational coordination of perspectives during his or her social interactions. They ideally lead to a universalist conception of morality that goes beyond any particular culture.

Piaget's research on moral development was published in his classic 1932 book, *The Moral Judgment of the Child*. He concluded that development moves toward (1) understanding the social nature and purpose of rules, (2) judging actions on the basis of the person's intentions, and (3) holding increasingly sophisticated ideas about justice. Overall, he suggested a developmental trend from (1) a heteronomous morality based on unilateral respect for authority and submission to external constraint to (2) an autonomous morality based on mutual respect and cooperation among equals. Piaget argued that interaction among peers is the key factor in moral development.

In an extension and revision of Piaget's theory, Lawrence Kohlberg has proposed six stages of moral development. In stage 1, children see certain things as inherently bad and show a naive respect for authority. In stage 2, there is recognition that others have their own needs and that deals must be made. Stage 3 morality emphasizes relationships and loyalty to others. The stage 4 individual views morality from the perspective of society as a whole. Stage 5 reasoning rationally evaluates laws and social structures from an even more abstract perspective outside of any particular society. Finally, stage 6 involves a conscious formulation of universal principles of justice, a formalized moral philosophy.

Kohlberg sees increasing perspective-taking ability as central to moral development. He and his associates use clinical interviews to assess a person's stage of moral reasoning, although a paper-and-pencil technique known as the Defining Issues Test is also available.

Cross-sectional and longitudinal research on Americans has supported Kohlberg's view that people do move through the stages in the order indicated. The precise rate of development varies widely, but on the average stage 2 reasoning develops during late childhood, stage 3 during adolescence, and stage 4 during early adulthood. It appears that most Americans never achieve stage 5 reasoning and none achieve stage 6 (which is therefore now considered a hypothetical end point of moral development rather than a demonstrated stage). Experimental studies have found that exposure to reasoning above one's stage can result in some advance in reasoning, and that progress is always to the next stage, even if the modeled reasoning was two stages up. Cross-cultural research has indicated that people in other cultures go through the same stages of moral development.

Recent work by Carol Gilligan has led psychologists to acknowledge that morality includes considerations of care, compassion, and personal responsibility that have been overlooked in Kohlberg's emphasis on justice. Current evidence, however, does not support Gilligan's contention that women are more oriented toward a morality of care and men toward a morality of justice. Other theorists and researchers have explored the complex interrelations of moral reasoning (as studied by Piaget and Kohlberg), moral feelings (e.g., empathy and guilt), and moral behavior (e.g., prosocial and antisocial actions). Educators have explored the possibility of facilitating moral development by having students discuss moral dilemmas and by setting up what Kohlberg calls "just communities."

Key Terms

absolutism	moral realism	individualism and exchange
ethical relativism	immanent justice	mutual expectations
cognitive-developmental approach	equity	social system
paradigm	heteronomous morality	social contract
justice	autonomous morality	prior-to-society perspective
perspective-taking	unilateral respect	utility
universality	constraint	universal ethical principles
motor rules	mutual respect	Defining Issues Test
coercive rules	cooperation	Standard Issue Scoring
rational rules	conventional morality	altruism
consequences	preconventional morality	empathy
intentions	postconventional morality	just community

Suggested Readings

Gilligan, C. (1982). *In a different voice: Psychological theory and women's development.* Cambridge, MA: Harvard University Press. This is one of those rare books that represents an important contribution to psychology but is aimed at, and accessible to, a broader audience. Recent research has cast doubt on Gilligan's conclusions about sex differences, but her insights into the nature and scope of morality remain enlightening.

Kohlberg, L. (1984). *Essays on moral development: Vol. II. The psychology of moral development.* New York: Harper & Row. This book is a collection of Kohlberg's writings on the psychology of moral development. It is the second volume of a three-volume series. Volume I, published in 1981, discussed the philosophy of moral development, and Volume III is to cover moral education.

Kurtines, W. M., & Gewirtz, J. L. (Eds.). (1984). *Morality, moral behavior, and moral development.* New York: Wiley. This edited volume includes chapters by most of the major theorists and researchers currently studying moral development, representing a wide diversity of perspectives.

Piaget, J. (1932). *The moral judgment of the child.* London: Routledge and Kegan Paul. This is Piaget's only book on moral development and is still widely read. Unlike most of Piaget's writings, it can be understood by a nonprofessional reader with no background in psychology or Piagetian theory.

Radke-Yarrow, M., Zahn-Waxler, C., & Chapman, M. (1983). Children's prosocial dispositions and behavior. In E. M. Hetherington (Ed.), P. H. Mussen (Series Ed.), *Handbook of child psychology: Vol. 4. Socialization, personality, and social development* (pp. 469–545). New York: Wiley. The chapter is a thorough synthesis of current research and theory on the development of altruism.

Reimer, J., Paolitto, D. P., & Hersh, R. H. (1983). *Promoting moral growth: From Piaget to Kohlberg* (2nd Ed.). New York: Longman. This is probably the best available introduction to moral education from a cognitive-developmental perspective. It is theoretically solid but also very clear and practical.

Rest, J. R. (1983). Morality. In J. H. Flavell & E. M. Markman (Eds.), P. H. Mussen (Series Ed.), *Handbook of child psychology: Vol. 3. Cognitive development* (pp. 556–629). New York: Wiley. Rest provides a thorough review of the literature on the development of moral reasoning.

Application Exercise

15-1 Stages of Moral Reasoning

Which of Kohlberg's first five stages is best illustrated in each of the following? (We have tried to set these examples up to be as clear as possible. Keep in mind that in real life isolated bits of moral reasoning are almost always ambiguous. This is why Kohlberg's assessment technique relies on detailed clinical interviews and complex scoring criteria.)

1. You should be helpful to others so that someday, when you need help, they will be helpful to you.
2. Civil disobedience—purposely breaking an immoral law to demonstrate one's moral objection to it—is justified in the case of laws inconsistent with a systematic analysis of fair ways for people to interact.
3. You should never break the law. Even if you dislike a particular law, keep in mind that if everyone broke laws they disliked the result would be utter chaos.
4. As a police officer you should arrest lawbreakers, even if you have sympathy in a particular case. The law may be harsh, but others are counting on you to fulfill your role.
5. Your brother has special obligations to you, as a brother, and you in turn have obligations to him as his sister.
6. Congress shall make no law respecting an establishment of religion or prohibiting the free exercise thereof; or abridging the freedom of speech or of the press, or the right of the people peaceably to assemble and to petition the government for a redress of grievances.
7. Murder is a crime because it is wrong.
8. You can't just do whatever you want because this may interfere with someone else doing what she wants. You have to look at it from her perspective too.
9. You shouldn't tattle on a good friend. It would destroy the relation of trust between the two of you.
10. You shouldn't tell people embarrassing things you know about a close friend, since she probably knows embarrassing things about you too.
11. You should always obey the teacher. Why? Because he's the teacher!
12. You should be helpful to others because it is important to be a moral person whom people can always count on.

CHAPTER 16

Personality Development

My self is Clem, a person who was born on the planet Earth.
   —Clem, age 10
   (Broughton, 1978, p. 86)

[The self is] a philosophical invention . . . somebody made up to sell deodorant.
   —Kathy, age 22
   (Broughton, 1978, p. 94)

You could ask me how is my integrity today. Well, maybe after lunch and a nap I will feel more like answering that.
   —Erik Erikson, age 77
   (Hulsizer et al., 1981, p. 257)

People are more than collections of cognitive abilities, emotions, social skills, and moral values. Psychologists are interested not only in the various dimensions on which people differ but in the unity of each individual—that is, his or her personality. Developmental psychologists are interested not only in the development of perception, memory, language, reasoning, emotions, social attachments, and moral orientations, but in how all these aspects of the developing person fit together: that is, in how the personality as a whole develops.

Studying the development of personality is a daunting task, however. Where do we even begin? One good starting point is to extend the idea of metacognition. We have seen in earlier chapters that children increasingly think about their memories, language, and reasoning. We will see in this chapter that, taking a broader perspective, they also think about *themselves*. Children's conceptions about themselves—their **self-concepts**—will be the focus for the first section of this chapter.

One particularly important aspect of self-concept is one's sense of maleness or femaleness. Psychologists have given much attention to how a child comes to understand that she is a girl or that he is a boy—a process known as **sex-typing**—and how she or he constructs ideas about **sex roles**, the views of society about the appropriate roles and behavior for each sex. The study of sex-typing and the development of sex roles is complicated by the fact that American society has evolved dramatically with respect to gender issues over the past 25 years. We will explore these issues in the second part of this chapter.

The remaining two sections of the chapter will consider two general theories of personality development. One will look at the psychoanalytic perspective, emphasizing the influential theory of Erik Erikson. The other will explore a cognitive-developmental perspective on personality development, emphasizing the recent work of Robert Kegan.

Development of Self-Concept

Imagine that you look into a mirror and see a smudge above your right eyebrow. You immediately wipe your forehead. This may seem a very ordinary occurrence, but in fact it shows a considerable degree of sophistication on your part. Why didn't you wipe the mirror, which is what you saw, rather than your forehead, which you did not actually see? Obviously, you know that what you saw in the mirror was neither a picture nor another person, but rather a reflection of *you*. Your reaction shows that you have a conception of yourself, an awareness of your *self*.

How do babies react to mirrors? This has been the focus of considerable research. In a recent review, Jeanne Brooks-Gunn and Michael Lewis (1984) concluded that, "the overwhelming response to a mirror is one of pleasure—smiling, vocalizing, and touching the mirror" (1984, p. 220). In a number of studies, the investigators have marked the infant's face (e.g., with rouge) and looked specifically at the infant's response to seeing the mark in a mirror. Infants under 15 months of age do not respond by touching the mark, whereas those at least 20 months old usually do (Lewis & Brooks-Gunn, 1979). Brooks-Gunn and Lewis (1984) reviewed other evidence that self-conscious reactions such as acting silly or coy or appearing embarrassed become increasingly common during this same time. The period around 18 months thus seems central in the initial formation of self-concept.

Self-concept continues to develop beyond infancy, however. William Damon and Daniel Hart (1982) provided a thorough review and imaginative synthesis of the relevant literature. The remainder of this section will present their model of the development of self-concept.

Self-Understanding and Self-Esteem

"Ellen is a happy and confident child because she has such a positive self-concept." "Brent does poorly in school because he has a negative self-concept." We hear statements like these all the time. Obviously, the term *self-concept* is used in a particular way in statements of this sort. We use the term to refer to children's evaluations of themselves, that is, whether they feel good or bad about themselves. In other words, we are talking about children's **self-esteem**.

But consider the following statements: "Arden thinks of himself as a helpful individual;" "Jane considers herself an athlete;" "Bob views himself as a hard-working student;" "George considers himself a very religious person;" "Clara thinks of herself as a radical political activist." All of the above statements concern people's cognitive conceptions about themselves—that is, how they *think* about themselves rather than how they *feel* about themselves. Thus, we are talking here not about self-esteem but about **self-understanding**.

Damon and Hart's model focuses on self-understanding. They point out that a 4-year-old and a 14-year-old with equally positive (or negative) feelings about themselves are likely to feel the way they do for very different reasons. Thus they argue that we cannot decipher children's self-esteem without first looking at developmental changes in their self-understanding.

"I" vs. "Me"

When you think about yourself, you are appearing twice in the same activity. First, there is the *you* doing the thinking, and second, there is the *you* being thought about. From your own point of view, we can say that "I think about me" includes an "I" that does the thinking and a "Me" that is thought about. In other words, the "I" is the subject and the "Me" is the object.

This distinction between the **"I"** and the **"Me"** was presented nearly a century ago by William James (1892), who is often considered the founder of American psychology. Damon and Hart proposed that self-understanding includes both an understanding of the characteristics of the self (the "Me") and an understanding of the self-as-knower (the "I"). We will see how they use this distinction as we consider their account of developmental trends from infancy through late adolescence.

Development of the "Me"

The "Me," according to Damon and Hart's analysis, includes four aspects of the self: the physical self, the active self, the social self, and the psychological self. The **physical self** includes one's name, bodily properties, and material possessions. The **active self** includes one's behavior and capabilities. The **social self** includes social characteristics, social relations, and group memberships. Finally, the **psychological self** includes feelings, thought processes, psychological traits, and belief systems.

Are all these selves equally prominent at all ages? Evidence reviewed by Damon and Hart shows they are not. The self-understanding of preschool children tends to stress the physical self. The self is considered to be part of the body, typically the head. Questions about the size, shape, or color of the self do not seem particularly odd to a child this age. Physical appearance and material attributes are what make you who you are: I am small, I am blond, I have a bike, I live in a big house, and so forth. Although young children may also talk about particular behaviors (active self), social interactions (social self), or feelings (psychological self), these are described as if they were physical attributes rather than general abilities or enduring social or psychological characteristics (e.g., "I ride my bike," "My friends are named Lucy and Jim," or "I have a funny feeling in my tummy," rather than "I am a good bike-rider," "I am very friendly," or "I am a sad person").

Development of Self-Concept

During the elementary years, the active self predominates. Moreover, the focus is not on particular behaviors but on general capabilities relative to others. An 8-year-old might define himself as the best bicycle-rider on his block. A 10-year-old might emphasize that she is the best home run hitter in her class. Again, characteristics of the physical, social, and psychological selves can be found, but the child stresses activity-related considerations in defining these aspects of who she or he is. This might, for example, include emphasis on physical characteristics such as strength or speed directly related to his or her activities.

In early adolescence, the focus moves to the social self. This emerges by emphasis on personality traits, such as being friendly or a good sport, that directly involve relations with other people. Considerations involving the physical, active, or psychological selves focus on social dimensions of these. Thus, being physically attractive or competent athletically might be central to an adolescent's self-concept if this is seen as the basis for his or her social popularity.

Finally, older adolescents stress deeper psychological characteristics. Their thought processes, belief systems, and personal philosophies are central to their conceptions of themselves: I am an intellectual, a nonconformist, a political activist, and so on. Physical, active, and social

In adolescence, the physical self is important primarily to the extent that it affects social relations.

"Wouldn't you know it! ... And always just before a big date!"

At all ages, the sense of self includes physical, active, social, and psychological dimensions.

characteristics are critical to the self only if they have psychological dimensions. Hairstyle, clothing, political activities, or group memberships may be central to the older adolescent's sense of herself if they reflect deeply rooted philosophical commitments.

In sum, the sense of self at all ages includes physical, active, social, and psychological considerations. The four considerations are not equally important at every age, however. In early childhood the physical self predominates and physical considerations color all four aspects of self. As development proceeds, the focus of self-concept shifts to the active self, then to the social self, and finally to the psychological self.

Development of the "I"

The "I" is the subjective self that organizes and interprets experience. Awareness of one's "I" is based on several dimensions: continuity, distinctness, volition, and self-reflectivity.

Continuity is the sense that I remain the same person over the course of time. I may be different in some ways a year from now but I describe that by saying that I will have changed, rather than by saying that I will cease to exist and be replaced by someone else. Last year I lived in a yellow house, this year I live in a brown house, and some day I may live in a different city; but it is still the same "I" in all three cases.

Distinctness refers to my sense of individuality. I may tell someone how things look or feel to me, but no one else can ever experience things from my perspective in the same direct way that I can. I experience a song or a sunrise differently from the way you do. No matter how clearly I describe my experience to you and no matter how insightful you are, my experience will always remain what *I* experience. You may figure it out to some extent, but you can never experience it in the same immediate way that I do.

Volition refers to my sense of myself as an active agent with free will: I can think, I can interpret, I can decide, I can act. If I decide to run to the corner instead of walking, it is *I* who makes that decision; it is not just something that happens to me.

Finally, **self-reflectivity** refers to the ability of the self to reflect on its continuity, distinctness, and volition. I understand that I am *I*, a distinct, continuing person with free will.

On the basis of a number of studies, Damon and Hart concluded that a concept of "I"—including senses of continuity, distinctness, volition, and self-reflectivity—is present even in young children. Over the course of development, however, radical changes occur in all four aspects of the "I."

Young children's sense of *continuity* is based on continuity of name and physical features: I am the same person I was last year because my name is still Jimmy and I still have red hair. With increasing age, the focus shifts to psychological characteristics (e.g., I am the same person because of consistencies in my underlying philosophy of life).

Similarly, young children see themselves as *distinct* from others because they have different names and physical features than other people. Psychological attributes distinguishing the self from the other are increasingly noted as children get older, leading ultimately to a sense of distinctness due to the inherent privacy and subjectivity of one's personal experience. Thus, a young child might see herself as different from Betty because she has a different name, an older child because she is smarter or nicer than Betty, and an adolescent because she understands that she has a personal, subjective point of view that Betty can learn about but can never directly experience.

For the young child, even free will (*volition*) is perceived in physical terms. "I am the boss of myself," said one child, because "my mouth told my arm and my arm does what my mouth tells it to do." (Selman, 1980, p. 95). As development proceeds, children increasingly view their behavior and experience in terms of active decisions and interpretations by a conscious mind and may even begin to understand the role of unconscious factors and self-deception. An older adolescent, for example, might notice that she has not been studying as hard as she used to and might think about unconscious factors that could be responsible (e.g., "Am I afraid of doing too well?" "Am I trying to teach my parents a lesson for pressuring me to succeed?"). Such questions would never occur to a younger child.

Finally, the self-reflection of young children is limited to awareness of body features and typical activities. With age, it increasingly includes behavioral capabilities and, eventually, recognition of conscious and unconscious psychological processes.

Conclusions: The Construction of Self

We have discussed the development of self-understanding in terms of four dimensions of "Me" and four dimensions of "I." Damon and Hart do not believe it is possible to reduce this complex picture to a simple sequence of overall stages. However, they also dismiss the idea that the development of self involves a number of completely independent changes. Rather, they suggest that the various dimensions of change, though distinct, are continually interacting in complex ways. Moreover, over the course of many years, the diverse aspects of self are increasingly integrated in a unified self-system. Thus, the development of self is a gradual construction of self-consistency. Of course, perfect consistency is never completely attained; it is merely an ideal.

One important limitation of Damon and Hart's model, which they themselves acknowledge, is that it is based entirely on studies of American students. It seems likely that development of self-concept in other cultures would be similar in some respects. It is highly improbable, for example, that any cultures exist in which young children think about themselves primarily in terms of their philosophical belief systems and only later in terms of their names and physical attributes. General principles of cognitive development simply would not allow such a pattern. On the other hand, there is no doubt that cultures have profound effects on how people perceive themselves. At what ages and to what extent children define themselves in social (rather than personal/psychological) terms, for example, might vary widely from one society to another. A great deal of further research must be done to see which aspects of the model are general and which are specific to cultures such as ours.

Another limitation of the model is that it purposely stops at the end of adolescence. Intuitively, it seems likely that our conceptions of ourselves continue to change in important ways as we move through adulthood and there is indeed some evidence supporting this view (Broughton, 1978). Again, we will need further evidence to determine whether changes in self-understanding beyond adolescence are common and what patterns they take.

Despite its limitations, Damon and Hart's model provides a thoughtful integration of a number of studies and a useful picture of the development of self-understanding. It makes it clear that although children may have high or low self-esteem at any age, the reasons for how they feel about themselves are likely to be quite different. Only by taking this into account can we address problems of self-concept sensitively and effectively.

Sex-Typing and the Development of Sex Roles

In the United States a *real* boy climbs trees, disdains girls, dirties his knees, plays with soldiers, and takes blue for his favorite color. A real girl dresses dolls, jumps rope, plays hopscotch, and takes pink for her favorite color. When they go to school, real girls like English and music and "auditorium"; real boys prefer manual training, gym, and arithmetic. In college the boys smoke pipes, drink beer, and major in engineering or physics; the girls chew Juicy Fruit gum, drink cherry Cokes, and major in fine arts. The real boy matures into a "man's man" who plays poker, goes hunting, drinks brandy, and dies in the war; the real girl becomes a "feminine" woman who loves children, embroiders handkerchiefs, drinks weak tea, and "succumbs" to consumption (Brown, 1965, p. 161).

One important aspect of self-concept is one's sense of oneself as female or male. *Sex-typing*, or learning to see oneself as male or female, is much more than a matter of recognizing one's physical characteristics or sexual preferences, however. Although Roger Brown's statement is a deliberate exaggeration, it makes the point that a great deal of psychological baggage is attached to maleness and femaleness in our culture. This raises a number of important questions: Do males and females really differ in the ways we think they do? Are young children aware of *sex roles*, or socially approved behaviors for males and females? Are sex differences due to biology, culture, or an interaction of both? How do sex differences and conceptions about sex roles develop? Is it possible for gender not to be a central psychological issue or for a person to have both male and female characteristics? Is this more or less healthy than having a strong identity as male or female? How do issues of individual gender development relate to broader cultural changes, such as those associated with the women's movement of the past 20 years? We will address all of these questions in the present section.

Stereotypes and Reality

Brown's exaggeration touches on many of the standard **stereotypes** about males and females. Are these stereotypes merely widespread myths, or do they reflect genuine differences between the sexes? There have been literally thousands of studies of sex differences exploring this question. A classic review of the literature by Eleanor Maccoby and

Carol Jacklin (1974) led to the conclusion that many widespread stereotypes are false. Four differences did hold up, however. It appeared that males are more physically aggressive, do better in mathematics, have better spatial skills, and have lower verbal skills than females. Other researchers have questioned Maccoby and Jacklin's conclusions, suggesting that they may have missed some important sex differences and that those they identified may not be well supported (Caplan, MacPherson, & Tobin, 1985; Linn & Peterson, 1985). Overall, it appears that sex differences between males and females are less common and smaller in magnitude than stereotypes suggest (Ruble, 1984). Even studies showing sex differences typically show that the difference *between* the average male and the average female is less than the variability *within* each sex. For example, although males may be more mathematically competent and females more verbally competent, on the average, it is clear that many girls are far better at math than the average boy and that many boys are more verbally capable than the average girl.

Young Children's Awareness of Sex Roles

When do children begin to think of themselves as girls or boys? At what age do they see particular objects or activities as "male" or "female"? How soon are they aware of distinct culturally defined roles for the two sexes? The answer to all these questions is the same: Very early. Sex-typing begins in infancy, and by age 2 or 3 children classify themselves and others as boys or girls, select "male" or "female" activities in their spontaneous play, and show considerable knowledge of cultural stereotypes (Fagot, 1985a; Huston, 1983, 1985; Perry, White, & Perry, 1984; Weinraub, Clemens, Sockloff, Ethridge, Gracely, & Myers, 1984). Although gender-related knowledge, traits, and preferences continue to develop, there is clearly a firm basis for them in early childhood.

Biological and Cultural Bases for Sex Differences

What accounts for sex differences? Are they due to biological factors, to cultural factors, or to an interaction of both? These have been exceedingly difficult questions to answer.

Although some researchers have argued for biologically based sex differences (Benbow & Stanley, 1980), most agree that available evidence must be interpreted cautiously (Moore, 1985; Ruble, 1984). For example, one might expect that a good way to study whether sex differences are innate would be to study very young infants. But this does not turn out to be very helpful. Consider two typical questions: Are boys innately more dominant? Are girls biologically predisposed to be more nurturant? It is difficult to see what behaviors we can observe in young infants relevant to these questions. Moreover, even if we did find sex differences at early ages, this would not prove the differences are innate rather than learned. As Diane Ruble (1984, p. 338) put it, "socialization can begin at birth, at the moment babies are wrapped in either pink or blue blankets."

Children learn the male and female roles of their cultures at very early ages.

Another approach to the question of biological bases of sex differences is to see whether similar sex differences can be observed in many cultures. Ruble concludes, for example, that women are primary caretakers and men fight the wars in virtually all cultures. But even perfect consistency would not prove a biological basis for these roles. There may be similarities in **sex-role socialization** in all the cultures studied. Moreover, detailed study shows that even where there do appear to be cross-cultural universals, variations among cultures are commonly greater than sex differences within any given culture. Thus cultural universals suggest a role for biological factors but are not conclusive.

Another way to show biological influence is to directly relate psychological differences to underlying biological mechanisms. For example, we saw in Chapter 7 that males and females have different hormones. We could look at the influence of hormones on aggression or mathematical ability. Unfortunately, researchers cannot usually manipulate biological variables in human beings (e.g., it would be unethical to inject people with hormones to see if this affects their math ability). Research with humans is thus limited to correlational evidence (Sanders & Soares, 1986). As we saw in Chapter 3, correlational evidence does not demonstrate cause and effect. If merely tells us whether two things are related or unrelated. Hence, even if we could show a correlation between male hormones and, say, aggression, this would not prove that the hormones are the *cause* of the aggression. It might be the case, for example, that just the opposite is true: Perhaps aggressive behavior causes the production of male hormones.

We *can*, of course, sometimes manipulate variables in animals (e.g., inject a rat with male or female hormones) and thus reach causal conclusions. But it is dangerous to generalize from animal results to human beings. Once again, we must be cautious in any conclusions we reach (Ruble, 1984).

The effects of social/cultural factors on sex differences and the development of sex roles (views about proper behavior for males and females) are easier to demonstrate. There is clear evidence that children are influenced by differences they observe in the behavior of males and females in real life, in books, and on television (De Lisi & Johns, 1984; Ruble, 1984). It also appears that boys and girls are treated differently by their parents and teachers and that this affects their development (Entwisle & Baker, 1983; Fagot, Hagan, Leinbach, & Kronsberg, 1985; Ruble, 1984). Boys, for example, are more often reinforced for physical activity and are given more freedom from adult supervision, whereas girls are more likely to be reinforced for playing with dolls and for showing dependency, affectionate behavior, and tender emotions (Huston, 1983). What remains unclear is how and to what extent these social influences interact with biological factors

Theories of Sex-Typing

Given the variety of interacting factors that may influence the development of sex differences and sex roles, it is not surprising to find that a number of theories of sex-typing have been proposed (Huston, 1983; Ruble, 1984). We will focus on three of the most important: social learning theory, Kohlberg's cognitive-developmental theory, and schema theory.

Social Learning Theory.. As we saw in Chapter 5, **social learning theory** emphasizes the modification of behavior as a result of models and reinforcement contingencies. Sex-typing is not seen as a unique topic requiring a special explanation. Sex differences in behavior are learned the same way any behaviors are learned. Boys tend to imitate males and to be rewarded for behavior considered "masculine" in their cultures; girls tend to imitate females and to be rewarded for "feminine" behavior.

Social learning theories emphasize that learning and behavior depend on the situation. Girls do not learn to be feminine and boys masculine in a general sense. Instead, girls learn to show "feminine" behaviors more often and in a wider variety of situations than "masculine" behaviors, whereas the reverse is true for boys. Although recent formulations of social learning theory emphasize cognitive considerations, the focus is still on gradual, specific changes in behavior as a

Research

Adult Reactions to Young Boys and Girls

It is clear that adults respond differently to boys and girls at very early ages and that this affects children's behavior. In order to study this phenomenon in more detail, one needs to select actual settings in which children spend a substantial portion of time and to observe systematically a carefully defined set of adult and child behaviors. This is a research technique known as naturalistic observation (see Chapter 3).

A recent study by Beverly Fagot, Richard Hagan, Mary Driver Leinbach, and Sandra Kronsberg (1985) illustrates this approach. A sample of 34 infants and their teachers were videotaped as they interacted in play groups of 6 to 8 infants each. The infants, all 13 to 14 months old, included 15 boys and 19 girls. Observers were carefully trained to code a variety of child behaviors falling in two categories: (a) physically assertive acts (e.g., shoving another child or grabbing an object) and (b) attempts to communicate with adults. They were also trained to code adult reactions.

Analyses of the results showed no differences between boys and girls in either assertive or communicative behavior. There were significant differences in adult reactions, however. With respect to communication attempts, girls were more likely than boys to get reactions when they talked or used gestures or gentle touches, whereas boys were more likely than girls to get attention when they cried, whined, screamed, or were physically assertive. Responses to girls also tended to be more positive and to lead to longer adult–child interactions.

An interesting aspect of this study is a longitudinal followup (see Chapter 3) of the same children about 10 months later. The pattern of results was now different. Whereas at the earlier age there had been no sex differences in children's actual behavior, several interesting sex differences now emerged. Specifically, girls talked to teachers more than boys did, whereas boys more often whined, cried, or screamed at teachers than did girls. Moreover, the frequency of physically assertive behavior declined for girls but not for boys so that at the later age girls were less likely than boys to be physically assertive. Interestingly, teachers responded to the toddlers on the basis of their behavior rather than on the basis of their sex. Talking, for example, resulted in positive reactions regardless of whether the talker was a boy or girl, whereas whining, crying, or screaming yielded negative reactions regardless of the child's sex.

How can this pattern of results be explained? The researchers suggest one plausible interpretation. The behavior of young infants is often ambiguous. In deciding what a child's behavior means and how to respond, teachers perhaps make use of their own stereotypes about boys and girls. The behavior of older children is more easily interpreted and so gender stereotypes play less of a role in guiding teachers' responses. By this age, however, real sex differences have appeared, perhaps due (at least in part) to adults' stereotyped responses at earlier ages. It thus appears that adults do influence the development of sex differences and sex roles, but the patterns of influence may be more complex than one would have guessed.

result of observational learning. The social environment defines what is masculine and feminine, and children pick this up through imitation and reinforcement. Recent research partially supports this view but suggests that cognitive factors are more important than social learning theorists acknowledge (Fagot, 1985b).

Kohlberg's Cognitive-Developmental Theory. Kohlberg (1966) agreed that the environment is an important source of information about sex roles in any given culture but put more emphasis on the activity of the child's mind in constructing ideas about sex roles. In particular, Kohlberg emphasized the idea of gender constancy. You will recall that, according to Piaget, children around age 7 (moving into concrete operations) construct concepts of conservation, involving the idea that things can stay constant even when they appear to be changing (see Chapter 8). Kohlberg believed that conservation of gender is a form of conservation in the social world that develops at about the same time. Younger children may know that they are boys and girls but do not understand that this is a "deep" characteristic that endures even if they wear different clothes, engage in activities popular with the other sex, wear their hair differently, or simply get older. Conservation of gender was seen by Kohlberg as a central issue in sex typing and an example of a concept that is not learned from the environment but rather is constructed (figured out) by the thinking child. Recent research (Wehren & De Lisi, 1983) has further elaborated Kohlberg's **cognitive-developmental approach.**

Schema Theory. Theorists taking an information-processing perspective have attempted to explain sex-typing using the concept of **schema** (Bem, 1981; Martin & Halverson, 1981). A schema is a cognitive structure used to organize and make sense of the world. A gender schema, then, is an interrelated set of views about males, females, masculinity, and femininity that determine what one perceives in a social situation, how one makes sense of that information, and what one does with it. Schema theories resemble cognitive-developmental theories in emphasizing the active knowing of the child. They differ in focusing more on the specific characteristics of the schemata involved rather than on global concepts such as gender constancy. In other words, they emphasize specific knowledge and individual differences among children rather than general stages of development.

Conclusion. All three of the above theories are helpful in understanding sex-typing. Cognitive-developmental theory emphasizes universal stages of development in children's construction of gender concepts. Schema theory focuses instead on differences among children's specific schemata. Finally, social learning theory highlights how children learn sex roles from their environments. Although no single theory is sufficient by itself, the three together provide substantial insight into the fundamentals of sex-typing.

Androgyny

In the early days of research on sex roles, it was assumed that strong sex-typing was a positive thing. Girls should be encouraged to be as feminine as possible and boys as masculine as possible. The only real question was how best to achieve this.

As a result of the contemporary women's movement, however, basic assumptions about sex roles have been questioned seriously in our society over the past two decades. This has affected the kinds of issues researchers address, the ways they interpret their results, and the practical applications of their conclusions. In particular, psychologists have become very interested in *androgynous* individuals, people who are not sharply masculine or feminine.

The term **androgyny** combines *andro*, referring to male (as in *androgens*, male hormones), with *gyn*, referring to female (as in *gyn*ecologist, a doctor specializing in women). What does it mean to be androgynous? One's first thought might be that it means being midway between masculine and feminine. That is, if we think of a line with high masculinity at one end and high femininity at the other, the androgynous person would be near the middle.

But this way of thinking about masculinity and femininity assumes that these are opposite ends of a single dimension. Is that a reasonable assumption? Consider the traditional stereotypes that men are logical and women emotional and that men are aggressive and women nurturant. Is being logical the opposite of being emotional? Is being aggressive the opposite of being nurturant? Couldn't a person be both logical and emotional—for example, being emotionally committed to the use of logic? Couldn't one be aggressively nurturant or aggressive in some situations and nurturant in others? Placing masculinity and femininity at opposite ends of a single dimension makes it difficult to resolve such questions.

One solution many psychologists have adopted is to think of masculinity and femininity as two dimensions at right angles to each other (see Figure 16-1). Thus, traditional masculinity would be a combination of high-masculine and low-feminine and traditional femininity would be high-feminine/low-masculine. Androgyny could now be defined as high-masculine *and* high-feminine. That is, the androgynous individual is not partly masculine and partly feminine or midway between the two but rather is high on both sets of characteristics. She or he is thus exactly the sort of person—logical *and* emotional as well as aggressive *and* nurturant—who led us to question the idea that masculinity and femininity are opposite ends of a single dimension.

Other psychologists (Bem, 1981) have taken a somewhat different approach. They define the androgynous individual as someone for whom the categories "masculine" and "feminine" are not very salient. In terms of schema theory, the strongly sex-typed person uses gender schemas to make sense of a wide variety of issues and experiences. The androgynous person, in contrast, uses gender schemas much more

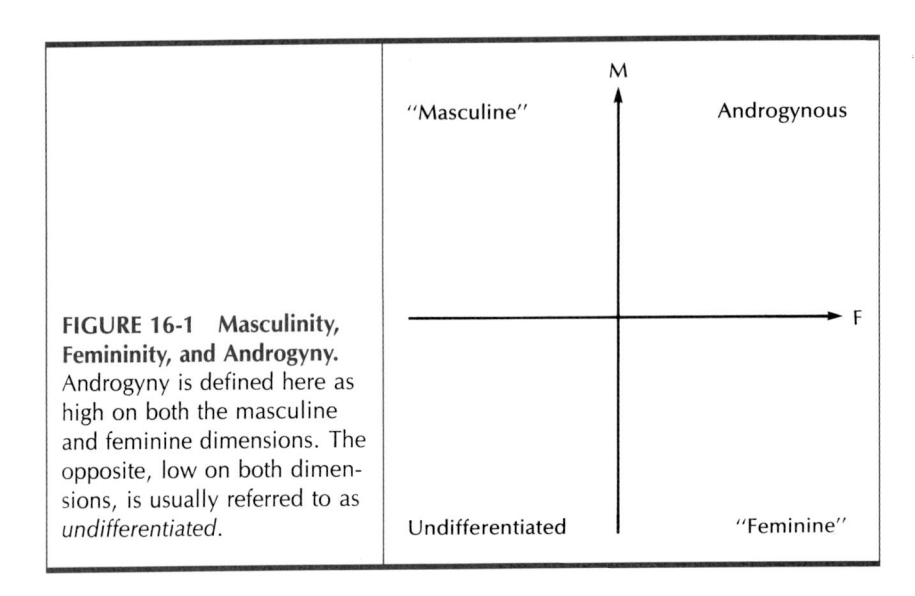

FIGURE 16-1 Masculinity, Femininity, and Androgyny. Androgyny is defined here as high on both the masculine and feminine dimensions. The opposite, low on both dimensions, is usually referred to as *undifferentiated*.

sparingly. Most of his or her perceptions and responses are based on considerations unrelated to masculinity or femininity.

Is it better to be androgynous? This is a very difficult question to answer scientifically. It might seem that all one needs to do is assess how androgynous various people are and see if high androgyny is correlated with being better off (Whitley, 1985). But even assuming we had accurate measures of androgyny, how can we objectively measure how well off people are? Do we ask them how happy they are? Do we measure success in jobs, success in relationships, or contributions to other people? Obviously researchers' judgments will vary depending on their own values. Most scientists admit that scientific research is not totally objective; the scientist's interpretations depend on his or her values. The study of sex-typing is a particularly clear example of how values can affect interpretations. Rigorous research on sex-typing is certainly possible, but we need to be especially careful in interpreting data and reaching conclusions in this area (Wittig, 1985).

A Dialectical Postscript There is one more reason to be cautious about research on sex roles. In Chapter 2, we discussed the dialectical paradigm as an alternative to learning and developmental approaches. A key emphasis of dialectical theorists is the continuing interaction between the individual and society. Not only do children develop in their ideas about sex roles, but our society itself has been changing rapidly and is continuing to change. Views about what women are like, what kinds of jobs they should have, and, more generally, how they should live their lives are very different in American society than they were 25 years ago. Partly as a result of

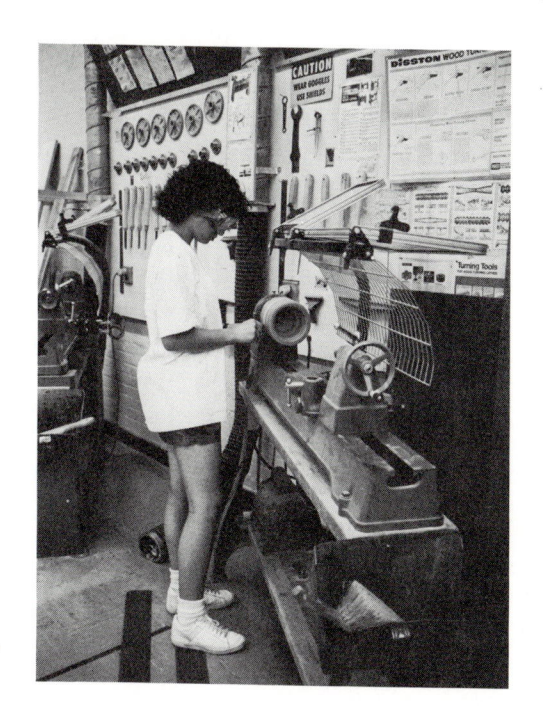

The roles of women in American society have changed dramatically over the past twenty-five years.

changing views about women, views about men have changed as well. Today's children are growing up in a very different society than their parents did and many are directly experiencing different family arrangements (e.g., working mothers). This will no doubt affect their development of sex role concepts or gender schemata.

But it would be too simple to say that society is now different and so will mold children differently. Society affects people, but it is equally true that people affect society. Views about sex roles in American society today will affect the current generation of children, but they in turn will influence those views, which will influence the next generation, and so forth. This interaction is what dialectical theorists have in mind when they emphasize that neither the individual nor society is a passive entity molded by the other. To understand sex role (or any other) issues, we must think about the continuing complex interactions between the developing individual and the changing social world.

A Psychoanalytic Approach to Personality Development

We have looked at people's self-concepts, both in a general sense of self-understanding and, more specifically, with respect to conceptions of the self as male or female. But your personality is not merely your conception of yourself: It *is* yourself, or, to put it another way, it is your *self*. Obviously, no theory of personality development can afford to be superficial. To say something worthwhile about personality, a theory must be able to look deeply into what it means to be a person.

One approach to the study of personality and its development is the **psychoanalytic approach**, a perspective that traces its roots to the work of Sigmund Freud (1856–1939). Although the specifics of Freud's theory have been questioned strongly by many psychologists, it is widely agreed that he was a brilliant and original thinker who looked at personality in a deep and interesting way. We will begin this section with a brief summary of Freud's theory. We will then turn to the work of Erik Erikson, a psychologist who disagreed with Freud on some specific issues and developed an alternative theory that preserves Freud's general perspective. Finally, we will consider the work of James Marcia, who has further developed many of Erikson's important ideas about the nature and development of identity.

Freud's Theory

Freud proposed that personality has three components: The id, the ego, and the superego. The **id** consists of the person's basic needs and desires. The **ego** is the component of personality that understands and deals with reality in order to satisfy the demands of the id. Finally, the **superego** is the moral aspect of the personality that causes the person to feel guilty for improper behavior. To put it simply, the id says, "I want this, and I want it *now*." The ego says, "I'm working on it but you'll have to be patient. The world is complicated. You can't always get what you want." The superego says, "That's not allowed, and if you do it I'll make us all feel guilty."

The newborn infant is pure id. If he feels hungry, he cries. Although this is initially automatic, the infant gradually learns that crying leads to being fed. As the ego develops, the infant learns increasingly subtle ways to get fed. By adulthood, this includes getting a job, earning money, and using the money to buy food. Of course, one can also get food by stealing it. As the ego develops, one gets better at using immoral as well as moral means for satisfying one's needs and desires. But development of the superego limits that. Some ways of satisfying the id are morally unacceptable to the superego, and it uses guilt to keep the ego in line.

According to Freud, the **libido**, or life force, underlies personality and its development. Freud conceived this life force in sexual terms. He believed children have sexual drives from birth and that the basic stages of personality development are based on shifts in the focus of sexual energy. With respect to personality development, the key period is the preschool years (around ages 3 to 5), during which the **Oedipal conflict** (or, for girls, the **Electra conflict)** takes place. At this time the child sexually desires the parent of the opposite sex but realizes that this desire cannot be fulfilled due to competition from the same-sex parent. The child deals with this by **identifying** with the same-sex parent and incorporating his or her sex role identity, moral values (superego), and personality.

You will notice that in our discussion of moral development (Chapter 15) we did not seriously consider Freud's view that morality is formed in early childhood. Similarly, our discussion of sex-typing earlier in this chapter did not include Freud's theory of identification among the major theories considered. The reason is that his specific views on these issues are not supported by current evidence. Similarly, Freud's conception that personality is simply taken in from the parent of the same sex is widely regarded as inadequate to explain personality development. Nevertheless, Freud's emphasis on the importance of childhood in shaping the adult was radical in its time and has exerted enormous influence on modern thinking about development. The most important theory of personality development to derive from Freud's approach has been that of Erik Erikson.

Erikson's Theory

Erikson (1950, 1968) proposed a stage theory of personality development that in some ways parallels Freud's theory but differs in two key respects. First, Erikson's stages are **psychosocial** rather than **psychosexual**; he believes Freud overemphasized children's sexuality and failed to recognize the importance of social factors. Second, Erikson believes that development continues throughout life, rather than ending (as Freud and many other psychologists have suggested) with adolescence.

Each of Erikson's eight stages represents a crisis or turning point in development. At each stage, development can move in either of two directions, one psychologically healthier than the other. The first stage is labeled **trust vs. mistrust**. Newborn babies obviously have no sense of what the world is like. If, during the course of infancy, their basic needs are met, they get the idea that they live in a predictable, secure world and feel a deep-seated sense of trust. If not, they approach the next stage—and perhaps their whole lives—with a basic sense of mistrust.

Erikson labels his second stage **autonomy vs. shame, doubt**. At this time, the toddler is developing the physical and cognitive abilities to act more and more independently and see the self as distinct from the parents. This can be seen in the negativism common in two-year-olds: To say "No" to someone else is an assertion of one's separateness and free choice. If parents provide reasonable support for independence (this does not necessarily mean giving in to all demands), the outcome is a feeling of self-confidence, pride, and control—in a word, autonomy.

Excessive restriction and punishment, on the other hand, can lead to lifelong feelings of shame and self-doubt.

Initiative vs. guilt is the third stage. The preschooler is curious about the world and active in exploring it. If all goes well, the outcome of this stage is a lasting sense of initiative and ambition. But if initiative regularly leads to trouble and punishment, the result can be an inhibited individual, who is immobilized by guilt or fear.

The fourth stage, occupying the elementary school years, is **industry vs. inferiority**. This is the period when children in all cultures are trained, either through formal schooling or informal observation and apprenticeship, in a variety of basic skills. Children who do well and are recognized for their achievements develop a sense of success, mastery, and accomplishment—what Erikson calls industry. The alternative is a general feeling of inferiority, uselessness, and futility.

Adolescence is the stage of **identity vs. identity confusion,** the period of **identity crisis**. The challenge is to construct an identity, a firm sense of who you are. The alternative is to go through life without this. We will consider identity issues in more detail shortly when we turn to the work of James Marcia.

True intimacy, according to Erikson, is not possible until one has a firm identity, since intimacy is defined by Erikson as the fusing of two identities. Therefore, the stage of **intimacy vs. isolation** does not occur until early adulthood, after an identity has been formed. The positive outcome is a capacity for a variety of intimate relationships, ranging from meaningful friendships to psychologically intimate sexual relationships. The alternative is broken relationships, loneliness, and a sense of isolation.

Generativity vs. stagnation is the developmental issue of middle adulthood. Generativity includes having children and guiding them toward adulthood. It also includes productivity and creativity in one's work. The generative person is genuinely interested in helping others and working toward ideals or goals in a way that shows a commitment to future generations. The alternative is absorption in the self, boredom, and a feeling of stagnation.

Finally, old age involves a confrontation with **integrity vs. despair**. Integrating the various aspects of one's life and coming to terms with one's limitations and mortality yield a sense of integrity. Feelings of failure, emphasis on missed opportunities, and fear of death constitute a sense of disgust and despair.

Obviously, development is not as simple as this sequence of eight stages may suggest. No one would accept the idea that one adresses one developmental issue at a time, resolves each once and for all, and then moves on to another issue. Erikson emphasizes, in fact, that all eight of these issues are involved in development throughout the life-

According to Erikson, the challenge of late adulthood is to develop a sense of *integrity,* a positive attitude toward life in general and the particular life you have lived.

span. Particular issues do tend to become more or less salient as one moves through life, however, and there is substantial regularity in the order in which various issues are addressed. The issue of "intimacy vs. isolation," for example, is important in some form for all ages but generally becomes particularly critical in the early adult years after one establishes a firm identity (Whitbourne & Tesch, 1985).

A challenge for Erikson's theory is whether it applies to all people in all cultures. There has been some question, for example, about whether the model fits women as well as men, especially with respect to the development of identity and intimacy (Marcia, 1980; Hulsizer, Murphy, Noam, Taylor, & Norman, 1981; Waterman, 1982, 1985; Schiedel & Marcia, 1985). Moreover, there is very little evidence regarding Erikson's stages in non-Western cultures.

Nevertheless, the theory has some important strengths that have kept it in the forefront of work on personality development for many years. One is that it provides some fascinating insights into relations between the generations. Successful resolutions to the early stages help an individual become a generative adult, which leads to precisely the sort of caring that the next generation needs in its early stages, which in turn leads to another generation of generative adults, and so forth. On the other hand, unfortunate childhoods can lead to adult stagnation, which has negative implications for the next generation. Personality development is not a purely personal matter. Erikson's theory helps us

Erikson stresses how closely each generation's development is related to the development of the generations before and after.

see how intimately the generations of humanity are linked. Positive or negative factors in a particular life can have long-term consequences for future generations.

Another strength of Erikson's theory is his influential account of identity. He has provided a strong theory of how one's concept of self plays a pivotal role in the development of personality (Logan, 1986). In the next section we will see how James Marcia has expanded this account.

Marcia's Theory of Identity Formation

Marcia (1980; Schiedel & Marcia, 1985; Waterman, 1982, 1985) has proposed that adolescents and adults can be divided into four categories. The **identity achieved** individual has been through an identity crisis and has successfully constructed a firm sense of who she is. She has made conscious, purposeful commitments with respect to occupation, religion, politics, sex role attitudes, and beliefs about personal sexuality. The key to determining whether a person is identity achieved is not the nature of her commitments but whether the commitments are strong and self-chosen. With respect to religion, for example, the identity achieved individual may be committed to Christianity, Judaism, Islam, or any other religion, or may be a committed atheist. What makes her identity achieved is that her beliefs concerning religion are a commitment she made after seriously thinking through the alternatives, rather than an unthinking continuation of what she learned as a child.

The person in the **moratorium** category is currently having an identity crisis. Note that for Marcia, as for Erikson, a crisis is not necessarily bad, or something to be avoided. On the contrary, it is the source of new commitments and is necessary to reach the status of identity achieved. An individual in moratorium does not have firm commitments but is actively trying to construct such commitments. He may, for example, be trying to decide what he wants to do for his life's work and struggling to select a major area of study with this in mind.

The **foreclosed** individual does have clear commitments, but these are not self-constructed. They are simply adopted from others, typically the person's parents, without serious questioning. They did not result from resolving an identity crisis. For example, a young woman who has never seriously considered sexual alternatives may be strongly opposed to premarital sex because of views taken from her parents. Note that it is not her specific beliefs that would lead Marcia to classify her as foreclosed; it is the fact that these beliefs come from her parents, not from personal questioning and serious consideration of possibilities.

Finally, **identity diffusion** is a category in which there are no current commitments, nor is there an attempt to construct them. Unlike identity achieved and foreclosed individuals, there is a lack of identity, and unlike the moratorium individual, there is no active search for identity. A person with no particular political views and no desire to think about political issues would be identity diffused with respect to politics.

In principle, at least, one can readily assign an individual to one of the four categories by considering a sequence of two questions (see Figure 16-2). First, are there strong commitments? If so, one then asks whether these are self-chosen commitments based on an earlier period of active search. If they are, the person is identity achieved. If not, the

FIGURE 16-2 **Criteria for Identity Statuses.** One determines a person's identity status by questioning him or her about religious, political, vocational, and sex role commitments.

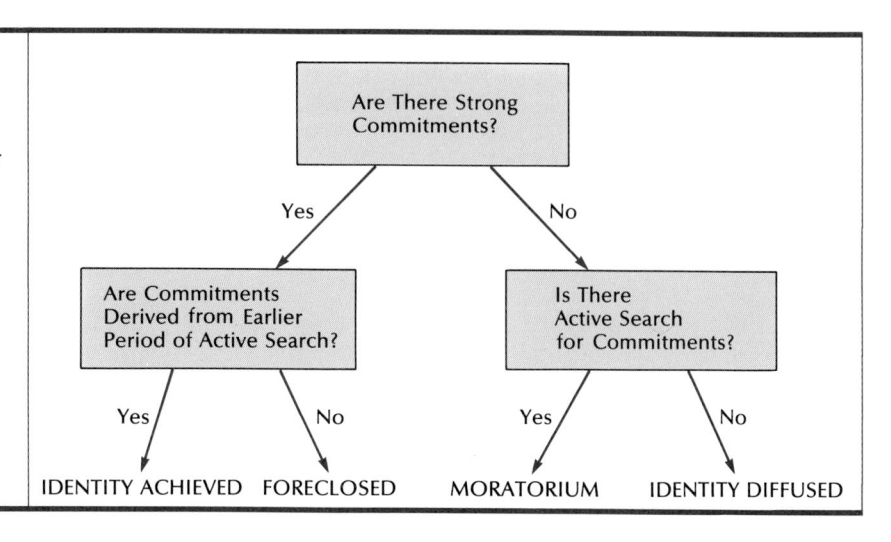

person is foreclosed. If there are no firm commitments, the followup question is whether there is an active search for such commitments. If so, the individual is in moratorium. If not, the person is identity diffused.

Actual research, of course, is much more complex than this. One cannot simply ask subjects whether they have commitments and how they got them. The nature, strength, and source of commitments can vary greatly and may be difficult to determine. A person may be more commited in one area (e.g., religion) than another (e.g., politics). Marcia has worked out detailed questions and procedures for assessing identity. His interviews have confirmed the value of these four identity categories in understanding adolescent and adult development and have indicated that identity issues are often particularly important for college students and young adults, rather than adolescents (Marcia, 1980; Schiedel & Marcia, 1985; Waterman, 1982, 1985).

It would be simple if young adolescents were diffused, adopted a foreclosed identity, went into moratorium, and finally emerged with a firm identity that would last through adulthood. Actual sequences that people go through, however, are far more complex (Waterman, 1982, 1985). Figure 16-3 illustrates the possible patterns. As you can see, the identity diffused individual may either blindly adopt a foreclosed identity or move into moratorium (crisis) by considering identity alternatives. The foreclosed individual can move back to diffusion by giving up externally imposed commitments or forward to moratorium by questioning those commitments and looking for alternatives. From moratorium, a person may move back to diffusion by giving up the search for

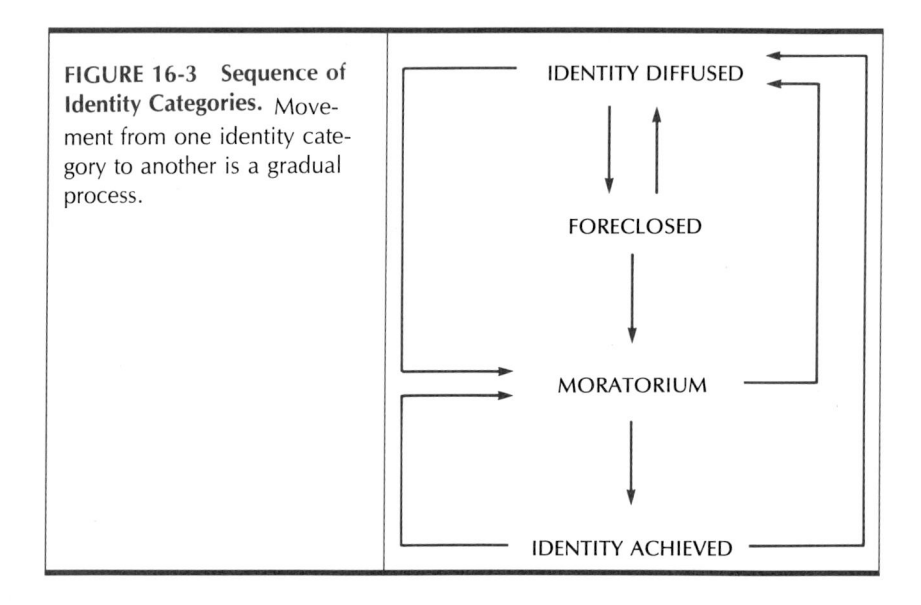

FIGURE 16-3 Sequence of Identity Categories. Movement from one identity category to another is a gradual process.

IDENTITY DIFFUSED

↓ ↑

FORECLOSED

↓

MORATORIUM

↓

IDENTITY ACHIEVED

commitment or forward to identity achievement by successfully constructing an identity of her own. But identity is not necessarily achieved once and for all. Commitments may lose their vitality, leading either to another moratorium (if the desire for commitment remains) or back to identity diffusion (if the desire for commitment is lost). Note that it is possible to remain indefinitely in any of the four categories except moratorium, which is a relatively unstable state. Application Exercise 16-1 provides some examples of transitions from one identity category to another.

Conclusion

Although many of Freud's specific ideas have been sharply questioned, his general approach to personality development has led to a number of important current theories. Erikson's is one of the most prominent. Research has supported Erikson's picture of development, especially his views—and those of Marcia—concerning identity (Damon, 1983; Marcia, 1980; Schiedel & Marcia, 1985; Waterman, 1982, 1985; Whitbourne & Tesch, 1985). The psychoanalytic perspective is not, however, the only useful framework for looking at personality development.

A Cognitive-Developmental Approach to Personality Development

In an important book entitled *The Evolving Self*, Robert Kegan (1982) proposes that Piaget's theory provides a strong basis for a theory of personality development. He readily acknowledges that this may seem an odd suggestion. Piaget's theory is not about personality, feelings, or social relations; it is a theory of intellectual development. Kegan, however, does not focus on Piaget's specific theory. Rather, he believes that Piaget's general perspective on the nature of development can serve as the grounding for a new theory of the evolving personality.

Figure 16-4 summarizes Kegan's analysis of Piaget. The Piagetian framework is simultaneously biological, psychological, and philosophical. The biological aspect is the relation of organism to environment, a question of adaptation. The psychological aspect is how one relates to other people, a matter of self or ego. The philosophical aspect is the relation of the subjective point of view to the objective nature of what is perceived, a matter of truth. But adaptation, ego, and truth (or, more broadly, biology, psychology, and philosophy) are not separate issues. They are three perspectives on the same basic process, what Kegan calls **meaning-constitutive development**.

As Kegan sees it, development is the process of making (constituting) meaning. The meaning of an object, event, or experience does not exist out in the world; it is provided by the person who perceives and

FIGURE 16-4 Kegan's Analysis of Piaget's Framework. Robert Kegan argues that Piaget's general framework is a useful starting point for a theory of personality development. *From Kegan, 1982.*

```
                        THE PIAGETIAN FRAMEWORK
                                  |
                                  is
                    ┌─────────────┼─────────────┐
                    ↓             ↓             ↓
              BIOLOGICAL    PSYCHOLOGICAL   PHILOSOPHICAL
                  |              |              |
               in that        in that        in that
              it studies     it studies     it studies
                  ↓              ↓              ↓
              THE RELATING   THE RELATING   THE RELATING
              OF ORGANISM  ← which is →  OF SELF  ← which is →  OF SUBJECT
              TO ENVIRONMENT  itself     TO OTHER    itself     TO OBJECT
                  |         related to      |      related to      |
               which is                  which is                which is
              the essence of           the essence of          the essence of
                  ↓                         ↓                       ↓
              ADAPTATION                   EGO                    TRUTH
                    └──────────────┬──────────────┘
                          and all three—
                       adaptation, ego, and truth—
                       are but different perspectives
                          on a single process,
                       the Piagetian object of study
                                  ↓
                    MEANING-CONSTITUTIVE DEVELOPMENT
```

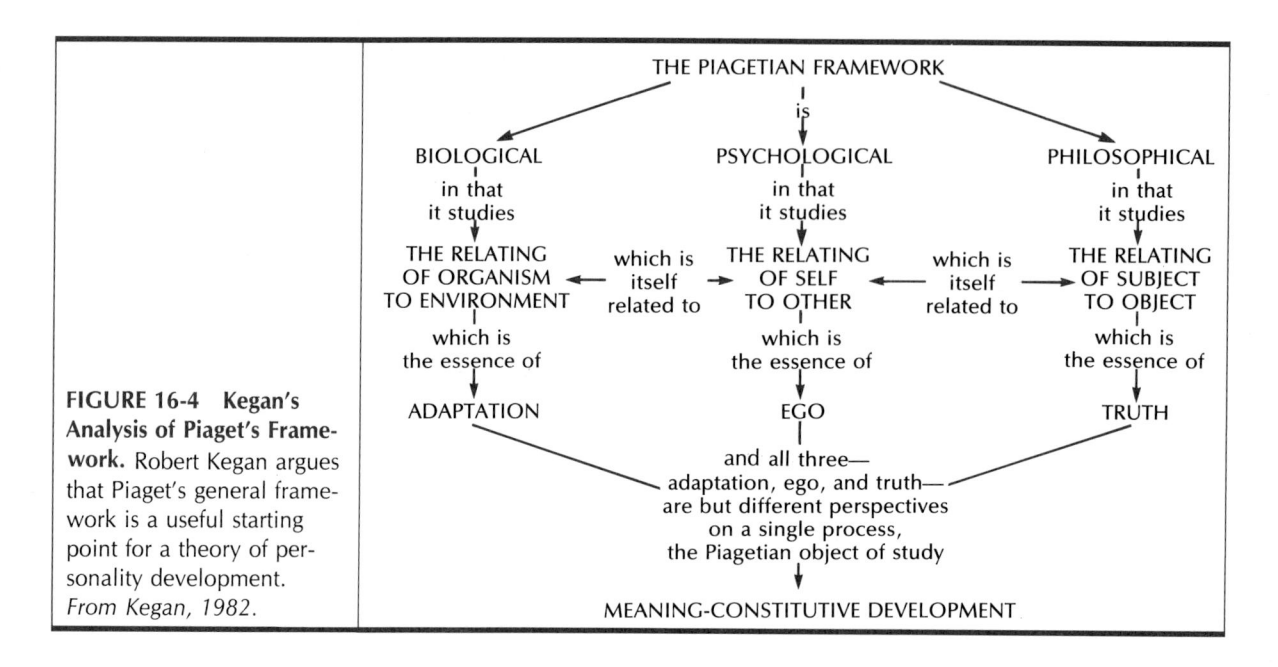

interprets the world. Developmental stages are different ways of knowing, or of constituting meaning.

Providing meaning is not a cold-blooded cognitive affair, however. Knowing and meaning have as much to do with how we *feel* about things as with how we *think* about them. When our way of construing something leaves us feeling uncomfortable or out of balance, we strive to create new meanings. But the new way of knowing is only a temporary truce, a momentary balance point in the continuing process of development.

In tracing the overall stages through which people pass in the construction of meaning, Kegan tries to focus our attention not on the person as an object but on what the world looks like from the person's subjective perspective. In terms of William James' distinction between the two aspects of self, Kegan's focus is not on the "Me" (the characteristics of the person) but rather on the "I" (the person's own way of making meaning of his or her experience). In other words, to understand the construction of meaning we must look at that construction not from the outside but from the inside, from the person's own point of view. Thus Kegan is less interested, for example, in what a child's parents are *really* like than in how the child perceives his or her relationship with them.

Stages of Personality Development

Kegan proposes that personality development proceeds through six stages (labeled 0 through 5). His stages are closely related to those proposed by Piaget, Kohlberg, and Erikson (see Table 16-1). Typical of developmental theorists, Kegan believes the sequence of development to be invariant, although the age at which a given stage is reached can vary widely, especially for the higher stages. Like Kohlberg, Kegan proposes that not everyone attains the highest possible stage.

Stage 0, corresponding to Piaget's sensorimotor period, is the **incorporative stage.** The infant, from its own point of view, does not *have* reflexes. It *is* its reflexes, its sensing and moving. This is a period of radical egocentrism in which the infant does not distinguish a "self" from an "other." The conception of other people as distinct from the self is being gradually constructed as the infant moves toward stage 1, the next period of temporary equilibrium.

Stage 1, corresponding roughly to Piaget's preoperational period, Kohlberg's stage 1 (Heteronomous morality), and Erikson's stage of initiative vs. guilt, is the **impulsive stage**. The preschool child, from her own point of view, is no longer her reflexes. Rather, she is now the coordination of those reflexes; she is her perceptions and impulses. She fails to show conservation because she has no way of integrating her various perceptions; she *is* her perceptions. She has limited self-control because she cannot step back from and deal with her impulses; she *is* her impulses. Any attempt to limit her acting on her impulses is a very personal threat to the impulsive child. Since she *is* her impulses, such

TABLE 16-1 Comparison of Piaget's, Kohlberg's, Erikson's and Kegan's Stages

	Theory			
Age Range	*Piaget*	*Kohlberg*	*Erikson*	*Kegan*
Infancy	Sensorimotor	—	Basic trust	Incorporative
Preschool	Preoperations	Heteronomy	Autonomy	Impulsive
			Initiative	
Elementary school	Concrete operations	Individualism and exchange	Industry	Imperial
Adolescence and beyond	Formal operations	Mutual expectations	—	Interpersonal
		Social system	Identity	Institutional
		Social contract	Intimacy	Interindividual
			Generativity	
			Integrity	

a restriction is not simply a limit on what she may do but a direct assault on her very self.

Stage 2, corresponding to Piaget's stage of concrete operations, Kohlberg's stage 2 (individualism and exchange), and Erikson's industry vs. inferiority, is the **imperial stage**. The imperial child can coordinate her impulses, feelings, and perceptions over a period of time to create enduring dispositions. Thus she is no longer those impulses and perceptions; she is her lasting needs, interests, and wishes. The child now "seals up," in a sense. She has a private world involving a relatively consistent self-concept. In taking command of her impulses—as opposed to simply *being* them—she feels a new freedom, power, and independence. She senses her increasing ability to *do* things, to make things happen.

Stage 3, corresponding to the beginning of formal operations and to Kohlberg's stage 3 (mutual expectations and interpersonal conformity), is the **interpersonal stage**. The interpersonal adolescent or adult thinks about her own needs, interests, and wishes in the context of her relationships with others who have their own needs, interests, and wishes. The interpersonal dimension is so central that, for her, she *is* her relationships. Deeper relationships are now possible, as is genuine guilt if she feels she has betrayed them. The self is a shared reality, and any threat to relationships is a direct threat to the self-concept.

Stage 4, corresponding to Kohlberg's stage 4 (social system), and Erikson's stage of identity formation, is the **institutional stage**. The institutional self is a coherent, self-contained person—an "executive" who runs and coordinates the various aspects of her life on the basis of her firm sense of who she really is, her identity. She is *in control* of her relationships rather than defining herself in terms of them. People are still important, but in a new way: They matter as others, rather than as part of the self.

Finally, stage 5, corresponding to Kohlberg's stage 5 (social contract), and Erikson's stage of intimacy vs. isolation, is the **interindividual stage**. The person now considers her identity from a broader point of view. Administering the various facets of one's life is no longer an end in itself. The self is seen in the broader context of relations with others. But these relations are not stage 3 relations in which one's identity is swallowed up. They are relations of genuine intimacy, in which individual identity (both your own and that of the other) is respected and given new meaning.

The Process of Personality Development

A common error in thinking about stage theories of development is to focus too strongly on the stages. Although the stages themselves are important, it is perhaps even more important to see how they are transformed into each other, that is, to understand the *process* of development.

How do Kegan's stages relate to each other? Kegan notes that from the point of view of the developing person, each of his stages can be seen as a theory of the previous stage. That is, each stage is a way of making sense of the world, and each new stage gets outside the previous one and makes new sense of it. In stage 0, I am my reflexes, my sensing and moving. In stage 1, I am my impulses and perceptions, which give meaning to my sensing and moving. In stage 2, I am my enduring needs, interests, and wishes, which give meaning to my immediate impulses and perceptions. In stage 3, I am my interpersonal relations, which give meaning to my needs, interests, and wishes. In stage 4, I am the coherent psychological organization that coordinates and gives meaning to my various interpersonal relations. Finally, in stage 5, we (not I, but *we*) are interacting self-systems, yielding a genuine intimacy that coordinates and imparts meaning to our individual identities.

Stage-to-stage progress is driven in large part by the continuing tension between two fundamental human yearnings: the desire for inclusion (integration, connection with others) and the desire for autonomy (differentiation, independence, and self-determination). In stage 0, self and other are not distinguished. Development moves toward

Kegan views personality development as a lifelong struggle to balance the needs for inclusion and autonomy.

inclusion (stage 1), toward a sealed-up self-sufficiency (stage 2), back toward interconnection (stage 3), back toward autonomous self-regulation (stage 4), and then back again toward interrelatedness (stage 5). But this is not simply a back and forth motion. The stage 4 self has a more sophisticated self-concept and a more genuine autonomy than the stage 2 self. Similarly, each return to interconnection with others (stages 1, 3, and 5) is at a higher level, ultimately reaching a genuine intimacy. The course of development can thus be seen as a spiral, involving a circular motion that keeps coming back to the same issues but each time at a higher level (see Figure 16-5). The struggle to balance the needs for inclusion and autonomy is the lifelong process of personality development. As Kegan (1982, p. 85) puts it, "each qualitative change, hard won, is a response to the complexity of the world, a response in further recognition of how the world and I are yet again distinct—and thereby more related."

We see clearly in Kegan's work, then, how cognitive, social, and emotional considerations interact in the fascinating process through which a human personality constructs itself. We see also that this process is potentially endless. Kegan's perspective challenges the traditional view that adulthood is the plateau of real life and childhood merely a preparation for that life. Childhood *is* life, a continuing sequence of changes, and that process continues through adulthood. The essence of human experience lies neither in the stages through which one passes, nor in the final stage attained, but rather in the process of development itself.

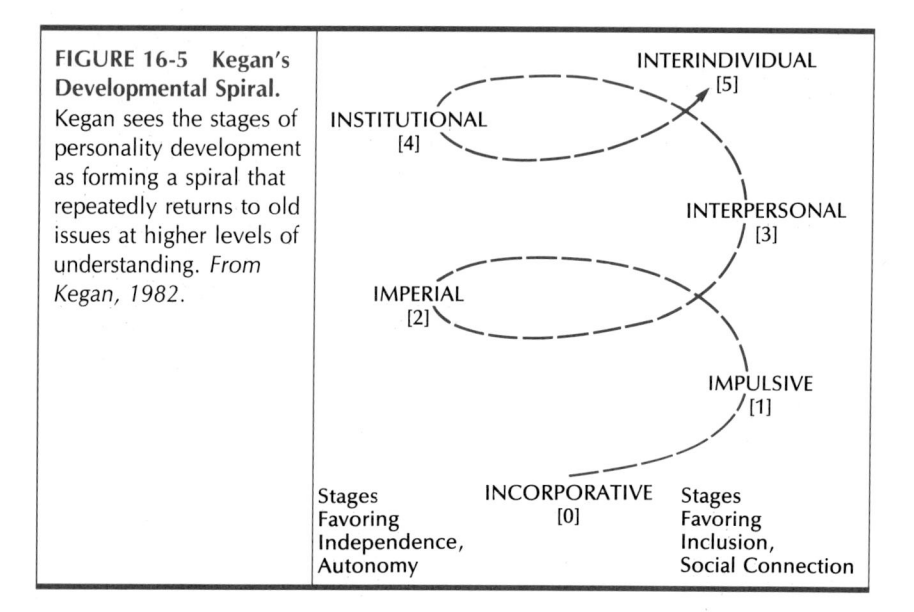

FIGURE 16-5 Kegan's Developmental Spiral. Kegan sees the stages of personality development as forming a spiral that repeatedly returns to old issues at higher levels of understanding. *From Kegan, 1982.*

INTERINDIVIDUAL [5]
INSTITUTIONAL [4]
INTERPERSONAL [3]
IMPERIAL [2]
IMPULSIVE [1]
INCORPORATIVE [0]

Stages Favoring Independence, Autonomy

Stages Favoring Inclusion, Social Connection

Applications

Knowledge about children's conceptions of themselves has important implications for parents and teachers. Insights into personality development across the lifespan are important not only for parents and teachers but for anyone who relates to other people. In this section, we will highlight a few of the major implications. You can probably think of many more.

1. *Consider children's self-understanding in trying to foster self-esteem.* Everyone wants children to have "positive self-concepts." It is important to recognize, however, that a child's self-concept may be based on very different considerations than an adult's. For example, you may see your psychological traits, your major beliefs and values, and/or your long-term goals as central to who you are, and consider how tall you are or how fast you can run as more superficial. A young child, however, may see her physical traits or abilities as central to who she is and these sorts of characteristics may thus be the basis for her self-esteem.

2. *Let individual interests and aptitudes, not gender stereotypes, determine children's activities and goals.* Available evidence does not provide any reason for channeling all boys in a certain direction or encouraging all girls to be a certain way. Consider, for example, the controversy about whether boys are better at math than girls and, if so, why. It may turn out that with suitable encouragement girls can do as well at math as boys. Even if there is a real and biologically based difference, however, it is clear that the range of abilities for boys greatly overlaps the range of abilities for girls. It is simply impossible to know, on the basis of a child's sex, whether that child is good at math. Children should be encouraged in their mathematical (and other) pursuits, regardless of gender.

3. *Teach children to analyze sex-role stereotypes.* It is naive to think children can be shielded from what you consider inappropriate or harmful stereotypes. Sex-role messages are widespread in our culture. You can, however, present your own views on these matters and help children understand what they encounter. For example, try watching television with a child and discussing differences in the behavior of male and female characters.

4. *Be skeptical of unquestioned or premature identity commitments.* Ask yourself why you believe and behave the way you do. Seek out new experiences and consider alternative possibilities. You do need to make commitments in life, but Erikson's theory suggests there is value in questioning childhood goals and beliefs and living through the uncertainties of moratorium in order to construct a firmer identity.

Highlights

The Construction and Limitations of Identity

An 8-year-old boy decided late one afternoon that he had had it with his parents and announced his intentions to leave home. The parents sympathized and watched him pack a few things into a bag. They told him how much they would miss him and bid him farewell. They watched discreetly from a window as their son walked away from the house and fell into playing with some friends from the neighborhood. Before too long it was dusk and dinnertime and the boy's friends headed off for home. The parents watched their son as he stood for a long while by himself, then stood for a long while by his little suitcase, and then slowly, dejectedly began to walk back home. . . . When their son returned they remained seated, kept their mouths closed, and offered the boy a quiet undemanding attention. They watched as he sat down in a chair opposite them, and then he too was quiet, pensive, self-absorbed. No one said a thing. Finally the family cat ran across the middle of the room. The boy looked up and said to his parents, "I see you still have that old cat." (Kegan, 1982, pp. 159–160).

We see here a boy working to establish the autonomy of Kegan's imperial stage. In essence, he is informing his parents that he has *not* failed to run away. He has indeed left and now is returning on his own terms. He remembers "that old cat," but his relationship to it, and to his parents, will have to be reestablished—a new relationship appropriate to his emerging imperial personality. If all goes well, he will reestablish his relationships not just once but several more times. His imperial personality will give way to an interpersonal orientation in which relations with others once again become central to the sense of self, and that in turn will be replaced by the institutional balance, a higher level of autonomy including what Erikson terms *identity*. But is that stage 4 institutional identity the last step?

5. *Schools should encourage complementary aspects of student and teacher development.* For example, a teacher with a sense of generativity (see Erikson's middle adulthood stage) may find it rewarding to help students develop their autonomy, industry, and identity (in Erikson's sense of these words). If the teacher can see the impact of his teaching on students' development, this may be encouraging to him and increase his commitment to and effectiveness in teaching, as well as his feelings of generativity. If administrative tasks put too much distance between teacher and student, however, then the fit of their developmental levels is likely to be missed.

Rebecca is an intensely self-sufficient woman in her mid-thirties. "I have very defined boundaries," she says, "and I protect them very carefully. I won't give up the slightest control. In any relationship I decide who gets in, how far, and when" (Kegan, 1982, p. 102). But she is beginning to see the limits of this stage. "How exhausting it's becoming holding all this together. And until recently I didn't even realize I was doing it" (p. 103). Moving on to the next stage, the interindividual balance, is not easy, however. As in any stage transition, the difficulty is not only in constructing a new orientation but in accepting the genuine risk and loss involved in giving up one's present self. We see this clearly in a dream she reports:

> I am in a crowded subway, rushing to get a train. I am standing. There is a woman next to me . . . asking me to identify myself. So I begin taking out all my cards—my social security card, my license, my work identification card, my health insurance—and I show them to the woman. All the while it is on my mind that I am late and might miss the train. While I am showing my cards the subway gets into the train station. I grab up all my cards and get off the subway. I run for the train. I come to a sort of revolving door and it closes on me with my arm outside, clutching all my cards, and the rest of me looking out toward the train. I feel just completely stuck. I know that if I could just let go of all these cards, just let them drop, I could get through and catch the train. But I am completely panicked. And I am panicked both at the idea of having to give up all these cards and at the idea of missing the train (p. 241).

Whether one is 8 years old or well past 30, development remains a challenge, both intellectually and emotionally.

6. *Look for both similarities and differences in developmental issues.* Regardless of age, other people are likely to be dealing with developmental issues that are in some ways similar to, and in some ways different from, those of central interest to you. A young child, for example, may be struggling to develop initiative (in Erikson's sense), whereas considerations of identity or intimacy may be more important to an adult's own life. In all likelihood, however, that child is dealing at her own level with issues of personal identity and relations with other people. There is both continuity and discontinuity in developmental issues across the lifespan.

7. *Think about adults as well as children in developmental terms.* Development may be more rapid and obvious in children but adults are developing as well. If you fail to see this, you may fail to address the issues of deepest importance for them.

Summary

Psychologists are interested not only in the various components of a person but also in people's developing conceptions of themselves. Babies' responses to mirrors show that they have some self-awareness by age 20 months. Damon and Hart have synthesized diverse evidence to show developmental changes in self-concept from infancy through adolescence.

Damon and Hart focus on self-understanding, the cognitive aspect of self-concept. Self-understanding includes awareness of the self as an object (the "Me") and of the self as a subject (the "I"). The "Me" includes the physical self, the active self, the social self, and the psychological self. Preschoolers tend to think about themselves in physical terms, with a focus on their names, bodily characteristics, and material possessions. Elementary school children focus more on the active self, including typical behaviors and capabilities relative to other children. In early adolescence, the self is defined socially, in terms of social characteristics, social relations, and group memberships. Finally, later adolescents stress their enduring psychological characteristics, including feelings, thought processes, psychological traits, and belief systems.

The "I" includes a sense that I remain the same person over time (continuity), that I have a unique perspective that no one else can ever fully share (distinctness), that I am an active agent with free will (volition), and that I am aware of all of the above (self-reflection). The self-understanding of young children includes all four of these aspects of the "I." The basis for each, however, shifts dramatically over the course of development from physical to psychological considerations. Further research is needed to explore how the various aspects of self-understanding interact over the course of development, to what extent development of self-understanding is similar or different in diverse cultures, and how self-understanding continues to change beyond adolescence.

A very important aspect of self-understanding is one's conception of oneself as female or male. Even children as young as 2 years of age use the dimension *male vs. female* in thinking about themselves and their environments, though sex differences in many respects are less dramatic than stereotypes might lead us to expect. The social environment greatly influences children's conceptions of sex roles, as well as sex differences in their actual behavior, though the interaction of cultural with biological factors is not yet well understood. Theories attempting to explain the development of sex roles include social learning theory, which emphasizes imitation and reinforcement; cognitive-developmental theory, which highlights the developing awareness that one's gender does not change; and schema theory, which postulates gender-related cognitive structures used to make sense of one's environment.

Psychologists have been increasingly interested in androgynous individuals. Some define androgyny as a combination of high masculinity *and* high femininity. Others define the androgynous person as one for whom the categories "feminine" and "masculine" are not relevant. Further research is needed on the characteristics of androgynous individuals and on how individuals' sex-role development interacts with changing conceptions about sex roles in society at large.

Personality development as a whole has been studied from many points of view. The psychoanalytic perspective traces its roots to Sigmund Freud. The most important current psychoanalytic view of personality development is that of Erik Erikson. Erikson postulates eight stages of personality, ranging from the formation of basic trust or mistrust in infancy to one's sense of integrity or despair in old age.

Erikson is best known for his work on the development of a sense of identity during adolescence. An expansion of this work by James Marcia distinguishes four identity categories. The identity-achieved individual has successfully constructed an identity. The moratorium individual is trying to do so. The foreclosed individual has accepted a ready-made identity from an external source, such as the parents. Finally, the identity-diffused person has no commitments and sees no need to form any.

Robert Kegan has recently developed an alternative conception of personality development based on the general approach of Jean Piaget. Kegan proposes six stages through which people pass in the process of making their experiences meaningful. The incorporative infant is her reflexes. The impulsive preschooler understands her reflexes from the point of view of her impulses and perceptions. The imperial child makes sense of her impulses and perceptions in terms of her enduring needs, interests, and wishes. The interpersonal adolescent or adult considers her needs and interests in the context of her relationships with others. The institutional adult construes her relationships and activities from the point of view of a coherent, self-contained executive. Finally, the interindividual self reconsiders the institutional self-system from the standpoint of a new kind of intimacy that respects, rather than swallows up, individual identity.

Kegan's view provides a picture of development based on the continuing tension between the human desire for inclusion with others and the equally strong need for autonomy. Like Erikson, he sees personality development as a lifelong process.

Key Terms

self-concept	social learning theory	industry vs. inferiority
sex-typing	cognitive-developmental theory	identity vs. identity confusion
sex roles	schema theory	identity crisis
self-esteem	androgyny	intimacy vs. isolation
self-understanding	psychoanalytic approach	generativity vs. stagnation
the "I"	id	integrity vs. despair
the "Me"	ego	identity achievement
physical self	superego	moratorium
active self	libido	foreclosure
social self	Oedipal conflict	identity diffusion
psychological self	Electra conflict	meaning-constitutive development
continuity	identification	incorporative stage
distinctness	psychosocial	impulsive stage
volition	psychosexual	imperial stage
self-reflectivity	trust vs. mistrust	interpersonal stage
stereotypes	autonomy vs. shame, doubt	institutional stage
sex-role socialization	initiative vs. guilt	interindividual stage

Suggested Readings

Damon, W., & Hart, D. (1982). The development of self-understanding from infancy through adolescence. *Child Development, 53,* 841–864. This article provides a thorough review and thoughtful synthesis of the literature on the development of self-understanding.

Erikson, E. H. (1968). *Identity: Youth and crisis.* New York: Norton. In this classic work, Erikson summarizes his eight stages of personality development and expands his account of the development of identity.

Huston, A. C. (1983). Sex-typing. In E. M. Hetherington (Ed.), P. H. Mussen (Series Ed.), *Handbook of child psychology: Vol. 4. Socialization, personality, and social development* (pp. 387–467). New York: Wiley. This chapter provides a thorough review of the extensive literature on sex-typing and the development of sex roles.

Kegan, R. (1982). *The evolving self: Problem and process in human development.* Cambridge, MA: Harvard University Press. George E. Vaillant writes, "If one could buy only one book on child development, *The evolving self* would be the book to buy. . . . It reflects the state of the art."

Marcia, J. E. (1980). Identity in adolescence. In J. Adelson (Ed.), *Handbook of adolescent psychology* (pp. 159–187). New York: Wiley. Marcia reviews the literature on the development of identity in adolescence, with a focus on his own important contributions.

Waterman, A. S. (Ed.) (1985). *Identity in adolescence: Processes and contents. New Directions for Child Development*, No. 30. San Francisco: Jossey-Bass. Five authors discuss identity development in adolescence, including its relation to vocational, religious, political, and sex-role issues.

Application Exercises

16-1 Determining Identity Status

Assign each of the following individuals to one of Marcia's four identity statuses: identity achieved, moratorium, foreclosed, or identity diffused. (You may find Figure 16-2 useful in working on this.)

1. George is a college freshman eager to experience new things. He is not sure what he wants to major in but is not especially concerned about it, nor is he particularly attached to any ideologies.

2. Martha is a high school junior who has never seriously doubted her parents' moral values and political views and who remains strongly committed to her childhood dream of becoming a nurse.

3. Jacob has dropped out of college, uncertain about his earlier plans to become an engineer, dubious of the political values that led him into engineering in the first place, and interested in moving to another part of the country and changing his life-style in order to "find himself."

4. Rachel, after exploring Buddhism for several years, has converted to that religion. She has also decided to apply to law school and focus on constitutional issues regarding the relations of church and state.

5. Four years later, George has graduated with a degree in sociology, is working for a large department store, and has joined the Libertarian party along with several of his friends. However, he is increasingly aware of conflicts between his sociological views and Libertarian ideology. Moreover, although he is earning enough money to live on, he would eventually like to find employment in a field he can be more committed to.

6. Martha, to her parents' dismay, has become active in a socialist organization at her college four years later. After thinking about what sort of vocation will make best use of her talents and also be consistent with her politics, she has decided to become a nurse after all.

7. Jacob has decided to remain in the rural environment he ended up in after dropping out of college four years ago. He has returned to college, however, to become a teacher, because he feels this will give him skills useful in his new surroundings.

8. Rachel, four years later, is thinking about quitting her new job at a prestigious law firm because she finds the work irrelevant to her moral and religious values. She wonders if any work in the field of law could possibly be defensible in terms of her other commitments and begins to wonder about those commitments as well and to look actively into new possibilities.

16-2 Personality Development

Think about people you know, including children, adolescents, and adults. Can you account for major aspects of their personalities in terms of Erikson's stages? Can you account for them in terms of Kegan's stages? Do the two theories give similar or disparate pictures? Do you find one more convincing than the other in helping you understand the people you know?

Glossary

absolutism. The view that certain ideas are inherently true or moral, cannot be seriously questioned, and do not need to be justified.

abstraction principle. The principle that a set of items can be counted even if they have nothing in common.

accommodation. In Piagetian theory, fitting or adjusting one's schemes to the aspect of the environment that one is assimilating.

acne. A severe inflammation of the oil glands on the face (and perhaps on the neck and shoulders as well). It may lead to large, painful cysts that may leave permanently disfiguring scars.

active environment. A view of development emphasizing the influence of the environment on the individual.

active person. A view of development emphasizing the influence of the person on the environment.

active self. An aspect of self-concept defining the self in terms of typical activities and special abilities.

adaptation. The tendency for a species or an individual to adjust increasingly to its environment.

adipocytes. Fat cells.

afferent fibers. PNS nerves that serve as conduits of incoming information.

aggression. Behavior aimed at harming or injuring another individual.

agonistic behavior. A cluster of behaviors that includes fighting, teasing, loud demands, tattling, and other negative behaviors.

alleles. Genes from both mother and father that govern a trait.

altruism. A concern for others and an inclination to act to further their welfare.

amniocentesis. Withdrawing a small amount of amniotic fluid from the mother's womb and subjecting this fluid to a series of tests.

amnion. The component of the blastocyst that forms the inner sac surrounding the embryo.

androgens. Male hormones.

androgyny. The state of being neither exclusively masculine nor exclusively feminine.

androsperm. Androsperm carry a Y chromosome and, if they fertilize ova, form a male zygote.

GLOSSARY

anorexia nervosa. An eating disorder characterized by refusal to eat and by extreme weight loss and not caused by an organic problem.

anoxia. Oxygen starvation. It can be a complication in the birth process if the umbilical cord is damaged.

antithesis. An idea or viewpoint contradicting an earlier view (the thesis).

Apgar Scale. A scale used in assessing the viability of newborns.

aqueous humor. A liquid that provides nutrition for the cornea and iris.

artificial insemination. Fertilization of the ovum with pre-selected sperm. This may be done in a test tube or in vitro through the use of a syringe.

assimilation. Fitting the environment to one's current knowledge in order to make sense of it. In Piagetian theory, a highly active process vital to all knowing.

asthma. Periodic difficulty in breathing because of the constriction of the lungs' bronchial passages.

astigmatism. A condition in which the lens of the eye is imperfect and, hence, vision is distorted.

asynchrony (in growth). The maturation of different parts of the body at different times.

attachment. An enduring social tie of a child to a specific person, such as the mother or father.

attachment stage. In emotional development, the attachment stage is thought to occur from 9 to 12 months of age. This stage is characterized by a preoccupation with the primary caregiver.

attention. Focusing consciousness on some aspects of the world and not on others.

auditory canal. A part of the outer ear that conducts sound to the tympanic membrane.

authoritarian-autocratic parenting. A parent-centered approach to child rearing, in which parents seek to assert their authority.

authoritative-reciprocal parenting. A parenting pattern in which the parent is strongly involved, but with two-way communication and respect for children's rights.

autism. A condition involving gross impairment in interpersonal relationships and communication, typically including bizarre reactions to the environment.

autonomic nervous system. The bodily system that controls basic life-support functions.

autonomous morality. A self-determined ethical orientation emphasizing mutual respect and rational cooperation among peers.

autonomy. Independence.

autonomy vs. shame, doubt. In Erikson's theory, a stage of personality development associated with toddlerhood in which emergence of a sense of independence is the primary psychological issue.

avoidant infants. A category of insecurely attached infants, avoidant infants seem relatively unconcerned about their mothers' whereabouts and ignore or avoid their mothers on reunion after separation.

awareness. A subcategory of metamemory, involving knowledge about when something needs to be remembered.

Glossary

babbling. Playful speech without meaning, in which children try out their sound-making ability.

Babinski reflex. The Babinski reflex in newborns is elicited by stroking the bottom of the foot. The baby responds by extending and fanning out its toes.

balance scale. A physical apparatus used by Piaget, Siegler, and many others for research on cognitive development.

baseline. The starting point of a single-subject experiment, in which one or more behaviors are observed prior to any intervention.

behavior coding. In research, prespecification of behavior that will be observed. If a behavior fits a prespecified category, then it is recorded.

behavior genetics. The study of the role of genes in behavior.

behaviorism. An approach to psychology focusing on observable behavior.

beriberi. A disease brought on by deficiency in vitamin B1. It causes heart and peripheral nerve damage.

blastocyst. When the zygote has grown via mitosis from a single cell into a ball of about 100 cells, this ball is referred to as a blastocyst.

bonding. Formation by a mother of an affectionate attachment to her infant immediately after birth.

bound morphemes. Morphemes, such as prefixes or suffixes, which must be linked to word stems to have meaning.

brain stem. A portion of the brain extending from the spine, including the midbrain, the pons varolii, and the medulla.

breech delivery. A birth in which the fetus is positioned buttocks down or even diagonally.

Broca's area. The part of the cerebral cortex (usually in the left hemisphere) that translates thought into speech.

bulimarexia. An eating disorder characterized by cycles of gorging and purging.

Caesarian section. A birth in which the baby is removed from the womb through surgical incisions made in the mother's abdomen and uterus.

canalization. Returning to a normal pattern of growth after serious illness or malnutrition.

cardinal principle. The principle that in counting a set of items, the number assigned to the last item counted is the total number of items in the set.

case study. A research method in which one individual is studied intensively.

causal attributions. Our analysis of situations for which we seek answers to the question "why?"

causality. In research, a situation in which changes in one variable are responsible for changes in the value of another.

causally linked emotions. Emotions determined by understanding the causes of some event.

central nervous system (CNS). The brain and spinal cord.

centration. In Piagetian theory, a tendency to focus on one aspect of a problem or situation.

cephalocaudal development. The tendency for development to proceed from head to foot.

cerebellum. The part of the brain that uses feedback from the body to coordinate and maintain balance, posture, and muscle control.

cerebral cortex. The surface of the cerebrum, the largest part of the brain. In the cerebral cortex thought, memory, language, and other sophisticated brain functions occur.

cerebral hemispheres. The cerebral cortex is divided into two hemispheres, right and left.

cerebrum. The largest part of the brain. Its surface, the cerebral cortex, is involved in the brain's most complex functions.

chorion. The component of the blastocyst that forms the outer sac surrounding the embryo.

chromosomes. The gene-bearing structures passed from parents to offspring that determine the offspring's characteristics.

classical conditioning. A learning process in which a neutral stimulus is paired with an eliciting stimulus until the neutral stimulus alone brings forth the response.

clause. A word combination that contains a verb.

clinical interview. A method of research, used especially by Piaget, involving flexible questioning of a child to determine how she or he is thinking.

clique. A close-knit group of individuals joined by similar interests and social values.

closure. The "law of closure" is one of the Gestalt "laws of perception" in which partially completed figures are seen as complete or closed.

cochlea. A hollow, liquid-filled structure of the inner ear that translates sound waves into neural impulses.

coercive rules. Rules that are seen as formulated by the authorities and thus absolute and unchangeable.

cognition. The processes of knowing, including perceiving, remembering, understanding, reasoning, and problem solving.

cognitive-developmental approach. A theoretical orientation, associated with Piaget, Kohlberg, and others, emphasizing the role of cognition and development in many types of psychological phenomena.

cognitive psychology. An area of study or theoretical approach focusing on mental processes or structures that cannot be directly observed.

cognitive structure. A postulated mental organization with which one knows one's environment.

cohesive devices. Mechanisms, such as conjunction and anaphora, for linking meaning in language.

cohort. A group of individuals of a given age or natural grouping (e.g., the class of 1988).

common ground. In children's communication, finding something to do together and exploring similarities and differences.

comparative research. Research comparing two or more species with each other.

conception. The moment at which the sperm and ovum join to form a zygote.

concrete operations. In Piaget's theory, a stage of advanced representational intelligence, postulated to begin about age 7, involving structured, reversible mental actions.

cones. Light-sensitive receptor cells at the back of the eye, associated primarily with color vision.

confidentiality. Keeping all research data secure, so that participants' privacy is protected.

connectedness. In John Gottman's research on friendship development, the extent to which children are able to relate effectively to each other.

consequences. The outcomes of one's actions, as distinguished from one's underlying intentions. According to Piaget, consequences are paramount to young children's judgments of morality.

conservation. An understanding that certain properties remain unchanged when others change.

consonant. Speech sound produced by stopping and releasing the airstream.

constraint. Obligations or limitations imposed by others, seen by young children (according to Piaget) as the basis for morality.

constructive views of memory. Models of memory that emphasize how social, cognitive, and emotional factors in children transform information into new forms.

constructivism. A theoretical approach to development emphasizing active construction of new concepts or abilities by the developing individual.

contemporary behaviorism. Contemporary behaviorism dates to the work of B. F. Skinner and focuses on how the antecedents and consequences of behavior influence behavior.

context cues. Indirect cues, such as pictures in a children's reader, which give clues to the meaning of things.

contextualism. A theoretical approach to development emphasizing the environmental context in which it takes place.

continuity. (1) In analyses of development, describes changes increasing or decreasing what was already present rather than adding something new. (2) An aspect of self-concept involving the sense that one remains the same person with passing time. (3) In perception, the Gestalt "law of continuity" holds that perceptual phenomena tend to be seen as continuous.

control of variables. The concept that to determine the effects of any variable one must hold all other variables constant.

conventional morality. A morality based on the values of one's peers or one's society.

conversational skills. Ability to talk with others, taking turns and exchanging information.

cooing. An early form of vocalization through which infants indicate their pleasure.

cooperation. Coordination of the ideas, values, or behaviors of two or more individuals, seen by Piaget as indispensable to mature morality.

cornea. A clear covering on the front of the eye important in focusing light.

corpus callosum. The structure that joins the two cerebral hemispheres.

correlation. A relationship between two variables.

correlation coefficient. A numerical index, ranging from -1.00 to $+1.00$, which indicates the strength of the relationship between two variables.

Cri du chat. A genetic abnormality caused by damage to (or partial absence of) the fifth chromosome. It is characterized by severe retardation.

critical period. The idea that a process (e.g., bonding) can develop only at a specific age or developmental period.
cross-cultural research. Research that compares development in different cultures around the world.
cross-pressures. Conflicts that arise when parents disapprove of adolescents' dress, grooming, or actions, while peers endorse them.
cross-sectional design. A research design in which individuals of different ages are observed at one time.
cross-sequential design. A combined research design in which individuals of different ages are observed at a given time but also followed as time passes.
crowd. A group of individuals who meet because of shared interest in an activity.
crying. Sounds produced by infants when they are uncomfortable, hungry, or want to be held.
culture. Qualities such as knowledge, beliefs, morals, and law, which individuals possess as members of a society.
cystic fibrosis. A fatal disease of the lungs and intestines associated with a recessive gene.
data. Observations, direct evidence (plural of *datum*).
dating. A date is a social engagement, an arrangement for two people to do something together. In the United States, dating is the major vehicle for fostering adolescent heterosexual relationships.
decentration (Piagetian theory). Considering two or more facets of a problem or situation simultaneously.
deep processing. In levels-of-processing theory, the more sophisticated and elaborate analysis of materials to be remembered that results in better memory.
Defining Issues Test (DIT). A paper-and-pencil assessment of moral development designed by James Rest.
deictic tutoring. An interaction pattern between parents and children, often used by middle-class American parents to teach children new words.
dependent variable. An outcome or consequent variable, presumed to be affected by one or more independent variables.
depression. A mental state characterized by very low moods and loss of enjoyment of activities that once were pleasurable.
depth perception. Perception of depth and relative distance among objects.
developmental behavior genetics. A branch of developmental psychology in which the emphasis is on how the genes influence behavior changes in development.
developmental norms. Ages at which various milestones of development are typically reached.
developmental theory. A theory specifically aimed at explaining development, especially one emphasizing inner-directed processes of change.
diagnosis. A subcategory of metamemory involving analysis of the items to be learned and of one's own memory ability to determine how difficult memory tasks really are.
dialectical theory. A theoretical approach to development emphasizing continuing interaction between person and environment.

Glossary

dialogue (in dialectical theory). An interaction between two equals, seen as critical to developmental progress.

diencephalon. The part of the brain just above the brain stem. It is made up of the thalamus and the hypothalamus.

differentiation. The increasing distinctness of concepts and abilities during development.

differentiation theory. A theory proposing that the separate emotions are derived from one emotion through differentiation.

disagreement chains. A failure in conflict resolution, in which children disagree repeatedly with one another.

discontinuity. A time in development at which a distinctly new concept or ability appears.

discrete emotions theory. Izard has developed a theory of emotional development he refers to as discrete emotions theory. In this perspective, each emotion is a separate system and emerges at a distinct point in development.

discrimination. The ability to distinguish among different stimuli.

disequilibration (Piagetian theory). A process in which one's cognitive balance is upset, thus creating disequilibrium.

disequilibrium. A state of imbalance, seen by Piaget as necessary for genuine development to take place.

distinctive features. Elements of complex stimuli that allow us to distinguish among them.

distinctness. An aspect of self-concept emphasizing the inherent uniqueness of one's experience.

DNA (Deoxyribonucleic acid). DNA molecules are complex organic molecules. Genes are DNA molecules or parts of them. It is the DNA molecules that carry information governing the structure of offspring.

dominant genes. Dominant genes are always expressed in the offspring's appearance.

Down's syndrome. Down's syndrome is trisomy 22. It is characterized by mental retardation and physical problems.

duos. Two-word sentences used by young children.

dyslexia. A form of learning disability in which readers have great difficulty dealing with letter orientations (e.g., *d* and *b*).

echoic memory. The brief, sensory-based memory for auditory information.

echolalia. A condition in which language use consists of simple repetition (echoing) of what is said.

ecological view of child development. The concept that children's development is affected by the context in which they develop.

ectoderm. The part of the blastocyst's inner cell mass that will ultimately form the skin, sense organs, and nervous system.

Edwards' syndrome. Edwards' syndrome is trisomy 18. It is characterized by severe retardation and multiple, severe malformations.

effectors. Parts of the body, such as muscles, which can act in response to stimuli encountered by receptors.

efferent fibers. PNS nerve fibers that carry information outgoing from the CNS.

ego. In Freudian theory, the executive component of the personality that coordinates the demands of the id, the superego, and reality.

elaborative recall. In recall, going beyond the information presented.

Electra conflict. In Freudian theory, a complex pattern of emotional interactions within the family resulting in the preschool girl's identifying with her mother.

elementarism. A theoretical view stressing the distinct elements that make up a complex concept or ability.

eliciting stimulus. An eliciting stimulus brings forth an unlearned, reflexive response.

embryonic period. The period of growth from two to eight weeks after conception.

emotions. Subjective experiences accompanied by physiological changes.

empathy. The ability to infer and experience the feelings of others.

empiricism. A philosophical view maintaining that all knowledge comes from the environment.

encoding. The process of representing information in one's mind, or the resulting mental representation.

encopresis. Voluntary or involuntary passage of feces that results in soiled clothing or occurs in a socially inappropriate place.

endocrine disorders. Problems with the endocrine glands. Two such disorders, simple diabetes and hypothyroidism, have been shown to adversely affect prenatal development.

endocrine system. The system of internal organs that secretes hormones.

endoderm. The part of the blastocyst's inner cell mass that will ultimately form the digestive system and other internal organs.

enuresis. Involuntary release of urine at an inappropriate time in the absence of any organic cause.

epigenesis. The process by which the genotype is transformed into the phenotype.

epistemology. The branch of philosophy dealing with the nature of knowledge.

equilibration. In Piaget's theory, the construction of new understandings that resolve disequilibrium and restore equilibrium.

equilibrium. In Piaget's theory, a consistency in one's knowledge allowing temporary cognitive stability.

equity. A mature view of justice recognizing that strict equality may be unfair in some situations.

estrogens. Female hormones.

ethical relativism. The view that what is morally right depends on one's personal perspective or on the values of one's society, or both.

eustachian tube. A tube connecting the middle ear to the very back of the nasal cavity.

evolution. The process by which a species progressively adapts to its environment over many generations. Sometimes, more generally, any process of change.

exosystem. In Bronfenbrenner's model of social influence, a system, such as parental workplace, which indirectly affects children's development.

experiment. A type of research involving systematic manipulation of variables in order to observe their effects.

extinction. Cessation of a response due to removal of reinforcement.

facial expressions. Expressions such as smiling or frowning.
Fallopian tubes. Tubelike structures running from the ovaries to the uterus, in which conception typically occurs.
falsification strategy. A strategy of testing a hypothesis by seeking cases that, if found, would prove it false.
family system. The family, characterized as two or more individuals interacting and affecting each other.
fetal alcohol syndrome. Severe malformations that occur among fetuses whose mothers regularly consume alcohol.
fetal period. The period of growth from the eighth week after conception until birth.
figurative component. The figurative component of perception refers to knowledge of what is being perceived.
first words. The initial words produced by children.
foreclosure. In Marcia's expansion of Erikson's theory of identity formation, an identity status in which one has strong commitments based on unquestioned ideas and values derived from one's childhood socialization.
form perception. Perception of (and distinction among) different visual forms.
formal operations. The final stage of cognitive development, according to Piaget, involving ability to reason about hypotheses and possibilities.
fovea. The part of the retina in which the sharpest vision occurs.
free morphemes. Morphemes that carry meaning by themselves.
gametes. Sex cells—the sperm and ovum.
gaze. Looking at objects or people; used by infants in their earliest social interactions.
generalization. In operant psychology, generalization refers to the appearance of a behavior learned in one situation in a new situation.
generalized excitement response. A precursor of true emotions.
generativity vs. stagnation. In Erikson's theory, the stage of personality development associated with middle adulthood, in which productive work and concern for future generations are leading issues.
genes. Molecules of DNA or parts of them that carry information from generation to generation governing the characteristics of offspring.
genetic counseling. Consultation aimed at helping prospective parents assess the potential risks of genetic problems in their offspring.
genetic epistemology (Baldwin, Piaget). Developmental epistemology, studying the origins and development of knowledge.
genetics. The study of how characteristics are transmitted from generation to generation.
genotype. A person's genetic constitution.
germinal period. The first two weeks after conception.
Gestalt psychology. Gestalt psychology was founded in Germany in 1912 by Max Wertheimer, Kurt Koffka, and Wolfgang Kohler. Primarily focusing on perception, Gestalt psychology was highly existential, arguing that the perceived world and the real world need not agree.
glial cells. Glial cells provide nutrition for neurons and form a sheath of myelin around each neuron.

grasping reflex. The grasping reflex occurs when the palm of a newborn's hand is pressed and the baby's fingers close around the object in its hand.

group. A social unit to which people belong.

group-based experimentation. A research method in which the researcher compares behaviors of groups of individuals under two or more conditions set up by the experimenter.

group structure. The patterns of power and influence in a group.

growth retarded babies. Full-term newborns who weigh less than five pounds eight ounces.

gynosperm. X-carrying sperm that, if they fertilize ova, result in female zygotes.

habituation. The process by which a stimulus becomes so familiar that it no longer brings about a response.

handedness. The fact that most people develop a dominant hand, right or left.

head movements. Turning or lifting the head; a part of infants' early social interactions.

heritability of intelligence. The degree to which individual differences in intelligence are inherited rather than due to the environment.

heteronomous morality. A moral orientation stressing obedience to authority.

heterozygotic. A heterozygotic zygote contains two alleles that possess different information from each parent.

hierarchical structure. A form of group structure in which the group is organized from top to bottom; that is, with leaders and followers.

hierarchic integration. The coordination of concepts or abilities that previously were differentiated.

historicism. A theoretical approach emphasizing that in order to genuinely explain something one must understand its developmental history.

holism. A theoretical approach that emphasizes understanding phenomena as wholes rather than breaking them down into their components.

holophrases. Single words used by very young children much like sentences.

homozygotic. A homozygotic zygote contains two alleles that possess the same information from each parent.

hormones. Chemical substances that govern the body's physiological activities.

hostile aggression. A cognitively based form of aggression in which children react to inferences that others are acting intentionally.

hyperactivity. A childhood problem characterized by short attention span and impulsive behavior.

hypothalamus. A part of the diencephalon that controls the autonomic nervous system, mediates emotional responses, controls body temperature, regulates hunger and thirst, and influences patterns of sleep and wakefulness.

hypothesis. A specific prediction about the results of a research study.

hypothesis testing. Seeking information to determine the truth or falsity of a hypothesis or theory.

hypothetico-deductive reasoning. Making inferences from hypotheses or possibilities rather than known facts.

iconic memory. The very brief sensory memory for visual information.

id. In Freudian theory, the aspect of personality related to one's most basic needs and desires.

identification. In Freudian theory, the process by which the young child incorporates the personality, sex role, and moral values of the same-sex parent.

identity achievement. In Marcia's expansion of Erikson's theory of identity formation, the consolidation of one's own self-chosen commitments to form a coherent identity.

identity crisis. A period in one's development in which the need to construct a clear sense of who one is, is primary.

identity diffusion. In Marcia's expansion of Erikson's theory of identity formation, a status in which one has no strong identity commitments and is not searching for any.

identity vs. identity confusion. In Erikson's theory, the stage of personality development, usually associated with adolescence or early adulthood, in which construction of identity is the primary issue.

imaginal coding. Retaining information by storing a picture or image of it.

imitation. Duplicating the actions of others.

immanent justice. A view, associated by Piaget with young children, that justice is automatic, a characteristic (like gravity) of the physical world.

immediate memory span. The capacity of short-term memory.

imperial stage. In Kegan's theory, the stage of personality development, usually associated with middle childhood, in which the child takes command of his or her impulses and develops some self-consistency and self-control.

impulsive stage. In Kegan's theory, the stage of personality development associated with the preschool years, in which the child is at the mercy of, rather than in control of, his or her impulses.

incorporative stage. In Kegan's theory, the stage of personality development associated with infancy, in which there is no sense of self.

independent variable. Antecedent or causal variable, presumed to affect other variables.

indifferent-uninvolved parenting. A parenting style in which parents minimize their contact with their children.

individualism and exchange. In Kohlberg's theory, stage 2 of moral development, in which morality is seen as involving deals between individuals.

indulgent-permissive parenting. A child-centered parenting pattern, with general avoidance of asserting parental authority and few restrictions on children's behavior.

industry vs. inferiority. In Erikson's theory, the stage of personality development, associated with middle childhood, in which development of a sense of competence is the major issue.

inferential recall. Recall of information not actually presented, but which is a logical extension of the material presented.

inferential validity. An argument is valid if its conclusion necessarily follows from the premises, regardless of whether the premises and conclusion are empirically true or false.

inflections. Particles added to words to change their meanings. English has inflections for tense, plurals, and possession.

information exchange. The degree to which children ask for and receive information.

information processing. A theoretical approach to cognition, increasingly influential since about 1960, emphasizing description and explanation of specific mental processes.

informed consent. Consent to participate in research, based on full information about research conditions and potential hazards.

initiative vs. guilt. In Erikson's theory, the stage of personality development, usually associated with the preschool years, in which active exploration of the world leads to a pervasive sense of initiative or guilt.

inner ear. The inner ear contains the cochlea, in which the mechanical energy of sound waves is transformed into neural impulses.

insecurely attached infants. Infants who are not securely attached, two categories of whom are avoidant and resistant.

institutional stage. In Kegan's theory, an adult stage of personality involving a coherent self in firm control of its relationships.

instruction. Education, especially where the teacher directly teaches the student.

instrumental aggression. A basic form of aggression, resulting simply from children's being blocked from attaining their goals.

integration. The tendency for newly differentiated actions and concepts to become coordinated.

integrity vs. despair. In Erikson's theory, the final stage of personality development, involving formation of a general perspective on one's life.

intelligence. The possession or use of cognitive abilities, especially those involving sophisticated reasoning and understanding.

intentions. The reasons for one's actions, seen by mature individuals (according to Piaget) as more important than consequences in making moral judgments.

interactionism. A theoretical approach that emphasizes the continuing interaction of factors (especially of heredity and environment) in determining the course of development.

interindividual stage. In Kegan's theory, the highest stage of personality development, involving a sophisticated coordination of identities to yield genuine intimacy.

interpersonal stage. In Kegan's theory, the stage of personality development, usually associated with adolescence, in which the self is defined in terms of relations with others.

intervention. In a single-subject experiment, the stage in which the experimental conditions are implemented.

interview. A research method in which individuals are asked a set of questions about aspects of their lives.

intimacy vs. isolation. In Erikson's theory, the stage of personality development following the formation of identity, in which genuine intimacy becomes the primary aim.

intimate friendship. A very close friendship that often appears for the first time in adolescence.

introspection. A research technique, used especially by early psychologists, involving careful observation and recording of one's own thoughts.

invariant sequence. A set of behaviors, strategies, or concepts that develop in the same order in all children.

iris. The round, colored part of the eye.

just community. A social group that determines its own rules and thus takes responsibility for its own behavior. The formation of such communities (e.g., in schools or prisons) is seen by Kohlberg as a key aspect of moral education.

justice. Basic fairness in human interactions, seen by Piaget and Kohlberg as the essence of morality.

karyotype. A photograph of an individual's complement of chromosomes.

knowing. In Ann Brown's analysis of memory development, the actual knowledge that children possess.

knowing about knowing. In Ann Brown's analysis of memory development, the knowledge that children have about their own memories; metamemory.

knowing how to know. In Ann Brown's analysis of memory development, children's use of strategies for enhancing their memories.

knowledge-acquisition components. In Sternberg's theory, the aspects of intelligence used in acquiring new knowledge.

kwashiorkor. A sometimes fatal disease caused by protein deficiency. It results in liver damage, severe diarrhea, and general weakening of resistance.

labor. The process of expelling the fetus from the womb. It is initiated by hormonal changes in the mother.

latchkey children. Children who spend large amounts of time alone without their parents, usually after school.

lateralization. The specialization of the two hemispheres of the cerebral cortex.

leadership. The ability to influence, guide, and direct others in groups.

learning theory. A theory focusing on changes induced by the environment and intended to explain those changes.

lens. The lens of the eye bends light to focus it on the retina.

levels-of-processing. A view of memory advanced by Craik and Lockhart that memory is a by-product of the perceptual analyses of the learner.

lexical meaning. Word meaning.

libido. In Freudian theory, the life force underlying personality and its development, seen by Freud as primarily sexual.

lightening. Birth is usually preceded by lightening, in which the fetus turns so that it is head down and prepared for exit from the womb.

limbic system. The limbic system includes the diencephalon, the amygdala, and the septum.

linguistic period. The period of language development from about one year onward, in which speech conveys meaning.

logical necessity. A conclusion is logically necessary if it follows necessarily from specific premises.

longitudinal design. A research design in which the same individuals are observed several times.

long-term store. The location of the permanent contents of memory.

macrosystems. In Bronfenbrenner's model, broad consistencies and shared beliefs at the subcultural or cultural level.

manner. In linguistics, differences in how sounds are produced.

maturation. An internally directed process of development, especially one guided primarily by heredity.

meaning-constitutive development. A Piagetian view highlighted by Kegan, in which development is seen as a continuing creation of new interpretations.

mechanisms of development. Processes that explain—rather than simply describing—developmental changes.

medulla oblongata (or, simply, the medulla). A part of the brain stem that contains all nerves passing from the spinal cord to the brain and back. It controls many important bodily processes.

meiosis. The process of cell division that forms the gametes. In meiosis, each cell divides twice but the chromosomes are doubled only once.

menarche. A girl's first menstrual cycle.

mental capacity. In information-processing theories, the upper limit on how much information can be processed at once.

mesoderm. The part of the blastocyst's inner cell mass that ultimately forms the muscles, circulatory system, and blood.

mesosystems. In Bronfenbrenner's model, the relationships among two or more systems.

metacognition. Cognition about cognition, or knowing about knowing. Includes the ability to understand and regulate one's own cognitive processes.

metacomponents. In Sternberg's theory, aspects of intelligence that activate and direct the other components in their processing of information.

metalinguistic awareness. Children's knowledge about their own use of language.

metamemory. The awareness children have about their own memories.

microgenesis (Werner). A brief repetition of a developmental process that earlier occurred much less rapidly.

microsystems. In Bronfenbrenner's model, the patterns of activities, roles, and relationships directly experienced by children as they develop.

midbrain. A part of the brain stem that conducts nerve impulses to the upper regions of the brain and back down the spinal cord and also serves as a reflex center for eye and head movements.

middle ear. The middle ear contains the eardrum and the ossicles.

mitosis. A cell division process in which the chromosomes double and then are divided into two cells.

mnemonic strategies. Purposeful methods children use to improve their chances of remembering something.

modeling. A learning process emphasized by social learning theory, involving imitation of others' behavior.

models of memory. Theoretical explanations for how memory works.

monitoring. A subcategory of metamemory that involves determining how well memory is progressing.

monozygotic twins. Identical twins, resulting when an original zygote divides into two identical zygotes.

moral realism. According to Piaget, an immature view of moral rules in which they are seen as absolute characteristics of reality rather than as social constructions.

moratorium. In Marcia's expansion of Erikson's theory of identity formation, a period during which one actively tries to make identity commitments.

Moro reflex. A startle response in newborns in which the arms are thrown out and brought back to the body.

morphemes. Minimal units of meaning; the building blocks of words.

morphology. The discipline that examines the formation of words.

motherese. The characteristic speech mothers and other adults use in talking to young children.

motor rules. According to Piaget, rules, followed by very young children, which are based on personal habits.

motor skills. The physical abilities of an individual.

multistore model. A model of memory that depicts it as consisting of separate stages through which information passes as it is processed.

mutation. A change in the hereditary materials that results in a change in the characteristics of offspring.

mutual expectations. In Kohlberg's theory, stage 3 of moral development, in which personal relationships are seen as vital to morality.

mutual respect. Respect between peers, seen by Piaget as indispensable to mature morality.

myelin. Myelin is formed by the glial cells and is a fatty material that insulates neurons and neural pathways.

myelinization. The process of covering the neurons and neural pathways with myelin.

nativism. A theoretical view emphasizing innate, hereditary factors as the guiding forces in development.

naturalistic observation. Observation of events as they occur in nature.

natural selection. A key evolutionary process in which characteristics favored by the environment become more frequent from generation to generation.

nature-nurture. The dispute over the extent to which development is guided by heredity (nature) or by environment (nurture).

negative correlation. A correlation in which values on two variables are inversely associated; high values on one variable are likely to be linked to low values on the second, and low values on the first to high values on the second.

neo-Piagetian theory. A theory differing from Piaget's on important points but consistent with his general theoretical perspective.

neurons. Nerve cells.

neutral stimulus. A stimulus that has little or no effect on behavior.

norms. Typical patterns of growth and development.

noun phrase. A set of words containing a noun and its modifiers.

novel productions. The unique things children say.

obesity. The condition of being 40 percent or more overweight.

object permanence. The understanding that the world consists of objects that continue to exist even when one is not perceiving them.

object play. An early form of play involving specific items such as balls, spoons, and cups.

observation. An approach to research emphasizing realistic settings and avoiding experimental manipulations.

observational learning. Learning by imitation.

Oedipal conflict. In Freudian theory, complex emotional interactions within the family resulting in identification of the preschool boy with his father.
one-one principle. The principle that in counting a set of items each must be assigned one and only one number name.
ontogeny. The development of an individual organism.
operant conditioning. A simple learning process in which behaviors are controlled by events that follow them.
operating space. In Case's theory, the amount of mental space used for processing information.
operative component. The operative component of perception refers to knowledge about how to perceive.
order-irrelevance principle. The principle that the order in which a set of items is counted makes no difference.
organization. In Piagetian theory, the fundamental tendency of knowledge to be integrated and internally consistent.
organizational strategy. Grouping information meaningfully to make it easier to remember.
orthogenetic principle (Werner). The principle that development consists of differentiation and hierarchic integration.
ossicles. Three tiny, connected bones in the middle ear.
ossification. Hardening of the bones.
outcome-dependent emotions. Emotions determined wholly by the results of some event.
outer ear. The external ear (pinna) and auditory canal.
ovum. The mother's egg. The ovum provides half of the genetic material for the offspring.
paradigm. A general approach to theory and research or a family of related theories and research methods.
parasympathetic nerve fibers. Autonomic nerves that deactivate various body systems.
parenting. The activities of child rearing.
parenting styles. Characteristic patterns of child rearing used by given parents.
pattern detection. The perception of specific patterns within complex stimulus situations.
peers. Children who are of approximately the same age as a given child.
pellagra. A disease caused by niacin deficiency, characterized by skin lesions, severe diarrhea, and irrational thought.
perception. Assignment of meaning to incoming stimuli.
perception of illusions. The perception of illusions refers to how people assign meaning to ambiguous stimuli that may be interpreted in different ways.
perceptual centration. Focusing on only one aspect of a stimulus.
performance components. In Sternberg's theory, the aspects of intelligence involved in solving problems.
peripheral nervous system (PNS). All the nerve tissue lying outside of the CNS.
perspective-taking. Looking at things from someone else's point of view.
phenotype. An individual's actual characteristics.
phobias. Irrational, overpowering fears.

phonemes. Meaningful sound units in a language that are perceived as distinctive.

phones. The technical name for language sounds.

phoneticians. Specialists who study the sounds of speech.

phonetics. The study of how human sounds are formed, transmitted, and heard.

phonology. The study of the sound systems of a language.

phylogeny. The evolution of a species.

physical aggression. Aggression involving physical action against others, such as hitting or kicking.

physical self. An aspect of self-concept, associated particularly with young children, stressing one's physical characteristics.

PKU. A serious metabolic disorder in which infants are unable to digest milk and several other foods. Caused by a recessive gene, PKU can result in severe retardation if not treated.

place. In linguistics, differences in where speech sounds are produced.

placenta. An organ that develops on the wall of the uterus during pregnancy. By means of the placenta the mother's system furnishes the embryo with oxygen and nutrients and removes wastes.

pons varolii. A part of the brain stem involved in the control of breathing and serving as a bridge between the spinal cord and the brain.

population. In research, the group of individuals to whom researchers hope to generalize their results.

positive affect stage. In emotional development, the positive affect stage occurs between 3 and 6 months of age. The major characteristic of this stage is the presence of positive emotions.

positive correlation. A correlation in which values of two variables are directly associated; high values on one variable are likely to be linked to high values on the second, and low values to low values.

positive reciprocity. In Gottman's research, the extent to which children were able to please one another.

postconventional morality. A moral orientation that goes beyond the conventions of one's society and may even reject some social traditions as immoral.

practicing stage. In emotional development, the practicing stage occurs from 12 to 18 months of age and is characterized by an exploration and mastery of the inanimate environment.

pragmatics. In linguistics, the study of how context affects language.

preconventional morality. A moral orientation that does not yet include understanding of social conventions.

prelinguistic period. The period of language development prior to one year in which speech does not yet convey meaning.

premature babies. Babies are considered premature when they are born earlier than 37 weeks following conception.

premises. Information used as a starting point in reasoning toward conclusions.

preoperational stage. In Piaget's theory, the first stage of representational intelligence.

presymbolic word use. Use of words by young children as an accompaniment to actions and objects.

pretend play. A form of play in which reality is suspended and objects often are used as symbols for other things.

primates. An order that includes homo sapiens, the great apes, and monkeys.

principles of counting. A set of principles necessary for mature counting.

prior-to-society perspective. A postconventional moral orientation that considers the rational basis for society and its conventions.

prosocial behavior. Positive interaction with others, including cooperation, sharing, and approval.

prosodic patterning. Patterns of stress and intonation in speech.

proximity. In perception, the Gestalt "law of proximity" holds that stimulus objects in a visual field tend to be grouped together on the basis of their proximity.

proximodistal development. A typical pattern of development, proceeding from the center of the body out to its extremities.

psychoanalysis. Freud's approach to personality and psychotherapy, emphasizing early childhood, sexuality, and unconscious motivation.

psychological self. A relatively mature aspect of self-concept focusing on one's thought processes and belief systems as the essence of who one really is.

psychophysiological disorders. See psychosomatic disorders.

psychosexual. A term used to refer to Freud's analysis of personality development, in which each stage has a strong sexual basis.

psychosocial. A term used to distinguish Erikson's analysis of personality from Freud's more sexually oriented approach.

psychosomatic disorders. Psychosomatic and psychophysiological disorders are conditions in which the body or body functions are adversely affected by the person's emotional state.

puberty. The time in life when a person becomes able to beget or conceive children.

punishers. Stimuli that weaken behaviors or decrease their likelihood of occurrence.

pupil. The very dark center of the eye formed by an opening in the iris.

qualitative change. A developmental change in which something distinctly new appears.

quantitative change. A developmental change in which something increases or decreases in strength or frequency but nothing genuinely new appears.

random assignment. In an experiment, using chance to determine which subjects will receive which experimental condition.

rationality. Reaching and justifying conclusions by applying good reasoning.

rational rules. According to Piaget, a mature conception of rules that takes into account their social functions and rational basis.

reading. The assignment of meaning to printed symbols.

reading readiness. The state of a child's perceptual, cognitive, and psychomotor skills prior to beginning reading instruction.

reasoning. Using available information to reach conclusions.

receptor cells. In perception, receptor cells respond to specific kinds of stimulation by producing neural impulses.

recessive genes. Genes not expressed in the offspring's appearance if paired with a dominant gene.

reciprocal determinism. In Bandura's theory of observational learning, the idea that there is a continuous interchange between individuals' actions and their environments, with each affecting the other.

reciprocity. The give and take between two individuals; cooperative support.

reductionism. A theoretical approach in which phenomena are understood by reducing them to their component elements.

referent. The object, event, or characteristic to which a word refers.

rehearsal strategies. Mnemonic strategies children use for keeping information alive in short-term memory and transferring it to long-term memory.

reinforcers. Stimuli that strengthen behaviors or increase their likelihood of occurrence.

relativism. A view that all knowledge and morality are relative to one's personal or cultural perspective and thus cannot be judged against any general standard.

replacement sequences. In children's speech, the phenomenon in which sequences of words are immediately replaced by more elaborate sequences.

representation. Something that stands for something else, such as a word or mental image representing a real object.

representational intelligence. In Piaget's theory, the level of intelligence encompassing all stages beyond the sensorimotor stage. Knowing, at this level, involves mental actions on mental representations.

representative sample. A small group of individuals that accurately represents some larger group or population.

research designs. Systematic frameworks used to make comparisons in research studies.

resistant infants. A category of insecurely attached infants, resistant infants seem simultaneously to seek and resist contact with their parent and are uneasy in new situations.

resolution of conflict. Successfully bringing a disagreement to a mutually satisfactory conclusion.

retina. The light-sensitive back surface of the eye.

retrieval strategies. Mnemonic strategies aimed at retrieving information already in memory.

reversibility. In Piaget's theory, the ability to grasp the relation between opposite transformations.

rhogam. An antibody-suppressing agent given to mothers to prevent problems associated with Rh protein.

Rh protein. A protein in the blood carried by about 85 percent of the population. When the mother does not possess the Rh protein and the fetus does, antibodies may be manufactured by the mother's immune system and attack the fetus's red blood cells.

rickets. A disease caused by a deficiency of vitamin D. It can lead to softening and distortion of bones.

rods. Light-sensitive receptor cells at the back of the eye that are primarily responsible for night and peripheral vision.

rooting reflex. The rooting reflex occurs when a hungry infant's face is touched. This produces quick, jerky movements of the baby's head until its mouth is lined up with the source of stimulation.

rule assessment. An information processing approach, used especially by Siegler, in which one determines the systems of rules used for solving various tasks at several levels of cognitive development.

S_D. An S_D is a discriminative stimulus indicating that previously learned responses will be reinforced in its presence.

S_Δ. An S_Δ is a discriminative stimulus indicating that previously learned responses will not be reinforced in its presence.

schema theory. An information processing perspective that explains behavior or development in terms of schemas (specific cognitive structures) for processing information.

scheme. In Piaget's theory, a physical or mental action that one can perform on the world in order to understand it.

sclera. The outer, white part of the eye.

scurvy. A disease caused by deficiency of vitamin C. It impedes skeletal growth, causes the gums to soften and swell, and can cause pain-induced paralysis.

second-order operations. Operations performed on other operations rather than on reality itself. In Piaget's theory, a key aspect of formal operations.

securely attached infants. Infants whose attachment is such that they react positively to strangers and use their parent as a secure base from which to explore.

selection task. A widely studied task in which the subject tests a hypothesis about four cards.

self-concept. One's conception of oneself.

self-concept stage. In emotional development, the self-concept stage occurs from 18 to 36 months of age. This stage is characterized by the beginnings of the formation of the self-concept.

self-disclosure. Expression of intimate thoughts and feelings.

self-esteem. One's positive or negative evaluation of oneself.

self-reflectivity. The ability of the self to reflect on its own continuity, individuality, and free will.

self-understanding. One's cognitive understanding of one's characteristics.

semantics. The study of meanings and their relations in language.

sensitive period. In perceptual development, sensitive periods refer to times in development during which certain kinds of stimulation must occur in order for the ability to perceive such stimuli to develop.

sensorimotor stage. In Piaget's theory, the period of infancy, when knowing involves physically acting on one's environment.

sensory coordination. The ability to coordinate different senses, such as looking for the source of a sound.

sensory deprivation. Sensory deprivation is the withholding of sensory stimulation. Pure instances of sensory deprivation are extremely difficult to locate because sensory deprivation is usually linked to other forms of deprivation.

sensory registers. Components of the multistore model, hypothesized to hold incoming information briefly until it can be picked up and processed by the rest of the information processing system.

sentence. Two or more words in a structured arrangement that conveys a unit of meaning.

separation anxiety. Fear of being separated from the mother or other well-known adults.

seriation. Placing items in order, a basic cognitive ability.

seven plus or minus two. The traditional view of the upper limit on the number of items of information human beings can process at once.

sex roles. Sets of socially approved behaviors for males and females.

sex role socialization. Learning the sex roles of one's culture.

sex-typed behaviors. Behaviors commonly associated with one sex or the other.

sex-typing. Coming to see oneself as male or female.

shallow processing. Nonmeaningful, rote processing of information to be learned.

shape constancy. Understanding that the actual shape of an object does not change regardless of how the object is rotated in a visual field.

short-term storage space. The number of items of information one can process at a given time.

short-term store. In the multistore model of memory, the location in which the current contents of consciousness are stored.

siblings. Brothers or sisters.

sickle-cell anemia. An occasionally fatal blood disease caused by a recessive gene.

similarity. In perception, the Gestalt "law of similarity" holds that similar objects tend to be perceived as related.

single-parent families. Families headed by one individual.

single-subject experimentation. An experimental method in which a subject's performances under experimental conditions are compared to his or her own performances under baseline conditions.

size constancy. Understanding that although far away objects look small, the actual size of an object does not vary with distance.

social behavior. The ways in which people relate to other people.

social cognition theory. A view of behavior as determined both by environmental events and individuals' interpretation of those events.

social contract morality. In Kohlberg's theory, stage 5 of moral development, in which morality is seen as a rational agreement among individuals.

social determinants of aggression. Sources of aggression in social factors, such as upbringing or situation-specific conditions.

social development. The changes that take place from infancy to adulthood in how individuals interact.

social cognition. Knowledge about people, social relationships, and social institutions.

socialization. The transformation of a child into an acceptable member of his or her society.

social learning theory. A theory of learning associated with Albert Bandura that stresses observation and imitation of others' behavior.

social play. Play involving more than one child in mutual interaction.

social self. The aspect of self-concept involving definition of oneself in terms of one's social relationships.

social smile. A smile used by babies to convey positive feelings.

social system morality. In Kohlberg's theory, stage 4 of moral development, in which the conventions of society are seen as determining what is moral.

speciation. The process by which one species becomes two.

species. A category of organisms that represents a natural, self-reproducing group distinct from others.

speech event. The total context of a language interaction.

sperm. The cell from the father that fertilizes the ovum, providing half of the genetic material for the offspring.

spinal reflexes. Involuntary CNS responses to various stimuli carried out by the spine.

stable-order principle. The principle that, in counting, one must apply a stable, consistent list of number names.

stage. A period of development involving general characteristics distinctly different from those of earlier and later periods.

standard issue scoring. The current scoring system used in analyzing Kohlbergian moral judgment interviews.

state of knowledge. A level of cognition with respect to either performance on a specific task or a more general stage of development.

stereotypes. Inaccurate but widely held views about particular groups of people, such as males and females.

story memory. Memory for the events in a typical story.

strabismus. A condition in which the muscles controlling the eyes do not allow the eyes to line up properly.

strange situation. An experimental arrangement used by Ainsworth and others to assess attachment.

subculture. The cultural ties shared by an identifiable group, such as an ethnic or religious group, within a larger culture.

sucking reflex. The innate tendency of newborns to suck on objects placed in their mouths.

superego. In Freudian theory, the moral component of the personality.

supraspinal activities. CNS responses involving the brain.

surfactin. A liquid that allows the lungs to transmit oxygen to the blood.

symbolic word use. Children's use of words independent of context to refer to things and events other than those in their immediate experience.

sympathetic nerve fibers. Nerve fibers in the autonomic nervous system that activate body systems.

syntactic stage. The stage of language development in which children begin to produce sentences.

syntax. The structure of sentences.

synthesis. In dialectical theory, a new idea or viewpoint that resolves an earlier contradiction between thesis and antithesis.

systematic desensitization. A process for treating fears.

systematic observation. Observation in research that includes a focus on variables, representative samples, and guidance by theory.

tabula rasa (Locke). A blank slate on which experience writes: an early view of the young child proposed by the philosopher John Locke.

Tay-Sachs disease. A degenerative nerve disorder caused by a recessive gene. It is fatal within the first three to four years of life.

temperament. One's natural disposition to be active or calm, irritable or easy to please, and so on.

teratogens. Factors that cause birth defects—drugs, chemicals, radiation, bacteria, viruses.

teratophobia. An irrational fear of potential birth defects.

testosterone. The male hormone produced by the testes. Testosterone stimulates rapid maturation of the genitals.

thalamus. A part of the diencephalon that relays all sensory information except smell to the cerebrum.

the "I". In William James's analysis, the subjective self that organizes and interprets experience.

the "Me". In William James's analysis, the characteristics of the self as a physical, active, social, and psychological being.

theory. A general account that explains a set of phenomena and predicts new observations.

thesis. An idea or point of view.

time sampling. A systematic observation technique in which individuals are observed in some but not all periods.

transduction. The conversion of light energy into neural impulses.

transitive inference. An inference in which the relation of two items is deduced from the relation of each to a third item (e.g., if A is bigger than B and B is bigger than C, then A is bigger than C).

trisomy. A condition occurring when the division process in meiosis is imperfect and an ovum or a sperm is formed that does not contain the normal 23 single chromosomes but instead has 22 single chromosomes and one chromosome pair.

trust vs. mistrust. In Erikson's theory, the first stage of personality development, in which the infant develops a deep-seated positive or negative sense of the world.

twin studies. Twin studies employ identical twins in order to determine the relative effect of environment and heredity on intelligence and other characteristics.

two-parent families. Families in which both parents are present.

tympanic membrane. The eardrum.

umbilical cord. The connection between the embryo (and later, the fetus) and the placenta. The umbilical cord carries oxygen and nutrients to the embryo and carries away waste.

unilateral respect. A naive submission to authority, seen by Piaget as underlying immature morality.

universal ethical principles. Ethical principles that hold for all societies.

universality. Consistency across cultures in the direction and stages of development.

uterus. A pear-shaped organ located in the pelvic cavity of female mammals. It receives and holds the fertilized ovum during prenatal development.

utility. A moral principle that emphasizes the greatest good for the greatest number of people.

variables. In research, factors that can take on different values.

verbal aggression. Aggression involving verbal actions against others, such as shouting or sarcasm.

verbal coding. Retaining information by storing a description of the event in words or phrases.

visual constancy. The ability to see an object as the same throughout a variety of spatial transformations.

vitreous humor. A clear liquid that provides nutrients to the inner eye as well as cushioning it against shock.

voicing. Production of speech sounds with vibration of the vocal cords; some phonemes are voiced and others unvoiced.

volition. Free will.

vowels. Speech sounds produced by the speaker's letting the airstream pass freely.

Wernicke's area. The part of the cerebral cortex in which thoughts are generated.

xerophthalmia. A nutritional deficiency stemming from lack of vitamin A. It can cause permanent eye damage.

zygote. The zygote is formed when the sperm fertilizes the ovum. It carries the full complement of chromosomal materials.

Answers to Application Exercises

Application Exercise 1–1

1. Baldwin and Piaget both proposed stages of intellectual development. S. Freud proposed stages of psychosexual development and A. Freud elaborated these.
2. Rousseau saw the child as a flowering seed; the later psychologists Preyer, Hall, and Gesell took a strongly maturational approach.
3. Locke was known for his view of the child as a blank slate and behaviorists such as Watson extended this idea.
4. Baldwin, Binet, Piaget, and Vygotsky focused strongly on intellectual development, though all had other interests as well.
5. Preyer published *The Mind of the Child* in 1882. Just remember that *Preyer* was *prior* to the other developmental psychologists.
6. Locke lived in the seventeenth century and Rousseau in the eighteenth. Darwin published *The Origin of Species* in 1859, shortly before the rise of scientific psychology in the 1860s and 1870s.
7. Shinn published this classic baby biography.
8. A. Freud, extending the work of her father, became a prominent child psychoanalyst.
9. Wundt, S. Freud, A. Freud, and Watson were all psychologists but are not generally considered developmental psychologists. Notice that the entire first generation of developmentalists—Preyer, Hall, Binet, and Baldwin—were broad-ranging psychologists who contributed to a variety of areas of psychology, but the second generation—Gesell, Werner, Piaget, and Vygotsky—though also broad-ranging, are more exclusively associated with developmental psychology. Thus one can see the tendency normal in all sciences toward increasing specialization.
10. Vygotsky put the most emphasis on this subject.
11. Darwin, of course, is the biologist on the list. Of the others, Preyer, Hall, Baldwin, Gesell, and Piaget were most explicit in using biological concepts to address psychological issues.
12. Locke and Rousseau were broad-ranging philosophers and Dewey was a philosopher of education. Others on the list, especially Baldwin and Piaget, directly addressed philosophical issues but are not primarily identified with this field.

Application Exercise 1–2

1. **e.** Mini-theories/broad theories. Essentially, in this question we ask whether mini-theories are possible. The question might also be seen as raising the related issue of holism (c), however.
2. **a.** Heredity/environment. In the question we assume that children have a basic hereditary nature.
3. **d.** Directionality of development. In other words, does development move in the direction of rationality? (We address this question in detail in Chapter 12, *Development of Reasoning*.)
4. **b.** Continuity/discontinuity. The question is whether a continuous (quantitative) change can account for intellectual development in this age range.
5. **a.** Hereditary/environment. This question is about how influential one's early environment is.
6. **c.** Elementarism/holism. In the question we suggest an elementaristic approach, in which component skills are taught and then integrated, rather than a holistic approach, in which one starts directly with "pitching" as a whole.
7. **e.** Mini-theories/broad theories. This question is about the feasibility of broad theories.
8. **d.** Directionality of development. In the question we raise the issue of whether Werner's conception of development is broad enough to include all the sorts of changes we intuitively feel are "developmental."
9. **c.** Elementarism/holism. An elementaristic view would suggest they are still the same perceptions, though perhaps combined differently, whereas a holistic view would suggest that because the perceptions reflect the new whole, they are now different perceptions.
10. **a.** Heredity/environment. With this question we address the roles of heredity and environment.
11. **b.** Continuity/discontinuity. In other words, is intellectual development discontinuous?
12. **b.** Continuity/discontinuity. To say children are essentially small adults implies that development is a matter of continuous, quantitative change rather than discontinuous, qualitative change.

Application Exercise 2–1

1. Developmental. Developmentalists emphasize universal sequences of development.
2. Learning. The emphasis here is on an active environment that gradually changes the child.
3. Dialectical. All psychologists would agree with this statement, but dialecticians put most emphasis on this sort of continuing interaction and make it a focus of their research and theorizing.
4. Dialectical. Again, most psychologists would agree that cultures may differ on what constitutes intelligence, but dialecticians emphasize most the cultural context of basic matters such as intelligence.
5. Learning. We can see an elementaristic approach here in the effort to understand memory by breaking it into component operations and carefully analyzing each operation.

6. Learning. All psychologists would agree that a child's ideas about sex roles (or anything else) may change as her environment changes. But a learning theorist would most emphasize the extent to which those changes directly reflect what she experiences.
7. Developmental. We see here the developmental emphasis on internally driven construction of new conceptions. A dialectician would have a similar view but would also emphasize the environment.
8. All three. Some psychologists are more oriented toward theory and some toward data, but all acknowledge that both are vital to scientific progress.
9. Developmental. We see here the idea of a general stage of development that is reflected in and thus can be inferred from specific behaviors.
10. Dialectical. The emphasis is not on any universal pattern of development (which would interest a developmentalist) but rather on a specific contradiction leading to a novel synthesis.
11. None. Though psychologists differ in the extent to which they emphasize the environment, all agree that it is very important.
12. Developmental. Neither learning nor dialectical theorists are comfortable with the idea of universal stages that are "natural" to the human species.
13. Learning. The emphasis here is that the observed environment impresses itself on our minds. Developmental theorists would see this attitude as downplaying knowledge that is either innate or self-constructed. Dialectical theorists would likewise be uncomfortable with the overemphasis on the environment.

Application Exercise 3–1

1. **d.** Correlational method. The intent here is to determine the degree of *association* among these variables. For example, do children from larger families have greater knowledge of kinship concepts? Do intelligent children have greater knowledge of kinship concepts?.
2. **f.** Group-based experimental method. Comparing two groups—an experimental and a control—is the classic experimental comparison. Of course, many experimental studies are far more complex, involving several groups, numerous conditions per group, and multiple measures of outcomes.
3. **a.** Case-study method. One child is intensively studied as the researcher attempts to build an in-depth model of how the child's knowledge is developing in this area.
4. **b.** Naturalistic observation method. The researcher does not intrude on the "natural" setting, but instead (by intensive observation) attempts to determine how children become friends.
5. **e.** Single subject experimental method. This example has the key elements of the single subject experiment: (1) focus on one subject; (2) focus on a specific behavior (oral reading rate); (3) observation of the behavior during a baseline period (the teacher secretly keeping a record of oral reading rate); and (4) an intervention (keeping a chart), in which the behavior continues to be recorded and, in fact, is improved.
6. **c.** Interview method. Specific questions are posed orally by the experimenter in this cross-cultural comparison. Responses to the questions are then compared across the national groups.

Application Exercise 4–1

1. Probably genetic. Thomas and Chess (1977) observed basic differences in temperament among infants. Rachel's actions fit within the definition of "easy babies."
2. Probably genetic. Baby Sam seems to have a basic temperament that fits what Thomas and Chess referred to as "difficult."
3. Probably environmental. A change such as this is probably due to an improved environment provided by the teacher.
4. The response to this item depends on which perspective you take. The general similarity in the measured levels of intelligence in the twins is probably due to genetic factors. Because the IQ scores differ more than we would expect of twins reared together, however, one could suppose that the difference probably results from environmental factors.
5. Probably environmental. Although we have basic genetic predispositions toward different weights, Angela is heavy because of her eating habits.
6. Probably environmental. Despite genetically based differences in infants' temperaments, parents can overcome the tendencies of "difficult" babies by carefully structuring their interactions with them.
7. This is our trick item in this set. No evidence in the literature seems to support genetic tendencies toward stubbornness, but the possibility is always there. More likely, Monica's stubbornness was learned from her parents and is thus environmental.
8. Probably environmental. The literature seems devoid of evidence substantiating innate tendencies among children toward thumb sucking and needing special blankets or dolls.

Application Exercise 4–2

1. Yes. PKU is a recessive gene disorder. Rodney may very well carry a recessive gene for PKU.
2. Yes. Women thirty-five and older are at somewhat greater risk than younger women for meiotic disorders.
3. No. Meningitis, whether bacterial or viral, is not genetic.
4. Yes. Mothers who have had spontaneous abortions are at high risk.
5. Yes. Related individuals run a higher than average risk of conceiving children with chromosomal damage.
6. Yes. Despite having had healthy babies, Mona's age indicates potential value for amniocentesis.
7. No. Although some have argued that XYY males are more prone to high levels of violence than other males, no evidence says that heredity is in any way related to the behavior of Andrew's brother.
8. Yes. Sickle-cell anemia is a dangerous gene disorder.
9. No. Malaria is not genetic.
10. Yes. Molly is a high-risk mother.

Application Exercise 5–1

1. a. Mesosystem. Rachel's parents are strengthening links between two microsystems: home and school. The two settings together and the links between them form a mesosystem.

2. **d.** Macrosystem. Roger's experiences in Indonesia all reflect the broad influence of the cultural context of that country.
3. **a.** Microsystem. A child and his babysitter form a microsystem.
4. **d.** Macrosystem. This is a general cultural effect that directly affects her. Popular music is likely to be heard in many settings and to influence the development of children's musical tastes.
5. **b.** Mesosystem. Jonas's mother is attempting to establish supportive links between two microsystems—home and preschool—in order to facilitate the transition from one to the other.
6. **c.** Exosystem. Andy has no awareness of his father's job, but it nonetheless affects important aspects of how he and his father will interact.
7. **a.** Microsystem. Lynette has found a new microsystem, for which her activities in drama provide the context.
8. **a.** Microsystem. Living with peers in a residence hall is a new sort of microsystem for many college students.
9. **b.** Mesosystem. For many students, both academic and family microsystems are enriched by establishing links between them. "Parents' days" are ways both of familiarizing parents with the academic world and vice versa.
10. **c.** Exosystem. School boards are systems that influence lives of countless children, even though most children have little, if any, knowledge about them.

Application Exercise 6–1

1. It is hard to say what effect diet pills may have on Robyn's fetus. No drug should ever be consumed during pregnancy, however, unless prescribed by a physician. The only effects here would be negative.
2. Although the research results are still preliminary, it is possible that Alex's drinking will contribute to a high-risk pregnancy. Alex would be well advised to abstain from alcohol.
3. Ellen is running the risk of a calcium deficiency in her child and in her own system. If she simply cannot consume milk products, she should talk to her physician about a dietary supplement in tablet form.
4. Mimi's age, seventeen, places her in the category of high-risk pregnancies.
5. Emotional stress is associated with high-risk pregnancies. Amy should seek professional help in working through the emotional trauma.
6. Andrea may or may not have a problem. First, it is not clear whether or not Andrea will contract the disease. Second, if she does contract measles, it may not occur during a critical period. In any event, Andrea's dilemma accentuates the need to be immunized against the disease.
7. If Nancy's baby is Rh positive, there may be a problem; Rh incompatibility is not typically encountered, however, until the second pregnancy and may be avoided by using rhogam.
8. If Laura continues her smoking, she may cause problems for the fetus. She should stop smoking.

Application Exercise 7–1

1. cerebral cortex
2. cerebral cortex

3. medulla
4. hypothalamus
5. spinal cord
6. medulla
7. cerebellum
8. Broca's area of the cerebral cortex
9. thalamus
10. midbrain

Application Exercise 8–1

1. Siegler
2. None of the four. Neither Piagetians nor information-processing researchers take this behaviorist approach to psychology. All hypothesize about cognitive structures and processes.
3. Case
4. Piaget. This is Piaget's idea of genetic (developmental) epistemology.
5. Sternberg
6. Piaget. Information-processing theorists do not generally disagree with this view, but this is Piaget's way of putting it.
7. All four. Piagetian and information-processing researchers express this idea in various ways, but it is vital to all of them.
8. Piaget
9. All four
10. None of the four. The four major theorists discussed in this chapter agree that knowledge is learned or constructed during interaction with the environment.
11. Sternberg
12. Case. Siegler and Sternberg do use Piagetian tasks and concepts, but only Case has tried to systematically synthesize Piaget's theory with information-processing conceptions.
13. Siegler
14. Piaget
15. Sternberg

Application Exercise 10–1

1. Knowing how to know. The girl shows clear signs of using memory strategies, albeit simple ones, by looking at her two friends and by saying the names to herself. Both strategies are likely to improve recall.
2. Knowing. Part of this girl's remarkable recall is due to her great familiarity with the items. This knowledge makes it easier for her to remember items than it would be if she were not so familiar with them.
3. Knowing how to know. The child interrupts his concentration by calling to the cat, indicating that he probably is not using any strategy to try to recall the information.
4. Knowing about knowing. In his statement, "I just don't get this stuff," the student shows clear indications of metamemory: he is clearly aware that his studying is getting him nowhere. Whether he will be able to take

advantage of what he knows and find an effective mnemonic strategy remains to be seen.
5. Knowing. This boy knows a great deal about needlepoint from his experience. His knowledge is the basis for his excellent memory about the prize winners and their work.
6. Knowing how to know. The older children's grouping of items is strong evidence for knowing how to know. They use the categories to aid their recall. The younger children do not seem to have developed the ability to use categorization in memory tasks.
7. Knowing how to know. Although we might find the categories a bit amusing, this child does have some categorization scheme and shows that he is using it to recall as he counts within each successive category.
8. Knowing about knowing. This example shows childrens' awareness of the need to remember. The afternoon class is able to ask more questions and remember more when told to remember, indicating that they are alert to some aspects of how to direct their memory.
9. Knowing about knowing. This too indicates a form of metamemory, diagnosing the task requirements. Because of her belief that some information will be tested, she concentrates her efforts on these areas.

Application Exercise 11–1

1. Morphemes. By adding *two* plural forms to the same word, this child clearly shows awareness of grammatical endings. Sometimes use of such endings is overgeneralized in the early stages of learning to use them.
2. Syntax. Children reach the syntactic stage when they begin to combine words. As stated in the chapter, correct word orders in early sentences seldom are violated.
3. Pragmatics. An indirect request such as this shows sophisticated pragmatic knowledge. Language is used pragmatically in trying to reach the goal of getting some cookie dough.
4. Phones. The baby is creating a wide range of sounds, but they are unconnected to any language. Babbling is phonetic but not phonemic.
5. Syntax. Children need to learn to comprehend the more complex forms of syntax. Whereas older children can unravel complicated expressions, younger ones cannot, as in this case, in which the younger child believes that Jodie bit the dog.
6. Semantics. "Rona" is a word with several meanings; word meaning is the realm of semantics.
7. Phones. The linguist has transcribed only the *sounds* of the Hopi language, not their meaning.
8. Phonemes. The difference between *d* and the *t* in *bad* and *bat* is a phonemic distinction in English. That is, the *d* and *t* are critical to understanding the meanings of these two words.

Application Exercise 11–2

1. Noam Chomsky. Key ideas referred to (1980, p. 35) are the discussion of a genetically determined language faculty determining the acquisition of

grammar. Acquisition occurs, says Chomsky, with minimal external stimulation.
2. Lev Vygotsky. The interactionist position of Vygotsky is evident in the statement about how thought affects language and vice versa (1962, p. 125).
3. Jean Piaget. Sensorimotor intelligence is seen as the key—creating the context in which language can exist (1980, p. 167).
4. Benjamin Whorf. In this statement (1952a, p. 21), Whorf clearly states his view that language is the framework through which the experience of the world can be understood.
5. Benjamin Whorf. Whorf amplifies his ideas about language affecting thought in this quotation. Thinking is seen as "following the network of tracks laid down by a given language" (1952b, p. 177).
6. Lev Vygotsky. In his *Thought and Language* (1962, p. 135), Vygotsky offers his view of egocentric speech: that it increasingly shows a child's ability to "think words" instead of pronouncing them.
7. Noam Chomsky. Here Chomsky says (1980, p. 313) that grammars are "built in" to the human brain and that language and communication are based on this built-in characteristic of the brain.
8. Jean Piaget. In his famous 1980 "debate" with Noam Chomsky, Piaget (1980, p. 167) clearly outlines his view that language is secondary to thought: "the formation of the symbolic function . . . allows the acquisition of language."

Application Exercise 12–1

1. Isolation of variables. Study technique is varied, whereas age and intelligence are held constant.
2. Transitive inference. This has the form A > B; B > C. Therefore, A > C.
3. Absolutism. This response shows naive belief in absolute truth and unquestioning reliance on authority.
4. Failure to apply falsification strategy. No matter how many cases we find that fit the hypothesis, we have not really tested it, for we are seeking information in such a way that falsification is highly unlikely.
5. Logical necessity. It follows from the premises that all Eps *must* be Bleps, and so there cannot be one that is not.
6. Metacognition. This suggests the value of actively thinking about one's problem-solving.
7. Order-irrelevance and one-one principles of counting. The order in which one counts each point does not matter, but it is critical to keep track of where one started so that each point is counted once and only once.
8. Relativism. Reasoning is seen as completely personal. There are no general standards.
9. Validity. The first argument reaches a true conclusion and the second a false conclusion. But both arguments have the same logical form and are equally valid in that each conclusion follows from the given premises.
10. Falsification strategy. Nonflying Ips are directly relevant, because if any can be found the hypothesis that all Ips fly will be falsified.

Application Exercise 14–1

1. **a.** Securely attached. Both securely attached and resistant infants are distressed on separation from their caregivers. Whereas securely attached babies are easily comforted on reunion, however, resistant infants are not.
2. **b.** Avoidant. Avoidant infants show little preference for caregivers over strangers, and they can be comforted just as easily by either.
3. **b.** Avoidant. *Gaze aversion* (looking away) in a situation like this is a common reaction of many infants to strangers but an uncommon one to mothers. It is seen almost entirely in avoidant infants. It differs, of course, from the reflexive head-turning seen in newborns.
4. **c.** Resistant. Resistant infants have great difficulty in separating from their caregivers to explore. They are often wary of novel situations.
5. **c.** Resistant. The simultaneous distress on separation, inability to be comforted, and anger on reunion are key characteristics of resistant infants.
6. **a.** Securely attached. More than either avoidant or resistant infants, securely attached babies seem to feel confident in exploring their world, using the caregiver as a secure base for this exploration.
7. **c.** Resistant. Excessive wariness of strangers, even when a caregiver is present, is a quality of resistant infants. In contrast, avoidant infants are not particularly anxious around strangers, whereas securely attached infants are reasonably comfortable with strangers when the caregiver is present.
8. **a.** Securely attached. Comforting *is* a comfort to securely attached babies. Contact with the caregiver is almost always effective in terminating distress.

Application Exercise 15–1

1. Stage 2. There is enough insight into others to see that doing good may be to one's own eventual advantage, but the morality is strictly tit-for-tat.
2. Stage 5. This clearly shows a prior-to-society perspective. Laws may violate rational principles of justice and, when they do, should be resisted and, ultimately, changed.
3. Stage 4. We see here stage 4 respect for the present social structure and commitment to preserving it.
4. Stage 4. Commitment to the social system takes the form of insisting on the importance of fulfilling abstract societal roles, regardless of personal feelings.
5. Stage 3. Again we see an emphasis on fulfilling one's role, but the roles now relate to immediate relationships.
6. Stage 5. This is the First Amendment to the U.S. Constitution. It shows a stage 5 perspective in specifying that Congress may not pass laws that violate fundamental rights of individuals, even if the majority supports those laws.
7. Stage 1. An example of moral realism. Nothing in this statement indicates more than the idea that murder is wrong because it is wrong. Of course, one should ask the person *why* it is wrong. If the reasoning is really stage

1, the person will have little more to say, failing to grasp the need for further justification.
8. Stage 2. This shows some degree of perspective-taking and thus goes beyond stage 1 but fails to show more abstract considerations of relationships (stage 3), social structure (stage 4), or social contract (stage 5).
9. Stage 3. The immorality is seen in the betrayal of the relationship.
10. Stage 2. Though an intimate relationship is at stake here, the rationale is based not on the relationship itself but on a more primitive tit-for-tat: I don't embarrass you and you don't embarrass me.
11. Stage 1. We see here a heteronomous respect for authority.
12. Stage 3. This shows a true conventional morality. The motivation to be helpful is not based simply on expectation of getting some return from the other person (as in stage 2). There is a genuine desire to be a good person who helps others. On the other hand, there is still no general grasp of social structure (stage 4) or social contract (stage 5) as a reason for moral behavior.

Application Exercise 16–1
1. Identity diffused. George lacks commitments and is not actively trying to do anything about this situation.
2. Foreclosed. Martha has moral, political, and vocational commitments that directly reflect parental and other childhood influences.
3. Moratorium. Jacob is actively trying to establish the commitments that he realizes he does not have.
4. Identity achieved. Rachel has self-determined religious and vocational commitments that reflect an earlier moratorium period.
5. Moratorium. George has no vocational commitment and senses ideological conflicts in his social and political views. His awareness of conflict and his interest in establishing commitments reveal him to be in a period of identity crisis.
6. Identity achieved. Martha has established political and vocational commitments. Her political commitment is apparently not a foreclosure, for it is a personal choice that goes against her parents' views. Although her vocational commitment is unchanged, it is now self-chosen rather than externally dictated.
7. Identity achieved. Jacob, after a period of searching, has made a commitment to a life-style and vocation.
8. Moratorium. Although Rachel has not given up all her commitments, she is aware of conflicts among them and of the resulting need to rethink major aspects of her identity. Thus, she is moving, at least partially, into a renewed identity crisis. This is not necessarily a step backward, because it may lead ultimately to a stronger, more coherent identity.

References

Aantaa, E. (1970). Light-induced and spontaneous variations in the amplitude of the electro-oculogram. *Acta Oto-Laryngolica, Supplementum, 267,* 114–126.

Abel, E. L. (1980). Fetal alcohol syndrome: Behavioral teratology. *Psychological Bulletin, 87,* 29–50.

Abramovitch, R., Pepler, D., & Corter, C. (1982). Patterns of sibling interaction among preschool children. In M. E. Lamb & B. Sutton-Smith (Eds.), *Sibling relationships: Their nature and significance across the lifespan.* Hillsdale, NJ: Erlbaum.

Achenbach, T. M. (1978). *Research in developmental psychology: Concepts, strategies, methods.* New York: Free Press.

Acheson, R. M. (1960). Effects of nutrition and disease on human growth. In J. M. Tanner (Ed.), *Human growth.* New York: Pergamon Press.

Acredolo, L. P., Pick, H. L., Jr., & Olsen, M. G. (1975). Environmental differentiation and familiarity as determinants of children's memory for spatial location. *Developmental Psychology, 11,* 495–501.

Ahlstrom, W. M., & Havighurst, R. J. (1971). *400 losers.* San Francisco: Jossey-Bass.

Ainsworth, M. D. (1967). *Infancy in Uganda: Infant care and the growth of love.* Baltimore: Johns Hopkins University Press.

Ainsworth, M. D. (1978). Infant-mother attachment. In M. Richards (Ed.), *The child's integration into the social world.* New York: Cambridge University Press.

Ainsworth, M. D. (1982). The development of infant-mother attachment. In J. Belsky (Ed.), *In the beginning: Readings on infancy* (pp. 135–143). New York: Columbia University Press.

Ainsworth, M. D., & Bell, S. M. (1969). Some contemporary patterns of mother-infant interaction in the feeding situation. In A. Ambrose (Ed.), *Stimulation in early infancy.* New York: Academic Press.

Ainsworth, M. D., Bell, S. M., & Stayton, D. J. (1971). In H. R. Schaffer (Ed.), *The origins of human social relations.* London: Academic Press.

Ainsworth, M. D., Blehar, M. C., Waters, E., & Wall, S. (1978). *Patterns of attachment.* Hillsdale, NJ: Erlbaum.

Alan Guttmacher Institute (1983). *Issues in brief* (Vol. 3, No. 3). Washington, DC: Author.

REFERENCES

Alan Guttmacher Institute (1984). *Issues in brief* (Vol. 4, No. 2). Washington, DC: Author.

Alan Guttmacher Institute (1985). *Issues in brief* (Vol. 5, No. 4). Washington, DC: Author.

Allaby, M., & Lovelock, J. (1983). *The great extinction: The solution to one of the great mysteries of science: The disappearance of the dinosaurs.* New York: Doubleday.

Allport, G. W. (1962). The general and the unique in psychological science. *Journal of Personality, 30,* 405–422.

American Psychiatric Association. (1980). *Diagnostic and statistical manual of mental disorders* (3rd ed.) (*DSM*-III). Washington, DC: Author.

American Psychological Association. (1982). *Ethical principles in the conduct of research with human participants.* Washington, DC: Author.

Anderson, J. R. (1980). *Cognitive psychology and its implications.* San Francisco: Freeman.

Anderson, R. C., & Ortony, A. (1975). On putting apples into bottles—A problem of polysemy. *Cognitive Psychology, 1,* 167–180.

Anisfeld, M. (1984). *Language development from birth to three.* Hillsdale, NJ: Erlbaum.

Annis, L. F. (1978). *The child before birth.* Ithaca, NY: Cornell University Press.

Apgar, V. (1953). A proposal for a new method of evaluation in the newborn infant. *Current Research in Anesthesia and Analgesia, 32,* 260.

Aries, P. (1962). *Centuries of childhood: A social history of family life.* New York: Vintage.

Aslin, R. N., Pisoni, D. B., & Jusczyk, P. W. (1983). Auditory development and speech perception in infancy. In M. M. Haith and J. J. Campos (Eds.), P. H. Mussen (Series Ed.), *Handbook of child psychology: Vol. 2. Infancy and developmental psychobiology* (pp. 573–687). New York: Wiley.

Atkinson, R. C., & Shiffrin, R. M. (1968). Human memory: A proposed system and its control processes. In K.W. Spence & J. T. Spence (Eds.), *The psychology of learning and motivation: Advances in research and theory* (Vol. 2). New York: Academic Press.

Atkinson, R. C., & Shiffrin, R. M. (1971). The control of short-term memory. *Scientific American, 225,* 82–90.

Auble, P. M., & Franks, J. J. (1978). The effect of effort toward comprehension on recall. *Memory and Cognition, 6,* 20–25.

Auble, P. M., Franks, J. J., & Soraci, S. S. (1979). Effort toward elaboration: Elaboration or "aha!"? *Memory and Cognition, 7,* 426–434.

Averbach, E., & Coriell, A. S. (1961). Short-term memory in vision. *Bell System Technical Journal, 40,* 309–328.

Ayala, F. J., & Valentine, J. W. (1979). *Evolving: The theory and processes of organic evolution.* Menlo Park, CA: Benjamin/Cummings Publishing Company.

Bachman, J. F., Johnston L. D., & O'Malley, P. M. (1980). *Monitoring the Future: Questionnaire responses from the nation's high school seniors.* Ann Arbor, MI: Institute for Social Research.

Baddeley, A. D. (1978). The trouble with levels: A reexamination of Craik and Lockhart's framework for memory research. *Psychological Review, 85,* 139–152.

Baker-Ward, L., Ornstein, P. A., & Holden, D. J. (1984). The expression of memorization in early childhood. *Journal of Experimental Child Psychology, 37,* 555–575.

Baldwin, J. M. (1985). *Mental development in the child and the race: Methods and processes.* New York: Macmillan.

Baltes, P. B. (1968). Longitudinal and cross-sectional sequences in the study of age and generation effects. *Human Development, 11,* 145–171.

Baltes, P. B., Cornelius, S. W., & Nesselroade, J. R. (1979). Cohort effects in developmental psychology. In J. R. Nesselroade & P. B. Baltes (Eds.), *Longitudinal research in the study of behavior and development.* New York: Academic Press.

Bandura, A. (1977). *Social learning theory.* Englewood Cliffs, NJ: Prentice-Hall.

Bandura, A. (1978). The self system in reciprocal determinism. *American Psychologist, 33,* 344–358.

Banks, M. S., Aslin, R. N., & Letson, R. D. (1975). Sensitive period for the development of human binocular vision. *Science, 190,* 675–677.

Banks, M. S., & Salapatek, P. (1983). Infant visual perception. In M. M. Haith and J. J. Campos (Eds.), P. H. Mussen (Series Ed.), *Handbook of child psychology: Vol. 2. Infancy and developmental psychobiology* (pp. 435–572). New York: Wiley.

Barcus, F. E. (1983). *Images of life on children's television: Sex roles, minorities, and families.* New York: Praeger.

Barker, R. G., & Wright, H. F. (1951). *One boy's day.* New York: Harper.

Barkley, R. A. (1983). Hyperactivity. In R. Morris & T. R. Kratochwill (Eds.), *The practice of child therapy.* New York: Pergamon.

Barrera, M. E., Rosenbaum, P. L., & Cunningham, C. E. (1986). Early home intervention with low birth-weight infants and their parents. *Child Development, 57,* 20–33.

Bartlett, F. C. (1932). *Remembering.* Cambridge: Cambridge University Press.

Basseches, M. (1985). *Dialectical thinking and adult development.* Norwood, NJ: Ablex.

Bates, E. (1976). *Language and context: The acquisition of pragmatics.* New York: Academic Press.

Bates, E., & MacWhinney, B. (1979). A functionalist approach to the acquisition of grammar. In E. Kennan (Ed.), *Developmental pragmatics.* New York: Academic Press.

Bates, J. E. (1980). The concept of difficult temperament. *Merrill-Palmer Quarterly, 26,* 299–319.

Bauer, D. H. (1976). An exploratory study of developmental changes in children's fears. *Journal of Child Psychology and Psychiatry, 17,* 69–74.

Baumrind, D. (1967). Child care practices anteceding 3 patterns of preschool behavior. *Genetic Psychology Monographs, 75,* 43–88.

Baumrind, D. (1971). Current patterns of parental authority. *Developmental Psychology Monographs, 4*(1, Pt. 2).

Baumrind, D. (1986). Sex differences in moral reasoning: Response to Walker's (1984) conclusion that there are none. *Child Development, 57,* 511–521.

Bayley, N. (1956). Individual patterns of development. *Child Development, 27,* 45–74.

Bayley, N. (1969). *Manual for the Bayley scales of infant development.* New York: The Psychological Corp.

Beall, P., & Nipp, S. (1983). *Wee sing silly songs.* Los Angeles: Price/Stern/Sloan Publishers.

Beardslee, W. R., & Mack, J. E. (1986, Winter). Youth and children and the nuclear threat. *Newsletter of the Society for Research in Child Development,* 1–2.

Bearison, D. J., Magzamen, S., & Filardo, E. K. (1986). Socio-cognitive conflict and cognitive growth in young children. *Merrill-Palmer Quarterly, 32,* 51–72.

Becker, W. C. (1964). Consequences of different kinds of parental discipline. In M. L. Hoffman & L. W. Hoffman (Eds.), *Review of child development research* (Vol. 1). New York: Russell Sage Foundation.

Bell, R. Q., & Harper, L. V. (1977). *Child effects on adults.* Hillsdale, NJ: Erlbaum.

Belsky, J. (1979). Mother-father-infant interaction: A naturalistic observational study. *Developmental Psychology, 15,* 601–609.

Bem, S. L. (1981). Gender schema theory: A cognitive account of sex typing. *Psychological Review, 88,* 354–364.

Benbow, C. P., & Stanley, J. C. (1980). Sex differences in mathematical ability: Fact or artifact? *Science, 210,* 1262–1264.

Benton, S. L., Glover, J. A., & Bruning, R. H. (1983). The effect of number of decisions on prose recall. *Journal of Educational Psychology, 75,* 382–390.

Bereiter, C., Hidi, S., & Dimitroff, C. (1979). Qualitative changes in verbal reasoning during middle and late childhood. *Child Development, 50,* 142–151.

Berkowitz, M. W. (Ed.) (1985). *Peer conflict and psychological growth.* San Francisco: Jossey-Bass.

Berkowitz, M. W., & Gibbs, J. C. (1983). Measuring the developmental features of moral discussion. *Merrill-Palmer Quarterly, 29,* 399–410.

Berkowitz, M. W., & Oser, F. (1985). *Moral education: Theory and application.* Hillsdale, NJ: Erlbaum.

Berne, R. M. (1983). *Annual review of physiology* (Vol. 45). Palo Alto, CA: Annual Reviews, Inc.

Bevan, J. (1983). *The Simon and Schuster handbook of anatomy and physiology.* New York: Simon and Schuster.

Bigelow, A. E. (1983). Development of the use of sound in the search behavior of infants. *Developmental Psychology, 19,* 317–321.

Binet, A. (1903). *L'étude experimentale de l'intelligence.* Paris: Schleicher.

Bisanz, G. L., Vesonder, G. T., & Voss, J. F. (1978). Knowledge of one's own responding and the relation of such knowledge to learning. *Journal of Experimental Child Psychology, 25,* 116–128.

Bjorklund, D. F., Ornstein, P. A., & Haig, J. R. (1977). Developmental differences in organization and recall: Training in the use of organization techniques. *Developmental Psychology, 13,* 175–183.

Blasi, A. (1980). Bridging moral cognition and moral action: A critical review of the literature. *Psychological Bulletin, 88,* 1–45.

Blasi, A. (1983). Moral cognition and moral action: A theoretical perspective. *Developmental Review, 3,* 178–210.

Blasi, A. (1984). Moral identity: Its role in moral functioning. In W. M. Kurtines & J. L. Gewirtz (Eds.), *Morality, moral behavior, and moral development* (pp. 128–139). New York: Wiley.

Blatt, M., & Kohlberg, L. (1975). The effects of classroom moral discussion upon children's level of moral judgment. *Journal of Moral Education, 4,* 129–161.

Block, J. H. (1978). Another look at sex differentiation in the socialization behaviors of mothers and fathers. In J. Sherman & F. L. Denmark (Eds.), *The psychology of women: Future directions of research*. New York:Psychological Dimensions.

Bloom, L. (1970). *Language development: Form and function in emerging grammars*. Cambridge, MA: MIT Press.

Bloom, L. (1973). *One word at a time: The use of single word utterances before syntax*. New York: Humanities Press.

Bloom, L., Lightbown, P., & Hood, L. (1975). Structure and variation in child language. *Monographs of the Society for Research in Child Development, 40*(2, Serial No. 260).

Boehm, C. D., Antonarakis, S. E., Phillips, J. A., Stetton, G., & Kazazian, H. H. (1983). Prenatal diagnosis using DNA polymorphisms: Report on 95 pregnancies at risk for sickle-cell disease or B thalassemia. *New England Journal of Medicine, 308*, 1054–1058.

Borman, K. M. (1982). *The social life of children in a changing society*. Hillsdale, NJ: Erlbaum.

Bornstein, M. H. (1975). Qualities of color vision in infancy. *Journal of Experimental Child Psychology, 19*, 401–419.

Bornstein, M. H. (1984). Perceptual development. In M. H. Bornstein and M. E. Lamb (Eds.), *Developmental psychology: An advanced textbook*. Hillsdale, NJ: Erlbaum, pp. 81–131.

Borstelmann, L. J. (1983). Children before psychology: Ideas about children from antiquity to the late 1800s. In W. Kessen (Ed.), P. H. Mussen (Series Ed.), *Handbook of child psychology: Vol. 1. History, theory and methods* (pp. 1–40). New York: Wiley.

Bousfield, W. A. (1953). The occurrence of clustering in the recall of randomly arranged associates. *Journal of General Psychology, 49*, 229–240.

Bower, T. G. R. (1966). The visual world of infants. *Scientific American, 215*, 80–92.

Bower, T. G. R. (1971). The object in the world of the infant. *Scientific American, 225*, 30–38.

Bower, T. G. R. (1977). *A primer on infant development*. San Francisco: Freeman.

Bower, T. G. R. (1979). *Human development*. San Francisco: Freeman.

Bowerman, M. (1978). Systematizing semantic knowledge: Changes over time in the child's organization of word meaning. *Child Development, 49*, 977–987.

Bowlby, J. (1951). *Maternal care and mental health*. Geneva: World Health Organization.

Bowlby, J. (1969/1982). *Attachment and loss: Vol. 1. Attachment*. New York: Basic Books.

Bowlby, J. (1973). *Attachment and loss: Vol. 2. Separation*. New York: Basic Books.

Bowlby, J. (1983). *Attachment and loss: Vol. 3. Loss, sadness and depression*. New York: Basic Books.

Boyd, D. R. (1984). The principle of principles. In W. M. Kurtines & J. L. Gewirtz (Eds.), *Morality, moral behavior, and moral development* (pp. 365–380). New York: Wiley.

Brabeck, M. (1983). Moral judgment: Theory and research on differences between males and females. *Developmental Review, 3*, 274–291.

Braine, M. D. S. (1971). The acquisition of language in infant and child. In C. E. Reed (Ed.), *The learning of language*. New York: Appleton-Century-Crofts.

Braine, M. D. S. (1976). Children's first word combinations. *Monographs of the Society for Research in Child Development, 41*(1, Serial No. 164).

Braine, M. D. S., & Rumain, B. (1983). Logical reasoning. In J. H. Flavell & E. M. Markman (Eds.), P. H. Mussen (Series Ed.), *Handbook of child psychology: Vol. 3. Cognitive development* (pp. 263–340). New York: Wiley.

Brainerd, C. J., & Kingma, J. (1984). Do children have to remember to reason? A fuzzy-trace theory of transitivity development. *Developmental Review, 4,* 311–377.

Brainerd, C. J., & Pressley, M. (Eds.) (1985). *Basic processes in memory development*. New York: Springer-Verlag.

Bransford, J. D., Barclay, J. R., & Franks, J. J. (1972). Sentence memory: A constructive versus interpretive approach. *Cognitive Psychology, 3,* 193–209.

Bray, N. W., Hersh, R. E., & Turner, L. A. (1985). Selective remembering in adolescence. *Developmental Psychology, 21,* 290–294.

Brazelton, T. B. (1983). Precursors for the development of emotions in early infancy. In R. Plutchik & H. Kellerman (Eds.), *Emotion: Theory, research, and experience* (Vol. 2). New York: Academic Press.

Breslow, L. (1981). Reevaluation of the literature on the development of transitive inferences. *Psychological Bulletin, 89,* 325–351.

Bretherton, I., & Waters, E. (Eds.) (1985). Growing points of attachment theory and research. *Monographs of the Society for Research in Child Development, 50*(1–2, Serial No. 209).

Bridgeman, D. L. (Ed.) (1983). *The nature of prosocial development: Interdisciplinary theories and strategies*. New York: Academic Press.

Bridges, K. M. B. (1932). Emotional development in early infancy. *Child Development, 3,* 324–341.

Brimblecombe, F., & Barltrop, D. (1978). *Children in health and disease* (formerly Patterson's sick children). London: Bailliere Tindall.

Bronfenbrenner, U. (1979). *The ecology of human development*. Cambridge, MA: Harvard University Press.

Bronson, W. (1975). Peer-peer interactions in the second year of life. In M. Lewis & L. A. Rosenblum (Eds.), *Friendship and peer relations*. New York: Wiley.

Bronson, W. (1981). *Toddlers' behavior with agemates: Issues of interaction, cognition, and affect*. Norwood, NJ: Ablex.

Brooks-Gunn, J., & Lewis, M. (1984). The development of early visual self-recognition. *Developmental Review, 4,* 215–239.

Brooks-Gunn, J., & Petersen, A. C. (1983). *Girls at puberty: Biological and psychosocial perspectives*. New York: Plenum.

Broughton, J. M. (1978). Development of concepts of self, mind, reality, and knowledge. In W. Damon (Ed.), *Social cognition* (pp. 75–100). San Francisco: Jossey-Bass.

Broughton, J. M. (1983). Women's rationality and men's virtues: A critique of gender dualism in Gilligan's theory of moral development. *Social Research, 50,* 597–642.

Broughton, J. M., & Freeman-Moir, D. J. (Eds.) (1982). *The cognitive-developmental psychology of James Mark Baldwin: Current theory and research in genetic epistemology.* Norwood, NJ: Ablex.

Brown, A. L. (1975). The development of memory: Knowing, knowing about knowing, and knowing how to know. In H. W. Reese (Ed.), *Advances in child development and behavior* (Vol. 10). New York: Academic Press.

Brown, A. L., Bransford, J. D., Ferrara, R. A., & Campione, J. C. (1983). Learning, remembering, and understanding. In J. H. Flavell & E. M. Markman (Eds.), P. H. Mussen (Series Ed.), *Handbook of child psychology: Vol. 3. Cognitive development* (pp. 263–340). New York: Wiley.

Brown, A. L., & DeLoache, J. S. (1978). Skills, plans and self-regulation. In R. S. Siegler (Ed.), *Children's thinking: What develops?* Hillsdale, NJ: Erlbaum.

Brown, F. G. (1983). *Principles of educational and psychological testing.* New York: Holt, Rinehart & Winston.

Brown, R. (1965). *Social Psychology.* New York: Free Press.

Brown, R. (1973). *A first language: The early stages.* Cambridge, MA: Harvard University Press.

Brown, R., & Bellugi, U. (1964). Three processes in the child's acquisition of syntax. *Harvard Educational Review, 34,* 133–151.

Brozan, N. (1983). New look at fears of children. *New York Times,* May 2, p. 20.

Bruner, J. S. (1978). From communication to language: A psychological perspective. In I. Markova (Ed.), *The social context of language.* New York: Wiley.

Bruner, J. S. (1983). *Child's talk.* New York: Norton.

Bruning, R. H., Murphy, C. C., Bishop, J., & Wingrove, L. (1985). Learning word meanings from reading in the classroom under incidental and intentional conditions. Paper presented at the Annual Meeting of the National Reading Conference, San Diego, CA.

Bryant, P. E., & Trabasso, T. R. (1971). Transitive inferences and memory in young children. *Nature, 232,* 456–458.

Buck, R. (1983). Emotional development and emotional education. In R. Plutchik & H. Kellerman (Eds.), *Emotion: Theory, research, and experience* (Vol. 2). New York: Academic Press.

Buechler, S., & Izard, C. E. (1983). On the emergence, functions, and regulation of some emotional expressions in infancy. In R. Plutchik & H. Kellerman (Eds.), *Emotion: Theory, research, and experience* (Vol. 2). New York: Academic Press.

Byrnes, J. P., & Overton, W. F. (1986). Reasoning about certainty and uncertainty in concrete, causal and propositional contexts. *Developmental Psychology, 22,* in press.

Cairns, R. B. (1979). *Social development.* San Francisco: W. H. Freeman.

Cairns, R. B. (1983). The emergence of developmental psychology. In W. Kessen (Ed.), P. H. Mussen (Series Ed.), *Handbook of child psychology: Vol. 1. History, theory, and methods* (pp. 41–102). New York: Wiley.

Calfee, R. C. (1977). Assessment of independent reading skills: Basic research and practical applications. In A. S. Reber & D. L. Scarborough (Eds.), *Toward a psychology of reading.* Hillsdale, NJ: Erlbaum.

Campbell, R. L., & Bickhard, M. H. (1986). *Knowing levels and developmental stages.* Basel: Karger.

Campos, J. J., Barrett, K. C., Lamb, M. E., Goldsmith, H. H., & Stenberg, C.

(1983). Socioemotional development. In M. M. Haith & J. J. Campos (Eds.), P. H. Mussen (Series Ed.), *Handbook of Child Psychology: Vol. 2: Infancy and developmental psychobiology* (pp. 783–915). New York: Wiley.

Campos, J. J., Hiatt, S., Ramsay, D., Henderson, C., & Sevja, M. (1978). The emergence of fear on the visual cliff. In M. Lewis & L. Rosenblum (Eds.), *The origins of affect*. New York: Plenum.

Candland, D. K. (1977). The persistent problems of emotion. In D. K. Candland, J. P. Fell, E. Keen, A. L. Leshner, R. Plutchik, & R. M. Tarpy (Eds.), *Emotion*. Belmont, CA: Wadsworth.

Caplan, P. J., MacPherson, G. M., & Tobin, P. (1985). Do sex-related differences in spatial abilities exist? A multilevel critique with new data. *American Psychologist, 40*, 786–799.

Caputo, D. V., & Mandell, W. (1970). Consequences of low birth weight. *Developmental Psychology, 3*, 363–383.

Carlson, N. R. (1977). *Physiology of behavior*. Boston: Allyn and Bacon.

Caron, A. J., Caron, R. F., Caldwell, R. C., & Weiss, S. J. (1973). Infant perception of the structural properties of the face. *Developmental Psychology, 9*, 385–389.

Case, R. (1972). Validation of a neo-Piagetian mental capacity construct. *Journal of Experimental Child Psychology, 14*, 237–302.

Case, R. (1974). Structures and strictures: Some functional limitations on the course of cognitive growth. *Cognitive Psychology, 6*, 544–573.

Case, R. (1978). A developmentally based theory and technology of instruction. *Review of Educational Research, 48*, 439–463.

Case, R. (1984). The process of stage transition: A neo-Piagetian view. In R. J. Sternberg (Ed.), *Mechanisms of cognitive development* (pp. 19–44). New York: Freeman.

Case, R. (1985). *Intellectual development: Birth to adulthood*. New York: Academic Press.

Cataldo, M. F., Bessman, C. A., Parker, L. H., Pearson, J. E., & Rogers, M. C. (1979). Behavioral assessment for pediatric intensive care units. *Journal of Applied Behavior Analysis, 12*, 83–97.

Cattell, P. (1940). *The measurements of intelligence of infants and young children*. New York: Psychological Corporation.

Chance, J. E., & Goldstein, A. G. (1984). Face-recognition memory: Implications for children's eyewitness testimony. *Journal of Social Issues, 40*, 69–85.

Chance, M. R. A. (1980). An ethological assessment of emotion. In R. Plutchik & H. Kellerman (Eds.), *Emotion: Theory, research, and experience* (Vol. 1). New York: Academic Press.

Charlesworth, W. R. (1986). Darwin and developmental psychology: 100 years later. *Human Development, 29*, 1–35.

Chi, M. T. H. (1978). Knowledge structures and memory development. In R. S. Siegler (Ed.), *Children's thinking: What develops?* Hillsdale, NJ: Erlbaum.

Chi, M. T. H. (1985). Changing conception of sources of memory development. *Human Development, 28*, 50–56.

Chi, M. T. H., & Koeseke, R. D. (1983). Network representation of a child's dinosaur knowledge. *Developmental Psychology, 19*, 29–39.

References

Chomsky, N. (1957). *Syntactic structures.* The Hague: Mouton.

Chomsky, N. (1965). *Aspects of a theory of syntax.* Cambridge, MA: MIT Press.

Chomsky, N. (1980a). On cognitive structures and their development: A reply to Piaget. In M. Piattelli-Palmarini (Ed.), *Language and learning: The debate between Jean Piaget and Noam Chomsky.* Cambridge, MA: Harvard University Press.

Chomsky, N. (1980b). The linguistic approach. In M. Piattelli-Palmarini (Ed.), *Language and learning: The debate between Jean Piaget and Noam Chomsky.* Cambridge, MA: Harvard University Press.

Chukovsky, K. (1963). *From two to five.* Berkeley, CA: University of California Press.

Cicchetti, D., & Hesse, P. (1983). Affect and intellect: Piaget's contributions to the study of infant emotional development. In R. Plutchik & H. Kellerman (Eds.), *Emotion: Theory, research, and experience* (Vol. 2). New York: Academic Press.

Claren, S. K., & Smith, D. W. (1978). The fetal alcohol syndrome. *New England Journal of Medicine, 298,* 1063–1067.

Clark, E. V. (1973). What's in a word? On the child's acquisition of semantics in his first language. In T. E. Moore (Ed.), *Cognitive development and the acquisition of language.* New York: Academic Press.

Clark, E. V. (1977). First language acquisition. In J. Morton & J. C. Marshall (Eds.), *Psycholinguistic series* (Vol. 1). London: Elek Science.

Clark, E. V. (1983). Meanings and concepts. In J. Flavell & E. Markman (Eds.), P. H. Mussen (Series Ed.), *Handbook of child psychology: Vol. 3. Cognitive development.* New York: Wiley.

Clark, E. V. (1985). How children create new words. Presentation to the University of Nebraska Reading Network, Lincoln, NE, May, 1985.

Clark, H. H., & Clark, E. V. (1977). *Psychology and language: An introduction to psycholinguistics.* New York: Harcourt Brace Jovanovich.

Clarke-Stewart, K. A. (1973). Interactions between mothers and their young children: Characteristics and consequences. *Monographs of the Society for Research in Child Development, 38*(6 & 7, Serial No. 153).

Clarke-Stewart, K. A. (1978). And daddy makes three: The father's impact on mother and young child. *Child Development, 49,* 466–478.

Clarke-Stewart, K. A. (1980). The father's contribution to children's cognitive and social development in early childhood. In F. A. Pederson (Ed.), *The father-infant relationship.* New York: Praeger.

Clarke-Stewart, K. A. (1984). Day care: A new context for research and development. In M. Perlmutter (Ed.), *Parent-child interactions and parent-child relations in child development: The Minnesota Symposia on Child Development* (Vol. 17). Hillsdale, NJ: Erlbaum.

Cohen, J., & Cohen, P. (1983). *Applied multiple regression: Correlational analysis for the behavioral sciences* (2nd ed.). Hillsdale, NJ: Erlbaum.

Cohen, L. J. (1981). Can human irrationality be experimentally demonstrated? *The Behavioral and Brain Sciences, 4,* 317–370.

Colby, A., & Kohlberg, L. (1986). *The measurement of moral judgment.* New York: Cambridge University Press.

Colby, A., Kohlberg, L., Gibbs, J., & Lieberman, M. (1983). A longitudinal study of moral judgment. *Monographs of the Society for Research in Child Development, 48*–(1, Serial No. 200).

Colman, A., & Colman, L. (1977). *Pregnancy: The psychological experience.* New York: Bantam.

Comer, J. P. (1980). Relations between school and family—Policy implications of an inner-city school program. In R. Raskins & J. J. Gallagher (Eds.), *Care and education of young children in America: Policy, politics and social science.* Norwood, N.J.: Ablex.

Commons, M. L., Richards, F. A., & Armon, C. (Eds.) (1984). *Beyond formal operations: Late adolescent and adult cognitive development.* New York: Praeger.

Condry, J., & Condry, S. (1976). Sex differences: A study in the eye of the beholder. *Child Development, 47,* 812–819.

Conger, J. J., & Peterson, A. C. (1984). *Adolescence and youth.* New York: Harper & Row.

Cooke, D. A. (1985). *The life and death of stars.* New York: Crown.

Coopersmith, S. (1967). *The antecedents of self-esteem.* San Francisco: Freeman.

Copans, S. A. (1974). Human prenatal effects: Methodological problems and some suggested solutions. *Merrill-Palmer Quarterly, 20,* 43–52.

Corbin, C. B. (1980). *A textbook of motor development* (2nd ed.). Dubuque: Wm. C. Brown.

Coren, S., Porac, C., & Ward, L. M. (1979). *Sensation and perception.* New York: Academic Press.

Cowan, W. M. (1979). The development of the brain. *Scientific American, 241,* 88–133.

Cowen, M. (Ed.) (1985). *Annual review of neuroscience.* Washington, DC: Annual Reviews, Inc.

Craik, F. I. M. (1973). A "levels of analysis" view of memory. In P. Pliner, L. Krames, & T. M. Alloway (Eds.), *Communication and affect: Language and thought.* New York: Academic Press.

Craik, F. I. M. (1977). Depth of processing in recall and recognition. In S. Dornic (Ed.), *Attention and performance: Vol. VI.* Hillsdale, NJ: Erlbaum.

Craik, F. I. M., & Lockhart, R. S. (1972). Levels of processing: A framework for memory research. *Journal of Verbal Learning and Verbal Behavior, 11,* 671–684.

Craik, F. I. M., & Tulving, E. (1975). Depth of processing and the retention of words in episodic memory. *Journal of Experimental Psychology: General, 104,* 268–294.

Crain, W. C. (1985). *Theories of development: Concepts and applications* (2nd ed.). Englewood Cliffs, NJ: Prentice-Hall.

Cravens, H. (1985). The wandering IQ: American culture and mental testing. *Human Development, 28,* 113–130.

Crick, F. H. (1979). The genetic code: III. In C. E. Folsolme (Ed.), *Life: Origin and evolution.* San Francisco: Freeman.

Crick, F. H. (1982). *Life itself: Its origin and nature.* New York: Simon and Schuster.

Cruttenden, A. (1985). Intonation comprehension in ten-year-olds. *Journal of Child Language, 12,* 643–661.

Crystal, D. (1976). *Child language, learning and linguistics.* London: Edward Arnold Ltd.

Daehler, M. W., & Bukatko, D. (1985). *Cognitive development.* New York: Knopf.

Dalby, J. T. (1978). Environmental effects on prenatal development. *Journal of Pediatric Psychology, 3,* 105–109.

Dally, P. (1969). *Anorexia nervosa.* New York: Grune & Stratton.

Damon, W. (1983). *Social and personality development: Infancy through adolescence.* New York: Norton.

Damon, W., & Hart, D. (1982). The development of self-understanding from infancy through adolescence. *Child Development, 53,* 841–864.

Dannemiller, J. L., & Banks, M. S. (1983). Can selective adaption account for early infant habituation? *Merrill-Palmer Quarterly, 29,* 151–158.

Dargassies, S. S. (1982). Developmental neurology from the fetus to the infant: Some French works. In W. W. Hartup (Ed.), *Review of Child Development Research.* Chicago: University of Chicago Press.

Darwin, C. (1859). *On the origin of species.* London: John Murray.

Davidson, E., & Benjamin, L. (in press). The child study movement. In J. A. Glover & R. R. Ronning (Eds.), *A history of educational psychology.* New York: Plenum.

Davies, P. (1983). *The edge of infinity: Where the universe came from and how it will end.* New York: Simon and Schuster.

DeCasper, A. J., & Fifer, W. J. (1980). Of human bonding: Newborns prefer their mothers' voices. *Science, 208,* 1174–1176.

DeLisi, R., & Johns, M. L. (1984). The effects of books and gender constancy development on kindergarten children's sex-role attitudes. *Journal of Applied Developmental Psychology, 5,* 173–184.

DeLoache, J. S. (1986). Memory in very young children: Exploitation of cues to the location of hidden object. *Cognitive Development, 1,* 123–137.

DeLoache, J. S., Cassidy, D. J., & Brown, A. L. (1985). Precursors of mnemonic strategies in very young children. *Child Development, 56,* 125–137.

Demkiw, P., & Michaels, C. F. (1976). Motion information in iconic memory. *Acta Psychologica, 40,* 257–264.

Dempster, F. N. (1981). Memory span: Sources of individual and developmental differences. *Psychological Bulletin, 89,* 63–100.

Denham, S. A. (1986). Social cognition, prosocial behavior, and emotion in preschoolers: Contextual validation. *Child Development, 57,* 194–201.

Dent, H. R. (1982). The effects of interviewing strategies on the results of interviews with child witnesses. In A. Trankell (Ed.), *Reconstructing the past* (pp. 279–298). Deventer, The Netherlands: Kluwer.

de Villiers, J. G., & de Villiers, P. A. (1978). *Language acquisition.* Cambridge, MA: Harvard University Press.

Dewsbury, D. A. (1984). *Comparative psychology in the twentieth century.* Stroudsburg, PA: Hutchinson Ross.

Diaz, R. M., & Berndt, T. J. (1982). Children's knowledge of a best friend: Fact or Fancy? *Developmental Psychology, 18,* 787–794.

Dick, A. O. (1974). Iconic memory and its relation to perceptual processing and other memory mechanisms. *Perception and Psychophysics, 16,* 575–596.

Dillon, L. S. (1978). *Evolution: Concepts and consequences* (2nd ed.). Saint Louis: Mosby.

DiLollo, V., Lowe, D. G., & Scott, J. P. (1974). Backward masking and interference with the processing of brief visual displays. *Journal of Experimental Psychology, 103,* 934–940.

Dixon, N. F. (1981). *Preconscious processing.* Chichester, England: Wiley.

Dixon, R. A., & Lerner, R. M. (1984). A history of systems in developmental psychology. In M. H. Bornstein & M. E. Lamb (Eds.), *Developmental psychology: An advanced textbook* (pp. 1–35). Hillsdale, NJ: Erlbaum.

Dixon, T., & Lucas, M. (1983). *The human race.* New York: McGraw-Hill.

Dmowski, W. P., Gaynor, L., Rao, R., Lawrence, M., & Scommegna, A. (1979). The use of albumin gradients for X and Y sperm separation and clinical experience with male preselection. *Fertility and Sterility, 31,* i.

Dodge, K. A. (1980). Social cognition and children's aggressive behavior. *Child Development, 51,* 162–170.

Dodge, K. A., & Frame, C. L. (1982). Social cognitive biases and deficits in aggressive boys. *Child Development, 53,* 620–635.

D'Odorico, L., & Franco, F. (1985). The determinants of baby talk: Relationship to context. *Journal of Child Language, 12,* 567–586.

Dore, J. (1985). Children's conversations. In T. A. van Dijk (Ed.), *Handbook of discourse analysis: Vol. 3. Discourse and dialogue.* London: Academic Press.

Dorval, B., & Eckerman, C. O. (1984). Developmental trends in the quality of conversation achieved by small groups of acquainted peers. *Monographs of the Society for Research in Child Development, 49*(2, Serial No. 206).

Eberhart, J. (1983). Another solar system. *Science News, 124,* 100.

Edwards, D. D. (1986). A common medical denominator. *Science News, 129,* 60–62.

Effron, R. (1970). The minimum duration of a perception. *Neuropsychologia, 8,* 57–63.

Egeland, B., & Vaughn, B. (1981). Failure of "bond formation" as a cause of abuse, neglect, and maltreatment. *American Journal of Orthopsychiatry, 51*(1), 78–84.

Ehri, L. C. (1978). Beginning reading from a psycholinguistic perspective: Amalgamation of word identities. In F. B. Murray (Ed.), *The recognition of words.* Newark, DE: International Reading Association.

Ehri, L. C. (1984). How orthography alters spoken language competencies in children learning to read and spell. In J. Downing and R. Valtin (Eds.), *Language awareness and learning to read.* New York: Springer-Verlag.

Ehri, L. C. (1985, April). *Learning to read and spell.* Invited address to the American Educational Research Association, Chicago.

Ehri, L. C., & Wilce, L. S. (1985). Movement into reading: Is the first stage of printed word learning visual or phonetic? *Reading Research Quarterly, 20,* 163–179.

Eich, J. M. (1985). Levels of processing, encoding specificity, elaboration, and CHARM. *Psychological Review, 92,* 1–38.

Eimas, P. D. (1985). The perception of speech in early infancy. *Scientific American, 252,* 46–52.

Eimas, P. D., Siqueland, E. R., Jusczyk, P. W., & Vigorito, J. (1971). Speech perception in infants. *Science, 171,* 303–306.

Eisenberg, J. F. (1983). *The mammalian radiations: An analysis of trends in evolution, adaptation, and behavior.* Chicago: Universitry of Chicago Press.

Eisenberg, N. (Ed.) (1982). *The development of prosocial behavior.* New York: Academic Press.

Eisenberg, R. B. (1970). The development of hearing in man: An assessment of current status. *Journal of the American Speech and Hearing Association, 12,* 119–123.

Eisenberg, R. B., Griffin, E. J., Coursin, D. B., & Hunter, M. A. (1964). Auditory behavior in the human neonate: A preliminary report. *Journal of Speech and Hearing Research, 7,* 245–269.

Ekman, P. (1972). Universals and cultural differences in facial expressions of emotion. In J. K. Cole (Ed.), *Nebraska symposium on motivation.* Lincoln: University of Nebraska Press.

Ekman, P. (1973). Cross-cultural studies of facial expression. In P. Ekman (Ed.), *Darwin and facial expression: A century of research in review.* New York: Academic Press.

Ekman, P., & Friesen, W. V. (1971). Constants across cultures in the face and emotion. *Journal of Personality and Social Psychology, 17,* 124–129.

Ekman, P., & Friesen, W. V. (1975). *Unmasking the face: A guide to recognizing emotions from facial cues.* Englewood Cliffs, NJ: Prentice-Hall.

Ekman, P., Sorenson, E. R., & Friesen, W. V. (1969). Pan-cultural elements in facial displays of emotion. *Science, 164,* 86–88.

Eldredge, N., & Tattersall, I. (1983). *The myths of human evolution.* New York: Columbia University Press.

Elkind, D. (1975). Perceptual development in children. *American Scientist, 63,* 533–541.

Elkind, D. (1978). *The child's reality: Three developmental themes.* Hillsdale, NJ: Erlbaum.

Elkind, D. (1979). *The child and society.* New York: Oxford University Press.

Ellngson, R. (1968). Clinical applications of evoked potential techniques in infants and children. *Electroencephalography and Clinical Neurophysiology, 24,* 293.

Ellingson, R., Lathrop, G., Nelson, G., & Donahy, T. (1971). Visual evoked potentials of infants. *Revue d'Électroencephalographie et de Neurophysiologie Clinique, 2,* 395–400.

Elliot, A. J. (1981). *Child language.* London: Cambridge University Press.

Ellis, H. C., & Hunt, R. R. (1983). *Fundamentals of human memory and cognition* (3rd. ed.). Dubuque, IA: Wm. C. Brown.

Emler, N. (1983). Morality and politics: The ideological dimension in the theory of moral development. In H. Weinreich-Haste & D. Locke (Eds.), *Morality in the making: Thought, action, and the social context* (pp. 47–71). New York: Wiley.

Engel, B. S. (1984). Between feeling and fact: Listening to children. *Harvard Educational Review, 54,* 304–314.

Engen, T., Lipsitt, L. S., & Peck, M. B. (1974). Ability of newborn infants to discriminate sapid substances. *Developmental Psychology, 10,* 741–744.

Entwisle, D. R., & Baker, D. P. (1983). Gender and young children's expectations for performance in arithmetic. *Developmental Psychology, 19,* 200–209.

Eriksen, C. W., & Collins, J. F. (1967). Some temporal characteristics of visual pattern perception. *Journal of Experimental Psychology, 74,* 476–484.

Eriksen, C. W., & Johnson, H. J. (1964). Storage and decay characteristics of non-attended auditory stimuli. *Journal of Experimental Psychology, 68,* 28–36.

Erikson, E. H. (1950). *Childhood and society.* New York: Norton.

Erikson, E. H. (1968). *Identity: Youth and crisis.* New York: Norton.

Eron, L. D. (1982). Parent-child interaction, television violence, and aggression of children. *American Psychologist, 37,* 197–211.

Eron, L. D., Huesmann, L. R., Brice, P., Fischer, P., & Mermelstein, R. (1983). Age trends in the development of aggression, sex typing, and related television habits. *Developmental Psychology, 19,* 71–77.

Ervin-Tripp, S. (1971). Wait for me, Roller Skate! In S. Ervin-Tripp & Y. C. Mitchell-Kernan (Eds.), *Child discourse.* New York: Academic Press.

Ervin-Tripp, S. (1977). Wait for me, Roller Skate! In S. Ervin-Tripp & Y. C. Mitchell-Kernan (Eds.), *Child discourse.* New York: Academic Press.

Ervin-Tripp, S. (1984). The art of conversation. (Commentary on Dorval, B., & Eckerman, C. O. Developmental trends in the quality of conversation achieved by small groups of acquainted peers.) *Monographs of the Society for Research in Child Development, 49*(2, Serial No. 206).

Evans, J. St. B. T. (1982). *The psychology of deductive reasoning.* London: Routledge & Kegan Paul.

Evans, J. St. B. T. (Ed.) (1983). *Thinking and reasoning: Psychological approaches.* London: Routledge & Kegan Paul.

Fagan, J. F. (1973). Infants' delayed recognition memory and forgetting. *Journal of Experimental Child Psychology, 16,* 424–450.

Fagan, J. F. (1975). Infants' delayed recognition memory and forgetting. *Journal of Experimental Child Psychology, 16,* 424–450.

Fagan, J. F. (1979). The origins of facial pattern recognition. In M. H. Bornstein & W. Kennen (Eds.), *Psychological development from infancy: Image to intention.* Hillsdale, NJ: Erlbaum.

Fagot, B. I. (1985a). Changes in thinking about early sex role development. *Developmental Review, 5,* 83–98.

Fagot, B. I. (1985b). Beyond the reinforcement principle: Another step toward understanding sex role development. *Developmental Psychology, 21,* 1097–1104.

Fagot, B. I., Hagan, R., Leinbach, M. D., & Kronsberg, S. (1985). Differential reactions to assertive and communicative acts of toddler boys and girls. *Child Development, 56,* 1499–1505.

Fantz, R. (1958). Pattern vision in young infants. *Psychological Review, 8,* 43–47.

Fantz, R. (1961). The origin of form perception. *Scientific American, 204,* 66–72.

Fantz, R. (1964). Visual experience in infants: Decreased attention to familiar patterns relative to novel ones. *Science, 146,* 668–670.

Fantz, R. (1965). Visual perception from birth as shown by pattern selectivity. *Annals of the New York Academy of Sciences, 118,* 793–814.

Fantz, R., & Fagen, J. F. III. (1975). Visual attention to size and number of pattern details by term and preterm infants during the first six months. *Child Development, 46,* 3–18.

Fantz, R., Fagen, J. F. III, & Miranda, S. B. (1975). Early visual selectivity. In L. B. Cohen and P. Salapatek (Eds.), *Infant perception: From sensation to cognition* (Vol. 1). New York: Academic Press.

Faust, M. S. (1977). Somatic development of adolescent girls. *Monographs of the Society for Research in Child Development, 42,* No. 1.

Fein, R. A. (1978). Research on fathering: Social policy and an emergent perspective. *Journal of Social Issues, 34,* 122–135.

Feldman, R. E. (1980). The promotion of moral development in prisons and schools. In R. W. Wilson & G. J. Schochet (Eds.), *Moral development and politics* (pp. 286–328). New York: Praeger.

Ferguson, T. J., & Rule, B. G. (1980). Effects of inferential set, outcome severity, and basis of responsibility on children's evaluations of aggressive acts. *Developmental Psychology, 16,* 141–146.

Ferrara, A. (1985). Pragmatics. In T. A. van Dijk (Ed.), *Handbook of discourse analysis: Vol. 2. Dimensions of discourse.* Orlando, FL: Academic Press.

Ferreira, A. J. (1969). *Prenatal environment.* Springfield, IL: Charles C. Thomas.

Feshbach, S. (1956). The catharsis hypothesis and some consequences of interaction with aggressive and neutral play objects. *Journal of Personality,* 1956, 24, 449–462.

Feshbach, S. (1970). Aggression. In P. H. Mussen (Ed.), *Carmichael's manual of child psychology.* New York: Wiley.

Fincher, J. (1982). *The brain: Mystery of matter and mind.* New York: Scribner.

Fischer, K. W. (1980). A theory of cognitive development: The control and construction of hierarchies of skills. *Psychological Review, 87,* 477–531.

Fishbein, H. D. (1976). *Evolution, development, and children's learning.* Pacific Palisades, CA: Goodyear.

Fisher, R. P., & Craik, F. I. M. (1980). The effects of elaboration on recognition memory. *Memory and Cognition, 8,* 400–404.

Flanery, R. C., & Balling, J. D. (1979). Developmental changes in hemispheric specialization for tactile spatial ability. *Developmental Psychology, 15,* 364–372.

Flavell, J. H. (1970). Developmental studies of mediated memory. In H. W. Reese & L. P. Lipsitt (Eds.), *Advances in child development and behavior* (Vol. 5). New York: Academic Press.

Flavell, J. H., Beach, D. R., & Chinsky, J. M. (1966). Spontaneous verbal rehearsal in a memory task as a function of age. *Child Development, 37,* 283–299.

Flavell, J. H., Friedrichs, A. G., & Hoyt, J. D. (1970). Developmental changes in memorization processes. *Cognitive Psychology, 1,* 324–340.

Flavell, J. H., & Wellman, H. M. (1977). Metamemory. In R. V. Kail, Jr., & J. W. Hagen (Eds.), *Perspectives on the development of memory and cognition.* Hillsdale, NJ: Erlbaum.

Flavell, J. H., Speer, J. R., Green, F. L., & August, D. L. (1981). The development of comprehension monitoring and knowledge about communication. *Monographs of the Society for Research in Child Development, 46*(Whole No. 192).

Fleming, A. T. (1980). New frontiers in conception. *The New York Times Magazine,* July 20.

Fodor, J. (1980). Fixation of belief and concept acquistion. In M. Piattelli-

Palmarini (Ed.), *Language and learning: The debate between Jean Piaget and Noam Chomsky* (pp. 143–149). Cambridge: Harvard University Press.

Foley, M. A., & Johnson, M. K. (1985). Confusions between memories for performed and imagined actions: A developmental comparison. *Child Development, 56*, 1145–1155.

Forman, G. E., & Hill, F. (1980). *Constructive play: Applying Piaget in the preschool.* Monterey, CA: Brooks/Cole.

Frankel, M. T., & Rollins, H. A., Jr. (1983). Does mother know best? Mothers and fathers interacting with preschool sons and daughters. *Developmental Psychology, 19*, 694–702.

Franks, B. A. (1986). Children's intellectual rights: Implications for educational policy. In D. Moshman (Ed.), *Children's intellectual rights.* San Francisco: Jossey-Bass.

Frazier, T. M., Davis, G. H., Goldstein, H., & Goldberg, I. O. (1969). Cigarette smoking and prematurity: A prospective study. *American Journal of Obstetrics and Gynecology, 81*, 988–996.

Freud, S. (1900). *The interpretation of dreams.* In J. Strachey (Ed.) (1953), *The standard edition of the complete psychological works of Sigmund Freud, Vols. 4–5.* London: Hogarth.

Freud, S. (1933). *New introductory lectures on psychoanalysis.* New York: Norton.

Freud, S. (1938). *The basic writings of Sigmund Freud* (trans. by A. A. Brill). New York: Random House.

Friedman, A. (1979). Framing pictures: The role of knowledge in automatized encoding and memory for gist. *Journal of Experimental Psychology: General, 108*, 316–355.

Fuller, R. G. (Ed.) (1980). *Piagetian programs in higher education.* ADAPT: University of Nebraska—Lincoln.

Furth, H. G. (1981). Jean Piaget: August 9, 1896–September 16, 1980. *Human Development, 24*, 77.

Futuyma, D. J. (1983). *Science on trial: The case for evolution.* New York: Pantheon.

Gallup, A. M. (1985). The 17th Annual Gallup Poll of the public's attitudes toward the public schools. *Phi Delta Kappan, 67*, 35–47.

Gardner, H. (1979). Developmental psychology after Piaget: An approach in terms of symbolization. *Human Development, 22*, 73–88.

Gardner, L. Deprivation dwarfism. *Scientific American*, 1972, *227*, 76–82.

Garvey, C. (1974). Some properties of social play. *Merrill-Palmer Quarterly, 20*, 163–180.

Garvey, C. (1977). *Play.* Cambridge, MA: Harvard University Press.

Garvey, C. (1983). Some properties of social play. In W. Damon (Ed.), *Social and personality development: Essays on the growth of the child.* New York: Norton.

Garvey, C. (1984). *Children's talk.* London: Fontana.

Gelles, R. J. (1975). Violence toward children in the United States. *American Journal of Orthopsychiatry, 48*, 580–592.

Gelman, R. (1980). What young children know about numbers. *Educational Psychologist, 15*, 54–68.

Gelman, R., & Baillargeon, R. (1983). A review of some Piagetian concepts. In J. H. Flavell & E. M. Markman (Eds.), P. H. Mussen (Series Ed.), *Handbook of child psychology: Vol. 3. Cognitive development* (pp. 167–230). New York: Wiley.

Gelman, R., & Gallistel, C. R. (1978). *The child's understanding of number.* Cambridge, MA: Harvard University Press.

Gelman, R., Meck, E., & Merkin, S. (1986). Young children's numerical competence. *Cognitive Development, 1,* 1–29.

Gentner, D. (1982). Why nouns are learned before verbs: Linguistic relativity versus natural partitioning. In S. A. Kuczaj, II (Ed.), *Language development: Vol. 2. Language, thought, and culture.* Hillsdale, NJ: Erlbaum.

Geschwind, N. (1979). Specialization of the human brain. *Scientific American, 241,* 180–201.

Gesell, A. L. (1925). *The mental growth of the pre-school child: A psychological outline of normal development from birth to the sixth year, including a system of developmental diagnosis.* New York: Macmillan.

Gesell, A. L. (1928). *Infancy and human growth.* New York: Macmillan.

Gibbs, J. C., Arnold, K. D., & Burkhart, J. E. (1984). Sex differences in the expression of moral judgment. *Child Development, 55,* 1040–1043.

Gibbs, J. C., Clark, P. M., Joseph, J. A., Green, J. L., Goodrick, T. S., & Makowski, D. G. (1986). Relations between moral judgment, moral courage, and field independence. *Child Development, 57,* 185–193.

Gibbs, J. C., & Schnell, S. V. (1985). Moral development "versus" socialization: A critique. *American Psychologist, 40,* 1071–1080.

Gibson, E. J. (1969). *Principles of perceptual learning and development.* New York: Appleton-Century-Crofts.

Gibson, E. J., Gibson, J. J., Pick, A. D., & Osser, H. (1962). A developmental study of the discrimination of letter-like forms. *Journal of Comparative and Physiological Psychology, 5,* 897–906.

Gibson, E. J., & Levin, H. (1975). *The psychology of reading.* Cambridge, MA: MIT Press.

Gibson, E. J., & Spelke, E. S. (1983). The development of perception. In J. H. Flavell and E. M. Markman (Eds.), P. H. Mussen (Series Ed.), *Handbook of child psychology: Vol. 3. Cognitive development* (pp. 1–76). New York: Wiley.

Gibson, E. J., & Walk, R. (1960). The "visual cliff." *Scientific American, 202,* 64–71.

Gibson, J. J., & Gibson, E. J. (1955). Perceptual learning: Differentiation or enrichment? *Psychological Review, 62,* 32–41.

Gilligan, C. (1982). *In a different voice: Psychological theory and women's development.* Cambridge, MA: Harvard University Press.

Ginsburg, D., Handin, R. I., Bonthron, D. T., Donlon, T. A., Bruns, G. A. P., Latt, S. A., & Orkin, S. H. (1985). Human von Willebrand factor (vWF): Isolation of complementary DNA (cDNA) clones and chromosomal localization. *Science, 228,* 1401–1406.

Gladwin, T. (1970). *East is a big bird.* Cambridge, MA: Belknap Press.

Gleitman, L. R., & Wanner, E. (1984). Current issues in language learning. In M. H. Bornstein & M. E. Lamb (Eds.), *Developmental psychology: An advanced textbook.* Hillsdale, NJ: Erlbaum.

Glover, J. A. (1981). *Becoming a more creative person.* Englewood Cliffs, NJ: Prentice-Hall.

Glover, J. A., Bruning, R. H., & Plake, B. S. (1982). Distinctiveness of encoding and recall of text materials. *Journal of Educational Psychology, 74,* 522–534.

Glut, D. F. (1983). *The new dinosaur dictionary.* Secaucus, NJ: Citadel.

Gnepp, J., & Hess, D. L. R. (1986). Children's understanding of verbal and facial display rules. *Developmental Psychology, 22,* 103–108.

Goetting, A. (1981). Divorce outcome research: Issues and perspectives. *Journal of Family Issues, 2,* 97–106.

Gofman, S., & DiVitto, B. A. (1983). *Born too soon: Preterm birth and early development.* San Francisco: Freeman.

Goldberg, S. (1983). Parent-infant bonding: Another look. *Child Development, 54,* 1355–1382.

Goldfield, E. C. (1983). The ecological approach to perceiving as a foundation for understanding the development of knowing in infancy. *Developmental Review, 3,* 371–404.

Goldin-Meadow, S., & Feldman, H. (1977). The development of language-like communication without a language model. *Science, 197,* 401–403.

Goldsmith, H. H. (1983). Genetic influences on personality from infancy to adulthood. *Child Development, 54,* 331–355.

Goldstein, E. B. (1980). *Sensation and perception.* Belmont, CA: Wadsworth.

Gollins, E. S. (1984). *Malformations of development.* New York: Academic Press.

Goodenough, F. L. (1931). *Anger in young children.* Institute of Child Welfare Monograph Series, No. 9. Minneapolis: University of Minnesota Press.

Goodman, C., & Gardiner, J. M. (1981). How well do children remember what they have recalled? *British Journal of Educational Psychology, 51,* 97–101.

Goodman, G. S. (1984). Children's testimony in historical perspective. *Journal of Social Issues, 40,* 9–31.

Goodman, G. S., & Goldstein, A. G. (1984). Face-recognition memory: Implications for children's eyewitness testimony. *Journal of Social Issues, 40,* 69–85.

Gorlin, R. J. (1977). Classical chromosome disorders. In J. J. Yunis (Ed.), *New chromosomal syndromes.* New York: Academic Press.

Gottesman, I. I. (1965). Personality and natural selection. In S. G. Vandenberg (Ed.), *Methods and goals in human behavior genetics.* New York: Academic Press.

Gottfried, A. W. (1984). *Home environment and early cognitive development.* New York: Academic Press.

Gottman, J. (1983). How children become friends. *Monographs of the Society for Research in Child Development, 48* (2, Serial No. 201).

Gould, S. J. (1982). Darwinism and the expansion of evolutionary theory. *Science, 216,* 380–387.

Gould, S. J. (1983). *Hen's teeth and horse's toes.* New York: Norton.

Graham, S. (1982). Communicated sympathy and anger as determinants of self-perception and performance. Unpublished doctoral dissertation, University of California, Los Angeles.

Graziano, A. M., DeGiovanni, I. S. (1979). The clinical significance of childhood phobias: A note on the proportion of child-clinical referrals for the treatment of children's fears. *Behavior, Research, and Therapy, 17,* 161–162.

Greeno, J. G. (1983). Response to Phillips. *Educational Psychologist, 18,* 75–80.

Greenfield, P. M., & Smith, J. H. (1976). *The structure of communication in early language development.* New York: Academic Press.

Greenwald, A. G., Pratkanis, A. R., Leippe, M. R., & Baumgardner, M. H. (1986). Under what conditions does theory obstruct research progress? *Psychological Review, 93,* 216–229.

References

Griffiths, R. (1954). *The abilities of babies.* New York: McGraw-Hill.

Griggs, R. A. (1983). The role of problem content in the selection task and in the THOG problem. In J. St. B. T. Evans (Ed.), *Thinking and reasoning: Psychological approaches.* London: Routledge.

Gross, T. F. (1985). *Cognitive development.* San Francisco: Brooks/Cole.

Gruber, H. E., & Voneche, J. J. (Eds.) (1977). *The essential Piaget.* New York: Basic Books.

Haber, R. N., & Nathanson, L. S. (1968). Post-retinal storage? Some further observations on Park's camel as seen through the eye of a needle. *Perception and Psychophysics, 3,* 349–355.

Hagen, J. W., & Stanovich, K. G. (1977). Memory: Strategies of acquisition. In R. V. Kail, Jr., & J. W. Hagen (Eds.), *Perspectives on the development of memory and cognition.* Hillsdale, NJ: Erlbaum.

Hainline, L. (1978). Developmental changes in visual scanning of face and nonface patterns by infants. *Journal of Experimental Child Psychology, 25,* 90–115.

Hainline, L., & Lemerise, E. (1982). Infants' scanning of geometric forms varying in size. *Journal of Experimental Child Psychology, 33,* 235–256.

Haith, M. M. (1966). The response of the human newborn to visual movement. *Journal of Experimental Child Psychology, 3,* 235–243.

Haith, M. M. (1980). *Rules that newborns look by.* Hillsdale, NJ: Erlbaum.

Haith, M. M., Bergman, T., & Moore, M. J. (1977). Eye contact and face scanning in early infancy. *Science, 198,* 853–854.

Hakes, D. T. (1982). The development of metalinguistic abilities: What develops? In S. Kuczaj, II (Ed.), *Language development: Vol. 2. Language, thought, and culture.* Hillsdale, NJ: Erlbaum.

Hales, D., & Creasy, R. K. (1982). *New Hope for problem pregnancies: Helping babies before they're born.* New York: Harper & Row.

Halford, G. S. (1984). Can young children integrate premises in transitivity and serial order tasks? *Cognitive Psychology, 16,* 65–93.

Halford, G. S., & Boyle, F. M. (1985). Do young children understand conservation of number? *Child Development, 56,* 165–176.

Halford, G. S., & Kelly, M. E. (1984). On the basis of early transitivity judgments. *Journal of Experimental Child Psychology, 38,* 42–63.

Halliday, M. A. K. (1975). *Learning how to mean: Explorations in the development of language.* New York: Elsevier.

Halpern, D. F. (1984). *Thought and knowledge: An introduction to critical thinking.* Hillsdale, NJ: Erlbaum.

Harlow, H. F., & Mears, C. E. (1983). Emotional sequences and consequences. In R. Plutchik & H. Kellerman (Eds.), *Emotion: Theory, research, and experience* (Vol. 2). New York: Academic Press.

Harris, P., & MacFarlane, A. (1974). The growth of the effective visual field from birth to seven weeks. *Journal of Experimental Child Psychology, 18,* 340–348.

Harrison, H., & Kositsky, A. (1983). *The premature baby book: A parents' guide to coping and caring in the first years.* New York: St. Martins Press.

Harter, M., & Suitt, C. (1970). Visually evoked cortical responses and pattern vision in the infant: A longitudinal study. *Psychonomic Science, 18,* 235–237.

Hartshorne, H., & May, M. A. (1928–30). *Studies in the nature of character* (3 Vols.). New York: Macmillan.

REFERENCES

Hartup, W. W. (1974). Aggression in childhood: Developmental perspectives. *American Psychologist, 29,* 336–341.

Hartup, W. W. (1983). Peer relations. In E. M. Hetherington (Ed.), P. H. Mussen (Series Ed.), *Handbook of child psychology: Vol. 4. Socialization, personality, and social development* (pp. 103–196). New York: Wiley.

Harway, M., Mednick, S. A., & Mednick, B. (1984). Research strategies: Methodological and practical problems. In S. A. Mednick, M. Harway, & K. M. Finello (Eds.), *Handbook of longitudinal research.* New York: Praeger

Hawkins, H. L., & Presson, J. C. (1977). Masking and preperceptual selectivity in auditory recognition. In S. Dornic (Ed.), *Attention and Performance VI.* Hillsdale, NJ: Erlbaum.

Hawkins, H. L., Thomas, G. B., Presson, J. C., Cozic, A., & Brookmire, D. (1974). Precategorical selective attention and touch specificity in auditory recognition. *Journal of Experimental Psychology, 103,* 530–538.

Hawkins, J., Pea, R. D., Glick, J., & Scribner, S. (1984). "Merds that laugh don't like mushrooms": Evidence for deductive reasoning by preschoolers. *Developmental Psychology, 20,* 584–594.

Hay, D. F. (1985). Learning to form relationships in infancy. Parallel attainment with parents and peers. *Developmental Review, 5,* 122–161.

Hearnshaw, L. S. (1979). *Cyril Burt, psychologist.* Ithaca, NY: Cornell University Press.

Heath, S. B. (1986). Composing as conversing: The linguistic connection. *Ethnography and education.* A symposium conducted at the University of Nebraska, April, 1986.

Heil, J. (1983). *Perception and cognition.* Berkeley: University of California Press.

Hellige, J. B., Walsh, D. A., Lawrence, V. W., & Prasse, M. (1979). Figural relationship effects and mechanisms of visual masking. *Journal of Experimental Psychology: Human Perception and Performance, 5,* 88–100.

Hentoff, N. (1980). *The first freedom: The tumultuous history of free speech in America.* New York: Delacorte.

Herbert, W. (1983). Lucy's uncommon forebears. *Science News, 123,* 88–92.

Hersen, M. & Barlow, D. H. (1976). *Single case experimental designs: Strategies for studying behavioral change.* New York: Pergamon.

Hershanson, M. (1964). Visual discrimination in the human newborn. *Journal of Comparative and Physiological Psychology, 58,* 270–276.

Hetherington, E. M., Cox, M., & Cox, R. (1976). Divorced fathers. *The Family Coordinator, 25,* 417–428.

Hetherington, E. M., Cox, M., & Cox, R. (1979). Play and social interaction in children following divorce. *Journal of Social Issues, 35,* 26–49.

Hetherington, E. M., Cox, M., & Cox, R. (1982). Effects of divorce on parents and children. In M. E. Lamb (Ed.), *Non-traditional families.* Hillsdale, NJ: Erlbaum.

Higgins, A., Power, C., & Kohlberg, L. (1984). The relationship of moral atmosphere to judgments of responsibility. In W. M. Kurtines & J. L. Gewirtz (Eds.), *Morality, moral behavior, and moral development* (pp. 74–106). New York: Wiley.

Hoffman, L. W. (1983). Increased fathering: Effects on the mother. In M. E. Lamb & A. Sagi (Eds.), *Fatherhood and family policy.* Hillsdale, NJ: Erlbaum.

Hoffman, L. W. (1984). Maternal employment and the young child. In M.

References

Perlmutter (Ed.), *Parent-child interactions and parent-child relations in child development: The Minnesota Symposia on Child Development* (Vol. 17). Hillsdale, NJ: Erlbaum.

Hoffman, M. L. (1975). Developmental synthesis of affect and cognition and its implications for altruistic motivation. *Developmental Psychology, 11*, 607–622.

Hoffman, M. L. (1984). Empathy, its limitations, and its role in a comprehensive moral theory. In W. M. Kurtines & J. L. Gewirtz (Eds.), *Morality, moral behavior, and moral development* (pp. 283–302). New York: Wiley.

Holstein, C. B. (1976). Irreversible, stepwise sequence in the development of moral judgment: A longitudinal study of males and females. *Child Development, 47*, 51–61.

Horn, J. M. (1983). The Texas adoption project: Adopted children and their intellectual resemblance to biological and adoptive parents. *Child Development, 54*, 268–275.

Horn, J. M. (1985). Bias? Indeed! *Child Development, 56*, 779–780.

Hottinger, W. (1980). Early childhood. In C. B. Corbin (Ed.), *A textbook of motor development* (2nd ed.). Dubuque, IA: Wm. C. Brown.

Hubel, D. D., & Wiesel, T. N. (1979). The brain. *Scientific American, 241*, 44–53.

Hughes, J. G. (1980). *Synopsis of pediatrics* (5th ed.). St. Louis: Mosby.

Hughey, L., & Weber, M. (1982). *The American Medical Association book of womancare*. New York: Random House.

Hulsizer, D., Murphy, M., Noam, G., Taylor, C., & Norman, D. (1981). On generativity and identity: From a conversation with Erik and Joan Erikson. *Harvard Educational Review, 51*, 249–269.

Huston, A. C. (1983). Sex-typing. In E. M. Hetherington (Ed.), P. H. Mussen (Series Ed.), *Handbook of child psychology: Vol. 4. Socialization, personality, and social development* (pp. 387–467). New York: Wiley.

Huston, A. C. (1985). The development of sex-typing: Themes from recent research. *Developmental Review, 5*, 1–17.

Iannotti, R. J. (1985). Naturalistic and structured assessments of prosocial behavior in preschool children: The influence of empathy and perspective taking. *Developmental Psychology, 21*, 46–55.

Inhelder, B., & Piaget, J. (1958). *The growth of logical thinking: From childhood to adolescence*. New York: Basic Books.

Inhelder, B., & Piaget, J. (1964). *The early growth of logic in the child: Classification and seriation*. London: Routledge.

Institute of Medicine. (1985). *Preventing low birthweight*. Washington, DC: National Academy Press.

Irvine, W. (1982). *Apes, angels, and Victorians*. Alexandria, VA: Time-Life.

Istomina, Z. M. (1975). The development of voluntary memory in preschool-age children. *Soviet Psychology, 13*, 5–64.

Ito, M. (1984). *The cerebellum and neural control*. New York: Raven.

Izard, C. E. (1977). *Human emotion*. New York: Plenum.

Izard, C. E., & Buechler, S. (1980). Aspects of consciousness and personality in terms of differential emotions theory. In R. Plutchik & H. Kellerman (Eds.), *Emotion: Theory, research, and experience*. New York: Academic Press.

Izard, C. E., Kagan, J., & Zajonc, R. B. (Eds.) (1984). *Emotions, cognition, and behavior*. New York: Cambridge University Press.

Jacoby, L. L., & Craik, F. I. M. (1979). Effects of elaboration of processing at encoding and retrieval: Trace distinctiveness and recovery of initial context. In L. S. Cermak & F. I. M. Craik (Eds.), *Levels of processing and human memory.* Hillsdale, NJ: Erlbaum.

Jacoby, L. L., Craik, F. I. M., & Begg, I. (1979). Effects of decision difficulty on recognition and recall. *Journal of Verbal Learning and Verbal Behavior, 18,* 585–600.

James, W. (1961/1892). *Psychology: The briefer course.* New York: Harper.

Jarvik, L. F., & Erlenmeyer-Kimling, L. (1967). Survey of familial correlations in measured intellectual functions. In J. Zubin and G. A. Jervis (Eds.), *Psychopathology of mental development.* New York: Grune and Stratton.

Jastrow, R. (1981). *The enchanted loom: Mind in the universe.* New York: Simon and Schuster.

Jenkins, J. J. (1974). Remember that old theory of memory? Well, forget it! *American Psychologist, 29,* 785–795.

Jensen, A. (1980). *Bias in mental testing.* New York: Free Press.

Jensen, A. (in press-a). A history of individual research on individual differences. In J. A. Glover and R. R. Ronning (Eds.), *A History of Educational Psychology,* New York: Plenum.

Jensen, A. (in press-b). The g beyond factor analysis. In R. R. Ronning, J. A. Glover, & J. Conoley (Eds.), *The influence of cognitive psychology on measurement.* Hillsdale, NJ: Erlbaum.

Jensen, D. (1980). *The human nervous system.* New York: Appleton-Century-Crofts.

Jensen, D., & Engel, R. (1971). Statistical procedures for relating dichotomous responses to maturation and EEG measurements. *Electroencephalography and Clinical Neurophysiology, 30,* 437–443.

Jersild, A. T. (1968). *Child psychology* (6th ed.). Englewood Cliffs, NJ: Prentice-Hall.

Jersild, A. T., & Holmes, F. B. (1935). *Children's fears.* Child Development Monographs, No. 20. New York: Teachers College, Columbia University.

Jersild, A. T., & Tasch, R. J. (1949). *Children's interests.* New York: Bureau of Publications, Teachers College, Columbia University.

Jessel, C. (1983). *The joy of birth: A book for parents and children.* New York: Dutton.

Johnson, C. N., & Wellman, H. M. (1980). Children's developing understanding of mental verbs: Remember, know, and guess. *Child Development, 51,* 1095–1102.

Johnson, M. K., & Foley, M. A. (1984). Differentiating fact from fantasy: The reliability of children's memory. *Journal of Social Issues, 40,* 33–50.

Jolley, A. (1985). The evolution of primate behavior. *American Scientist, 73,* 230–239.

Jones, M. C. (1957). The later careers of boys who were early- or later-maturing. *Child Development, 28,* 113–128.

Jones, M. C. (1965). Psychological correlates of somatic development. *Child Development, 36,* 899–911.

Jones, M. C., & Bayley, N. (1950). Physical maturity among boys as related to behavior. *Journal of Educational Psychology, 41,* 129–148.

Jones, O. H. M. (1977). Mother-child communication with pre-linguistic Down's Syndrome and normal infants. In H. R. Schaffer (Ed.), *Studies in mother-infant interaction.* London: Academic Press.

References

Juel-Nielsen, N. (1965). Individual and environment: A psychiatric-psychological investigation of monozygotic twins reared apart. *Acta Psychiatrica et Neurologica Scandinavia (Monograph Supplement)*, Whole Number 183.

Kagan, J. (1958). The concept of identification. *Psychological Review, 65,* 296–305.

Kagan, J. (1976). Emergent themes in human development. *American Scientist, 64,* 186–196.

Kagan, J. (1981). Universals of human development. In R. H. Munroe, R. L. Monroe, & B. B. Whiting (Eds.), *Handbook of cross-cultural human development.* New York: Garland STPM Press.

Kagan, J., & Brim, O. (1981). *Change and continuity in development.* New York: Basic Books.

Kail, R. V., Jr. (1984). *The development of memory in children* (2nd ed.). New York: Freeman.

Kail, R. V., Jr., & Hagen, J. W. (Eds.). (1977). *Perspectives on the development of memory and cognition.* Hillsdale, NJ: Erlbaum.

Kamin, L. J. (1975). *The science and politics of IQ.* New York: Wiley.

Kaplan, B. (1984). *Development and growth.* Hillsdale, NJ: Erlbaum.

Kaslow, N. J. & Rehm, L. P. (1983). Childhood depression. In R. J. Morris & T. R. Kratochwill (Eds.), *The practice of child therapy.* New York: Pergamon.

Kaye, D. B. (1986). The development of mathematical cognition. *Cognitive Development, 1,* 157–170.

Kaye, K. (1980). Why we don't talk "baby talk" to babies. *Journal of Child Language, 7,* 489–507.

Kegan, R. (1982). *The evolving self: Problem and process in human development.* Cambridge, MA: Harvard University Press.

Keil, F. C. (1981). Constraints on knowledge and cognitive development. *Psychological Review, 1981, 88,* 197–227.

Kennell, J. H., & Klaus, M. H. (1984). Mother-infant bonding: Weighing the evidence. *Developmental Review, 4,* 275–282.

Kerlinger, F. H. (1979). *Behavioral research: A conceptual approach.* New York: Holt, Rinehart & Winston.

Kimura, M. (1979). The neutral theory of molecular evolution. *Scientific American, 241* (5), 98–130.

Kintsch, W. (1979). On modeling comprehension. *Educational Psychologist, 14,* 3–14.

Kisker, E. E. (1985). Teenagers talk about sex, pregnancy and contraception. *Family Planning Perspectives, 17*(No. 2).

Kitchener, K. S., & King, P. M. (1981). Reflective judgment: Concepts of justification and their relationship to age and education. *Journal of Applied Developmental Psychology, 2,* 89–116.

Kitchener, R. F. (1978). Epigenesis: The role of biological models in developmental psychology. *Human Development, 21,* 141–160.

Kitchener, R. F. (1980). Predetermined versus probabilistic epigenesis. A reply to Lerner. *Human Development, 23,* 73–76.

Kitchener, R. F. (1986). *Piaget's theory of knowledge: Genetic epistemology and scientific reason.* New Haven, CT: Yale University Press.

Klatzky, R. L. (1980). *Human memory: Structures and processes* (2nd. ed.). San Francisco: Freeman.

Klaus, M. H., & Kennell, J. H. (1976). *Mother-infant bonding.* St. Louis: Mosby.

Klaus, M. H., & Kennell, J. H. (1982). *Parent-infant bonding.* St. Louis: Mosby.

Klopfer, P. H. (1971). Mother love: What turns it on? *American Scientist, 59,* 404–407.

Kobasigawa, A. (1974). Utilization of retrieval cues by children in recall. *Child Development, 45,* 127–134.

Kobasigawa, A. K. (1977). Retrieval strategies in the development of memory. In R. V. Kail, Jr., & J. W. Hagen (Eds.), *Perspectives on the development of memory and cognition.* Hillsdale, NJ: Erlbaum.

Kohlberg, L. (1966). A cognitive-developmental analysis of children's sex-role concepts and attitudes. In E. E. Maccoby (Ed.), *The development of sex differences* (pp. 82–172). Stanford: Stanford University Press.

Kohlberg, L. (1973). Continuities in childhood and adult moral development revisited. In P. B. Baltes & K. W. Schaie (Eds.), *Life-span developmental psychology: Personality and socialization.* New York: Academic Press.

Kohlberg, L. (1984). *Essays on moral development: Vol. II. The psychology of moral development.* New York: Harper & Row.

Kohlberg, L. (in press). *Essays on moral development: Vol. III. Education and moral development.* New York: Harper & Row.

Kohlberg, L., & Candee, D. (1984). The relationship of moral judgment to moral action. In W. M. Kurtines & J. L. Gewirtz (Eds.), *Morality, moral behavior, and moral development* (pp. 52–73). New York: Wiley.

Kohlberg, L., & Kramer, R. (1969). Continuities and discontinuities in childhood and adult moral development. *Human Development, 12,* 93–120.

Kohlberg, L., Levine, C., & Hewer, A. (1983). *Moral stages: A current formulation and a response to critics.* Basel: S. Karger.

Kohlberg, L., & Mayer, R. (1972). Development as the aim of education. *Harvard Educational Review, 42,* 449–496.

Kolata, G. (1978). Behavioral teratology: Birth defects of the mind. *Science, 202,* 732–734.

Kolata, G. (1984). Studying learning in the womb. *Science, 225,* 302–303.

Kolata, G. (1985). How safe are engineered organisms? *Science, 229,* 34–35.

Konner, M. J. (1981). Evolution of human behavior development. In R. H. Munroe, R. L. Munroe, & B. B. Whiting (Eds.), *Handbook of cross-cultural human development.* New York: Garland STPM Press.

Kornblith, H. (Ed.) (1985). *Naturalizing epistemology.* Cambridge, MA: MIT Press.

Kremnitzer, J. P., Vaughan, H. G., Kurtzberg, D., & Dowling, K. (1979). Smooth-pursuit eye movements in the newborn infant. *Child Development, 50,* 442–448.

Kreutzer, M. A., Leonard, C., & Flavell, J. H. (1975). An interview study of children's knowledge about memory. *Monographs of the Society for Research in Child Development, 40* (1, Serial No. 159).

Kuhn, D. (1986). Education for thinking. *Teachers College Record, 87,* 495–512.

Kuhn, D., & Brannock, J. (1977). Development of the isolation of variables scheme in experimental and "natural experiment" contexts. *Developmental Psychology, 13,* 9–14.

Kuhn, D., & Phelps, E. (1979). A methodology for observing development of a formal reasoning strategy. In D. Kuhn (Ed.), *Intellectual development beyond childhood.* San Francisco: Jossey-Bass.

References

Kunzinger, E. L., III (1985). A short-term longitudinal study of memorial development during early grade school. *Developmental Psychology, 21,* 642–646.

Kurtines, W. M., & Gewirtz, J. L. (1984). Certainty and morality: Objectivistic versus relativistic approaches. In W. M. Kurtines & J. L. Gewirtz (Eds.), *Morality, moral behavior, and moral development* (pp. 3–23). New York: Wiley.

LaBerge, D., & Samuels, S. J. Toward a theory of automatic information processing in reading. *Cognitive Psychology,* 1976, *8,* 283–323.

Labouvie, E. W., & Nesselroade, J. R. (1985). Age, period, and cohort analyses and the study of individual development and social change. In J. R. Nesselroade & A. von Eye (Eds.), *Individual development and social change: Explanatory Analysis.* Orlando, FL: Academic Press.

Lamb, M. E. (1977a). Father-infant and mother-infant interactions in the first year of life. *Child Development, 48,* 167–181.

Lamb, M. E. (1977b). The development of mother-infant and father-infant attachments in the second year of life. *Developmental Psychology, 13,* 637–648.

Lamb, M. E. (1980). The development of parent-infant attachments in the first two years of life. In F. A. Pedersen (Ed.), *Developmental psychology: An advanced text.* Hillsdale, NJ: Erlbaum.

Lamb, M. E. (1984). Social and emotional development in infancy. In M. A. Bornstein & M. E. Lamb (Eds), *Developmental psychology: An advanced text.* Hillsdale, NJ: Erlbaum.

Lamb, M. E., Thompson, R. M., Gardner, W., Charnov, E. L., & Estes, D. (1984). Security of infantile attachment as assessed in the "Strange Situation": Its study and biological interpretation. *The Behavioral and Brain Sciences, 7,* 127–171.

Lamb, M. E., Thompson, R. M., Gardner, W., Charnov, E. L., & Estes, D. (1985). *Infant-mother attachment.* Hillsdale, NJ: Erlbaum.

Langlois, J. H., & Downs, C. A. (1979). Peer relations as a function of physical attractiveness: The eye of the beholder or behavioral reality? *Child Development, 50,* 409–418.

Langlois, J. H., & Downs, C. A. (1980). Mothers, fathers and peers as socialization agents of sex-typed play behaviors in young children. *Child Development, 51,* 1217–1247.

Langsdorf, P., Izard, C. E., Rayias, M., & Hembree, E. A. (1983). Interest expression, visual fixation, and heart rate changes in 2- to 8-month-old infants. *Developmental Psychology, 19,* 375–386.

Lasky, R. E., Syrdal-Lasky, A., & Klein, R. E. (1975). VOT discrimination by four to six and a half month old infants from Spanish environments. *Journal of Experimental Child Psychology, 20,* 215–225.

Lawlor, R. W. (1981). The progressive construction of mind. *Cognitive Science, 5,* 1–30.

Leakey, R. E. (1982). *Human origins,* New York: Dutton.

Lederberg, A. J. (1982). A framework for research on preschool children's speech modification. In S. A. Kuczaj, II (Ed.), *Language development: Vol. 2. Language, thought, and culture.* Hillsdale, NJ: Erlbaum.

Leon, M. (1984). Rules mothers and sons use to integrate intent and damage information in their moral judgments. *Child Development, 55,* 2106–2113.

Lerner, R. M. (1978). Nature, nurture, and dynamic interactionism. *Human Development, 21,* 1–20.

Lerner, R. M. (1980). Concepts of epigenesis: Descriptive and explanatory issues: A critique of Kitchener's comments. *Human Development, 23,* 63–72.

Lerner, R. M., Skinner, E. A., & Sorell, G. T. (1980). Methodological implications of contextual/dialectic theories of development. *Human Development, 23,* 225–235.

Lesgold, A. M., Levin, J. R., Shimron, J., & Guttman, J. (1975). Pictures and young children's learning from oral prose. *Journal of Educational Psychology, 67,* 636–642.

Leshner, A. I. (1977). Hormones and emotions. In D. K. Candland et al. (Eds.), *Emotion.* Belmont, CA: Wadsworth.

Levitan, S. A., & Belous, R. S. (1981). *What's happening to the American family?* Baltimore, MD: Johns Hopkins University Press.

Levitt, M. J., Weber, R. A., Clark, M. C., & McDonnell, P. (1985). Reciprocity of exchange in toddler sharing behavior. *Developmental Psychology, 21,* 122–123.

Lewin, R. (1983). Were Lucy's feet made for walking? *Science, 220,* 700–702.

Lewis, M., & Brooks-Gunn, J. (1979). *Social cognition and the acquisition of self.* New York: Plenum.

Lewis, M., & Michalson, L. (1983). *Children's emotions and moods.* New York: Plenum.

Liben, L. S. (1977). Memory in the context of cognitive development: The Piagetian approach. In R. V. Kail, Jr., & J. W. Hagen (Eds.), *Perspectives on the development of memory and cognition.* Hillsdale, NJ: Erlbaum.

Liebert, R. M. (1984). What develops in moral development? In W. M. Kurtines & J. L. Gewirtz (Eds.), *Morality, moral behavior, and moral development* (pp. 177–192). New York: Wiley.

Lieven, E. V. M. (1980). *Language development in young children: Children's speech and speech to children.* Unpublished doctoral dissertation, Cambridge University.

Linn, M. C., & Peterson, A. C. (1985). Emergence and characterization of sex differences in spatial ability: A meta-analysis. *Child Development, 56,* 1479–1498.

Lipsitz, J. S. (1979). Adolescent development: Myths and realities. *Children Today, 31,* 2–7.

Locke, D. (1983a). Theory and practice in thought and action. In H. Weinreich-Haste & D. Locke (Eds.), *Morality in the making: Thought, action, and the social context* (pp. 157–170). New York: Wiley.

Locke, D. (1983b). Moral reasons and moral action. In H. Weinreich-Haste & D. Locke (Eds.), *Morality in the making: Thought, action, and the social context* (pp. 111–124). New York: Wiley.

Lockhart, A. (1980). Motor learning and motor development during infancy and childhood. In C. B. Corbin (Ed.), *A textbook of motor development* (2nd ed.). Dubuque: Wm. C. Brown.

Loehlin, J. C., & Nichols, R. C. (1976). *Heredity, environment, and personality: A study of 850 sets of twins.* Austin: University of Texas Press.

References

Loftus, E. T., Green, E., & Smith, R. H. (1980). How deep is the meaning of life? *Bulletin of the Psychonomic Society, 15,* 282–284.

Logan, R. D. (1986). A reconceptualization of Erikson's theory: The repetition of existential and instrumental themes. *Human Development, 29,* 125–136.

Long, F., Peters, D. L., & Garduque, L. (1985). Continuity between home and day care: A model for defining relevant dimensions of child care. In I. E. Sigel (Ed.), *Advances in applied developmental psychology* (Vol. 1). Norwood, NJ: Ablex.

Long, J., & Baddeley, A. (1981). *Attention and performance IX.* Hillsdale, NJ: Erlbaum.

Lopreato, J. (1984). *Human nature and biocultural evolution.* New York: Allen & Unwin.

Lorenz, K. (1965). *Evolution and modification of behavior.* Chicago: University of Chicago Press.

Lorenz, K. (1966). *On aggression.* New York: Harcourt, Brace & World.

Lotter, V. (1978). Follow-up studies. In M. Rutter & E. Schopler (Eds.), *Autism: A reappraisal of concepts and treatment.* New York: Plenum.

Lucariello, J., & Nelson, K. (1985). Slot-filler categories as memory organizers for young children. *Developmental Psychology, 21,* 272–282.

Lumsden, C. J., & Wilson, E. O. (1983). *Promethean fire: Reflections on the origins of mind.* Cambridge: Harvard University Press.

Lund, N. J., & Duchan, J. F. (1983). *Assessing children's language in naturalistic contexts.* Englewood Cliffs, NJ: Prentice-Hall.

Luria, A. R. (1982). *Language and cognition.* New York: Wiley.

Maccoby, E. E. (1980). *Social development: Psychological growth and the parent-child relationship.* New York: Harcourt Brace Jovanovich.

Maccoby, E. E., & Jacklin, C. N. (1974). *The psychology of sex differences.* Stanford: Stanford University Press.

Maccoby, E. E., & Martin, J. A. (1983). Socialization in the context of the family: Parent-child interaction in E. M. Hetherington (Ed.), P. H. Mussen (Series Ed.), *Handbook of child psychology: Vol 4. Socialization, personality, and social development.* New York: Wiley.

Macnamara, J. (1972). Cognitive basis of language learning in infants. *Psychological Review, 79,* 1–13.

MacWhinney, B. (1982). Basic syntactic processes. In S. Kuczaj, II (Ed.), *Language development: Vol. 1. Syntax and semantics.* Hillsdale, NJ: Erlbaum.

Malatesta, C. Z., & Izard, C. E. (Eds.) (1984). *Emotion in adult development.* Beverly Hills, CA: Sage.

Malina, R. M. (1979). Secular changes in size and maturity: Causes and effects. In A. F. Roche (Ed.), Secular trends in human growth, maturation, and development. *Monographs of the Society for Research in Child Development, 44,* Nos. 3–4.

Malina, R. M. (1980). Factors influencing motor development: Introductory comments and biologically related correlates to motor development and performance during infancy and childhood. In C. B. Corbin (Ed.), *A textbook of motor development* (2nd ed.). Dubuque: Wm. C. Brown.

Mandler, G. (1980). The generation of emotion: A psychological theory. In R.

Plutchik & H. Kellerman (Eds.), *Emotion: Theory, research, and experience* (Vol. 1). New York: Academic Press.

Mandler, J. M., & Johnson, N. S. (1977). Remembrance of things parsed: Story structure and recall. *Cognitive Psychology, 9,* 111–151.

Maratsos, M. (1983). Some current issues in the study of the acquisition of grammar. In J. Flavell & E. Markman (Eds.), P. H. Mussen (Series Ed.), *Manual of child psychology: Vol 3. Language and cognitive development.* New York: Wiley.

Marcia, J. E. (1980). Identity in adolescence. In J. Adelson (Ed.), *Handbook of adolescent psychology* (pp. 159–187). New York: Wiley.

Margolin, G., & Patterson, G. R. (1975). Differential consequences provided by fathers and mothers for their sons and daughters. *Developmental Psychology, 11,* 537–538.

Markman, E. M. (1979). Realizing you don't understand: Elementary school children's awareness of inconsistencies. *Child Development, 50,* 643–655.

Markman, E. M. (1981). Comprehension monitoring. In W. P. Dickson (Ed.), *Children's oral communication skills.* New York: Academic Press.

Marr, D. (1982). *Vision: A computational investigation into the human representation and processing of visual information.* San Francisco: Freeman.

Martin, C. L., & Halverson, C. F., Jr. (1981). A schematic processing model of sex typing and stereotyping in children. *Child Development, 52,* 1119–1134.

Martin, J. A. (1981). A longitudinal study of the consequences of early mother-infant interaction. A microanalytic approach. *Monographs of the Society for Research in Child Development, 46*(3, Serial No. 190).

Massaro, D. W. (1972). Stimulus information vs. processing time in auditory pattern recognition. *Perception and Psychophysics, 12,* 50–56.

Massaro, D. W. (1979). Preperceptual auditory images. *Jounal of Experimental Psychology, 85,* 411–417.

Massaro, D. W., & Idson, W. L. (1978). Target-mask similarity in backward recognition masking of perceived tone duration. *Perception and Psychophysics, 24,* 225–236.

Masur, E. F., McIntyre, C. W., & Flavell, J. H. (1973). Developmental changes in apportionment of study time among items in a multitrial free recall task. *Journal of Experimental Child Psychology, 15,* 237–246.

Matas, L., Arend, R. A., & Sroufe, L. A. (1978). Continuity of adaptation in the second year: The relationship between quality of attachment and later competence. *Child Development, 49,* 547–556.

Matheny, A. P. (1983). A longitudinal twin study of stability of components from Bayley's infant behavior record. *Child Development, 54,* 356–360.

Matheny, A. P., & Dolan, A. B. (1975). Persons, situations and time: A genetic view of behavioral change in children. *Journal of Personality and Social Psychology, 32,* 1106–1110.

Matthews, G. B. (1980). *Philosophy and the young child.* Cambridge, MA: Harvard University Press.

Maurer, D. (1975). Infant visual perceptions: Methods of study. In L. B. Cohen & P. Salapatek (Eds.), *Infant perception: From sensation to cognition, basic visual processes:* Vol. 1. New York: Academic Press.

Mayer, R. E. (1983). *Thinking, problem solving, cognition.* San Francisco: Wadsworth.

McBurney, D. H., & Collings, V. B. (1984). *Introduction to sensation/perception* (2nd ed.). Englewood Cliffs, NJ: Prentice-Hall.

McCabe, M. P., & Collins, J. K. (1979). Sex role and dating orientation. *Journal of Youth and Adolescence, 8,* 407–425.

McCall, R. B. (1977). Challenges to a science of developmental psychology. *Child Development, 48,* 333–344.

McCune-Nicolich, L. (1981). The cognitive bases of relational words in the single word period. *Journal of Child Language, 8,* 15–34.

McGurk, H., & Lewis, M. (1974). Space perception in early infancy: Perception within a common auditory-visual space? *Science, 186,* 649–650.

McKeever, W. F., & Hoff, A. L. (1983). Further evidence of the absence of measurable interhemispheric transfer time in left-handers who employ an inverted writing position. *Bulletin of the Psychonomic Society, 21,* 255–258.

McKnew, D. H., Cytryn, L., & Yahraes, H. (1983). *Why isn't Johnny crying?* New York: Norton.

McNeill, D. (1970). *The acquisition of language.* New York: Harper & Row.

Medinnus, G. R. (1976). *Child study and observation guide.* New York: Wiley.

Mednick, B., Hocevar, D., Baker, R., & Teasdale, T. (1983). Effects of social, familial, and maternal state variables on neonatal and infant health. *Developmental Psychology, 19,* 752–765.

Mednick, S. A., Harway, M., & Finello, K. M. (Eds.) (1984). *Handbook of longitudinal research.* New York: Praeger.

Mehan, H. (1985). The structure of classroom discourse. In T. A. van Dijk (Ed.), *Handbook of discourse analysis: Vol. 3. Discourse and dialogue.* London: Academic Press.

Mehler, J., & Fox, R. (1985). *Neonate cognition: Beyond the blooming buzzing confusion.* Hillsdale, NJ: Erlbaum.

Melamed, B. G., & Siegel, C. J. (1975). Reduction of anxiety in children facing hospitalization and surgery by use of filmed modeling. *Journal of Consulting and Clinical Psychology, 1975, 43,* 511–521.

Melton, G. B. (1983). Toward "personhood" for adolescents: Autonomy and privacy as values in public policy. *American Psychologist, 38,* 99–103.

Melton, G. B. (Ed.) (1986). *Adolescent abortion: Psychological and legal issues.* Lincoln: University of Nebraska Press.

Melton, G. B., Koocher, G. P., & Saks, M. J. (Eds.) (1983). *Children's competence to consent.* New York: Plenum.

Mezynski, K. (1983). Issues concerning the acquisition of knowledge: Effects of vocabulary training on reading comprehension. *Review of Educational Research, 53,* 253–279.

Michaels, C. F., & Carello, C. (1981). *Direct perception.* Englewood Cliffs, NJ: Prentice-Hall.

Milewski, A. E., & Siqueland, E. R. (1975). Discrimination of color and pattern novelty in one-month human infants. *Journal of Experimental Child Psychology, 19,* 122–136.

Miller, G. A. (1956). The magical number seven, plus or minus two: Some limits on our capacity for processing information. *Psychological Review, 63,* 81–97.

Miller, G. A. (1981). *Language and speech.* San Francisco: W. H. Freeman.

Miller, J. A. (1983a). The brain is behind evolution's drive. *Science News, 124,* 101.
Miller, J. A. (1983b). Toward gene therapy: Lesch-Nyman syndrome. *Science News, 124,* 90–91.
Miller, J. A. (1983c). The littlest babies. *Science News, 124,* 250–253.
Miller, J. A. (1983d). Small-baby biology. *Science News, 124,* 266–267.
Miller, J. A. (1983e). Alcohol damage at time of conception. *Science News, 124,* 214.
Miller, J. A. (1985a). Common ground for X, Y chromosomes. *Science News, 127,* 374.
Miller, J. A. (1985b). Sperm sort: On the road to sex selection. *Science News, 127,* 310.
Miller, J. R., & Kintsch, W. (1980). Readability and recall of short prose passages: A theoretical analysis. *Journal of Experimental Psychology: Human Learning and Memory, 6,* 335–353.
Miller, K., Perlmutter, M., & Keating, D. (1984). Cognitive arithmetic: Comparisons of operations. *Journal of Experimental Psychology: Learning, Memory, and Cognition, 10,* 46–60.
Mills, M., & Melhuish, E. (1974). Recognition of mother's voice in early infancy. *Nature, 252,* 123–124.
Milton, S. (1983). *Daytime star: The story of our sun.* New York: Scribner.
Minuchin, P. P., & Shapiro, E. K. (1983). The school as a context for social development. In E. M. Hetherington (Ed.), P. H. Mussen (Series Ed.), *Handbook of child psychology: Vol. 4. Socialization, personality, and social development.* New York: Wiley.
Mirga, T. (1983). Panel hears children tell of nuclear war fears. *Education Week,* Sept. 28, 12–13.
Mistry, J. J., & Lange, G. W. (1985). Children's organization and recall of information in scripted narratives. *Child Development, 56,* 953–961.
Mitchell, D. E., Freeman, R. D., Millodot, M., & Haegerstrom, G. (1973). Meridional amblyopia: Evidence for modification of the human visual system by early visual experience. *Vision Research, 13,* 535–558.
Moates, D. G., & Schumacher, G. M. (1980). *An introduction to cognitive psychology.* Belmont, CA: Wadsworth.
Moely, B. E., Olson, F. A., Halwes, T. G., & Flavell, J. H. (1969). Production deficiency in young children's clustered recall. *Developmental Psychology, 1,* 26–34.
Molfese, D. L., & Molfese, V. J. (1979). Hemisphere and stimulus differences as reflected in the cortical responses of newborn infants to speech stimuli. *Developmental Psychology, 15,* 505–511.
Moore, C. L. (1985). Another psychobiological view of sexual differentiation. *Developmental Review, 5,* 18–55.
Morris, R. J., & Kratochwill, T. R. (1983). Childhood fears and phobias. In R. J. Morris & T. R. Kratochwill (Eds.), *The practice of child therapy.* New York: Pergamon.
Moshman, D. (1979a). Development of formal hypothesis-testing ability. *Developmental Psychology, 15,* 104–112.
Moshman, D. (1979b). To *really* get ahead, get a metatheory. In D. Kuhn (Ed.), *Intellectual development beyond childhood.* San Francisco: Jossey-Bass.

Moshman, D. (1981). Jean Piaget meets Jerry Falwell: Genetic epistemology and the anti-humanist movement in education. *The Genetic Epistemologist, 10*(3), 10–13.

Moshman, D. (1982). Exogenous, endogenous, and dialectical constructivism. *Developmental Review, 2,* 371–384.

Moshman, D. (1985a). Faith Christian v. Nebraska: Parent, child, and community rights in the educational arena. *Teachers College Record, 86,* 553–571.

Moshman, D. (1985b). Individual differences, competence-performance and human rationality. *New Ideas in Psychology, 3,* 345–350.

Moshman, D. (1986). Children's intellectual rights: A First Amendment analysis. In D. Moshman (Ed.), *Children's intellectual rights.* San Francisco: Jossey-Bass.

Moshman, D., & Franks, B. A. (1986). Development of the concept of inferential validity. *Child Development, 57,* 153–165.

Moshman, D., & Timmons, M. (1982). The construction of logical necessity. *Human Development, 25,* 309–323.

Motti, F., Cicchetti, D., & Sroufe, L. A. (1983). From infant expression to symbolic play: The coherence of development in Down Syndrome children. *Child Development, 54,* 1168–1175.

Moynihan, D. P. (1986). *Family and nation.* San Diego: Harcourt Brace Jovanovich.

Muir, D., & Field, N. (1979). How infants orient to sounds. *Child Development, 50,* 431–436.

Murchison, C. (1931). *A handbook of child psychology.* Worcester, MA: Clark University Press.

Murdock, B. B., Jr. (1961). The retention of individual items. *Journal of Experimental Psychology, 62,* 618–625.

Murphy, L. B. (1983). Issues in the development of emotion in infancy. In R. Plutchik & H. Kellerman (Eds.), *Emotion: Theory, research, and experience* (Vol. 2). New York: Academic Press.

Murray, A. W., & Szostak, J. W. (1983). Construction of artificial chromosomes in yeast. *Nature, 305,* 189–198.

Murray, L., & Trevarthen, C. (1986). The infant's role in mother-infant communication. *Journal of Child Language, 13,* 15–19.

Mussen, P. H. (1973). *The psychological development of the child.* Englewood Cliffs, NJ: Prentice-Hall.

Mussen, P. H., & Cover, M. C. (1957). Self-concepts, motivation, and interpersonal attitudes of late- and early-maturing boys. *Child Development, 28,* 243–256.

Myers, B. J. (1984a). Mother-infant bonding: The status of this critical-period hypothesis. *Developmental Review, 4,* 240–274.

Myers, B. J. (1984b). Mother-infant bonding: Rejoinder to Kennell and Klaus. *Developmental Review, 4,* 283–288.

Myers-Walls, J., & Fry-Miller, K. M. (1984). Nuclear war: Helping children overcome fears. *Young children,* May, 27–32.

Myles-Worsley, M., Cromer, C. C., & Dodd, D. H. (1986). Children's preschool script reconstruction: Reliance on general knowledge as memory fades. *Developmental Psychology, 22,* 22–30.

Nagy, W., & Anderson, R. C. (1984). The number of words in printed school English. *Reading Research Quarterly, 19,* 304–330.

REFERENCES

Nagy, W., & Herman, P. A. (1984). Grade and reading ability effects on learning words from context. Paper presented at the Annual Meeting of the National Reading Conference, St. Petersburg Beach, FL.

Nagy, W., & Herman, P. A. (1985). The influence of word and text properties on learning words from context. Paper presented at the Annual Meeting of the American Educational Research Association, Chicago, IL.

Nagy, W., Herman, P. A., & Anderson, R. C. (1985). Learning words from context. *Reading Research Quarterly, 20,* 233–253.

Nathan, P. (1983). *The nervous system.* London: Oxford University Press.

National Institute of Mental Health (1982). *Television and behavior: Ten years of scientific progress and implications for the Eighties* (Vol. 1). Washington, DC: U.S. Government Printing Office.

Neisser, E. G. (1951). *Brothers and sisters.* New York: Harper.

Neisser, U. (1979). The control of information pickup in selective looking. In A. D. Pick (Ed.), *Perception and its development: A tribute to Eleanor Gibson.* Hillsdale, NJ: Erlbaum.

Neisser, U. (1982). *Memory observed: Remembering in natural contexts.* San Francisco: Freeman.

Nelson, K. (1973). Structure and strategy in learning to talk. *Monographs of the Society for Research in Child Development, 38*(1–2, Serial No. 149).

Nelson, T. O. (1977). Repetition and depth of processing. *Journal of Verbal Learning and Verbal Behavior, 16,* 151–171.

Nerlove, S. B., & Snipper, A. S. (1981). Cognitive consequences of cultural opportunity. In R. H. Munroe, R. L. Munroe, & B. B. Whiting (Eds.), *Handbook of cross-cultural human development.* New York: Garland STPM Press.

Nesdale, A. R. Herriman, M. L. & Tunmer, W. E. (1984). Phonological awareness in children. In W. E. Tunmer, C. Pratt, & M. Herriman (Eds.), *Metalinguistic awareness in children: Theory, research, and implications.* Berlin: Springer-Verlag.

Nesselroad, J. R., & Baltes, P. B. (Eds.) (1979). *Longitudinal research in the study of behavior and development.* New York: Academic Press.

Newman, H. H., Freeman, F. N., & Holzinger, K. J. (1937). *Twins: A study of heredity and environment.* Chicago: University of Chicago Press.

Newport, E. L., Gleitman, H., & Gleitman, L. R. (1977). Mother, I'd rather do it myself: Some effects and non-effects of maternal speech style. In C. E. Snow & C. A. Ferguson (Eds.), *Talking to children: Language input and acquisition.* New York: Cambridge University Press.

Ninio, A., & Bruner, J. S. (1978). The achievement and antecedents of labelling. *Journal of Child Language, 5,* 1–15.

Nisan, M., & Kohlberg, L. (1982). Universality and variation in moral judgment: A longitudinal and cross-sectional study in Turkey. *Child Development, 53,* 865–876.

Nitko, A. J. (1983). *Educational tests and measurement: An introduction.* New York: Harcourt Brace Jovanovich.

Nowlis, G. H., & Kessen, W. (1976). Human newborns differentiate differing concentrations of sucrose and glucose. *Science, 191,* 865–866.

Noyes, R. W. (1982). *The sun, our star.* Cambridge: Harvard University Press.

Nunnally, J. C. (1980). The study of human change: Measurement, research strategies, and methods of analysis. In B. B. Wolman & G. Stricker (Eds.), *Handbook of developmental psychology.* Englewood Cliffs, NJ: Prentice-Hall.

Nunner-Winkler, G. (1984). Two moralities? A critical discussion of an ethic of care and responsibility versus an ethic of rights and justice. In W. M. Kurtines & J. L. Gewirtz (Eds.), *Morality, moral behavior, and moral development* (pp. 348–361). New York: Wiley.

Oakhill, J. (1984). Why children have difficulty reasoning with three-term series problems. *British Journal of Developmental Psychology, 2,* 223–230.

Oakley, A. (1984). *A history of the medical care of pregnant women.* New York: Blackwell.

O'Brien, D. P. (1986). The development of conditional reasoning: An iffy proposition. In H. W. Reese (Ed.), *Advances in child development and behavior,* Vol. 20. New York: Academic Press.

Offer, D., & Sabshin, M. (1984). *Normality and the life cycle.* New York: Basic Books.

O'Neil, R. M. (1981). *Classrooms in the crossfire: The rights and interests of students, parents, teachers, administrators, librarians, and the community.* Bloomington: Indiana University Press.

Olson, S. L., Bayles, K., & Bates, J. E. (1986). Mother-child interaction and children's speech progress: A longitudinal study of the first two years. *Merrill-Palmer Quarterly, 32,* 1–20.

Olweus, D. (1980). Familial and temperamental determinants of aggressive behavior in adolescent boys: A causal analysis. *Developmental Psychology, 16,* 644–666.

Olweus, D., Mattsson, A., Schalling, D., & Low, H. (1980). Testosterone, aggression, physical and personality dimensions on normal adolescent males. *Psychosomatic Medicine, 42,* 253–269.

Ornstein, P. A. (1978). *Memory development in children.* Hillsdale, NJ: Erlbaum.

Ornstein, P. A., & Corsale, K. (1979). Process and structure in children's memory. In G. J. Whitehurst & B. J. Zimmerman (Eds.), *The functions of language and cognition.* New York: Academic Press.

Ornstein, P. A., Medlin, R. G., Stone, B. P., & Naus, M. J. (1985). Retrieving for rehearsal: An analysis of active rehearsal in children's memory. *Developmental Psychology, 21,* 633–641.

Ornstein, P. A., & Naus, M. J. (1978). Rehearsal processes in children's memory. In P. A. Ornstein (Ed.), *Memory development in children.* Hillsdale, NJ: Erlbaum.

Ornstein, P. A., Naus, M. J., & Liberty, C. (1975). Rehearsal and organization processes in children's memory. *Child Development, 26,* 818–830.

Ornstein, R., & Thompson, R. F. (1984). *The amazing brain.* Boston, MA: Houghton Mifflin.

Ortony, A. Beyond literal similarity. *Psychological Review, 86,* 161–180.

Osherson, D., & Markman, E. (1975). Language and the ability to evaluate contradictions and tautologies. *Cognition, 3,* 213–226.

Ottoson, D. (1983). *Physiology of the nervous system.* London: Oxford University Press.

Overton, W. F. (1984). World views and their influence on psychological theory and research: Kuhn—Lakatos—Laudan. In H. W. Reese (Ed.), *Advances in child development and behavior,* Vol. 18. New York: Academic Press.

REFERENCES

Overton, W. F., & Newman, J. L. (1982). Cognitive development: A competence-activation/utilization approach. In T. M. Field, A. Huston, H. C. Quay, L. Troll, & G. E. Finley (Eds.), *Review of human development* (pp. 217–241). New York: Wiley.

Palmere, M., Benton, S. L., Glover, J. A., & Ronning, R. R. (1983). Elaboration and recall of main ideas in prose. *Journal of Educational Psychology, 75,* 898–907.

Paris, S. G., & Lindauer, B. K. (1976). The role of inference in children's comprehension and memory for sentences. *Cognitive Psychology, 8,* 217–227.

Paris, S. G., & Lindauer, B. K. (1977). Constructive aspects of children's comprehension and memory. In R. V. Kail, Jr., & J. W. Hagen (Eds.), *Perspectives on the development of memory and cognition.* Hillsdale, NJ: Erlbaum.

Parke, R. D. (1978). Children's home environment: Social and cognitive effects. In I. Altman & J. F. Wohlwill (Eds.), *Children and the environment.* New York: Plenum.

Parke, R. D., & Slaby, R. G. (1983). The development of aggression. In E. M. Hetherington (Ed.), P. H. Mussen (Series Ed.), *Handbook of child psychology: Vol. 4. Socialization, personality, and social development.* New York: Wiley.

Pascal-Leone, J. (1970). A mathematical model for the transition rule in Piaget's development stages. *Acta Psychologica, 63,* 301–345.

Patterson, G. R. (1982). *Coercive family process.* Eugene, OR: Catalia Press.

Pawson, M., & Morris, N. (1972). *Psychosomatic medicine, obstetrics, and gynecology.* New York: Karger.

Pedersen, F. A. (1982). Mother, father, and infant as an interactive system. In J. Belsky (Ed.), *In the beginning: Readings in infancy.* New York: Columbia University Press.

Pederson, F. A., Cain, R. L., Zaslow, M. J., & Anderson, B. J. (1982). Variation in infant experience associated with alternative family roles. In L. Laosa & I. Sigel (Eds.), *Families as learning environments for children.* New York: Plenum.

Pellegrino, J. W., & Goldman, S. R. (1983). Developmental and individual differences in verbal and spatial reasoning. In R. F. Dillon & R. R. Schmeck (Eds.), *Individual differences in cognition.* New York: Academic Press.

Perry, D. G., White, A. J., & Perry, L. C. (1984). Does early sex typing result from children's attempts to match their behavior to sex role stereotypes? *Child Development, 55,* 2114–2121.

Perry, W. G. (1970). *Forms of intellectual and ethical development in the college years.* New York: Holt, Rinehart & Winston.

Persky, H., Smith, K. D., & Basu, G. K. (1971). Relation of psychological measures of aggression and hostility to testosterone production in man. *Psychosomatic Medicine, 33,* 265–277.

Peters, R. S. (1981). *Moral development and moral education.* London: Allen & Unwin.

Phillips, D. C. (1983). On describing a student's cognitive structure. *Educational Psychologist, 18,* 59–74.

Piaget, J. (1932). *The moral judgment of the child.* London: Routledge & Kegan Paul.

Piaget, J. (1954). *The construction of reality in the child.* New York: Basic Books. (Orig. pub. 1937.)

Piaget, J. (1962). *Play, dreams, and imitation in childhood.* New York: Norton. (Orig. pub. 1945.)
Piaget, J. (1963). *The origins of intelligence in children.* New York: Norton. (Orig. pub. 1936.)
Piaget, J. (1965). *The child's conception of number.* New York: Norton. (Orig. pub. 1941.)
Piaget, J. (1969). *The mechanisms of perception.* New York: Basic Books.
Piaget, J. (1978). *Behavior and evolution.* New York: Pantheon.
Piaget, J. (1980). Schemes of actions and language learning. In M. Piattelli-Palmarini (Ed.), *Language and learning: The debate between Jean Piaget and Noam Chomsky.* Cambridge, MA: Harvard University Press.
Piaget, J., & Inhelder, B. (1973). *Memory and intelligence.* New York: Basic Books.
Piattelli-Palmarini, M. (Ed.) (1980). *Language and learning: The debate between Jean Piaget and Noam Chomsky.* Cambridge, MA: Harvard University Press.
Pick, A. D. (1979). *Perception and its development.* Hillsdale, NJ: Erlbaum.
Pick, H. L., & Macleod, R. B. (1974). *Perception: Essays in honor of James J. Gibson.* Ithaca, NY: Cornell University Press.
Pick, H. L., & Saltzman, E. (1978). *Modes of perceiving and processing information.* Hillsdale, NJ: Erlbaum.
Pick, H. L., & Walk, R. D. (1981). *Intrasensory perception and sensory integration.* New York: Plenum.
Pieraut-Le Bonniec, G. (1980). *The development of modal reasoning: Genesis of necessity and possibility notions.* New York: Academic Press.
Piers, M. W. (1978). *Infanticide.* New York: Norton.
Plomin, R., & DeFries, J. C. (1983). The Colorado adoption project. *Child Development, 54,* 276–289.
Plomin, R., DeFries, J. C., & McClearn, G. E. (1980). *Behavioral genetics.* San Francisco: Freeman.
Plomin, R., Loehlin, J. C., & DeFries, J. C. (1985). Genetic and environmental components of "environmental" influences. *Developmental Psychology, 21,* 391–402.
Plutchik, R. (1980a). *Emotion: A Psychoevolutionary synthesis.* New York: Harper & Row.
Plutchik, R. (1980b). A general psychoevolutionary theory of emotion. In R. Plutchik & H. Kellerman (Eds.), *Emotion: Theory, research, and experience* (Vol. 1). New York: Academic Press.
Plutchik, R. (1983). Emotions in early development: A psychoevolutionary approach. In R. Plutchik & H. Kellerman (Eds.), *Emotion: Theory, research, and experience* (Vol. 2). New York: Academic Press.
Pratt, M. W., Golding, G., & Hunter, W. J. (1984). Does morality have a gender? Sex, sex role, and moral judgment relationships across the adult lifespan. *Merrill-Palmer Quarterly, 30,* 321–340.
Pressley, M. (1977). Imagery and children's learning: Putting the picture in developmental perspective. *Review of Educational Research, 47,* 585–622.
Pressley, M., & Brainerd, C. J. (Eds.) (1985). *Cognitive learning and memory in children.* New York: Springer-Verlag.
Priess, B. (Ed.) (1980). *The dinosaurs.* New York: Bantam.

Pyroos, R. S., & Eth, S. (1984). The child as witness to homicide. *Journal of Social Issues, 40,* 87–108.

Rader, N., Bausano, M., & Richards, J. E. (1980). On the nature of the visual-cliff response in human infants. *Child Development, 51,* 61–68.

Radke-Yarrow, M., Zahn-Waxler, C., & Chapman, M. (1983). Children's prosocial dispositions and behavior. In E. M. Hetherington (Ed.), P. H. Mussen (Series Ed.), *Handbook of child psychology: Vol. 4. Socialization, personality, and social development* (pp. 469–545). New York: Wiley.

Ramer, A. L. H. (1976). Syntactic styles in emerging language. *Journal of Child Language, 3,* 49–62.

Rawls, J. (1971). *A theory of justice.* Cambridge, MA: Harvard University Press.

Rawls, J. (1980). Kantian constructivism in moral theory. *The Journal of Philosophy, 77,* 515–572.

Reese, H. W., & Overton, W. F. (1970). Models of development and theories of development. In L. R. Goulet & P. B. Baltes (Eds.), *Life-span developmental psychology: Research and theory.* New York: Academic Press.

Reid, E. (1975). Anomalies in development. In F. D. Horowitz (Ed.), *Review of child development research.* Chicago: University of Chicago Press.

Reimer, J., Paolitto, D. P., & Hersh, R. H. (1983). *Promoting moral growth: From Piaget to Kohlberg* (2nd Ed.). New York: Longman.

Rescorla, L. A. (1980). Overextension in early language development. *Journal of Child Language, 7,* 321–335.

Rest, J. R. (1979). *Development in judging moral issues.* Minneapolis: University of Minnesota Press.

Rest, J. R. (1983). Morality. In J. H. Flavell & E. M. Markman (Eds.), P. H. Mussen (Series Ed.), *Handbook of child psychology: Vol. 3. Cognitive development* (pp. 556–629). New York: Wiley.

Rest, J. R. (1984). The major components of morality. In W. M. Kurtines & J. L. Gewirtz (Eds.), *Morality, moral behavior, and moral development.* New York: Wiley.

Reynolds, A. G., & Flagg, P. W. (1983). *Cognitive psychology* (2nd ed.). Boston: Little, Brown.

Reynolds, C. R. (1981). The problem of bias in psychological assessment. In C. R. Reynolds and T. B. Gutkin (Eds.), *Handbook of school psychology.* New York: Wiley.

Rheingold, H. L., & Adams, J. L. (1980). The significance of speech to newborns. *Developmental Psychology, 16,* 397–403.

Rheingold, H. L., & Eckerman, C. O. (1970). The infant separates himself from his mother. *Science, 168,* 78–83.

Riegel, K. F. (1979). *Foundations of dialectical psychology.* New York: Academic Press.

Rivlin, R., & Gravelle, K. (1985). *Deciphering the senses: The expanding world of human perception.* New York: Simon and Schuster.

Roche, A. F. (Ed.). (1979). Secular trends in human growth, maturation, and development. *Monographs of the Society for Research in Child Development, 44,* Nos. 3–4.

Rock, I. (1984). *Perception* (2nd ed.). San Francisco: Freeman.

Rodman, H., & Griffith, S. B. (1982). Adolescent autonomy and minors' legal rights: Contraception and abortion. *Journal of Applied Developmental Psychology, 3,* 307–318.

Rogoff, B., Gauvain, M., & Ellis, S. (1983). Development viewed in its cultural context. In M. H. Bornstein & M. E. Lamb (Eds.), *Developmental psychology: An advanced textbook.* Hillsdale, NJ: Erlbaum.

Rogoff, B., & Mistry, J. (1985). Memory development in cultural context. In M. Pressley & C. Brainerd (Eds.), *Cognitive learning and memory in children.* New York: Springer-Verlag.

Rose, R. J., & Ditto, W. B. (1983). A developmental-genetic analysis of common fears from early adolescence to early adulthood. *Child Development, 54,* 361–368.

Rosenblatt, J. S., & Siegel, H. I. (1981). Factors governing the onset and maintenance of maternal behavior among nonprimate mammals: The role of hormonal and nonhormonal factors. In D. J. Gubernick & P. H. Klopfer (Eds.), *Parental care in mammals.* New York: Plenum.

Rosenhahn, D. L., & Seligman, M. E. P. (1984). *Abnormal psychology.* New York: Norton.

Ross, B. H. (1981). The more, the better? Number of decisions as a determinant of memorability. *Memory and Cognition, 9,* 22–33.

Ross, R. D., & Slaby, R. G. (1983). The development of aggression. In E. M. Hetherington (Ed.), P. H. Mussen (Series. Ed.), *Handbook of child psychology: Vol. 4. Socialization, personality, and social development.* New York: Wiley.

Rowland, W. (1983). *The politics of TV violence.* Beverly Hills: Sage.

Rubin, J. Z., Provenzano, F. J., & Luria, Z. (1974). The eye of the beholder: Parents' view on sex of newborns. *American Journal of Orthopsychiatry, 43,* 720–731.

Rubin, K. H., Fein, G. G., & Vandenberg, B. (1983). Play. In E. M. Hetherington (Ed.), P. H. Mussen (Series Ed.), *Handbook of Child Psychology: Vol. 4. Socialization, personality, and social development.* New York: Wiley.

Rubin, Z. (1980). *Children's friendships.* Cambridge: Harvard University Press.

Rubin, Z. (1983). What is a friend? In W. Damon (Ed.), *Social and personality development: Essays on the growth of the child.* New York: Wiley.

Rubinstein, E. A. (1983). Television and behavior: research conclusions of the 1982 NIMH Report and their policy implications. *American Psychologist, 38,* 820–825.

Ruble, D. N. (1984). Sex-role development. In M. H. Bornstein & M. E. Lamb (Eds.), *Developmental psychology: An advanced textbook.* Hillsdale, NJ: Erlbaum.

Rugh, R., & Shettles, L. B. (1971). *From conception to birth.* New York: Harper & Row.

Rumelhart, D. C. (1975). Notes on a schema for stories. In D. G. Bobrow & A. Collins (Eds.), *Representation and understanding: Studies in cognitive science.* New York: Academic Press.

Rumelhart, D. C. (1980). Schemata: The building blocks of cognition. In R. J. Spiro, B. C. Bruce, & W. F. Brewer (Eds.), *Theoretical issues in reading comprehension.* Hillsdale, NJ: Erlbaum.

Rumelhart, D. E., & Ortony, A. (1977). Representation of knowledge in memory. In R. C. Anderson, R. J. Spiro, & R. E. Montague (Eds.), *Schooling and the acquisition of knowledge.* Hillsdale, NJ: Erlbaum.

REFERENCES

Russell, J. A., & Bullock, M. (1986). On the dimensions preschoolers use to interpret facial expressions of emotion. *Developmental Psychology, 22,* 97–102.

Russell, M. J. (1976). Human olfactory communication. *Nature, 26,* 520–522.

Salapatek, P. (1977). Stimulus determinants of attention in infants. In B. B. Wolman (Ed.), *International encyclopedia of psychiatry, psychology, psychoanalysis, and neurology* (Vol. 10). New York: Aesculapius.

Salapatek, P. H., & Kessen, W. (1966). Visual scanning of triangles by the human newborn. *Journal of Experimental Child Psychology, 3,* 155–167.

Santrock, J. W. (1984). *Adolescence* (2nd ed.). Dubuque, IA: W. C. Brown.

Sakitt, B. (1975). Locus of short-term visual storage. *Science, 190,* 1318–1319.

Sakitt, B. (1976). Iconic memory. *Psychological Review, 83,* 257–276.

Sakitt, B., & Long, G. M. (1978). Relative rod and cone contributions in iconic storage. *Perception and Psychophysics, 23,* 527–536.

Sakitt, B., & Long, G. M. (1979). Spare the rod and spoil the icon. *Journal of Experimental Psychology: Human Perception and Performance, 5,* 19–30.

Sanders, B., & Soares, M. P. (1986). Sexual maturation and spatial ability in college students. *Developmental Psychology, 22,* 199–203.

Sarafino, E. P. (1985). Peer-peer interaction among infants and toddlers with extensive daycare experience. *Journal of Applied Developmental Psychology, 6,* 17–29.

Saywitz, K., & Wilkinson, L. C. (1982). Age-related differences in metalinguistic awareness. In S. Kuczaj, II (Ed.), *Language development: Vol. 2. Language, thought, and culture.* Hillsdale, NJ: Erlbaum.

Scarr, S. (1966). Genetic factors in activity motivation. *Child Development, 37,* 663–673.

Scarr, S. (1969). Social introversion-extroversion as a heritable response. *Child Development, 40,* 823–832.

Scarr, S. (1984). *Mother care/Other case.* New York: Basic Books.

Scarr, S., & Kidd, J. (1983). Developmental behavior genetics. In M. M. Haith & J. J. Campos (Eds.), P. H. Mussen (Series Ed.), *Handbook of child psychology: Vol. 2. Infancy and developmental psychobiology* (pp. 345–433). New York: Wiley.

Scarr, S., & Salapatek, P. (1970). Patterns of fear development during infancy. *Merrill-Palmer Quarterly, 16,* 53–90.

Scarr, S., & Weinberg, R. A. (1983). The Minnesota adoption studies: Genetic differences and malleability. *Child Development, 54,* 260–267.

Schaie, K. W. (1965). A general model for the study of developmental problems. *Psychological Bulletin, 64,* 92–107.

Schaie, K. W., & Baltes, P. B. (1975). On sequential strategies in developmental research: Description or explanation? *Human Development, 18,* 384–390.

Schaie, K. W., & Hertzog, C. (1980). Longitudinal methods. In B. B. Wolman & G. Stricker (Eds.), *Handbook of developmental psychology.* Englewood Cliffs, NJ: Prentice-Hall.

Schallert, D. L. (1980). The role of illustrations in reading comprehension. In R. J. Spiro, B. C. Brure, & W. F. Brewer (Eds.), *Theoretical issues in reading comprehension.* Hillsdale, NJ: Erlbaum.

Schank, R. C. (1982). *Reading and understanding.* Hillsdale, NJ; Erlbaum.

Schiedel, D. G., & Marcia, J. E. (1985). Ego identity, intimacy, sex role orientation, and gender. *Developmental Psychology, 21,* 149–160.

Schlaefli, A., Rest, J. R., & Thoma, S. J. (1985). Does moral education improve

References

moral judgment? A meta-analysis of intervention studies using the Defining Issues Test. *Review of Educational Research, 55,* 319–352.

Schriebman, L., Charlop, M. H., & Britten, K. R. (1983). Childhood autism. In R. S. Morris & T. R. Kratochwill (Eds.), *The practice of child therapy.* New York: Pergamon.

Schulman, C. (1973). Eye movements in infants using dc recording. *Neuropaediatric, 4,* 76–87.

Schulsinger, F., Mednick, S. A., & Knop, J. (Eds.) (1981). *Longitudinal research: Methods and uses in behavioral science.* Boston: Martinus Nijhoff.

Schultebrand, J. G., & Raskin, A. (Eds.) (1977). *Depression in childhood: Diagnosis, treatment, and conceptual models.* New York: Raven Press.

Science (1986). Obese children: A growing problem. *Science, 232,* 20–21.

Science News (1984). Teen suicide and "masked" depression. *Science News, 126,* 266.

Scott, J. P. (1980). The function of emotions in behavioral systems: A systems analysis. In R. Plutchik & H. Kellerman (Eds.), *Emotion: Theory, research, and experience* (Vol. 1). New York: Academic Press.

Scrimshaw, N. S. (1969). Early malnutrition and central nervous system function. *Merrill-Palmer Quarterly, 15,* 375–388.

Searle, J. (1969). *Speech acts: An essay in the philosophy of language.* London: Cambridge University Press.

Sears, P. S., Maccoby, E. E., & Levin, H. (1957). *Patterns of child rearing.* Evanston, IL: Ron Peterson.

Seitz, V. (1984). Methodology. In M. H. Bornstein & M. E. Lamb (Eds.), *Developmental psychology: An advanced textbook,* Hillsdale, NJ: Erlbaum.

Selman, R. (1980). *The growth of interpersonal understanding.* New York: Academic Press.

Serpell, R. (1979). How specific are perceptual skills? A cross-cultural study of pattern reproduction. *British Journal of Psychology, 70,* 365–380.

Sewall, M. (1930). Two studies in sibling rivalry: I. Some causes of jealousy in young children. *Smith College Studies in Social Work, 1,* 6–22.

Shavelson, R. J. (1983). On quagmires, philosophical and otherwise: A reply to Phillips. *Educational Psychologist, 18,* 81–87.

Sherif, M., Harvey, O. J., White, B. J., Hood, W. R., & Sherif, C. W. (1961). *Inter-group conflict and cooperation: The Robber's Cave experiment.* Norman: University of Oklahoma Press.

Sherman, J. A. (1973). *On the psychology of women: A survey of empirical studies.* Springfield, IL: Charles C. Thomas.

Sherrod, L. R. (1978). *Social cognition in infants: Developmental perception of the human face.* (Doctoral dissertation, Yale University.) *Dissertation Abstracts International, 39,* 2548B.

Sherrod, L. R. (1981). Issues in cognitive-perceptual development: The special case of social stimuli. In M. E. Lamb & L. R. Sherrod (Eds.), *Infant social cognition.* Hillsdale, NJ: Erlbaum.

Sherzer, J. (1985). Puns and jokes. In T. A. van Dijk (Ed.), *Handbook of discourse analysis: Vol. 4. Discourse and dialogue.* London: Academic Press.

Shields, J. (1962). *Monozygotic twins: Brought up apart and brought up together.* London: Oxford University Press.

Shinn, M. (1900). *Biography of a baby.* Boston: Houghton Mifflin.

Shultz, T. R., Wright, K., & Schleifer, M. (1986). Assignment of moral responsibility and punishment. *Child Development, 57,* 177–184.

Shute, G. E. (1983). The assessment of formal-operational reasoning: A caution. *The Genetic Epistemologist, 12*(4), 6–7.

Sidman, M. (1960). *Tactics of scientific research.* New York: Basic Books.

Siegel, H. (1986). Critical thinking as an intellectual right. In D. Moshman (Ed.), *Children's intellectual rights.* San Francisco: Jossey-Bass.

Siegel, H. (1987). *Educating reason: An essay on rationality, critical thinking, and education.* London: Routledge & Kegan Paul.

Siegel, L. J. (1983). Psychosomatic and psychophysiological disorders. In R. J. Morris & T. R. Kratochwill (Eds.), *The practice of child therapy.* New York: Pergamon.

Siegler, R. S. (1976). Three aspects of cognitive development. *Cognitive Psychology, 8,* 481–520.

Siegler, R. S. (1980a). Recent trends in the study of cognitive development: Variations on a task-analytic theme. *Human Development, 23,* 278–285.

Siegler, R. S. (1980b). When do children learn: The relation between existing knowledge and learning. *Educational Psychologist, 15,* 135–150.

Siegler, R. S. (1983a). Five generalizations about cognitive development. *American Psychologist, 38,* 263–277.

Siegler, R. S. (1983b). Information processing approaches to development. In W. Kessen (Ed.), P. H. Mussen (Series Ed.), *Handbook of child psychology: Vol. 1. History, theory, and methods* (pp. 129–211). New York: Wiley.

Siegler, R. S. (1984). Mechanisms of cognitive growth: Variation and selection. In R. J. Sternberg (Ed.), *Mechanisms of cognitive development* (pp. 141–162). New York: Freeman.

Siegler, R. S., & Richards, D. D. (1982). The development of intelligence. In R. J. Sternberg (Ed.), *Handbook of human intelligence* (pp. 897–971). Cambridge: Cambridge University Press.

Simon, H. A., & Chase, W. G. (1973). Skill in chess. *American Scientist, 61,* 394–403.

Sinclair, H. The role of cognitive structures in language acquistion. In E. H. Lenneberg & E. Lenneberg (Eds.), *Foundations of language development: A multidisciplinary approach (Vol. 1)* (pp. 223–238). New York: Academic Press.

Singer, D. G. (1983). A time to reexamine the role of television in our lives. *American Psychologist, 38,* 815–816.

Singer, J. L., & Singer, D. G. (1983). Implications of childhood television viewing for cognition, imagination, and emotion. In J. Bryant & D. R. Anderson (Eds.), *Children's understanding of television: Research on attention and comprehension.* New York: Academic Press.

Skinner, B. F. (1938). *The behavior of organisms.* New York: Appleton-Century-Crofts.

Skinner, B. F. (1956). A case history in scientific methods. *American Psychologist, 11,* 221–233.

Skinner, B. F. (1957). *Verbal behavior.* New York: Appleton-Century-Crofts.

Skinner, B. F. (1971). *Beyond freedom and dignity.* New York: Knopf.

Skinner, B. F. (1974). *About behaviorism.* New York: Vintage.

Skinner, B. F. (1981). Selection by consequences. *Science, 213,* 501–504.

Skipper, J. K. & Nass, G. (1966). Dating behavior: A framework for analysis and an illustration. *Journal of Marriage and the Family, 28,* 412–420.

Slackman, E., & Nelson, K. (1984). Acquisition of an unfamiliar script in story form by young children. *Child Development, 55,* 323–340.

Slobin, D. I. (1973). Cognitive prerequisites for the development of grammar. In C. A. Ferguson & D. I. Slobin (Eds.), *Studies of child language development.* New York: Holt, Rinehart & Winston.

Smetana, J. G. (1984). Morality and gender: A commentary on Pratt, Golding, and Hunter. *Merrill-Palmer Quarterly, 30,* 341–348.

Smetana, J. G. (1985). Preschool children's conceptions of transgressions: Effects of varying moral and conventional domain-related attributes. *Developmental Psychology, 21,* 18–29.

Smith, D. W. (1977). *Growth and its disorders.* Philadelphia: W. B. Saunders.

Smith, F. (1983). *Essays into literacy.* Exeter, NH: Heinemann.

Smith, S. D., Kimberling, W. J., Pennington, B. F., & Lubs, H. A. (1983). *Science, 219,* 1345–1346.

Snarey, J. R. (1985). Cross-cultural universality of social-moral development: A critical review of Kohlbergian research. *Psychological Bulletin, 97,* 202–232.

Snarey, J. R., Reimer, J., & Kohlberg, L. (1985a). Development of social-moral reasoning among Kibbutz adolescents: A longitudinal cross-cultural study. *Developmental Psychology, 21,* 3–17.

Snarey, J., Reimer, J., & Kohlberg, L. (1985b). The kibbutz as a model for moral education: A longitudinal cross-cultural study. *Journal of Applied Developmental Psychology, 6,* 151–172.

Snow, C. E. (1977). The development of conversation between mothers and babies. *Journal of Child Language, 4,* 1–22.

Snow, C. E., & Ferguson, C. A. (Eds.) (1977). *Talking to children: Language input and acquisition.* New York: Cambridge University Press.

Snyder, M., & Campbell, B. (1980). Testing hypotheses about other people: The role of the hypothesis. *Personality and Social Psychology Bulletin, 6,* 421–426.

Somerville, S. C., Hadkinson, B. A., & Greenberg, C. (1979). Two levels of inferential behavior in young children. *Child Development, 50,* 119–131.

Spache, G. D., & Spache, E. B. (1977). *Reading in the elementary school* (4th Ed.). Boston: Allyn & Bacon.

Speer, J. R., & Flavell, J. H. (1979). Young children's knowledge of the relative difficulty of recognition and recall memory tasks. *Developmental Psychology, 15,* 214–217.

Spelke, E. S., & Cortelyou, A. (1981). Perceptual aspects of social knowing: Looking and listening in infancy. In M. E. Lamb & L. R. Sherrod (Eds.), *Infant social cognition.* Hillsdale, NJ: Erlbaum.

Sperling, G. (1960). The information available in brief visual presentations. *Psychological Monographs, 74* (Whole Number 498).

Sperling, G. (1963). A model for visual memory tasks. *Human Factors, 5,* 19–31.

Sperry, R. (1982). Some effects of disconnecting the cerebral hemispheres. *Science, 217,* 1223–1226.

Spiegler, M. D. (1983). *Contemporary behavioral therapy.* Palo Alto, CA: Mayfield.

Spoehr, K. T., & Lehmkuhle, S. W. (1982). *Visual information processing.* San Francisco: Freeman.

REFERENCES

Sroufe, L. A. (1979a). Socioemotional development. In J. D. Osofsky (Ed.), *Handbook of infant development*. New York: Wiley.

Sroufe, L. A. (1979b). The coherence of individual development: Family care, attachment, and subsequent developmental issues. *American Psychologist, 34,* 834–841.

Sroufe, L. A., & Waters, E. (1977). Attachment as an organizational construct. *Child Development, 48,* 1185–1199.

Sroufe, L. A., & Wunsch, J. P. (1972). The development of laughter in the first year of life. *Child Development, 43,* 1326–1344.

Stark, R. E. (1979). Prespeech segmental feature development. In P. Fletcher & M. Garman (Eds.), *Language acquisition: Studies in first language development* (pp. 15–32). New York: Cambridge University Press.

Stein, N. L., & Glenn, C. G. (1979). An analysis of story comprehension in elementary school children. In R. O. Freedle (Ed.), *Discourse processing: Advances in research and theory* (Vol. 2). Norwood, NJ: Ablex.

Steptoe, A., & Mathews, A. (1984). *Health care and human behavior.* New York: Academic Press.

Stern, D. (1977). *The first relationship: Mother and infant.* Cambridge, MA: Harvard University Press.

Sternberg, R. J. (1982). A componential approach to intellectual development. In R. J. Sternberg (Ed.), *Advances in the psychology of human intelligence,* Vol. 1 (pp. 413–463). Hillsdale, NJ: Erlbaum.

Sternberg, R. J. (1983). Criteria for intellectual skills training. *Educational Researcher, 12*(2), 6–12; 26.

Sternberg, R. J. (1984a). What should intelligence tests test? Implications of a triarchic theory of intelligence for intelligence testing. *Educational Researcher, 13*(1), 5–15.

Sternberg, R. J. (1984b). Mechanisms of cognitive development: A componential approach. In R. J. Sternberg (Ed.), *Mechanisms of cognitive development* (pp. 163–186). New York: Freeman.

Sternberg, R. J. (1984c). Toward a triarchic theory of human intelligence. *The Behavioral and Brain Sciences, 7,* 269–315.

Sternberg, R. J. (1984d). *Beyond IQ: A triarchic theory of human intelligence.* New York: Cambridge University Press.

Sternberg, R. J., & Gardner, M. K. (1983). Unities in inductive reasoning. *Journal of Experimental Psychology: General, 112,* 80–116.

Sternberg, R. J., Powell, J. S., & Kaye, D. B. (1983). Teaching vocabulary-building skills: A contextual approach. In A. C. Wilkinson (Ed.), *Communicating with computers in the classroom: Prospects for applied cognitive science.* New York: Academic Press.

Sternberg, R. J., & Rifkin, B. (1979). The development of analogical reasoning processes. *Journal of Experimental Child Psychology, 27,* 195–232.

Sternberg, S. (1966). High-speed scanning in human memory. *Science, 153,* 652–654.

Stewart, M. J. (1980). Fundamental locomotor skills. In C. B. Corbin (Ed.), *A textbook of motor development* (2nd ed.). Dubuque: Wm. C. Brown.

Stirnimann, F. (1944). Über das farbempfinden neugeborener. *Annales Paediatrici, 163,* 1–25.

References

Stone, J. (1983). *Parallel processing in the visual system.* New York: Plenum.

Straughan, R. (1983). From moral judgment to moral action. In H. Weinreich-Haste & D. Locke (Eds.), *Morality in the making: Thought, action, and social context* (pp. 125–140). New York: Wiley.

Strauss, M. S., & Cohen, L. B. (1980). Infant immediate and delayed memory for perceptual dimension. Paper presented at the International Conference on Infant Studies.

Streeter, L. A. (1976). Language perception of 2-month-old infants shows effects of both innate mechanisms and experience. *Nature, 259,* 39–41.

Suomi, S. (1977). Development of attachment and other social behaviors in rhesus monkeys. In T. Alloway, P. Pliner, & L. Krames (Eds). *Attachment behavior.* New York: Plenum.

Suomi, S., & Harlow, H. (1972). Social rehabilitation of isolate-reared monkeys. *Developmental Psychology, 6,* 487–496.

Super, C. M., & Harkness, S. (1982). The development of affect in infancy and early childhood. In D. A. Wagner & H. W. Stevenson (Eds.), *Cultural perspectives on child development.* San Francisco: Freeman.

Surgeon General's Scientific Advisory Committee on Television and Social Behavior (1972). *TV and growing up: The impact of televised violence. Report to the Surgeon General, U.S. Public Health Service.* Washington, DC: U.S. Government Printing Office.

Svedja, M. J., Campos, J. J., & Emde, R. H. (1980). Mother-infant "bonding": Failure to generalize. *Child Development, 51,* 775–779.

Tallman, I., Marotz-Baden, R., & Pindas, P. (1983). *Adolescent socialization in cross-cultural perspective.* New York: Academic Press.

Tanner, J. M. (1978). *Fetus into man: Physical growth from conception to maturity.* Cambridge, MA: Harvard University Press.

Taylor, G. R. (1983). *The great evolutionary mystery.* New York: Harper and Row.

Taylor, P. M., & Hall, B. L. (1979). Parent-infant bonding: Problems and opportunities in a perinatal center. *Seminars in Perinatology, 3,* 73.

Taylor, S. G., & Brown, D. R. (1972). Lateral visual masking: Supraretinal effects when viewing linear arrays with unlimited viewing time. *Perception and Psychophysics, 12,* 97–99.

A teen-pregnancy epidemic (1985, March 25). *Newsweek,* p. 90.

Thayer, E. S., & Collyer, C. E. (1978). The development of transitive inference. *Psychological Bulletin, 85,* 1327–1343.

The Diagram Group. (1982). *The brain: A user's manual.* New York: Putnam.

Thoma, S. J. (1986). Estimating gender differences in the comprehension and preference of moral issues. *Developmental Review, 6,* 165–180.

Thomas, A., & Chess, S. (1977). *Temperament and development.* New York: Brunner/Mazel.

Thompson, R. A. (1983). The father's case in child custody disputes: The contributions of psychological research. In M. E. Lamb & A. Sagi (Eds.), *Fatherhood and family policy.* Hillsdale, NJ: Erlbaum.

Thompson, R. A. (1986a). Temperament, emotionality, and infant social cognition. In J. V. Lerner & R. M. Lerner (Eds.), *Temperament and social interaction in infants and children* (pp. 35–52). San Francisco: Jossey-Bass.

Thompson, R. A. (1986). The development of children's inferences of the emotions of others. *Developmental Psychology, 22,* in press.

Thompson, R. A., & Paris, S. G. (1981). *Children's inferences about the emotions of others.* Unpublished manuscript. University of Michigan.

Thomson, D. (1984). Historians of the future. *The Humanist,* March/April, 11, 40.

Tighe, T. J. & Shepp, B. E. (1983). *Perception, cognition, and development: Interactional analysis.* Hillsdale, NJ: Erlbaum.

Tobin, K. G., & Capie, W. (1981). The development and validation of a group test of logical thinking. *Educational and Psychological Measurement, 41,* 413–423.

Tortora, G. J., & Anagnostakos, N. P. (1981). *Principles of anatomy and physiology* (3rd ed.). New York: Harper & Row.

Travers, R. M. W. (1982). *Essentials of learning* (5th ed.). New York: Macmillan.

Trevarthen, C. (1979). Communication and cooperation in early infancy: A description of primary intersubjectivity. In M. Bullowa (Ed.), *Before speech: The beginning of interpersonal communication.* New York: Cambridge University Press.

Tronick, E. Z. (1982). *Social interchange in infancy.* Baltimore: University Park Press.

Tunmer, W. E., & Bowey, J. A. (1984). Metalinguistic awareness and reading acquisition. In W. E. Tunmer, C. Pratt, & M. L. Herriman (Eds.), *Metalinguistic awareness in children.* Berlin: Springer-Verlag.

Tunmer, W. E., & Herriman, M. L. The development of metalinguistic awareness: An overview. In W. E. Tunmer, C. Pratt, & M. L. Herriman (Eds.), *Metalinguistic awareness in children.* Berlin: Springer-Verlag.

Tunmer, W. E., Pratt, C, & Herriman, M. L. (Eds.) (1984). *Metalinguistic awareness in children.* Berlin: Springer-Verlag.

Turiel, E. (1974). Conflict and transition in adolescent moral development. *Child Development, 45,* 14–29.

Turiel, E. (1977). Conflict and transition in adolescent moral development II: The resolution of disequilibrium through structural reorganization. *Child Development, 48,* 634–637.

Turiel, E. (1983). *The development of social knowledge: Morality and convention.* New York: Cambridge University Press.

Turkington, C. (1983). Lifetime of fear may be legacy of latchkey children. *American Psychological Association Monitor,* November, p. 19.

Turkington, C. (1984). Support urged for children in mourning. *American Psychological Association Monitor,* December, pp. 1, 16–17.

Tylor, E. B. (1871). *Primitive culture.* London: John Murray.

Tzeng, O. J. L., & Hung, D. (1981). Linguistic determinism: A written language perspective. In O. J. L. Tzeng & H. Singer (Eds.), *Perception of print: Reading research in experimental psychology.* Hillsdale, NJ: Erlbaum.

Tzeng, O. J. L., & Wang, W. S-Y. (1981). The first two R's. *American Scientist, 71,* 238–243.

Umezaki, H., & Morrell, F. (1970). Developmental study of photic evoked responses in premature infants. *Electroencephalography and Clinical Neurophysiology, 28,* 55–63.

U.S. Bureau of the Census (1984). *Statistical abstract of the United States: 1985* (105th ed.). Washington, DC: Author.

Vandell, D., & Mueller, E. C. (1980). Peer play and friendships during the first two years. In H. C. Foot, A. J. Chapman, & J. R. Smith (Eds.), *Friendship and social relations in children*. New York: Wiley.

Vandell, D., Wilson, K., & Buchanan, N. (1980). Peer interaction in the first year of life: An examination of its structure, content, and sensitivity to toys. *Child Development, 51*, 481–488.

Vandenberg, S. G. (1968). The nature and nurture of intelligence. In D. C. Glass (Ed.), *Genetics*. New York: Rockefeller University Press.

Vaughan, V. C., McKay, J. R., & Behrman, R. E. (1984). *Nelson textbook of pediatrics* (12th ed.). Philadelphia: W. B. Saunders.

Venezky, R. L. (1975). Prereading skills: Theoretical foundations and practical applications. In T. A. Brigham, R. Hawkins, J. W. Scott, and T. F. McLaughlin (Eds.), *Behavior analysis in education: Self-control and reading*. Dubuque, Iowa: Kendall/Hunt.

Vernon, P. (1979). *Intelligence: Heredity and environment*. San Francisco: Freeman.

Vincze, M. (1971). The social contacts of infants and young children reared together. *Early child development, 1*, 99–109.

Vine, I. (1983). The nature of moral commitments. In H. Weinreich-Haste & D. Locke (Eds.), *Morality in the making: Thought, action, and social context* (pp. 19–45). New York: Wiley.

Von Bargen, D. M. (1983). Infant heart rate: A review of research and methodology. *Merrill-Palmer Quarterly, 29*, 115–150.

von Wright, J. M. (1972). On the problem of selection in iconic memory. *Scandinavian Journal of Psychology, 13*, 159–171.

Vurpillot, E. (1968). The development of scanning strategies and their relation to visual differentiation. *Journal of Experimental Child Psychology, 6*, 632–650.

Vurpillot, E. (1976). *The visual world of the child* (W. E. C. Gillham, trans.). New York: International Universities Press.

Vygotsky, L. S. (1962). *Thought and language*. Cambridge, MA: MIT Press.

Vygotsky, L. S. (1976). Play and its role in the mental development of the child. In J. Bruner, A. Jolly, & K. Sylva (Eds.), *Play: Its role in development and evolution*. New York: Basic Books.

Vygotsky, L. S. (1978). *Mind in society: The development of higher psychological processes*. Cambridge: MA: Harvard University Press.

Wagner, D. A., & Stevenson, H. W. (Eds.) (1982). *Cultural perspectives on child development*. San Francisco: Freeman.

Wagner, K. R. (1985). How much do children say in a day? *Journal of Child Language, 12*, 475–487.

Wagner, R. K., & Sternberg, R. J. (1984). Alternative conceptions of intelligence and their implications for education. *Review of Educational Research, 54*, 179–223.

Wagoner, R. V., & Goldsmith, D. W. (1983). *Cosmic horizons: Understanding the universe*. San Francisco: Freeman.

Walk, R. D. (1981). *Perceptual development*. Monterey, CA: Brooks/Cole.

Walk, R. D., & Gibson, E. (1961). A comparative and analytical study of visual depth perception. *Psychological Monographs, 75* (15, Whole No. 519).

Walker, E., & Emory, E. (1985). Commentary: Interpretive bias and behavioral genetic research. *Child Development, 56,* 775–778.

Walker, L. J. (1982). The sequentiality of Kohlberg's stages of moral development. *Child Development, 53,* 1330–1336.

Walker, L. J. (1984). Sex differences in the development of moral reasoning: A critical review. *Child Development, 55,* 677–691.

Walker, L. J. (1986a). Experimental and cognitive sources of moral development in adulthood. *Human Development, 29,* 113–124.

Walker, L. J. (1986b). Sex differences in the development of moral reasoning: A rejoinder to Baumrind. *Child Development, 57,* 522–526.

Walker, L. J., de Vries, B., & Bichard, S. L. (1984). The hierarchical nature of stages of moral development. *Developmental Psychology, 20,* 960–966.

Walters, J., Pearce, D., & Dahms, L. (1957). Affection and aggressive behavior of preschool children. *Child Development, 28,* 15–26.

Wason, P. C. (1983). Realism and rationality in the selection task. In J. St. B. T. Evans (Ed.), *Thinking and reasoning: Psychological approaches.* London: Routledge & Kegan Paul.

Wason, P. C., & Johnson-Laird, P. N. (1972). *Psychology of reasoning: Structure and content.* Cambridge, MA; Harvard University Press.

Waterman, A. S. (1982). Identity development from adolescence to adulthood: An extension of theory and a review of research. *Developmental Psychology, 18,* 341–358.

Waterman, A. S. (Ed.) (1985). *Identity in adolescence: Processes and contents.* San Francisco: Jossey-Bass.

Waters, E., & Sroufe, L. A. (1983). Social competence as a developmental construct: Perceiving the coherence of individual differences across age, across situations, and across behavioral domains. *Developmental Review, 3,* 79–97.

Waters, E., Wippman, J., & Sroufe, L. A. (1979). Attachment, positive affect, and competence in the peer group: Two studies in construct validation. *Child Development, 50,* 821–829.

Waters, H. S., & Tinsley, V. S. (1982). The development of verbal self-regulation: Relationship between language, cognition, and behavior. In S. Kuczaj, II (Ed.), *Language development: Vol. 2. Language, thought, and culture.* Hillsdale, NJ: Erlbaum.

Watson, J. B. (1913). Psychology as the behaviorist views it. *Psychological Review, 20,* 158–177.

Watson, J. B. (1919). *Conditioning of fear responses.* Philadelphia: Lippincott.

Waugh, N. C., & Norman, D. A. (1965). Primary memory. *Psychological Review, 72,* 89–104.

Wehren, A., & De Lisi, R. (1983). The development of gender understanding: Judgments and explanations. *Child Development, 54,* 1568–1578.

Weiner, B. (1980a). *Human motivation.* New York: Holt, Rinehart, & Winston.

Weiner, B. (1980b). May I borrow your class notes? An attributional analysis of judgments of help giving in an achievement-related context. *Journal of Educational Psychology, 72,* 676–681.

Weiner, B. (1982). The emotional consequence of causal attributions. In M. S.

Clark & S. T. Fiske (Eds.), *Affect and cognition: The 17th annual Carnegie Symposium on cognition.* Hillsdale, NJ: Erlbaum.

Weiner, B., & Graham, S. (1984). An attributional approach to emotional development. In C. E. Izard, J. Kagan, & R. B. Zajonc (Eds.), *Emotions, cognition, and behavior.* New York: Cambridge University Press.

Weiner, B., Graham, S., Stern, P., & Lawson, M. E. (1982). Using affective cues to infer causal thoughts. *Developmental Psychology, 18,* 278–286.

Weiner, B., Kun, A., & Benesh-Weiner, M. (1980). The development of mastery, emotions, and morality from an attributional perspective. In W. A. Collins (Ed.), *Minnesota Symposium on Child Psychology* (Vol. 13). Hillsdale, NJ: Erlbaum.

Weiner, H. M. (1977). *Psychology and human disease.* New York: Elsevier.

Weinraub, M., & Frankel, J. (1977). Sex differences in parent-infant interaction during free play, departure, and separation. *Child Development, 48,* 1240–1249.

Weinraub, M., Clemans, L. P., Sockloff, A., Ethridge, T., Gracely, E., & Myers, B. (1984). The development of sex role stereotypes in the third year: Relationships to gender labeling, gender identity, sex-typed toy preference, and family characteristics. *Child Development, 55,* 1493–1503.

Weinrich, J. D. (1980). Toward a sociobiological theory of emotion. In R. Plutchik & H. Kellerman (Eds.), *Emotion: Theory, research, and experience* (Vol. 1). New York: Academic Press.

Weir, R. H. (1962). *Language in the crib.* The Hague: Mouton.

Weisskopf, V. F. (1983). The origin of the universe. *American Scientist, 71,* 473–480.

Welfel, E. R., & Davison, M. L. (1986). The development of reflective judgment during the college years: A 4-year longitudinal study. *Journal of College Student Personnel, 27,* 209–216.

Welsh, R. S. (1985). Spanking: A grand old American tradition. *Children Today, 14,* 25–29.

Werner, E. E., & Smith, R. S. (1982). *Vulnerable but invincible: A longitudinal study of resilient children and youth.* New York: McGraw-Hill.

Werner, H. (1965). *Comparative psychology of mental development.* New York: Science Editions.

Wertheimer, M. (1961). Psychomotor coordination of auditory and visual space at birth. *Science, 134,* 1692.

Wertheimer, M. (1978). *A brief history of psychology.* New York: Holt, Rinehart & Winston.

Whelan, E. (1975). *A baby? . . . maybe.* New York: Bobbs-Merrill.

Whitbourne, S. K., & Tesch, S. A. (1985). A comparison of identity and intimacy statuses in college students and alumni. *Developmental Psychology, 21,* 1039–1044.

Whitley, B. E., Jr. (1985). Sex-role orientation and psychological well-being: Two meta-analyses. *Sex roles, 12,* 207–225.

Whorf, B. L. (1952a). *Collected papers on metalinguistics.* Washington, DC: Department of State, Foreign Service Institute.

Whorf, B. L. (1952b). Language, mind and reality. *Etc.: A Review of General Semantics, 9,* 167–188.

Whorf, B. L. (1956). Science and linguistics. In J. B. Carroll (Ed.), *Language, thought, and reality: Selected writings of Benjamin Lee Whorf.* Cambridge, MA: MIT Press.

Wieman, L. A. (1976). Stress patterns in early child language. *Journal of Child Language, 3,* 283–286.

Wiggins, J. A. (1983). Family violence as a case of interpersonal aggression: A situational analysis. *Social Forces, 62,* 102–123.

Wilkinson, L. C., & Rembold, K. (1982). The communicative context of early language development. In S. Kuczaj, II (Ed.), *Language development: Vol 2. Language, thought, and culture.* Hillsdale, NJ: Erlbaum.

Willems, E. P., & Alexander, J. L. (1980). The naturalistic perspective in research. In B. B. Wolman & G. Stricker (Eds.), *Handbook of developmental psychology.* Englewood Cliffs, NJ: Prentice-Hall.

Wilson, P. T. (1985). *Amount of reading, reading instruction, and reading achievement.* Paper presented at the Annual Meeting of the National Reading Conference, San Diego, CA.

Wilson, R. S. (1977). Twins and siblings: Concordance for school age mental development. *Child Development 48,* 211–216.

Wilson, R. S. (1978). Synchronies in mental development: An epigenetic perspective. *Science, 202,* 939–948.

Wilson, R. S. (1983). The Louisville twin study: Developmental synchronies in behavior. *Child Development, 54,* 298–316.

Wimmer, H., Gruber, S., & Perner, J. (1985). Young children's conception of lying: Moral intuition and the denotation and connotation of "to lie." *Developmental Psychology, 21,* 993–995.

Winsom, S. (1985). *Brain and psyche: The biology of the unconscious.* New York: Doubleday.

Wittig, M. A. (1985). Metatheoretical dilemmas in the psychology of gender. *American Psychologist, 40,* 800–811.

Wood, G. (1983). *Cognitive psychology: A skills approach.* Monterey, CA: Brooks/Cole.

Wright, B. J., & Bell, S. R. (1984). Item banks: What, why, how. *Journal of Educational Measurement, 21,* 331–345.

Wright, J. C., & Huston, A. C. (1983). A matter of form: Potentials of television for young viewers. *American Psychologist, 38,* 835–841.

Wyatt, R. J. (1985). *A physician's guide to staying healthy while growing older.* New York: McGraw-Hill.

Yando, R., Seitz, V., & Zigler, E. (1978). *Imitation: A developmental perspective.* Hillsdale, NJ: Erlbaum.

Yang, R. K., Zweig, A. R., Douthitt, T. C., & Federman, E. J. (1976). Successive relationships between maternal attitudes during pregnancy, analgesic medication during labor and delivery, and newborn behavior. *Developmental Psychology, 12,* 6–14.

Yerushalmy, J. (1971). The relationship of parents' smoking to outcome of pregnancy: Implications as to the problem of inferring causation from observed effects. *American Journal of Epidemiology, 93,* 443–456.

Yerushalmy, J. (1972). Infants with low birth weight born before their mothers started to smoke cigarettes. *American Journal of Obstetrics and Gynecology, 112,* 277–284.

Youniss, J. (1978). Dialectical theory and Piaget on social knowledge. *Human Development, 21,* 234–247.

Yudkin, M. (1984). When kids think the unthinkable. *Psychology Today, 18,* 18–25.

Yussen, S. R., & Bird, J. E. (1979). The development of metacognitive awareness in memory, communication, and attention. *Journal of Experimental Child Psychology, 28,* 300–313.

Yussen, S. R., & Levy, V. M., Jr. (1975). Developmental changes in predicting one's own span of short-term memory. *Journal of Experimental Child Psychology, 19,* 502–508.

Zaporozhets, A. V. (1965). The development of perception in the preschool child. In P. H. Mussen (Ed.), European research in child development. *Monographs of the Society for Research in Child Development, 30,* No. 100, 82–101.

Zaslow, M. J., Pederson F. A., Suwalsky, J. T. D., Cain, R. L., & Fivel, M. (1985). The early resumption of employment by mothers: Implication for parent-infant interaction. *Journal of Applied Developmental Psychology, 6,* 1–16.

Zelnik, M., & Kim, Y. J. (1982). Sex education and contraceptive education in U. S. public high schools. *Family Planning Perspectives* (Vol. 14, No. 6.).

Zimmerman, B. J. (1981). Social learning theory and cognitive constructivism. In I. E. Sigel, D. M. Brodzinsky, & R. M. Golinkoff (Eds.), *New directions in Piagetian theory and practice* (pp. 39–49). Hillsdale, NJ: Erlbaum.

Zinn, H. (1980). *A people's history of the United States.* New York: Harper & Row.

Photo Credits

Title page and Part I Opener: pp. ii and 4, Erica Stone.

Chapter 1: p. 8, "Mrs. Elizabeth Freake and Baby Mary" by an unknown artist. Worcester Art Museum, Worcester, Mass.; p. 9, "Boy with Squirrel (Henry Pelham)" by John Singleton Copley. Museum of Fine Arts, Boston; p. 10, "Susanna Fourment and Her Daughter" by Sir Anthony van Dyck. National Gallery of Art, Washington D.C., Andrew W. Mellon Collection; p. 12, "Mother and Child" by Mary Cassatt. Museum of Fine Arts, Boston, Gift of Miss Aimee Lamb in memory of Mr. and Mrs. Horatio A. Lamb; p. 31, "Rocking Chair #2" by Henry Moore. Hirshhorn Museum and Sculpture Garden, Smithsonian Institution, Washington, D.C.

Chapter 2: p. 45, Peter Vandermark/Stock Boston; p. 48, Michal Heron/Woodfin Camp & Associates; p. 55, Lynn McLaren/Photo Researchers; p. 56, Suzanne Szasz/Photo Researchers; p. 60, Lionel J. M. Delevingne/Stock Boston.

Chapter 3: p. 72, William Vandivert; p. 83 Howard B. Moshman; p. 85, Bob Bouchal; p. 88, Ulrike Welsch; p. 93, Jason Laure/Woodfin Camp; p. 96, Victor Englebert/Photo Researchers.

Part II Opener: p. 104, Timothy Eagan/Stock Boston.

Chapter 4: p. 122, Photo Researchers; p. 124, Erica Stone; p. 131, Bruce Roberts/Photo Researchers.

Chapter 5: p. 141, Michael Hayman/Photo Researchers; p. 147, Renee Lynn/Photo Researchers; p. 152, Patrica Agre/Photo Researchers; p. 169, Ann Holmes/Photo Researchers; p. 182L, James Holland/Stock Boston; p. 182R, Erica Stone.

Part III Opener: p. 186, Art Attack/Photo Researchers.

Chapter 6: p. 193, Lennart Nilsson A CHILD IS BORN © 1965 Dell Publishing Co, N.Y.C.; p. 194 James Holland/Stock Boston; p. 204, Jim Harrison/Stock Boston; p. 205, Stan Goldblatt/Photo Researchers; p. 209, Suzanne Szasz/Photo Researchers; p. 211, Courtesy Massachusetts General Hospital.

Chapter 7: p. 219, Elizabeth Crews/Stock Boston; p. 234, Jean B. Hollyman/Photo Researchers; p. 237, Peter Vandermark/Stock Boston; p. 253, Jean Claude Lejeune/Stock Boston; p. 254, Ira Berger/Woodfin Camp.

Part IV Opener: p. 258, Jim Anderson/Woodfin Camp.

Chapter 8: p. 267, Michael Weisbrot/Stock Boston; p. 269, Burk, Uzzle/Woodfin Camp; p. 271, Jean Claude Lejeune/Stock Boston; p. 274, Donald Dietz/Stock Boston; p. 281, Yves De Braine/Black Star; p. 292, Sybil Shelton/Peter Arnold.

Chapter 9: p. 309L, Thomas Russell/The Picture Cube; p. 309R, Glenn Engman/The Picture Cube; p. 312, Suzanne Szaz/Photo Researchers; p. 320, Sepp Seitz/Woodfin Camp; p. 326, Jean Claude Lejeune/Stock Boston; p. 327, Peter Menzel/Stock Boston.

Chapter 10: p. 335, Peter Menzel/Stock Boston; p. 348, Roger H. Bruning; p. 353, Charles Gatewood/Stock Boston; p. 356, Ulrike Welsch; p. 362, Barbara Rios/Photo Researchers.

Chapter 11: p. 371, Ulrike Welsch; p. 377, Hazel Hankin/Stock Boston; p. 395L, Erica Stone; p. 395R, Hella Hammid/Photo Researchers; p. 399L, Drawing by David B. Kyle; p. 399R, Drawing by Libby Glover.

Text Credits

Chapter 12: p. 406, Erica Stone; p. 423, Erica Stone; p. 434, Michal Heron/Woodfin Camp.

Part V Opener: p. 438 © *Boston Globe,* photo by Ulrike Welsch

Chapter 13: p. 446, Erica Stone; p. 448, Peter G. Aitken/Photo Researchers; p. 459, Jerry Berndt/Stock Boston; p. 462, Neal Benzi/The New York Times Pictures; p. 465, David M. Grossman/Photo Researchers; p. 470, Howard B. Moshman; p. 476, Richard Hartman/Photo Researchers.

Chapter 14: p. 489, Suzanne Szasz/Photo Researchers; p. 492, Charles Gatewood/Stock Boston; p. 500, Elizabeth Hamlin/Stock Boston; p. 506, Peter Vandermark/Stock Boston; p. 513, Ulrike Welsch; p. 518, Erica Stone.

Chapter 15: p. 529, Owen Frankin/Stock Boston; p. 533, Lionel J. M. Delevingne; p. 541, UPI; p. 549, Eugene Gordon/Photo Researchers; p. 553, Bettye Lane/Photo Researchers.

Chapter 16: p. 570, Owen Franken/Stock Boston; p. 575, Boston Globe Photo; p. 581, Robert H. Bruning; p. 585, Michal Heron/Woodfin Camp; p. 586, Alice Kandell/Photo Researchers; p. 593, Erica Stone/Photo Researchers.

Text Credits

Chapter 1: pp. 26–28, excerpts from *The Essential Piaget* edited by Howard E. Gruber and J. Jacques Voneche. Copyright © 1977 by Basic Books, Inc., Publishers. Reprinted by permission of Basic Books, Inc. and Routledge & Kegan Paul Ltd.

Chapter 3: p. 92, Fig. 3–2, from Cataldo, M. F., Bessman, C. A., Parker, L. H., Pearson, J. E. R., & Rogers, M. C. (1979). Behavioral assessment for pediatric intensive care units. *Journal of Applied Behavioral Analysis, 12,* 83-97. Reprinted by permission.

Chapter 4: p. 110, Fig. 4–2, from Lawrence J. Dillon (1978). *Evolution: Concepts and Consequences.* St. Louis: C. V. Mosby. Used by permission.

Chapter 5: p. 155, Table 5–1, from E. E. Maccoby and J. A. Martin, "Socialization in the context of the family: Parent–child intreaction," in E. M. Hetherington (Ed.), P. H. Mussen (Series Ed.), *Handbook of Child Psychology: Vol. 4: Socialization, Personality, and Social Development,* 4th ed. © 1983 by John Wiley & Sons, Inc. Reprinted by permission; p. 168, Tables 5–2, adapted from Konner, M. J. (1981). Evolution of human behavior development. In R. H. Munroe, R. L. Monroe, and B. B. Whiting (Eds.), *Handbook of Cross-Cultural Human Development.* Reprinted by permission of Garland Publishing Inc.

Chapter 6: p. 192, Fig. 6–3, from *Human Development: From Conception to Development* by Kurt Fischer and Arlyne Lazerson. W. J. Freeman and Company. Copyright © 1984. Reprinted by permission; p. 207, Fig. 6–4, from David A. Schulz and Stanley F. Rogers, *Marriage, the Family, and Personal Fulfillment,* © 1985, p. 162. Reprinted by permission of Prentice-Hall, Inc., Englewood Cliffs, New Jersey; p. 208, Table 6–2, from Apgar, V. (1953). A proposal for a new method of evaluation in the newborn infant. *Current Research in Anesthesia and Analgesia, 32,* 260. Reprinted by permission of the International Anesthesia Research Society.

TEXT CREDITS

Chapter 7: p. 218, Fig. 7–1, adapted from C. M. Jackson, "Some aspects of form and growth" in W. J. Robbins et al, *Growth* (New Haven: Yale University Press, 1929); p. 247, Table 7–2, abridged from Dennis, W. (1934). A description and classification of the responses of the newborn infant. *Psychological Bulletin, 31,* 5–22; p. 250, Table 7–3, abridged from Bayley, N. (1935). The development of motor abilities during the first three years. *Monographs of the Society for Research in Child Development, 1,* 1–26. Copyright 1935 The Society for Research in Child Development, Inc. Reprinted by permission.

Chapter 8: pp. 276–277, "The Stage Beyond" by Dave Moshman. Reprinted by permission of the author; p. 286, Fig. 8–4, from Siegler, R. S. (1976). Three aspects of cognitive development. *Cognitive Psychology, 8,* 481-520. Reprinted by permission of Academic Press and the author.

Chapter 9: p. 307, Fig. 9–2, from R. L. Fantz, "The Origin of Form Perception," *Scientific American,* May 1961. Reprinted by permission of W. H. Freeman Company; p. 308, Fig. 9–3, from Zaporozhets, A. V. (1985). The development of perception in preschool children. In P. H. Mussen (Ed.), European research in child development, *Monographs of the Society for Research in Child Development,* 9 (2), #100. © 1985 The Society for Research in Child Development, Inc. Reprinted by permission; p. 310, Fig. 9–4, from Gibson, J. J., & Gibson, E. K. (1955). Perceptual learning: Differentiation or enrichment. *Psychological Review, 62,* p. 36; p. 328, Fig. 9–13, from Eleanor Gibson, *Principles of Perceptual Learning and Development,* © 1969, p. 88. Reprinted by permission of Prentice-Hall. Inc., Englewood Cliffs, New Jersey; p. 332, Fig. 9–14, from Bugelski (1961). *Canadian Journal of Psychology, 15.* Copyright (1961) The Canadian Psychological Association. Reprinted by permission.

Chapter 10: p. 341, Table 10–1, from Ornstein, P. A., Naus, M., & Liberty, C. (1975). Rehearsal and organization processes in children's memory. *Child Development, 26,* 818–830. © 1975 The Society for Research in Child Development, Inc. Reprinted by permission; p. 352, Fig. 10–2, from Chi, M. (1978). Knowledge structures and memory development. In R. Siegler (Ed.), *Children's thinking: What develops?* Hillsdale, NJ: Erlbaum. Reprinted by permission of the author and Lawrence Erlbaum Associates, Inc.

Chapter 11: p. 372, Fig. 11–1, from Crystal, D. (1976). *Child learning: Language and linguistics,* p. 26. London: Edward Arnold (Publishers) Ltd. Reprinted by permission; p. 373, Table 11–1, from Anisfeld, M. (1984). *Language development from birth to three,* Table 8–1. Hillsdale, NJ: Erlbaum. Reprinted by permission of the author and Lawrence Erlbaum Associates, Inc.; p. 388, Table 11–2, from Erica Werner and Bernard Kaplan, *Symbol Formation.* New York: Wiley, 1966. Adapted by permission of the authors; p. 390, Fig. 11–2, adapted from Anisfeld, M. (1984). *Language development from birth to three,* Fig. 6–1. Hillsdale, NJ: Erlbaum. Reprinted by permission of the author and Lawrence Erlbaum Associates, Inc.

Chapter 12: p. 413, Fig. 12–2, from Kuhn, D., & Brannock, J. (1977). Development of the isolation of variables scheme. *Developmental Psychology, 13,* 9–14. Copyright 1977 by the American Psychological Association. Reprinted by permission of the authors; p. 417, cartoon panel by Gary Larson. Copyright, 1985, Universal Press Syndicate. Reprinted with permission. All rights reserved.

Text Credits

Chapter 13: p. 443, Fig. 13–1, from A. I. Leshner (1977). Hormones and emotions. In D. K. Candland et al (Eds.), *Emotion*. Reprinted by permission of Brooks/Cole Publishing Company; pp. 460–461, excerpt reprinted with permission from Richard J. Morris and Thomas R. Kratochwill, "Childhood fears and phobias" in Morris and Kratochwill, eds., *The Practice of Child Therapy*, copyright 1983, Pergamon Press; p. 471, Fig. 13–2, from Paul Ekman, *Darwin and Social Expression: A Century of Research in Review* (Orlando, FL: Academic Press, 1973). Reprinted by permission of the publisher and the author; p. 472: cartoon panel by Gary Larson. Copyright, 1985, Universal Press Syndicate. Reprinted with permission. All rights reserved.

Chapter 14: p. 493, Fig. 14–1, from Jerome Kagan, "Emergent Themes in Human Development," *American Scientist* 64:186–96 (1976). Reprinted by permission; p. 496, Fig. 14–2, from Clarke-Stewart, K. A. (1973). Interactions between mothers and young children: Characteristics and consequences. *Monographs of the Society for Research in Child Development, 38* (6 & 7, Serial No. 153). © 1973 The Society for Research in Child Development, Inc. Reprinted by permission; p. 517, "The Far Side" cartoon panel by Gary Larson is reprinted by permission of Chronicle Features, San Francisco. All rights reserved; p. 519, Table 14–1L, from Bachman, J. F., Johnston, L. D., & O'Malley, P. M. (1980). *Monitoring the future: questionnaire responses from the nation's high school seniors*. Ann Arbor, MI: Institute for Social Research. Reprinted by permission; p, 520, Fig. 14–3, copyright 1986, by Newsweek, Inc. All Rights Reserved. Reprinted by Permission; p. 522, Table 14–2, from M. P. McCabe and J. K. Collins, "Sex role and dating orientation," *Journal of Youth and Adolescence, 8,* 407-425. Reprinted by permission of the authors and Plenum Publishing Corporation.

Chapter 15: p. 527, "The Exception" from The Talk of the Town in *The New Yorker*, September 18, 1954. Reprinted by permission. © 1954, 1982 The New Yorker Magazine, Inc.; p. 543, Dilemma II (pp. 640–641) from *The Psychology of Moral Development: Essays on Moral Development*, Volume II by Lawrence Kohlberg. Copyright © 1984 by Lawrence Kohlberg. Reprinted by permission of Harper & Row, Publishers, Inc.

Chapter 16: p. 569, "The Far Side" cartoon panel by Gary Larson is reprinted by permission of Chronicle Features, San Francisco. All rights reserved; p. 590, Fig. 16–4, from Robert Kegan, *The Evolving Self: Problems and Process in Human Development* (Cambridge, MA: Harvard University Press, 1982). Reprinted by permission; p. 594, Fig. 16–5, from Robert Kegan, *The Evolving Self: Problems and Process in Human Development* (Cambridge, MA: Harvard University Press, 1982). Reprinted by permission.

Name Index

A

Aantaa, E., 304
Abel, E. L., 200
Abramovitch, R., 149, 150
Achenbach, T. M., 79, 90, 102
Acheson, R. M., 240
Acredolo, L. P., 357
Adams, J. L., 381
Adelson, J., 600
Ahlstrom, W. M., 155
Ainsworth, M. D., 491, 494, 495
Alexander, J. L., 84, 102
Allport, G. W., 91
Anagnostakos, N. P., 221, 222, 225, 228, 232
Anderson, B. J., 164
Anderson, J. R., 321
Anderson, R. C., 347, 376, 394
Anisfeld, M., 373, 375, 380, 381, 382, 387, 388, 389, 390, 401
Annis, L. F., 133
Apgar, V., 208
Aries, P., 8
Armon, C., 276
Arnold, K. D., 550
Aslin, R. N., 314, 316, 318
Atkinson, R. C., 337–338
Auble, P. M., 346–347
Ault, R. L., 298
Ayala, F. J., 119

B

Bachman, J. F., 519
Baddeley, A., 321, 345
Baillargeon, R., 280, 430
Baker, D. P., 576

Baker, R., 90
Baldwin, J. M., 18, 21–23, 29, 32, 49, 61, 65
Balling, J. D., 228
Baltes, P. B., 75, 76, 79, 102
Bandura, A., 34, 44, 46, 62, 179, 181, 184, 512
Banks, M. S., 305, 306, 308, 309, 318
Barclay, J. R., 346
Barcus, E., 174–175
Barker, R. G., 84
Barkley, R. A., 466
Barltrop, D., 196, 197, 198, 201
Barrera, M. E., 212
Barrett, K., 123
Bartlett, F. C., 346
Basseches, M., 276
Basu, G. K., 511
Bates, E., 377
Bates, J. E., 159, 387, 392
Bauer, D. H., 452
Baumgardner, M. H., 53
Baumrind, D., 155, 158, 550
Bausano, M., 71
Bayles, K., 387, 392
Bayley, N., 16, 218, 229, 238, 250, 316
Beach, D. R., 354
Beardslee, W. R., 454
Bearison, D. J., 433, 538
Becker, W. C., 155
Begg, 343
Behrman, R. E., 197, 198
Bell, R. Q., 145
Bell, S. M., 491, 494
Bellack, 93
Bellugi, U., 84
Belous, R. S., 143, 148, 151, 153

Bem, S.L., 578, 579
Benbow, C. P., 574
Benesh-Weiner, M., 449
Benjamin, L., 17, 19
Benton, S. L., 343
Bereiter, C., 408
Bergman, T., 306
Berkeley, G., 42
Berkowitz, M. W., 433, 538, 556, 558
Berndt, T. J., 517
Bessman, C. A., 91
Bichard, S. L., 547
Bickhard, 296
Bigelow, A. E., 316
Binet, A., 18, 20–21, 23, 30
Bird, J. E., 340
Bisanz, G. L., 361
Bjorklund, D. F., 342
Blackburn, G., 243
Blasi, A., 552, 554–555, 559
Blatt, M., 558
Blehar, M. C., 491, 494
Block, J. H., 512
Blume, J., 432
Boehm, C. D., 132
Bonthorn, D. T., 135
Borman, M. H., 236
Bornstein, M. H., 37, 107, 304, 308, 309, 310, 311, 314, 335
Borstelmann, L. J., 8, 9, 36
Bousfield, W. A., 341
Boveri, T., 118
Bower, T. G. R., 309, 315
Bowlby, J., 40, 491, 495
Boyd, D. R., 530
Boyle, F. M., 420
Brabeck, M., 550, 551

691

Braine, M. D. S., 389, 407, 436
Brainerd, C. J., 334, 345, 365, 407
Brannock, J., 413, 415
Bransford, J. D., 346, 426
Bray, N. W., 355
Brazelton, T. B., 444
Breslow, L., 407
Bretherton, I., 491, 497
Brice, P., 74
Bridgeman, D. L., 556
Bridges, K. M. B., 466
Brim, O., 497
Brimblecombe, F., 196, 197, 198, 201
Britten, K. R., 465
Bronfenbrenner, U., 102, 141–144, 151, 155, 159–163, 168, 173, 184
Bronson, W., 494, 509
Brooks-Gunn, J., 235–238 passim, 256, 567
Broughton, J. M., 21, 22, 23, 36, 49, 427–428, 550, 572
Brown, A. L., 346, 352, 354, 355, 357, 426
Brown, R., 84, 384, 390, 401, 573
Brownell, K., 243
Brozan, N., 452, 453
Bruner, J. S., 378, 381, 388–389
Bruning, R. H., 343
Bruns, G. A. P., 135
Bryant, P. E., 406–407
Buck, R., 469
Buechler, S., 445, 466, 474
Buhler, C., 16
Bukatko, D., 227, 322, 324
Bullock, M., 470
Burkhart, J. E., 550
Burt, C., 126
Byrnes, J. P., 409

C

Cain, R. L., 162, 164
Cairns, R., 14, 17, 18, 19, 20, 36, 511
Caldwell, 306
Campbell, B., 470
Campbell, R., 296
Campione, J. C., 426
Campos, J. J., 71, 123, 490
Candee, D., 552, 553
Candland, D. K., 441, 443
Capie, W., 280
Caplan, 574

Caputo, 213
Carello, C., 326
Caron and Caron, 306, 308
Case, R., 32, 284, 290–294, 295, 298, 339
Cassidy, D. J., 354, 357
Cataldo, M. F., 91–92
Cattell, P., 229
Chance, J. E., 359
Chapman, M., 556, 563
Charlesworth, W. R., 12
Charlop, M. H., 465
Charnov, E. L., 491
Chase, W. G., 327
Chess, S., 121–123, 137
Chi, M. T. H., 82, 339, 351–352, 366
Chinsky, J. M., 354
Chivian, E., 454, 455
Chomsky, N., 50, 282, 295, 370, 383, 385
Chukovsky, K., 82, 401
Cicchetti, D., 444, 469
Claren, S. K., 200
Clark, E. V., 371, 376, 384, 386, 389, 394
Clark, H. H., 376
Clark, M. C., 556
Clark, P. M., 552
Clarke-Stewart, K. A., 142, 145, 147, 151, 164, 495, 496, 497
Cleese, J., 41
Clemens, L. P., 574
Cohen, J., 90
Cohen, L. B., 336
Cohen, L. J., 431
Cohen, P., 90
Colby, A., 77, 78, 79, 546
Collings, V. B., 315, 321, 328, 332
Collins, J. K., 522
Collyer, C. E., 407
Colman, A., 204–206, 214
Colman, L., 204–206, 214
Comer, J. P., 160, 162
Commons, M. L., 276
Condry, J., 512
Condry, S., 512
Conger, J. J., 518, 519
Constantian, 159
Coopersmith, S., 159
Copans, S. A., 196
Corbin, C. B., 252
Coren, S., 315

Cornelius, S. W., 75
Corsale, K., 334
Cortelyou, A., 486
Corter, C., 149
Coursin, D. B., 314
Cowan, W. M., 224, 227, 302
Cox, M., 154
Cox, R., 154
Craik, F. I. M., 342, 343, 347
Crain, W. C., 24, 36, 65
Creasy, R. K., 200, 201, 214
Crick, F. H., 118
Cruttenden, A., 341, 398
Crystal, D., 370, 372, 375, 381, 382, 389, 391, 393
Cunningham, C. E., 212
Cytryn, L., 464, 481

D

Daehler, M. W., 227, 322, 324
Dahms, L., 453
Dalby, J. T., 200
Dally, P., 461
Damon, W., 485, 487, 494, 495, 497, 504, 505, 516, 520, 524, 567, 568, 571, 572, 589, 600
Dannemiller, J. L., 306
Dargassies, S. S., 196, 218
Darwin, C., 11, 13, 18, 82, 108–111, 115
Davidson, E., 17, 19
Davies, P., 137
Davis, G. H., 201
Davison, M. L., 430
DeCasper, A. J., 314
DeFries, J. C., 127, 137
DeGiovanni, I. S., 461
De Lisi, R., 576, 578
DeLoache, J. S., 352, 354, 357
Dempster, F. N., 339, 351
Denham, S. A., 556
Dennis, W., 249
Dent, H. R., 358
de Vries, B., 547
Dewey, J., 17
Dewsbury, D. A., 22
Diaz, R. M., 517
Dietz, W., 242
Dillon, L. S., 109, 110, 111
Dimitroff, C., 408
Ditto, W. B., 121
DiVitto, B. A., 201, 211

Name Index

Dixon, R. A., 11, 12, 37
Dmowski, W. P., 133
Dodge, K. A., 513, 514
D'Odorico, L., 377–378
Dolan, A. B., 123
Donahy, T., 304
Donlon, T. A., 135
Dorval, B., 378, 396–397
Douglas, W. O., 433
Douthitt, T. C., 211
Dowling, K., 306
Downs, C. A., 148, 236
Drage, J. S., 256
Duchan, J. F., 374, 375, 377–379

E

Eckerman, C. O., 37, 396–397, 491
Egeland, B., 490
Ehri, L. C., 391
Eich, J. M., 343
Eimas, P. D., 315, 369, 370, 381
Einstein, A., 73
Eisenberg, J. F., 8
Eisenberg, N., 556
Eisenberg, R. B., 314
Ekman, P., 470
Eldredge, N., 114, 115
Elkind, D., 143, 184, 311
Ellingson, R., 304
Elliot, A. J., 384, 385
Ellis, S., 96
Emde, R. H., 490
Emler, N., 534
Emory, E., 127, 128
Engel, B. S., 455
Engen, T., 317
Entwisle, D. R., 576
Erikson, E. H., 14, 34, 50, 54, 59, 545, 566, 583–589, 591–592, 595, 599
Eron, L. D., 74
Ervin-Tripp, S., 378
Estes, D., 491
Eth, S., 359
Ethridge, T., 574
Evans, J., 423, 431

F

Fagan, J. F., 334, 336, 486
Fagot, B. I., 574, 576–577
Fantz, R., 306, 307, 334–335

Faust, M. S., 229, 232
Federman, E. J., 211
Fein, G. G., 505, 507
Fein, R. A., 147
Feldman, H., 560
Fell, J. P., 443
Ferguson, C. A., 378, 510
Ferrara, A., 376, 377
Ferrara, R. A., 426
Ferreira, A. J., 201
Feshbach, S., 456–457
Field, N., 316
Fifer, W. J., 314
Filardo, E. K., 433, 538
Fincher, J., 227, 256
Finello, K. M., 77, 79
Fischer, K. W., 282, 295
Fischer, P., 74
Fishbein, H. D., 108
Fisher, R. P., 343
Fivel, M., 162
Flanery, R. C., 228
Flavell, J. H., 85, 331, 340, 352, 354, 355, 360, 361, 366
Fleming, A. T., 133
Fodor, J., 283, 295
Foley, M. A., 358
Forman, G. E., 278
Fox, R., 224, 240
Frame, C. L., 513
Franco, F., 377, 378
Frankel, J., 84, 148
Franks, B. A., 410–412, 432
Franks, J. J., 346–347
Frazier, T. M., 201
Freeman, F. N., 125
Freeman, R. D., 318
Freeman-Moir, D. J., 21, 22, 23, 36, 49
Freud, A., 16
Freud, S., 14, 20, 49, 61, 177, 474, 582–583, 589
Friedrichs, A. G., 340, 360
Friesen, W. V., 470
Fry-Miller, K. M., 455
Fuller, R. G., 278
Furth, H. G., 298
Futuyma, D. J., 137

G

Gallistel, C. R., 282, 421
Gallup, A. M., 521

Gardiner, J. M., 361
Gardner, H., 280
Gardner, L., 244
Gardner, W., 491
Garduque, L., 144, 163
Garvey, C., 396, 505, 507
Gauvain, M., 96
Gaynor, L., 133
Gelles, R. J., 206
Gelman, R., 280, 282, 421–423, 430, 436
Geschwind, N., 227
Gesell, A. L., 23–24, 29, 49, 229
Gewirtz, J. L., 528, 563
Gibbs, J., 77, 531, 546, 550, 552, 558
Gibson, E., 71, 309–310, 321, 324, 325–329, 331
Gibson, J. J., 309–310, 325
Gilligan, C., 544, 548–551, 563
Ginsburg, D., 135
Ginsburg, H., 298
Gladwin, T., 166
Gleitman, H., 378, 379
Gleitman, L. R., 378, 379
Glenn, C. G., 347, 348
Glick, J., 407
Glover, J. A., 343, 478
Gnepp, J., 470
Goetting, A., 154, 155
Gofman, S., 201, 211
Goldberg, I. O., 201
Goldberg, S., 145, 490
Goldfield, E. C., 325, 326, 331
Golding, G., 550
Goldsmith, H. H., 121, 123
Goldstein, A. G., 359
Goldstein, E. B., 304, 313
Goldstein, H., 201
Goodenough, F. L., 16, 453, 510
Goodman, C., 361
Goodman, G. S., 358
Goodrick, T. S., 552
Gorlin, R. J., 131
Gottesman, I. I., 123
Gottfried, A. W., 244, 256
Gottman, J., 84, 499, 502, 524
Gould, S. J., 110–113, 137
Gracely, E., 574
Graham, S., 449–451, 459, 481
Gravelle, K., 304, 321
Graziano, A. M., 461
Green, E., 345
Green, J. L., 552

Greenberg, C., 409
Greenfield, P. M., 386
Greenwald, A. G., 53
Greenwood, M. R. C., 243
Griffin, E. J., 314
Griffith, S. B., 418
Griffiths, R., 229
Griggs, R. A., 418
Gross, T. F., 321, 324
Gruber, H. E., 26, 27, 28, 299
Gruber, S., 536, 538
Guttmacher, A., 520, 521
Guttman, J., 347

H

Hadkinson, B. A., 409
Haegerstrom, G., 318
Hagan, R., 576, 577
Hagen, J. W., 345
Haig, J. R., 342
Hainline, L., 308
Haith, M. M., 107, 306, 308, 486
Hales, D., 200, 201, 214
Halford, G. S., 407, 420
Hall, B. L., 490
Hall, G. S., 18, 19–20, 21, 23, 29, 49
Halliday, M. A. K., 390
Halpern, D. F., 423
Halverson, C. F., 578
Handin, R. I., 135
Hardy, J. B., 256
Harkness, S., 166, 168
Harlow, H., 469
Harper, L. V., 145
Harris, P., 304
Harrison, H., 211
Hart, D., 567, 568, 571, 572, 599
Harter, M., 30
Hartshorne, H., 528
Hartup, W. W., 149, 498, 499, 502, 503, 504, 510, 516, 517
Harvey, O. J., 503
Harway, M., 77, 79
Havighurst, R. J., 155
Hawkins, J., 407
Hay, D. F., 485, 494, 498
Hearnshaw, L. S., 126
Heath, 388
Hegel, G. W. F., 55, 61
Heil, J., 325, 326, 328, 332
Hembree, E. A., 76, 94, 306

Henderson, C., 71
Hentoff, N., 432, 433
Herbert, W., 114, 199
Herman, P. A., 347, 376, 394
Herriman, M. L., 376, 392, 398, 401
Hersen, M., 93
Hersh, R. E., 355
Hersh, R. H., 559, 563
Hershanson, M., 305
Hertzog, C., 79
Hess, D. L. R., 470
Hesse, P., 469
Hetherington, E. M., 154, 155
Hewer, A., 551
Hiatt, S., 71
Hidi, S., 408
Higgins, A., 560
Hill, F., 278
Hillis, C. B., 17
Hocevar, D., 90
Hoff, A. L., 227
Hoffman, L. W., 144, 148, 149, 163
Hoffman, M. L., 556–557
Holmes, F. B., 452
Holstein, C. B., 545
Holzinger, K. J., 125
Hood, W. R., 503
Horn, J. M., 125–127, 128
Hottinger, W., 246, 249, 251
Hoyt, J. D., 340, 360
Hubel, D. D., 227
Huesmann, L. R., 74
Hughes, J. G., 193–197, 200, 201, 227, 231, 240, 241
Hughey, L., 195, 200, 202, 203–205, 214
Hulsizer, D., 585
Hume, D., 42
Hunter, M. A., 314
Hunter, W. J., 550
Huston, A. C., 148, 170, 173, 574, 576, 600
Hwang, 490

I

Ianotti, R. J., 556
Inhelder, B., 261, 262, 284, 285, 319, 406, 409, 414
Irvine, W., 108, 137
Istomina, Z. M., 352
Ito, M., 224, 225
Izard, C. E., 76, 94, 306, 444, 445, 458, 466, 474, 481, 512

J

Jacklin, C. N., 150, 511, 574
Jackson, C. M., 218
Jackson, E. C., 256
Jacoby, L. L., 343
James, W., 568
Jenkins, J. J., 62, 346
Jensen, A., 125, 126
Jensen, D., 220, 227, 228
Jersild, A. T., 452, 453, 457, 458, 459, 477, 481
Jessel, C., 203–208 passim, 210
Johns, M. L., 576
Johnson, C. N., 357
Johnson, L. D., 519
Johnson, M. K., 358
Johnson, N. S., 347
Johnson-Laird, P. N., 416
Jolly, A., 114, 115
Jones, M. C., 16, 238
Joseph, J. A., 552
Juel-Nielsen, N., 125
Jusczyk, P. W., 314, 315

K

Kagan, J., 167, 177–179, 481, 493, 495, 497, 512
Kail, R. V., 336, 339, 345, 356, 357, 360, 361, 366
Kamin, L. J., 125, 126
Kant, I., 24, 49
Kaplan, 234, 235–238 passim
Kaslow, N. J., 458, 463
Kaye, D. B., 394, 422
Kaye, K., 381
Keen, E., 443
Kegan, R., 527, 566, 589–594, 596–597, 600
Keil, F. C., 50, 295
Kelly, M. E., 407
Kennell, J. H., 145, 489–491
Kerlinger, F. H., 69
Kessen, W., 36, 308, 317
Kidd, J., 120
Kim, Y. J., 521
Kimberling, W. J., 135
King, P. M., 429, 430, 436
Kingma, J., 407
Kintsch, W., 62
Kisker, E. E., 521
Kitchener, K. S., 429, 430, 436

Name Index

Kitchener, R. F., 120, 283
Klaus, M. H., 145, 489–491
Klein, R. E., 315
Klopfer, P. H., 488
Knop, J., 79
Kobasigawa, A. K., 355
Koeseke, R. D., 83
Koffka, K., 322
Kohler, W., 322
Kohlberg, L., 51, 57, 59, 77–78, 432, 527, 530–531, 534, 539–560, 563, 578, 591–592
Kolata, G., 119, 136, 202, 211, 314
Konner, M. J., 167, 168
Koocher, G. P., 418
Kornblith, H., 283
Kositsky, A., 211
Kramer, R., 545, 549
Kratochwil, T. R., 460–461
Kremnitzer, J. P., 306
Kretchmer, N., 198
Kreutzer, M. A., 85–86, 360, 366
Kronsberg, S., 576, 577
Kuhn, D., 413–416
Kuhn, T. S., 65
Kun, A., 449
Kunkel, 175
Kunzinger, E. L., 341
Kurtines, W. M., 528, 563
Kurtzberg, D., 306

L

Laberge, D., 220
Labouvie, E. W., 81
Lamaze, F., 200
Lamb, M. E., 37, 123, 147, 148, 447, 490, 491, 494, 495, 497
Lange, G. W., 346, 347
Langlois, J. H., 148
Langsdorf, P., 76, 94, 236, 306
Lasky, R. E., 315
Lathrop, G., 304
Latt, S. A., 135
Lawlor, R. W., 83
Lawrence, M., 133
Lawson, M. E., 449
Leakey, R. E., 114, 115
Lederberg, A. J., 378
Lehmkuhle, S. W., 302, 304
Leinbach, M. D., 576, 577
Leippe, M. R., 53

Lemerise, E., 308
Leon, M., 538
Leonard, C., 85, 366
Lerner, R. M., 11, 12, 37, 59, 62, 120
Lesgold, A. M., 347
Leshner, A. I., 443
Letson, R. D., 318
Levin, H., 158, 310, 329
Levin, J. R., 347
Levine, C., 551
Levitan, S. A., 143, 148, 151, 153
Levitt, M. J., 556
Levy, V. M., 360
Lewis, M., 315, 441, 445, 481, 567
Liben, L. S., 349
Liberty, C., 340, 341
Lieberman, M., 77, 546
Liebert, R. M., 529, 534
Lindauer, B. K., 345, 346, 347
Linn, M. C., 574
Lipsitt, L. S., 317
Lipsitz, J. S., 238
Locke, D., 552, 553
Locke, J., 10, 42, 61, 107
Lockhart, A., 252
Lockhart, R. S., 342, 343, 347
Loehlin, J. C., 125, 127
Loftus, E. T., 345
Long, F., 144, 163
Long, J., 321
Lopreato, J., 114
Lorenz, K., 50, 511
Lotter, V., 465
Low, H., 511
Lubs, H. A., 135
Lucariello, J., 346, 347
Lumsden, C. J., 114, 137
Lund, N. J., 374, 375, 377–379
Luria, A. R., 386
Luria, Z., 512

M

McBurney, D. H., 315, 321, 328, 332
McCabe, M. P., 522
McCarthy, D., 16
McClearn, G. E., 137
McClelland, 159
Maccoby, E. E., 143, 145–148, 150, 155, 156–158, 184, 487, 490, 491, 492, 494, 509, 510, 511, 524, 573
McCune-Nicolich, L., 387

McDonnell, P., 556
MacFarlane, A., 30
McGraw, M., 16
McGurk, H., 315
McIntyre, C. W., 361
Mack, J. E., 454
McKay, J. R., 197, 198
McKeever, W. F., 227
McKnew, D. H., 464, 481
Macleod, R. B., 326
Macnamara, J., 384
McNeill, D., 84, 370, 389
MacPherson, 574
MacWhinney, B., 375, 377
Magzamen, S., 433, 538
Makowski, D. G., 552
Malatesta, C. Z., 458
Malina, R. M., 217, 239, 252, 253
Mandell, 213
Mandler, G., 441, 444, 473–474
Mandler, J. M., 347
Marcia, J. E., 584–589
Margolin, G., 84, 85
Markman, E. M., 274, 331, 376, 397, 412
Marotz-Baden, R., 140
Marr, D., 308
Martin, C. L., 578
Martin, J. A., 143, 145–148, 155, 156–158, 184, 487, 490, 492, 494
Marx, K., 29, 55, 61
Masur, E. F., 361
Matheny, A. P., 121, 123
Mathews, A., 244
Matthews, G. B., 428, 436
Mattsson, A., 511
Maurer, D., 304
May, M. A., 528
Mayer, R., 432
Mears, C., 469
Meck, E., 421
Medinnus, G. R., 84, 102
Medlin, R. G., 340
Mednick, B., 90
Mednick, S. A., 77, 79
Mehler, J., 224, 240
Melamed, B. G., 475
Melhuish, E., 381
Melton, G. B., 418, 419
Mendel, G., 115–117
Merkin, S., 421
Mermelstein, R., 74

NAME INDEX

Mezynski, K., 394
Michaels, C. F., 326
Michalson, L., 441, 445, 481
Milewski, A. E., 304
Miller, G. A., 290, 339, 352, 370, 380, 401
Miller, J. A., 111, 132, 133, 135, 194–195, 200, 211, 213
Millodot, M., 318
Mills, M., 381
Minuchin, P. P., 144, 160
Miranda, S. B., 334
Mirga, T., 454
Mistry, J. J., 161, 346, 347
Mitchell, D. E., 318
Molfese, D. L., 228
Molfese, V. J., 228
Monroe, R. H., 168
Monroe, R. L., 168
Monty Python, 41
Moore, C. L., 574
Moore, M. J., 306
Morrell, F., 304
Morris, N., 210
Morris, R., 460–461
Moshman, D., 62, 64, 65, 276–277, 410–412, 418–420, 431, 432, 433, 436
Motti, F., 444
Moynihan, D. P., 153
Muchow, M., 16
Mueller, E. C., 498
Muir, D., 316
Murchison, C., 28
Murphy, L., 16
Murphy, L. B., 446, 448, 458
Murphy, M., 585
Murray, A., 136
Murray, L., 381
Mussen, P. H., 36, 184, 236, 238, 436, 563, 600
Myers, B., 145, 146, 488, 490–491, 524, 574
Myers-Walls, J., 455

N

Nagy, W., 347, 376, 394
Nass, 519
Naus, M. J., 340, 341
Neisser, E. G., 457
Neisser, U., 358

Nelson, G., 304
Nelson, K., 346, 347, 387
Nelson, T. O., 345
Nerlove, S. B., 166
Nesdale, A. R., 392
Nesselroade, J. R., 75, 79, 81, 102
Newman, H. H., 125
Newman, J. L., 282
Newport, E. L., 378, 379
Nichols, R. C., 125
Ninio, A., 378, 388–389
Nisan, M., 548
Noam, G., 585
Norman, D., 585
Nowlis, G. H., 317
Nunnally, J. C., 77
Nunner-Winkler, G., 550

O

Oakhill, J., 407
Oakley, A., 135
O'Brien, D. P., 419
Offer, D., 447
Olsen, M. G., 357
Olson, S. L., 387, 392
Olweus, D., 159, 511
O'Malley, P. M., 519
O'Neil, R. M., 432
Opper, S., 298
Orkin, S. H., 135
Ornstein, P. A., 220, 222, 334, 340, 341, 342, 354
Ortony, A., 347, 377
Oser, F., 556
Osherson, D., 274, 376, 397, 412
Osofsky, J. D., 481
Osser, H., 310
Overton, W. F., 62, 64, 282, 409

P

Palmere, M., 343
Paolitto, D. P., 559, 563
Paris, S. G., 345, 346, 347
Parke, R. D., 75, 156, 169, 172, 175, 508–509, 512, 513
Parker, L. H., 91
Patterson, G. R., 84, 85, 156, 157, 159
Pavlov, I. P., 467
Pawlby, 469

Pawson, M., 210
Pea, R. D., 407
Pearce, D., 453
Pearson, J. E., 91
Peck, M. B., 317
Pederson, F. A., 145, 151, 162, 164
Pennington, B. F., 135
Pepler, D., 149
Perner, J., 536, 538
Perry, D. G., 574
Perry, L. C., 574
Perry, W. G., 427
Persky, H., 511
Peters, D. L., 144, 163
Peters, R. S., 555
Peterson, A. C., 235–238 passim, 256, 518, 519, 574
Phelps, E., 416
Piaget, J., 22, 23, 26–28, 29, 30, 32, 34, 49, 50, 51, 52, 54, 56, 59, 61, 62–63, 86, 97, 111, 246, 262–285, 294–297, 321, 322, 324, 349, 377, 384, 385, 386, 404–409, 414, 420, 508, 527, 530–531, 532–538, 539, 544, 563, 578, 589, 591–592
Piattelli-Palmarini, M., 283
Pick, A. D., 310, 325, 326
Pick, H. L., 357
Pieraut-Le Bonniec, G., 409
Piers, M. W., 8
Pindas, P., 140
Pisoni, D. B., 314
Plake, B. S., 343
Plomin, R., 127, 131, 137
Plutchik, R., 441–442, 443, 469
Porac, C., 315
Powell, J. S., 394
Power, C., 560
Pratkanis, A. R., 53
Pratt, C., 376, 398, 401
Pratt, M. W., 550
Pressley, M., 334, 345, 365
Preyer, W., 18–19, 21, 23
Priess, B., 113
Provenzano, F. J., 512
Pyroos, R. S., 359

Q

Quilligan, E. J., 198
Quine, W. V., 65

R

Rader, N., 71, 73, 93
Radke-Yarrow, M., 556, 563
Ramer, A. L. H., 390
Ramsay, D., 71
Rao, R., 133
Raskin, A., 458
Rawls, J., 530, 542
Rayias, M., 76, 94, 306
Reese, H. W., 62, 65
Regalado, 159
Rehm, L. P., 458, 463
Reid, C. E., 132
Reimer, J., 548, 550, 559, 560, 563
Rembold, K., 378
Rest, J. R., 538, 539, 543, 544, 552, 553–555, 558, 563
Reynolds, C. R., 126
Rheingold, H. L., 381, 491
Richards, D. D., 404
Richards, F. A., 276
Richards, J. E., 71
Riegel, K. F., 57, 65
Rifkin, B., 289
Rivlin, R., 304, 321
Robbins, W. J., 218
Robinson, J., 9
Roche, A. F., 229, 239
Rock, I., 321, 324
Rodman, H., 418
Rogers, M. C., 91
Rogoff, B., 96, 97, 161
Rollins, H. A., Jr., 84
Ronning, R. R., 343
Rose, R. J., 121
Rosenbaum, P. L., 212
Rosenblatt, J. S., 488
Rosenhahn, D. L., 457, 460, 461, 463, 464, 465, 468
Ross, B. H., 343
Ross, R. D., 74
Rousseau, J.-J., 9–10, 49, 61
Rubin, J. Z., 512
Rubin, K. H., 505, 507, 508
Rubin, Z., 499, 524
Rubinstein, E. A., 172–175
Ruble, D. N., 574–576
Rugh, R., 193
Rule, 510
Rumain, B., 407, 436

Rumelhart, D. C., 347
Russell, J. A., 470
Russell, M. J., 317

S

Sabshin, M., 447
Saks, M. J., 418
Salapatek, P., 304, 305, 308, 309, 447
Saltzman, E., 326
Samuels, S. J., 220
Sanders, B., 575
Santrock, J. W., 515, 516, 517, 519
Saywitz, K., 398
Scarr, S., 120, 123, 127, 142, 144, 151, 156, 159, 162, 163, 447
Schaie, K. W., 79
Schallert, D. L., 347
Schalling, D., 511
Schank, R. C., 310
Schiedel, D. G., 585, 586, 588, 589
Schlaefli, A., 543
Schliefer, M., 538
Schnell, S. V., 531
Schreibman, L., 465
Schulman, C., 304
Schulsinger, F., 79
Schultebrand, J. G., 458
Scommegna, A., 133
Scribner, S., 407
Scrimshaw, N. S., 240
Searle, J., 378
Sears, P. S., 158
Seitz, V., 69, 75, 76, 79, 83, 84, 179, 513
Seligman, M. E. P., 457, 460, 461, 463, 464, 465, 468
Selman, R., 517, 577
Serpell, R., 167
Sevja, M., 71
Sewall, M., 457
Shapiro, E., K., 144, 160
Shepp, B. E., 309, 313
Sherif, C. W., 503
Sherif, M., 503
Sherman, J., 232
Sherrod, L. R., 306, 486
Sherzer, J., 394
Shettles, L. B., 193
Shields, J., 125
Shiffrin, R. M., 337–338
Shimron, J., 347

Shinn, M., 16
Shultz, T. R., 538
Shute, G. E., 280
Sidman, M., 91
Siegel, C. J., 475
Siegel, H., 432, 488
Siegel, L. J., 462–463
Siegler, R. S., 47, 284–288, 292, 293, 295, 352, 404
Simon, H. A., 327
Sinclair, H., 384
Singer, D. G., 169, 170, 173, 175, 176
Singer, J. L., 170, 175, 176
Siqueland, E. R., 304, 315
Skinner, B. F., 43, 46, 91, 370, 468–469, 529
Skinner, E. A., 59, 62
Skipper, J. K., 519
Slaby, R. G., 74, 156, 169, 172, 175, 508–509, 512, 513
Slackman, E., 346
Slavin, R., 102
Slobin, D. I., 384
Smetana, J. G., 538, 550
Smith, D. W., 200, 217, 218, 229, 230, 231, 232, 240, 241, 244
Smith, F., 330, 332
Smith, J. H., 386
Smith, K. D., 511
Smith, R. H., 345
Smith, S. D., 135
Smith, 497
Snarey, J. R., 548, 550, 560
Snipper, A. S., 166
Snow, C. E., 146, 378
Snyder, M., 420
Soares, M. P., 575
Sockloff, A., 574
Somerville, S. C., 409
Soraci, S. S., 347
Sorell, G. T., 59, 62
Sorensen, E. R., 470
Spache and Spache, 329
Speer, J. R., 360
Spelke, E. S., 326, 327, 331, 486
Sperry, R., 227
Spiegler, M. D., 241, 475, 476, 477
Spock, B., 24
Spoehr, K. T., 302, 304
Sroufe, L. A., 441, 444–448, 466, 474, 481, 495, 496

Stanley, J. C., 574
Stark, R. E., 381
Stayton, D. J., 491, 494
Stein, N. L., 347, 348
Stellar, E., 243
Stenberg, C., 123
Steptoe, A., 244
Stern, D., 486–487
Stern, P., 449
Sternberg, R. J., 284, 288–290, 293, 294, 299, 338, 394, 404, 424, 426
Stevenson, H. W., 165
Stewart, M. J., 252
Stirnimann, F., 306
Stolz, L. M., 16
Stone, B. P., 340
Stone, J., 332
Stone, 159
Straughan, R., 552
Strauss, M. S., 336
Streeter, L. A., 315
Stunkard, A., 242
Suitt, C., 304
Suomi, S., 497, 511
Super, C. M., 166, 168
Sutton, W. S., 118
Suwalsky, J. T. D., 162
Svejda, M. J., 490
Syrdal-Lasky, A., 315
Szostak, J., 136

T

Tallman, L., 140
Tanner, J. M., 230, 231, 236, 240, 241
Tarpy, R. M., 443
Tasch, R. J., 459
Tattersall, I., 114, 115
Taylor, C., 585
Taylor, G. R., 111, 112
Taylor, P. M., 490
Teasdale, T., 90
Tesch, S. A., 585, 589
Thayer, E. S., 407
Thoma, S. J., 544
Thomas, A., 121–123, 137
Thompson, R. A., 121, 148, 153, 449, 466
Thompson, R. F., 220, 222
Thompson, R. M., 491
Thomson, D., 455

Tighe, T. J., 309, 313
Timmons, M., 412
Tinsley, V. S., 377
Tobin, K. G., 280, 574
Tortora, G. J., 221, 222, 225, 228, 232
Trabasso, T. R., 406–407
Trevarthen, C., 381
Tulving, E., 343
Tunmer, W. E., 376, 392, 398, 401
Turiel, E., 538, 545
Turkington, C., 163, 464
Turner, L. A., 355
Tylor, E. B., 164

U

Ullian, J. S., 65
Umezaki, H., 304

V

Valentine, J. W., 119
Vandell, D., 498
Vandenberg, B., 505, 507
Vandenberg, S. G., 123
Vaughan, H. G., 306
Vaughan, V. C., 197–202 passim, 210–211, 225, 231, 232, 234, 237–241 passim
Vaughn, B., 490
Venezky, R. L., 329, 330
Vernon, P., 126
Vesonder, G. T., 361
Vigorito, J., 315
Vincze, M., 498
Vine, I., 534
Von Bargen, 305
Voneche, J. J., 26, 27, 28, 299
Vonnegut, K., 432
Voss, J. F., 361
Vurpillot, E., 311–313
Vygotsky, L. S., 23, 28–29, 56–57, 61, 63, 295, 377, 384–385, 507

W

Wagner, D. A., 165
Wagner, R. K., 426
Walk, R. D., 71, 316, 318, 326
Walker, E., 127, 128
Walker, L. J., 542, 547

Wall, S., 491, 494
Walters, J., 453
Ward, L. M., 315
Wason, P. C., 416, 418
Waterman, A. S., 585, 586, 588, 589, 600
Waters, E., 491, 494, 495, 497
Waters, H. S., 377
Watkins, 175
Watson, J. B., 15, 16, 24, 43, 61, 467–468
Watson, J. D., 118
Weber, M., 195, 202, 203–205, 214
Weber, R. A., 556
Wehren, A., 578
Weinberg, R. A., 127
Weiner, B., 449–451, 456, 457, 459, 466, 481
Weiner, H. M., 463
Weinraub, M., 148, 574
Weiss, 306
Welfel, E. R., 430
Wellman, H. M., 352–355, 357
Welsh, R. S., 156
Werner, H., 23, 24–26, 29, 34, 49, 61, 497
Wertheimer, M., 15, 315, 322
Whelan, E., 133
Whitbourne, S. K., 585, 587
White, A. J., 574
White, B. J., 503
Whiting, B. B., 168
Whitley, B. E., 580
Whorf, B. L., 383–384, 385
Wieman, L. A., 390
Wiesel, T. N., 227
Wiggins, J. A., 156
Wilce, L. S., 391
Wilkinson, L. C., 378, 398
Willems, E. P., 84, 102
Wilson, E. O., 114, 137
Wilson, P. T., 394
Wilson, R. S., 125, 127
Wimmer, H., 536, 538
Winsom, S., 220, 222, 224, 232
Wippman, J., 495
Wittig, M. A., 580
Wolman, B. B., 102
Wright, H. F., 84
Wright, J. C., 170, 173
Wright, K., 538

Name Index

Wundt, W., 14, 43, 61
Wunsch, J. P., 444
Wyatt, R. J., 135

Y

Yahraes, H., 464, 481
Yando, R., 179, 513
Yang, R. K., 211

Yerushalmy, J., 201
Youniss, J., 62
Yudkin, M., 454, 455
Yussen, S. R., 340, 360

Z

Zahn-Waxler, C., 556, 563
Zajonc, R. B., 481, 512

Zaporozhets, A. V., 308
Zaslow, M. J., 162, 163, 164
Zelnik, M., 521
Zigler, E., 179, 513
Zimmerman, B. J., 46, 295
Zinn, H., 7
Zweig, A. R., 211

Subject Index

A

Absolutism, 428–429
   moral, 528, 558
Accommodation of schemes, 263, 264
Acne, 235
Active self, 568
Adaptation, 110
   of schemes, 263, 264
Adipocytes, 232, 241
Adolescence
   civil rights, in, 418–419
   emotional development in, 450–452
   growth in, 232–235, 237–238
   moral development in, 546
   pregnancy in, 520–521
   reasoning in, 418–419
   self-concept in, 569–570, 571
   sexuality in, 519–523
   social development in, 515–524
Afferent fibers, 221
Age norms, 282
Aggression
   biological factors, 511
   children, 510–515
   cultural factors, 512
   development of, 508–515
   family and, 512
   infancy, 509–510
   instinct and, 511
   parental influence on, 156, 159
   peers and, 512
   sex typing and, 575–576
   and social cognition theory, 513
   social determinants, 511–515
   and social learning theory, 512
   sources of, 510–515
   television and, 171–172, 514

Agonistic behavior, 149
Alcoholism, effect on fetus, 198, 200–201
Alleles, 116
Altruism, 556–557
Amniocentesis, 134–135
Amnion, 189
Amphetamines, effect on fetus, 198, 201
Androgens, 233
Androgyny, 578–580
Anemia, effect on fetus, 198
Anger, 453, 456–457, 477–478
Anorexia nervosa, 461
Anoxia, 210–211
Apgar scale, 208–209
Aphasia, 225
Aqueous humor, 303
Artificial insemination, 133
Assimilation of schemes, 263, 264
Asthma, 463
Astigmatism, 318
Asynchrony, in growth, 235
Attachment, 491–498
   effects of, 495–498
   family and, 497
   father and, 497
   insecure, 494–495
   intensity of, 495
   isolation and, 497–498
   secure, 494
Attention, 179–180
Auditory canal, 313
Autism, 465
Autonomic nervous system, 221, 473
Avoidance of attachment, 494
Awareness, as metamemory, 356–357

B

Babinski reflex, 249
Balance scale task, 284–286
Bayley Scales of Infant Development, 316, 392–393
Behavior
   coding, 84
   and evolution, 111–112
   sex-typed, 148
Behavioral genetics, 119–128
Behaviorism, 15, 43–44, 46, 467–473, 529
Beriberi, 240
Birth, 207–213
   breech delivery, 210
   Caesarean section, 210
   complications of, 209–211
   forceps delivery, 210
   Lamaze method, 210
   midwives and, 210
Blastocyst, 189
Bonding, 488–491
Brain, 220, 222–228
   cerebellum, 224
   cerebral cortex, 223–224
   cerebrum, 223–224, 225–228
   corpus callosum, 227
   diencephalon, 222–223
   hemispheres of, 225–228
   hypothalamus, 223
   lateralization, 227–228
   limbic system, 444
   medulla oblongata, 222
   midbrain, 222
   pons varolii, 222
   stem of, 222
   thalamus, 222

701

SUBJECT INDEX

Breech delivery, 210
Broca's area, 225, 227
Bulimarexia, 461–462

C

Caesarean section, 210
Caffeine, effect on fetus, 198
Canalization, 232
Case study, 82–83
Causal attribution, 451–452
Causality, 88–90
Central nervous system, 220, 222–225
Centration, 264, 271, 322
Cephalocaudal development, 217–218
Cerebellum, 224
Cerebral cortex, 223–224, 224–225
Cerebrum, 223–224, 225–228
Child care, 162–163
Children
  aggression and, 510–515
  anger and, 477–478
  fear and, 475–477
  friendship in, 499–502
  groups, 503–505
  moral development and, 545–546
  play among, 505–508
  self-concept of, 568, 571
  and sex roles, 574, 577
  social development of, 491–508
  as witnesses to crime, 358–359
Chorion, 189
Chromosomes, 117
Cigarette smoking. *See* Tobacco
Clinical interview, 86, 264, 279–280
Closure principle, 322–323
Cochlea, 314
Coding, 180
Cognition, 20
  and emotion, 473–474, 475
  and morality, 531
  Piagetian theory of, 261–283
Cognitive abilities, identification of, 280
Cognitive change, Piagetian theory of, 283
Cognitive-developmental approach to morality, 531–555, 558
Cognitive-developmental theory, 578, 589–594
Componential analysis, 288–290
Concrete operations, 264, 270–273

Conditioning
  classical, 467
  operant. *See* Operant conditioning
Cones of eye, 304
Conferences, research, 98–99
Conservation, 264, 271
Constancy, size and shape, 308–309
Constructive model, of memory, 345–350
Constructivism, 50, 51, 263, 264, 321, 324
  moral development, 532
  paradigm of, 283
Context, 347
Contextualism, 57
Continuity
  vs. discontinuity, 32–33
  of personality, 570
  principle of, 322–323
Control, of variables, 412–416
Conversational skills, 395–397
Coordination, of senses, 315–316
Corpus callosum, 227
Correlation, 86–90
  causality and, 89–90
Cortex, cerebral, 223–224, 224–225
Counting, principles of, 421–422
Cross-cultural research, 96–97, 165–169, 548
Cross-sectional research, 76–77, 79–81, 544–545
Cross-sequential research, 79–81
Cultural norms, and school, 161
Culture, 164–165
  and aggression, 512
  and child development, 165–169
  values of, 528–529
Cystic fibrosis, 131, 132

D

Darwinian theory. *See* Evolution
Dating, 518–519
Decentration, 264, 271–272
Deep processing, 343, 344, 347
Deictic tutoring, 388–389
Depression, 463–464
Depth perception, 308
Development
  of aggression, 508–515
  attention and, 179–180
  cephalocaudal, 217–218

  coding and, 180
  constructivist view of, 50, 51
  differentiation and, 219
  of hearing, 314–316
  identification and, 177–178
  imitation and, 178
  integration and, 219–220
  intellectual, 263–275
  language, 368–400
  mechanisms of, 287
  of memory, 334–364
  moral, 527–562
  motivation and, 181
  motor, 217–220, 246–255
  motor skills and, 180–181
  nativist view of, 49–50, 51
  observational learning and, 178–183
  personality, 566–598
  physical, 217–220
  prenatal, 189–206
  proximodistal, 218–219
  psychoanalysis and, 50–51
  of reasoning, 404–435
  reciprocal determinism and, 181–182
  retention and, 180
  sequences of, 51–52, 59
  of smell, 316–317
  social, 485–508, 515–523
  social influences on, 177–183
  of taste, 316–317
  theories of, 49–52, 61–64
  of touch, 316–317
  visual, 304–313
Developmental norms, 23–24
Developmental psychology
  behaviorism, 15, 43–44, 46, 467–473, 529
  constructivism, 50, 51, 263, 264, 321, 324
  development of, 11–30
  ecological view of, 141–142
  history of, 7–9
  information processing theory, 44, 284–295
  operant conditioning, 43–44, 468–469
  paradigms for, 62–64
  psychoanalytic theory, 474
  research designs, 74–82
  social learning theory, 44, 46–47, 469–473, 512, 529, 576–577
  theories of, 41–64

in USSR, 56–57
women and, 16
Diabetes, effect on fetus, 198, 199
Diagnosis, as metamemory, 356, 357, 360
Dialectical theory, 54–64
   contextualism and, 57
   dialogue and, 60
   interactionism and, 58
Diencephalon, 222–223
Differentiation, 219
   theory of, 325–329, 466–467
      detection of patterns, 326–327
      distinctive features and, 327
Discrete emotions theory, 474
Discrimination, 469
Disequilibrium, 54, 264
Distinctiveness, of personality, 571
Divorce, 153–155
DNA, 118–119
Down's syndrome, 129–130
Drug use, effect on fetus, 198, 200–201

E

Ear, 313–314
Eating disorders, 461–462
Echoic memory, 338
Ecological view of development, 141–142
   exosystems, 144
   macrosystems, 144–145
   mesosystems, 143–144
   microsystems, 142–143, 145–159
Ectoderm, 191
Education
   development of reason and, 432–433
   and growth of developmental psychology, 15–17
   and moral development, 555–561
   and personality development, 596
   See also School
Effector, 220
Efferent fibers, 221
Ego, 582
Electra conflict, 582–583
Elementarism, 46
Elimination disorders, 462–463
Emotion
   anger, 453, 456–457, 477–478
   biological bases for, 441–444
   causally linked, 449–450

cognition and, 473–474, 475
defined, 441
discrete theory of, 474
evolutionary basis for, 441–443, 474
expression of, 470–472
fear, 452–453, 454–455, 468, 475–477
grief, 458
jealousy, 457–458
objects of, 472–473
outcome-dependent, 449, 450
physiological basis for, 443–444
positive, 458–460
Emotional development
   active participation stage, 446–447
   adolescent, 450–452, 457, 458, 459–460
   attachment stage, 447
   behavioral view of, 467–473
   of children, 448–450, 452, 453, 454–455, 456, 457, 458, 459, 475–478
   differentiation theory of, 466–467
   in infants, 444–448
   positive affect stage, 445–446
   practicing stage, 447
   self-concept stage, 448
   social smile, 445
Emotional problems, 460–466
   asthma, 463
   autism, 465
   depression, 463–464
   eating disorders, 461–462
   elimination disorders, 462–463
   hyperactivity, 465–466
   phobias, 460–461
   psychosomatic and psychophysiological, 461–463
   suicide, 464
Emotional stress. See Stress
Empathy, 448, 556–557
Empiricism, 46, 283
Encoding, 287, 355
Encopresis, 462–463
Endocrine system, 232–235
Endoderm, 191
Enuresis, 462
Environment
   vs. heredity, 22, 24, 30–31, 125–127
   and individual, 51, 61
Epigenesis, 120–121
Epistemology, 27
Equilibration, 265
Equilibrium, 264, 265

Equity, and moral development, 537
Eriksonian theory of personality, 583–586
Estrogens, 233, 234
Evolution, 11–14, 108–115
   adaptation, 110
   behavior and, 111–112
   emotion and, 441–443, 474
   human, 112–114
   mutation and, 111
   natural selection, 108–109
   speciation, 109–110
Excitement response, 466
Exosystems, 144, 162–164
Expectant parents
   emotions of, 203–207
   guidelines for, 202–203
   preparation of, 206
Experiment, group-based, 93–96
   methods of, 90–96
   single-subject, 91–93
Experimental research, 546–548. See also Research
Extinction, 469
Eye, 302–304

F

Fallopian tubes, 189
Falsification strategy, 419
Family
   and aggression, 512
   and attachment, 497
   single-parent, 152–155
   structure of, 151–155
   two-parent, 151–152
Father
   and attachment, 497
   and child development, 147–149
Fear, 452–453, 454–455, 468, 475–477
Fetal alcohol syndrome, 200
Figurative component, 321
Forceps delivery, 210
Form perception, 309–310
Formal operations, 265, 273–275, 276–277
Fovea, 304
Freudian theory of personality, 582–583
Friendship, 499–502
   common ground and, 500–501
   conflict resolution and, 501

SUBJECT INDEX

Friendship (continued)
  connectedness in, 500
  cross-sex, 518
  dating, 518–519
  disagreement chains and, 501
  information and, 500
  intimate, 517
  positive reciprocity and, 501–502
  same-sex, 518
  self-disclosure and, 502

G

Gametes, 116
Gender, genetic determination of, 118
Generalization, 469
Genes. See Genetics
Genetic counseling, 133–134
  amniocentesis, 134–135
Genetic disorders, 129–132
  meiosis and, 129–130
  recessive genes and, 131–132
Genetic engineering, 135–136
Genetic epistemology, 22, 265, 275, 283
Genetics, 115–136
  behavioral, 119–128
  concepts of, 115–119
  counseling in, 133–134
  and development, 52
  DNA, 118–119
  and gender, 118
  genes and, 116
  and intellectual development, 123–127
  and personality development, 121–123
  and selection of child's sex, 133
Genotype, 120
Gestalt psychology, 322–323
Glial cells, 224
Grasping reflex, 246
Grief, 458
Groups
  children in, 503–505
  influence of, 505–506
  structure of, 504
Growth, 228–245
  asynchrony in, 235
  illness and, 241
  nutrition and, 240–241, 244–245
  psychological aspects of, 235–238

  rates of, 229–231
  sex differences and, 231
  socioeconomic status and, 241
  stress and, 241, 244

H

Habituation, 305, 335–336
Hearing, 313–316
  development of, 314–316
  and vision, 315–316
Hemispheres, of brain, 225–228
Hemoglobin, 193
Hemophilia, 132, 134
Heredity vs. environment, 22, 24, 30–31, 125–127
Herpes viruses, effect on fetus, 198
Hierarchic principle, 25
Historicism, 11
Holism, 51
Hormones, 232–234
  and sex typing, 574–576
Humans, evolution of, 112–114
Hyperactivity, 465–466
Hypothalamus, 223
Hypothesis testing, 73, 416–420
Hypothetico-deductive reasoning, 265, 273, 274–275
Hypothyroidism, effect on fetus, 199

I

Iconic memory, 338
Id, 582
Identification, 177–178
Identity crisis, 587
Identity formation, 586–589
Illness, childhood, 241
I/me distinction, 568–573
Imitation, and development, 178
Immediate memory span, 339
Immunization, 199, 245
Incus, 314
Infant
  aggression and, 509–510
  Apgar scale score, 208–209
  avoidant, 494
  bonding, 488–491
  development of, 16
  emotional development of, 444–448
  facial expression of, 487–488
  growth-retarded, 212–213

  head movements of, 487
  hospital care of, 209
  memory of, 334–337
  newborn, 208–209
  peer relations of, 498–499
  perception by, 304–308
  premature, 211–213
  reflexes in, 246–249
  resistant, 495
  responses of, 247–249
  securely attached, 494
  self-concept of, 567
  size of, 194
  social development of, 486–491
  vision in, 304–308
  See also Prenatal development
Infectious diseases, and fetus, 198, 199
Inference, 346–347
Inferential validity, 409–412
Inflections, 374
Information processing theory, 44, 284–295
  applications of, 293–294
  evaluation of, 294–295
  paradigm in, 292–293
Informed consent, 98–99
Inner ear, 313, 314
Insecure attachment, 494–495
Instinct, and aggression, 511
Instruction, 49
Integration, 219–220
Intelligence, 262–263
  genetics and, 123–127
  and IQ testing, 20–21, 288–289
  mental capacity, 291
  Piagetian theory of, 282
  representational, 265, 267–275
  twin studies and, 123–124
Intelligence quotient. See IQ testing
Interactionist approach, 29–30, 58
Interviews, 85–86
  clinical, 86, 264, 279–280
Intimate friendship, 517
Introspection, 43
Inversion of reality and possibility, in Piagetian theory, 273–274
Iodides, effect on fetus, 198
Iowa Child Welfare Research Station, 17
IQ testing, 20–21, 288–289
Iris, 303

Subject Index

J
Justice, 532
  human, 536
  immanent, 536

K
Klinefelter's syndrome, 130
Knowledge
  levels of, 350–361
  phonological, 391–392
  reasoning about, 429
  states of, 287
Knowledge-acquisition components, 289
Kwashiorkor, 240

L
Labor, 207–208
Lamaze method, 210
Language, 107
  babbling as, 381
  cohesive devices in, 379–380
  conversational skills, 395–397
  cooing as, 381
  crying as, 380
  development of, 269, 368–400
  inflections in, 374
  instruction, 160–161
  lexical meaning, 376
  listeners to, 378
  morphemes, 374–375
  phonemes, 373–374
  phonetics, 372–373
  pragmatics, 377–380
  semantics, 375–377
  social factors and, 392–393
  speakers of, 378
  syntactic stage, 389
  syntax, 375, 393–394
  theories of, 50
  and thought, 383–385
  vocabulary, 394
Language acquisition device, 383
Lanugo, 193
Latchkey children, 163–164
Lateralization, 227
Learning
  behaviorism and, 43–44, 46
  in information processing theory, 44
  operant conditioning and, 43–44
  in social learning theory, 44, 46–47
  theories of, 42–49, 61–64
Lesch-Nyhan syndrome, 134, 135
Levels of processing, 342–345
Libido, 582
Lightening, 207
Limbic system, 444
Linguistic period, 380, 382
Logical necessity, 408–409
Longitudinal research, 77–79, 79–81, 545–546
Long-term store, 337, 339
Love, as adaptive trait, 442
LSD, effect on fetus, 198

M
Macrosystem, 144–145, 164–176
  television as, 169–176
Malleus, 314
Maturation, historical trends in, 239
Meaning-constitutive development, 589
Medical care, 245
Medulla oblongata, 222
Meiosis, 117
  problems in, 129–130
Memory
  application of, 361–364
  constructive model of, 345–350
  context and, 347
  development of, 334–364
  echoic, 338
  iconic, 338
  immediate, 339
  inference and, 346–347
  levels of knowing and, 350–361
  levels-of-processing model of, 342–345
  multistore model of, 337–342
  Piagetian theory of, 349
  story, 347–348
Menarche, 234, 239
Mercury, effect on fetus, 198
Mesoderm, 191
Mesosystems, 143–144, 159–162
  linkages in, 160–162
Metacognition, 423–426, 566
Metacomponents, 289–290
Metalinguistic awareness, 397–398
Metamemory, 85, 355–361
Microsystems, 142–143
  family structure, 151–155
  parenting styles, 155–159
  parents, 145–149
  siblings, 149–151
Midbrain, 222
Middle ear, 314
Midwives, 210
Mnemonic strategies, 354
Monitoring, as metamemory, 361
Moral development
  absolutist approach to, 528, 558
  in adolescence, 546
  of children, 545–546
  cognition and, 531
  cognitive-developmental approach to, 531–555, 558
  consequences vs. intentions, 535–536
  constructivist view of, 532
  education and, 555–561
  equity and, 537
  heteronomous vs. autonomous, 537
  justice and, 532, 536–537
  Kohlbergian stages of, 539–541
  Kohlbergian theory of, 539–555
  perspective-taking and, 533
  Piagetian model of, 534–538
  play and, 535
  rationality and, 533, 542–544, 547, 551–555
  realism and, 536
  relativist approach to, 528–530, 558
  rules and, 535, 538
  sex roles and, 548–551
  social interaction and, 533
  stages of, 531
  structure of, 532
  study of, 528–534
  universality and, 534
Moral reasoning, 542–544, 547, 551–555
Morality, 539. See also Moral development
Moro reflex, 246
Morphemes, 374–375
Morphology, 374
Mother
  and attachment, 491–495
  and bonding, 488–491
  and child development, 145–146

SUBJECT INDEX

Mother (continued)
  effects of on fetus. See Prenatal development
  "motherese," 378
Motivational processes, 181
Motor development, 246–255
  patterns of, 217–220
  practice and, 251–252
  race and, 253
  and self-image, 254–255
  sex and, 252–253
  timetable of, 250, 251
Motor skills, 180–181
Multistore model of memory, 337–342
Mumps, effect on fetus, 198
Mutation, 111
Myelin, 224

N

Nativism, 49–50, 51, 283
Natural selection, 108–109
Nature vs. nurture. See Heredity
Nerve fibers, 221
Neurons, 224, 291
Norms, 503
Nuclear war, fear of, 454–455
Numbers
  principles of counting, 421–422
  understanding of, 420–423
Nutrition and growth, 240–241, 244–245

O

Obesity, 237, 241, 242–243
Object permanence, 268
Object play, 505
Observation, 68–72, 83–85
  behavior coding and, 84
Observational learning, 178–183, 512, 529
Oedipal conflict, 582–583
Operant conditioning, 43–44, 468–469
Operating space, 291
Operative component, 324
Opiates, effect on fetus, 198, 201
Organizational strategies, 341–342
Organization of schemes, 263, 265
Orthogenetic principle, 25
Ossicles, 314
Outer ear, 313

P

Paradigm, 531
Parasympathetic nerve fibers, 221
Parents, 145–149, 150–151
  authoritarian-autocratic, 155, 156–157
  authoritative-reciprocal, 155, 158–159
  and child care, 162–163
  indifferent-uninvolved, 155, 157
  indulgent-permissive, 155, 157–158
  and moral development, 538
  work and roles of, 162
  See also Expectant parents
Patterns, detection of, 326–327
Pearson Product-Moment correlation, 86
Peers
  and aggression, 512
  infants and, 498–499
  and moral development, 537–538
Pellagra, 241
Perception
  defined, 302
  and development, 143
  of form, 311
  of illusion, 311
  research in, 317–320
  speech, 314–315
  theories of, 320–330
Perceptual centration, 322
Performance components, 288–289
Peripheral nervous system, 220, 221–222
Personality
  of adolescents, 569–570, 571
  of children, 568, 571
  cognitive-developmental theory of, 589–594
  development of, 592–594
  Eriksonian theory of, 583–586
  Freudian theory of, 582–583
  genetics and, 121–123
  identity formation theory, 586–589
  psychoanalytic approach to, 581–589
  self-concept, 567–573
  self-esteem, 567, 595
  self-understanding, 567–568
  sex roles and sex typing, 566, 595
  stages of development, 590–592
Perspective-taking, 533
Phenotype, 120

Phenylketonuria, 131–132, 134
  effect on fetus, 198
Philosophical reasoning, 426–429
Phobias, 460–461
Phonemes, 373–374
Phonetic symbols, 373
Phonetics, 372–373
Phonology, 373–374, 391–392
Physical development, patterns of, 217–220
Physical growth. See Growth
Physical self, 568
Piagetian theory
  and age norms, 252
  applications of, 278–279
  cognitive abilities and, 280
  of cognitive change, 283
  of intelligence, 282–283
  of memory, 349
  methodology of, 280–281
  of perception, 321, 324
  of reasoning, 62–63, 261–283
  stage theory in, 281–282
  terms of, 264–265
Pinna, 313
Placenta, 189–190, 208
Play, 505–508
  and moral development, 535
Pneumonia, effect on fetus, 198
Pons varolii, 222
Pragmatics, 377–380
Prelinguistic period, 380
Premature infants, 211–213
Prenatal development
  conception, 189–190
  critical periods of, 196–197
  embyronic period, 191, 192
  fetal period, 191–194
  germinal period, 189–191
  guidelines for expectant parents, 202–203
  maternal age and, 195–196
  maternal diseases and, 197–199
  maternal drug use and, 198, 200–201
  maternal emotions and, 196
  maternal endocrine disorders and, 199
  maternal nutrition and, 194–195
  maternal socioeconomic level and, 195
  negative influences on, 196–202
  teratogens and, 197

Subject Index

Preoperational stage, 265, 267–268
Pretend play, 505
Privacy, 97–98
Processing
 deep, 343, 344, 347
 shallow, 343, 344
Prosocial behavior, 149, 514–515
Proximity principle, 322–323
Proximodistal development, 218–219
Psychoanalysis, 14, 50–51
Psychoanalytic approach to personality, 581–589
Psychoanalytic theory, 474
Psychological self, 568
Psychology
 cognitive, 15
 early, 13–14
 See also Developmental psychology
Psychosomatic and psychophysiological disorders, 461–463
Puberty, 232
Publication of research, 75
Punishers, in operant conditioning, 468
Pupil of eye, 303

Q

Quinine, effect on fetus, 198

R

Race, and motor development, 253
Radiation, effect on fetus, 198, 201–202
Rationality, 429–431
 and moral development, 533
Reading, readiness for, 329–330
Realism, moral, 536
Reasoning
 absolutism vs. relativism, 428–429
 adolescent, 418–419
 control of variables, 412–416
 defined, 404
 development of, 431–435
 falsification strategy, 419
 hypothesis testing, 416–420
 hypothetico-deductive, 265, 273, 274–275
 inference, 409–412
 knowledge and reality, 429
 logical, 408–409

metacognition, 423–426
numerical, 420–423
philosophical, 426–429
rationality and, 429–431
selection task and, 416
transitivity, 404–407
Recall
 elaborative, 348
 inferential, 348
Receptor cells of eye, 304
Recessive genes, and genetic disorders, 131–132
Reciprocal determinism, 181–182
Reciprocity, and friendship, 501–502
Reductionism, 46
Reflexes, 246, 249
Rehearsal strategies, 340–341, 354–355
Reinforcers, in operant conditioning, 468
Relativism, 428–429
 moral, 528–530, 558
Replacement sequences, 389
Representation, 265, 269
Representational intelligence, 265, 267–275
Research, 68–100
 case study methods, 82–83
 correlational methods, 86–90
 cross-cultural, 96–97, 165–169, 548
 cross-sectional, 76–77, 79–81, 544–545
 cross-sequential, 79–81
 design of, 74–82
 ethical questions, 73–74, 97–101, 126
 experimental, 546–548
 experimental methods, 90–96
 hypothesis testing, 73
 informed consent and, 98–99, 100
 interview methods, 85–86
 longitudinal, 77–79, 79–81, 545–546
 methods of, 48, 52–53, 59–60
  listed, 82
 observation and, 68–72
  methods of, 83–85
 perception, 317–320
 privacy and, 97–98, 101
 protection of subjects, 99–100, 101
 publication of, 75
 sampling and, 70
 theory and, 53, 59, 71–72
 variables and, 69–70
Research conferences, 98–99

Resistance to attachment, 495
Retention, and coding, 180
Retina, 302–303, 304
Retrieval strategies, 355
Reversibility, 265
Rh Factor, 199–200
Rickets, 240
Rods and cones of eye, 304
Rooting reflex, 107, 249
Rubella, effect on fetus, 198
Rule assessment, 284

S

Sampling, 70
Scarlet fever, effect on fetus, 198
Schema theory, of sex typing, 578
Schemes, cognitive, 262, 265
School
 cultural norms in, 161
 language instruction in, 160–161
 as mesosystem, 159–162
Science
 role of data in, 40–41, 52, 59
 role of theory in, 39–41, 52, 59
 See also Education
Sclera, 303
Scurvy, 241
Second-order operations, 265, 273, 275
Secure attachment, 494–495
Self
 construction of, 572–573
 development of, 568–573
 types of, 568
Self-concept, 447–448, 567–573
Self-esteem, 567, 595
Self-image
 in adolescence, 235–238
 and motor development, 254–255
 obesity and, 237
 size and physique and, 235–237, 245
Self-reflectivity, 571
Self-understanding, 567–568
Semantics, 375–377
Sense receptors, 337–338
Sensorimotor stage, 265, 266
Sensory deprivation, 318
Sensory register, 337, 338
Separation anxiety, 447, 493, 494
Sex bias, in research, 548–551
Sex differences
 and aggression, 511

Sex differences *(continued)*
    and growth rate, 231, 234–235, 237–238
    and motor development, 242–253
Sex education, 521
Sex roles, 566, 573–581, 595
Sex typing, 148, 566, 573–574, 595
    androgyny, 578–580
    biological bases for, 574–576
    cultural influences on, 576
    television and, 173
    theories of, 576–578
Sexuality
    adolescent, 519–523
    sexual behaviors, 522
Shallow processing, 343, 344
Short-term storage space, 291, 337, 338–339
Siblings, and child development, 149–151
Sickle-cell anemia, 131, 132, 134
Similarity principle, 322–323
Single-parent families, 152–155
Size
    historical trends in, 239
    and self-image, 235–237
Smell, 316–317
Social cognition theory, 513
Social development, 485–508, 515–523
    of adolescent, 515–524
    attachment, 491–498
    bonding, 488–491
    of child, 491–508
    cliques in, 515–516
    crowds and, 515
    and friendship, 499–502
    group interaction and, 503–505
    of infant, 486–491
    peers and, 498–508
    play in, 505–508
    sexuality and, 519–523
Socialization, 38–39, 140–141
Social learning theory, 44, 46–47, 469–473, 512, 529, 576–577
Social play, 505–508
Social self, 568
Social services, 245
Social smile, 445
Society for Research in Child Development, 17

Speciation, 109–110
Speech
    events, 378
    patterns of, 370
    perception of, 314–315, 381–382
    production of, 380–381
Spinal cord and reflexes, 222
Stage theory, 281–282
Stapes, 314
States of knowledge, 287
Stereotypes, sexual. *See* Sex typing
Stimulus, 467
Storage of information, 355
Story memory, 347–348
Strabismus, 318
Strategies
    mnemonic, 354
    organizational, 341–342
    rehearsal, 340–341, 354–355
    retrieval, 355
Stress, and growth, 241, 244
Sucking reflex, 246
Suicide, 464
Superego, 582
Supraspinal activities, 222
Surfactin, 193
Survival, as adaptive trait, 442
Sympathetic nerve fibers, 221
Syntax, 375, 393–394
Syphilis, effect on fetus, 198, 199

T

Taste, 316–317
Tay-Sachs disease, 131, 132, 134
Television
    aggression and, 171–172, 514
    and child development, 153
    children's, 174–175
    effects of, 172–173, 175–176
    as macrosystem, 169–176
    potential of, 173–174
    stereotypes, 173, 174–175, 176
Temperament, 121
Teratogens, 197
Testosterone, 234
Thalamus, 222
Thalidomide, effect on fetus, 198, 201
Thought, and language, 383–385
Tobacco, effect on fetus, 198, 201

Touch, 316–317
Toxoplasmosis, effect on fetus, 198
Transduction, 302
Transitivity, 404–407
Trisomy, 129
Tuberculosis, effect on fetus, 198
Turner's syndrome, 130
Twins, intelligence studies of, 123–124
Two-parent families, 151–152
Tympanic membrane, 313

U

Umbilical cord, 189
UNESCO, 170–171
UNICEF, 170–171
Uterus, 189

V

Values, 528–529
Variables, independent and dependent, 69–70
Vernix, 193
Vision, 302–304
    constancy of, 308–309
    development of, 304–313
    and hearing, 315–316
    of infant, 304–308
Vitreous humor, 303
Vocabulary growth, 394
Volition, and personality, 571

W

Wernicke's area, 225, 227
Witnesses, children as, 358–359
Words
    presymbolic, 382
    symbolic use of, 386–388
Work
    economic effects of, 164
    and parent roles, 162

X

Xerophthalmia, 241